THE LIFE OF RICHARD WAGNER
1859-1866

ERNEST NEWMAN

The Life of

RICHARD

WAGNER

VOLUME III   1859–1866

CAMBRIDGE UNIVERSITY PRESS

CAMBRIDGE

LONDON · NEW YORK · MELBOURNE

Published by the Syndics of the Cambridge University Press
The Pitt Building, Trumpington Street, Cambridge CB2 1RP
Bentley House, 200 Euston Road, London NW1 2DB
32 East 57th Street, New York, NY 10022, USA
296 Beaconsfield Parade, Middle Park, Melbourne 3206, Australia

This paperback edition first published by the Cambridge University Press, 1976

Printed in Great Britain
at the
University Printing House, Cambridge
(Euan Phillips University Printer)

Library of Congress Cataloguing in Publication Data
Newman, Ernest, 1868–1959
The life of Richard Wagner.
Reprint of the ed. published by Knopf, New York.
Includes bibliographies and indexes.
CONTENTS: v. 1. 1813–1848. – v. 2. 1848–1860. – v. 3. 1859–1866. – v. 4. 1866–1883.
1. Wagner, Richard, 1813–1883.
ML410.WIN532   782.1'092'4 [B]   76-22682
ISBN 0 521 29094 5   Volume I
ISBN 0 521 29095 3   Volume II
ISBN 0 521 29096 1   Volume III
ISBN 0 521 29097 X   Volume IV
ISBN 0 521 29149 6   set of four volumes

FOREWORD

IT WILL perhaps come as a shock to the reader to discover that another volume of this Life of Wagner is to follow the present one. He need feel no apprehension, however, as to the total demand to be made on his staying-power. He will not be compelled to read a page more than was contemplated by the publishers and myself when the work was originally planned; the change from three volumes to four is merely a matter of convenience in book-making and in intervals of publication.

The writing of the present volume has been one of peculiar difficulty owing to the immense number of new first-hand documents pertaining to the period that have come to light during the last few years. Never until now have I realised how right Anatole France was when he said ironically that the events in history about which we can be surest are those for which we have the testimony of only one witness. In Wagner biography our problems increase with the number of witnesses and of documents. It becomes more and more difficult even to establish such apparently simple things as the dates of events that occurred not in the dim and distant past but almost within living memory. Wagner's own records are a mass of wrong dates. Letters from all and sundry are sometimes mis-dated, sometimes not dated at all. Every variety of pitfall awaits the feet of the unsuspecting researcher: a man, for instance, will date his letter from a particular hotel in a particular town, not because he is there at the time of writing — he may be a couple of hundred miles away — but because he expects to be there by the time a reply can reach him. Or he writes that " tomorrow " he intends to go to such and such a place, and then calmly postpones his departure for a day or two without the smallest thought for the future biographer, whose whole theory regarding something or other must stand or fall by the accuracy of his attribution of an event to this day or that.

Documents again, have first of all to pass through the hands of editors; and these gentlemen are often a sore trial to the historian and the biographer. Many vital letters are suppressed; others are given in an incomplete form without even a hint being vouchsafed that something has been omitted. Others, again, are deliberately garbled to suit the prepossessions of the editor or the supposed interests of some living or recently dead third party. Men whose sense of honour in other matters is beyond question will sometimes indulge in the most amazing deceits where letters are concerned: not content with suppressing something which they do not think it desirable for us to know, they will on occasion actually conceal the fact of the concealment by linking up the severed sentences of the original with words of their own.

Even as regards the mere establishment of facts, then, a multiplicity of documents often merely increases dubiety instead of diminishing it. And naturally what holds good of the facts is still more true of the interpretation of them. It is for this reason, among others, that I would humbly ask the reader of the present volume not to jump to the conclusion that I am mistaken in this or that opinion merely because it runs counter to what he has long been accustomed to believe. The same facts are often capable of interpretation in more than one way; and more than one judgment in this volume will perhaps take the reader by surprise. But the interpretation, such as it is, will have been based on the careful consideration of every known fact relating to the matter; and anyhow, whether success or failure attends the attempt, it is worth while to try to clear away from certain aspects of the Wagner story the errors, some of them gross, that have gathered about them in the course of time.

I desire to express my warm thanks for help of various kinds from Dr. Otto Strobel — at once the best-informed and the most scrupulous of all Wagner editors, past or present — Mr. Robert Lorenz, Mr. W. R. Steinway, Dr. Willi Schuh, editor of the *Neue Zürcher Zeitung*, and Dr. Franz Beidler, of Zürich. Dr. Beidler, who is the son of Wagner's and Cosima's daughter Isolde, has in hand a study of Cosima that should prove of exceptional interest and value.

E. N.

Tadworth, 22nd May, 1940.

CONTENTS

ADDITIONAL SOURCES AND REFERENCES

A

APA   =   Juliette Adam: *Mes premières armes littéraires et politiques.* Paris, 1904.

B

BAR   =   Charles Baudelaire: *L'art romantique, in Oeuvres complètes,* ed. by Jacques Crépet. Paris, 1925.

BATC   =   Hector Berlioz: *A travers chants.* 4th ed. Paris, 1886.

BBFL   =   *Briefe an Hans von Bülow von Ferdinand Lassalle, 1862–1864.* Dresden, 1893.

BCWH   =   *Briefwechsel zwischen Cosima Wagner und Fürst Ernst zu Hohenlohe-Langenburg.* Stuttgart, 1937.

BFWB   =   *Bayreuther Festblätter in Wort und Bild.* Munich, 1884.

BLE   =   Robert Bory: *Liszt et ses enfants . . . d'après une correspondance inédite avec la Princesse Marie Sayn-Wittgenstein.* Paris, 1936.

BLKB   =   Gottfried von Böhm: *Ludwig II, König von Bayern, sein Leben und seine Zeit.* 2nd ed. Berlin, 1924.

BRWP   =   *Briefe Richard Wagners an eine Putzmacherin, veröffentlicht von Daniel Spitzer.* Vienna, 1906.

C

CLEO   =   *Correspondance de Liszt et de sa fille Madame Emile Ollivier, 1842–1862; publiée par Daniel Ollivier.* Paris, 1936.

F

FEL   =   Julius Fröbel: *Ein Lebenslauf.* 2 vols. Stuttgart, 1890/1.

FKLB   =   Eugen Frantz: *König Ludwig II von Bayern, das königliche Kabinett, das Ministerium und das bayerische Volk, 1864–1866.* (In *Staat und Volkstum,* a volume of historical studies by various authors, issued as " Festgabe " in honour of Karl Alex. von Müller). Munich, 1933.

G

GIS   = C. H. N. GARRIGUES: *Ein ideales Sängerpaar, Ludwig Schnorr von Carolsfeld und Malvina Schnorr von Carolsfeld, geborne Garrigues*. Copenhagen and Berlin, 1937.

GSRC   = JUDITH GAUTIER: *Le second rang du collier*. Paris [1903].

H

HERW   = MARIE FÜRSTIN ZU HOHENLOHE: *Erinnerungen an Richard Wagner*. Weimar, 1938.

HMP   = FRIEDRICH HERZFELD: *Minna Planer und ihre Ehe mit Richard Wagner*. Leipzig, 1938.

HNBW   = ARTHUR HÜBSCHER: *Neues aus den beiden Wagnerjahren*. (In the Munich *Süddeutsche Monatshefte* for June, 1932).

HRWV   = JULIUS HEY: *Richard Wagner als Vortragsmeister, 1864–1876; herausgegeben von Hans Hey*. Leipzig, 1911.

HSM   = *Memoirs of Prince Chlodwig of Hohenlohe-Schillingsfürst, edited by Friedrich Curtius . . . translated by George W. Chrystal*. 2 vols. London, 1906.

J

JNRW   = ANNA JACOBSON: *Nachklänge Richard Wagners im Roman*. Heidelberg, 1932.

K

KBWP   = LUDWIG KARPATH: *Zu den Briefen Richard Wagners an eine Putzmacherin: Unterredungen mit der Putzmacherin Berta*. Berlin, n.d. [1907?].

KJR   = THEODOR KROYER: *Joseph Rheinberger*. Regensburg, 1916.

KLRWB = *König Ludwig II und Richard Wagner Briefwechsel, bearbeitet von Otto Strobel*. 5 vols. Karlsruhe, 1936, 1939.

KPWA   = JULIUS KAPP: *Der Privatdruck von Richard Wagners Autobiographie; in Die Musik*, July, 1930.

KUD   = JULIUS KAPP: *Unterdrückte Dokumente aus den Briefen Richard Wagners an Mathilde Wesendonk; in Die Musik*, Sept., 1931.

L

LIK   = FRITZ LINDE: *Ich, der König: Der Untergang Ludwigs des Zweiten*. Leipzig, 1928.

SOURCES AND REFERENCES

M

MGW   = MALWIDA VON MEYSENBUG: *Genius und Welt: Briefe von Richard Wagner;* in *Cosmopolis,* August, 1896.

MMCW = MAX MILLENKOVICH-MOROLD: *Cosima Wagner, ein Lebensbild.* Leipzig, 1937.

MMKB = *Marie von Mouchanoff-Kalergis, geb. Gräfin Nesselrode, in Briefen an ihre Tochter: herausgegeben von La Mara.* Leipzig, 1907.

MVWR = E. MICHOTTE: *La Visite de R. Wagner à Rossini (Paris 1860).* Paris, 1906.

O

OIRF   = ALDO OBERDORFER: *Il Re folle, Luigi II di Baviera.* Milan, 1935. (A French translation of this work — *Louis II de Bavière, la Légende et la Vérité* — was published in Paris in 1937).

P

PEE   = ERNST VON POSSART: *Erstrebtes und Erlebtes, Erinnerungen aus meiner Bühnentätigkeit.* 2nd ed. Berlin, 1916.

PRW   = T. PUSCHMANN: *Richard Wagner, eine psychiatrische Studie.* 3rd ed. Berlin, 1873.

PW   = GUY DE POURTALÈS: *Wagner.* Paris, 1932.

R

RRWM = SEBASTIAN RÖCKL: *Richard Wagner in München: ein Bericht in Briefen.* Regensburg, 1938.

RVPW = SEBASTIAN RÖCKL: *Von der Pfordten und Richard Wagner.* (*Süddeutsche Monatshefte,* April, 1928).

RWAN = *Richard Wagner und Albert Niemann . . . herausgegeben von Wilhelm Altmann.* Berlin, 1924.

RWHR = *Richard Wagner Briefe an Hans Richter, herausgegeben von Ludwig Karpath.* Berlin, 1924.

RWMM = *Richard Wagner an Mathilde Maier, 1862–1878, herausgegeben von Hans Scholz.* Leipzig, 1930.

RWSK = *Richard Wagner an seine Künstler, herausgegeben von Erich Kloss.* 3rd. ed. Leipzig, 1911.

S

SEHM = GEORGES SERVIÈRES: *Episodes d'histoire musicale.* Paris, 1914.

SFCW = WALTHER SIEGFRIED: *Frau Cosima Wagner.* Stuttgart, 1930.

[xiii]

SOURCES AND REFERENCES

SHB   = LUDWIG SCHEMANN: *Hans von Bülow im Lichte der Wahrheit*. Regensburg, 1935.

SLD   = LUDWIG SCHEMANN: *Lebensfahrten eines Deutschen*. Leipzig, 1925.

SMF   = MANFRED SEMPER: *Das Münchener Festspielhaus: Gottfried Semper und Richard Wagner*. Hamburg, 1906.

STP   = EDUARD SCHELLE: *Der Tannhäuser in Paris und der dritte musikalische Krieg: eine historische Parallele*. Leipzig, 1861.

SWMZ   = OTTO STROBEL: *Wagners Münchener Zeit, im Lichte unveröffentlichter Briefe des Meisters*. (In *Nationalsozialistische Monatshefte*, Heft 40, July, 1933).

T

TALKB   = *Tagebuch-Aufzeichnungen von Ludwig II, König von Bayern, herausgegeben von Edir Grein*. Schaan-Liechtenstein, 1925.

W

WFL   = COSIMA WAGNER: *Franz Liszt, ein Gedenkblatt von seiner Tochter*. 2nd ed. Munich, 1911.

WKLW   = GEORG JACOB WOLF: *König Ludwig II und seine Welt*. Munich, 1922.

Z

ZUBW   = *Zwei unveröffentlichte Briefe Richard Wagners an Robert von Hornstein, herausgegeben von Ferdinand Freiherr von Hornstein*. Munich, 1911.

THE LIFE OF RICHARD WAGNER
1859-1866

CHAPTER I

THE SECOND ASSAULT ON PARIS

1

THE PARIS musical venture of 1860/1, like that of twenty years earlier, was to prove a turning-point in Wagner's fortunes not only as composer but as man: and the Spirit of History seemed bent on stressing the line of transition between past and present by removing from the scene, about this time, several of the figures who had not only played a considerable part in the first half of Wagner's life but had been, in their several ways, typical of the departing order of things. The trusty old Dresden stage-manager and chorusmaster Fischer, whom Wagner had not seen since his flight from Germany in May, 1849, died on the 3rd November, 1859, before a letter could reach him in which Wagner had expressed his concern at the news of his old friend's illness. Spohr had passed away a fortnight earlier; and on the 28th January the troubled life of Wilhelmine Schröder-Devrient came to a close. Wagner paid a warm tribute to the memory of Fischer and Spohr in an article that appeared in the Dresden *Konstitutionelle Zeitung* of the 25th November, 1859 and in the *Neue Zeitschrift* of the 2nd December: [1] these two men and Schröder-Devrient were symbols of a musical Germany that was now no more. [2]

Even before he had made an open attempt to interest the French public in his music Wagner had to contend with the enmity of the corrupt Paris Press, which, it is no secret today, was handsomely taken care of by the rich Meyerbeer. So far had the campaign of

[1] Reprinted in RWGS, V, 105 ff.

[2] So, in his way, was Reissiger, Wagner's former chief in the Dresden theatre, who died on the 7th November, 1859. Bülow, in a letter of a couple of days later to Bronsart, took it for granted that his correspondent would be "delighted with the news" of the death of this opponent of Wagner and Liszt. Wagner was no less ironically outspoken in a letter to Minna: "I suppose *I* am really to blame for R.'s death, for when Fischer died I said to myself, 'Ach, that a man like that must die, and such a —— remain alive!'"

calumny already gone by December, 1859 that in that month Wagner was compelled to publish a protest — in French, perhaps drafted by Gasperini — in the friendly-disposed *L'Europe artiste*.

> "For ten years", he said, "I have been an exile from Saxony and consequently barred from setting foot anywhere in Germany. . . . I have come to France in order to perform, if possible, my music before a few friends. I shun noisy *réclame*. A foreigner and a proscript, I looked forward to a friendly reception as a guest in France. I am called the Marat of music. My works, however, have no such subversive tendency as it pleases people to ascribe to them: even the monarch who has banished me listens to my operas in Dresden and applauds them. The French Press can surely wait a little while; perhaps it will then judge me on the strength of something else than what appears in certain German papers. I ask for nothing but impartiality."

How little he could expect in the way of impartiality from the professional musical world in Paris, however, he was soon to discover. Baudelaire tells us that at the end of the rehearsals for the Wagner concerts he saw

> " one of the accredited Paris critics plant himself pretentiously before the ticket office, preventing the crowd from getting out, and laughing like a maniac, like one of those unfortunates who are known in hospitals as *agités*. This poor man, believing his appearance to be familiar to everyone, seemed to be saying, ' See how I am laughing, I, the celebrated S. [Scudo?]; so conform your judgment to mine." [3]

As already told,[4] both Wagner and Lucy were left so long without official replies to their petition for the use of the Opéra for the projected three concerts that Wagner had to make arrangements with Calzado for the use of the Théâtre Italien (the Salle Ventadour): the Emperor did indeed, in the end, place the Opéra at his disposal, but it was then too late. There was a touch of ominous irony in the fact that this Théâtre Italien was the old Théâtre de la Renaissance under another name — the selfsame building in which Wagner's hopes for a production of *Das Liebesverbot* had come to nothing in 1840.[5] The orchestral rehearsals for the concerts were held, under

---

[3] BAR, p. 210.

[4] See Vol. II, p. 602.

[5] See Vol. I, p. 280. The director of the Italien, Calzado, seems to have been an interesting if dubious character. He was intimately associated with the most famous gambler of that epoch, Thomas Garcia, whose fabulous exploits at Monte-Carlo and elsewhere are known to all students of the history of roulette and baccara. We

Wagner himself, in the Salle Herz. With the strings, which numbered sixty-four, he was very pleased. The wood wind and brass were less satisfactory; particularly informative is his criticism of the oboe playing, which, he told Frau Wesendonk, " remained pastoral all the time, never rising to passion." Bülow, who had come to Paris partly for Wagner's sake, partly to give some piano recitals on his own account, took the choral rehearsals in the Salle Beethoven: the choir was made up mostly of German amateurs living in Paris. Bülow, now and for weeks to come, was of the utmost service to Wagner in many other ways: he not only helped to keep the master's heart up by his sympathy and understanding but pulled all kinds of wires for him in the high social circles to which his introductions gave him access. The concerts were given on three successive Wednesdays, the 25th January and 1st and 8th February, 1860, the programmes being virtually the same on each occasion [6]

read of a party at the Paris house of one Madame Julia Barucci, at which the presence was noticed of "a certain Signor Calzado, the manager of a theatre in Paris, whom everyone disliked except Garcia. Nothing definite was known against him, but he had an unsavory reputation as a gamester, and no one liked playing with him." Some years before that there had been a colossal card-swindle in Havana, the mastermind in which was one "Bianca": there are grounds for believing that this "Bianca" was none other than Calzado. At a rather later period than the present point of our story, Garcia and Calzado, at a private gambling party in Paris, fleeced one of the guests of 130,000 francs by ingeniously slipping cards of their own into the shoe at baccara. Calzado was arrested and sent to prison for thirteen months: Garcia, who had fled, was sentenced to five years imprisonment *in absentia*. (See Frédéric Loliée's *La Fête Impériale*, pp. 259–262, and Prince Pierre Polotsoff's entertaining *Monte-Carlo Casino*, London, 1937, p. 169 ff.).

Verdi had come into collision with the unscrupulous Calzado in 1855. (See the *Copialettere di Giuseppe Verdi*, Milan, 1913, p. 163 ff.). But even a Paris operatic impresario would have had to get up very early in the morning to score off Verdi!

[6] At the second and third concerts Wolfram's song to the evening star was added as a *bonne bouche*. The singer was the Richard Lindau who has already been mentioned in connection with the French translation of *Tannhäuser*. (See Vol. II, p. 592). According to Wilhelm Altmann (*Mein Leben*, II, 1053), Lindau, though he had studied music to some extent, was not a professional singer but a business man: he died in 1900 as German Consul in Barcelona. There exist a number of unpublished letters from Wagner to him. Wagner, in *Mein Leben*, is very contemptuous about his amateurish performance of the *Abendstern* song. Lindau had only undertaken it after the French singer engaged for the concerts had failed Wagner.

For the *Tristan* Prelude Wagner had already made an ending for concert purposes, a copy of which he sent to Mathilde Wesendonk on the 19th December, 1859. The quaint belief still persists in some quarters that this ending was the work of Bülow. This delusion had its origin in the fact that when Bülow thought of giving the Prelude at a concert of his own in Prague, on the 12th March, 1859, Wagner had told him that he had no objection to his doing so, but that he (Bülow) would have to rig up a concert ending for it himself: "you mustn't expect one from me!" His reason for his refusal, as he explained later to Mathilde, was that at that time he could not quite

— (1) The *Flying Dutchman* Overture, (2) Selections from *Tann-häuser* (the March and Chorus, the introduction to the third act, the Pilgrims' Chorus and the Overture, (3) the Prelude to *Tristan*, (4) Selections from *Lohengrin* (the Prelude, the Bridal Procession, the Prelude to the third act, and the Bridal Chorus with the ending he had devised for this at his Zürich festival of May, 1853.[7]

The theatre, which held about 1550 people, was well filled at the first concert, the excited and polyglot audience consisting apparently in about equal parts of devotees, declared enemies or underground ill-wishers, the open-minded, and the merely curious. Meyerbeer was there, along with Berlioz, Reyer, Gounod, the Belgian composer and musicologist Gevaert, and the venerable Auber. Wagner conducted the whole programme without a score — a novelty in those days that always aroused comment. All the pieces created the utmost enthusiasm with the exception of the *Tristan* Prelude, which was beyond the comprehension of the average French music-lover of the period. A curious light on the habits of audiences in that epoch is thrown by a circumstance which Wagner remembered, apparently with approval, in later years. In his articles on *Public and Popularity*, which appeared in 1878 in the *Bayreuther Blätter*, he recalled that after the sixteenth bar of the *Tannhäuser* March the French audience, which, as he says, had been assured that he was " lacking in melody ", burst into applause. A similar experience, the reader may remember, had befallen Mozart in Paris in 1778 during the performance of his " Paris " symphony. One would have thought that the naïve ancient practice of breaking in upon a piece of music with applause had died out by the mid-nineteenth century, or at any rate was confined by that time to Paris. But Wagner gave another instance from his Vienna concert of the 8th January, 1863.

---

see how the thing should be done; since then, however, having completed the third act of the opera, the solution of his problem had become clear to him. (See RWHB, p. 118, and RWMW, pp. 201–2). A facsimile of the manuscript sent to Frau Wesendonk will be found at the end of the volume of Wagner's letters to her. On the 25th December he sent a copy of the concert close to Breitkopf and Härtel, asking them to bring out a special edition of the Prelude with this ending, for the benefit of concert conductors. (See RWBV, I, 182–3).

The provisional ending concocted by Bülow for his Prague concert must have been a rather lamentable piece of hack-work, judging from the seven bars of it which he himself quotes in his letter to Wagner of the 4th March, 1859. (See BNB, p. 431).

[7] See Vol. II, p. 180.

"Here", he says, "it was manifest that everyone was following intently the development of a diversely-articulated melodic idea, so that at the conclusion of the phrase they broke out into expressions of delight. Nowhere else in Germany have I met with anything else of this kind: there it was only, for the most part, from summary explosions of enthusiasm that I was able to gather that, in the mass, I had met with a general susceptibility." [8]

Oddly enough, he seems not to have frowned on a practice that is an abomination to the music-lover of today. We shall see later that he even indulged in it to a small extent himself in Bayreuth!

2

With his usual contempt for the critics, Wagner sent out no tickets for the Press. The journalists were there in full force, however, and their comments were almost wholly unfavourable: Wagner had for him virtually only his friend Gasperini and a writer personally unknown to him at that time — Emile Perrin, of the *Revue Européenne,* who had been Director of the Opéra-Comique, and was later to become the Director of the Grand Opéra.[9] Azevedo complained that he had heard only two good phrases the whole evening, " and two good phrases in three hours is rather little." Another critic plaintively wondered why Wagner, instead of losing himself in abstruse harmonies and modulations, did not elect to " write music like other people ": were he to do that, he would " take a high place in art." " If this is true music ", cried another, " I prefer the false." " Fifty years of this music ", wailed the critic of the *Ménestrel,* " and music is dead; for melody will have been slain, and melody is the soul of music." Others opined that there was the making of quite a good composer in this Richard Wagner if only he would not " reject the past absolutely " and work on a " system ".

Besides Perrin, two distinguished Frenchmen whom Wagner did not know personally testified their admiration and their sympathy. One was Champfleury, who published, shortly after the concerts, a brochure which showed so much genuine understanding of Wagner

---

[8] *Public and Popularity*, in RWGS, X, 73–4. Apparently the incident occurred during the orchestral preamble to Pogner's Address: before the singer could strike in, the audience insisted on an encore! See RWML, II, 960.

[9] Forgetting Perrin's many services to him, Wagner had the bad taste, in 1870, to make him one of the characters in the farcical *A Capitulation.*

and so much decent human feeling in the recognition of what his idealism must have cost him in suffering that Wagner always remembered it and its author with gratitude.[10] The other was Baudelaire, who had been so moved by Wagner's music that after the third concert he wrote him a letter of generous thanks.[11] He was a Frenchman, he said, —

" that is to say, a man scarcely constructed for enthusiasm, and born in a country where poetry and painting are hardly better understood than music is. I am of an age at which one no longer amuses oneself by writing to eminent men; and I should have hesitated for a long time to send you a letter expressive of my admiration if my eyes did not light, day after day, on absurd and shameful articles in which every possible attempt is made to defame your genius. You, sir, are not the first man in connection with whom I have had to suffer and blush for my country. In the end, my indignation has driven me to testify to you my gratitude: I said to myself, ' I want to mark myself off from all these imbeciles! ' "

He went on to say that he had gone to the Théâtre Italien prejudiced against Wagner, prepared in advance for another of those deceptions in which his life as an artist had been so rich. But he had at once been vanquished and convinced by the spirit of Wagner's music, its grandeur, its naturalness. " There can be no doubt that there are others like me ", he concluded. " All in all, you have reason to be satisfied with the public, whose instinct has risen superior to the wretched learning of the journalists." He signed his name, but refrained from adding his address in order that Wagner might not think he wanted anything of him. Wagner, however, had

---

[10] The brochure was also published in Leipzig, in a German translation (*Richard Wagner in Paris*), in the same year. Champfleury was not a musician but a painter and sculptor, and could therefore do no more than record the tremendous emotional effect the concerts had on him and on the audiences in general. What touched Wagner so deeply was the author's sympathy with him in his struggles. "It is said," writes Champfleury, "that the composer is exhausted, and that his face shows marked traces of mental strain. This is due not to his exertions in connection with these concerts — his reception by the public was too enthusiastic and too decisive for that — but to fifteen years of troubles and bitternesses which time will find it difficult to heal. . . . In vain I try to recall a martyrdom that could be compared with that of Richard Wagner: yet of all this there is not a hint in his works." The study was reprinted in Champfleury's *Grandes figures d'hier et d'aujourd'hui* (1861).

[11] Altmann, in his edition of *Mein Leben*, says that the letter has never been published. It is easily accessible, however, in TLFW, p. 198 ff. It is dated the 17th February, 1860: apparently it was sold to Jacques Doucet by Cosima during the period of post-war inflation in Germany.

no difficulty in finding him, and Baudelaire soon became a more or less regular attendant of his receptions on Wednesday evenings.[12]

3

Wagner's social backers in Paris belonged in large part to the republican and liberal parties and to that section of artists of all kinds which had anti-imperial leanings. He felt himself an alien in this milieu, however. He was aware how little the majority of these people really understood him: it was never his way to endure with patience the ordinary fribble-frabble of " society "; and his energies were almost wholly taken up with the business details in which his attempt to establish himself in the Parisian musical world involved him. So it was no wonder that he made few real friends, and that several of those who could make no impression on his intense self-concentration called him " egoistic " and " ungrateful ". Juliette Lamber, who was later to win a European celebrity as Madame Adam,[13] has described for us his " strange smile ", his " enormous

---

[12] Baudelaire had taken the trouble to read not only Liszt's brochure on *Lohengrin et Tannhäuser* but the English translation of *Opera and Drama*. He could not read *The Art-Work of the Future* or *Art and Revolution*, as he knew no German. Though he was not a musician, he wrote more intelligently about Wagner's novel aims than the great majority of the music critics of the period did. Like many other people, he thought that Berlioz had shown less cordiality towards Wagner than he might have done in his *Débats* article of the 9th February, though he praised his "magnificent eulogy of the *Lohengrin* Prelude from the technical point of view."

Jacques Crépet, in his annotated edition of Baudelaire's brochure *Richard Wagner et Tannhäuser à Paris*, mentions an unpublished letter of Baudelaire's of the 13th July 1849(?) from which it would appear that already at that time the poet was interested in Wagner, though he could have known nothing at first hand either of his music or his theories. The letter is a recommendation of some German critic or other who wished to publish, in Paris, a study of *Tannhäuser:* "you will be serving", said Baudelaire, "the cause of one whom the future will consecrate as the most illustrious among the masters." BAR, p. 509. But is 1849, one cannot help wondering, the real date of the letter?

[13] This remarkable woman, who, in the course of her long life, met almost everyone of importance in European literature and politics, died on the 24th August 1936, within a few weeks of her hundredth birthday. She was the last survivor of those who were associated with Wagner in Paris in 1860–1. Her reminiscences had an astonishing range: she had spoken, in her youth, to one who was present at the execution of Louis XVI.

We will do well to remember that Madame Adam's book was not published until 1904, and that in the 1880's she had been a violent opponent of Wagner: she particularly resented, as so many French patriots rightly did, the farce (*A Capitulation*) in which he made merry at the expense of the Parisians who suffered so much during the siege of 1870. When, in 1885, it was proposed to give *Lohengrin* in Paris, Madame

head " with its great forehead, his " enquiring eyes, by turns very gentle and very hard "; " but his unpleasant mouth ", she adds, " forced back his cheeks, and, with a sarcastic movement, brought his authoritative chin near his haughty nose. A strange face, as anti-pathetic as Bülow's appearance was attractive. Biting, clever, talk-ing on all subjects, for he understood them all, then suddenly com-mon, self-assertive, such was Wagner as he appeared at that time." [14] He was probably not seen at his best among these new acquaintances: he was embarrassed in his expositions of his own aesthetic by his none too fluent French, and the sense of being at war with the world undoubtedly gave the peculiar twist to his face at this time that is noticeable in the photograph reproduced as the frontispiece of this volume. (This is the portrait which, he told Frau Wesendonk, was " abhorrent " to him, for it made him " look like a sentimental Marat." [15] The fault was not, as he imagined, en-tirely that of the photographer who posed him: the bitterness of his existence at that period had brought out everything that was hard in his nature).

Wagner's contacts with Paris musicians were necessarily limited. With Meyerbeer, of course, personal intercourse was out of the question. Of the others of the older school, Halévy and Auber were the most friendly. The amiable Halévy, now sixty-one, gladly took up once more the acquaintance which had lapsed since Wagner's sojourn in Paris twenty years earlier. Though it is hardly likely that he had much understanding of Wagner's new aesthetic, Halévy stoutly refused to join in the general hue-and-cry against him. Hearing of this, Wagner called on him at the Institute, of which Halévy was the permanent secretary. The composer of La Juive had liked such fragments of his German colleague's music as he had heard, and he was keen to have Wagner's own explanation of the new " system " with which the journalists persisted in crediting

Adam organised a movement to prevent this. The generally unfriendly tone she adopts towards Wagner in her book seems to have been the result in part only of her personal dislike of him: she was unable to forgive him for having frequented, in 1860, the "Opposition" circle of the Countess d'Agoult. Edouard Dujardin acquaints us with a curious and little-known fact: Juliette Lamber's mother had been the Countess d'Agoult's governess, and Juliette herself had been the Countess's demoiselle de compagnie. See RMWF, p. 155.

[14] APA, pp. 219, 220.
[15] See Vol. I, p. 3

him. Wagner parted from him with a feeling of regret that a man of Halévy's undoubted talent should have lapsed into such moral and artistic enervation. Auber also had given up the struggle, but, thanks to his gay cynicism, was still able to turn an interested and amused eye upon the spectacle of the Parisian world. He had been born nearly ten years before the death of Mozart; and it was as long ago as 1828 that he had shown such decided possibilities in his *Masaniello*. Since then he had mostly been content to exploit his lighter vein; and Wagner, who had a sincere admiration for his gifts, and regretted that they had not come to finer fruition, could only regard him as another sacrifice to the declining French taste of his day. But the sprightly old man — he was now seventy-eight, and had still eleven years to live — was always cheerful over his ice at Tortoni's, where Wagner met him frequently. He still went regularly to the Opéra, where as a rule he fell asleep in his box. He asked Wagner to expound to him the subject of the much-discussed *Tannhäuser;* impressed by the amount of what seemed to him promising incident of a certain kind in it, he rubbed his hands cheerfully, and said, " Ah, il y aura du spectacle; ça aura du succès, soyez tranquille! "

Of the younger composers, Saint-Saëns, then only twenty-five, impressed Wagner by his technical assurance, especially his facility in score-reading. In those days Saint-Saëns was an ardent Wagnerite: Wagner was astonished to find that he knew *Tristan* by heart. Another enthusiastic admirer was Gounod: Wagner took to him as a man and was duly grateful for his social support, but, like most Germans at that time and since, could not forgive him his *Faust,* which had started on its triumphal career in March 1859. Before he left Paris in 1861 Wagner presented Gounod with the full score of *Tristan,* " being all the more pleased with his behaviour ", he says, " because no considerations of friendship had been able to induce me to hear his *Faust.*" [16]

---

[16] He attended a performance of it, however, in Wiesbaden in February 1862. He would perhaps have done better not to do so; for no doubt it was the irritation set up in him by this travesty of Goethe that accounted, in large part, for his display of ill temper over Gounod in the following November. The Hamburg theatre had recently not only produced *Faust* but had given the French composer a great ovation and presented him with a laurel wreath. With the best intentions the theatre authorities now proposed to fête Wagner in the same way if he would conduct *Tannhäuser* in Hamburg in return for his travelling expenses and his hotel board. To a man so

4

It was in March 1860 that Wagner and Rossini met for the only time in their lives. In 1906 one E. Michotte published a brochure [17] in which he claimed that he had been a member of the small circle of literary men who gathered round Wagner in Paris in 1860, that it was he who took Wagner to Rossini's house and introduced him, and that his brochure is based on notes made at the time of the conversation between the two. Wagner nowhere makes any mention of Michotte: perhaps he had forgotten his existence when he came to write *Mein Leben*. But his own accounts of his meeting with Rossini — in the autobiography and in the *Recollections of Rossini* which he wrote for the Augsburg *Allgemeine Zeitung* of the 17th December, 1868, a month after the Italian master's death — agree in essence with that of Michotte. The latter could hardly have known *Mein Leben*, which was not published until 1911; but he had obviously read the *Recollections*. His little book contains many errors on points of fact; but biographers and historians will hardly expect from any man a minutely accurate recollection of a conversation of nearly half a century earlier. All in all, however, when full allowance has been made for Michotte's mistakes and embroideries, there seems little reason to doubt that he was present at the interview, and that the talk was substantially as he represents it to have been.

Many malicious witticisms at the expense of Wagner and the " music of the future " were circulating in Paris; and Rossini being the accredited wit of the day, it was natural that they should mostly be fathered upon him. One story had become especially popular — that his friend Carafa [18] having declared himself to be on Wagner's side, Rossini invited him to dinner, served him with fish sauce but no fish, and told the protesting Carafa that sauce without fish was the right thing for any man who liked music without melody. This

chronically impecunious as Wagner was, this, of course, seemed not merely a gaucherie but an insult. He wrote back, he told Minna, declining the invitation, adding that "since the Hamburgers had already be-laurelled my friend Gounod I would regard that honour as simultaneously conferred on me, and would thank them for the railway and hotel expenses."

[17] MVWR.

[18] Thus in *Mein Leben:* in the *Recollections of Rossini* and elsewhere the story is told of Mercadante.

story having come to Rossini's ears, he wrote to a Paris paper protesting vigorously against being made responsible for what he called the *mauvaise blague:* he knew nothing of Wagner's music, he said, beyond the *Tannhäuser* March, which had pleased him very much when he heard it at a German watering-place: for the rest, he had too much respect for an artist who was trying to enlarge the scope of his art to permit himself jests at his expense. Encouraged by this, Wagner called on Rossini.

We can imagine, without difficulty, the conversation running on very much the lines indicated by Michotte. Wagner would be sure to thank the older man for his generous courtesy, to pay him a few tactful compliments on his finest work, and to ask for details of his famous visit to Beethoven in 1822. Rossini was certain to have sought information about Wagner's " system ", to have wondered what would become of the older type of melody, ensembles, and so on, in this new " system "; and Wagner must then have expounded, as well as he could in his none too fluent French, the essential principles of music drama as distinct from those of opera. When Wagner reminded him of certain scenes in *William Tell* and other works in which the Italian himself had broken with the conventions of his day, we can see Rossini saying with his sardonic smile, " So I have been writing music of the future without knowing it? " The two men parted with mutual respect: Rossini told Michotte afterwards that he was astonished to find in Wagner, instead of the intellectually-befogged Teuton he had been led to expect by his friends, a mind of the utmost lucidity and rationality, while Wagner assured Michotte that Rossini was " the only really great musician he had met in Paris." This agrees in essence with Wagner's account of the matter in the *Recollections:* Rossini, it appears, had spoken so sanely and so modestly of his own achievements and his limitations that he gave Wagner " the impression of the first really great and respectworthy man I had met with till then in the world of art."

Malice was soon at its favourite work again, however. Reports were carried to Rossini of imaginary attacks made on him by Wagner. Whether he believed them or not we do not know; but he certainly refused to take any step unfriendly to his German colleague. Wagner, for his part, felt that if Rossini could not of himself see the falsity of these reports, for him to go out of his way to allude to them would only be to increase whatever misunderstanding there might already be: he accordingly declined the suggestion of his friends that he should call on Rossini once more.[19] In 1861 Liszt was in Paris. He too urged Wagner to see Rossini, who, he assured him, remained correct and loyal in his attitude. Wagner's resolution, however, was unalterable: even when, after Liszt's departure from Paris, Rossini sent to Wagner's house some scores that Liszt had left behind him, with an accompanying letter in which he said that he would have brought them personally had his health allowed him to do so, Wagner still made no move towards a second meeting: " and thus ", he says, " I took it upon myself to bear the self-approach of behaviour difficult to judge, towards a man whom I honoured so sincerely." [20] The explanation of it all probably is that in that hotbed of envy, hatred, malice and all uncharitableness he felt it useless to struggle against the powers of evil; it was less trouble to curl a contemptuous lip at slander than to waste himself in trying to dissipate it. An attempt to enter into closer personal relations with Rossini would merely have led to an intensification of the campaign against himself. It was better to leave things as they were: if Rossini was the man of sense Wagner thought he was, he would not lend an ear to these calumnies; if he was not, explanation would be useless. Rossini can certainly be acquitted of any ill-will towards Wagner: he was neither fool enough to be blind to the fact that there must be something in the man who could win such admiration from men of the quality of Liszt, Bülow and many others, nor base enough to see merely an occasion for witticisms in the spectacle of an idealist fighting for his very life against journalistic gangsters the real character of whom no one knew better than Rossini himself.

5

One of the bitterest ingredients in Wagner's cup was Berlioz's manifest lack of cordiality. There was no personal unfriendliness and no sense of artistic rivalry on Wagner's part: what " rivalry ",

[19] "I see a good deal of Wagner and of Rossini, who can hardly endure each other", Mme. Kalergis writes to her son-in-law in June 1860. (MMKB, p. 81). Probably this relates to the weeks following the conversation between the pair, when friends of both parties were no doubt trying to make mischief between them.
[20] RWGS, VIII, 224. See also Wagner's letter to Minna of the 21st May, 1862.

indeed, could there be, he would have asked, between two men whose respective paths in music crossed each other at so few points as theirs? About the middle of January 1860, Breitkopf and Härtel had sent Wagner the first three copies of the engraved full score of *Tristan;* he immediately sent one to Berlioz (on the 21st), inscribed " Au grand et cher auteur de *Roméo et Juliette,* l'auteur reconnaissant de *Tristan et Isolde* ", with a covering letter that read: " Dear Berlioz, I am enchanted to be able to offer you the first copy of my *Tristan.* Accept it and keep it out of friendship for me." It was three weeks before Berlioz even acknowledged receipt of the score. " I know nothing more heartless — and to the other man [Wagner] it was a stab in the heart — than this three-weeks' silence ", Bülow wrote to Richard Pohl on the 2nd October, 1861. Berlioz was ageing now and incurably sick, nursing an inappeasable grievance against Paris for its long neglect of him and especially for the apathy of the authorities towards his still unperformed *Troyens,* and harried incessantly by the waspish woman he had taken as his second wife, whose venomous pin-point of a mind could see nothing in Wagner but a " rival " and a " traitor ". Berlioz had not been spiritually big enough, or he had lacked the physical health, to bear his disappointments with philosophy; and he now looked with an unfriendly eye on Wagner's efforts to make a place for himself in Paris. The musician Wagner he never understood: *Tristan* in particular would be completely beyond him, for he knew no German, while his own ideals of harmony, form and so on were so fundamentally different from Wagner's that on that account alone the score was bound to be mostly incomprehensible to him.[21] He lived now entirely wrapped up in himself, letting his accumulated grievances rankle in him, cold and suspicious towards not only Wagner but everyone in the Wagner circle.

---

[21] His copy of it is now in the Bibliothèque Nationale. Berlioz's marginal comments would make interesting reading today if published in full.

Berlioz insisted, in a letter of the 30th August, 1864 to Princess Wittgenstein, that he always kept his personal feelings and his artistic judgments in separate compartments — that he could no more help "adoring a sublime work of art by my greatest enemy" than "execrating some horrible absurdity by my most intimate friend." (BBCS, p. 141). This was written, however, some four years later. It may be freely granted that Berlioz's honest dislike of *Tristan* in 1860 had its roots in his very nature as a musician. But his general behaviour to Wagner at that time was influenced much more by personal than by artistic considerations.

"I will give Berlioz's works in my [Berlin] concerts", Bülow told Pohl in October 1861. ". . . Do not misunderstand me if I drag in personal matters: I attach no more to these than they objectively deserve. We cannot, however, ignore the fact that Berlioz has behaved as the more ungrateful, the more egoistic of the two [Wagner and Berlioz]: the third [Liszt] is not to be brought into comparison with them as a man. . . . Various other things [besides Berlioz's discourtesy in the matter of the *Tristan* score], which I will pass over to avoid fruitless chatter, were of a kind of which the German [Wagner] never *could* have been guilty. . . . How he [Berlioz] behaved to me in Paris! He did not, it is true, wound my self-respect; but his omissions of every kind were something I certainly had not expected!" [22]

Several people, among them, apparently, Berlioz, attended all three of Wagner's concerts. Juliette Adam tells us that at the second of them Paul Challemel-Lacour drew her attention to Berlioz applauding: "He is taken in spite of himself", he said to her. Whether Madame Adam's memory was at fault in later years, so that she confused the second concert with the third, or whether a somewhat similar incident happened on both occasions, is a minor matter. What is certain, from a contemporary letter of Challemel, is that Berlioz *was* "taken in spite of himself" under the immediate impact of some of Wagner's music, and that his jealousy of the composer was no secret to his friends. Challemel's letter of the 10th February 1860 to Emma Herwegh is interesting as evidence of how Wagner struck the average French listener of the period:

"Yesterday we went to Wagner's last concert. The hall was practically full, but there were evidently many free tickets. It seems to me beyond doubt that there is something in him — power, an absolute horror of the conventional, possibly genius. This will perhaps be disputed, for there is no limit to the venality, the ignorance, the spirit of routine, in a word the infamy of our journalism — the *Débats* excepted. I saw Berlioz: he seemed to me to be applauding heartily. As for a success in the theatre, that is another matter. The Parisian public is neither musical nor religious nor artistic: it merely wants to be amused. Wagner has not descended, and for his own sake I hope he never will descend, low enough to become a purveyor to our pleasures. Another trouble is that Wagner has a system: this would be no more than an inconvenience for his talent if he merely demonstrated it in his works, but he has made himself the theoretician of it. Now nothing frightens a timid public, the slave of success and tradition, so

---

[22] BB, III, 435–7.

much as the idea that someone is trying to impose a system on it. It will be in vain that Wagner has written beautiful, superb music, such as the overture to *Tristan and Isolde:* the imbeciles, that is to say the public, will always be afraid that they are going to listen to a pleading instead of to hear an opera." [23]

Like almost everyone else in Paris at that time, Challemel shuddered at the mistaken notion that Wagner worked to a " system " that was cramping his genius; but at any rate he had ears for what he heard, and a comprehensive contempt for the " imbeciles " who could not or would not see the composer as he really was. The sad thing was that Berlioz had already ranged himself, in the judgment of posterity, among these " imbeciles ".

His article appeared in the *Débats* on the 9th February.[24] He began in a quite eulogistic tone. He expressed a good deal of admiration, though with certain reservations, for the *Flying Dutchman* overture, the *Lohengrin* prelude, and certain other pieces. The *Tannhäuser* overture did not greatly appeal to him: he could not stomach the reiterated violin figure, nor what he called the " chromatic sequences, the extremely rough modulations and harmonies." His tone became less and less friendly as he went on; and by the time he had arrived at the *Tristan* prelude he was in full opposition. How far he had read in the score, which, by the time he wrote his article, had been in his hands more than a fortnight, it is impossible to say; but one surmises that he had not got much further than the prelude, which was evidently beyond not only his poetic but his musical comprehension, partly, no doubt, because harmonically it ran counter to his own prepossessions: all he could see in it was a long crescendo and diminuendo of the same type as that in the *Lohengrin* prelude, " without any theme but a sort of chromatic moan, filled, however, with dissonances the cruelty of which is increased by long appoggiature that take the place of the real note of the harmony. I have read and re-read this strange piece of music ", he continued, in a passage that has become historical; " I have listened to it with the profoundest attention and a lively

[23] HBD, p. 70.
[24] Champfleury was wrong when he said, in his brochure of 1860, that Berlioz delayed publication of his feuilleton until a month after the first concert, "fearing, with reason, to draw attention to so redoubtable a rival." From the 25th January to the 9th February was only a fortnight. Champfleury, however, was no doubt voicing contemporary Parisian opinion as to Berlioz's uncordial attitude towards Wagner.

desire to discover the sense of it; well, I have to admit that I still
have not the least notion of what the composer was driving at."

Then Berlioz proved himself to be a victim of the current delusion that Wagner wrote to a " system ". He could have had little,
if any, first-hand acquaintance with Wagner's theory of opera and
drama; but he blindly accepted the popular journalistic misrepresentation of it, and, having set up a scarecrow of his own in what
he took to be the image of Wagner, he proceeded to demolish it in
the belief that he was disposing of his rival. Beginning with the
protestation of a sincere desire to examine impartially " the theories of the Wagner school, which is generally known today as the
school of the music of the future ", he soon lost himself in misrepresentation of fact and sophistry of dialectic. If, he argued, the
school of the future says so-and-so, then he and all the rest of them
belong to that school heart and soul, Berlioz's so-and-so consisting
of pious platitudes which no one would dream of countering —
that contemporary music must be " free ", that the old " rules "
have no validity now, that the singers exist for the opera, not the
opera for the singers, that the music in opera must be everywhere
congruous with the character who is speaking, and so on. But if, he
continues, the musical code of the school of the future is that one is
tired of melody and of rational harmony; that only the " idea "
matters, the effect on the ear of the tones in which it is expressed
being of no concern; that the ear is to be abused by bad harmonies,
bad modulations and conflicting tonalities; that no consideration is
to be given to the art of singing; that only declamation is to be employed, and the uglier the better; that music is to be read rather
than performed; that " if it costs the singers as much trouble to
memorise and perform a work as to learn by heart a page of San-
scrit or swallow a handful of nutshells, so much the worse for them
— they are paid for their work, they are slaves "; that " if the
witches in *Macbeth* are right, and the beautiful is horrible and the
horrible beautiful "; then " if this is the new religion, I am far
from professing it: I have never professed it, I do not profess it
now, and I will never profess it: I raise my hand and swear, *Non
credo*." [25]

---

[25] BATC, pp. 305–317. We are inclined today to forget that Berlioz, for all his
marvellous originality in some fields of musical expression, was conservative almost

To such lamentable depths of foolishness can an intelligent man sink when he allows his personal prejudices and his artistic jealousies, working hand in glove with his limitations, to get the whip hand of his reason. If Berlioz had had the smallest understanding of Wagner's aesthetic he must have known that his own version of it was the crudest parody: if he had no direct knowledge of that aesthetic he had no business to represent it as he merely imagined it to be, and, for his own ill-natured journalistic purposes, would fain have it be.

6

Wagner was wounded by this exhibition not so much of honest obscurantism as of sheer ill-will on the part of one for whom, in spite of the unbridgeable gulf between their respective ideals of music, he had considerable respect as an artist and profound sympathy as a man. But he kept his temper, and his reply, which appeared in the *Débats* of the 22nd February and the *Presse théatrale* of the 26th, is a model of dignity and restraint. He begins by pointing out that he happens to be more fortunate than his French colleague in one respect — the mainly instrumental character of so much of Berlioz's music makes it possible for *him* to understand it, whereas his own work will always be, in large part, a sealed book to Berlioz by reason of the fact that it is organically interwrought with a language foreign to him. He then proceeds to correct Berlioz's misrepresentation of his " theories ". He himself is not even, he says, the inventor of the absurd term " music of the future "; that ridiculous phrase was the coinage of a German journalist, Herr Professor Bischoff, of Cologne; it had its origin in a mistaken reading of Wagner's *Art-Work of the Future* of 1849, the central thesis of which had been that true art was now so out of touch with the practice of the theatres that only a revolution in public opinion could bring about the needed reform: the new art-work he had in mind

---

to the point of being a reactionary in the matter of form. He was even capable of finding fault with Gounod for having, in his *Sapho*, sacrificed "form" to "the faithful expression of sentiments and passions"! His conception of form was evidently a very narrow one. Nor was his taste in contemporary opera particularly good, judging from the eulogies of Meyerbeer in his feuilletons and his correspondence: the man who could rhapsodise over the "grand", the "magnificent", the "sublime" in Meyerbeer could never have breathed easily in the mental atmosphere of a Wagner.

[19]

was nothing more dreadful than the drama restored, by means of music, to its ancient rights in men's souls.

" Judge then, my dear Berlioz, what my feelings must be when, after ten years, I find myself reproached with the phrase ' music of the future ' — that most nonsensical misunderstanding of an idea of mine which, even if erroneous, was at any rate deep-probing — and this time not by obscure scribblers, not by the herd of half or wholly inane wags, not by the chatter of the blind masses, who only repeat what they have heard, but by a man so earnest, an artist so uncommonly gifted, a critic so honest, a friend so sincerely valued as yourself; and that upon assumptions which, had I really any share in the formation of that absurd thesis, would suffice to rank me among the silliest of mankind. As my book will no doubt continue to be unknown to you, please take my word for it that there was not a syllable in it about music in itself and its grammar, or as to whether one should use it to write nonsense or folly. . . . For myself, I heartily regret having ever made public the ideas set forth in that book, for when the artist is so little understood, even by the artist, as has just now proved to be once more the case; when even the most cultivated critic is so much the victim of the prejudices of the half-educated amateur that, when he hears an art-work, he sees and hears things in it that as a matter of fact are not in it at all, while at the same time he misses what is the essence of it, — how is the thinker about art ever to be understood by the public, except much as my essay was understood by Professor Bischoff of Cologne? " [26]

He expressed the dual hope that his own works might obtain a hearing on French soil and that he might hear " the first, and, let us hope, the thoroughly successful performance of your *Troyens.*" The letter concluded with an assurance that *Les Troyens* would undoubtedly prove to be of significance in the world of contemporary music, and that he looked forward to it " because of the particular importance attaching to it from the point of view of the ideas and principles that have always guided me." These final sentences Wagner deleted when reprinting the *Letter* in after years in his collected works. They were merely a polite formula dictated by the circumstances of the moment, for, as he himself tells us in *Mein Leben,* what he had seen of the libretto of Berlioz's work had not made much impression on him; in later years there could have been no point, for him, in reprinting this somewhat irrelevant passage.

---

[26] *A Letter to Hector Berlioz*, in RWGS, VII, 82–86.

There was no personal breach between the two men: **Wagner**, indeed, still did what he could to keep alive the friendship, such as it had ever been. On the 22nd May he read an article by Berlioz on *Fidelio* which pleased him so much that he sent him a letter of warm appreciation. On the same day he wrote to Liszt, enclosing a copy of this letter, expressing sympathy with Berlioz in all his troubles, domestic and artistic, and ending with the remark that " in the world of the present only we three belong to each other — you, he, and I. But that is what one simply mustn't say to him: he kicks up his heels when he hears it."

> " Since my concerts ", says Wagner in the same letter to Liszt, " I have not met Berlioz: even before then it was always I who had to seek him out or invite him: he never troubled himself about me. It made a sad impression on me. I was not offended: I merely ask myself whether the good God would not have done better to leave women out of his scheme of creation; for they are rarely of much use, while as a rule they work us much mischief without in the end doing themselves any good. The Berlioz case has shown me once more, with anatomical accuracy, how a malignant woman can ruin a brilliant man to her heart's delight and make him ridiculous."

All we know of Berlioz's reply to Wagner's friendly letter is the extract given from it in Wagner's letter to Otto Wesendonk of the 5th June: " Berlioz has replied, and indeed very nicely: my lines seem to have made a great impression on him. But among other things the strange fellow says, ' I do not know if you have any illusions left; but as for myself, for many years now I have seen things as they are. . . . You are at any rate full of ardour, ready for conflict; I am ready for nothing but to sleep and die.' " Berlioz and the world had indeed little in common at this time; but one feels that had it not been for the malignant Mme. Berlioz he and Wagner might possibly have drawn closer together than they did.

In the following summer, by way of compliment to Madame Kalergis, who had helped him so generously to liquidate the debt [27] in which his concerts had involved him, Wagner gave a quasi-performance of the second act of *Tristan* in Pauline Viardot-Garcia's house, the great singer herself taking the female parts and

---

[27] See *infra*, p. 29. Wagner further presented Mme. Kalergis with the orchestral sketches for *Tristan*.

Wagner the others: Klindworth, who had come specially for the purpose from London at Wagner's expense, accompanied on the piano. Besides Madame Kalergis the only auditor present was Berlioz, who, seemingly, had been invited by Madame Viardot " with the avowed object of restoring harmony " between the two composers. The music evidently made no impression on Berlioz, who merely complimented the composer on " the warmth of his delivery ". Wagner may have expected no more from his French colleague than this; but he was plainly disturbed, as his account of the matter in *Mein Leben* shows, by the attitude of Madame Kalergis, who, as he says, " remained dumb ". The episode is interesting as showing the difficulty even some of his most cordial well-wishers had at that time in grasping the new musical and poetical idiom of *Tristan:* a year later Madame Kalergis wrote to her daughter, " *Tristan* is quite plainly impossible; it is an abstraction, intriguing to study, and with beauties in it in which one can perceive a sound idea; but as a dramatic work it will be rejected by the public everywhere." [28]

To a man of Wagner's simplicity in business matters it was the most natural thing in the world that he should now imagine he could recoup his losses on one set of concerts by giving another. The idea of repeating the Paris concerts in Brussels seems to have been suggested to him, with the best intentions, by Giacomelli; and as the terms, on the face of them, appeared to be favourable he jumped at the idea. There were to be three concerts in the Théâtre de la Monnaie, half of the net receipts of which were to go to him; he himself, he thought, could in no case lose anything, while he might possibly make a little. With an innocent of his type, everything was delightfully easy for his agent. Wagner's heart no doubt leaped within him when he found the first Brussels concert on the 24th March — for which the theatre abonnement was suspended, — so well patronised; but he soon discovered that owing to his misunderstanding of a clause in the contract the cost of the musical part of the proceedings, which was exceptionally high, fell to *his* account, so that virtually nothing of the receipts would come his way. He was assured that the second concert would make amends for this. But at that concert the abonnés exercised their rights in such

---

[28] MMKB, p. 96.

numbers that although the house was full the net receipts were practically nil; and as so far he had not made enough to cover even his
own travelling and hotel expenses, to say nothing of those of his
servant and his Paris agent, the idea of a third concert had to be
abandoned. " At Brussels ", he told Hans Richter more than nine
years later,

> " I was engaged for three concerts on the basis of half the receipts
> after expenses had been paid. The hall was crowded; but after the
> second concert I denied myself the advantage of a third, as it ap-
> peared, according to the computation of my agent, that while, to be
> sure, I did not owe him anything, I had to pay my travelling and hotel
> expenses out of my losses on my Paris concerts. . . . We can't count
> on any country in which French is spoken: take my word for that!
> We certainly don't get any money out of them. It has never yet been
> my experience to receive from a Frenchman five francs by way of
> earnings; it seems to go incredibly against the grain with them — to
> be quite insane indeed — to fork out money. Strangely enough, even
> my excellent friend Truinet [Nuitter] has become remarkably silent
> and mysteriously retiring ever since it became a matter of sending me
> the trifle due to me in respect of my Paris *Rienzi* royalties: he ap-
> pears to regard it as an absurdity." [29]

7

Brief as his stay in Brussels was, Wagner had time to make some
new acquaintances and enjoy a few fresh experiences. He met the
veteran critic Fétis *père*, who was reputed to have accepted, in years
gone by, bribes from Meyerbeer to attack him and " the music of
the future ": [30] Wagner had an argument with the old dogmatist
and succeeded in bringing him round to his own way of thinking —
which was decidedly an achievement where Fétis was concerned.
He also met a remarkable old diplomatist, Councillor Klindworth,

[29] RWHR, pp. 43–44. *Rienzi* had been produced in the Théâtre Lyrique by
Pasdeloup, with great success, on the 6th April, 1869; performances were given to
full houses between that date and the early part of June.
   [30] This François Joseph Fétis (1784–1871), who is remembered now mainly by his
Biographie universelle des musiciens, was an extraordinary character. He had the
courage to begin writing a history of music when he was about eighty! The first of
the five volumes to see the light was issued in 1869, when Fétis was eighty-four:
the fifth, bringing the story down to the fifteenth century, appeared posthumously
in 1876. An amusing account of the tough old fellow will be found in one of the essays
in the first volume of the *Bunte Blätter* (1872) of Ambros, who knew him well.

and his daughter Agnes Street — the latter a former pupil and love
of Liszt (she is the " Friend " to whom the letters in the third volume of Liszt's collected correspondence are addressed). Klindworth, who was a relation of Wagner's friend Karl Klindworth, the
pianist, had been a considerable figure in international politics in
the pre-1848 Metternich days, and Wagner found his reminiscences
entertaining. He was destined to come into the Wagner story again
in a curious way some four or five years later.[31] At the Klindworth
house Wagner met Madame Kalergis' daughter Marie and her husband, Count Franz Coudenhove. By the 30th March he was back
once more in Paris. Perhaps his greatest disappointment in Belgium had been the sight of the " citadel " of Antwerp. He had expected something answering more closely to the romantic conception he had formed of it when writing *Lohengrin,* but all he saw
from the other side of the Scheldt was a monotonous plain with
some sunken fortifications; and in later years he could never see a
performance of *Lohengrin* without a smile at the scene-painter's
too-imaginative creation of an imposing citadel on a mountain
height in the background of the scene.

His plans for paving the way for a production of *Tristan* by
means of his Paris concerts seemed to have failed utterly, and for
a time he looked like cracking under the strain of so much uncongenial labour and so many annoyances of all kinds. " Wagner ",
Bülow wrote to Raff on the 29th February, " is in such a state of
agitation as to cause me the gravest concern for his health. He
would gladly give himself up to the executioner the next day if
only he could have conducted a good performance of his *Tristan*
the night before." One of the most ironic features of the affair had
been that old M. Lucy, whose purse, it was hoped, would open wide
for the larger undertaking when he saw the success of the smaller
one, had been unable to come to Paris until the final concert; and
even to that, owing to the competition of a big dinner party the same
evening, he had been able to devote only an hour. He was highly
pleased with what he heard, but did not conceal from Wagner his
scepticism with regard to a German opera season in Paris. On the
1st January Wagner had been so confident of the success of the
coming concerts that he told Frau Wesendonk that he counted on

---

[31] See *infra,* p. 397.

[24]

opening his season of German opera in the Salle Ventadour on the 1st May: he would begin with *Tannhäuser* and *Lohengrin*, and *Tristan* would follow between the 1st and 16th June. Long before his third concert had been given he must have recognised that there was not the least hope of this dream coming true. The *Tristan* scheme was in any case full of difficulties, not the least of which concerned the German singers who would have to be imported: as time went on it seemed more and more unlikely that, with the best will in the world, they could all obtain leave from their respective theatres at the same time. As a result, however, partly of the sensation made by the concerts, partly of the activities of powerful friends at Court, Wagner was now beginning to be noticed favourably in high quarters. The Emperor had belatedly placed the Opéra at his service for a fourth concert on the 28th February, but Wagner did not accept it. Although he had himself conceived the idea of now making *Tannhäuser* the spearpoint of his attack on Paris, he was as astonished as other people when, about the middle of March, the imperial command went forth that the work was to be produced at the Opéra. Political considerations no doubt played a large, if not the largest, part in this sudden decision of Napoleon. The Saxon ambassador in Paris, Baron von Seebach, who had married a cousin of Madame Kalergis, was a Wagner enthusiast who lost no opportunity of sounding his praises at the French Court. Wagner's most influential patron there, however, was Princess Pauline Metternich, to whose husband (a son of the more famous Metternich, and in 1860 Austrian ambassador in Paris), he had been given a letter of introduction by Klindworth senior in Brussels.[32]

She was one of the most notorious figures in the higher Parisian society of the Second Empire. Partly out of crude animal spirits, partly out of a desire, as an aristocrat *pur sang*, to show her contempt for a parvenu Court, she distinguished herself, even in that milieu of extravagance and vulgarity, by the freedom of her tongue and the pert audacity of her behaviour. To beauty she never had the slightest pretensions. Her sycophants, as might have been expected, used to speak of her as a *jolie laide*, a description which, it

---

[32] Pauline, who was born in 1836 and died in 1921, was the daughter of a Hungarian magnate, Maurice Sándor, and a grand-daughter of the great Metternich. She had married Prince Richard Metternich, her uncle, in 1856.

has to be admitted, was at any rate fifty per cent accurate. Her face was that of an impudent urchin; [33] and the nearest she ever approached to being made a subject for the fine arts was when the sculptor Carpeaux modelled the ears of one of his statues upon hers. Her adorers, both in her lifetime and after her death, have grown lyrical over her gifts of mind and of spirit. But there is nothing either in her memoirs or in her recorded sayings to give posterity a lofty opinion of either her intelligence or her character: most of her belauded exploits were of the kind that are regarded as dashing only in " society " and by the literary parasites and vulgarians who in every age have gasped ecstatically on the fringes of " society ".[34] What in one of the Princess Pauline Metternich's maidservants would have been taken merely as evidence of a brain of feathers and a front of brass was lauded, in the Princess Pauline herself, as high spirits and a charming petulance. But she certainly did Wagner, and, so, indirectly, the cause of music, a considerable service when she helped to turn the Emperor's thoughts in his direction, even though, as one may not uncharitably suspect, her original motive was no more than the sufficiently common one among her feminine type of stealing a march on her social rivals and posing as the patroness of the coming man in opera. As might have been expected, however, her partisanship ultimately did Wagner as much harm as good. Even in Court quarters she was cordially disliked by many people not only for her own sake but as an Austrian whose mission, as everyone knew, was to bring about a rapprochement between France and Austria after the defeat of the latter in the Italian campaign of 1859. She was in too high favour with both Napoleon and the Empress for her own position at Court to be assailable by her rivals; but they could at least strike at her through the German musician whom she had taken under her wing.[35] " She was obsti-

---

[33] Her favourite description of herself was "le singe à la mode."

[34] She was cordially despised by those of her acquaintance whose standards of breeding were more exacting than her own. Count Horace de Viel Castel makes no attempt to conceal his contempt for her in his diary: "Princess Metternich", he notes in July 1860, "who has adopted the manners and the tone of the commonest sort of lorette, is a favourite of the Empress, who invites her to all her parties; she drinks, she smokes, she swears, she is as ugly as sin, and she tells stories!" *Mémoires sur le règne de Napoléon III, 1851–1864* (1883–4), VI, 81. Viel Castel gives us an edifying specimen of her "stories".

[35] Interesting light on the feminine personalities of the Court of the Second Empire, their vulgarities and inanities, will be found in Frédéric Loliée's *Les Femmes*

nately bent on imposing Wagner on France ", says Henri d'Alméras; " she did so, and got him hissed, which proves that at that
time there were in France, if not as many imbeciles as there are
today — that would be impossible — almost as many."

---

du Second Empire (Papiers intimes), in the same author's La Fête Impériale, and in
Henri d'Alméras' La Vie Parisienne sous le Second Empire. The real French aristocracy mostly cold-shouldered the Court, at which the dividing line between the
monde and the demi-monde was never very clear.

Princess Metternich's memoirs, which were published in 1920 (they were Eng-
lished in 1921 as The days that are no more), labour under the double handicap of a
shallow intelligence and an infirm memory. The chapter on her relations with Wagner
is an incredible farrago of errors of fact, of scene, and of date; the only place for such
rubbish is the waste-paper basket.

While it is true that Pauline's influence at Court must have counted for a good
deal in the Tannhäuser matter, it now seems probable that one of the prime movers
in it was Count Hatzfeld, an attaché in the Prussian embassy in Paris. In later years
Hatzfeld became German ambassador in London, where his Legation Secretary was
the Prince Ernst zu Hohenlohe-Langenburg whose correspondence with Cosima
Wagner has been published recently. In 1894 Hatzfeld gave Hohenlohe his account
of the pre-history of the Tannhäuser production. At a masked ball in the Tuileries,
he said, he recognised, under her mask, the Empress Eugénie, in whose favour he
stood high. She took him into a less crowded room to talk over a personal matter;
and he seized the opportunity to enlist her sympathies with the scheme for giving
Tannhäuser at the Opéra. At her request he afterwards submitted a written statement of details, which she brought before the Emperor. See BCWH, pp. 88–89.
Wagner himself says, in Mein Leben, that it was Hatzfeld who first brought him the
news that "on the preceding evening the Emperor had given orders for the production of Tannhäuser", though he adds that the prime motive force in the matter had
been the Princess Pauline.

That Hatzfeld played a considerable part in the affair is evident from Mein Leben;
but perhaps the first cause of all was Bülow. The Princess Augusta of Prussia had
given him a letter of introduction to Count Pourtalès, who, however, showed no
particular interest in either him or Wagner. At last Bülow invited Pourtalès and
Hatzfeld to a luncheon at Vachette's, a fashionable restaurant of the period: there he
presented Wagner to them. Pourtalès was greatly taken by Wagner: Hatzfeld was
henceforth a regular frequenter of Wagner's Wednesday evenings, and he was soon
able to inform Wagner that there was "a decided movement in his favour at the
Tuileries." (See the story as told in Mein Leben, and the contemporary letter of
Bülow to Bronsart, in BB, III, 301).

In 1877 the eternally feather-brained Pauline asked Liszt to play for her "the
sublime melodies" of Parsifal — before a page of these "sublime melodies" had been
written! See LZB, VII, 189.

CHAPTER II

THE YEAR 1860

1

WAGNER'S SOLE object in going to Paris, he had told Otto Wesendonk, was to win there a success with *Tristan* that would force the German theatres to take up the *Ring:* the result of it all, as it turned out, was not a success with *Tristan* but a failure with *Tannhäuser*. Yet paradoxically this failure in Paris became a success for him in Germany. It had half-amused, half-angered him to find himself once more, when he went to Paris in 1859, in what had become for him " the eternally youthful state of a débutant ". It had been so for a long time in Germany, he told Otto; then, just when he was establishing himself in the German repertory, he had had to fly to Zürich, where he had to begin over again once more; and no sooner had he persuaded the Zürichers to take him seriously than he found himself at the foot of the ladder again in Paris. " Always I am the beginner, who has to make himself known "; perhaps, he added humorously, it was because age and its rewards never came to him that he kept so young. " I seek neither applause nor triumphs ", he wrote to Otto later, " only the chance to put my new works before a few people, but adequately, so that I may die in peace." When he arrived in Paris he was known only to a handful of music lovers there who happened to possess a vocal score of one of his earlier operas or had heard one of these in Germany. For the French, opera still meant, in the main, Meyerbeer and Verdi.[1] During the next decade Wagner was to become the centre, if only the storm centre, not only of German but of European music. The Paris period of 1859/61, disastrous as it was in almost every respect, was really the turning-point in his fortunes, if only for the reason that during that period the ban on his residence in Germany

[1] "Today", Charles de Boigne wrote in 1857, "Verdi and Meyerbeer are the leading composers of France, Germany and Italy; but Meyerbeer is getting old, while Verdi is in his prime." BPMO, p. 336.

was in part removed. But during those two years he was as near shipwreck as he had ever been in the worst storms of his life until then; and, as usual with him, the reef on which he was in constant danger of foundering was finance.

At this time, be it remembered, he had nothing that could be called a regular income; and he was considerably richer in hopes than in assets. Little more money could now be expected from the German theatres in respect of his earlier operas; Paris would probably open up a new source of income for him if only he could float the older works there, but the local difficulties in his path could hardly be removed in less than three or four years. It would be many years yet before the *Ring* could be produced anywhere. A success with *Tristan* might mean money for him; but the larger German theatres showed no great anxiety to be the first to have the honour of producing the work, and in any case Wagner shuddered at the thought of its being given anywhere without himself being there to drill the meaning of it into singers, conductors and stage managers — which was one of the main reasons why he had planned to give it first of all, with German artists, in Paris. The economic consequences of his three concerts, given under such conditions as reigned in the Paris of 1860, had of course been disastrous. According to a letter of Minna's to Emma Herwegh, the rent of the Théâtre Italien, not including light and service, came to 8,000 francs, the orchestra cost as much, and the chorus 3,000 francs: in addition there was the advertising and the cost of the smaller halls for rehearsals.[2] The total deficit was in the neighbourhood of 11,000 francs. It was not until much later in the year that Madame Kalergis, having heard the extent of the disaster, presented Wagner of her own accord with 10,000 francs; at the moment there was nothing for it but to tap every possible or probable source to save himself from complete ruin. He angled for 5,000 francs for the first performance of *Tristan* in Vienna, but was told that the Vienna Opera was under the necessity of practising all-round economy just then. He next turned to Hanover, where the leading tenor was Albert Niemann, whom he had in view for the performance which he still thought might be possible in Paris. On the 27th January he

---

[2] HBD, p. 67. Minna repeats these figures, with one or two slight variants, in a letter to a Dresden friend, given in HMP, p. 282.

wrote to the Hanover Intendant, Count Platen, offering him the first German performance of *Tristan* on the same terms as those he had desired from Vienna, and stipulating that the Hanover Kapellmeister and the singers to whom would be allotted the two chief parts should attend the Paris performance in the following May, to receive the benefit of his personal training. Once more his hopes were dashed: Platen could neither afford the desired fee nor spare any of his company for a trip to Paris. Wagner now realised the final impossibility of carrying through his Paris project with regard to *Tristan*, for he had learned that neither Frau Bürde-Ney (Dresden) nor Frau Dustmann (Vienna) would be free in May.[3] For a moment he reverted to his old idea of producing *Tristan* in Strassburg; but this also came to nothing.

2

The reader will recall that Otto Wesendonk had agreed to advance him 6,000 francs on the score of each completed section of the *Ring*, and that Wagner had already received 12,000 francs in respect of the *Rhinegold* and the *Valkyrie* before leaving for Paris in the autumn of 1859. By the spring of 1860 he had further received payment from Otto for the still unfinished *Siegfried* score. During the winter of 1859/60 it occurred to Franz Schott, at that time sole partner in the Mainz firm of B. Schott's Söhne, that an opera by Wagner would lend distinction to his list of publications. Through the instrumentality of his friend Heinrich Esser, at that time Hofkapellmeister in Vienna, he got into communication with Wagner, who offered him the German, French and English publishing rights of the full score of the *Rhinegold*, together with Klindworth's piano arrangement, for 10,000 francs, the composer to retain the right to performing fees. Schott tried, on various pretexts, to beat him down to 7,500 francs, but in the end agreed to Wagner's terms; the publisher was further to have the first refusal of the remaining portions of the tetralogy. (At that time Wagner was confident that he would be able to produce the *Rhinegold* in the Salle Ventadour, in Paris, with " the best German singers ", in May

---

[3] RWAN, p. 95 ff. Wagner makes no mention in *Mein Leben* of these negotiations with Vienna and Hanover.

1861). Wagner received from Schott the 10,000 francs, in two instalments, in the latter half of January 1860. He ought, of course,
to have devoted part of this sum to repaying Otto Wesendonk's
first advance of 6,000 francs; but almost before Schott's money was
in his hands he realised that every franc of it had been lost on his
three Paris concerts. And once more hope flattered only to deceive.
About the end of May the Director of the Imperial Opera in Petersburg, General von Sabouroff, came to Paris with a dazzling offer
from the institution of which he was the head — Wagner was to
spend the following winter in Petersburg, conducting concerts and
producing *Tannhäuser*, at a fee of 50,000 francs, 25,000 of which
would be paid him in advance immediately the contract was signed.
The ironic Fates had seen to it, however, that by this time Wagner
had become inextricably involved in the preparations for the production of *Tannhäuser* at the Paris Opéra. Every suggestion he
could put forward as to fitting in the one engagement with the other
was turned down: the Petersburg proposal had either to be accepted
at once, just as it stood, or be rejected *en masse*. " I remained true
to Paris ", Wagner wrote to Wesendonk on the 5th June, " shoul-
dered the immeasurable misery of my Parisian existence down to
the period of the performances of my opera . . . and went back
to my Rue Newton." Unfortunately, he goes on to say, the deficit
on his concerts and the failure of the Petersburg negotiations had
made it impossible for him to repay Otto, as he had intended to do,
his 6,000 francs for the *Rhinegold* score out of the 10,000 francs
received from Schott. But a brilliant idea strikes him: he will give
Otto now a receipt for the money due to him some day for the fourth
section of the *Ring*, " and ask you to regard it as paying back to
you the 6,000 francs for the *Rhinegold*." Otto, as a simple business
man, must have smiled to himself at this ingenious financial plan
for feeding the dog its own tail; but he evidently raised no objection
to it. He could never have looked upon his agreement with Wagner
as anything more than a way of lending — or giving — him a considerable sum of money in his need without it looking too obviously
like charity.[4]

---

[4] According to Altmann (RWBA, II, 395) Wesendonk "wrote on the 23rd
November 1860, on the promissory note given him by Wagner on the 1st February
1860 in connection with *Siegfrieds Tod*, that he had released against this the first
section of the *Ring*."

It goes without saying that Wagner had to resort for financial help not only to several of his friends and acquaintances but to moneylenders. Through Malwida von Meysenbug he obtained from an English widow, one Madame Salis-Schwabe, a loan of 5,000 francs that was to cause him some bitter moments a few years later.[5] In the hope that the French rights in his earlier operas might be turned to some account he sounded the Paris publisher Flaxland with regard to these; and early in 1860 he was able to contract with Flaxland for the sale of his French publishing rights in the *Flying Dutchman, Tannhäuser* and *Lohengrin:* he was to receive 1,000 francs down for each of these works, with another 1,000 francs after the first ten performances in Paris, and a further 1,000 after the twentieth. Complications soon developed: Müller, his Dresden publisher, claimed that the French rights in the *Flying Dutchman* and *Tannhäuser* were not Wagner's to sell, threatened Flaxland with an action, and in the end had to be bought off with 6,000 francs. Pusinelli's " interests ", of course, had to go by the board in the difficult situation in which Wagner found himself just then. In *Mein Leben* he tells us that he duly notified Pusinelli of the agreement with Flaxland, but asked to be allowed, in consideration of his distressful situation, to retain the first payment received. To this, he says, his old friend consented. The letters to Pusinelli that have survived, however, are silent on this matter; there is a gap in the published-correspondence between the pair, indeed, from December 1859 to June 1862.

3

Wagner has been gleefully accused, by the type of person who is never happy unless he is accusing him of some crime or other, not only of failing, in *Mein Leben*, to give Flaxland due credit for all his kindnesses to him but of having, in effect, cheated him in the business deal. It is true that Flaxland (an Alsatian who had settled in Paris, where he opened a small shop in the Place de la Madeleine in 1848), was of considerable service to Wagner not only in large financial matters but in small — we find Wagner nobly offering on

[5] See *infra*, p. 371. For some of his letters connected with finance in 1860 see TLFW, p. 206 ff.

one occasion to repay a sum of five francs lent him by Flaxland to settle a bill at the " Glacier " — and that he deserved rather more mention than is accorded him in the autobiography. But we must remember that that work does not profess to be a detailed record of Wagner's borrowings during the fifty-one years of his life which it covers. For that record, indeed, there would have been all too little space: *Mein Leben* runs only to some nine hundred pages. Granting, however, that in the Flaxland case Wagner, as usual, failed to soar to the supreme heights of enthusiasm at the recollection of a one-time creditor — though as a matter of fact he has more praise for Flaxland than for most of the fauna — a conscientious biographer cannot allow to pass unchallenged the allegation that he deliberately and knowingly sold the French publisher something it was not within his competence to sell.

Wagner had a magnificent head for figures — if he often forgot to pay a debt he at least remembered the amount of it for years after payment of it was due — but in some departments of business he was as innocent as a child. Apparently he never scrutinised as closely as he should have done his agreements with publishers and others, or took expert advice before signing them; with the result that more than once in the course of his life he found that a contract committed him to rather more than he had contemplated at the time of signing it. He was ill-acquainted, too, with the intricacies of the copyright laws of his own and other countries, those amazing laws which often look to the innocent literary and musical victim of them as if they had been enacted by parliaments of fools for the benefit of gangs of rogues. It was over a nicety of international copyright that he tripped in the Flaxland case. He had never doubted, from the far away days when he first began to issue his scores through Meser, that a contract with a German publisher applied to Germany only, leaving him free to arrange on his own account for separate publication abroad. This question, of course, could not become one of practical importance until a foreign demand for his scores appeared to be likely, which became the case, so far as France was concerned, towards the end of the 1850's. Sooner or later, it seemed certain at that time, *Tannhäuser* would be given in Paris; and in the event, about which Wagner had no doubt, of its success there, a demand would spring up for the piano score and for " arrangements ". There was always the danger of pirated editions if he did not take in time the necessary steps to protect his French rights, either by the publication of an authorised French edition of the score or by complying with certain legal formalities in anticipation of this.

Through Meser he had published *Rienzi*, the *Flying Dutchman* and *Tannhäuser: Lohengrin* had been issued by Breitkopf and Härtel. With *Rienzi* he had no particular concern at the time we are now considering; he had almost lost interest in this work of his callow youth, and certainly had no desire to see himself introduced by it to a foreign public. *Tannhäuser*, which had been an astonishing success in Germany, was obviously the opera most likely to be taken up first by a French theatrical manager; and if this went well in Paris, presumably the *Flying Dutchman* and *Lohengrin* would follow it. To Flaxland, accordingly, he sold the French publishing rights in these three works in the early weeks of 1860. His complete honesty in the matter is shown by his at once informing Breitkopfs of his negotiations with Flaxland. He soon found that there was rather more in his contract of 1851 with the great Leipzig house than he had imagined. He became involved in a network of legal complications which the firm tried to elucidate for him in letter after letter, with the utmost patience and courtesy. It is unnecessary to go over this technical ground in detail here; suffice it to say that Breitkopfs gently but firmly insisted on their international rights as against Flaxland. But as the latter had no thought of issuing *Lohengrin* immediately, or indeed for some time to come — for everything depended on the Paris success or failure of *Tannhäuser* — there could be no actual collision between the French firm and the German one just then. The gist of it all was that Breitkopf and Härtel had no objection whatever to Wagner's arranging for an independent French edition of the opera, which, indeed, it is clear from the correspondence, he had the legal right to do: they merely insisted that as the Franco-German copyright laws gave them the right to sell their own publications in France and Belgium, French edition or no French edition, they would not tolerate any attempt on Flaxland's part to deprive the French music shops of these, and if necessary they would invoke the law against him.

4

Wagner recognised that Breitkopfs had a perfectly good case, so far as it went — not against himself but against Flaxland. But with *Tannhäuser*, which was what Flaxland was naturally anxious to take in hand first, it was quite another story. Whether the German publisher of this had really any foreign rights in it at all it is impossible now to say; but certainly Wagner received notice of the claiming of these rights with a dazed incredulity that endured with him to the distant days when he came to write his autobiography.

By his arrangement with Meser in 1844, Wagner was to provide the necessary capital for the publishing of his own scores, which Meser was to market for a commission of ten per cent on sales to the music-dealers. The reader will remember that after Wagner had abandoned hope of getting enough from the profits of the business to pay off his debts to his Dresden friends within a reasonable time he had assigned, in 1853, his " literary property " in the three early operas to Pusinelli, Hiebendahl and Kriete — that is to say, the publishing rights of scores and text books, but not the performing fees from theatres. In 1856 Pusinelli became sole proprietor of the business. Meser died in the same year; and in 1859 Pusinelli sold out for 3,000 thalers to the man who had managed the business for the preceding three years, one Hermann Müller.[6]

Now nothing can be more certain that not only did Wagner regard the foreign publishing rights of *Rienzi*, the *Flying Dutchman* and *Tannhäuser* as still his but this claim was tacitly admitted all along by the other people concerned. It was he, not the publisher, who went to Paris in January 1858 to guard against the possibility of the French copyright being filched from him by some pirate or other; it was he, not Pusinelli or Müller, who had all the trouble and expense connected with that matter. His correspondence with Pusinelli shows him repeatedly assuring his Dresden friend that he is doing all this in the interest of both of them, for he hopes some day to pay off Pusinelli out of the proceeds of the sale of his French rights. On the 17th January, 1858, for instance, he tells Pusinelli that a performance of *Tannhäuser* in Paris is probable within a year or so. If this materialises and the work proves a success, he

[6] See Vol. II, p. 421.

will be able to sell the copyright of a French version to a French publisher; " I then promise ", he continues, " to turn over to you the purchase price of this opera, and possibly of the other two, to the extent of your claims outstanding against me." He repeats this promise a year later; " the fees of the music-dealers for the French editions of my operas shall be ceded to you and Kriete . . . until you are both completely repaid." The sale of the business by Pusinelli to Müller had taken place in May 1859; five months after that we once more find Wagner telling Pusinelli that he " hopes to bring off a performance of *Tannhäuser* in Paris this winter ", in which case " I may have the good fortune to sell the opera to a Paris publisher, and hence have the satisfaction . . . of promptly repaying a surely not small part of my pecuniary debt to you." [7] In *Mein Leben* Wagner says categorically that in the interests of Pusinelli he expressly reserved to himself, at the time of the sale of the business to Müller, the right to dispose of the French copyright, and that according to Schmidt, the Dresden lawyer who had acted for Müller in the matter, this reservation had been accepted.

5

M. A. Dubuisson, in his article *Wagner et son éditeur parisien* in the *Revue Musicale* of the 1st October, 1923, gives us a highly-coloured account of what he alleges to have happened after the conclusion of the agreement between Wagner and Flaxland. The latter, it seems,

"had hardly signed the contract for the purchase of the scores of the *Flying Dutchman*, *Tannhäuser* and *Lohengrin* when a letter from Germany warned him, under the threat of an action, not to publish anything (*sic*) of Wagner's in France, for the excellent reason that Wagner had already sold to the German publishers (*sic*) the property in the scores in question not only for Germany but for all foreign countries. Astonished and perturbed, Flaxland informed the Master of these pretensions on the part of the German publishers (*sic*). Wagner pretended to be overwhelmed, cried aloud, and cursed, as he so well knew how to do in moments of rage, those stupid Dresden people who had made him sign an agreement that was incomprehensible to him. In order to put an end to the trouble Flaxland went to Dresden, dis-

---

[7] The correspondence with Pusinelli will be found in full in RWAP.

cussed the matter with the German publishers (*sic*), and finally repur-
chased the rights in the three (*sic*) operas for France. On his return
to Paris he told Wagner the result of his journey, entered the affair
in his profit-and-loss account, and said no more about it."

It is difficult to make this circumstantial story fit in with all the
known facts. Has M. Dubuisson, perchance, achieved the feat of
merging Müller of Dresden and Breitkopf and Härtel of Leipzig
into a single firm? He speaks of the " publishers " in the plural —
a mode of reference that would apply to the Leipzig firm but not to
Müller, who still traded alone as " C. F. Meser ". M. Dubuisson
appears to be under the impression throughout that the three operas
had all been published by the same German house, whereas Müller
was concerned only with the *Flying Dutchman* and *Tannhäuser*,
Breitkopfs only with *Lohengrin;* and a visit " to Dresden " and a
talk with the " publishers " there about an " incomprehensible
agreement " foisted on Wagner by " stupid people " would have
no applicability to Leipzig and *Lohengrin,* nor could Flaxland " repurchase " the rights in all three operas in France from anyone
whatever in Dresden. The remark about Flaxland having " hardly
signed " the contract with Wagner when a letter from Germany
threatened him with an action would appear to apply to the case of
Breitkopf and Härtel. But it was Wagner himself who had told
Breitkopfs *in advance* (on the 25th December, 1859) of his plan for
a French edition of both *Lohengrin* and *Tristan,* and had asked
their advice as to the best way to go about this. Their reply was
not the threat of an action against either him or Flaxland, but a
cordial approval of the plan — so long as an understanding could
be arrived at with Flaxland that would protect their own legal rights
in France. Again there is no necessity for us to spend any time
over the copyright technicalities of the matter as elucidated in
Breitkopfs' letters. These are not the subject now under discussion.
All we are concerned with is the moral aspect of Wagner's conduct
in his dealings with Flaxland; and it has to be said that from first
to last in Breitkopfs' letters there is not the faintest suggestion that
they regarded him as having done anything he ought not to have
done: they merely explained to him, as experts, the bearing of the
law of international copyright on a case of this kind.

As regards the *Flying Dutchman* and *Tannhäuser,* it is quite possible that Flaxland went to Dresden to have a little talk with Müller about that matter. The problem is, when did he go? M. Dubuisson conveys the impression that he did so, as a consequence of Müller's threats, immediately after the signing of the agreement. If that were so, and Flaxland had then had to " repurchase " the French rights in these operas, and had written off the sum (6,000 francs, as we learn from *Mein Leben*) in his profit-and-loss account, it is difficult to understand why there is no reference whatever to this awkward little matter in the further letters from Wagner to Flax-land printed by M. Dubuisson. In December 1860 — i.e., a year or so after the conclusion of the deal with Flaxland — we find Wagner saying that he has been re-reading the contract and has recognised that, owing to the financial embarrassments in which he was involved at that time, he had parted with his French rights for less than they would probably turn out to be worth. Flaxland, apparently, had shown signs of a willingness to be accommodating in this regard in the event of sales (presumably of arrangements of " morceaux ") coming up to expectation. This has actually been the case, says Wagner. He turns a deaf ear, he continues, to the friends who advise him to try to have the contract revised; he pre-fers to believe that in the event of a continuing success Flaxland will spontaneously do the handsome thing by him. Meanwhile Flax-land can do him an immediate and real service by giving him bills for 4,000 francs in anticipation of the fees the publisher has con-tracted to pay him in virtue of future performances of *Tannhäuser* (250 francs a performance): these bills M. d'Erlanger is willing to discount for Wagner. In the following June we find him pro-posing another deal to Flaxland. According to their contract, the publisher was to pay him, in all, a further 2,000 francs for *Tann-häuser*, 4,000 for *Lohengrin*, and 4,000 for the *Flying Dutchman*, after so many performances of each of these works. He will be willing to compound here and now, he says, for 7,000 francs for the three operas for all time, though it will suit him still better if Flaxland will allow him to throw in *Rienzi* also for another 3,000 francs, making a total immediate payment of 10,000 francs for the right for all time to issue these four works of his in France. Seven months later, in January 1862, he makes yet another desperate attempt to induce Flaxland to come to his aid. The publisher's replies to these letters have not been made public, but M. Dubuisson assures us that after the failure of *Tannhäuser* in Paris in March 1861 (it was withdrawn after only three performances), the generous Flaxland of his own accord sent Wagner, of whose desperate situation he was well aware, a purse containing 3,000 francs — i.e., 750 francs in fulfilment of his contract as regarded these three performances, the remainder amounting to what, in the circumstances, was either a long loan or a gift pure and simple, according to how one prefers to look at it. It is difficult to believe that business and friendly relations between the two men in 1860 and 1861 were of the kind suggested by the letters and events described above had Flaxland, in the early part of 1860, been compelled to pay Müller 6,000 francs owing to shady conduct on Wagner's part: alternatively, if he *had* been mulcted in this sum by that time he must surely have been convinced that Wagner had acted honestly according to his lights and was in no way to blame for the unfortunate turn that events had taken in Dresden.

6

It seems probable, however, on the evidence available, that it was not until some time in 1863 that Müller began to make real trouble with Flaxland. For in September of that year Wagner, who was at that time living in Penzing, near Vienna, addressed an urgent request to Franz Adolf Schmidt, the Dresden lawyer who had arranged matters between the creditors and Müller in the sale of the Meser business in 1859.[8] He appeals to Schmidt for legal attestations (1) that at the time of the sale to Müller he (Wagner) had given him a written assurance that he would pay over to his Dresden creditors any sums received by him for a French edition of the

---

[8] In *Mein Leben* Wagner says that Müller "at once" began to complain that his rights in France were being prejudiced, "and so pestered Flaxland over the affair that the latter felt justified in raising difficulties against me." Presumably the point at which Flaxland was compelled to buy peace for 6,000 francs came much later: for Wagner says that when, as a result of this payment, Flaxland alleged that the composer now possessed no French rights at all in his early works, he "repeatedly" asked the Dresden lawyer, Adolf Schmidt, for a copy of the correspondence relating to his reservation of certain rights in the sale to Müller in 1859, but received no answer to any of his letters. This is confirmed by his letter of the 2nd September 1863 to Schmidt, which makes it probable that it was about this time that Müller brought the matter to a head with Flaxland.

three operas, with the object of making good to those creditors whatever difference there might be between the amount due to them and
the amount realised by the sale of the Meser business to Müller,
(2) that Schmidt had told him in writing that the creditors had
assented to this proposal, (3) that in the early months of 1860 he
had written to Schmidt, from Paris, informing him, as the creditors'
lawyer, that he had made an arrangement with Flaxland for a
French edition of his works. Wagner, it appears from this letter,
has already made similar applications to Schmidt, but has received
no reply. " As Herr H. Müller ", he concludes, " is now contemplating bringing an action against Herr Flaxland, it behoves me to
prove that when I conveyed to this Paris publisher the right to publish a French edition of my operas I acted legally and with a clear
conscience; and consequently, as my honour is at stake, I appeal
to *your* sense of honour to let me have your testimony on the three
above points as quickly as possible."

This surely places it beyond question that Wagner had done nothing in any way dishonourable in the matter. What he is now saying
to Schmidt is in complete consonance with everything he had had
to say on the subject to Pusinelli in years gone by. Obviously it
never occurred to him that there could be the slightest doubt as to
his legal right to the French copyright; [9] he had informed Schmidt
himself, as representing Pusinelli's interests, of the negotiations
with Flaxland; and now that Müller is threatening Flaxland with an
action in connection with these French rights he feels that all he
has to do is to appeal to the attorney's sense of honour to obtain
the declarations he wants. Schmidt's reply is curious. He begins
by reminding Wagner that in the sale of 1859 he had been the
lawyer for the creditors and had acted solely according to their
instructions. Evidently Pusinelli had handed over to him at that
time (or earlier) the letters of Wagner to him that bore on the
question of the debt, for the passages that Schmidt quotes from
these are in accordance with the text of the Wagner-Pusinelli letters

[9] It is beyond question that his original agreement with Meser left the foreign
rights of publication in Wagner's possession. This is proved by his letter of February
1844 to Avenarius: "I am publishing my operas, under the most advantageous conditions and with the best prospects: my publisher, Meser of Dresden, advises me to
secure the French and English copyright against all future eventualities. . . . (RWFB,
p. 128).

published in recent years by Mr. Elbert Lenrow: these quotations
relate to the steps taken by Wagner in 1858 to protect his French
copyright, and to his promise to devote the receipts from a French
edition of the three operas to reducing his debt to Pusinelli and
others. After giving Wagner a short exposition of the copyright law
as between Saxony and France, Schmidt coolly informs him that

" the case therefore stood thus after your Paris journey of January
1858: (1) a contract was to be made, and was later made, with Müller
for the marketing of the operas in question, at the cost of the conces-
sionaires of your property; (2) the property rights of the concession-
aires . . . had already by that time been ceded by you *for France
also* and their legal validity has not been called in question, although
you yourself were willing to see to the *execution* of this matter; (3) it
was doubtful whether there would be any further returns to the creditors from the German market, you yourself, indeed, centreing all hope
in a sale of the operas in France." [10]

So that was that! The lawyer, for all his professional verbiage,
did not make it clear to Wagner just how or when he had forfeited
his French copyright: he merely informed him, in 1863, that he
had forfeited it. On the face of it it looks as if somehow or other,
at some stage or other, Wagner had been jockeyed — on strictly
legal lines, of course — out of his property. Precisely what had
happened it is difficult to decide without a knowledge of all the legal
documents concerned; but it is easy to see that with Wagner in
Switzerland and the others in Dresden, with his rights and reservations as regards Pusinelli never put into precise legal form, with
a vendor (Pusinelli) to Müller unversed in the technicalities of
international copyright, with a shrewd business man (Müller) who
could be counted upon to see that any agreement for purchase did
not operate to his own disadvantage, and with a lawyer who, on his
own showing, was not concerned in the least with Wagner's interests
but only with those of the Dresden people, it would have been a
miracle had the contract for sale contained nothing that could be
made to operate to Wagner's disadvantage in the future. It is quite
possible that had the matter come into court in 1863 it would have
been found that Müller was claiming rather more than he was en-

---

[10] See Ludwig Schmidt's article, *Wagner-Akten*, in ZIMG, 1901, pp. 4–8. Apparently the author of this article was a descendant of the attorney Franz Adolf Schmidt,
whose papers relating to Wagner are now in the Dresden Public Library.

titled to under the agreement for sale to him. Wagner never wavered in his assertion that he had reserved the French copyright to himself, and he seems to have consulted a legal luminary in Vienna — presumably in 1863 — with the object of compelling the reluctant Schmidt to supply him with a copy of the correspondence that had passed between them in 1859: he was told, however, that he " must give up hoping to get this kind of evidence ", as he " had no legal means in his possession to force the lawyer to give it if he were not inclined to do so ".

Whether Wagner had or had not inadvertently signed away his French rights, it is clear to anyone who will take the trouble to read all the tiresome documents relating to the case that there is not the smallest basis in fact for the insinuation that he had knowingly misled Flaxland at the time of the sale to him of the *Flying Dutchman* and *Tannhäuser*. His letters over a longish period consistently show that he looked upon the foreign copyright in these early operas of his as his one ewe lamb, the one piece of solid property he could call his own after all his years of struggle, a possible source of income to him some day when his debts in Dresden should be liquidated; and he was manifestly not only surprised but shocked to be told that the lamb had somehow or other ceased to be his. Apparently he could never be convinced that Müller was doing anything more than bluffing Flaxland with his threats of legal action: in October 1864 we find him telling Pusinelli that Flaxland had been induced to pay Müller — who was by this time doing very well out of the business he had acquired so cheaply — " behind his [Wagner's] back ". It is not improbable, indeed, that Wagner wanted to fight the case in 1863 or 1864, but that Flaxland had decided to pay Müller for mere peace' sake. Flaxland's warm friendship for Wagner in later years, it may be added, is not quite consistent with the theory that he believed the composer to have practised a trick on him in connection with the agreement of 1860.[11]

---

[11] A few years later Müller sold his Wagner rights to the publisher Adolph Fürstner, and this worthy had the gay assurance, in 1876, to claim from Wagner a share in the royalties from *performances* of *Tannhäuser*, to which he must have known he had not the smallest title. For well over thirty years that unfortunate Dresden publishing venture of Wagner's youth was the source of nothing but worry to him; and when at last the profits from the scores began to come in, owing to the spread of his fame, it was not he who benefited most by them.

7

In the midst of all the anxieties that were accumulating about him in the early part of 1860, Wagner discovered that in taking the Rue Newton house for three years and paying the rent for the two final terms in advance [12] he had been bamboozled by his landlord. In a letter to this gentleman of the 17th February, 1860 we find him expressing his great concern at the rumours which have reached him that in a little while the house will be impossible of habitation.[13] He soon discovered what was afoot. The authorities had long ago resolved to sweep away the Rue Newton in order to lay out the neighbourhood on its present broad lines, but had refrained from making their plans public earlier so as not to attract inconvenient claims for compensation. The rebuilding scheme involved a sinking of the street level of the Rue Newton some ten or eleven feet; very soon Wagner's friends could call on him only at the risk of their lives, and finally the house was approachable neither by carriage nor on foot. The landlord, who seems to have known well enough what was in the wind when he let the house on terms so advantageous to himself, blandly suggested that Wagner should bring an action against him for damages, whereupon he in turn would sue the municipality. Wagner duly brought his action, but of course obtained nothing: and in October, with some two years of his lease still to run, he had to take a fresh apartment in the Rue d'Aumale. He not only lost everything he had expended on making the dilapidated Rue Newton house inhabitable, but had the costs of a futile legal action to pay in addition to the expense of yet another removal.[14]

A curious episode of this period that has not yet been fully elucidated was that connected with a young Paris banker, Emile[?]

---

[12] See Vol. II, p. 589. The house had only been in existence since 1856. Apparently Wagner had taken over part of the still unexpired lease of Octave Feuillet; in the municipal survey of 1860 the tenant's name is given as "M. Feuillet Octave, homme de lettres"; underneath this is "Vaegner, artiste". It was a novelist, again, whom Wagner succeeded at No. 2 Rue d'Aumale, his predecessor there being Amédée Achard. See RMWF, p. 172.

[13] TLFW, p. 209.

[14] In the Burrell Collection is a bill of one Monsieur Churnis, decorator, Rue de Ponthieu, for decorations in the Rue Newton house from October 1859 to January 1860. The account occupies eleven and a half folio pages. See CBC, No. 344.

Erlanger.[15] Wagner was informed by a friend, towards the end of 1860, that this gentleman would like to make his acquaintance. He was on the point, he says in *Mein Leben*, of answering jestingly that he took no interest in any banker except for his money when the intermediary hinted that it was precisely in this way that Erlanger contemplated being of some use to him. He found him a pleasant young man who had heard and liked Wagner's music in Germany and was sympathetic towards him personally. Erlanger suggested becoming, in a sense, Wagner's French business man: he was to advance him, then and in the future, whatever funds he might require for his maintenance, against the security of an assignment of Wagner's theatre receipts from his operas in Paris. (From some letters summarised in Altmann's *Richard Wagners Briefe nach Zeitfolge und Inhalt*, however, it would appear that it was Wagner who approached the banker with a request for assistance). On the 20th December we find him asking Erlanger for an advance of 4,000 francs against Flaxland's bills for that amount: this is evidently the transaction to which reference has already been made on p. 38. As we shall see later, the business connection with Erlanger did not last long; but the young banker evidently served for the time being to stop one of the leaks in Wagner's finances, and in *Mein Leben* Wagner recognises his services, and the goodness of heart that had prompted them, with a warmth of tone that is somewhat unusual with him where creditors are concerned.

According to the Countess d'Agoult (in a letter to Emma Herwegh) he petitioned the French Emperor for a pension of 6,000 or 7,000 francs, but was merely laughed at at the Tuileries.[16] It is not at all improbable that he may have naïvely suggested something of the kind in confident anticipation of his royalties from the Opéra. There is no evidence that he indulged himself in any particularly oriental " luxuries " in Paris, though for appearances' sake he had to keep up a certain style and entertain fairly generously.[17] His financial stringency towards the end of 1860 can per-

---

[15] On an envelope which has survived Wagner addresses him, perhaps in error, as Victor Erlanger.

[16] HBD, p. 74.

[17] The Rue Newton house consisted of an entrance hall, a drawing room and a dining room on the ground floor, a large room and two smaller ones on the first floor, and a large room and three smaller ones on the second. Minna occupied the top floor and Wagner the first.

haps be accounted for, in the main, by the loss on his concerts and the legal and other expenses connected with the Rue Newton house and the removal to the Rue d'Aumale. Between the autumn of 1859 and the end of 1860 he had had 18,000 francs from Otto Wesendonk, 6,000 from Schott, about 3,000 from Madame Schwabe, perhaps 3,000 from Flaxland, and various loans the amount of which we cannot trace. If we rule out the 10,000 francs given him later by Madame Kalergis, as merely off-setting the loss on his concerts, it would appear that he had got through some 30,000–35,000 francs in rather less than eighteen months, which, in the circumstances, cannot be called grossly excessive, at any rate for Wagner. Generally speaking he could raise money only by pledging the future of his works; and as he had by now sold or hypothecated almost every publishing right he possessed, obviously the outlook for some distance ahead was black unless the Paris royalties for *Tannhäuser* should prove considerable. The strain of all these worries, in addition to the labour imposed on him by the supervision of the *Tannhäuser* translation and by his participation in the Opéra rehearsals, finally brought on a serious illness at the end of October. He went down with some form of fever which he calls typhoid, though it would probably not be called that today, during which he developed brain-fever; he suffered from hallucinations, and plagued poor Minna and the faithful Gasperini with all kinds of crazy demands, among them that he should be taken to Naples, where he would be cured by conversing with Garibaldi. The illness, which lasted some weeks, left him extremely weak, and partially blind for a time. In December he had reluctantly to ask Wesendonk for a loan — against those always hypothetical Paris *Tannhäuser* royalties ! — which the illimitably good Otto supplied as usual.

It is an ironic reflection that Wagner could easily have become a rich man before he was fifty, and thereby not only saved himself a great deal of suffering but protected his memory against much unkind criticism on the score of his manifold borrowings, had he only had the foresight to be born not a German but an Italian composer. It was by taking that simple precaution that Verdi amassed a fortune so early. " In ten years ", said Charles de Boigne, writ-

---

The apartment in the Rue d'Aumale was smaller, consisting, as far as one can gather, of a drawing room, a dining room, a large bedroom and two smaller rooms.

ing in 1857, " Verdi has acquired one of those colossal fortunes which as a rule can be made only on the Bourse." For each of his recent scores Ricordi had paid Verdi 60,000 francs; in addition there were the " composer's rights ", which in Italy were very valuable.

> " A composer writes an opera ", explains de Boigne; " he sells the score to a publisher, who hires it out for a three months' season to various theatres. Verdi gets half of whatever is received in this way. *Il Trovatore* cannot be had for less than 5,000 francs a season: there are eighty theatres in Italy and four seasons in the year: work it out for yourself! Not all the theatres are in a position to pay 5,000 francs for the hire of a score: if they were, the composer would be too well off! For all that, *Trovatore* itself has brought Verdi 80,000 francs in a single year."

While the poor German composer, exploited by both theatres and publishers, looked longingly toward Paris as likely to afford him wealth beyond the dreams of *his* avarice, Verdi could afford to curl a contemptuous lip at Paris, where the composer's profits were cut into by the singers.

> "During a period of twenty-five years the four hundred perform-ances of *Robert the Devil,* the greatest success ever known, brought Meyerbeer only 45,000 francs. . . . Compare the twenty-five years of *Robert* with a single year of *Trovatore!* Yet while the composer is so shabbily rewarded, the four hundred performances of *Robert* have certainly brought the Opéra more than 3,000,000 francs; and the singers have made far more in one year by singing Meyerbeer's music than the composer himself has made out of it in twenty-five." [18]

Wagner would have been well content to have drawn from the Paris performances of *Tannhäuser* in twenty-five years the paltry 45,000 francs that Meyerbeer had drawn from *Robert:* we shall see shortly how much *Tannhäuser* actually brought him.

8

The one relatively bright spot on the year 1860 was the ending of his exile from Germany. It came with what was on the whole surprising suddenness. All through 1859 the King of Saxony and his ministers had clung obstinately to their rigid legalistic formula

---

[18] BPMO, pp. 335–6.

— there could be no question of a pardon for Wagner until he complied with the law by returning to Dresden and standing his trial as the other participants in the rising of 1849 had had to do.[19] To this it was impossible for him to consent: neither would his health, he said, be able to endure the strain of a trial, nor could his memory, after eleven years, be expected to serve him faithfully with regard to many of the matters about which he would presumably be examined. In none of his appeals, be it observed once more, does he deny that he had done enough in 1849 to make him liable to arrest and trial along with Röckel, Heubner and the others. He unreservedly acknowledged, he had written to the new Saxon Minister of Justice, von Behr, in February 1859, the justice of the conditions laid down for the grant of a pardon, and confessed, " as I did years ago, my punishable conduct with sincere repentance." Against the abstract rightness of the King's attitude towards him he had nothing to urge; he merely pleaded special consideration in view of his health and of his lamentable position as a German artist excluded from his fatherland. As neither he nor the authorities would or could give way, the situation by the end of 1859 was one of seemingly permanent deadlock. Yet even at that time, strangely enough, he indulged himself in the hope that the ban might be lifted, if only for a little while, to permit of his producing *Tristan* in Dresden; Lüttichau appears, in fact, to have looked not unfavourably on this scheme. It came to nothing, however; and it seemed, at the beginning of 1860, as if Wagner's sole sheet-anchor now was Paris. But the financial failure of his concerts there, meaning, as it did, not only an aggravation of his private embarrassments but the ruin of all his hopes for a *Tristan* production to be financed by Lucy, drove the despairing man to think once more of Germany and its many opera houses, and almost to believe now that any danger, any humiliation, would be better than utter frustration as an artist to the end of his mortal days.

On the 3rd March, by which time his disillusionment with regard to his concerts was complete, he wrote to Frau Wesendonk that now he could have but one goal in view — the production of his *Tristan* somehow, somewhere: that achieved, he is willing to die. But *Tristan* would be possible in Paris only by way of further trials, further

---

[19] See Vol. II, p. 536 ff.

humiliations, on his part; and rather than undergo these he is thinking seriously of shouldering his cross, going to Dresden, standing his trial, and being pardoned or sentenced — it is all one to him — merely in order that afterwards he may be able to find somewhere in Germany where his new work can be brought into being. The German in him was just then in full revolt against everything foreign: " I have no belief in my operas in French ", he tells Mathilde; " everything I do to that end is against the inner voice which I can silence only with levity or with violence. I believe neither in a French Tannhäuser nor a French Lohengrin, and least of all in a French Tristan. . . ." In any case, he continues, only as the result of a despot's command could the Paris Opéra be opened to him, and he lacks zeal to work to bring that about. Moreover, his old operas have become almost matters of indifference to him now, while the mere thought of a French translation of one of them reduces him to despair.

In little more than a week after this letter was written the seemingly incredible and impossible had happened: the " despot's order " regarding *Tannhäuser* had gone forth. To Wagner's friends this must have looked like salvation for him at long last; but he himself was too thoroughly German at heart to believe that his cause could be finally won anywhere but on German soil. He was tired of Paris and the Parisians, and in his heart of hearts would almost have preferred, just then, not to have been made the subject of Napoleon's unexpected benevolence.

" God knows ", he wrote to Liszt on the 29th March, " what will come out of this projected *Tannhäuser:* inwardly I have no faith in it, and that for good reasons. What is of greater moment to me is the possibility of producing *Tristan* in Germany, and I am seriously thinking of settling my old differences with Dresden if they will only make some sort of reasonable concessions. If that should come about, then I have my eye on Vienna as the theatre with the best singers, and — a unique phenomenon of its kind — a competent musician at its head. . . ."

9

Paradoxically, it was during the very days of this inner revolt of his against the idea of *Tannhäuser* in Paris, and to a great degree as the result of the imperial order to produce the work, that there

came a change of heart towards him in Dresden. The scattered
forces working in his favour suddenly converged and carried the
stubbornly-held official fortress almost at a single assault. It was
a piece of good luck for Wagner that the Saxon Ambassador in
Paris, Baron von Seebach, happened to be a man of culture with
a sympathetic understanding of him; further, as we have seen, Seebach's wife was a cousin of the influential Madame Kalergis. Count
Pourtalès, the Prussian Ambassador, and his attaché, Count Hatzfeld, were both of them prepossessed in Wagner's favour as man
and artist. With the Metternichs also on his side, he was now surrounded by German friends of the highest social standing in Paris
and of undoubted political influence. It may have been principally
to ingratiate himself with the foreign diplomatic corps for his own
political ends that Napoleon had given the order for the production
of *Tannhäuser:* but once that order had been given, it was obviously
policy on the part of the German diplomatists in Paris to take the
favoured German composer under their protection also. In Berlin
the Princess Augusta of Prussia had long been an admirer of Wagner's music; and it may be assumed that about this time some hints
were given her by Pourtalès of the way things were shaping at the
Tuileries. Almost in a moment it became evident to all impartial
observers that the Saxon Court could not decently maintain much
longer its stonewall attitude towards this greatest of living German
musicians, who was now turning the eyes of the whole musical world
upon a foreign capital. Almost simultaneously we find Seebach,
who had returned on leave to Dresden in the early summer of 1860,
urging the Saxon ministers to reconsider Wagner's case, and the
Princess Augusta pleading his cause in person with the King of
Saxony in Baden-Baden, where various German princes had fore-
gathered for the meeting of Napoleon and the King of Prussia in
June of that year. It was no doubt on a friendly unofficial hint from
Seebach, on his return to Paris, that Wagner wrote him a long letter
in which he protested once more that he had years ago ceased to
be interested in politics or to associate with revolutionaries, and
pledged his word that if the King of Saxony would permit him to
return to Germany he would take care that no complaint could ever
again be levelled against him on either of these counts. Seebach,
for his part, thereupon respectfully assured Baron von Beust, the

THE LIFE OF RICHARD WAGNER

President of the Saxon Council and Minister for Foreign Affairs, that he had no doubt of the genuineness of Wagner's assurances, in face of which he could not bring himself to " deny him all hope of his Majesty's pardon."

In view of the bitter opposition of the King and the Saxon Government during so many years to every plea for consideration for Wagner, it is unlikely either that Seebach would have ventured to raise the question afresh purely on his own initiative or that Beust would have shown any more consideration now than had been done on previous occasions, unless the pressure of events had by this time forced the King's hands — though he would naturally insist that Wagner should once more approach him as a humble petitioner for the royal bounty. But even now the thin-lipped and narrow-souled monarch could not bring himself to do the inevitable thing amiably and gracefully. With manifest reluctance he consented to raise the eleven-year-old ban on Wagner's re-entry into Germany in general, but he still refused to grant him a formal pardon, nor would he raise the ban at all so far as Saxony was concerned. Beust, who certainly had no liking for Wagner and no understanding of him, showed a better spirit in the affair than his royal master. The draft, in Beust's own handwriting, of the letter he proposed to send in reply to Seebach's is still in the Saxon archives: it shows the minister's idea to have been that Wagner, whenever he might want to go to any place within the German Federation, should himself apply to the Saxon Government for formal permission to do so. But this, in the King's opinion, was making things too easy for the " revolutionary ". He would not allow him to approach even as closely as that to his own offended majesty: he altered with his own hand the wording of Beust's draft, making it necessary for Wagner to apply not to the Saxon Government but to that of the particular State in which he might wish to produce one of his works; that State would then pass the application on to Dresden, and " should the Government of the State concerned ", wrote the King, " refrain from proposing his extradition, his Majesty is inclined to accede to such a request. This concession is of course to be regarded as revocable, and liable to be withdrawn if Wagner's conduct gives occasion for doing so." [20] The royal terms were conveyed to See-

[20] Most of the documents in the case will be found in LWV, Chapters V and VI.

bach in a letter from Beust of the 15th July. Wagner thanked his
" Most Serene Monarch, Most August King and Lord " in his best
formal style on the 26th July, assuring him that he would " make
use of his Majesty's gracious permission only for the furtherance
of his artistic interests." And there, for the present, the matter
rested.

10

Characteristically enough, he found that no sooner had he obtained the long-coveted fruit than it had lost its savour for him:
it had been gained at the cost of too many annoyances and humiliations for him to be able to appreciate it just then. He foresaw, too,
as he told Mathilde Wesendonk wearily, that with freedom to re-
enter Germany a new world of suffering was opening out to him
as an artist, a world of fresh struggles, vain compromises, heart-
breaking disappointments. The news of the removal of the ban
left him, he said, cold and unmoved: he replied to none of the telegrams of felicitation that poured in on him. All the same, he was
glad to take advantage of the permission to re-enter Germany to
snatch a few days' relaxation before embarking in earnest on the
business of preparing *Tannhäuser* for the Opéra. Minna had gone
at the beginning of July to Soden, in the Taunus, to take one of her
cures. Wagner had received a hint from Seebach that it would not
only gratify the Princess Augusta but placate the King of Saxony
if on his first visit to Germany he would see the royal lady and
thank her for her exertions on his behalf. Expecting to find her in
Coblentz he made his way thither in August, via Cologne, only to
discover that she was in Baden-Baden. He accordingly went on to
Soden, collected Minna, and took her with him to Frankfort, where
he saw his brother Albert again for the first time since the Dresden
days, and where he half-thought of calling on Schopenhauer. But
something within him, an instinct that in his then untuneful mood
the old philosopher would not be good company for him or he for
the philosopher, kept him from calling. Another opportunity for
meeting the sage of Frankfort never occurred; the old man died
on the 21st September of this same year.

From Frankfort the pair went on to Baden-Baden, accompanied
by a friend of Minna's, one Mathilde Schiffner, of Dresden, a bour-

geoise of Minna's own type, whose influence upon his wife's mind Wagner had plentiful reason to deplore later.[21] Armed with a letter of introduction from Count Pourtalès to the Princess's lady-in-waiting, Countess Hacke, he presented himself to his royal bene-factor in the Trinkhalle at five o'clock one afternoon: " It was a cold wet day ", he says, " and at that hour the whole surroundings of the place seemed as quiet as the grave. . . ." If his account of the interview in *Mein Leben* is to be trusted, his reception was as cold and cheerless as the day. The Princess's conversation

" consisted almost wholly of assurances that she was completely pow-erless in every respect; in reply to which I was imprudent enough to refer to the hint received from the King of Saxony that I ought to thank her for the favour that had been extended to me. This mani-festly annoyed her, and she dismissed me with listless assurances of a sympathy that did not seem to amount to much. My old friend Alwine Frommann [the Princess's reader] told me that she did not know what it was about me that presumably displeased her, but thought it might have been my Saxon accent."

Possibly Alwine was merely being tactful: the real cause of the Princess's coldness may have been a suspicion that Wagner was ex-pecting further favours of her. Seebach, he had told Liszt before the interview, had merely suggested his sending the lady a letter of thanks, but he himself thought a personal meeting would be better, at which, without asking definitely for anything, he might be able to discover whether Augusta was willing to be of service to him in connection with the production of his new works in Berlin. In a further letter to Liszt, written after his return to Paris, he points out sadly how little real improvement the King of Saxony's " clem-ency " has effected in his situation as an artist. He has been neither amnestied nor pardoned, but merely told that if he applies to some German State other than Saxony for permission to enter it, and that State in turn passes the application on approvingly to Saxony, the latter will not interpose any obstacle! Not only did this regulation make a sudden visit on his part to a particular town for a mere day or two difficult, if not actually impossible, but — which was more important — no German ruler could take the initiative with regard to him, so that the omens for the production of his new works under

[21] She seems to have been a dressmaker. In *Mein Leben* Wagner rather conveys the impression that she and Minna had first met not long before the period of which he is now speaking; but her name figures in his letters as early as July 1853.

his own guidance were not much better than before. In any case, he tells Liszt, the condition of the larger German theatres is appalling; Berlin in particular is out of the question, so far as he is concerned, without a complete overthrow of the present management. He had not been bold enough, he continues, to approach the Princess with any great expectations in that respect, because he knows that his own ideas would be frankly incomprehensible to people such as those in power in Berlin. He had been pleased, however, to find her as lively and intelligent a woman as he had expected; and he had contented himself with thanking her for her constant interest in his works, without telling her any of his wishes or putting forward any particular plan. He told Otto Wesendonk also that the Princess had made a good impression on him, and had " assured him warmly of her adherence ", but that in view of the unfavourable accounts he had recently had of the state of the Berlin Opera he did not feel impelled to go into details regarding possible performances of his new works there. All this conflicts somewhat with the account he gives of the meeting some years later in his autobiography, an account which is no doubt coloured by subsequent hard experiences and disappointments in Berlin. But perhaps we may assume that at some stage or other of the conversation, emboldened by the Princess's obvious interest in him, he *had* thrown out a hint or two concerning Berlin and its present unfitness for his purposes, whereupon, having no desire to become mixed up with matters of practical theatrical politics of that kind, she may have thought it prudent to assure him that she " was completely powerless in every respect ": some remark of that nature had manifestly persisted in his memory of the conversation in after years.

11

Though Wagner had more than once crossed the Rhine, he had never, till this six-days' excursion of his in August 1860, travelled up or down it; and in spite of the fact that, as he assured Wesendonk, he had not felt the faintest spark of emotion at treading German soil once more, he was interested and even " stimulated " by what he saw. On his return to Paris he found plenty to occupy his attention. There was now a rehearsal of one kind or another for *Tannhäuser* every day of the week, in addition to daily conferences with the scene painters, the regisseur, the costumier, and others. It had been represented to him in the earlier part of the year, apparently by Frédéric Villot, that he ought to do something to remove from the French mind the impression that his works were written to a " system "; and it seemed to him that the best way to do this would be to bring out translations (without the music) of the *Flying Dutchman, Tannhäuser, Lohengrin* and *Tristan,* together with a foreword explaining his attitude towards the problem of the fusion of music and poetry in the music drama. A verse translation of the poems was not to be thought of; his experiences in that field with *Tannhäuser* alone had been sufficient to cure him of all desire to go through anything of the same kind on a still larger scale. A prose version was accordingly decided upon; this was entrusted to his and Herwegh's Paris friend Paul Challemel-Lacour, of whose competence in both languages there could be no doubt. Wagner gratefully remembers in *Mein Leben* Challemel's intelligent services to him in this matter. We know now that Challemel, conscientiously as he fulfilled his task, was not fanatically in love with it.

> "Paul has just begun his translation of the libretto", Madame Eugénie Fétis wrote to Emma Herwegh in the spring of 1860, " and I judge Wagner's work by the grimaces he makes. Sometimes he sighs in a fashion that is anything but flattering, sometimes he throws the book aside and runs into the garden to shake himself free of this sham poetry by admiring the greatest poetry of all."

Paul, for his part, confessed that his job amounted to not much more than manual labour, which was all the better for him, he said, in that it left his mind neutral: " I translate very much as I would rule paper, turning the ecstasies of *Tristan* into French as best I can and thinking all the while of Garibaldi." Madame Fétis found it positively amusing that Wagner should occasionally venture to plead for a little more fire in the French version, claiming that in the German there was more energy and subtlety; " what do you think of this modesty and this blindness? " [22] But Madame Fétis, writing as one woman to another, about a man whom neither of them understood or greatly liked, always indulged herself in the luxury of a little malice where Wagner was concerned.

---

[22] HBD, p. 73 ff.

The Foreword to the opera poems — it too was translated, by the way, by the grimacing Challemel-Lacour — took the form of an " Open Letter to a French Friend (Frédéric Villot) ". It deals on quite a large scale with the history of opera in general and with Wagner's own artistic evolution in particular. He scouts the popular notion, which was doing him so much harm in Paris, that his works had been written to demonstrate a theory; with the artist, he says, theorising comes after creation, not before it. In the main he traverses what for modern readers of his prose works is familiar ground: he shows that while the French and Italians have always had an opera of their own, the product of the specific national mentality of each of them and of the historic national culture, the Germans had so far not succeeded at all in solving *their* problem, which was to re-express their great dramatic poets in the musical language of their great composers, especially Beethoven. He summarises, as best he can in so little space, the long argument of his *Opera and Drama*, traces the main line of his own poetic and musical evolution, disposes of the foolish charge against him that he " despises melody ", demonstrates the potentialities that have existed for opera, since 'Beethoven, in the " symphonic " handling of the orchestra, and ends by assuring his French readers that he has confidence in their judgment of his *Tannhäuser*, in which he has tried to develop a dramatic action without " any sort of concession to the banal requirements of an opera libretto ", and to employ music as a means to make that action intelligible and interesting. The Letter, which is dated the 15th September, 1860, was admirably calculated to appeal to the more intelligent section of the Paris public; but whether it had much circulation at the time among the general opera public may be doubted. The volume was published towards the end of November, during that illness of Wagner to which reference has already been made: the translator's name was not given in connection with either the poems or the Foreword. This latter was published very soon afterwards in Leipzig, by J. J. Weber, under the title of " *Zukunftsmusik* " — in ironic reference to that " music of the future " of which Wagner was supposed by ill-informed professors and journalists to plume himself on possessing the sole patent.

[55]

CHAPTER III

EN ROUTE TO "TANNHÄUSER"

1

WHEN WAGNER left Switzerland for Paris in the autumn of 1859 his prime purpose, of course, had not been to give concerts there but to float himself as an opera composer; and after the shelving of *Tristan* by the Karlsruhe management this new work of his was of necessity included in his Paris plans. Adequate production of a work so much at variance with all current conceptions of opera would be impossible anywhere without his personal supervision; and as he was barred from going to any of the German theatres the only thing to do was to bring, in a sense, the German theatres to him. As early as November 1859 we find him telling the Hanover tenor, Albert Niemann, of his plan for assembling a "model German company" to perform some of his operas, including *Tristan*, in Paris from about the end of next April to the middle of June. In view of the length of the proposed season he would of course need an alternative singer for each of the principal parts; and in further view of the great expense of such an undertaking and his difficult position as an exile from his own country he hoped the artists would not be too exacting in their terms. For the tenor parts he wanted the two leading German tenors of the period, Tichatschek and Niemann; for the chief soprano rôles, Frau Bürde-Ney, of Dresden, and Luise Meyer-Dustmann, of Vienna. Niemann was to be the Tannhäuser, Tichatschek the Lohengrin, each replacing the other in case of necessity: *Tristan* they were to share between them.[1] The singers, for the most part, met him cordially enough so far as they were personally concerned, but the possibility of their co-operation depended, of course, largely

---

[1] The Meyer-Dustmann is the Luise Meyer already mentioned in Vol. II, pp. 512, etc. She had married a bookseller named Dustmann in 1858, and added her husband's name, in German fashion, to her own.

on the good will of their directors. In February 1860 Wagner informed Breitkopf and Härtel of his intention to give *Tristan* in Paris in May with Niemann as Tristan and Bürde-Ney as Isolde, and asked the publishers to send each of these people a proof copy of the vocal score as quickly as they could. Breitkopfs were further to use their influence with Wirsing, the director of the Leipzig theatre, to obtain from him a modification of Frau Bürde-Ney's "guest" agreement with Leipzig for the coming spring, so as to permit of her being in Paris from the 16th April to the beginning of June. Wagner admits that this may be a little awkward for Wirsing, but not so awkward as it will be for *him*, he pleads, if his request is not granted. As compensation for any inconvenience to which the director may be put by the release of Frau Bürde-Ney he offers Leipzig the first German performance of *Tristan* later in the year, with Bülow as conductor, and with the singers who will already by that time have sung the work under himself in Paris. Breitkopfs did their best with Wirsing, but were unable to obtain the desired favour: the lady, it seems, had been expressly engaged for the Leipzig Fair season, when the town would be full of visitors from all quarters, and to part with her just at that time would mean a loss to the theatre which Wirsing saw no reason to incur merely for Wagner's sake.

The disastrous financial results of his Paris concerts and the consequent cooling of M. Lucy's ardour made a German Wagner-season in Paris highly problematic. As we have seen, he now offered the first German performance of *Tristan* to Hanover, on the condition, among others, that the local Kapellmeister and the two chief singers should be released in May in order to rehearse the work in Paris under himself. The Hanover Intendant professing himself unable to make that sacrifice, Wagner now realised that his scheme for a season of his own in Paris, with *Tristan* as the centrepiece of it, was beyond the range of practicability. For a moment he reverted to a former idea of his [2] — to give *Tristan* in Strassburg in the summer, at a time when he could count on Niemann and Luise Dustmann being free of their respective theatres. But even before he

---

[2] See Vol. II, p. 520. Strassburg had three points in its favour. It was handier for the German singers than Paris; it was largely German in language and in spirit; yet, being in French territory, it was open to the as yet unamnestied Wagner.

had mentioned this plan to Breitkopf and Härtel he had told Otto Wesendonk that his hopes for *Tristan* in Paris were at an end, and that his objective now was the securing of an imperial order for the production of *Tannhäuser* at the Opéra. For such a production, he thought, he could confidently count on Niemann, who, after one of his periodical quarrels with the Hanover management, was thinking of leaving that town. By the 8th March Wagner could tell Niemann that a Paris performance of *Tannhäuser* was virtually assured. In the main he could " cast " the work well enough, he said, from the personnel of the Opéra; all he would need from Germany was a Tannhäuser, the typically French tenor being antipathetic to him. In case of Niemann breaking with the Hanover management, therefore, he would be able to offer him a lucrative temporary engagement in Paris. But within a few days of his telling him this he is able to inform him of the magical transformation in his fortunes. He has suddenly become, he says, a " power " at the Opéra: *Tannhäuser* is definitely commanded, he has been given *carte blanche* in the matter of the singers, and his first recommendation has been Niemann.

2

The reader will remember that Albert Niemann had visited Wagner in the Asyl in the summer of 1858. Wagner had heard a good deal from his friends of this rising young tenor, whose voice was on the same generous scale as his physique: and as Niemann was at that time only twenty-seven, while Tichatschek, though still in amazingly good condition, was fifty-one, it was naturally the younger man whom Wagner, looking well ahead, had in view at that time for his Siegfried.[3] He had invited him to the Asyl with the object of hearing him as well as seeing him; but as Tichatschek also was his guest at the time, and each tenor shrank coyly from singing in the presence of the other, Wagner, in 1860, had still

---

[3] It is generally forgotten today, not only by opera directors and the public but by the Heldentenor himself, that Wagner wanted as boyish-looking a singer as possible for his Siegfried. Niemann was at the height of his reputation in 1876, and, at the age of forty-one, in the fullest possession of his vocal powers; but Wagner thought him too mature to convey the illusion of his young Siegfried, though he entrusted him with the part of Siegmund in Bayreuth.

nothing but hearsay to go upon for his judgment of him as a singer, though he had been impressed in 1858, he tells us, by the young man's " almost superhuman build ". The typical French tenor and baritone timbre seems, in general, to have been repugnant to Wagner, at any rate where his own music was concerned; while he had always shuddered at the thought of his Siegmund or Siegfried or Tristan being sung by a tenor of the " eunuch " type, as he disrespectfully described the lighter tenor voice of his period.[4] Apart from Ludwig Schnorr von Carolsfeld, who in 1860 was only twenty-four years old, there was no tenor in all Germany of the " heroic " calibre of Niemann and Tichatschek: and not only was Schnorr relatively immature in 1860 but, being a member of the Karlsruhe company, he was under the control of Eduard Devrient, with whom Wagner was by now on almost the worst terms possible. For his Paris Tannhäuser, then, Wagner had hardly any choice but Niemann. With this young man he was to have before long some of the bitterest experiences of his artistic life.

In a Foreword to Wagner's letters to Niemann,[5] published in 1924, Dr. Gottfried Niemann, the second son of the singer, paints a not unattractive portrait of his father, who died on the 13th January, 1917, two days before completing his eighty-sixth year. Albert Niemann's father had died young; his mother, who lived to be ninety, is described as " of almost unwomanly hardness ". From her, no doubt, he inherited not only his exceptional vitality but some of the less admirable constituents of his being. The mature Niemann, as depicted for us by the son, was a many-sided creature, with a good deal both of the primitive German of the field and the forest and of the modern student and recluse about him. He was at once a great hunter and an assiduous reader of history, philosophy and science. Although the theatre had brought him wealth and fame, and though he had always taken his profession seriously, it would seem that he never really liked his life as an opera singer; after his retirement he not only associated as little as possible with actors, but forbade the other members of his household to talk about the stage in his presence; and even at the height of his career he so

---

[4] "A pure mezzo-castrato" was an English wit's description of a certain tenor of this sort.
[5] RWAN.

greatly disliked having any of them in the theatre when he was singing that on one occasion, having learned accidentally that his wife
had smuggled herself into a box without his consent, he refused to
go on the stage until after she had left. He was never particularly
tactful or sociable, was brusque in manner and blunt of speech, and
was given to throwing his weight about in a style that as often as
not put him on the worst of terms with the people with whom he
came into the closest contact in the theatre. In the days when Wagner first had anything to do with him he was undoubtedly, at
bottom, an arrogant, ill-conditioned boor, with all the vanity and
other notorious failings of his tribe.

After going the usual round of the smaller German theatres and
singing for a little while in Berlin he had been engaged as principal
tenor at Hanover in September 1854. There he remained, the favourite of the King and the idol of the public, for several years; after
the war of 1866 between Bavaria and Prussia, as a sequel to which
Hanover became a Prussian dependency, he removed to Berlin. He
had been singing, after his own fashion, Tannhäuser since 1854,
Lohengrin since 1855, Rienzi since 1859, so that he was no stranger
to the Wagner rôles when he was invited to Paris. With all of them
he had had a great popular success in Germany; perhaps this had
turned his head and made him less amenable than he should have
been to Wagner's criticisms and suggestions with regard to the true
meaning of the part of Tannhäuser. The curious thing is that
while, as his diary shows, Niemann was willing enough to observe
and analyse critically this or that of his professional rivals in one
rôle and another, with a view to improving himself in it, he was
reluctant to admit the possibility of a creator, even a creator so im-
measurably his intellectual superior as Wagner was, being able to
teach *him* anything where the " interpretation " of a part was concerned.

Although the Opéra authorities had of course accepted Wagner's
nomination of him for Tannhäuser, Niemann was expected, as a
matter of routine, to " prove " himself at an official trial in Paris.
It was a little while, however, before he was free to make the journey. On the 18th March he had become involved in one of those
incidents with his colleagues to which his overbearing temper always made him peculiarly liable. During the interval between the

first and second acts of *Lohengrin,* in a quarrel with the Kapellmeister, Bernhard Scholz, he had gone so far as to commit a minor
assault on him — he had snatched Scholz's hat off his head. This
kind of thing was frowned upon in Germany, where it was almost
as grave a crime to show disrespect towards a functionary's office
as to assault the functionary's person. Scholz having appealed to
the law, Niemann was sentenced to an apology and four weeks'
imprisonment. His captivity, however, seems to have been more of
the operatic than the penal order: he used to amuse himself by
standing at the window and singing at the top of his voice, to the
great enjoyment of the passers-by, the prison scene from *Il Trovatore.* He was free again on the 19th May, the King having gra-
ciously knocked a week off his admired tenor's term of detention.
Even before this awkward little affair he had been seriously thinking of treating his written engagement with the Hanover theatre
as a mere scrap of paper and absconding to Paris. This course, however, proved unnecessary, the King and the theatre directorate
treating him, after his release from captivity, with greater consideration than ever — impressed, perhaps, by the compliment paid
not only to him but to Hanover by Wagner's selection of him as
his Paris Tannhäuser. The King granted him in June a year's leave
for Paris.

3

He arrived there at the end of June; and from the moment of
their first meeting Wagner had cause to feel a little perturbed about
him. " I was astounded ", said Wagner in *Mein Leben* many years
later, " at his manner, and the way in which he presented himself
at my door with the question, ' Well, do you want me or don't
you? ' " The mentality of the man is revealed in his cool assertion,
in later years, that Wagner asked him to " create " the part of
Tannhäuser. As Glasenapp points out, in the whole of his correspondence and prose writings Wagner uses that fatuous theatrical
expression only once, and then ironically, " as a quotation from the
jargon of the theatre." Wagner's view of these matters was that
of all rational people — that a Don Giovanni, a Florestan, a Tannhäuser is " created " not by some strutting stage peacock or other
who happens to have the luck to be the first singer of the part, but

by a Mozart, a Beethoven or a Wagner. On the 2nd July Niemann sang, as his "trial", Tannhäuser's song in praise of Venus and the story of Tannhäuser's pilgrimage, from the stage of the Opéra, before a select audience that included Prince and Princess Metternich, Count Hatzfeld and Madame Kalergis: the piano accompaniment was supplied by Karl Klindworth. All were impressed by the powerful voice and the huge stature of the singer. Niemann was given a nine months' engagement, from the 1st September, 1860 — at which time the rehearsals for *Tannhäuser* were to begin — to the 31st May, 1861, at a monthly salary of 6,000 francs.[6] He had no duties whatever in all that time but to prepare himself for the one part for which he had been brought to Paris. Wagner had insisted on a clause to that effect going into the contract: he wished, says Gasperini, to guard himself against the smallest possibility of his tenor being " compromis par des cabales souterraines ". Niemann's as yet imperfect French was at once taken in hand by " nombreux professeurs ", while Wagner, who found him " almost raw ", " doing everything solely by instinct ", undertook his musical and dramatic education. Wagner had no need to hurry anyone: the performance could not take place until he himself sanctioned it, so absolute was his authority in the theatre.

For his Venus, Wagner would have liked Madame Gueymard of the Opéra; but to this, for some reason or other which he never understood, Royer would not consent. Wagner probably lost nothing by not being able to obtain Madame Gueymard; seemingly she was a person of so little importance even in her own day that the modern encyclopaedias of music do not so much as mention her name. Royer probably acted in Wagner's and the theatre's interests, for manifestly he had orders from the Emperor to meet the composer's wishes in every detail. Wagner had now, much against his will, to spend several nights at the Opéra, listening to *La Favorita, Semiramide, Il Trovatore,* and much more of that sort

---

[6] Wagner's memory was at fault when he said, in *Mein Leben*, that Niemann was engaged for eight months at 10,000 francs a month. Niemann was also in error when, in some reminiscences published in 1895, he said he received "a year's engagement at 6,000 francs a month — an unheard-of salary at that time." His leave of absence from Hanover was for a year; but his Paris engagement was for nine months. The contract, which is apparently still in the possession of the family, was signed by Royer, the Director of the Opéra, in Paris on the 9th July and by Niemann in Interlaken on the 12th. See RWAN, p. 114.

of thing; the result of these painful attempts to decide whether a passable Leonora or Semiramide or Luna could be transformed into an ideal Venus or Elisabeth or Wolfram was generally to send him home vowing he would wash his hands of the whole business of *Tannhäuser* in Paris. For the Venus, Royer suggested the engagement of an Italian soprano, Fortunata Tedesco, whose voluptuous appearance was deemed particularly appropriate to the part. Wagner described her to Frau Wesendonk as " especially engaged for me — has a superb head for her rôle, though the figure is just a shade too sumptuous: talent very considerable and suitable." [7] For his Elisabeth he accepted, at Royer's suggestion, a promising young " half-novice " [8] with a " beautiful " voice, Mademoiselle Sax. As he could not endure any of the " sickly " French baritones, he was lucky to find in an Italian, Morelli, the presence and the vocal sonority he desired for his Wolfram. Gasperini and other friends doubted whether Morelli's purely Italian artistic heredity could adapt itself to the Wagnerian style; but Wagner merely laughed and assured them that he would " cure him of his bad habits ". " And indeed ", says Gasperini, " he managed to obtain from Morelli sacrifices in the matter of phrasing, placing the voice, and linking the tones, which must have cost this worthy son of Italy a good deal." [9] Bülow gave his correspondents in Germany his own impression of the singers shortly before the first performance: Marie Sax, " splendid " . . . " ideally fresh, brilliant and poetic "; Tedesco, " excellent in person and in voice " . . . " sings with a purity of intonation and a vitality that rejoices both heart and ear "; Morelli, " no Mitterwurzer, but a glorious organ and a fair amount of understanding "; Cazaux (the Landgraf),

---

[7] Glasenapp ungallantly speaks of her as "no longer in her first youth"; but she was only in her thirty-fourth year in 1860. She retired from the stage in 1866.

[8] "Halbwilde" is Wagner's adjective; perhaps Ellis's "half-novice" meets the case better than any other word. Marie Sax, who was only twenty-two in 1860, had begun as a café singer, had been "discovered" by someone or other and trained for opera, and had begun her genuine career in 1859 as the Countess in *Figaro*. Wagner's "halbwilde" may refer either to her temperament, or to her relative lack of experience, or to both. Her real name was Sass. When Adolph Sax, the famous inventor of a notorious instrument, obtained a court order prohibiting her use of the name Sax, she added a final "e" to her spelling of the word; later she reverted to her true name.

[9] GW, p. 60. Gasperini's account of Wagner's transformation, in a few weeks, of the inexperienced Mademoiselle Sax into an intelligent dramatic artist is interesting.

" everywhere applaudable "; Coulon (Biterolf), " rather rough "; the Walther, "very mediocre "; [10] Mademoiselle Reboux (the Shepherd Boy), "uncertain ".[11] The chorus (trained by Victor Massé, the famous light opera composer), Bülow thought " magnificent ". The singer who found no favour at all in Bülow's eyes or ears was Niemann. His uncomplimentary opinion of him may have been coloured to some extent by resentment of Niemann's loutish behaviour towards Wagner; [12] but he seems never to have liked his voice, which he describes as a " toneless baritone ". That Niemann was what is known as " a forced-up baritone " seems not unlikely from all we read about him.

4

The story of Wagner's first difficulties over the translation of *Tannhäuser* has already been told.[13] When the question of a practicable French version became one that concerned the Opéra as well as Wagner, Royer ran a critical eye over the results obtained by Lindau and Roche; and as they did not meet with his approval [14] he suggested the collaboration of his own and Emile Ollivier's friend Charles Truinet, an amiable person who had been trained, more or less, for the law, but had preferred to become archivist of the Opéra and to write vaudevilles for the minor Paris theatres under the anagrammatic pseudonym of Nuitter. As soon as the order had gone forth to produce *Tannhäuser*, Royer had told Wagner that he would be expected to comply with the traditions of the house by inserting a ballet in the second act. That, of course, Wagner refused to do; but as he had long been secretly dissatisfied with the opening scene of this old work of his it now occurred to him to rewrite it in

[10] See *infra*, p. 85.

[11] This little piece of casting was evidently one of Wagner's mistakes. "He could find no one at the Opéra", says Gasperini (writing in 1866), "to whom he could entrust the small part of the young shepherd. After a number of experiments he allowed himself, I do not know why, to be captivated by the voice of a Conservatoire pupil, Mademoiselle Reboux, who was manifestly unequal to the task set her. This young person sang out of tune as gaily as you please at the rehearsals. It was still worse at the first performance. . . ."

[12] A number of Bülow's references to him are said to have been omitted from the imprint of the letters.

[13] See Vol. II, pp. 591–2.

[14] For one thing, Roche's lines were unrhymed; Royer insisted on a rhymed version, in conformity with the practice of the Opéra.

a form that would at once satisfy his artistic conscience and meet the requirements of Royer. In particular he wanted to give a larger development to the part of Venus and to the psychological reactions of Tannhäuser in the first scene between them.

" The only scene I mean to recast entirely is the one with Venus ", he told Frau Wesendonk: " Frau Venus strikes me as stiff — a few good touches, but no real life. Here I have composed a fair number of new verses: the Goddess of Delight herself becomes affecting and Tannhäuser's agony real, so that his invocation of the Virgin Mary bursts like a cry of profound anguish from the depths of his soul. At the time I wrote the work I could not manage this."

Scared, no doubt, at the thought of having to supervise line by line yet another French translation of a poem of his, he merely gave Truinet the German sketch of the new matter, to be turned by him into French verses; and to these he composed the new music for the first act, leaving to a later time the shaping of the German-text into its definitive form. Truinet seems to have done his part of the work quite to Wagner's satisfaction. The Fates, however, saw in this business of the *Tannhäuser* translation yet another opportunity for harassing Wagner. In the early days of 1861, when the date of the performance seemed at last to be drawing near, Lindau put in a claim to " author's rights " in the libretto, as one of the three collaborators in the French version. When the case came into court, Lindau's advocate took the ingenious line of arguing that according to Wagner's own principle the important thing was not the melody but the correct declamation of the words, the credit for which, in the present instance, was virtually all Lindau's, since neither Roche nor Truinet understood German! Emile Ollivier, who appeared for Wagner, " seemed to be on the point ", the latter tells us, " of proving the purely musical essence of my melody by singing the ' Star of Eve '." Convinced by Ollivier's eloquence, as Wagner implies in *Mein Leben,* or, it may be, appalled by the prospect of his bursting into song, the court non-suited Lindau, but at the same time suggested that Wagner might like to pay him something for the work he appeared to have done in connection with the translation. Wagner having refused to do anything of the kind after the fiasco at the Opéra, Lindau sent him a lawyer's letter; this, on Ollivier's advice, he merely ignored, and never heard any more of the matter. When the time for the performance at last arrived, Roche declared that he did not wish his name to appear on the playbills; as Truinet thereupon declined to let his own name stand alone in connection with the translation, it came about that the *affiches* contained no mention of anyone at all as being responsible for the French version.

Having a work produced at the Paris Opéra was not all plain sailing for a foreign composer; and least of all for a German composer who, like Wagner, prided himself on the poetic validity of his text, who was accustomed to conducting and producing his own works, and for whom an opera of his was a creation with an organic unity of its own, not an amorphous compromise that could without any particular damage to it be adapted to the local taste of this or that theatre. As far as the actual production of *Tannhäuser* was concerned Wagner had no cause for complaint from first to last: the imperial protection had given him an authority in the Paris Opéra more absolute than anything he had previously enjoyed anywhere, even in Dresden during the period of his Kapellmeistership. But the written laws of the institution not only prohibited performance of a foreign work in any language but French but barred a composer, whether French or not, from conducting his own work, however superior he might be as a conductor to the functionary who bore that title at the Opéra. The unwritten law as to a ballet in the second act was, however, the most difficult hurdle that Wagner had to take.

He probably did not take Royer very seriously when the latter first told him that his second act would have to be rearranged, because of the " indispensability of a grand ballet " at some point in it. " M. Royer wants a grand ballet for the second act of *Tannhäuser:* you can imagine how that makes me feel at home! ", he wrote to Liszt on the 29th March, 1860. " My refuge against such demands is for the present Princess Metternich, who has made herself uncommonly respected by Fould.[15] So I will see if she can save me from this ballet; if not, then of course I would withdraw *Tannhäuser*." To Frau Wesendonk he was similarly confident. A ballet, he had been told, there absolutely had to be, and that in the second

---

[15] Secretary of State and Minister of the Household to Napoleon III. He had so far been hostile to Wagner, owing, it is said, to his friendship with Meyerbeer. He was succeeded in his offices by Count Walewski in the autumn of 1860.

act, as the aristocratic subscribers never arrived until then, after dining themselves well. " I have declared ", he said, " that I could not
take orders from the Jockey Club, and would withdraw my work.
However, I mean to help them [i.e. the Opéra direction] out of
their difficulty; the performance need not begin until eight o'clock,
and then I will amplify the unhallowed Venusberg in a suitable
way." In other words, as he put it about the same time to Bülow,
his idea was to enrich the opening scene for his own sake with a new
choregraphic representation of the splendours of the court of Venus,
and to placate the abonnés by calling this a ballet.

People who knew Paris better than himself, however, could not
share his complacent belief in so easy a way out of the difficulty.
The Jockey Club — composed mainly of rich young men of fashion
— did not know much or care much about art, but it knew what it
wanted after dinner and could be trusted to see that it got it. No
matter what the opera of the evening and no matter at what hour
it commenced, it began to exist, for these gentlemen, only with the
second act, and in that second act there had to be a ballet.[16] On not
a single occasion when they met, Wagner tells us, did Royer fail to
urge him to introduce a ballet into the second act. It was in vain
that Wagner pointed out, again and again, that a ballet in the second
act of *Tannhäuser* would be a dramatic absurdity: Royer was not
concerned with dramatic consistency, but only with his aristocratic
abonnés and their power for evil.

Already in June, 1860, nine months before the *Tannhäuser* performances took place, the problem had become a critical one.
Wagner, feeling that he had the Emperor at his back, refused point-
blank to insert a ballet in the second act: Royer, for his part, as
emphatically declined to regard the proposed new Venusberg scene

---

[16] Berlioz's *Les Troyens*, which was originally planned as an opera in five acts,
contains two ballets: (A) Act I, Scene 5 consists of a mimic "Combat de ceste (Pas de
lutteurs)", followed by the long dumb-show of Andromache and the little Astyanax.
(B) Act IV, Scene 3 contains a series of dances in celebration of the return of Aeneas
from his victory over Iarbas. The work was later divided into two operas, *La Prise
de Troie* (three acts) and *Les Troyens à Carthage* (four acts) of which the second only
was given during Berlioz's lifetime. In this arrangement each of the two operas has
its ballet in the second act, (A) occupying that position in *La Prise de Troie*, (B) in
Les Troyens à Carthage. It looks, therefore, as if from the beginning Berlioz had
foreseen the possibility of being obliged to give the work on two successive evenings,
and had accordingly provided for each occasion a ballet that would occupy the
traditional place in the second act.

in the first act as likely to meet the requirements of his patrons. He suggested a compromise: *Tannhäuser* was to be given just as the composer had written it, but between the first and second acts there was to be inserted a " Dance-Intermezzo ", quite independent of the opera, in which a number of the ballerine who were especially dear to the Jockey Club could display their art; alternatively, the second act was to be divided into two scenes, the first of them closing with a ballet! Rumours of the conflict spread as far as Berlin, where it was confidently reported in the Press that Wagner himself had agreed to find a place for a ballet in his *Tannhäuser*. Wagner found himself compelled to send a denial of these and other absurd rumours to the *Journal des Débats* on the 23rd July; " Believe me to be as cowardly as you please ", he said, " but rest assured that only ignorance of my work has been able to give the semblance of possibility to what is absolutely impossible." In his idealistic innocence it seemed to him that the Jockey Club had only to be told that the question, for him, was one of artistic integrity for it to be decided in his favour. He was soon to be disabused; the Jockey Club was not in the least interested in the psychological actions and reactions of Venus and Tannhäuser, or in ideals of musical and dramatic form, or even, in the present instance, in a mere assertion of its traditional right to a ballet where and when it wanted one. The artistic question, it turned out in the end, was only the façade of a political and social question: the production of *Tannhäuser* was a heaven-sent opportunity for striking a blow at Princess Metternich and at this alien protégé of hers who had not only been so unduly favoured in Court circles but was held to be still a political revolutionary at heart, as in 1849. It had done Wagner no good to be taken up in Paris, for the most part, by opponents of the imperial régime; Emile Ollivier in particular was at that time in bad odour in high quarters.[17] When Baudelaire asked his friend Charles As-

---

[17] A thumb-nail sketch of him will be found in the *Souvenirs d'un homme de lettres* of Alphonse Daudet, who had known him since about 1858. At that time the rising young lawyer was known as "One of the Five" — "one of the five deputies who, alone, dared to defy the Empire." "About thirty-three years old, leader of the most popular party among the youthful republicans, who were proud to have a chief of his age, he was in the full glare of glory." Not many years later Ollivier, who had made his peace with the Second Empire, became Minister of Justice. "To sum up", says Daudet, "he was but an indifferent statesman, full of impulse and devoid of reflection; but withal an honest man, a poet full of ideals strayed into public busi-

selineau, who was something of a musician, why he had not attended any of the Wagner concerts, Asselineau excused himself on the grounds that (a) " it was too far away for him ", (b) "he had been told that Wagner was a republican." A contemporary Swiss journalist no doubt expressed the current view of the matter when he said that " it is hardly necessary to observe that the imperial interests were more fundamentally concerned with politics than with the music of the future. Napoleon had heard that Richard Wagner belonged to an influential set of German democrats. He hoped, by taking him under his protection, to facilitate somewhat the Bonapartist propaganda among the democratic party beyond the Rhine: it was as if he had said to this party, ' See how I humour and uphold one of your chiefs, whom the German princes have banished! Could you do better than range yourselves on my side? ' " [18]

5

Wagner had had it in his mind for a long time to remodel the opening scene of *Tannhäuser*, in order to make more convincing to the spectator the conflict between the sensual and the ideal in Tannhäuser's soul. For this purpose he would first of all have to paint the attractions of the court of Venus in more voluptuous colours than he had been able to do in 1845. For one thing, in the Dresden theatre of that period there had been no dancers or choregraphic designers capable of any greater effect, intellectual or technical, than he had demanded of them in his first score. He had gone frequently to the Opéra since his arrival in Paris in September 1859, and there for the first time he had realised the possibilities of ballet both as an art in itself and as an ingredient in a musical-dramatic action. Had he been able to obtain a production of *Rienzi* in Paris in 1841 he might possibly have had his imagination fired by the ballet to such an extent as to influence to some degree his later operatic thinking. A few pages of *Opera and Drama* show him to have had an intuition, though of the vaguest kind, of a dramatic idea express-

ness. . . . While posing as a republican he attempted to consolidate the dynasty by splashing over it a rough-cast of liberty; later on he wished for peace yet declared war . . ." Wagner seems to have respected Ollivier but never to have been greatly attracted by him: he found him "dry and superficial."

[18] HBD, p. 78.

ing itself through the dual medium of orchestral music and choregraphy; but what he has to say on the subject is plainly that of a man of very limited experience of ballet as an art. The choregraphic resources of practically every German theatre at the time of Wagner's Dresden Kapellmeistership must have been extremely limited: a " ballet " probably meant nothing more than a moderately competent solo dancer and half a dozen assistants striking a few conventional attitudes. In Switzerland, where the last ten years of Wagner's life had been mostly spent, he had, of course, seen nothing even remotely deserving the name of ballet.

This new perception of the expressive possibilities of choregraphic miming seems to have come to Wagner just about the time when his imagination had begun once more to work at high pressure. Since the completion of the *Tristan* score in August 1859 his creative faculty had for the most part lain fallow; but in the summer of the following year it began to be stirred to its depths again. His *Tristan*, he wrote to Frau Wesendonk in August, 1860, after reading through the score, was a perpetual wonder to him; " it is becoming ever more incomprehensible to me how I managed to create a thing like that ". The *Parsifal* subject was also germinating afresh within him, the character of Kundry especially beginning to take definite shape. As a musician he was conscious of an immense recent access of power, and of a longing to utilise some of it in creation. It was only after completing *Tristan*, as he said to Frau Wesendonk, that he understood how to solve some of the problems that had hitherto evaded him — to find the right music, for example, for the apotheosis at the end of the *Flying Dutchman* overture and for the re-writing of the bacchanal and the opening scene of *Tannhäuser*. When the opportunity came to him to marshal the whole forces of the Paris Opéra for the realisation of his old dream of a new and wilder bacchanal, a long procession of voluptuous stage pictures began to file through his mind. We first hear of his plans in a letter to Mathilde Wesendonk of the 10th April, 1860, that contains a detailed sketch for the proposed new Venusberg scene. This he developed further, a few weeks later, in a long memorandum that is now available in his Collected Writings.[19] Some of

---

[19] RWGS, XI, 414–419. See also DM, February 1905. The scenario given in the new vocal scores of *Tannhäuser* differs at several points from both these sketches.

his first intentions were not carried out in the final version — the introduction, for instance, of a Strömkarl (a Northern water-sprite) fiddling furiously for the dancers, and of a tableau representing Diana and Endymion. Wagner would almost seem, indeed, to have made up his mind to introduce into his bacchanal as much of classical and northern mythology and as varied a menagerie as he could while he had the chance: one gets a little dizzy as one reads of all these Cupids, Graces, sirens, nymphs, satyrs, bacchantes, goddesses, water-sprites, slaughtered rams, fauns, maenads, sphinxes, great cats, tigers, panthers, griffins, and what not. Two of the cloud-pictures familiar to the opera-goer of today — that of Europa and the bull and that of Leda and the swan — do not appear in the first sketch; Wagner's imagination evidently grew, where ballet was concerned, with what it fed on.

His enthusiasm received many a damper from the ballet-master of the Opéra, the famous Petipa, who first of all pointed out to him that by placing his " ballet " at the commencement of the first act he had forfeited his claim upon the services of the regular female dancers of the Opéra; it might be possible, however, said Petipa, to engage three Hungarians from the Porte St. Martin Theatre to play the parts of the three Graces. Wagner thought he would be able to get the rèsults he wanted by a careful training of the rank and file; but excuse after excuse was made for doing nothing, subterfuge after subterfuge was practised on him, until it became perfectly clear to him that there was no real intention of doing anything to meet his unheard-of wishes as far as the ballet was concerned. By the end of 1860 the situation had obviously become critical. Everyone deplored what was regarded as Wagner's mulish obstinacy over an absurdly trifling matter. The new Minister of the Household, Count Walewski, went so far as to get Prince Metternich to arrange a meeting between him and Wagner, at which a last attempt was made to get this idealist from beyond the Rhine to see reason. The authorities were perfectly willing, here as in the matter of the singers, the orchestra, the scenery, the number of rehearsals and so on, to take any trouble and spend any amount of money for his sake if only he would not continue to stand in his own light.

He was told he could have any dancers he chose, from the best theatres in Europe, for a ballet in the second act. The whole wearisome ground was gone over once more, for the thousandth time, and with the usual result. Wagner argued that a ballet in the second act of *Tannhäuser* would be pure nonsense, whereas one could be inserted in the first act without any harm being done to the dramatic idea, and a ballet was surely a ballet wherever it might be placed. To this Walewski urged once more that the most influential habitués of the Opéra, caring as they did for little else but ballet, were not in the habit of coming to the theatre before ten o'clock or so, when the performance was half over. Wagner countered with the remark that for his part he could manage quite well without the company of the gentlemen in question, and that he hoped to interest a totally different section of the public by means of the ballet he had in mind for it; whereupon there followed the regulation rejoinder, from the Minister's side, that the Jockey Club could make or mar the performance, as it was powerful enough to defy even the Press. Walewski was kind and courteous, sincerely anxious to make the production a success; Wagner, of course, was immovable. " My authority remains as great as ever ", he wrote to Otto Wesendonk on the 16th December, evidently after his conference with the Minister, " and in fact is stronger than ever, as the Princess Metternich (who becomes more and more attached to me) and Walewski are especially friendly. So — as God wills! " One has the suspicion that he never quite realised the hard actualities of the situation — that he trusted overmuch in the ability of the Princess and the Court to see him through any difficulty. It seems likely, also, that he was asking too much from the ballet-master in too short a time. In this same letter to Wesendonk he confesses that owing to his illness, his incessant overwork, and one thing and another he is much behindhand with the new music he had to write for *Tannhäuser;* " the dance-scene isn't begun, and I have no idea as yet how I shall do it." [20] As the opera was by that time nearly ready for perform-

---

[20] He had not quite finished the music of the long scene between Venus and Tannhäuser, he told Otto Wesendonk, when his work was interrupted by his removal to the Rue d'Aumale (the 15th October). This refers only to the *composition:* there was still the orchestration to be done. His illness in October and November must have thrown him still further back with the work. As late as the 15th December we find him telling Liszt that he "still has the long new scene for Venus to score, and the whole of the Venusberg dance-music to compose. How all this is going to be ready at the right time, without a miracle, I don't know!" The first performance of the opera was at that time fixed provisionally for the last week of January! It

ance in every respect except that of the changed opening scene, and as the Venusberg bacchanal, in its expanded literary and musical form, set the ballet-master a host of problems the like of which he could never have been faced with before, Petipa could be forgiven for thinking that not merely the unreasonable but the impossible was being demanded of him. When the bacchanal actually came to rehearsal, Wagner pointed out the woeful discrepancy between the frenzied music he had written for his maenads and bacchantes and the silly stereotyped steps of the dancers, and asked the ballet-master if he could not devise something bolder, wilder, yet elevated in style, something more in keeping with the bacchantes portrayed on ancient reliefs. Petipa merely whistled through his fingers and said, " Oh, I understand quite well; but for that I would need all premières danseuses. If I were to say a word to my people about it, and suggest to them the attitudes you want, we should get the cancan right away, and we should be ruined." [21]

6

It is the peculiar misfortune of the operatic composer that what he has to say in his work cannot be communicated to the world without the co-operation, often at great expense, and never without infinite trouble and anxiety on his part, of a small army of operatives of all sorts. It would not be true to say that Wagner never found any satisfaction at all in bringing his works to performance: exhausting as the labour was, and grievous as were the disappointments he had to undergo in the process, there was naturally a certain pleasure for him in re-living, this time in an externalised form, the inner artistic delight he had experienced in the creation of an opera: this beating of an at first inchoate mass

---

certainly looks as if Petipa were given quite insufficient time to design and rehearse a ballet in any degree worthy of Wagner's ambitious scenario.

[21] *On Conducting*, in RWGS, VIII, 315. The new ballets produced at the Opéra during and shortly after the period when *Tannhäuser* was in hand were those in Rossini's *Semiramide* (9th July), *Le Papillon*, to music by Offenbach, choregraphy by Marie Taglioni (26th November), *Graziosa*, to music by Labarre, choregraphy by Petipa (25th March), and *Le Marché des Innocents*, to music by Pugni, chore-graphy by Petipa (29th May). It is doubtful, therefore, if either Petipa or the ballet troupe had very much time to spare for designing and rehearsing so elaborate a pantomime as that sketched by Wagner for his Venusberg.

of human material into shapes of beauty was in its own way also creation, bringing with it, for the moment, a rich sense of power. But in the depths of that strangely complex soul of his the rehearsing and producing of one of his works in the theatre was generally the cause of a profound unhappiness. He was susceptible in these matters to none of the simple self-satisfactions and ambitions which act as a tonic to other composers. Fame and money from his works were always secondary considerations with him; for neither of them would he have sacrificed his idealism. It is true that his attitude in these matters, especially that of money, occasionally involved him in contradictions from which there was no way out by the route of reason.[22] Money he needed like the rest of mankind; and what would have satisfied most ordinary men was insufficient for him. The world would do well to remind itself constantly, when contemplating half-amusedly, half-censoriously his passion for luxury, that by some curious kink or other in his constitution a certain luxury in his domestic surroundings was necessary to him if he was to create, and it was always in times of intensive creation, or when he was planning to settle down to a period of intensive creation, that he plunged most recklessly into a domestic expenditure beyond his means.[23] It had been so in Dresden during the period of high-powered creation that saw the production of *Tannhäuser* and *Lohengrin*. It was so in the Rue Newton, which he had furnished with some elegance, as well as comfort, because he planned to remain there for three years in order to complete the *Ring* and, if possible, get to grips with the other dramatic schemes

---

[22] Bayreuth itself was and is, strictly speaking, a contradiction in terms: claiming that his art was for the German "people", Wagner demanded so much in the way of singers, players, stage material and so on that the sheer expense of it all made it prohibitive for the "people" proper. The contradiction was gleefully pointed out by his enemies even in his own lifetime: writing of the — necessarily expensive — *Ring* performances given by Angelo Neumann in Berlin in 1881, a writer of the period asked ironically, "Is *this* a folk-stage-festival (Volksbühnenfestspiel)? Only people in a position to pay a large sum for an evening in the theatre can go to it. Among these there are many people of culture. But is a stage performance at such prices really open to the majority of men of learning and culture? And the Folk, the great Folk of the middle class, is it not excluded, individually and collectively?" (Paulus Cassel, *Der Judengott und Richard Wagner*, Berlin, 1881, p. 26).

[23] See, on this point in general, Vol. II, pp. 398, 408, where it is suggested that the sumptuousness of his household decorations, and especially that of the room in which he had to work, were not merely useful but perhaps essential in that they gave him a feeling of complete insulation from the unfriendly outer world.

which at that time were only dimly stirring within him. The high cost of this Paris house of his was due in part to its garden — and a garden, ensuring him as it did a certain amount of protection from the incessant piano-playing that had made his life a misery to him in many places, was really more of a necessity than a luxury in his case. The same craving for an insulating space about him and for a further luxurious entrenchment of himself in the centre of that space manifested itself again in each later period of his life when he wished to concentrate on his creative work — in Biebrich and Vienna in 1863, when he was occupied with the *Meistersinger,* in Munich in 1864–5, when he hoped to sink himself in the *Ring* and complete it within three years or so, and again in Triebschen and in Bayreuth, where once more he hoped to be able to forget the outer world for long stretches of time and lose himself in the divine joy of composition.

He was himself fully aware of this peculiarity of his being, and on several occasions made open confession of it to his correspondents. When Malwida von Meysenbug returned from London to Paris in the autumn of 1860 and found that he was no longer in the pleasant, tranquil haven of the Rue Newton but in an apartment on the second floor of a large building in the Rue d'Aumale, one of the noisiest and darkest streets in Paris, she felt a pang of pity for him.[24] He had been compelled to go there, she says, for pecuniary reasons. Another consideration had been operative, however — the proximity of the Rue d'Aumale to the Opéra made his daily journeys there less exhausting for him. With his energies sure to be drained to the last drop for months to come by the *Tannhäuser* rehearsals, there could be no thought for the present of resuming work on the *Ring:* it was therefore a matter of almost entire indifference to him where or how he dragged out his mere bodily existence. " From next October ", he wrote to Wesendonk in June, when it had become clear to him that he could not remain much longer in the Rue Newton,

" I shall rent a smaller lodging in the town, much nearer to the Opéra, abandoning all ideas of peace and comfort, as I shall have to bid good-

---

[24] MMI, II, 190. Malwida's reminiscences of Wagner in this period of his life are of exceptional interest.

bye to the Muse for some time. When I fitted up that last little house for myself I had nothing else in my mind . . . than soon taking up my work again, and having a place in which I could live in peace and quiet for it. Only when I want to conjure the Muse to me and bind her fast, however, do I seriously think of arranging my house for quiet and cosiness: as soon as I give her up, all that kind of thing has no longer any meaning for me. If it is just a matter of attending to business, making myself dog-tired and coming home half-dead, then the tiniest nook suffices for my rest, for this rest is something of far less importance than rest for creating. As I am not composing at present, everything that has the appearance of the superfluous oppresses me: and if I ever give up all hope of meeting the Muse again, some people will be astonished how little I need for the other sort of rest! "

7

People who had eyes only for the outer man at that time were astonished at his elasticity under the tremendous strain: some of them were even under the delusion that he was happy, and put it down to his " good fortune " in the matter of *Tannhäuser* at the Opéra. Of all his associates just then, only Malwida saw beneath the surface and understood something of his inner misery; and she, as we have seen, did not return to Paris until the autumn. By then he was almost crushed under his financial cares; he was doing three men's work in the way of rehearsing, organising and letter-writing; and his general health and vitality, quite apart from his actual illness towards the end of the year, must have suffered terribly by the change from Switzerland and Venice to the bad air and incessant racket of Paris. At one time he had hardly a franc in his pocket; a letter written in June to Serov in Russia, in connection with the invitation from Sabouroff to St. Petersburg, remained on his hands for more than a month because he lacked the money to pay for the franking of it.

As usual when his life took a turn of this kind, he was at a loss to understand why the world should be so hard a place for one who, like himself, was capable of conferring so much beauty upon it. As he saw the matter, he wrote to Malwida on the 22nd June,[25] all he needed was " credit during a standstill " — i.e., until his royalties for the Paris *Tannhäuser* should come in.

[25] RWFZ, p. 275.

> "I must confess that I have never been in a situation such as this in all the eight years that my operas have been performed in Germany: I was always drawing something from them on which I could exist. But now all my older operas are completely exhausted, my new ones are impeded, I have enormous losses, and — no one who helps me!"

To Agnes Street he wrote on the same day in the same depressed strain:

> "How do you imagine I feel when I look at the world to which I might be so much, and then at myself, to whom, meanwhile, existence is being made simply impossible? Believe me, nobody can fathom the bitterness that people like myself experience; but believe me when I say that there is no helping the world in its stupid blindness — this world whose eyes open only when its treasure is lost!" [26]

And again to Malwida, on the 20th May,

> "I assure you that for my part I only turn my eyes upon the world to learn by experience how it behaves towards a man of my sort and understands how to profit by him — whether it grants him the sole scope defined for him by the laws of his own being for the development of his activity, or how much of this it can cheat him of. . . . This much is certain, that already I have created more than was necessary had I wanted to feel comfortable myself at times." [27]

"God knows for what I still exist!", he cried out to Mathilde Wesendonk in a letter of the 2nd May that lets us into the secret of his misfortune and his misery as a writer of operas. He has the choice, he says, of producing (in the theatre) his old works or creating new ones. The former means for him the expenditure of the last ounce of his vitality in the attempt to secure an adequate performance, a struggle in which the turning of his soul's eye inward upon himself is treason to the task in hand — he must look only outwards, belong solely to the world, let it betray him, humiliate him, torture him, destroy him, in order that he may pass over into its conscience. The alternative is that he shall renounce all possibility of ever hearing his works, and consequently of ever revealing them to the world as they really are. That would mean a sacrifice for him, and yet, perhaps, a satisfaction also: for his inner voice tells him that never will he find contentment through the performance of his works — "always there will be a secret pain

---

[26] GRW, III, 264.   [27] RWFZ, pp. 269–270.

that tortures me all the more because I must conceal it and deny it, if I am not to be regarded as an utter madman." Yet such a sacrifice would mean, in a way, happiness for him —

> " in the first place, complete, absolute personal poverty; never again the smallest care about possessions; some family that will harbour me, satisfy my very modest needs, in exchange for which I will assign to it all that may ever be mine; there to do nothing, have no other aim beyond the writing of my final works, everything I still have in my head. And then I shall leave it also to my protecting daemon to summon the man who shall one day reveal these works of mine to the world " —

it being left open to him, however, to accept this interpreter or to reject him if he thought him impossible.

8

All the while that he was flinging himself into the routine business of rehearsing *Tannhäuser* with an energy that surprised everyone, and, indeed, assuring his friends abroad that the performance would be the best he had ever known of any of his works, within himself he was dead to the world of reality. In June, the reader will recall, he had had to ask Wesendonk to allow him to retain for his own immediate needs the fee received from Schotts for the *Rhinegold,* to be set off against the future delivery of the score of the fourth section of the *Ring.*

> " I shall certainly produce this last piece [the *Götterdämmerung*] some day; for if that were not reserved for me I know not what mission could still hold me to life, daily longing for death as I do with all my heart. It is very possible that you will have reproaches to make me; impossible also, however, that you will not save them for a later time, when they could no longer serve to increase the greatest bitterness towards life that any man could feel."

As was to be the case again later, in the Munich years, contact with the theatrical world, even though it brought with it a temporary heightening of all his energies and ultimately the joy of triumph, caused also an instinctive protective withdrawal of himself to the inner citadel of his being, gazing out from which upon the ordinary world of men everything seemed curiously unreal to him. The feeling, during these Paris days, that happiness for the artist is to be achieved only by the denial of the will to live brought to the surface, as of old, all that was mystical in his temperament. He took refuge again, as in the Venice period, in Schopenhauer and the Buddha; and, by a natural transition, he turned once more to Mathilde Wesendonk as a mirror in which he might the better contemplate himself. It is exceedingly doubtful whether she ever had any real comprehension of his philosophising. But it has already been argued in these pages that in the Asyl and the Venice days he had idealised her not because she had " inspired " *Tristan* but because, full of *Tristan* as he was, he saw her with a spiritual aura about her head that emanated from nothing really within herself but was only a projection from the tropical heat-haze in which his music enveloped them both. Now, in the summer of 1860, when the Tristan-Schopenhauer-Buddhistic mood again floods the innermost chamber of his soul, he instinctively turns once more to Mathilde as the recipient of his confidences. For a few weeks his letters to her read like a continuation of those of 1858 from Venice — a continuation, it is true, that lacks most of the tense poetic quality of the earlier letters, for the emotional heat of *Tristan* was no longer in him except as a memory, but unmistakably the same in psychological essence. To others also of his correspondents he can bewail his misery, his sense of strangeness in an irrational, incomprehensible world; but to none of them does he use quite the same language as to Mathilde.

The more the world, especially the theatrical world in which so much of his time is now spent, envies him for his " good fortune ", his " power ", his " fame ", the more it sees him as a man inordinate in his personal desires and in his demands upon others, the more strangely, he tells her, does he despise all that the world is offering him. Even bitterness towards it he does not feel as of old: bitterness is being replaced by contempt.

" So I reveal myself less and less in speech, reflecting that I am not a man to be understood through my actions, and hoping that some day something at least of my works will meet with understanding. But to you I say this — only the sense of my purity confers on me this power. I feel myself pure: I know in the innermost depth of me that I have never wrought for myself, but only for others; and my perpetual sufferings are my witnesses."

[79]

The justice of that proud sad claim an understanding world will not deny him now: there is murk enough about him as a man in his relations with individuals, but as an artist facing a world that is ceaselessly trying to corrode the ideality and integrity of every artist there has never been an example of higher courage or cleaner conscience.

To Mathilde he talks once more of Schopenhauer, and reincarnation, and *Die Sieger,* and Day's illusion and Night's redemption, and all the old esoteric things with which, in days of trial gone by, he had built for himself a golden bridge to his own spirit in the belief that he was building one to hers.

" When all has withdrawn inwards, unsatisfied, the life within grows warmer and brighter. This is the night of *Tristan:* ' Barg im Busen uns sich die Sonne, leuchten lachend Sterne der Wonne! ' . . . . A life-course such as mine must always be illusory to the onlooker; he sees me engaged in acts and undertakings he imagines to be my own, whereas at bottom they are utterly alien to me; who perceives the repugnance that often fills my soul? All this will remain uncomprehended until the day comes when the sum is cast and the balance struck."

The nearer the time came for the performances that promised to be a supreme triumph for him, the more illusory all this ant-like activity in the theatre appeared to him. " How strangely it all fares with me now ", he wrote to Mathilde just before Christmas.

"Towards everything which, generally speaking, sets the world in motion I remain cold and unmoved. Fame has no power at all over me, and Profit only so far as I may need it to keep me independent: of taking any serious step to win either I am quite incapable. Getting my own way is also a matter of indifference to me, since I know how incredibly few people are capable of even the beginning of an understanding of their fellows. The profound longing, natural and pardonable, to see a fully representative performance of each of my works has very much cooled down of late, especially during this last year: this mixing again with singers, players, and so on has wrung many a sigh out of the depths of me, nourished my resignation mightily on this side also."

Resignation will be more than ever necessary to him in the future, he continues, for when he looks at the operatic world as it is, and then at his own newest works, he has to admit frankly to himself that these are " unperformable ". What keeps him going through this inwardly repugnant business of producing *Tannhäuser* is merely the necessity imposed on him of captaining his forces. In the theatre itself he is for the time being stimulated, in spite of himself, by the artistic problems that come up for solution; before each rehearsal, however, he has to goad himself to feel an interest in his work, and after it he asks himself the reason for it all. " I squander myself and my energies — and for a thing that really leaves me indifferent! " This was the mood in which he faced the final stage of the preparations for *Tannhäuser*.

CHAPTER IV

GATHERING CLOUDS

1

FOR THE *Tannhäuser* settings and costumes, apparently, Wagner could hardly wish for anything better than those used in the original Dresden production of 1845.[1] As Desplechin no longer possessed the sketches for these décors, Wagner obtained them in July from the Dresden theatre through his old friend Wilhelm Heine, as also Heine's own sketches for the costumes. Presumably both costumes and settings had been designed in 1845 in accordance with Wagner's indications. He had heard, he tells Heine, that the Berlin setting for the Hall of Song had been very fine, and if Heine could obtain drawings of this for him he would see if it were possible to improve on the Dresden design by means of them at any point: but, he adds, " I certainly do not believe that it answers to my scenic demands — for I simply cannot consent to give up the open archway with the stairway and tower." [2] We may probably assume that the Paris settings were finally a compromise between those of Dresden and those submitted by the Opéra artists, for we find Wagner telling Frau Wesendonk, in September, that he had " thrice rejected the plans for the scenery before they produced what I wanted." On the theatre bill for the first performance, Cambon, Desplechin and three others are mentioned as responsible for the décors.

Wagner had nothing but praise for the zeal and industry shown by the personnel at the rehearsals until these reached the point at which the Opéra conductor, Dietsch, took charge. In all there were

---

[1] See Vol. I, p. 394.

[2] An aquarelle by Heine of the Dresden setting for the Hall of Song is reproduced in JKRW, p. 37. Figurines showing Heine's costume designs for some of the leading characters (now in the Richard Wagner Museum in Eisenach) will be found in ERWL, p. 145 ff. The "open arch with the stairway and tower" are striking features of the aquarelle.

one hundred and sixty-three rehearsals of one kind and another, in most of which Wagner took an active part: [3] in addition he was constantly coaching individual singers in the Rue d'Aumale. Of the orchestra, he assured Mathilde Wesendonk, he could " ask anything: it is the best in the world." Even in departments in which he was conscious of a secret lack of sympathy with his ideals he had no complaint to make on the score of conscientiousness. From Vauthrot, the chorus-master, for instance, he never heard a word of enthusiasm; yet Vauthrot made up in discipline for what he lacked in warmth. Cormon, the stage-manager, was equally scrupulous; while to the mise en scène, says Wagner, " a care was given of which I had never had any conception before."

By the end of September the verses for the remodelled and ex-panded scene in the first act between Venus and Tannhäuser were finished, and he had even been able to make a start with the music. Other portions of the score had also been touched up where neces-sary: " for instance ", he wrote to Frau Wesendonk, " at Tann-häuser's outburst at the end of the second act I have replaced a very tame passage for the violins by a new one, which is very diffi-cult, but the only thing that will suffice." [4] In his letter of the 30th September he sets forth in detail for Mathilde's benefit the changes he has made in the text of the Venus-Tannhäuser scene.[5] The new matter commences with Venus's cry of " Zieh' hin, Wahnsin-niger! ", at the conclusion of the third stanza (in E flat major) of Tannhäuser's song. After Venus's " Suche dein Heil, und find' es nie " the dialogue between the pair is greatly extended, the four pages or so from this point to the end of the scene in the original vocal score now becoming twelve. The text printed in the Collected Edition of Wagner's prose and poetical works agrees, apart from two or three trifling variants, with that in the letter to Mathilde. The text in the new vocal scores, however, differs widely from this; the reason being that, having written his music to the French

---

[3] For further details see *infra*, p. 107.
[4] He is referring to the passage immediately following the conclusion of the Pil-grims' Song, where, a few bars before the curtain falls, Tannhäuser cries out "To Rome!". In the original version there are four rather conventional bars for the violins at this point: in the Paris version the four bars become eight, and the whole character of the violin figure is altered and improved.
[5] The verses are omitted from the English version of the letters.

words, Wagner found, when he came to make a German performing version, that numerous verbal changes were necessary if the
melodic shape was to be preserved intact. A single example will
suffice to show the difficulties in which this task involved him. In
the draft that he gave to Truinet to turn into French, Venus thus
describes the hypothetical pleading of Tannhäuser to be taken
into her favour again:

" O fändest du sie wieder,
die einst dir gelacht!
Ach, öffneten sich wieder
die Thore ihrer Pracht! " —
Da liegt er vor der Schwelle,
wo einst ihm Freude floss:
um Mitleid, nicht um Liebe,
Fleht bettelnd der Genoss!

in the German singing version this becomes:

" O fändest du sie wieder,
die einst dir gelächelt!
Ach, öffnete sie dir wieder
die Tore ihrer Wonnen! " —
Auf der Schwelle, sieh' da!
ausgestreckt liegt er nun,
dort wo Freude einst ihm geflossen!
Um Mitleid fleht er bettelnd,
nicht um Liebe!

The formal symmetry of the first version has had to be sacrificed;
the lines are now cut to irregular lengths, and the rhymes have
disappeared.[6]

With the singers, in general, Wagner had little trouble in the
earlier stages; they seem to have been fascinated by a type of
music that was new to most of them, and to have thrown themselves
into the study of it heart and soul. Wagner's tuition worked wonders with some of them; they shed all their faults and mannerisms

---

[6] A study of the differences between the Dresden and the Paris *Tannhäuser* will
be found in an essay on *A Neglected Page of Wagner's*, in Lawrence Gilman's *The
Music of Tomorrow*.

for the time being. " The French singers ", Bülow wrote to Kalli-woda in February, 1861 after seeing a full rehearsal,[7] " are as if transformed: there is no longer a trace of tremolando or vibrato — only beautiful, expressive singing." The Italian Madame Tedesco, he told Raff, had convinced him that " a German soprano must be very poor if she can't master the part of Isolde." We have already seen that Bülow did not think very much of the tenor chosen to play Walther von der Vogelweide. In the end Walther's solo in the tournament of song was cut out, the two sections of Tannhäuser's outburst now being fused into one, " with an orchestral prelude or interlude ", says Bülow, " making it apparent that Tannhäuser has suddenly become the victim of an enchantment that snatches him away from his bodily surroundings and ' magnetises ' him into a reminiscent dream-state ". " The mounting ", he added, " defies description — a thing of such marvellous beauty that it has to be seen to be believed. In comparison with this, everything that the German stages have done is merely puerile."

2

Wagner's most grievous disappointment came from the quarter in which he had expected, and had the right to expect, the greatest faith and loyalty, — from the one German singer in the com-pany. He was for a time very enthusiastic over Niemann, believ-ing that he had at last found the Heldentenor of his heart's desire — raw enough at the moment, it is true, but presumably capable of shaping and polishing into first-rate Wagner material. It took him only a few weeks to realise his mistake. Niemann had come to Paris entirely for his own sake, not for Wagner's. He had the usual crude notions of his species as to what was " effective ", and bridled at Wagner's hints that something more than " effect " was required to play Tannhäuser as his creator had conceived him. The tenor's vanity and his anxiety for a " success " had led him to make acquaintances in the Parisian journalistic world, from whom he discovered that underground forces were already at work

---

[7] He had gone to Paris in the belief that the first performance would take place on the 25th February. At the rehearsal of which he is speaking, the whole time from seven-thirty to midnight was devoted to the second act and the first half of the first. "Never a sign, even to the very end, of inattention or slackening." BB, III, 382.

bent on ruining Wagner and his opera. He saw himself condemned to return to Germany without the " triumph " for himself that he had counted on; and he became the victim of a nervous depression from which Wagner in vain tried to rescue him. Of a generous thought for Wagner, of respect for him as a composer, of courtesy to him as an older man and a great figure, of sympathetic understanding of his trials and cares, he seems never to have given the least evidence, or indeed shown the smallest capacity, from first to last. " Courage, friend! ", Wagner had written him on the evening of the 1st October, no doubt after a discouraging afternoon with him in the theatre; " everything will turn out splendidly. Take this from one who himself has his bad hours! "

The situation, so far from improving, grew worse the nearer the time for the first performance drew: Niemann, thinking now only of what he personally could save from what he was convinced was doomed to be a wreck, entrenched himself all the more obstinately in the crude theatrical routine he had brought with him from Germany, and refused to adopt any suggestions made by Wagner. By the third week in February, 1861 — only three weeks before the first performance — Wagner had to write him a long letter, running to twelve printed pages, in which we see him asking as a favour, almost at the eleventh hour, for an understanding and a trust that ought to have been granted him as a matter of course from the first. The letter, in spite of the fatigue from which Wagner must have been suffering, in spite of his manifest heartbreak over the turn for the worse that the *Tannhäuser* affair was indisputably taking now, is a model of patience and reasonableness. The suffering which prompted it, however, is unmistakable. In later years, particularly in the first Bayreuth period, Wagner sometimes had cause to complain of the behaviour of a singer towards him; but never, in the whole course of his life as an artist, was he so grievously wounded as now by Niemann. It was something he never forgot to the end of his days.

He begins his letter by asking the singer to turn to the last page first, and then to read the remainder or not, according to his mood. The last lines run thus: " Be tranquil! Take care of yourself, and — if that be possible — come to an opinion about me that will allow you in future to show me rather more consideration than is evident in the tone of your letter to me of today." Wagner's letter is exceptionally interesting not only for the insight it gives us into his difficulties with Niemann but for the light it throws on what had been from the very beginning the cause of the trouble the German tenors had with the part of Tannhäuser.

It is manifest that all through the rehearsals the fatuous self-esteem of the twenty-nine-years old Niemann had made it impossible for him to take advice from the composer of forty-seven.

> " Since our study of *Tannhäuser* began, six months ago ", says Wagner, " I have had the satisfaction of working so advantageously on singers who, until then, had not the least idea of how to sing my music, that everyone is astounded at the success achieved, as shown by their performances. But whereas in that quarter everything improves and fills me with joy and hope, *you* show yourself smaller and smaller, and, receding from me step by step, rob me of the satisfaction of feeling that I have had any influence at all upon you."

While a Tedesco and a Sax have been glad to act upon his suggestions as to phrasing and breath-taking, he has not been able to persuade Niemann to take his advice even in so small a matter as the division of two phrases by a breath in the first stanza of Tannhäuser's song to Venus, so as to secure at once a better musical shape and give a more intimate meaning to the melodic line.[8]

His confident selection of Niemann to sing Tannhäuser, he says, had drawn the eyes not merely of Germany but of Europe upon the ambitious young tenor, yet this " blind trust " on his part has not met with the smallest return:

> " Never, since your arrival in Paris, have I succeeded in obtaining the slightest trust from your side. You have held aloof from me in a fashion that has been well-nigh insulting, and have gone to almost excessive trouble to avoid taking any advice whatever from me. You had the indelicacy to tell me, long before there was any necessity to do so, that at the end of May you would finish for good and all with *Tann-*

---

[8] The passage in question is evidently the transition from the last line of the first section of the song — "Gab deine Gunst mir Sterblichem dahin" — to the first line of the second section — "Doch sterblich, ach! bin ich geblieben". One conjectures that Wagner wanted a strict observance of the fermata over the last syllable of "dahin", and the commencement not merely of a new verbal sentence but of a new musical sentence with the "Doch" of the next line; whereas Niemann joined the C of the "Doch" to the D flat of the "-hin" in the fashion still affected by Italian and Italianised singers in cases of this kind.

häuser in Paris,[9] and indeed that in future you wished to have as little to do with my operas as possible. . . ."

Although from the beginning Niemann had shown himself reluctant to take hints as to the interpretation of his part, Wagner had still trusted to his " sound artistic receptivity " to effect an understanding between them on various points of detail. Now, after working with him for six months, he sees that Niemann is stubbornly bent on singing Tannhäuser in Paris precisely as he had sung it in Germany. He gives the tenor generous credit for many things in his performance; but he feels bound to ask him to take his word for it that the idea of the part he had brought with him to Paris is not ideally complete. " It was the product of an immense talent operating on the foundation of a first youthful conception "; the object of his studying the part with the composer should be to ripen this conception intellectually, and, at the same time, to help him to find the technical means by which certain difficulties of execution were to be surmounted.

3

There had always been a difference of opinion between Wagner and the German tenors as to what constituted the essence of *Tannhäuser*. The tenors, thinking, as tenors everywhere are inclined to do, only of making a big impression on the audience before the fall of the final curtain, and more especially with a shrewd professional eye for the easy " effect " to be achieved in Tannhäuser's story of his pilgrimage to Rome, had come to believe, and had persuaded their audiences to believe, that the act which mattered most was the third. In the opinion of the creator of the work, however, — who, after all, might be supposed to know something about the matter — the dramatic crux of the opera was in the first two acts, particularly the second. It was here that every tenor, from Tichatschek onwards, had disappointed Wagner. They had all begged for a cut in the great finale of the second act because, for one thing, they wanted to save their voices for the third. It was in vain that Wagner argued that the pilgrimage was something that any tenor worthy of the name ought to be able to sing without the smallest

---

[9] Niemann's contract bound him to the Opéra until then.

sense of fatigue, and that if they found the Tannhäuser part too
exacting in the choral and orchestral ensembles at the end of the
second act, this was purely and simply because they had not grasped
the meaning of the part *dramatically;* once they understood the
true import of the passage that frightened them, they would find
that the mere vocal power to deal with the situation would come
of itself. The crucial episode in this finale was that commencing
with Tannhäuser's words " Zum Heil den Sündigen zu führen "
and culminating in his agonised cry of " Erbarm' dich mein, der
ach! so tief in Sünden, schmachvoll des Himmels Mittlerin ver-
kannt! " Delete or weaken this passage, and, as is implicit in all
that Wagner says on the subject, the psychological life-nerve of
the drama has been severed. From the very commencement he had
had trouble with Tichatschek over this episode; having more voice
than brains, as is suspected in some quarters to have been the case
with more than one tenor since opera began, the worthy Tichatschek " could not succeed in grasping the characteristic nature of
a demand addressed more to his capacity as an actor than to his
talent as a singer." [10]

In some of the older vocal scores of *Tannhäuser,* at the point
where the tenor enters with his " Zum Heil den Sündigen zu
führen ", we find a footnote to the effect that " if necessary, the
other voices can be silent (leaving Tannhäuser singing alone) " for
some twenty following bars. This cut was made in practically
every German performance of the opera, being everywhere regarded as " sanctioned by the composer ".[11] It was " sanctioned "
by Wagner only in sheer despair of ever getting the passage interpreted as he intended it to be. Since everyone on the stage took
part in this finale, they assumed it to be, says Wagner, " an ordinary
concerted piece, in which no single individual thinks himself en-

[10] *On the Performing of Tannhäuser,* in RWGS, V, 133–4. One wonders how many
of those who are engaged today in "the performing of *Tannhäuser*" have ever cast
an eye on that pregnant treatise. Not many, it is to be feared, judging by what one
still sees and hears in the average opera house! And when we see the fatuities perpetrated — with the best intentions, of course — in the name of Wagner in *Tristan*
and the *Ring* and other works of his in most opera houses today, after all that Wagner
wrote and said on these matters, and after countless reprints and discussions of what
he wrote and said, we have an almost terrified sense of the imbecility that must
have characterised most of the earlier performances of his works.

[11] There is no mention of such a cut in the *original* score published by Wagner
himself.

titled to make himself especially prominent " — a conventional " adagio-ensemble ", in fact, " of the type we are accustomed to in operatic finales just before the concluding stretto ". Performed in this unintelligent fashion, the episode seemed too spun-out: and so, when the theatres began asking for cuts, these half-dozen pages were among those sacrificed by Wagner. But he never ceased to plead that he had done so under compulsion, and to insist that as these pages were perhaps the most important of all to the true understanding of his work, they ought to be restored to any performance of *Tannhäuser* that professed to be in accordance with his intentions.

> " Wherefore my prayer goes out to every future player of the part of Tannhäuser to lay the utmost weight on the passage in question. . . . The cries of ' Ach! erbarm' dich mein! ' demand so poignant an accent that it is not sufficient here for him to be merely a well-trained singer; the highest dramatic art alone will endow him with the necessary energy of grief and desperation for an expression that must seem to burst forth from the very bottom of a heart in the direst pain, like a cry for redemption. It is the conductor's duty to see that the desired effect is made possible to the chief singer by means of the most discreet accompaniment on the part of the rest of the voices and the orchestra."

All this, and much more to the same effect, had been in print since 1852, apparently without anyone whose special business it was to read it taking much notice of it: the tenors in particular would have small use for it, it being the notorious privilege of these gifted creatures to be better judges than the composer himself of the correct way of interpreting a work. Niemann had been singing Tannhäuser since 1854, with, of course, the traditional cuts.

Wagner's letter to him shows us clearly enough what the source of the trouble was between them. Not merely had the tenor only the minimum of notion what the drama of *Tannhäuser* as a whole was about, but even had he understood it better he was technically too undeveloped to give Wagner all he wanted. Evidently he relied, as operatic tenors of his " heroic " type are always inclined to do, on weight of metal rather than finesse in the use of it: so long as he could make the desired and admired " effect " in this or that major moment, the minor moments did not greatly matter. Wagner, it is obvious, tried to convince him that it was not enough merely to flash a light from mountain top to mountain top: the valleys in between also required illumination. This is clear enough from Wagner's delicate hint that Niemann should " apply the polishing file to his voice, especially when it was a matter of soft tones ", and aim at " effecting the proper connection between the brilliant individual moments." He hoped, he added, that Niemann would not counter this criticism with " the usual theatre-jargon of ' effects ' and ' thunder-claps ' "; to that sort of thing he would not reply. Wagner, with his long experience of opera singers, surely might have known that it was useless to appeal to them, or at any rate to more than two or three of the exceptionally intelligent among them, on purely artistic grounds such as these. It was particularly futile in the case of Niemann because his professional vanity was bound to be sorely bruised by Wagner's criticisms. His crude Tannhäuser had been over-praised in Hanover and elsewhere by critics and audiences who knew even less about the true essence of the work than he did. He himself, in his diary, complacently notes that in Hanover he had " made his greatest effect " in this rôle, and that it " established " him in his new job there.[12] After seven years of uncritical adulation for his Tannhäuser — adulation in the bestowal of which he himself had been by no means niggard — it must have been a shock to him to discover that Wagner did not think very highly of much of it. He had seen himself, in advance, " triumphing " in Paris with the " effects " that had gone down so well in the German provinces: to be told that the first things he had to do were to rid himself of the notion that these superficial " effects " were everything and to devote himself seriously to a fresh study of the work from the foundations up, was more than his self-esteem could stand.

---

[12] See the entry for the 21st January, 1855, in RWAN, p. 42. Niemann had made his début in Hanover in the preceding September. He had sung Tannhäuser for the first time in July 1854, in Insterburg; and the young man of twenty-three had been so naïvely satisfied with his performance that he assured the Hanover Intendant that "Tannhäuser might have been written for me". Which reminds one of the priceless remark of an admirer of a certain notorious German conductor of the present day, whom we will call X.: "Beethoven ist der richtige X.-Komponist". Could there be higher praise for Beethoven?

4

He had told Wagner that in Germany it was only in the third act that he was conscious of being at his best. Wagner's reply to that naïve confession was his usual one — that even mediocre singers everywhere had found it easy to be quite " effective " in this act, just as the first tenor you happened to light upon could not help being " effective " in the frenzy scene in *Masaniello*. " Let me assure you, however, that I will make you a present of this third act if only you will do the finale of the second act as I want it ", for *this* is the central point of the whole work considered not merely as an opera for the glory of the singers but as a drama. He harks back again to that cut in the finale which, to his enduring sorrow, he had made in days gone by for Tichatschek, and that had by this time become *de rigueur* in the theatres, the innocent notion of both tenors and conductors being that if a Tichatschek could not sing the crucial passage in the finale no one could. Wagner tells Niemann that it was not because of the strain the passage imposed on Tichatschek's voice that he had consented to delete it — regarded from the vocal standpoint alone it was child's play to the Dresden giant. The trouble had been that Tichatschek, by reason of his intellectual limitations, had not been able to make the passage " tell " through the choral texture purely and simply by an intensity of sorrowful expression which could make itself felt even in a subdued tone. At that time the simple expedient, which Wagner adopted later, of dispensing with the other voices, leaving Tannhäuser singing alone for these few bars, had not occurred to him: and so he had sanctioned that cutting out of the whole episode that was afterwards such an annoyance to him.[13] Niemann had shown conclusively, in his rehearsals with Wagner, that he had at his command the very tones required for the " Erbarm' dich

---

[13] He found it a pure impossibility to make any impression on the indolence and stupidity of the operatic world where this *Tannhäuser* cut was concerned. The trouble had begun with Tichatschek in 1845. In 1852–3 Wagner had gone carefully over the whole ground in the essay *On the Performing of Tannhäuser*. In 1860 he had to go over it again verbally with Niemann. And in 1875 we find him telling Richter that either the Vienna tenor, Leonhard Labatt, will sing the passage in the second finale without the usual cut or he [Wagner] will wash his hands of the "model production" of *Tannhäuser* which the Vienna Opera was planning to give. See RWHR, p. 134.

mein! ". All he had to do was to employ these tones in the actual performance, and to sing the finale of the second act as if the evening were to end with this, calmly confident that after it he would find the third act, sung as Wagner wished it to be sung, a bagatelle to a tenor of his herculean power.

But all this, of course, cut straight across every instinct of Niemann as a " star " tenor for whom the third act of any opera, seeing that here was *his* farewell to the audience for the night, was by that very fact more important than any imaginable first or second act. The difference between the points of view of the two men must have become still more glaring when Wagner made it clear to Niemann that the very virtues which, in the tenor's opinion, rendered his third act so " effective " and had made it go down so well in such centres of culture as Insterburg and Gumbinnen, were from the composer's point of view deplorable psychological errors. If one could persuade oneself that it is any use talking reason to the average tenor, one might urge him, if he should be thinking of playing Tannhäuser, to read and ponder what Wagner had to say to Niemann about the third act. The things that seemed to the Hanover singer the most important of all — brilliance and power of tone — were precisely what Wagner did *not* want here.

" In the third act ", he writes to Niemann, " you are much too vigorous for my liking, too sensuously strong; in vain I have waited hitherto for the nuances I desire. In this act I do *not* want any exhibition of sensuous power of voice: everything you do here is too material. To keep level with you I would have to re-orchestrate my music completely from the moment of your entry. Everything is calculated here [14] in terms of a ghostlike tonelessness, with a gradual rise to no more than an expression of affecting softness. The whole narration, as far as the arrival in Rome, is sung by you too loudly and with too sensuous a tone-quality: it is not thus that one who has just awakened from madness and attained to a few lucid minutes narrates his experiences, one whom the passer-by instinctively shuns, one who for months past has hardly known what it is to eat, and whose very life is kept in being only by the last tiny flicker of an insane longing."

[14] I.e., in the first few minutes of Tannhäuser's scene with Wolfram. The directions for Tannhäuser's first words are "mit matter Stimme": the voice, that is to say, is to be feeble, weary, lustreless, in keeping with the physical and mental condition of the character. Apart from a bar or two, this colour has to be maintained through the whole of the first part of the scene.

The Pope's excommunication, as Niemann delivered it, has an energy that is indeed of overwhelming " effect "; but the employ-ment of a smaller tone would not merely not weaken this effect but positively increase it, by giving it the right psychological tinge. It is not for a purely vocal " effect " such as Niemann is aiming at here that Wagner can consent to sacrifice the vital finale to the sec-ond act: if Tannhäuser has not been able to win the proper sympa-thetic interest of the audience there, the capturing of that interest by tenoristic " effect " in the third act means nothing at all. There follow some detailed instructions as to Tannhäuser's acting in the scene with Wolfram, and as to the general melodic and verbal nuancing required in the third act and elsewhere. Wagner con-cludes with some tactful but obviously sincere compliments to Nie-mann's natural gifts as a singer, and a final exhortation to him to be faithful and of good courage. He has been hurt by the tenor's re-fusal to sing the new stanza he has written for Tannhäuser in the Contest of Song,[15] but on this point he is prepared to give way: as regards the finale of the second act, however, there can be no com-promise on his part, no sacrifice of this vital episode to Niemann's " momentary discouragement ".

5

When Wagner had arrived at this point in his letter, there ar-rived at the Rue d'Aumale one from the tenor.

"I had got thus far", says Wagner in his postscript, "when your letter reached me.[16] I see where you have now got to: you employ towards me a manner of speech which I find myself able to under-stand only by casting my mind back to the very first period of my painful career. Permit me to say that you are mistaken when you

[15] In the original Dresden version, the procedure after Wolfram's song in praise of love is (A) a song by Tannhäuser, commencing "Auch ich darf mich so glücklich nennen"; (B) Walther's song — "Den Bronnen, den uns Wolfram nannte"; (C) a second outburst from Tannhäuser — "O Walther, der du also sangest"; (D) the wrathful intervention of Biterolf. As already mentioned, in the Paris version B was cut out; A and C were fused into one. Tannhäuser now *begins* with C, addressing his words this time not to Walther but to Wolfram, and concludes with the main strain of A. This change of procedure necessitated a number not only of melodic but of verbal alterations, which Niemann, like a true "star" tenor, refused to learn.

[16] Presumably this is the letter, dated the 20th February, that is now in the Burrell Collection.

speak of having laid yourself open to ridicule, and I can only wonder who has been repeating the chatter of the boulevards to you. I ask myself doubtfully whether this letter of mine can still serve any good purpose with you, or whether it will only make matters worse. However, I will not all at once give up the last hope concerning my art. From this letter you can see how very high my opinion is of you, and the sure consciousness of this must preserve you from a superficial misunderstanding of the spirit in which I have addressed myself to you. But on one point I withdraw what I have said in this letter of mine: I am prepared to cut the passage in question. May you find peace! Take care of yourself, and — should that be possible — form an opinion of me that in future will ensure for me rather more regard on your part than is evident in the tone of your letter of today." [17]

This, then, was the situation, so far as his compatriot and leading singer was concerned, on almost the eve of the first performance. Niemann had come to Paris filled only with thoughts of his own glory, not of serving Wagner; and to lack of all conscience in the matter of art he had added an arrogance and a boorishness towards the Master himself such as Wagner had never met with before in the smallest provincial theatre. Wounded vanity was no doubt largely answerable for it all, though account must also be taken of Niemann's peculiar temperament. As is frequently the case with men of his physical build, there was a womanish strain in him that ran to hysteria in times of trial. It was in vain that Wagner had tried to guard in advance against his tenor being " compromis par des cabales souterraines." He could indeed insist on his not singing anywhere else in Paris until he had concluded his engagement with the Opéra; but he could not prevent him from being subtly wrought on in private by the enemy. Long before the work came to performance Niemann had had it drummed into him that a fiasco was certain; and in face of that fiasco he had no thought for anyone but himself. His rudeness to Wagner was mostly the effect of vanity and fear working on a mentality that was never particularly remarkable for refinement.

There were other hints, towards the end, of coming evil. Wagner began to have his doubts about one or two of the other singers, notably Madame Tedesco. Gasperini, who was in close touch with him and with the Opéra all this time, suggests that Wagner, in his first

[17] RWAN, pp. 129–130.

enthusiasm, had over-estimated the quality of his Venus: " as the production drew nearer, he realised little by little that he had expected too much of her." Apparently the clouds began to form when she discovered that Wagner had re-written her first scene and that consequently she had a quantity of new music to learn. Worse still, from the point of view of that day this new music was exceedingly difficult. Gasperini, who knew Wagner's works better than most Frenchmen of that epoch, and was thoroughly sympathetic towards both the man and his theories, shook his head in what seems to us now comic despair over the Paris revision of *Tannhäuser*. By a supreme exercise of the historical imagination we can just manage to realise that even in its Dresden form the opera was a difficult problem for French singers and a French audience of 1860: the new portions, in a style which we can now see to have many affinities with that of *Tristan*, must have complicated their problem immensely. Even Gasperini completely failed either to grasp the idiom of the new music or to comprehend the necessity for this expansion of the original. To Wagner it was the simplest matter in the world. Partly because of the lack of the right human material in the Dresden of 1845, partly because of his own relative artistic immaturity at that time, he had written a first scene that no longer satisfied him. He had always wanted to improve it; and now that the opportunity came his way to do so he naturally seized upon it. As Gasperini — and no doubt the other French friends of Wagner — saw the matter, however, the new bacchanal and the revised scene between Tannhäuser and Venus were

" perhaps the greatest mistake Wagner had ever made in all his career as a composer. The success he saw so close to him had literally intoxicated him. It occurred to him one day that his work was not on the level of all that was being done for it, that he must not miss so fine an opportunity to try out before the French public the ideas that had been fermenting in his head for years; so he formed the bizarre, extravagant, crazy resolution to re-touch his *Tannhäuser*, to add a whole new scene, and to write this scene — could he do otherwise? — in his latest style. Such a resolve was manifestly the death-blow to *Tannhäuser*. I made some friendly representations to him on the subject; nor was I the only one to do so. I implored him, in the name of art itself, in the name of the success assured for him, in the name of all his own interests which he was so gaily compromising, to change his mind, not to disrupt violently the unity of a work of his youth that was well-conceived and was quite homogeneous. All in vain! He completely re-wrote the words of his first scene, gave them to Nuitter . . . and a few days later the first scene between Tannhäuser and Venus was composed and sent out to the copyists. . . . The Opéra direction was not at all pleased about this drastic alteration in the original work: the singers were worried by it — especially Madame Tedesco, whom Wagner had confronted with many terrible difficulties of intonation: and from that moment she began to be doubtful about success. The rehearsals had to be begun all over again: they dragged on for some months; one postponement of the first performance followed on another: in a word, dissatisfaction broke out everywhere. Meanwhile Wagner fell ill, and had to keep to his bed for some weeks: and so — fresh obstacles, more delays." [18]

Wagner himself tells us, in *Mein Leben*, that when he returned to the theatre after his illness he found a marked change in the atmosphere. That illness, indeed, could not have come at a more unfortunate time. Had he been able to attend daily at the Opéra during the first few days when the singers and the orchestra were suddenly faced with these terrifying new problems of style, his energy and his personal magnetism might have helped them all to win through. As it was, they had to learn as best they could, without his help, a quantity of new music in an idiom that must have seemed immensely complex to singers who had been trained on Rossini, Meyerbeer, Verdi and Auber. Worst of all, when at last he managed to creep back to the theatre he was an exhausted man, unable to rekindle in others the fire that had died down, for the time being, to a dull smoulder even within himself. In his heart of hearts he seems to have already sensed in December that, as he puts it, " the affair had collapsed ", though he tried to persuade himself that it could not be so. The report had gone round, during his illness, that he was as good as dead; his coming back to the Opéra was that of a ghost to a hearth that had almost forgotten him, and, all in all, would not have been sorry now for an excuse to forget him. The rehearsals had been spun out too long: it would have been difficult in any case to maintain everyone's interest at so high a tension for months on end; and once the bow had been suffered to relax, as it had done during Wagner's absence, to get it back to its former tautness was virtually

---

[18] GW, pp. 61-2.

impossible. Bit by bit, however, the old demoniac energy returned to him, and with it the power to drive others even against their will. But he could not close his eyes to the fact that a subtle change had come over it all: while on the surface there was the same activity as at first, the same unquestioning obedience, the same complaisance towards him, at the back of everyone's mind now was the feeling that they were fighting merely a rearguard action in a battle already lost. He himself, and a few of his friends such as Bülow, could still persuade themselves, under the immediate thrill of a rehearsal, that it would all result in an incomparable performance. But even they, in cooler moments, were conscious of the storm-wind blowing up more violently day by day from two quarters — the Jockey Club and the Press.

CHAPTER V

THE STORM BREAKS

1

IN THE early weeks of 1861 Wagner's position was very much
that of the last heroic defender of a fort which he alone is unaware is undermined, the explosion being now only a matter of a
few hours more. He astonished his enemies and dismayed his
friends by refusing to employ the claque, the head of which was the
redoubtable David: and soon the wits were passing the word round
that the days of the German Goliath were numbered. In spite of
the arduous work put in by everyone since the beginning of September, by January 1861 a production was even yet hardly in
sight. Singers and orchestra were struggling with the new music
written for them. The problem of the ballet was still unsolved, in
spite of Walewski's friendly intervention about this time. Wagner's
newest suggestion was that if the balletomanes really could not get
through an evening without their usual ballet, one might be given
entirely for their benefit at the end of the performance; it would
have to be understood, however, that the opera was not to be cut in
any degree to find time for this, and that the divertissement [1] was
to be independent of the opera in every respect: moreover, even
this divertissement was not to be given in connection with the first
three performances, Wagner hoping that by that time his own
bacchanal would have made such an appeal that the Paris public

---

[1] One of the best touches of unconscious humour in the Opéra playbill is the description of Wagner's carefully planned dramatic bacchanal as a "divertissement
par M. Petipa". Another is the headline "Débuts de M. Niemann", dominating
the "Première Représentation, *Tannhäuser*, Opéra en trois actes et quatre tableaux,
de M. Richard Wagner" — with Niemann's name in letters twice the size of anything else on the bill except the name of the opera! The mere composer is fobbed off
with letters the same size as those thought good enough for the chief singers other
than Niemann. At the foot of the historic document is an announcement suggesting
the shape of things to come: "En attendant, 27me représentation, LE PAPILLON,
ballet-pantomine en 2 actes et 4 tableaux de *Marie Taglioni* et *M. de St.-Georges*, mus.
de *M. J. Offenbach*".

would not desire anything else in the same line. All his suggestions, of course, fell on deaf ears.

In December he was optimistically calculating, he told Otto Wesendonk, on a first performance by the end of January. In January the date was provisionally fixed for some day between the 15th and the 20th February. Early in February the definitive date was first given as the 25th, then the 27th. The next " definitive " date was the 8th March; but an illness of Madame Tedesco necessitating a postponement for nearly another week, the actual first performance did not take place until the 13th. All this time Wagner was doing three men's work in the theatre and elsewhere, and, though worn almost to a shadow with anxieties of all kinds and unable to get a single night's decent sleep, sustained even yet by the last shreds of his elastic optimism. In January he still felt justified in promising Wesendonk " a fine, highly-finished performance, even if the talents employed are not in every respect the ideal ones — non-existent! " In mid-February, no doubt after a rehearsal at which his tenor had shown some willingness to take advice, he even went so far as to describe him to Mathilde as " really grand — a great artist of the rarest kind ". About the others he is not so certain now as he was at the beginning, though he hopes for the best: he is a trifle perturbed about his Venus, whose contours, always ample, were now becoming redundant: Wagner goes so far as to hint that she is " rather stouter " than he could wish his Venus to be. He confidently invites Otto to Paris, telling him that if he is not inclined to make the journey in winter he can safely put it off till the summer, for *Tannhäuser* will be given " almost without interruption " until at least the end of May, when Niemann's contract expires.[2]

Wagner's and Bülow's hopes of a successful ending to the long and exhausting adventure gradually faded away from the moment the full rehearsals began. The first of these took place on the 19th

---

[2] Otto went to Paris towards the end of February, in the belief that the first performance would take place about the 25th or 27th; but owing to the postponement to the 13th March he was able to attend only a rehearsal or two before having to return to Zürich. Mathilde did not accompany him, obviously because a meeting with Minna would have been awkward for everyone.

Liszt, to Wagner's disappointment, did not go to Paris. The excuse was that his affairs detained him in Weimar; but the real reason was the Princess Wittgenstein's dislike of Wagner, which had by now become an obsession.

February. In accordance with the rules of the Opéra, Dietsch now took control of the orchestra. This Pierre Louis Philippe Dietsch, who in 1861 was in his fifty-third year, had apparently so far profited by the lesson of his fiasco with *Le Vaisseau Fantôme* in 1842 as to see the inadvisability of ever writing another opera,[3] though he continued to turn out a quantity of church music and works for the organ. (The spurious Ave Maria masquerading under the name of the sixteenth century composer Arcadelt, which figures so regularly in the programmes of our popular concerts, is gen-

---

[3] The curious reader will find amusing details of Dietsch's opera in an article on *Les deux 'Vaisseau-Fantôme'* in SEHM, pp. 257–270, and in one by Xavier de Courville — *Deux parodies françaises de Wagner* — in RMWF, p. 178.

The French librettists were Bénédict-Henri Révoil and Paul Foucher, the former shaping the plot, the latter being responsible for the verses. Révoil "improved" upon Wagner in many places. The Dutchmen now became Norwegians, and the Norwegians Shetlanders. The phantom seaman, who bears the name of Troïl, has not merely offended heaven and hell by rounding the Cape but has killed the pilot who tried to dissuade him. In the third act a monastery is added to the setting, in which, when the scene opens, the monks are heard welcoming in chorus a postulant who proves to be none other than Magnus, the former lover of Minna (Senta). When Minna comes to say her prayers in the church the monk raises his hood and discloses his identity; the spirit of his father, it appears, has come to him in a dream and told him to renounce love, become a monk, and perform the marriage ceremony between Minna and Troïl. It seems, however, that the pilot who not only had his good advice rejected but was killed by Troïl was Magnus's father. The dreadful deed had left on the murderer's hand a scar that would never heal; and when Troïl — who now calls himself Waldemar — is compelled by the monk to remove his glove in order to exchange rings with Minna, the blood-stained hand reveals to Magnus the assassin of his father! In the end, Minna "redeems" Troïl in the approved fashion, by jumping into the sea.

In an article in *Nord und Süd* in 1884, Ernst Pasqué told the story of the acquisition of Wagner's scenario as given him by Révoil himself four years before that date. According to this, Wagner, when he asked Pillet for news of his scenario, was informed that it had been passed on to Foucher and Révoil, and that he was not being defrauded in any way, as the legend already existed in a story by Heine. Pillet, however, kindly "took five napoleons out of his pocket" and handed them to Wagner, "not as a recognition of author's property but as an act of charity." Georges Servières examined the correspondence and the accounts of the Opéra for the period 1840–1842, and found no mention in either of them of the five hundred francs which Wagner says he drew from the theatre cashier on Pillet's order. It is quite possible, therefore, that Révoil's account of the affair is substantially correct. But even if Pillet put the transaction through as a personal one between Wagner, Révoil, Foucher and himself, we may respectfully be permitted to doubt whether, in compensating Wagner, he was weakly obeying the dictates of a too generous heart. Behaviour of that kind on the part of a French theatre director of that epoch would almost have justified his fellow-practitioners in striking him off the rolls for unprofessional conduct.

Dietsch's opera, given as a curtain-raiser before a ballet divertissement, had a run of eleven performances. Berlioz is said to have been accommodating enough, in his notice in the *Débats*, to find a good word for the cavatina sung by the monk.

erally blamed now on the gifted Dietsch). The famous Habeneck
had been succeeded at the Opéra in 1846 by Narcisse Girard, who
died suddenly in January 1860 while conducting a performance
of *Les Huguenots.* Berlioz had hoped to succeed Habeneck; had
he done so, the piquant situation might have arisen in 1861 of his
having to conduct *Tannhäuser,* for it was a rule of the Opéra that
the official musical head of the institution was to conduct every
new work. How the singularly incompetent Dietsch had managed
to obtain the appointment is not clear: anything, however, seems to
have been possible in the Paris Opéra of that epoch, provided only
it was sufficiently absurd. He held his post only until July 1863,
and died in February 1865. Like most of his French predecessors
and contemporaries he seems to have been incapable of reading
a full score: Berlioz assures us that Habeneck himself always conducted from a first violin part at the Conservatoire concerts, and
that " his successors have taken care to imitate him ". A Providence with a most misguided sense of humour had seen fit to ordain
that the destinies of Wagner and his *Tannhäuser* in the Paris of
1861 should lie in the hands of a Dietsch.

2

A few of Wagner's friends, among them Malwida von Meysenbug and, probably, Baudelaire, were present at the first full rehearsal, which lasted until one in the morning. To the casual spectator all seemed reasonably well on the surface: the effect of the
previous eight orchestral rehearsals under Wagner himself could
not be dissipated in a moment, even with a Dietsch now in command.
After the septet in which the Landgraf and the minstrels welcome
Tannhäuser back again to their midst the orchestra itself broke
into applause. No technician, however, could fail to perceive that
with the passing of the baton into the hands of Dietsch most of what
had been so painfully acquired during the last five months was already well on the way towards being completely lost. Full rehearsals would now have to be held not so much for the work's sake
as in order that the conductor might learn something of the score.
There was a second rehearsal on the 24th, after which the exasperated Bülow poured out his feelings in a letter to Raff. The post-

ponement of the first performance to some quite indefinite date or other had upset all poor Bülow's plans. He should already have been on his way back to Germany to fulfil concert engagements and attend to his teaching duties in Berlin; but the loyal creature could not reconcile himself to deserting Wagner in the hour of his great need. The sole cause of all the new trouble, he writes, is

> " that pitiful creature Dietsch, the most asinine, thickest-skinned, most unmusical of all the Kapellmeisters I ever came across in Germany. Under no circumstances is the composer to be allowed to conduct the first few performances, or even a full rehearsal: ' usus-tyrannus ' will not hear of it. Dietsch is afraid that, notoriously incompetent as he is, non-observance of this rule may cost him his post. It is monstrous that singers, chorus and orchestra, all of whom know their job inside out and are as safe as houses, should be put out of their stride by this ' Schöps [duffer] d'orchestre ', as Wagner calls him, with his wretched memory and his imbecile fumbling."

After this second exhibition of incompetence on Dietsch's part, Wagner felt it was time for him to act, and vigorously. On the 25th he sent Royer an ultimatum: " I decidedly cannot consent ", he wrote, " to have the results of the unprecedented zeal of so many artists and répétiteurs left to the mercies of a conductor who is incompetent to take charge of the definitive performance of my work." Dietsch has rejected a well-meant offer on Wagner's part to take a rehearsal himself, at which he would have been able to indicate the nuances he desires. It therefore becomes necessary for him to go further, and to

> " convey to you the irrevocable decision I have taken after yesterday's rehearsal. I now demand to conduct not only a rehearsal, which must be the final one, but also the three first performances of my work, the production of which I regard as impossible if you cannot find a way to meet my legitimate requirements. It is not for me to go into the difficulties that stand in the way of granting my request: all I can do is to impress on you the absolute necessity for it. . . . You will understand that, things being as they are, this question should be settled promptly. To prolong the rehearsals, even on the supposition that the conductor would benefit by them, is impossible. The artists are worn out; as for myself, I no longer feel within me the courage to undertake the education of the conductor in any other way than by inviting him to be present at the final rehearsal and the three performances under myself." [4]

[4] TLFW, pp. 231–2.

On the 7th March we find Bülow telling a Berlin friend that the problem can be solved only by " a sort of musical or theatrical coup d'état ". On that day Wagner made a direct appeal to Count Walewski. The Minister replied the next day. He welcomed politely the phrases in which Wagner had commended and thanked the whole of the personnel apart from Dietsch. But it was a rule in France, he continued, that the conductor should in no circumstances be deprived of the right " to remain at the head of his phalanx of executants "; indeed, a conductor who gave up his seat on one of " these solemn and decisive days " would be regarded as guilty of dereliction of duty, and would lose all future " prestige of authority ".[5] Wagner's coup d'état had thus failed. " Alas! ", Bülow wrote to Alexander Ritter on the 9th; " it is all settled. Wagner is not to conduct. ' Usus-tyrannus '. One of the wretchedest of blockheads, in comparison with whom the merest Schindelmeisser is a Franz Liszt, this Herr Dietsch, an old man [6] without intelligence, without memory, utterly unteachable — as has been proved at the numerous rehearsals that have been held solely for his instruction — destitute of an ear, is to conduct." Bülow discusses the singers and the orchestra, and concludes, " And all this will be practically ruined by this ass of a chef d'orchestre . . . who conducts from a first violin part! Who never gives the orchestra a single entry! Frightful! " The official view of the matter is reflected in a letter from Dietsch to his brother Joseph in Dijon. He had been summoned to the Minister's office, he says, where he had half-an-hour's talk with the Secretary-General.

" I saw that I was much stronger and more highly esteemed than I had ventured to hope. He complimented me on the firmness and decision of my character; and I confessed to him that the whole personnel of the Opéra, with the director at its head, had counselled me to give way. But I have fought them all. After Wagner had exhausted his intrigues at Court he tried to work on me by sending to me the Prussian and Austrian ambassadors, Prince Poniatowsky, and several other highly-placed Germans. To all of them my answer was ' No! No! ' "

The man's vanity was evidently on a par with his stupidity.

---

[5] BFWB, p. 38.
[6] Dietsch was only fifty-three.

3

It is difficult for us today to understand why the Emperor, after having conferred virtually unlimited power on Wagner, did not choose to exercise his authority in this one vital matter of the conducting of the final rehearsal and the first few performances of *Tannhäuser*. Not a single individual in the theatre could have had the smallest doubt about Dietsch's incompetence. Until the last rehearsals of all, Wagner, from his place on the stage, had conducted not only the performers but Dietsch; it was he who had given the tempi and indicated the nuances, and he had hoped that these would remain so fixed in the singers' and players' memory that they could defy the worst that Dietsch could do. It was not so, however; from the moment Dietsch assumed full control the whole machine became disorganised. Wagner now at last realised the danger of his position. There were some things, he said later, which, though making against an ideal performance, did not rule out the possibility of a good one — his singers were not all he could have desired, the spirit of his poem, which made an instinctive appeal to every German audience, could not be counted on to have the same effect in Paris,[7] and the absence of a ballet of the regular type was not a factor in the opera's favour. But as against all this he had reckoned confidently on the effect, even on a French audience, of the orchestral part of the score, interpreted by so fine a body of players. And it was precisely here, he says, that under Dietsch's touch he " saw everything melt away into a colourless chaos, with every line of the drawing obliterated ". The rot spread from the orchestra to the stage: the singers lost confidence in themselves, and even the poor ballet dancers could not keep time in their trivial steps. Yet, oddly enough, as soon as he appealed over Dietsch's head to the Minister the clan-spirit of the orchestra caused it to turn against him.

---

[7] Eduard Schelle, who was present at the performances, testifies that the French critics regarded the Tannhäuser legend as "an absurdity", "la chose la plus idiote qu'on ait jamais entendue." The average Parisian could not understand how the mere sound of a bell could tear Tannhäuser out of the arms of Venus. There was, indeed, a good deal of sympathy expressed with Venus: the general French feeling was that the poor dear had behaved so nicely towards Tannhäuser that she deserved rather better treatment from him. See STP, p. 15.

" This declaration of mine [that Dietsch was so incompetent that he himself would have to take charge of the opera] brought to a climax the confusion that had gathered about me: even the orchestra, which had long recognised and derided the incompetence of its conductor, took sides against me now that it had become a matter of its authorised chief. The Press foamed at the mouth over my ' arrogance '; and . . . Napoleon III could give me no better advice than to desist from my demands, as I was only endangering to the utmost my position and the chances of my work."

Once more he was assured that if the trouble were simply one of more rehearsals, he could have as many as he liked.

Perhaps the Dietsch problem would have been settled in Wagner's favour had he had the foresight to make it the crucial issue at the very beginning of the undertaking, refusing to let his work go into rehearsal at all unless he himself were allowed to conduct it. When the question finally came up for decision it was at the wrong psychological moment: by February, 1861, after some six months of unprecedented labour for everyone in the theatre, the one desire in the minds of all of them — of Napoleon and the Ministers no less than of the singers and players and dancers and designers — must have been to get the opera on to the stage now by hook or by crook and have finished with it and with its pest of a composer. The early enthusiasm of Royer and the others had not been altogether disinterested: they had regarded *Tannhäuser* as a first-rate business proposition for the Opéra, what with the fame — or notoriety — of Wagner as the leading German representative of " the music of the future ", and the exceptional publicity conferred on the undertaking by the carte blanche in the matter of trouble and expense given the composer by the Emperor. But by March, 1861 most of the keenness of the first few months had disappeared. Singers and administration alike wanted to get back to the old comfortable routine. The attitude of the Press and of the Jockey Club had made it practically certain that the production would end in a fiasco: but even if *Tannhäuser* were destined to prove a success, the longer the production was postponed the less profit the Opéra would reap from that success, for Niemann's contract expired on the 31st May.

Nor did Wagner himself now wish for any further delay. His experienced eye saw that the whole company was going stale, like an overtrained athlete; more rehearsals would mean simply an aggravation of the evil. The orchestra, in fact, as he says, " was the first to break out into rebellion against the ' excessive ' number of rehearsals." Faced with the alternatives of letting Dietsch ruin his work there and then or of exhausting the company with more and more rehearsals, with the certainty of merely the same result in the end, he decided to withdraw his score. He wrote to that effect to Walewski. The Minister's reply was that in view of the trouble and expense to which the theatre had been put, such a withdrawal could not be permitted. Wagner now summoned a conference of his friends, including Erlanger, Hatzfeld, and Wesendonk, to help him to find a way of compelling the authorities to grant his request. The appeal went to the Emperor, who, as usual, tried to conciliate both sides — *Tannhäuser* could not be withdrawn, but the composer was to have as many more rehearsals as he might deem necessary.[8] " At last ", says Wagner, " tired to the very depths of

---

[8] Interesting details of the production are given by Nuitter in an article on *Les 164 Répétitions et les 3 représentations du Tannhäuser à Paris*, in BFWB, pp. 38–40. The figures were compiled from the official records.

There were 73 piano rehearsals, 45 choral rehearsals, 27 rehearsals for stage details (without orchestra), 4 for the décors, and 14 of various kinds for the orchestra. (This totals 163 only: apparently Nuitter gets the "164" of his title by including an orchestral rehearsal called for the 14th February, but cancelled because of the indisposition of Niemann and Mdlle. Sax). Wagner was at every rehearsal except nine of those with piano (during his illness in October and November), and those of the 5th, 7th and 8th February on the stage without the orchestra.

The *special* expenses of the production ran to 100,000 francs, the décors and accessories accounting for 35,000 francs, the costumes and arms for 52,000, copying the music for 7,000. Extra choralists, and instruments on or under the stage, meant a further expense of 860 francs a performance. Niemann's salary was 6,000 francs a month, Mme. Tedesco's 6,000, Morelli's 3,000 and Mdlle. Sax's 1,000.

A note in Wagner's writing shows him asking, for the hunting scene in the first act, for 12 horns, to be doubled at the end of the act. As the resources of Paris were unequal to this unexampled demand, Wagner suggested that Adolphe Sax should be commissioned to substitute for some of the horns "instruments of the same timbre, perhaps saxophones." (Sax was paid 3,000 francs for his services). For the second act Wagner desired 12 trumpets "off"; in the third act, for the scene of the approach of Venus and her court he asked for a complete orchestra below the stage, consisting of 2 piccolos, 4 flutes, 4 oboes, 2 D clarinets, 4 other clarinets (4 cors à pistons), 4 bassoons, 1 tambourine, 1 pair of cymbals, à triangle and 4 trombones. Pencillings on the memorandum suggest that Wagner abated these demands somewhat, no doubt in response to Royer's protests.

Four horses and ten dogs appeared in the hunting scene. At the second performance the dogs and the hunting horns were omitted. The three performances that were given of the work brought more than 26,000 francs into the house, of which some 5,700 represented the abonnement; so that the management's belief that *Tannhäuser* would prove a money-maker would certainly have justified itself had the performances, instead of ending summarily on the 24th March, been allowed to continue for the remaining ten weeks of Niemann's engagement.

my soul, I decided, pessimistically clear as I now was about it all, to let the thing run its outer course."

Even now his troubles were not at an end. He had had, one would think, enough to endure from his enemies: now it was his friends' turn to plague him. All of them wanted tickets for the first night. He was anxious to oblige them, especially those who would be coming from places far afield. As early as the 4th February he had found these requests more numerous than he himself could cope with: he had accordingly constituted Giacomelli his man of affairs in this matter, and had instructed the theatre management to deal directly with him as such.[9] He soon discovered that the mere composer's interests in a thing of this kind took only second place; apart from the traditional prior claims of all sorts of people from the Court downwards, everyone in the theatre, as he told Pauline Viardot, from the director to the comptroller, was in the habit of speculating in tickets.[10] Several of his best friends, he says, saw fit to resent what they imagined to be his neglect of them.

" Champfleury sent me a letter complaining of this flagrant breach of friendship; Gasperini went so far as to start an open quarrel with me because I had not reserved one of the best boxes for his Marseilles patron and my creditor Lucy. Even Blandine, who had been filled with the most generous enthusiasm for my work at the rehearsals she had attended, could not repress the suspicion that I was slighting my best friends when I was unable to offer her and Ollivier anything better than a couple of stalls." [11]

The only one who never misunderstood him, never complained, and never failed him was Bülow — who happened also to be the only one of them all who was making what, for him, were serious sacrifices for Wagner's sake.

4

Inside the theatre, the nearer the day of performance approached the deeper became the conviction of them all, Wagner included, that the result would no longer answer to the time and trouble

---

[9] See his letter of the 4th February to Royer, in TLFW, p. 236.
[10] TLFW, p. 238.
[11] No. 371 in the Catalogue of the Burrell Collection is a two-page letter from Princess Metternich dated the 30th January 1861, in which she asks "dear Wagner" to reserve two stalls for her for the first performance.

taken. The final rehearsals had degenerated into something like a farce. From his place in the orchestra Dietsch beat time according to his own notions: a couple of paces away from him, in a seat on the stage by the prompter's box, was Wagner, giving singers and orchestra his own tempi not only with his hands but with his feet, raising clouds of dust in the process. The work itself, he told Mathilde Wesendonk when the long nightmare was over, had become so unrecognisable by him and alien to him during these final rehearsals that the brutalities to which the actual performances were subjected left him almost unmoved — they were like purely physical blows " that merely woke me from my soul's distress to consciousness of my wretched outer existence: the blows themselves I felt only superficially."

He wished the last rehearsal but one to be of so intimate a nature that he denied even Minna permission to attend it. To his astonishment he found the theatre full of strangers of all sorts, chiefly representatives of the more unfriendly Press, who, like vultures, scenting death from afar, had more or less forced their way into the Opéra to stake out for themselves a claim on the carrion. For the final rehearsal Wagner insisted, as some kind of counterpoise to this evil band, on a hundred seats being occupied by his own friends. At this rehearsal, on the 10th March, the gigantic Niemann, who had no doubt been for a long time asking himself whether it was for something so unpromising for his personal glory as this that he had come to Paris, had an attack of vertigo which made it necessary for him to leave the stage at the end of the first act: the remainder of the rehearsal had to go on as best it could without him. Malwida, who had been present, met Wagner afterwards outside the theatre, where he was waiting for Minna: from the cloud on his brow, she says, she saw how deep was his discontent with it all.

There cannot be much doubt that the first performance, on the 13th, would have been, so far as the majority of the spectators was concerned, a triumph for Wagner had the circumstances been normal. The house was as brilliant a one as the Opéra had ever seen: the Court was there in full strength, no doubt hoping that its presence would impose some degree of decency on the aristocratic ruffians and their Press hirelings, who had made no secret of their intention of ruining Wagner and his work. All accounts agree that things were shaping excellently until the commencement of the " open landscape " scene in the first act; and it was probably the uncomfortable feeling that a great success was preparing for Wagner that brought his enemies into the open at the first real opportunity that presented itself — the episode of the shepherd boy and his pipe. Malwida tells us that " the overture and the first scene were got through without any disturbance; and though the execution of the spectral dance of the divinities [12] in the Venusberg fell far short of Wagner's conception — the three Graces appearing in pink ballet skirts — I began to breathe again and to hope that our fears had been superfluous." The whistling and the shouting began with the cor anglais melody of the shepherd boy; Wagner's first innocent conjecture was that the Emperor had arrived. The disturbance called forth protests from those members of the public who wished to listen to the opera; and as they were in the majority, says Malwida, they were able to silence the interrupters for a while. So it went on until the evening's end; victory remained with those who demanded fair play for Wagner, but victory at what a cost! The work " was so deranged and mangled that not even for the well-disposed was there the least possibility of forming a right conception of it as a whole." [13] One is mildly surprised to learn that they were able to form any conception of it at all, what with the malcontents, in massed formation, raising their white-kid-gloved hands to their lips and blowing their whistles at each signal from the leader of the squadron, and the more decent members of the audience shouting them down and threatening to throw them out.

Wagner himself, one gathers, came away with the feeling that, all in all, this first battle had left him in possession of the field. In the *Report on the Production of Tannhäuser in Paris* which he published in the *Deutsche Allgemeine Zeitung* on the 7th April,[14] he

---

[12] I translate faithfully, though I do not quite know what Malwida is referring to. Glasenapp evidently felt the same difficulty in connection with the passage, for he changes Malwida's "obwohl die Anordnung des gespenstischen Götterreigens im Venusberg" into a simple "ihre Anordnung".

[13] Malwida's reminiscences of the *Tannhäuser* rehearsals and performances will be found in MMI, II, 194 ff.

[14] It was reprinted in the *Neue Zeitschrift für Musik* of the 12th. He had finished it on the 27th March, within a fortnight of the first performance.

was at pains to correct the impression current in Germany that the production had been a fiasco from the first and the general reception of the work a reflection on French taste. On the contrary, he praised the " quick responsiveness " of the Paris public and its " truly magnanimous sense of justice ". It had filled him with gratitude to see this public, which knew nothing of him at first hand, and had been fed daily by the Press with slanders about him, repeatedly doing battle for him on that evening against the clique that caused the disturbance, " with repeated outbursts of applause a quarter of an hour long ". (Presumably this means during the actual performance: if so, it is hardly to be wondered at that those who did not already know *Tannhäuser* could get no connected idea of it!). Yet in spite of everything, he told his German readers, " I think I have a right to speak of a great victory when I tell you the simple truth — that this by no means enchanting performance [15] of my work met with louder and more unanimous applause than I have ever experienced in Germany." It had been, he said, precisely because the performance threatened to prove a brilliant success for him that the opposition, including the journalists, had been scared into acting as it did from the middle of the first act onwards. If later they concentrated their worst fury on the third act, that was simply because this act was the one richest in elements making for a popular success. Desplechin's setting for this act, says Wagner, had charmed everyone at the rehearsals; the Pilgrims' Chorus was always impeccably sung; Mlle. Sax was admirable in Elisabeth's Prayer and Morelli in the " Abendstern " scene; while " the best part of Niemann's performance, his story of Tannhäuser's pilgrimage, always brought this artist the warmest commendation." [16] The

---

[15] To his sister Luise Brockhaus he wrote that he had not spoken *all* his mind in the article with regard to the weak spots in the performances: it was these, not the brutalities of the Jockey Club, that had made him really unhappy.

[16] Wilhelm Altmann (RWAN, pp. 130–1), regards this passage in Wagner's *Report* as correcting, to some extent at least, Bülow's unflattering opinion of Niemann. But apparently Dr. Altmann has forgotten that Wagner himself told Niemann that virtually any tenor with a voice could win a success of "effect" with the story of the pilgrimage, whereas the really difficult movements of the rôle came in the first and second acts. For him to say, then, that it was in the narration of the pilgrimage that Niemann always won most applause at rehearsals, and that it was in this that he was at his best in the performance, was surely a criticism of Niemann of which the tenor, if he had any intelligence at all, should have been the first to perceive the veiled irony.

opposition therefore did its worst in the third act: yet, says Wagner, it succeeded neither in putting the singers out nor in quelling the enthusiasm of the audience: " and at the end, when the performers were tumultuously called before the curtain, the opposition was finally and completely beaten ".[17]

5

Bülow's *compte rendu* to his friend Alois Schmitt, of Schwerin, was not written until the 26th March, two days after the third (and last) performance; it therefore summarises the affair as a whole rather than describes specifically the events of any one night. Incidentally, however, it supports Malwida's and Wagner's view that, in spite of the organised opposition, the first performance could be regarded as a triumph for the work.

" The talk of the German journalists ", says Bülow, " who repeat only the enemy reports from Paris of a fiasco, is mendacious, or at any rate most premature. By the sixth performance [18] the *whole* work will have completely established itself, to the benefit of the Académie Impériale. Even at the first performance many things in it decidedly struck home: the overture, the septet in the first act, the duet, the march and chorus, the adagio of the second finale, the ' Abendstern ', the prayer, and the first section of the pilgrimage were enthusiastically applauded without any opposition.[19] I left Paris with this firm conviction [of an ultimate triumph]. The performance was most excel-

---

[17] To Agnes Street he wrote, "Be reassured somewhat! The papers love to give only bad news where I am concerned. They mention only the cabal, but forget to add that I conquered. The first performance was a battle in which I kept the field; and it would simply serve to cheer me if only — I could be sure of my tenor and had the ministry on my side! My greatest danger is in Countess Walewski's hatred of Princess Metternich." GRW, p. 305.

[18] Bülow, who was by this time back in Berlin, evidently did not know, at the time of writing his letter, that Wagner had withdrawn the work after the third performance.

[19] Eduard Schelle, in his contemporary report of the performances to the German public, pointed out that naturally the most applauded pieces were the "melodious" ones in the more "routine" vein. STP, p. 13.

We are not surprised at the difficulty the ordinary Parisian had with the long first scene of *Tannhäuser* — which is really in the *Tristan* manner — when we find Marie Kalergis writing to her daughter, in April 1861, "Wagner's reverse grieves me very much. He made a great mistake in allowing his work to be mutilated, and in elongating the first scene beyond measure. May his recent calamity enlighten him as to the danger his own genius creates for him — too deep a sinking of himself in a subject." MMKB, p. 96. Yet when asked by Princess Bismarck whether she believed in papal infallibility she could reply, "I believe in three infallibilities — in the church, the Pope; in politics, Bismarck; in art, Wagner."

lent: the one blot on it was Herr Niemann, whose toneless baritone
. . ."[20] was a bitter disappointment to both the Master and the public.
Formes, Schnorr, Tichatschek, even the mediocre Gueymard [hus-
band of the Madame Gueymard mentioned on an earlier page] would
have been of more service to the work." [21]

It is interesting to compare with these reports that of Niemann,
in a letter to a Berlin friend:

"At yesterday's performance *Tannhäuser* made a fiasco such as
has probably never been known in Paris before. It was literally hissed
off, hooted off, and finally laughed off. I am speaking of the *opera*
called *Tannhäuser*: the *player* of Tannhäuser, God be praised, saved
his artistic honour, and in the second and third acts reduced the hissing, the whistling and the laughing to silence, and won the loudest
applause not only from the whole of the public but again and again
from his Majesty the Emperor.

"The row was beyond belief; even the presence of the Emperor
could not keep it within bounds. Princess Metternich, to whose patronage the production of the opera is mainly due, was compelled to
leave the theatre after the second act, the audience continually turning
round towards her box and jeering at her at the top of its voice.

"Spare me further details about this lively evening, and rejoice,
with me, that at any rate I personally managed to save myself in this
shipwreck.

"At the end the Emperor and the public recalled the *performers*.
Please tell the Princes this.

"I have just heard from a person of standing, whose name I do not
know — he is a friend of Count Walewski — that at the conclusion of
the opera the Emperor, by his applause, particularly recalled *me*." [22]

Of all the foul things in connection with the production of *Tannhäuser* in Paris this letter of Niemann's is perhaps the foulest. Of
sympathy with the composer, of respect for his work, of the indignation one might expect from an " artist " at so gross an insult to
a work of art, there is not a hint from first to last in Niemann's
letter. There is no thought in it for anyone but himself. It is some
small satisfaction for us to know that before the curtain rang down
on the final catastrophe the obscene mob rolled him in the mire
along with Wagner and his work.[23]

---

[20] Evidently the editor of the letters has discreetly omitted something here.
[21] BB, III, 394.
[22] RWAN, pp. 131–2.
[23] Niemann himself has told us that when, many years later, personal relations

The French and Italian singers had behaved more decently than this German. At the end of the performance Wagner had chaffed Mlle. Sax about being whistled off: " with proud dignity she replied, ' Je le supporterai cent fois comme aujourd'hui. Ah, les misérables! " Morelli had no sooner taken up his harp to commence the " Abendstern " song than someone shouted, " Ah! il prend encore sa harpe "; this was followed by an outburst of laughter lasting so long that Morelli, to be heard at all, had to ignore Wagner's instructions to address himself solely to the retreating form of Elisabeth, lay aside his harp, come down to the footlights, and sing his song straight at the audience. This he did unaccompanied, Dietsch not being able to find his place again until the tenth bar.

Malwida called on Wagner the day after the first performance. She found him, she says, calm and courageous, as indeed he had been all through the storm of the night before. He spoke of preventing another performance by withdrawing his score. From this she and other friends managed to dissuade him.

6

The second performance had been fixed for the 15th March, but an indisposition of Niemann's necessitated a postponement to the 18th. Meanwhile Royer, who had got it into his head that the opposition on the first night had been due to the boredom of the audience with the work, had begged the composer to make a few cuts. Wagner reluctantly did so, feeling, perhaps, that nothing that could

---

were resumed with Wagner, the latter never once, in all their conversations, referred to the events of 1860–1. In the following decade Niemann seems to have developed an artistic conscience that was only embryonic in him in the Paris *Tannhäuser* days. The reason for Wagner's almost complete silence about Niemann from 1861 onwards was simply that he had been too deeply hurt even to cry out. We find, however, a brief reference to the tenor in a letter of the 1st May, 1866 to King Ludwig. Apart from Frau Schnorr, says Wagner, there is no one now capable of playing his characters as he had conceived them: "Niemann, though gifted in some respects, is a crude effect-snatcher, whom I detest from the bottom of my soul." KLRWB, II, 30.

Eduard Schelle, writing immediately after the third performance, and describing how, for some time before the production, certain Paris papers had denigrated Wagner almost every day, — a process described locally, he says, as "faire la scie" — says that the journalists were supplied with material by a "dissatisfied part" of the Opéra personnel. The only seriously dissatisfied part of the personnel seems to have been Niemann.

happen now to his work could matter very much one way or another. The cuts were made at a piano rehearsal in the foyer of the Opéra on the 16th; the sacrifices included a portion of Venus's music in the first scene, the whole episode of her re-appearance in the third act, the instrumental ritornelli in the shepherd's song, and the new violin passage at the end of the finale of the second act that had so greatly pleased Wagner.[24] Poor Royer complained pathetically, in his report to Walewski, of the trouble he had had with Wagner: it was " very difficult ", he wrote, to get " a man so convinced of the merit of his work as M. Wagner is to consent to cuts: those who know him are astonished at his conceding so much." Had *Tannhäuser* been a spoken play, Royer continued, he would have exercised his authority and made the cuts himself; but in a musical score, unfortunately, deletions involve " a joining up of tonalities " to which he confesses he does not feel equal.

At the second performance, at which Napoleon and Eugénie were once more present, all went well for a time. The overture was applauded; so was the septet, at the end of which Mme. Tedesco, who was sitting with Wagner in Royer's box, called out to them joyously that the victory was won. It was not until the middle of the second act that the shock troops of the Jockey Club went into action. At the first sound of their whistles Royer said resignedly to Wagner, " It's the Jockeys: we are lost! " According to Wagner, the Emperor had tried to conclude a truce with them, the terms of which were that they should allow three performances to take place, after which *Tannhäuser* would be cut down to such an extent as to be no more than a curtain raiser for a ballet. These terms had been rejected because in the first place the Jockeys' hatred of Wagner and of Pauline Metternich had in no way abated, and in the second place because it seemed certain that if the opera were given fair play it would score a success with the public. And so, in spite of the presence of the imperial pair, the more the audience applauded the more gaily did these gallant gentlemen of France unleash their dog-whistles and cat-calls and the rest of their mechanical menagerie. In the third act the aristocratic ruffians, divesting themselves of the last shreds of decency, even showed themselves lacking in respect for something so sacred as

[24] See *supra*, p. 83.

the " artistic honour " of a tenor. Niemann was so exasperated at finding that they would not listen even to him in his big scene in the third act that he threw his broad-brimmed pilgrim's hat at them. Sheer astonishment at such conduct on the part of a singer silenced the opposition, we are told, for the time being; and Niemann, " stepping forward with his hand on his breast, bowed to the imperial box with a mute gesture which the good Kietz, from whom the story comes and who was an eye-witness of the episode, took to signify, ' *I* can't do anything if the opera is no good ' ". According to another version of the story the tenor shouted abuse at the interrupters, whereupon a voice from the audience kindly assured him that the demonstration was not against him.

The performance was somehow or other carried through to the end, but what the average spectator could have made of it all is simply beyond one's comprehension. By all accounts the audience was as vocal as the singers for the greater part of the time. Malwida, who occupied a box with Minna, found herself near a posse of the whistlers. " So this ", she shouted at them, " is the public that claims to set the standards of taste for the whole world! A rabble of street urchins, without even manners enough to let people who differ from them listen in peace and quiet! " Poor Bülow broke into sobs when it was all over.

Once more Wagner wanted to withdraw his score, and once more his friends persuaded him to consent to at least a third performance. Royer, one gathers, had asked, after the second performance, for still more cuts, in order to make time for a divertissement at the end of the opera. A letter to the Director, now in the archives of the Opéra, shows how utterly weary of it all Wagner now was. Had *Tannhäuser* been a new work, he said, he would certainly have withdrawn his score. But the sixteen-year-old *Tannhäuser* now belongs to the world rather than to him; whatever the Paris Opéra may do to it cannot affect it in its essentials. Everywhere in Germany it has for a long time been given without him, and he feels as good as dead towards it. It was only chance that brought him and it to Paris. He now retires from the affair, leaving the process of making the opera " conform to the ruling practice of your theatre " to those who have " so well entered into the spirit of it." As it is now merely a matter of keeping the thing going for the satisfaction of those who have shown an interest in it, he authorises Royer to do what he likes with the work in order to satisfy the people who have not been able to find in it what constitutes their usual pleasure in opera. " Regard me as dead, — as I really am, dead to this *Tannhäuser* so far as performances in other theatres are concerned." The bitter irony of the letter was probably lost on Royer.

Wagner stipulated that the third performance should take place on a Sunday — a day not included in the abonnement, and on which the box-holders especially were in the habit of surrendering their tickets for sale to the general public. Royer agreed to this, though he would not permit the performance to be advertised as the last. The sequel showed that he and the others might as well have saved themselves the trouble of repeating the farce. Wagner wisely resolved to remain at home with Minna on the night of this third performance, the 24th March. The Jockeys, contrary to expectation, had not stayed away: this time, indeed, they were in their seats at the commencement, determined not to give the work the smallest chance. The hopes of Wagner's friends rose when, on arriving at the theatre, they found strong bodies of police scattered about the corridors. They were there, however, to protect not the performance from the Jockeys but the Jockeys from the indignant public, for many of these chivalrous gentlemen were attached to the imperial household. Wagner was assured later that in the first act alone the performance had twice been suspended by fights lasting a quarter of an hour each. The tactical advantages were all on the side of the opponents: they had only to wait till the respectable part of the audience had silenced one outburst of rowdyism to begin the hullabaloo all over again with their dog whistles.[25] As Baudelaire said, " ten obstinate people armed with shrill whistles can put the actors out, overcome the good will of the public, and even cut through the voice of an orchestra as power-

---

[25] The receipts for the three performances were (1) 7,491 francs, (2) 8,415 francs, (3) 10,764 francs. The smaller receipts on the first night were partly accounted for by the number of free tickets allotted to the Press, the artists and others. On the first two nights the abonnement accounted for 2,770 and 2,758 francs respectively. For the third night this sank to 230 francs; and as the total receipts for that night were the largest of all, it is evident that the public proper was sincerely interested in the work. See BFWB, p. 40.

ful as that of the Opéra." By this time all the hawkers of toys on the boulevards were selling " Wagner whistles ".

7

Malwida was one of the few friends of Wagner who had the heart to attend this third performance. The imagination boggles at the thought of what it must have been like: in Malwida's account of the evening, and elsewhere, we read of the singers sometimes waiting as long as fifteen minutes for the storm to die down, then patiently resuming where they had left off. Baron von Seebach, the Saxon ambassador, could hardly speak when he met Wagner the next day; he had lost his voice shouting at the interrupters the night before. Princess Metternich was not there. She had had enough of insults; and one can forgive her many things for her contemptuous retort to some of her noble French friends who had sided with the Jockey Club: " Don't talk to me about your free France! In Vienna, where at least there is a genuine aristocracy, it would be unthinkable for a Prince Liechtenstein or Schwarzenberg to whistle from his box for a ballet in *Fidelio*." [26] The performance somehow or other reached its appointed end; but this time no one could delude himself that the evening was a victory for Wagner. The malignant opposition had had its full revenge upon everything it so hated — upon Princess Metternich and through her upon Austria, upon this alien composer who had had the temerity to flout them and their notions of art, who was suspected of democratic leanings and was known to despise Meyer-

---

[26] Frédéric Loliée's account of the performances is rather fanciful; but he seems to be correct in saying that not long after the fiasco some of Pauline's friends consoled her for her chagrins over *Tannhäuser* by means of a parody of Wagner performed in her own house: the Wartburg was transformed into the Johannisberg (Prince Metternich had a castle and vineyards bearing that name), and Tannhäuser was shown draining a bottle of Johannisberger and singing:

> Dieu, quelle veste
> Pour Wagner et son Vénusberg!
> Noyons du moins leur sorte funeste
> À grands flots de Johannisberg
> Sur cette veste!

According to Loliée, "some people insinuated that the *Tannhäuser* production was one of the secret clauses of the Treaty of Villafranca, while others maintained that Wagner had been sent to the Parisians to make them admire Berlioz." (*Les Femmes du Second Empire*, pp. 180–1).

beer. They left the stricken field in triumph: the honour of France had been vindicated by the gentlemen of France.

At two in the morning Malwida and a few friends left the theatre together to call upon Wagner in the Rue d'Aumale. They found him smoking his pipe and drinking tea with Minna. He put a brave face on it all, smiling at their story of the events in the theatre, and teasingly accusing little Olga Herzen [27] of having hissed him. But from the trembling of the hand he gave to Malwida she could see how profoundly he was suffering.

That night he sent out a note to a few of his friends, asking them to confer with him at noon the next day (Monday). After that meeting he wrote to Royer once more withdrawing his work, " as the members of the Jockey Club will not allow the Paris public to hear my opera, for lack in it of a ballet at the hour when they are accustomed to enter the theatre." He learned later that Royer, in spite of everything, was planning to give a fourth performance on the 12th April, on the grounds that the Friday subscribers were no less entitled than those of Monday and Wednesday to hear the work. Wagner at once protested both to Royer and to Walewski. Nuitter's hand is evident in the letter of the 9th April to the Minister: we can hardly credit Wagner with the delicate Gallic irony of the remark that he is reluctant to see either his opera or the singers subjected once more to disturbances " that go beyond the limits of ordinary criticism ": these disturbances have " degenerated into a veritable scandal against which the administration has been powerless to protect those spectators who wished to listen and judge." If the Opéra persists in giving the work again, says Wagner, he will inform publicly " both those who like my music and those who do not that this performance takes place contrary to my clearly expressed wish." The Minister, in his reply of the 14th, again insisted, for appearances' sake, that " a composer, having once handed in his work to a theatre, cannot withdraw it of his own volition." After careful consideration, however, he continues, he has come to the conclusion that a fourth performance would

---

[27] The daughter of the Russian revolutionary Alexander Herzen. Malwida had undertaken the care and education of Olga after Herwegh had broken up Herzen's home by an intrigue with Mme. Herzen. (See Vol. II, p. 460). Olga subsequently married Gabriel Monod.

result in more inconveniences than advantages; it is therefore a pleasure to him to know that his own decision to close down there and then on the performances is in accord with Wagner's wishes.

That was the end of *Tannhäuser* in Paris. The reader already knows how financially profitable the affair had been to the singers. The composer did not come out of it so well. Nominally his fee from the Opéra was to have been 500 francs a performance; but as regards the first twenty performances, half this sum was to go to the French translators of the text. As against the 54,000 francs, then, drawn by the vain young lout of a tenor who had so basely betrayed Wagner in his hour of need, the mere creator of *Tannhäuser* received, in respect of the three performances given, only 750 francs; and even these he handed over to poor Roche, whose economic situation seemed to him even more pitiable than his own.[28]

8

Towards midnight on the day of the last general rehearsal, says Judith Gautier, she and her father Théophile were waiting outside the Opéra for Mme. Gautier, for whom Wagner had obtained a ticket for the rehearsal. An excited crowd was issuing from the theatre, gesticulating, debating: little Judith, who as yet knew nothing of the battle that was already raging round *Tannhäuser* in Paris, gazed around her uncomprehendingly. Suddenly

" a man of original and striking appearance ", she says, " stopped to greet my father. He was small, lean, with bony cheeks, a nose like an eagle's beak, a great forehead with piercing eyes, a ravaged, passionate look. He had been at the rehearsal, at which there had been an indescribable tumult: they had hissed prodigiously. This gave him a ferocious pleasure, and he talked about it violently, spitefully. I looked at him with the fixed, staring gaze habitual with me when astonished. Something within me, I do not know what, impelled me suddenly to break through the silence and reserve proper to my age, and say to him, with incredible impertinence, ' It is easy to see that you are talking about a colleague! And, no doubt, of a masterpiece! ' My father, amazed at me, scolded me aloud, but laughed softly to himself. ' Who was that? ' I asked when the man had left us. ' Hector Berlioz '. I have often admired, in later years, this great artist, who also was unappreciated and derided; but I have never forgotten this

---

[28] Roche died, of consumption, in the following December.

incident, and there seems to me to have been a presentiment in my quickness to defend this Richard Wagner, who was one day to inspire me with such enthusiasm, and whose name I heard that night for the first time. In the carriage my mother gave us an account of the terrible evening. She was beside herself over the cabal, and still stunned by the tumult. She could say nothing about the music, for the good reason that it had been impossible to hear any of it." [29]

As Judith was only eleven years old at that time, and she was fifty-three when *Le Second Rang du Collier* was published (in 1903), her memory is not wholly to be trusted on points of detail. She may have confused a rehearsal with one of the performances: there is no record of an " indescribable tumult " at the final rehearsal, though it is quite on the cards that at the end of the *last rehearsal but one,* at which the journalists were present in full force, there was a demonstration of some sort against Wagner; and Berlioz would presumably be present at that rehearsal in his capacity of music critic of the *Journal des Débats*. There is no reason to doubt that something answering broadly to Judith's description occurred on some night or other.[30] For unfortunately there is ample evidence as to Berlioz's rancorous jealousy of Wagner and his malignant joy over the indignities inflicted by the cabal on his " rival ". Berlioz was at that time moving heaven and earth to have his *Troyens* taken up by the Opéra, and it had infuriated him to see his path blocked for the time being by this intruder from Germany.

" I had a long talk a week ago with the Minister of State about this matter [the *Troyens*] ", he wrote to his son on the 14th February; " I told him of all the basenesses of which I have been the victim. He said he would like to see my poem: I took it to him the next day, and since then I have heard nothing more about the affair. Public

[29] GSRC, pp. 173–4.
[30] In her earlier *Richard Wagner et son œuvre poétique* (1882) Judith had told substantially the same story in connection with the *first performance* of Tannhäuser. She and her father, it appears, were not waiting for Mme. Gautier, but Théophile and she were "crossing by chance the passage de l'Opéra during an entr'acte" when Berlioz accosted them. Judith's memories of what had happened in 1861 were more likely to be true to the facts in 1882 than in 1903. Why she should have altered her original version twenty-one years later is a mystery.

Théophile always plumed himself on having been "the first to talk about Tannhäuser in Paris". He had heard the work in Wiesbaden in 1857, and had written enthusiastically about it in the *Moniteur* of the 29th September of that year. He ended his article with the hope that Tannhäuser might be given at the Opéra.

THE LIFE OF RICHARD WAGNER

opinion is becoming more and more indignant at my being shut out from the Opéra while the protection of the Austrian ambassador's wife has so easily obtained the entry there for Wagner."

A week later he wrote:

" Wagner is turning the singers, the orchestra and the chorus of the Opéra into goats. . . . The final general rehearsal, it is said, was atrocious; it lasted until one in the morning. . . . I will not do the article on *Tannhäuser* myself: I have asked d'Ortigue to take charge of it. This will be better in every way, and it will disappoint them more. Never have I had so many windmills to fight as this year: I am surrounded by fools of every sort: there are times when my rage suffocates me."

Even Berlioz could not be blind to the fact that *Tannhäuser* was creating enormous interest in Paris; but he took a morbid pleasure in trying to persuade himself and other people that everyone was as prejudiced against the German composer as he was.

" There is much excitement in our musical world ", he wrote to his son on the 5th March, " over the scandal the production of *Tannhäuser* is going to cause. Everyone I meet is furious: the Minister came away from the rehearsal the other day in a rage! The Emperor is dissatisfied; and yet there are some enthusiasts in all good faith, even among the French. Wagner is plainly mad. He will die as Jullien did last year, of a brain fever. . . . As I have told you, I will not write about it myself; I will let d'Ortigue do the notice. I want to protest by my silence, leaving myself free to say what I think later, if I am driven to it."

On the morrow of the first performance he gave full vent to his ignoble *Schadenfreude*:

" God in heaven! " he wrote to a lady friend; " what a performance! what outbursts of laughter! The Parisian showed himself yesterday in an entirely new aspect; he laughed at the bad musical style, he laughed at the absurd vulgarities of the orchestration, he laughed at the naïvetés of an oboe; he now realises that there is such a thing as style in music. As for the horrors, they were splendidly hissed."

On the 21st he had still not exhausted his venom.

" The second performance ", he assured his son, " was worse than the first. This time the audience did not laugh so much; it was furious, it hissed enough to bring the roof down, in spite of the presence of the Emperor and Empress.[31] On the staircase, as people were going out, they openly treated this wretched Wagner as a rogue, an insolent fellow, an idiot. If they go on like this, one of these days the performance will not finish, and there will be nothing more to be said. The Press is unanimous as to exterminating him. As for myself, I am cruelly avenged." [32]

Did Berlioz, one wonders, remember his horrible exultation over Wagner's defeat when, two-and-a-half years later, *Les Troyens à Carthage* was produced at the Théâtre-Lyrique? He too, when that happened, was pestered by the management to cut and re-arrange his darling score; he too was insulted and reviled not only in the theatre but in the Press of which he was so distinguished an ornament — " five papers insulted me ", he complains indignantly in his *Memoirs,* " in terms expressly chosen to wound my feelings as an artist "; [33] he too had to endure the sight and sound of the boulevard wits making merry over naïvetés in his text and his score.

9

Berlioz, in his attitude towards Wagner in those fateful weeks, represented only the worst side of the Parisian culture of the day. Wagner probably never knew how meanly Berlioz had behaved, while to the flood of ignoble letters, signed and anonymous, that reached him he was indifferent by long practice. The " immensity of the injustice " perpetrated by the Jockey Club, said Baudelaire, created sympathy for Wagner on all sides. The finer Parisian spirits, in particular some of the younger men, burned with a

---

[31] Berlioz, it will be observed, has not even the honesty to tell his distant correspondents that the disturbance came only from one section of the audience, and was angrily resented by the remainder. Or was he so blinded by envy and hatred of Wagner that he saw and heard on those evenings only what he would have liked to see and hear?

[32] BCI, pp. 277–280.

[33] BMEN, p. 449. This time, however, Berlioz takes pains to remind his readers what he had forgotten in the case of Wagner, that he and his work had many well-wishers whose friendliness "was ample compensation for the insults of my enemies — people whose enmity was due less to my criticisms than to my musical tendencies, and whose hatred, indeed, was such as to honour me, resembling as it did the hatred of the street-walker for the honest woman."

generous indignation against the cowardly malefactors. Expressions of sympathy and suggestions for help reached Wagner from many quarters. In April Baudelaire produced his famous brochure, *Richard Wagner et Tannhäuser à Paris.*[34] Jules Janin, Berlioz's collaborator on the *Débats,* seized upon the famous episode of Pauline Metternich furiously smashing her fan on the ledge of her box at one of the performances as a pretext for one of his best articles, in which he suggested a coat of arms for the Jockey Club — " un sifflet sur champ de gueules hurlantes, et pour exergue, ' Asinus ad lyram '." The young Catulle Mendès, at that time only in his teens but already a strong Wagnerite, invited Wagner to contribute an article to the *Revue fantaisiste.* Victor Cochinat, the editor of *La Causerie,* denounced the cabal against *Tannhäuser,* and placed his columns at Wagner's service should he have a message for the French public. Gustave Doré, whose acquaintance Wagner had made through Ollivier, carried his enthusiasm to the point of proposing to do a series of drawings illustrating the *Ring:* by way of initiating him into the world of the Teutonic sagas Wagner presented him in the following summer with the recently published piano score of the *Rhinegold.*[35] Wagner selections proved the greatest attractions at the Musard and the Pasdeloup concerts

---

[34] Now included in the volume entitled *L'art romantique.* The bulk of it had already appeared in the *Revue Européenne* of the 1st April: the postscript — *Encore quelques mots* — is dated 8th April. Apparently the brochure did not enjoy a large sale. His friend Félix Tournachon (who wrote under the pseudonym "Navar"), finding himself next to Princess Metternich at dinner, spoke to her about the brochure. She "expressed a lively desire to read it". He sent her a copy the next day. Many weeks afterwards she returned it with "a gracious expression of thanks": unfortunately she had forgotten to cut the pages. BAR, pp. 514–5, 519.

A re-issue of *Richard Wagner et Tannhäuser à Paris* was not called for until 1868.

It is interesting to compare Baudelaire's view of the performances, as representing that of the ordinary intelligent amateur, with the more professional one of Wagner and Bülow. Baudelaire found the mise en scène, so far at any rate as Cormon was responsible for it, "inadequate". The orchestral playing was "flabby and incorrect." The Venus, made up into a bundle of white rags, suggested neither Olympus nor the Middle Ages. The "German tenor" on whom such great hopes had been built "sang out of tune with deplorable assiduity." Baudelaire praises Mlle. Sax and Morelli: "but what is to be said about M. Niemann, of his weaknesses, his swoons, his tantrums of a spoiled child . . . ? The so-called ballet consisted of Prussian regiments in short petticoats, making the mechanical gestures of the military school." BAR, pp. 245–6.

[35] So says Wagner in *Mein Leben.* According to TLFW, p. 253, there exists also a score of *Tannhäuser,* with the inscription " À Monsieur Gustave Doré, son admirateur le plus sincère, Richard Wagner. Paris, le 23 Juillet 1861."

during the next few months. Carvalho was only restrained from producing *Tannhäuser* at the Théâtre-Lyrique by the fact that he could not find a suitable tenor. Roger, though hampered by the loss of his arm, was still bravely trying to continue his career; and for his benefit at the Opéra-Comique he chose the third act of *Tannhäuser*, with the overture as introduction — an unmistakable sign of the interest Paris still took in the work. To the director of a Festival Orphéonique Wagner had to explain that none of his operatic choruses was adapted for performance at a meeting of that kind, but that he would be happy to compose a piece for it if he could find a suitable poem.

The interest he had excited in the French musical world was perhaps most conclusively shown by the eagerness of a number of people to put him to sound commercial use. Beaumont, the director of the Opéra-Comique, making a last desperate effort to stave off bankruptcy, tried to get Wagner to interest Princess Metternich, and through her the Emperor, in a plan for producing *Tannhäuser* at his theatre. Wagner says in *Mein Leben* that he gave the proposal a chilly reception, as he himself was unable to share Beaumont's optimism in the matter. His memory, however, was a little at fault here. A letter to Bülow [36] shows that at first he was all in favour of the scheme, which, on the face of it, promised to relieve him from his financial embarrassments, and he only allowed his secret weariness of the whole subject of a Paris *Tannhäuser* to turn him against it when Erlanger, who was willing enough to guarantee the undertaking for Wagner's sake, refused to do so merely for Beaumont's. A still more ambitious plan was hatched by a certain M. Chabrol, a journalist who wrote under the pseudonym of Lorbac. A company with an " enormously rich man " at the head of it, it appeared, was willing to found a " Théâtre Wagner " in Paris. A scheme of this kind, holding a promise for the production at any rate of *Tristan* among his newer works, naturally made more appeal to Wagner than one concerned merely with *Tannhäuser*, of which he was now thoroughly tired. He gave the project his blessing, only stipulating that a competent person should be installed as director. The choice fell on Perrin, who was for a time most enthusiastic about the scheme, in which, with his eye per-

[36] RWHB, p. 157.

petually on the reversion of Royer's post at the Opéra,[37] he thought
he saw his chance to prove that Royer had bungled the flotation
of *Tannhäuser*. On the 3rd May Wagner could confidently inform
Bülow that everything was going swimmingly. Ministers and cap-
italists were willing to co-operate. The general idea was to open
with performances of German and some of the older Italian operas,
these to be succeeded by new contemporary works conceived in a
style consistent with the ends of such a theatre, the slogan for the
house being, " Good music — first-rate performances ".

Wagner had promised to take an active part both in the general
direction and, occasionally, in the performances, on the condition
that a permanent conductor agreeable to himself was appointed.
His choice, of course, was Bülow; and he exhorted Hans to think
the matter over seriously, for

> " nowhere in Germany, particularly in any of the large towns, is a
> theatre possible that will set itself such a mission as the one projected
> here. A theatre the normal function of which is to devote itself en-
> tirely to good music is conceivable only in Paris, where all the special
> requirements can be met; whereas Berlin and Vienna will always have
> to perform a certain amount of trash along with what is good."

Like so many other admirable plans for the reform of the operatic
theatre, however, this one came to nothing. According to *Mein
Leben*, Perrin first of all became suspicious of Lorbac, whom he
suspected of feathering his own nest with secret commissions, after
a fashion said to be still not entirely unknown in opera houses and
other temples of the Muses. Perrin thereupon resolved to found
the " Wagner Theatre " according to his own notions, with the financial backing of Erlanger, who thought he could raise, in conjunction with nine or ten other bankers, a capital of half a million francs
for the project. The end of all these too sanguine hopes might have
been anticipated: Perrin soon found that while the speculators
were not unwilling to risk their money for a theatre after their
own hearts, they were decidedly unwilling to risk it for anything
so idealistic as art in general and Wagnerian art in particular.
That the idea of a Wagner theatre was seriously entertained in

---

[37] He superseded Royer as administrator general of the Opéra in December 1862.
In April 1866 he became "directeur-entrepreneur", which office he held until the war
of 1870.

Paris circles is shown by Baudelaire's remark, at the end of his brochure, that *Tannhäuser* would be heard again " in a place to which the abonnés of the Opéra will have no interest in pursuing it." [38] According to Glasenapp the scheme for such a theatre occupied the minds of Wagner's French friends for several years, and was actually not far from realisation when the war of 1870 gave it its death-blow. As for *Tannhäuser*, Paris was destined not to hear the opera again until 1895.

10

" Mais que voulez-vous? " Wagner had asked in his letter to Cochinat the day after the final performance of *Tannhäuser;* " je suis à jamais perdu pour la France." He had his livelihood to earn, he added; but who, after this disaster, would take him seriously? The brief spell of optimism with regard to the " Wagner Theatre " at an end, he could no longer conceal from himself that his cause was lost in France, if not for ever, at any rate for a considerable time. The enemy, indeed, not only remained in possession of the Parisian field but did his best to cut Wagner's communications with his homeland: Meyerbeer's journalistic myrmidons saw to that. The anonymous author of a friendly article in the *Neue Zürcher Zeitung* of the 19th March drew attention to the almost literal correspondence between various reports of the Paris fiasco that had appeared in foreign journals. " Are they not as like each other ", he asked, " as one egg is like another? Assuredly if it was not the same hen that laid them, the paternity of them is traceable to the same cock — and that, without a doubt, not a Gallic cock but a Semitic one [Meyerbeer]. . . . Everywhere Moses and the prophets, or rather *Moïse* and *Le Prophète!* ". Dietsch, said the writer, was only " a non-commissioned officer

---

[38] Baudelaire had already pointed out the dangers inherent in a system which, by means of a yearly abonnement, "creates a sort of aristocracy which, at any given moment, from this or that motive or for this or that interest, can exclude the big public from participation in the judging of a work." Such a system in the Comédie-Française, he said, would produce the same disorders as at the Opéra.

M. Jacques Crépet, in his valuable notes on *L'art romantique*, says that Baudelaire's references to a production of *Tannhäuser* in "another place" are to be read in the light of his own life-long desire to be a theatre director. See BAR, pp. 242–3, 512–3.

of Meyerbeer "; while Niemann had been craftily worked upon by the assurance of the French critics that " he is a great singer, if only they would give him music to sing. It is said that he is already studying the part of John of Leyden [in *Le Prophète*] ".[39] " Niemann ", the *Revue et Gazette des Théâtres* had said, " is a singer of talent; he has a fine and powerful tenor voice which would be much more comfortable in our own great repertory." According to the *Figaro*, " Niemann is entitled to his revenge: the Opéra owes that to him on the grounds of hospitality and humanity. He knows the repertory: he has sung in Germany in the *Huguenots, Robert,* and *William Tell.* See to it that he is quickly washed clean and baptised in the holy waters of genius. . . . M. Meyerbeer is reserving for him the tenor part in *L'Africaine."* [40] When the Meyerbeerian Press did agree, its unanimity was wonderful! Sure enough, Niemann's first rôle after his return to Hanover was that of Raoul in the *Huguenots* — a baptism in the holy waters of genius which no doubt washed him clean of all Wagnerian defilements and left him pure as " any christom child ". As for Paris, already by the 1st April many of the *Tannhäuser* costumes were being used for a revival of *Robert the Devil.* They also, perhaps, were in need of baptism.

---

[39] GRW, III, 482. Glasenapp attributes the article to Herwegh: so does the poet's son (HBD, p. 75). An article in the *Zürcher Intelligenzblatt* of the 31st March undoubtedly came from Herwegh's pen. In this we see the real Herwegh, especially in a remark so characteristic of him as this: "Wagner's friends in Zürich explain, in part, the inimical attitude of the Parisians towards him by his intractability, which, even before the first performance, had given personal offence to all kinds of people and created trouble." (HBD, p. 79). The tone of the anonymous article in the *Neue Zürcher Zeitung* is so entirely different from that of Herwegh in the *Intelligenzblatt* that one has always suspected it to have come from some truer "Zürich friend" of Wagner then Herwegh occasionally proved himself to be. This suspicion has recently been revived on the excellent authority of Dr. Max Fehr, who knows the Zürich environment of Wagner better than anyone else. "It unfortunately cannot now be established", he writes, "who was the author of this spirited little defence: it might have been Franz Hagenbuch, Wilhelm Baumgartner, or Kapellmeister Louis Müller; anyhow not Georg Herwegh. . . .' (BFF, 1938, pp. 122–3).

[40] RWAN, p. 133.

CHAPTER VI

BETWEEN PARIS AND VIENNA

1

ON THE 17th March, 1861 Liszt wrote to his patron, the Grand Duke Carl Alexander of Weimar, reminding him that three months earlier Liszt had suggested the conferring of an order on Wagner, in spite of the fact that a fiasco in connection with *Tannhäuser* in Paris seemed probable. Since then the probability, said Liszt, had become reality; but as " this brutal fact " did not in the least affect Wagner's standing as an artist, he once more asked his Royal Highness " to confer on my noble and illustrious friend R. Wagner the Chevalier Cross as an appropriate and timely sign of your sovereign favour." In the following autumn the Weimar princeling sent the desired order to Liszt, asking him to hand it to Wagner, and assuring him that he made him his intermediary because above all " I think I am giving *you* pleasure in conferring it on the composer of the *Nibelungen*." [1]

This was the end of a rather curious story. Already in 1860 the signal favour shown Wagner by the French Emperor had made a few German consciences feel a trifle uneasy.

" It behoves me ", Carl Alexander had written towards the end of that year, " as Grand Duke of Weimar, to recognise all true merit in the realms of science, art and industry. Wagner especially deserves my full recognition, for in the world of music his greatness gives him a place apart. We are proud to be able to say that his works, so preeminently German in character, have for years found shelter on the Weimar stage. He is now about to produce *Tannhäuser* in Paris, and no doubt the Emperor who invited him to do so in his capital will reward him. I should not like it to be said that the great German composer possessed no German honour, or even that he should receive a French order before a German one." [2]

[1] LZCA, pp. 101–3.
[2] LWV, pp. 237–8.

The Grand Duke had planned, therefore, conformably with Liszt's suggestion, to confer on Wagner the Cross of the First Class of the Weimar Order of the Falcon. Lippert, who cites this letter, does not give the name of the addressee, but one surmises it to have been the Grand Duke's Minister, Bernhard von Watzdorf, who seems to have counselled caution in the matter. Enquiries were made in Dresden as to the possible reception there of such an act on the Duke's part; and as various Saxon holders of Weimar orders threatened to return their decorations if Wagner were thus honoured, the Grand Duke had thought it unwise to proceed further with his plan just then.

Although, as we have just seen, the amiable Carl Alexander had summoned up courage enough by the summer of 1861 to nominate Wagner for the order and to entrust Liszt with the delivery of it — perhaps during the Tonkünstlerverein festival to be held at Weimar in the first week of August, at which Wagner intended to be present — for some reason or other the order was never bestowed. That, of course, would not have distressed Wagner in the least: he was never tainted with Liszt's curious reverence for titles and " honours ". It was not trash of that sort that he wanted from the German princes, but help of a practical kind — money to keep him alive while he wrote his works, and facilities for producing them at the Court theatres after they were written. The significant thing, however, is that by the summer of 1861, after having hesitated so many years to set his fellow princes an example by honouring, in spite of his revolutionary past, the composer of the popular *Tannhäuser* and *Lohengrin*, even the timorous Carl Alexander had at last decided that it was safe to do so.

Napoleon III had, in fact, without knowing it and without intending it, not only forced the hands of some of the German rulers but given a new turn to Wagner's fortunes in his native land. It was mainly the imperial favour shown to Wagner in the spring of 1860 by the order to the Opéra to produce *Tannhäuser* that shamed, in the summer of that year, the Saxon monarch into partially withdrawing the ban upon the exile. And oddly enough, the *Tannhäuser* fiasco was perhaps more advantageous to Wagner in the end, so far as Germany was concerned, than a success would have been. Resentment of the outrages inflicted on their compatriot now became, in many quarters, a point of German national honour. Carl Alexander's newly-found courage was, in its mouse-like way, evidence of this: the plunge, he saw, was not going to be quite as cold a one as he had feared. All in all, the Fates, we now recognise, dealt not altogether unkindly with Wagner over the Paris affair, brutal as the hand they laid on him had seemed to him and his friends at the time. " What will Europe think of us? " Baudelaire had cried out in his distress over the blackguardism of the Parisian cabal. " What will they say of Paris in Germany? A handful of rowdies has disgraced us *en masse!* " [3] What Germany had to say about Paris did not long remain in doubt.

2

It was financially, of course, that Wagner was hardest hit by the Paris catastrophe: not only had he not profited to the extent of a single franc by all his labour during the last eighteen months but he had perforce piled up a mass of new debts. His German friends in Paris seem to have rallied round him, and, at his suggestion, to have sounded the Emperor as to some sort of monetary compensation for the immense amount of work Wagner had put in at the Opéra purely for the Opéra's benefit. *Mein Leben* is rather ambiguous on this point, but we may surmise that a fund was somehow raised to meet at any rate his immediate necessities. Erlanger, he says, " withdrew from all further participation in my fate " after the collapse of the scheme to float a " Wagner Theatre " in Paris: " from a mercantile point of view he regarded the arrangement made with me [4] as a sort of business deal that had just not succeeded." Precisely what that may mean is not made clear; but the indications are that as Wagner was already considerably in Erlanger's debt, the young banker, while not pressing for payment of what was owing to him, politely declined to make any further advances. That he had solid legal claims which he forbore from pressing while Wagner was in difficulties, but which he thought himself justified in reviving in later years when the Wahnfried fortunes were flourishing, is suggested by a passage in Du Moulin Eckart's biography of Cosima relating to 1892 —

[3] BAR, p. 251.   [4] See *supra*, p. 44.

nine years after Wagner's death, and more than thirty after the debts were incurred. In 1892 the trusty Adolf von Gross [5] went to Paris to see the first production there of *Lohengrin*. " In Paris ", says Du Moulin, " tough work was awaiting him. It was still a question of an orderly settlement with the banker Erlanger of difficulties that dated back to the time of the *Tannhäuser* performances in Paris. He accomplished this in a way that was not without its humorous side, but that signified a substantial success for Wahnfried." [6] It was rather characteristic of Wagner to lay more stress, in *Mein Leben*, upon what some of his Paris friends and acquaintances did *not* do for him than on what they had done.

The essential thing now, from every point of view, was to get *Tristan* upon the boards of some German theatre. The most immediately likely place for that was Karlsruhe. Bülow spent a few days there on his way back from Paris to Berlin — " diplomatising ", as he put it to a correspondent, on Wagner's behalf at the Court. His object was not only to prepare the ground for a production of *Tristan* in Karlsruhe but to secure a domestic " Asyl " there for Wagner. He came away believing he had definitely succeeded in the latter aim, if not entirely in the former. On the 15th April, only three weeks after the last performance of *Tannhäuser* in Paris, Wagner himself went to Karlsruhe for some ten days, expressly to discuss the *Tristan* question with the art-loving young Grand Duke Friedrich of Baden. He found him even better-disposed towards him than in the past, manifestly because of Wagner's woeful experiences in Paris. It was arranged that *Tristan,* under Wagner's direction, should be produced on the Grand Duke's thirty-fifth birthday, the 9th September. " The example of Napoleon the Great is having its effect ", Bülow wrote to Alexander Ritter; " the singers whom Wagner regards as necessary are to be specially engaged from outside." Wagner tells us in *Mein Leben* that he believed Eduard Devrient, the director of the theatre, to be still inimical to him, but he admits that he was soon able to win him over to the Grand Duke's plan, " at any rate in appearance ". It is not at all improbable that Devrient's lack of en-

[5] Son-in-law of the banker Feustel, who had so staunchly stood by Wagner during the difficult early years of the Bayreuth theatre. Adolf von Gross was a tower of strength to Cosima in her business dealings with the world.

[6] MECW, II, 390.

thusiasm for the *Tristan* project had been due to the clear perception that the resources of the Karlsruhe theatre alone were inadequate to the realisation of it. That this was the case became evident the moment the idea of a production in the following September began to be considered seriously: hence the permission granted to Wagner to engage the necessary singers wherever he thought he could find them.

As luck would have it, the one singer in Germany potentially able and not unwilling to sing Tristan — Ludwig Schnorr von Carolsfeld,[7] who had been a member of the Karlsruhe company when Wagner first hoped to produce his new work there in 1860 — had left the town for Dresden: had he still been resident in Karlsruhe in 1861 the whole course of Wagner's existence during the next three years might have been radically altered.[8] Wagner had been first told of the promising young Karlsruhe tenor by Tichatschek in 1856. In his *Recollections of Ludwig Schnorr von Carolsfeld* (1868) he says that in 1859, when he was hoping to have *Tristan* produced in Karlsruhe, Schnorr had confessed that in spite of his devotion to the composer he did not feel equal to the task; he found the third act particularly exhausting. That may well be; but Malvina maintained in later years that it was really she who had been answerable for *Tristan* being shelved. According to her, Ludwig was threatened in 1859 with a dangerous affection of the heart: to protect him from the strain she knew that *Tristan* would impose on the young man of twenty-three she told the management that the part of Isolde was too much for her.[9] It may have been as the result of this that Wagner could at that time congratulate

---

[7] His culture, which was superior to that of the average tenor of his epoch, he owed in part to the fact that he was the son of the famous painter Julius Schnorr von Carolsfeld (1794–1872).

[8] Both Schnorr and his future wife Malvina had been located in Karlsruhe since 1854, in which year Ludwig was no more than eighteen, while Malvina was some ten years older. They first appeared together in October, 1854, when Malvina sang Valentine in *Les Huguenots*, Ludwig figuring as a soldier. Three years later he was singing Tannhäuser to her Elisabeth. They became engaged in December 1857. In May, 1860 Schnorr was given a three years' engagement at the Dresden Opera; and although Malvina's contract in Karlsruhe still had some years to run she decided to follow Ludwig to Dresden, and to sacrifice her own career as an opera singer in order to foster his exceptional talent. They married in April, 1860. In 1862 the Dresden management signed a new contract with Schnorr to run for seven years from the 1st May, 1863. It was from Dresden that Wagner obtained him to sing Tristan in Munich in 1865.　　　　　[9] GIS, p. 107.

himself, as we have seen, on not having to produce his work with " a voiceless Isolde ". In the *Recollections* he never once mentions Malvina, for reasons with which the reader will be made acquainted later; and we have to bear in mind that in April, 1861, when the Grand Duke of Baden authorised him to engage whatever singers he liked for *Tristan*, Wagner had never seen or heard Schnorr, while he had heard Malvina only once in his life — as long ago as September, 1848, when, as a beginner of twenty-two, she had made a " guest " appearance in Dresden as Norma.

3

Devrient had been authorised by the Grand Duke to borrow Schnorr from Dresden for the projected performances; but even now, though the young man was generally regarded in German musical circles as the destined successor of Tichatschek, Wagner was reluctant to entrust the part of Tristan to him; he had heard so much, indeed, of Schnorr's corpulence — the result of some unalterable physical idiosyncrasy — that he told Devrient outright he had no desire even to make the singer's personal acquaintance. The reports he had received must have been quite horrific to prejudice him to that extent, for there could be no doubt either as to Schnorr's vocal endowment or his intellectual calibre. As is the case with so many " heroic " tenors, one cannot be quite sure that nature had not originally intended him for a baritone; but he evidently had a command of the finer shades of expression that one does not usually associate with singers of his robust vocal type. At his first appearance in Dresden (as Lohengrin) in 1860 a critic described his voice as " of unusual power ", of " noble timbre ", " of baritone quality, and predominantly brilliant "; " fortunately ", the critic added, " this exceptional vocal material was played upon by the singer in a musical, cultivated style "; he praised also Schnorr's " taste and nobility " as an actor.[10] Robert Prölss, the historian of the Dresden theatre, described the tenor's tone in retrospect (1878) as " curiously elegiac, somewhat veiled ", but flashing out triumphantly, when required, " like the sun breaking through passing clouds "; Schnorr further had " an

---

[10] GIS, p. 120, quoting the *Signale* of the 7th June, 1860.

exquisite portamento and a splendid cantilena "; his bearing, in spite of his abnormal bulk, was " distinguished ", his acting full of expression ".[11]

As for Malvina, if she could sing Isolde's music to Wagner's satisfaction in Munich in 1865, as we know she did, she could presumably have sung it even better in Karlsruhe when she was four years younger: both she and Schnorr soon discovered that it required only a little help, of the peculiar kind that Wagner was so skilled in giving his singers, for difficulties which they had thought insuperable to vanish into thin air. Had they both been located in Karlsruhe in the summer of 1861, then, *Tristan* would have been a practical certainty there, for an adequate Brangaene, Marke and Kurvenal could easily have been found somewhere or other in Germany or Austria. All this would probably have meant Wagner's settling down for a considerable time in Karlsruhe under the protection of the Grand Duke; in which case the long Vienna episode, with its ruinous effects on both his finances and his character, would have been avoided. How the siren Vienna lured him on to a disaster worse than anything even he had ever yet experienced will appear shortly.

With a new hope in his heart he went back to Paris for a few days, partly to regularise his economic affairs as well as he could for the time being, partly because of the prospect of a meeting with Liszt, whom he had not seen since the Zürich days of October 1856. Precisely how he managed to raise funds for the Vienna journey that now lay before him is not known: according to *Mein Leben* " the operations begun by Princess Metternich to obtain some sort of compensation for me dragged along with mysterious slowness ", and it was a merchant named Stürmer, whom he had known in Zürich, and who had all along taken a sympathetic interest in his Paris fortunes, whose timely help enabled him first to set his household affairs in some sort of order and then to depart for Vienna. As regards a meeting with Liszt he was not so fortunate. Whether by accident or design, Liszt did not arrive in Paris till a few hours after Wagner had left. One suspects that it was by design: Liszt was probably unwilling to do anything just then to annoy his Carolyne, whose prejudice against Wagner was by this time develop-

[11] PGHD, p. 610.

ing into monomania. There can be no doubt that for one reason or another, or for a combination of reasons, Liszt had been for some time out of tune with his old friend, and was to remain so for a considerable time to come.[12] " Certainly no one could be more *devoted* (to employ a banal locution) than I am ", Liszt had written to Agnes Street in the spring of 1861. " I really wish I could be of service to him in some way or other; but unfortunately the means necessary for that are not at my disposition. He is in need of a great deal of money: where can it be found? " There certainly is no hostility towards Wagner in any of Liszt's letters of this period; but there is as certainly very little of the old cordiality.

Matters had not been improved by a piece of extraordinary stupidity on Bülow's part in October, 1859. On the 7th of that month Wagner had poured out his soul to Hans regarding Liszt, whom he suspected of cooling towards him, and against whom, he felt, he had certain legitimate small grievances. Bülow, with the tactlessness that came so easily to him, and that sometimes raises a faint doubt in us whether a man so thick of skin and so heavy of hand could really have been a Prussian, sent the letter to Liszt. The latter, who by that time had had more than one piece of evidence that some of his friends were rather less infatuated with Princess Wittgenstein than he was, saw in it, of course, a veiled attack on his Carolyne. " He seems to insinuate to Hans ", he wrote to her *à propos* of Wagner's letter, " that you exercise a regrettable influence over me, and one contrary to my true nature "; this is a " falsity " Liszt has met with in other quarters, and one with which he will have no truck. He piously exhorted the Princess, who was in Paris at the time, to call on Wagner and be very gentle with him, " for he is sick, and incurable; for that reason one must just love him, and try to serve him as well as one can." The Princess, however, studiously avoided Wagner, though she called on Berlioz; and for all Liszt's fine sentiments he himself made no serious attempt to close the breach that had already opened out between

[12] See Vol. II, pp. 530–554. Their correspondence between the summer of 1849, when Wagner fled from Dresden, to the autumn of 1859, when he settled in Paris, occupies some 570 pages in the second edition. A mere 30 pages or so suffice for the letters between October, 1859 and the 7th July, 1861; and the next letter after that is Wagner's of the 18th May, 1872.

himself and Wagner. It was a situation in which each of them suffered profoundly, for each, in his heart of hearts, had an unbreakable regard and affection for the other.

It was not only in Karlsruhe that Wagner found a new interest being taken in him. From Thomé, the director of the Prague National Opera, he received a suggestion that the *Rhinegold* should be given there, under Wagner himself, on the 21st August, during the festivities in connection with the coronation of the King of Bohemia. Wagner's original intention, of course, had been to perform the *Ring* in its entirety before permitting a production of any single section of the tetralogy. The prospects of his completing the huge work, however, were remote at this time; and he had begun seriously to ask himself whether it would not be advisable to get the already complete *Rhinegold* and *Valkyrie* into theatrical circulation. His reply to Thomé — transmitted through his Prague friend Franz Apt [13] — suggests that he would have had no fundamental objection just then to floating the individual operas of the *Ring* one by one, providing only that the first production in each case were entirely under his control, and that the technical staff of any other theatre that might wish to give one of the works later should have been present at the " model " performance: evidently it was in the stage handling of the *Ring*, even more than in the singing and playing of the score, that he anticipated having trouble with the German opera houses. As it happened, he went on to say, his co-operation in a Prague production of the *Rhinegold* in August would be impossible, as the *Tristan* production in Karlsruhe would tie him to that town all through the summer of 1861; while he was planning to give the *Rhinegold* also there in the summer of 1862 — a clear indication that he thought of making the Baden capital his headquarters for some time to come.

4

Disappointed in his hope of seeing Liszt, he left Paris for Vienna, in quest of singers for *Tristan*, at the beginning of the second week

---

[13] This Franz (Anton) Apt is not to be confused with Franz Abt, the composer of "When the swallows homeward fly". Apt was the conductor of the Prague Cecilia Society, and a great admirer of Wagner. The latter's personal relations with Thomé were none of the friendliest; hence the use of Apt as an intermediary.

in May, calling at Karlsruhe en route for another conference with the Grand Duke. Karl Eckert, who had been both Kapellmeister and technical director at the Vienna Opera for some years, had left that town for Stuttgart in 1860, where we shall find Wagner resuming acquaintance with him later. He had been succeeded in the Vienna management by Matteo Salvi, and as conductor by Heinrich Esser, who, while never a true-blue Wagnerian, seems always to have tackled with the utmost conscientiousness any Wagnerian problem that formed part of his professional duties. The Vienna Opera seized the opportunity of Wagner's presence in the town not only to show what it could offer him in the way of singers for *Tristan* but to demonstrate its sympathy with him after the Paris outrage. The Opera was rather proud of its Wagner performances: and the most graceful form in which it could express its admiration for the composer of *Lohengrin* was to let him hear, for the first time in his life, this work of his that had been written no less than thirteen years before.

He arrived in Vienna on the 9th May, and settled in the " Erzherzog Karl " Hotel, in the Kärntnerstrasse, not far from the Opera (the Kärntnertor Theatre). A full stage rehearsal — though the principal singers were not in costume — was called for the 11th: Salvi introduced him, from the stage, to the assembled company. He was given a very cordial reception, for which he thanked them all in a short speech. With the rehearsal as a whole he was enchanted; the playing of the orchestra in particular moved him deeply. His highly emotional mood found expression a couple of days later in a letter to Minna.

" Words cannot convey the profound, completely unalloyed joy I felt: orchestra, singers, chorus, all excellent, incredibly fine . . . I sat quite motionless through it all; merely one tear chased another down my cheek. The good people came and silently embraced me: finally orchestra and chorus broke into loud applause."

He was particularly interested in the tenor, Aloys Ander, and the soprano, Luise Meyer-Dustmann, whom he had in view for his Karlsruhe Tristan and Isolde. Luise Dustmann, he told Minna, had " a heavenly, soulful voice, capable of anything ", and in addition " an excellent dramatic delivery " and a great range of nuance: there would be little, he thought, he would have to teach her. Ander

was " quite perfect; the voice not merely sufficient but of brilliant
energy when needed; a conscious artist through and through, admirable both in delivery and in his acting, completely absorbed in
what he is doing, full of life and fire ". He had reason to modify
his opinion of Ander in the sequel. It may have been that his emotion on hearing his *Lohengrin* for the first time had slightly dulled
his critical faculty, though it has to be borne in mind that it had
always been in the part of Lohengrin that Ander had been at his
best.[14]

On the 13th Wagner was presented to the Intendant of the Opera,
Count Lanckoronski, who showed himself so friendly that, as we see
from Wagner's letter of the same day to Minna, doubts about Karlsruhe already began to take root in him.

"He has placed his theatre at my disposal for all my works; and I
am told that he doesn't trifle, but means what he says and keeps to it
literally. Truly, I cut quite a comic figure in my own eyes now with
my laborious Karlsruhe model-performance, for which I have first
of all to assemble my forces; and indeed I almost believe I shall
have to seize hold where I find *everything, everything* ready to my
hand [i.e. in Vienna], and in addition a big, enthusiastic public, very
fond of me, at my back."

Manifestly the same idea had struck him and the Intendant simultaneously; since the singers for *Tristan* are all here in Vienna, why
drag them off to Karlsruhe, where the orchestra is inferior to that
of Vienna, while there is no comparison between the financial and
other resources of the two theatres? Wagner assures Minna, however, that he " sticks to our plan for Karlsruhe as a residence. . . .
In any case a favourable and lasting change is coming over our
prospects in life."

The performance of *Lohengrin,* originally arranged for the 12th

[14] He was in his forty-fourth year at this time. He enjoyed immense popularity
in Vienna, where he had been stationed since 1845. Luise Dustmann was thirty. A
Karlsruhe or Vienna production of *Tristan* in 1861 would thus have given Wagner a
Tristan older by fifteen years and an Isolde younger by nine years than Schnorr and
his wife were at the time of the Munich performances of 1865.

The French tenor Gustave Roger, who heard Ander in Vienna in 1858, described
him as "bawling at the top of his voice", "utterly lacking in nuances", and trusting
to "the thunder of his voice" to make "effects" instead of interpreting the poet and
the composer. This, says Roger, is all that is required in Germany. (RCT, p. 341).
A German writer of about the same period, however, speaks of Ander's voice as
"soft and lyrical" rather than powerful or brilliant. (NULT, I, 232-3).

May, had to be postponed, by reason of the indisposition of the
Ortrud, until the 15th. It was made the occasion of a demonstration of respect and affection such as Wagner had never experienced before, even in the days of his greatest popularity in Dresden. The evening was one long triumph for him. At the end of
the performance he made a short speech to the audience, in a voice
trembling with emotion:

> "Tonight I have heard my work for the first time, performed by an
> ensemble of artists the equal of whom I do not know, and received by
> the public in a way that well-nigh overwhelms me. What can I say?
> Let me bear in all humility the burden you have thus laid on me; let
> me go on striving towards the goal of my art. I beg you to support me
> in doing so, by continuing in your good will towards me."

Three days later the *Flying Dutchman* was given in his honour,
with Beck in the title part.[15]   To avoid such another demonstration
as that on the night of the *Lohengrin* performance Wagner had it
given out that he had left Vienna, and hid himself at the back of a
parquet box. He was recognised, however, and was once more
called and recalled by a huge audience that seemingly could not do
enough to show its regard for him. At the conclusion of the *Lohengrin* prelude he had had to acknowledge the applause five times
from his box in the second tier: after the *Flying Dutchman* overture he was brought upon the stage to bow his thanks: and, strangest
thing of all to us of today, he had had to go to the front of the box
and bow, he told Minna, after " each of the principal musical pieces
in each act " of *Lohengrin*. Evidently a long course of education
was needed before even Wagnerian audiences developed the habit
of listening to a whole act of an opera in silence.

5

As Bülow had foreseen at the time, the most serious after-effect
of the Paris *Tannhäuser* disaster was in connection with Wagner's
finances. He had already sold the publishing rights of *Tristan* and

---

[15] Johann Nepomuk Beck (1827–1904) was a favorite member of the Vienna company from 1853 till his retirement in 1885. Wagner had a fair amount of trouble with
him in later years, though he greatly admired his voice and actually cast him for the
first King Marke in *Tristan* in 1865; the part was ultimately taken, however, by
Zottmayer.

of so much of the *Ring* as he had completed, and he had spent the proceeds. In the way of performing rights from the German theatres he had virtually nothing, and for some time to come would have nothing, but *Tristan* to look to; and whatever good fortune he might have once *Tristan* was floated, his position till then was critical. Had he realised all that lay before him even his inveterate optimism would probably have failed him. For more than three years after the Paris catastrophe he was a wanderer on the face of the earth, his main occupation, during a large part of that time, being a desperate hunt for money — money from anyone, extracted by any means, at whatever cost of decency or dignity. And they were years not of careful economy but of the most reckless expenditure at other people's expense. Yet oddly enough these three years, as the pages of *Mein Leben* show, were years of a feverish gaiety that surprised everyone who knew him. Nature had provided him at his birth with a beneficent compensatory principle which, in times of stress, enabled him not so much to bear his burden philosophically as to convert it into a spring-board for a leap into a delightful world of his own making, in which the writ of crude reality did not run. It was only at the end of these three years that he seemed, even to himself, to be really beaten; and by that time the Fates, who had obviously had a sneaking affection for their victim all the while they had been sporting with him, thought it time at last to play their master-stroke in his favour.

He returned from Vienna to Paris towards the end of May. There he found Liszt, from whom, apparently, he managed to extract a small grant in aid. The two saw little of each other, however, for Liszt, as Wagner puts it in *Mein Leben,* had " fallen back into his old current ", frequenting for preference the rich and aristocratic circles in which he could be sure of the adulation that was as the breath of his nostrils to him, and neglecting even his daughter Blandine, who " could only manage to get a word with him in his carriage, between one visit and another." [16] Through

---

[16] "*He was just pitched about from one prince, countess, emperor and minister to another*", Wagner wrote to Mathilde Wesendonk. "*And he went on with it all with incredible zeal. He tried to make me understand that it was in order to achieve something.* No one knows better than himself what can be achieved there; and so I judge him more justly when I assume that, since the real thing is denied him, he loves to intoxicate himself now and then with the semblance. *He even finds pleasure in being fêted*

the Metternichs he managed to get himself invited to the Tuileries, where, Wagner notes caustically, they had not deemed it necessary to invite *him:* and though his difficulties were evidently discussed by Liszt and the Emperor, the latter had no idea of helping him financially, which was the only help that Wagner wanted just then. Other friends besides Liszt came to his help, among them a Mlle. Eberty, Meyerbeer's niece, the publisher Flaxland, and certain sympathisers who " desired to remain unknown ", but who were manifestly associated with the Austrian, Prussian and other embassies. As the result of it all Wagner was able to clear off some of his more pressing debts, sub-let the apartment in the Rue d'Aumale, store his furniture, and send Minna off to Soden on the 12th July for a cure. A few weeks before she left Paris their little dog Fips died rather suddenly, presumably from having picked up some poison in the street during a walk with Minna.[17] The charitable suggestion was made by Ashton Ellis that Minna herself had poisoned the dog, being unable to endure it because it had been a present to Wagner from Frau Wesendonk. Wagner himself does not so much as hint at this, nor is there the faintest supporting evidence for the malicious charge. What Wagner does say is that in the case of this childless couple the loss even of such a link between them as poor little Fips had been was enough to mark the end of a chapter: nothing was said between them, Wagner tells us, but the dog's sudden death " came as the last cleavage in a union that had long ago become impossible." With the touching devotion to his dogs and his fidelity to the memory of them that is one of the most likeable features of his character, he saved the pathetic little body from the normal fate of dead dogs in Paris — the gutter and the scavenger's cart — by burying it with his own

---

like this, and will confess as much when the wine begins to have an effect on him over dessert. When that happens he lavishes benedictions on me, and describes himself as totally lost. What is one to make of it? God knows! I could not accompany him anywhere, and so I saw little of him." The passages here italicised were suppressed in the official edition of the letters. See Julius Kapp's *Unterdrückte Dokumente aus den Briefen Richard Wagners an Mathilde Wesendonk,* in DM, September, 1931, p. 883.

What Liszt was trying to "achieve" in Paris was election to the Institute. This meant a good deal of personal canvassing for votes.

[17] Thus in *Mein Leben,* in a passage dictated about 1880. In his letter of the 12th July, 1861 to Frau Wesendonk, written some three weeks after the death of the animal, he presumed Fips to have been struck by a cart wheel.

hands beneath a bush in the garden of his friend Stürmer's house, Stürmer being conveniently away from home at the time.

Wagner had undertaken the supervision of the French translation of the *Flying Dutchman* which Truinet was making for Flaxland. As the task would occupy him for some time, and his apartment was now denuded of its furniture, Count Pourtalès placed at his disposal a pleasant room in the Prussian embassy, facing the garden, with a view over the Seine as far as the garden of the Tuileries. Here he was virtually one of the family; at the daily " diplomatic dinner " he met a number of interesting people, some of them old acquaintances, such as the Metternichs and the two attachés, Prince Reuss and Count Dönhoff, others new, such as the former Prussian minister Bethmann-Hollweg, whom he describes as " the father of Countess Pourtalès ".[18] In the evenings he could now and then hold forth to a numerous company, as he so loved to do, upon art and philosophy as he conceived them, though apparently without making any converts; and on one occasion the Neapolitan Princess Campo-Reale sang Isolde's Liebestod in excellent style to the skilled accompaniment of Saint-Saëns. Outside the embassy there were plenty of friends of his own kind to whom he could give, or from whom he could receive, farewell dinners — Champfleury, Flaxland, Truinet, Gasperini, Gustave Doré and others.

In a pool in the garden of the embassy there were two black swans that had a peculiar fascination for him. He has conferred immortality on these birds in an *Albumblatt* for piano in A flat major — *Ankunft bei den schwarzen Schwänen* — which he wrote by way of a compliment to his hostess. The manuscript of this having been mislaid for a long time the little work was not published until 1897: it is based on the " Sei mir gegrüsst " motive from Elisabeth's Hall of Song aria. A companion piece in C major, intended for Princess Metternich, was published in 1871. Its central motive, he tells us, is " a pretty theme which had been floating about in my mind for a long time."

After three weeks in the Prussian embassy he went to Weimar,

---

[18] The Countess Pourtalès described by Frédéric Loliée was, however, the daughter of Baron Alfred Renouard de Bussière, an Alsatian manufacturer. Count Pourtalès came of a family of Swiss bankers domiciled in Paris. See *Les Femmes du Second Empire*, pp. 309–332.

arriving there on the 2nd August. He had gone by way of Soden, where his main object had been to try to persuade Minna to settle in Dresden as soon as she could, leaving him to seek his fortune elsewhere, and first of all in Vienna. (At this time, of course, Saxony was still barred to him; he had even to travel with a Prussian passport supplied by Count Pourtalès, an attempt to procure him a Saxon passport having failed). He promised to provide Minna, in all circumstances, with a steady income of 3,000 marks a year — a promise which, by hook or by crook, he seems to have kept to the end.

6

As was often the case with him, the Wagner with whom friends and acquaintances rubbed shoulders at this time and the Wagner he felt himself to be deep down within him were two very different beings. Happy as he seemed in his retreat in the embassy, he told Malwida, his eyes often filled with tears at the thought of the futility of everything and the sense of his utter loneliness in the world. "Two whole years absolutely wasted, and I feel exceedingly weary. But what I have lost, so far as art is concerned, I have perhaps won in the sphere of life: an ultimate, profoundly-rooted experience — not to try to compel what does not come of itself." Even the thought of producing *Tristan* alienated him as much as it attracted him.

> "God knows ", he wrote to Mathilde Wesendonk on the 25th July, "whether *Tristan* will resuscitate me: if I dip into the score by accident I am often appalled at the thought that I may have to hear it soon. Once more I am astonished how little, strictly speaking, people can know of one — how completely different I am when I am alone and when I go among others; often I cannot help laughing at the phantom that steps before them! "

The phantom, however, had willy-nilly to go to the meeting of the Tonkünstlerverein in Weimar, where some works of Liszt were to be given. It went sorely against the grain with him, for he never had much appetite for miscellaneous and generally futile music-makings of this sort; but to have refused meant offending Liszt. His later description of the festival to Malwida von Meysenbug would apply to most gatherings, ancient or modern, of the kind —

" rather too many people . . . mostly ridiculous . . . little talent but much inanity . . . music often very bad." Liszt's *Faust
Symphony* he thought " really excellent "; but he must have found
such things as Weissheimer's ballad *Das Grab im Busento* and the
Germania Marsch of Dräseke a sore trial. He found himself, however, among a crowd of admirers and well-wishers whose cordiality
must have heartened him for the time being. Most of the " New
German " musicians and journalists and dilettanti were there —
Tausig, Cornelius, Bülow, Brendel, Dräseke, Leopold Damrosch,
Lassen, Alwine Frommann and many others. Cosima was absent;
she was taking a milk cure in Reichenhall. Blandine and Ollivier,
however, had come to do honour to Liszt, and Blandine in particular Wagner found very agreeable company. To the public that
attended the four days' festival — from the 5th to the 8th August
— a public drawn from Germany in general rather than from
Weimar itself, the greatest attraction was undoubtedly Wagner.
Enthusiasts burst into song under his window; they toasted him
at a banquet; and they only refrained from a torchlight procession
in his honour because he implored them to spare him that.

The festival was marred by some characteristically neurotic behaviour on Liszt's part. Dräseke's over-ambitious March had been
coldly received. This annoyed Liszt, who had never forgiven Weimar for its hissing of Cornelius's *Barber of Bagdad* in December,
1858, and of himself as the conductor of it, and had seemingly
managed to persuade himself that any work by a protégé of his
that did not go down well in Weimar must necessarily be good.
Red with anger he leaned out of the stage box, ostentatiously clap-
ping and shouting " Bravo! " It developed into what Wagner calls
" an out-and-out fight between him and the audience." Blandine
was as shocked by this sorry spectacle as Wagner was; and it was
long after the concert was over before any of them recovered their
equanimity.

The Ollivier's objective after the festival was Reichenhall. Wagner accompanied them there, travelling by way of Munich, where,
he says, he ran across an old acquaintance, the young Baron von
Hornstein. In *Mein Leben* he jeers at him, after an interval of
nearly twenty years, for what he calls his " droll figure and doltish
behaviour ", and gives us the impression that his own, Ollivier's

and Blandine's not very refined amusement consisted largely in making a butt of the young man. The real reason for Wagner's inappeasable animus against Hornstein will appear later. At Reichenhall the trio found Cosima rather better in health than they had expected. In a few days Wagner was on his way to Vienna again, receiving, he tells us, " a look of almost timid questioning from Cosima " as they parted.[19]

In Vienna a house had been placed at his disposal [20] by his friend Adolph Kolatschek, whom the reader will remember as a co-exile with Wagner from Saxony in the Zürich days. But Kolatschek, who had left Vienna for the summer, had forgotten to make any provision of comforts or service for his guest, while the house, as Wagner soon discovered, stood in a suburb inconveniently remote from the centre of the town. On a previous visit to Vienna he had made the acquaintance of a Dr. Joseph Standhartner, a physician with an extensive practice in Court circles, who was destined to prove one of Wagner's most faithful friends for the remainder of his life — one more illustration of his power to win occasionally the friendship and retain the life-long devotion of men of the finest type. Sitting disconsolately in a café after his disillusioning inspection of Kolatschek's house, he was surprised to see Standhartner enter, the coincidence being all the more remarkable in that the physician had never in his life been in that café until then. Standhartner, as it happened, was also on holiday with his family. He placed his home [21] at Wagner's service for six weeks: the housekeeping was done by a young niece of his, one Seraphine Mauro, about whom Wagner says little in *Mein Leben*, but with whom, we gather, he carried on a very agreeable flirtation, much to the chagrin of Cornelius; for Cornelius himself was at that time in love with the pretty little Seraphine, whose figure had won her the affectionate title, among her intimates, of " the doll ". Six years later, writing to his fiancée, Bertha Jung, Cornelius says that Wagner " was at that time as much in love with Seraphine as he is now with Cosima." The infatuation lasted quite a while: in January, 1862 we find him writing to Cornelius from Paris, *à propos*

---

[19] See *infra*, p. 302.
[20] Gumpendorferstrasse 368, now Gumpendorferstrasse 88, Webgasse 2.
[21] The third floor of Seilerstätte 806, now Seilerstätte 4, Singerstrasse 32

of his plans for settling down somewhere on the Rhine, " Good
Lord, how I should like to have the poor *Puppe* with me! ", and regretting his own " incredible, naïve morality ". He cannot see why
the girl should not come to him and be to him what her sweet nature
so well fits her to be. " But how to find the *terminus socialis?* Ach
Himmel, I'm amusedly sorry! " [22]

The poor man certainly deserved whatever consolation the bright
Seraphine could give him, for his general situation was becoming
daily more desperate. *Tristan* was no nearer performance in Vienna than it had ever been. With Ander he had an experience that
was to be repeated again and again during the next couple of years:
the tenor had temporarily lost his voice, and lived in growing terror
of the difficult part. Wagner's enemies, of whom he had plenty in
Vienna, spread the story that Ander's troubles all came from the
" impossible " nature of the *Tristan* music; the tenor himself was
prone to believe this, and with each fresh attack of hoarseness or
of general malaise he became more and more convinced that *Tristan* would kill him.[23] As yet there was no trouble with Frau Dustmann, who, indeed, was keen enough about the part of Isolde and
was working conscientiously at it; but the time was not far distant
when she too would fail Wagner. The Press was already making
it clear that it had no particular affection for either Wagner or his
Tristan; and the Opera management, while cordiality itself with
Wagner to his face, was already regretting its promises to him and
only looking round for a valid pretext for not carrying them out.
He was soon to realise that the far-famed Viennese charm was not
much more than skin-deep. It had never occurred to the Opera
people that Wagner would take quite literally their request to him
to be back in Vienna by the 14th August, in order to start rehearsals
for a production alleged to be contemplated in early October!

Wagner's strange optimism with regard to *Tristan* during this
long time was perhaps only the reverse side of his desperation. Not
only had he a pathetic longing to hear this favourite work of his; a

[22] The "lächerlich" in RWFZ, p. 292 is an error. It should be "lächelnd".

[23] Although he made several successful appearances in other parts during the next
couple of years there was plainly something wrong with him. At last, in a performance
of *William Tell* in which he could not remember his music, the indications of mental
disturbance became unmistakable. He never recovered his sanity, and died on the
11th December, 1864.

production of it was imperative if royalties were to begin to come in again, and at the moment a production seemed possible nowhere but in Vienna. Only on the theory of his utter despair can we account for the concessions he showed himself willing to make to the singers. The copy of the score used by Ander is still in existence, and from this and other sources we realise how considerable these concessions were. From the big scene in the third act in which Tristan calls down curses on love, Wagner deleted, for Ander's sake, no less than 142 bars. Notes that lay too low for the tenor he transposed for him, sometimes as much as a whole octave higher. If a re-arrangement of the vocal line disturbed the verbal values, Wagner altered the words. As these changes in words and music extend only about as far as the episode that precedes the joyful signal of the shepherd, the presumption is that the attempt to accommodate the part to Ander's capacity was given up as hopeless at that point. In addition to all this, he had apparently been pestered to re-cast the part of Kurvenal for a bass, as it did not meet with Mayerhofer's approval in its original form. Wagner refused to make the change; " the baritone nature of the rôle is too pronounced for that ", he said; and if Mayerhofer could not or would not sing it as it was written he suggested Beck, or the Karlsruhe Franz Hauser. Particularly interesting is his specification, in a letter to Esser, for the horn on which the shepherd was to blow his jubilant melody: it was to be " of wood, at least three feet long, almost trumpet-like, but with a rather crooked curve at the end, so that the bell faces sideways "; the tone was to be " that of a medium-sized Alpine horn, fairly powerful, even rough, but in any case of a natural naïveté." [24]

7

Standhartner and his family having returned to Vienna, Wagner had to take up his autumn quarters in the " Kaiserin Elisabeth " Hotel, in the Weihburg Gasse, which he found very expensive. Nothing like the full story of his frantic efforts to raise money anywhere and by any means is told us in *Mein Leben;* but even from his own sketchy account of the matter we can see how desperate

[24] In his manuscript score he had prescribed a "cor anglais behind the scenes".

his position was, and how grievously his character must have deteriorated under the incessant strain of borrowing, or trying to borrow, on a scale that was staggering even for Richard Wagner. About the beginning of June, after his temporary return from Vienna to Paris, he had received a very cordial letter from an admirer in Prague, a merchant named Bergmann, whom he at once tried to put under contribution to the tune of 10,000 francs, the repayment of which, he said, he would regard as an " obligation of honour " when his circumstances improved. The practical result of this request is not known for certain; but the indications are that it was unsuccessful. He made a passionate appeal to the Grand Duke of Baden for a pension of 2,400 marks with which to secure for himself a " modest refuge " in or near Karlsruhe. The request was refused, ostensibly on the grounds that at Karlsruhe he might interfere with Devrient's management of the theatre to such an extent as to hinder the smooth working of that institution: at the back of the Grand Duke's mind, however, there was probably the feeling — shared by numberless other people after coming into close contact with Wagner — that as a man, and especially as an economic man, he was hopeless, and that to help him once was to burden oneself with him in perpetuity.

So everyone who could not or would not give him money passed him on to someone else. Princess Metternich, for instance, gave him an introduction to the Hungarian Count Coloman Nákó, who had an estate some miles distant from Vienna. Thither Wagner betook himself one fine day in the company of Prince Rudolph Liechtenstein, an amiable young dilettante, studying musical theory with Cornelius, whom he had met through Standhartner. Wagner's account of the visit to Schwarzau, which lasted a day and a night, is not lacking in frankness. He had no sooner arrived at the Nákó estate than he began to spy out the land for his own peculiar purposes. At breakfast the next day he broke out into what he no doubt regarded as subtly tactful comments on the great size of the château, in which, he tells us, he had already privately speculated which might be his room on the occasion of another and longer visit; whereupon his hosts, with a technique in no way inferior to his own, hastened to assure him that, large as the place seemed, it no more than sufficed for the family and their depend-ants. No man or woman of the world, indeed, could look at this time into that hungry, coldly calculating eye without sensing in it, with an apprehensive shiver, the impending "touch" of the professional borrower. He soon came to the conclusion that he had nothing in common with Count and Countess Nákó and the local gentry he met at their table. They talked a great deal, but always about the wrong things, about pictures, or Hungarian melodies, or horses, about anything, in fact, but the one thing it was their plain duty to talk about — Richard Wagner and his ideals and necessities. He left Schwarzau baffled and depressed.

Attempts at one time or another to speed up the production of *Tristan* by obtaining another tenor all failed; he tried to procure from Dresden first Tichatschek, then Schnorr, but neither was available. From somewhere or other he managed to obtain money enough to keep going for a while in Vienna; and with no pressing duties at the theatre and no inclination to start composing again just yet he had plenty of leisure for amusement and for social intercourse. An enthusiastic article in the *Oesterreichische Zeitung* of the 8th October on a new ballet, *Gräfin Egmont*, was certainly from his pen, though it was published under the initials "P.C." [25] For genuine companionship there were always Standhartner, Cornelius and Tausig. A half-hearted attempt to cultivate the acquaintance of Hebbel broke down through fundamental incompatibility of temper; Wagner had never anything but contempt for the poet's dramas, and was probably at no great pains to conceal the fact. Hebbel, for his part, could make nothing of Wagner's theoretical writings, while of the operas only the *Flying Dutchman* had any attraction

---

[25] It will be found in Cornelius's *Literarische Werke* (CABT, III, 72 ff.); it has not so far been included in Wagner's Collected Works. The style is unmistakable, and Standhartner's step-son, Gustav Schönaich, has testified that for secrecy's sake he himself took Wagner's manuscript to the newspaper office and read the proofs.

The editor of Vol. III of CABT, Edgar Istel, says that "of course" there was an understanding between Wagner and Cornelius that the former should use the latter's initials. Cornelius's son, however, shows that this was not so. Peter was known to the editor of the paper. Wagner was not; and he made use of his friend's name without his knowledge or consent, no doubt thinking he was being both humorous and clever. Peter was very angry at first, but relented when Wagner assured him that perhaps the fate of *Tristan* depended on the article. Ostensibly written to compliment the Opera director, Salvi, on his fine production of *Gräfin Egmont*, the article had gone on to speak of Salvi's courage and taste in deciding to give *Tristan*, and of the necessity of finding another tenor for the work if Ander's indisposition should continue.

for him, and that solely because of its drama. *Lohengrin* he could not endure, for the curious reason that a dog of his had been killed by a swan! Wagner found his old friend Laube again, whom he had not seen since 1846. Laube now held the important position of Director of the Burg Theatre. At his house Wagner was always sure of meeting the leading members of the Vienna theatrical, literary and musical worlds; but their conversation generally failed to interest him, concerned as it was for the most part with other subjects than himself. Another former acquaintance whom Fate threw his way again in Vienna was the pianist Winterberger, the one-time pupil of Liszt, with whom he had had some sort of contact in Zürich and later in Venice,[26] but towards whom he had never felt particularly drawn. He found Winterberger in circumstances that aroused his envy; the pianist, who seemed to have a natural genius for this kind of thing, was living in clover in the house of the Countess Banfy. There is a potential good fairy of this sort somewhere on earth for every really deserving pianist, fiddler, tenor and conductor; but the competition for them in the profession is fierce, and other arts than that of music pure and simple are sometimes necessary to capture the auriferous bird. Wagner had the misfortune to be merely a creative genius, not an " artist ".

It may have been the sight of Winterberger's felicity, and the remembrance of happier days of his own which it brought with it, that turned Wagner's thoughts once more in the direction of the Wesendonks. When he had left Vienna in the preceding May for Paris, he tells us, he made a détour to take in Zürich, impelled, he would have us believe, by the desire to spend his birthday there. Precisely why this nostalgia for Zürich should overwhelm him just then in that connection he does not explain; but as he spent a day in the Wesendonk villa we may perhaps assume, without doing him any great injustice, that one of his objects had been to discover if the much-enduring Otto's purse was as wide open as it used to be. If so, he was probably disappointed, for just about that time a crisis in America looked like causing Otto the loss of his fortune. In November he once more felt an urge to see the Wesendonks, who, with their minds free of financial cares again, were now in Venice and seemingly anxious for his company. Thither he be-

[26] See Vol. II, pp. 561, 584.

took himself for about a week, from the 7th to the 13th, the funds for the trip having been opportunely provided by the Brunswick theatre with a fee of twenty-five or thirty louis for a performance of *Tannhäuser*.

" Heaven knows what was in my mind ", he tells us, when he " casually " boarded the train for Trieste. Perhaps what was in his mind was clearer to him at the time than he was willing to admit in *Mein Leben* later. Otto and Mathilde, however, though cordiality itself, seemed to have been sadly unresponsive to hints of the usual kind on Wagner's part. So much, at any rate, we surmise from his plaintive remark in *Mein Leben* that " they seemed to have no desire to realise my position in Vienna "; " indeed ", he continues, " after the sad collapse of the glorious hopes with which I had entered upon my Paris undertaking I had to recognise a tacit, resigned abandonment, on the part of the majority of my friends, of all further hope of my succeeding." His letters of the period, however, present the matter in rather a different light. Writing a few weeks later to Mathilde he says quite frankly that he had gone to Venice cherishing the hope of being able to take up his residence once more at the Asyl, but that a single hour with them had been " enough to shatter that last fond illusion ": he had, it appears, recognised that

> " the freedom which is needful to you, and to which you must hold fast for your very existence' sake, you cannot maintain so long as I am near you: only my being at a distance can give you the power to move freely at your own will. . . . I cannot bear, as the price of my proximity, to see you straitened, constrained, governed, dependent. . . ."

And so he is " fully resigned " — for neither the first nor the last time in his life. This is certainly a more delicate and a more generous note than the one sounded years later in *Mein Leben*. But can we be sure that the picture of his feelings given there is not, after all, the more veracious one of the two — that in his letter to Mathilde he was not merely writing " literature ", savouring, in a way not unusual with him, the double luxury of self-pity and self-approval?

8

In his autobiography he tells us that it was when he was standing, in Venice, before Titian's picture of the Assumption of the Virgin that he sank into a mood of sublime absorption, out of which there came to him, in a flash, the resolve to set to work once more upon his *Meistersinger*. His contemporary letters, however, prove that his memory betrayed him here; the resolution to embark on his comic opera had been taken at least a fortnight before he went to Venice. On his way from Weimar to Vienna in August he had spent a day in Nuremberg, the sight of which could hardly fail to send his mind back to that sixteen-year-old plan of his for a comic opera on the subject of the Mastersingers. In September he had evidently been doing some hard thinking about his economic situation, and had come to the conclusion that Schotts now constituted his last line of defence. The 5,000 francs he was to receive from the Vienna Opera as the first fee for *Tristan* kept receding further and further into the distance as Ander's hoarseness increased. For a time Wagner had built new hopes on an Alsatian tenor who, though named Schrumpf, called himself Morini; but this gentleman's intellectual deficiencies soon became only too apparent to him. The orchestra, it is true, was keenly interested in *Tristan*. On the 26th October Wagner took a rehearsal, at which Princess Metternich was present, of selected passages from the opera: he had every reason to be satisfied with Frau Dustmann, and with the Brangaene, Fräulein Destinn, who had been coached by Cornelius; and the orchestra itself approached him afterwards with a request for another rehearsal of the same kind.[27] But he could no longer persuade himself that *Tristan* would be possible in Vienna within any reasonable period; and meanwhile he had to live. On the 17th October we find him asking Schott for an advance of 3,000 francs on nothing in particular; then, on the 30th, he sets before them a new plan — that for the *Meistersinger*.

---

[27] The prima ballerina of the Opera, Signora Couqui, tells us in her reminiscences that Wagner stopped the rehearsal when she chanced to step on the stage, saluted her with his baton, and called out "Saluto la diva della danza!" The orchestra, we are further asked to believe, echoed his inspired cry, and Frau Dustmann was so annoyed that the rehearsal terminated there and then. The fair Couqui's imagination seems to have been stronger than her memory. See NFF, pp. 178–9.

Around this scheme his optimism begins at once to play in its usual airy fashion. The work, he assures Franz Schott, will be light, popular, and easy to produce. Unlike the unfortunate *Tristan*, it will not call for either " a so-called first tenor " or " a great tragic soprano "; as for his jovial Hans Sachs, any reasonably good bass or baritone will be able to do him justice. While the work will be well within the capacity of the smallest German theatre, the bigger ones can let themselves go to their heart's content on the massive choruses. If only he can count on money enough to ensure him a year's material maintenance and peace of mind he can promise to complete the opera in that time: he specifically promises Schott the poem in January, 1862, the full score of the first act at the end of March, of the second by the end of July, and of the third by the end of September. The theatres can take it in hand in October, and by December it will be on the boards everywhere. A curious prophetic instinct made him suggest Munich as the place of the first performance of all — in November, 1862; it was indeed in Munich that the *Meistersinger* was destined first to see the light, but not until the summer of 1868. Of Wagner's optimistic timetable only one item worked out according to schedule: he actually finished the poem in the following January. Though he was quite mistaken when he said, in *Mein Leben,* that he " decided to write the *Meistersinger* " after contemplating Titian's picture, he had obviously talked the scheme over with Frau Wesendonk while in Venice, if for no other reason than that she possessed the manuscript of the sketch he had made for the work in 1845. This she sent to him, at his request, at Christmas.[28] It " afforded him ", he told her, " little or nothing ". For one thing, the episodic details of it must have been fixed firmly enough in his memory; for another, he found, when he came to draft the poem, that his view of some of the characters had changed somewhat since 1845. That his mind was full of the new subject when he left Venice is shown by the fact that during the return journey to Vienna he drafted " the principal part [Hauptteil] of the overture in C major." [29]

[28] See her letter to him of the 25th December, 1861, in RWMW, p. 346.
[29] *Mein Leben,* II, 906, RWMW, p. 289. It is not clear whether "Hauptteil" here means "the major part" in the dimensional or merely the thematic sense.
It has frequently been said that he could not possibly have drafted the overture as a whole during the return journey from Venice, because at that time he was not

Schott proved exceedingly accommodating; realising, no doubt, that the prospect of his getting back very much of his money on the *Ring* was now rather remote, he turned a credulous ear towards Wagner's siren song of a comic opera in a popular style, easy for the theatres, and likely to become marketable quickly. By the 3rd December Wagner had managed, after a personal discussion with Schott in Mainz, to get from him no less than 10,000 francs " as payment in advance for works of mine to be delivered ": thus forti-fied, he went to Paris a few days later in order to set to work at the *Meistersinger*. There was no sense in his continuing to live in an expensive hotel in Vienna, as it would obviously be a long time before *Tristan* became even a probable possibility; and the Metter-nichs had offered him a suite of rooms in the Austrian embassy in Paris. But before he left Mainz he received a letter from Princess Metternich in which she regretted being unable at the moment to keep her promise to him. Her mentally unhinged and almost un-governable father, Count Sándor, had long been amenable to no influence but that of his wife. The Countess having recently died,

acquainted with the genuine Mastersinger melody — associated in the opera with the Guild — that first appears in bar 48 of the overture. It was not until after his return to Vienna that he obtained from the Imperial Library, through Cornelius, the copy of Wagenseil's book from which he made the copious notes appended to his second Prose Sketch. The melody in question is described by Wagenseil as "Heinrich Mügling's Long Tone". Wagner uses only the second to the seventh notes inclusive: the first note he sinks a fourth.

But may not Wagner have known this "Tone" before he began systematic work on Wagenseil in November 1861? Is it wholly credible that, having sketched an opera dealing with the Mastersingers in great detail in 1845, from that time until 1861 he never once troubled to learn something about the actual music of these worthies? May he not have come across the Mügling "Tone" long before 1861 in some book or article or other?

There is now a large literature, from Kurt Mey's *Der Meistergesang in Geschichte und Kunst* (1901) to Alfred Lorenz's *Der musikalische Aufbau von Richard Wagners 'Die Meistersinger von Nürnberg'* (1931), dealing with Wagner's indebtedness to predecessors for certain details of his text. He drew, for one purpose or another and to one degree or another, on several earlier works, in particular E. T. A. Hoffmann's stories *Meister Martin* and *Signor Formica*, the dramas *Hans Sachs* (1828) and *Salvator Rosa* (1845) of Deinhardstein, and Philipp Reger's libretto for Lortzing's opera *Hans Sachs* (1840). The most penetrating study of his indebtedness to these and other forerunners is that of Professor Gustav Roethe in a paper, *Zum dramatischen Aufbau der Wagnerschen 'Meistersinger'*, read at a meeting of the Prussian Akademie der Wissenschaften on the 19th December, 1918. It is a pity that this excellent study not only of the *Meistersinger* but of Wagner's dramatic technique as a whole should be buried among the Proceedings of a learned Society.

Analyses of Deinhardstein's *Hans Sachs* and Reger's libretto will be found in Kurt Mey's book, pp. 272–301.

Princess Metternich felt compelled to take personal charge of the intractable old gentleman; and the only rooms in the embassy available for that purpose were those she had intended for Wagner. The latter had to be satisfied with uncomfortable quarters in the Hôtel Voltaire (19, Quai Voltaire), where his spirits were sustained only by the joy his new work brought him. For on the face of it this last journey to Paris seemed even fuller of ill omens than any of its predecessors. He had not been there many days when he read in the papers of the sudden death, from heart disease, of his good friend Count Pourtalès; while temporarily strained relations between Pauline Metternich and the young Countess Pourtalès made it diplomatically inadvisable for him to call on the latter just then. Other friends, such as the Olliviers, greeted his return to Paris in what Kai Lung would have called a spirit of no-enthusiasm; they no doubt dreaded a request on his part to be allowed to quarter himself on them. But what with the company of Truinet, Flaxland and a few others of his old friends, and above all with his delight in the way the *Meistersinger* poem, which had already been begun in Vienna, was now shaping, he found life in the Hôtel Voltaire more tolerable than he had expected; later, indeed, he could assure Malwida von Meysenbug that these few weeks had been the happiest of his life. Everything seemed to augur well for the completion of the new score before the end of 1862, and, after that, a most welcome inflow of theatre royalties.

9

We possess three Prose Sketches by Wagner for the *Meistersinger* — (A) the original one of July 1845, (B) one that bears no date, but was evidently made in the autumn of 1861, at the time when he decided to take up again this old scheme of his for a comic opera, (C) one dated " Vienna, 18th November, 1861 ", a copy of which he sent to Schott on the 19th.[30] B and C are virtually identical: at the end of the manuscript of B there are several pages of notes on the Meistersinger rules and practices, made after Wagner had become acquainted with old Wagenseil's so-called " Nurem-

---

[30] The three Sketches will be found in RWGS, XI, 344–394.

berg Chronicle ",[31] in which the Mastersingers and their art are discussed at some length. Not only do B and C differ considerably from A in matters of stage detail, but they breathe a somewhat different atmosphere. In his first form Wagner's Sachs was a rather cynical, ironic, embittered character, who, apart from his advocacy of the cause of the young Knight, reminds us comparatively little of the wise, kindly, mellow poet-philosopher he ultimately became in Wagner's treatment of him. In *A Communication to my Friends* (1851) Wagner had explained why, instead of setting to work at the *Meistersinger* immediately after sketching it in 1845, he had put it aside in favour of *Lohengrin.* He had become conscious, he said, of an impulse in him to evade the tragedy of the world by a resort not merely to cheerfulness, but to cheerfulness expressing itself in irony; and " my nature at once reacted against the imperfect attempt to unburden myself by means of irony of the contents of my mirthful urge ". His daemon beckoned him away from the Mastersingers and their grotesque failings to the more ideal and more tragic world of *Lohengrin.* Nothing in his career is more remarkable than the way in which, in obedience to the inner voice, he postponed the completion of each of his dramatic schemes in turn until life had made him poetically and musically ripe for the perfect handling of it.

In A, the only characters to bear the names by which we now know them are Sachs, David and Magdalena: Walther is as yet only " the young man " or " the lover ", Beckmesser is simply " the Marker ", Pogner is " the elder ", Eva " the daughter " or " the maiden ". In B the characters hitherto anonymous all receive names, though not the ones they now bear: the senior member of the Guild becomes Bogler (in C, Thomas Bogler, goldsmith), his daughter is Emma (she becomes Eva in C), the Knight is Konrad von Stolzing, Eva's maid changes her name in B to Kathrine, but reverts to Magdalena in C, and the Marker is labelled, with the broadest intention, Hanslich (in C, Veit Hanslich). In A and B the action takes place in St. Sebald's Church. In C this becomes

---

[31] *De Sacri Rom. Imperii Libera Civitate Noribergensi Commentatio. Accedit, De Germaniae Phonascorum von Der Meister-Singer Origine, Praestantia, Utilitate et Institutis, Sermone Vernaculo Liber:* Nuremberg, 1697. The *Buch von der Meister-Singer Holdseligen Kunst, Anfang, Fortübung, Nutzbarkeiten und Lehr-Sätzen* occupies pp. 433–576.

simply " the church "; and it was no doubt when Wagner transferred the opening scene of his opera to St. Catharine's that he
decided against " Kathrine " as the name of the waiting-woman.

In A, the hero, who is the son of an impoverished nobleman, has
come to Nuremberg, aflame with youthful enthusiasm for art, expressly to seek admission to the Mastersingers' Guild; for this purpose he has naturally gone to the senior of the Guild, and, in the
course of time, has fallen in love with the latter's daughter. In B
it is simply Konrad's poverty that has brought him to Nuremberg,
apparently to do business with Bogler; and he had arrived in the
town only the day before the opera opens. He feels the urge to become a Mastersinger only after hearing of the coming contest of
song for the hand of Emma, of whom he has caught a glimpse at
Bogler's house. Wagner's original intention had been to give the
Folk the first vote in deciding the result of the contest, the Mastersingers having only the second, and the maiden herself a casting vote
in case the other parties should not agree. In B, Bogler having insisted that the Guild shall be the judges, it is left to Sachs to suggest
that the Folk shall decide the result of the contest — a suggestion
which is scouted by the Masters.

Apparently Wagner had no very definite ideas, even when making his second Sketch, as to the individualisation of the Masters,
apart from Bogler, Sachs and the Marker. In A it is Sachs who
reads the rules of the Guild to the Knight in the church scene; in B
and C we are merely told that " the rules of the tabulatur are
read ". Presumably it was while working at the poem itself that
the racy figure of Kothner sprang into separate life in Wagner's
brain.[32]

---

[32] Wagner's supplementary notes to B, made after reading Wagenseil, begin with
a list of names of "twelve old Nuremberg Masters" — exclusive of Sachs. These
names agree in the main with those of the present libretto, except that Wagner
improves "Fritz Zorn" into Balthasar Zorn. It is noticeable that although "Sixtus
Beckmesser" figures in this list, Wagner has seemingly not thought even yet of
conferring this name on the Marker, whom he continues to call Hanslich in C. Included in the list is a Nikolaus Vogel, whom Wagner does not use in the opera. It
may have been the fact that the worthy tinsmith Nachtigall had Konrad for his
Christian name that ultimately decided Wagner to rename his young hero Walther;
and perhaps "Veit Pogner" had a realistic ring about it that made it inevitable
that this character should displace the fictive Thomas Bogler as head of the guild.

Wagner made also, at the end of his second Sketch, copious extracts from Wagenseil concerning the rules of the guild, its quaint terminology, its forms of versification,
and so on. The reprint of these jottings in RWGS Vol. XI is a rather negligent piece

It is interesting to trace the gradual perfecting of one of the most charming episodes of the opera — the birth of the lyric that is afterwards to become the Prize Song. In A, when the Knight enters Sachs's room in the third act the pair discuss the former's chances of winning the maiden for bride. After his rejection by the Masters on the previous day he is rather bitter: he had come to Nuremberg, he says, hoping to find there the remains of the old Thuringian spirit in art; but he has been disappointed and disillusioned. " What then have you written? " asks Sachs. The young man shows him various poems; among them is his latest Minnelied. While Sachs reads this through, the orchestra plays the melody. After musing for a while he declares the Knight to be a true poet, pours out a bitter lament of his own over the degeneration of the times in general and of art in particular, and ends by advising the young man to go back to his castle, study Ulrich von Hutten and the Wittenberger (Luther), and, if the need should arise, defend what he has learned with his sword. For what immediately follows this episode Wagner, in 1845, was unable to decide between two procedures: either (I) the Marker, entering the room after Sachs and the Knight had gone, was to appropriate the song, which had been left on Sachs's table, and afterwards, on the cobbler's return, confess the theft (" perhaps ", Wagner notes, " Sachs can pretend not to have the least idea whose song it is — perhaps it may be the young man's, who by now is over the hills and far away "): or (2) the Marker having reproached Sachs with ruining, the night before, the song with which he had intended to woo the maiden, Sachs offers him one of his own, written in his young days, and unknown to anyone. After some hesitation the Marker accepts this offer, and Sachs hands him the Knight's poem. In B and C all this is changed. The Knight, having been unable to sleep, had spent part

---

of editorial work: mistakes of spelling are fairly frequent, Wagner's handwriting seems to have been misread at times, and bad alignment obscures the point of some of Wagenseil's antitheses.

The *Meistersinger* scores and text-books still dutifully give the last of the grotesque titles in David's catalogue of the "tones" as "die buttglänzende Drahtweis". The mysterious "butt" has been the object of a good deal of learned discussion. It is now agreed, however, that it is simply a misprint in Wagenseil for "gutt"; other records associate a "guttglänzende Drahtweis" ("bright-shining-thread mode") with one Jobst Zolner. Wagner innocently transferred the "butt" to his notes, and thence to his poem and his score.

of the night writing a poem to his beloved. Sachs asks for this, reads it approvingly, and leaves it behind him on the table, where, in due time, it is discovered by the Marker. It was not until Wagner was engaged on the poem itself that the device occurred to him of letting the Knight launch his love song in the form of the description of a dream which he had had, Sachs taking it down on paper as he sings it.

10

We have seen, in connection with the *Ring* poem,[33] Wagner realising at this point or that that a slight modification of his original scheme in one respect had involved him in an inconsistency elsewhere, taking what he no doubt regarded as a reasonable amount of trouble to reconcile the two procedures, and then, if he had not fully succeeded in this, leaving the small resulting discrepancy as it stood and trusting to the spectator's either not becoming too aware of it or extending his tolerance towards it. There is another minor case of the same kind in the second act of the *Meistersinger*.

A change of outer garments between Eva and Magdalena there had to be at some point in this act, for two excellent reasons — (1) to make Eva's escape with Walther more plausible, (2) to bring about, by making David imagine that Beckmesser is serenading Magdalena, the hurly-burly that is necessary not simply for its own effective sake but to afford a cover under which Eva can slip into her own house and Sachs can drag Walther into his. In A, shortly after the second act opens, Magdalena tells Eva of Beckmesser's request that she (Eva) shall appear at her window that night and listen to his rehearsal of the song he intends to sing on the morrow. But Eva is too agitated just then to feel any interest, and particularly a friendly interest, in the Marker, who, as she has learned, has disqualified the Knight: her only reply to Magdalena is a tart " Ich werd' ihm dienen! " " She is exceedingly troubled and does not know what to do ", the stage directions run. " The two women go into the house." It is not until much later, after a scene between the lovers, that Magdalena appears at the door of Pogner's house and reminds Eva of the Marker's message; whereupon Eva

---

[33] See Vol. II, chapter XVII.

suggests that her servant shall impersonate her at the window. Magdalena asks what she is to do there, and is told to express dislike of the song. " Magdalena agrees, for reasons of her own "; and Eva, having re-entered the house for a moment, returns in other clothes.

That Wagner, even in 1845, was not quite satisfied with this plan is shown by a jotting of his own in the margin (or at the foot of the page) of his first Sketch: " The beloved and Magdalena exchange their outer garments after the former has advised the maid not to show herself at the window until the Marker has begun. (All this can be narrated by the beloved after she has emerged from the house)." Wagner makes no provision for this " narration " — intended for the audience's benefit — in his Sketch. He recognises, however, that the young man will ask, as any young man would in the circumstances, the meaning of this unexpected change of costume; and so he suggests that Eva shall explain, in answer to Walther's astonished enquiry, that " she perceives in this disposition of events heaven's favour on their plan for flight." That is not very convincing; evidently Wagner did not quite see, at that time, just how to handle this episode of the exchange of clothes, with which he might have dispensed, if need were, so far as Eva was concerned, but that was absolutely indispensable to his drama so far as David and the Marker were concerned.

So in B and C he tries another plan [34] — when Magdalena tells Emma of the Marker's desire that she shall listen to his serenade, " Emma, in great agitation, will not hear of such a thing; she implores Kathrine to exchange clothes with her and appear instead of her at the window. Kathrine undertakes to do this, in the hope of arousing the jealousy of David, who sleeps opposite, and so bring

---

[34] His handling of this episode in the long summary he had given of the *Meistersinger* plot in *A Communication to my Friends* is of itself proof conclusive that he was up against a problem which he had not quite solved even by 1851. There is no mention there of any change of clothes: we are merely told that the Marker serenades the maiden, that Sachs reduces the performance to a farce, and that finally the Marker "makes a shocking mess of the remainder of the song", falling into despair over "the violent head-shakings of the female figure at the window". No one who did not know the present *Meistersinger* text could have the slightest inkling, from this, that the figure at the window was that of the servant. The suppression of the change-of-clothes episode in the *Communication* necessitates the further suppression of the story of David's assault on the Marker, and the omission of any indication of how Sachs frustrates the flight of the lovers.

him to declare his love." She goes into Pogner's house, while Emma runs to meet the approaching Konrad; after a few words with him she also enters the house, and returns " in Magdalena's cloak and head-gear ". This scheme, surely, was both practical and sufficient: the plan for exchanging clothes is agreed upon the very moment Kathrine gives Emma the Marker's message, it is acted upon almost instantly, and the audience hears and sees all that is necessary to explain what happens later.

Why then did Wagner see fit, when he came to write his poem, to discard this simple and rational procedure and involve himself once more in the difficulties of the first Sketch? In the poem he makes Eva say, at an early stage in the second act, that she will try to learn from Sachs what had happened to Walther at the trial. Magdalena warns her not to arouse her father's suspicions by staying out for this purpose now, but to wait till after supper, when, moreover, Magdalena will have a secret to tell her which " someone " entrusted to her lately. " Who? " Eva asks eagerly. " The Knight? " " No, no! Beckmesser! " " A nice sort of secret that must be! ", says Eva contemptuously; and the pair go into the house together, Eva not returning until after Sachs has sung his " Wie duftet doch der Flieder ". Next comes the long scene between Sachs and Eva, after which Magdalena calls Eva to her and tells her, at last, the Marker's " secret " — that he intends to serenade her. Even yet, apparently, the scheme for the change of clothes does not occur to Eva; all she says in reply to Magdalena is, in effect, " That's the last straw! (Das fehlte auch noch!). If only he [Walther] would come! " She refuses to go into the house until she has seen the Knight, and it is left to Magdalena to hint that it is really time something was done about the Marker: " Let us think out how we can get rid of Beckmesser." " Go you to the window in my place ", says Eva — a proposal which Magdalena joyfully adopts for the reason we now know. But even yet there is no suggestion on Eva's part of any exchange of clothes. Walther enters; in due course the night-watchman's horn is heard, followed by the appearance of that functionary. At this point Wagner seems to realise that so far as that awkward but vital change of costume is concerned it is now or never; so he resorts to the lame device of making Magdalena call to Eva from the house, and to this still lamer piece of dialogue:

Walther. Thou fliest?
Eva.   Must I not fly?
Walther. Escapest?
Eva.   From the Masters' tribunal!

She disappears into the house with Magdalena — what Walther is supposed to make of all this we are not told! — returns in a minute or two in Magdalena's cloak, throws herself into the Knight's arms, and is on the point of eloping with him when Sachs frustrates their plan by directing the light of his lamp on the alley.

11

Now why did Wagner resort, in his poem, to all this slow-moving, creaking, and in the end not quite adequate machinery in order to do what he had done more swiftly and efficiently in another way in his Sketches? The explanation is simple. In none of the Sketches is there any hint of the long scene between Sachs and Eva early in the second act of the opera — just as there is no provision, it may be added, for the quintet in the third. The Sachs-Eva dialogue was evidently something that occurred to Wagner for the first time when he was writing his poem; he no doubt felt it to be necessary in order to let us into the secret of the love, of its own type, between the old cobbler and the girl. But obviously Eva could not appear in *this* scene in Magdalena's clothes and head-gear: Sachs would certainly have wanted to know the reason for that masquerade! And so, in the preceding scene, in which Magdalena had told Eva that she has a secret message for her from the Marker, Wagner had no alternative but to make Eva profess indifference to the message; and although the two women go into the house at this point, so as to leave Sachs free for his " Wie duftet doch der Flieder ", Magdalena does not succeed in getting any further with her message during all the time they are indoors together! In any case, for Magdalena to tell Eva of Beckmesser's plan *behind the scenes* would, of course, not enlighten the audience; so an opportunity for the open communication has to be manufactured later. Sketch B had handled the whole motive much more logically; when Magdalena, early in the act, had told Emma of the coming serenade, Emma had brushed the subject aside with an impatient " I can't be bothered with all this: we will exchange clothes, and *you* will appear at the window." In the poem, that opportunity having been forfeited owing to the insertion of the Eva-Sachs scene, a situation has to be created later in which Magdalena comes out of the house while Eva is waiting for Walther, and rather irrelevantly takes up again the Beckmesser question where it had been dropped some time before. " Ah, how I fear! " says Eva; to which Magdalena can think of nothing to say more appropriate to the occasion than " Also let us confer as to how we are to get rid of Beckmesser."

That Wagner was well aware that he had got himself into a mess is shown not only by the fumbling way he handles what was originally a simple situation but by the lame doggerel he is compelled to put into his characters' mouths here and there. But at all costs his new scene, exquisite both poetically and musically, between Sachs and Eva had to go in. If the dislocations in his original scenario caused by the insertion of that scene could be soundly repaired, well and good; if not, they would just have to be patched up as best they could, with a prayer to Providence that the audience, with so many other things to engage its attention in an act that is in general a marvel of close construction, would not be too conscious of the patches.

CHAPTER VII

THE MINNA CRISIS

1

ON THE 3rd December 1861 Wagner had received 10,000 francs from Schott — a not inconsiderable sum in those days. He evidently foresaw that it would not last him very long, however, for only a week later we find him trying to lay Hornstein under contribution. His treatment of this young man in *Mein Leben* affords one of many illustrations of the souring his temper underwent later, and his regrettable proneness, perhaps under Cosima's influence, to speak maliciously of everyone who, in his opinion, had not sacrificed himself to the cause of Richard Wagner as he ought to have done.

Hornstein had visited him in Zürich in 1855; Wagner found him on that occasion " intelligent and agreeable ", and was particularly pleased with the way he took to the study of Schopenhauer. But only a few pages later in *Mein Leben* we learn that during another visit in the following autumn Hornstein had told him that he dreaded the loss of his reason, his mother having died insane. " Although this made him to some extent interesting," says Wagner superciliously, " there was blended so much weakness of character with his intellectual capacity that we soon came to the conclusion he was rather hopeless, and were not inconsolable when he suddenly left Zürich." Hornstein, for his part, though he duly admired Wagner, saw him steadily and saw him whole during these visits. One of Wagner's little foibles his whole life long was the desire to read to the company — he knew his exceptional talents as a reader — and then expound; the rôle of the others, whoever they might be, was to listen reverently. Voltaire was asked what he thought of Diderot, after a meeting in which the latter had talked so incessantly that Voltaire could hardly get a word in. " A wonderful man! " he replied. " There's only one art he doesn't understand — the art of dialogue." Wagner suffered from a cognate disability. One evening when Hornstein, the Wesendonks, the Heims, Karl Ritter, and perhaps a few others were with Wagner in Zürich, and everyone was quietly talking to his neighbour, there suddenly came from Wagner a scream that made them all jump with fright — " a short, shrill yell ", says Hornstein,

> " that was like a pistol shot. Everyone stared at him. He then told us quietly that he was very fond of Hoffmann's *Der goldene Topf,* and would like to read it to us. He did so, from A to Z. It got very late. At the end of the reading, Wesendonk permitted himself a not unwarranted observation about this romantic genre, of which he was no admirer. Thereupon Wagner fell on him furiously, and it was solely due to Wesendonk's moderation that the evening did not end in a quarrel. But another surprise was in store for us. Before we broke up he burst out into laments that his creditors were pressing him hard on account of the lumber he had in the place. Next day Wesendonk settled the bills. It took all a young man's enthusiastic attachment to make him forget this impression! " [1]

The youngster of twenty-two had received some plain warnings from Karl Ritter that if Wagner did not " pump " him then it was only because he was holding him in reserve; and the " sudden departure " from Zürich, which Wagner tries to represent in a light so unfavourable to Hornstein in *Mein Leben,* had been the result of an unpleasant scene in which Wagner had been ill-bred enough to fall foul of Hornstein and Baumgartner, who were dining with him, for not providing his table with champagne.[2] Baron Hornstein, who was still no more than twenty-eight when Wagner ran into him again in Munich in the summer of 1861, recalled at that time Ritter's warning that " Wagner knows your circumstances and is sure to follow you up later: he is waiting for a more favourable moment ", and was consequently on his guard. Whether Wagner threw out any hints in Munich that it was time for all good men to come to the aid of his exchequer we do not know; but by the

---

[1] HM, pp. 139–40.

[2] Hornstein tells the story in connection with Wagner's birthday, but on this point his memory was seemingly at fault.

He forebore to narrate this and several other Wagnerian experiences of a disagreeable kind in his Memoirs, though he had recorded them in his private papers. They were published for the first time by his son, Friedrich von Hornstein, in 1911, by way of correction of some of Wagner's remarks about his father in *Mein Leben.* See ZUBW, p. 7 ff., and NW, p. 9 ff.

following December he had evidently decided that the time had come to tap Hornstein if that were possible. For in Munich the young man had been indiscreet enough to inform him of the recent death of his father, of his inheritance of a small property, and of his marriage.[3]

It was Schott, according to Wagner, who told him that Hornstein had " a nice property " in the neighbourhood of Mainz. " I really thought I was conferring an honour on him ", he calmly informs us in *Mein Leben*, " when I wrote to him, in Munich, asking if I might take up my abode for a time at his place in the Rhine district; and I was therefore extremely disconcerted when I received an answer expressing terror at my presumption." He would have done well, when dictating this passage in his autobiography, to stay his unkind hand; for after the appearance of *Mein Leben* Baron Friedrich von Hornstein published the actual correspondence concerning this matter that had passed between his father and Wagner in December, 1861. "Dear Hornstein", is the airy preamble to Wagner's letter of the 12th, " I hear you have become rich." There follows the usual pathetic story of care and suffering and the desire to find salvation in a new work, for the realisation of which desire, however, he requires "an immediate advance of 10,000 francs ". To provide him with this sum will perhaps be a little difficult for Hornstein: but he hopes the *will* to make the sacrifice is there. He promises to repay the loan within three years " out of my receipts ". " Now let us see if you are the right sort of man! " But even this is not all. " If you prove to be this for me . . . the assistance you give me will bring you into very close touch with me, and next summer you must be pleased to have me for three months at one of your estates, preferably in the Rhine district." It would be a great relief to him to receive 6,000 francs immediately; the remaining 4,000, he hopes, will not be needed till March.

Not only the largeness of the sum but the tone of the letter, says Hornstein, made a refusal easier to him. He knew he had to deal with a " bottomless cask, — that while 10,000 francs were a great deal for me, they were simply nothing to him. I knew that Na-

---

[3] HM, p. 211 ff. It is interesting to compare Hornstein's account of the time he spent with Wagner, Ollivier and Blandine in Munich with the story told in *Mein Leben*.

poleon, Princess Metternich, Morny and Erlanger had all been bled of large sums that were simply like drops of water falling on a hot stone." He replied politely enough, however, to the effect that Wagner had a false idea of his " riches ", and that he possessed merely a modest competency on which to maintain himself, his wife and his child; but if it were possible for him later to arrange for a long visit on Wagner's part to " one of his estates " he would let him know. Meanwhile he suggested that Wagner should appeal to some really rich people, of whom there were plenty among his admirers all over Europe. He ended with a hope that the production of *Tristan* would not be much longer delayed. Wagner's answer to this, dated the 27th December, is a gem that deserves citation in full:

" Dear Herr von Hornstein, — It would be wrong of me to pass by without censure an answer such as you have given me. Though it will probably not happen again that a man like me will apply to you, yet the mere realisation of the impropriety of your letter ought to be a good thing for you.

" It was not for you to take upon yourself to advise me in any way whatever, even as to who is really rich; and you should have left it to myself to decide why I do not apply to the patrons and patronesses to whom you refer.

" If you are not in a position to have me at any of your estates, you could have seized the opportunity I indicated to you to enable me to provide myself with what is necessary in some place of my own choice. It is consequently insulting of you to say you will let me know when you will be in a position to receive me.

" You should have omitted the wish you express with regard to my *Tristan:* your answer could come only from one who is totally indifferent to my works.

" Let this end the matter. I reckon on your discretion, as you can on mine." [4]

To this masterpiece of courtesy Hornstein made no reply.

2

The pages of *Mein Leben* give us many a hint of the desperate efforts Wagner was making in January, 1862 to find some spot on

---

[4] ZUBW, pp. 15–21.

earth where he could live in peace and quiet, and, of course, without too much expense to himself, until he had finished the music of the *Meistersinger*. No one in Paris showed any particular desire to be burdened with him. Remembering a " pressing invitation " of long ago on the part of Agnes Street that he would pay her and her father a visit in Brussels he wrote to her asking if she could house him for a time. The lady was politely unable to oblige. He thought for a moment of quartering himself on the Bülows in Berlin, but the suggestion frightened Cosima: poor Bülow found it difficult enough to keep even his modest household going on what he earned. Someone who figures in Wagner's letters to Minna as " St.", — probably Stürmer — could not offer him hospitality as he was " expecting relatives ". His brother-in-law Eduard Avenarius, who now lived in Berlin, was not unwilling to harbour him; but as either Cäcilie was not keen to have Minna, or Minna would not go to Cäcilie,[5] this plan also came to nothing. From the Wesendonks there was nothing on a large scale to be hoped for just then: Mathilde sent him not an invitation to the Green Hill but a cast-iron paperweight she had bought for him in Venice. It was in the form of the winged lion of San Marco, his paw resting on the book: the implication was that Wagner should try to emulate the lion in fortitude and patience.

It took him no more than thirty days to complete the poem of the *Meistersinger;* and, as always when he was engaged in creative work, these were days of extraordinary elation. The friends whom he saw in Paris were astonished at his gaiety; but, as Berthold Kellermann observed of him in later years, his mood was always cheerful or sombre not according to the circumstances of his outer life but according to the colour of the work he had in hand at the moment.[6] The poem was no sooner finished [7] than, of course, he was consumed with impatience to read it to all his friends. The first to make its acquaintance was Countess Pourtalès, to whom its old-world humours came as a gleam of sunshine in her bereave-

---

[5] The reader can take his choice of the alternatives. *Mein Leben* and Wagner's letter to Minna of the 1st February are not in agreement on this point.

[6] See the quotation from KEK in Vol. II, p. 553. This pupil of Liszt, by the way, is generally regarded now as the hero of Ernst von Wolzogen's novel *Der Kraft-Mayr.*

[7] On the 25th January.

ment. Wagner tells us, in *Mein Leben*, of the pleasure it gave her; but he does not mention her loan — or gift — of 1,200 thalers some three months later. His memory for an injury or what he took to be neglect was always more lively than his memory for benefits received.

He left Paris on the 1st February, with, as yet, no definite idea where he would next pitch his tent. He went first of all to Karlsruhe, where he was kindly received by the Grand Duke and Duchess. The subject of a pension for him, to be paid jointly by some of the German princes, seems to have been broached; but when Wagner was next in Karlsruhe, where he read his poem to the Duke on the 9th March, nothing more was said about this. By the 4th February he was in Mainz, where he read the *Meistersinger* to Schott and other friends; among them was Cornelius, who had come all the way from Vienna expressly to hear it. Peter being as poor as a church mouse, the journey had been made possible only by a remittance of a hundred francs from Wagner; [8] and it is typical of the latter's nonchalant way of managing his finances that while he could spare money for pure luxuries of this kind he should be trying, in March, to borrow two hundred thalers from Bülow, one hundred of which were to be sent to Minna. All through the years, indeed, between the Paris *Tannhäuser* affair and the final catastrophe in Vienna in the spring of 1864 one wonders how Wagner managed to get through the large sums that kept accruing to him from one source and another.

3

The poem which Wagner read at Schott's house, and a copy of which he had already sent to Frau Wesendonk, differs in some respects from the libretto as we now have it. The Prize Song is entirely different; in the 1862 version this consists of a long poem of good imaginative quality if somewhat artificial construction, commencing thus:

---

[8] If, indeed, it was he who provided the funds, as he alleges in *Mein Leben!* His letter of the end of January to Cornelius shows him unable to send any money: Peter is to borrow it from Standhartner, and Wagner will make it good in Mainz. It is to be hoped he did.

Fern
meiner Jugend gold'nen Toren
zog ich einst aus
in Betrachtung ganz verloren:
väterlich Haus,
kindliche Wiege,
lebet wohl! ich eil', ich fliege
einer neuen Welt nun zu!

Much the same basic metrical pattern is preserved throughout the various stanzas. In this first form of the Prize Song the young Knight tells how he once left " the golden portals of his youth " and ventured out in search of a new world: night sank, and in a dream the beloved appeared to him in the form of a dove. Now the reader who knows his *Meistersinger* will remember that after Walther has sung his dream to Sachs, in an early scene of the second act, the latter conducts his guest from the room, bidding him array himself in the gay clothes in which he had planned to appear at his wedding feast — for, as Sachs goes on to explain, the Knight's trusty squire has found his way to the cobbler's house with them. " No doubt ", says Sachs, " a little dove directed him to the nest in which his master was dreaming." This is obviously a roguish reference on Sachs's part to the " Täubchen " and the Dream about which Walther, in the 1862 version, has just been singing. More than one student of the *Meistersinger* must have wondered why this somewhat curious image was introduced into the *present* text to explain the fact of the squire's tracing the Knight to Sachs's abode. The " Täubchen ", we are apparently meant to understand, is Eva; obviously the squire would first seek his master at Pogner's house, whence he would be re-directed by Eva, who alone, with the exception of Sachs, knew where Walther had found refuge for the night. The strange thing is that Wagner should still retain the reference to the dove in his *final* version of his poem, in which the Knight makes no reference whatever to such a bird. It turns out, on examination, to be one more illustration of Wagner's relative indifference to small discrepancies in his libretti brought about by a change of plan at some point or other.[9]

[9] Frederick Jameson, in his excellent translation of the *Meistersinger* libretto, obscures the point for English readers by rendering Sachs's lines thus:

In a letter of the 12th March, 1862 to Frau Wesendonk, Wagner says that though she necessarily lacks the melody of the Prize Song, this is " indispensable ". It may surprise those who take too literally his theorising, in *Opera and Drama*, about the necessity of the music of an opera flowering directly from the poem, to find him adding, " I set these verses to the melody already in my head." On this matter there will be something more to be said later, *à propos* of the final form of the music of the Prize Song. Here it will be sufficient to quote the melody to which, he assures Frau Wesendonk in 1862, he had written the words of Walther's song, and to congratulate ourselves that some years later he discarded it: [10]

Wagner then goes on to propound an enigma that has not yet been solved. " Of the whole thing ", he tells Mathilde after quoting the first seven bars with the accompanying words, " the Folk hears only the melody: guess my secret who can! " A German tenor, Carl Clewing, who has sung the part of Walther at Bayreuth and elsewhere, has made a gallant attempt to solve this mystery.[11] He finds

Some *bird*, sure, must have shown the nest
wherein his master dreams.

[10] See *infra*, p. 188.
[11] In an article on *Walthers erstes Preislied und sein 'Geheimnis'*, in DM, May, 1938, pp. 505–514.

significant analogues to the first three bars of the melody in two of the songs — *Der Engel* and *Stehe still* — which Wagner had written to words by Frau Wesendonk in 1857–8, and draws the inference that the composer intended the Prize Song to be a secret homage to Mathilde. It may or may not have been; but Professor Clewing's argument is anything but conclusive. For the type of melodic phrase referred to occurs frequently in Wagner's operas, in various contexts that have not the remotest reference to Mathilde Wesendonk: this descending line ending in a sort of musical spondee (or a trochee) at the interval of a falling second constitutes, in fact, one of the fingerprints of his style. We get what is essentially the same procedure in the music to the opening words of Elsa's monologue on the balcony — " Euch Lüften, die mein Klagen ", — in the orchestral melody which accompanies the words " Denn so kehrt der Gott sich dir ab ", in Wotan's farewell to Brynhilde, in the " Lass mich im Staub vor dir vergehen " of Elisabeth's prayer, and in scores of other places; while we frequently meet with the same basic figure in what may be called a secondary form — for example, in the opening phrase of the introduction to the third act of the *Meistersinger*.

4

Several things had to be taken into consideration in the choice of a domicile for the composition of the music of the *Meistersinger:* the place must be cheap, it must offer reasonable quietness for work, and it must be central. Biebrich on the Rhine struck Wagner as ideal for his purpose. It was about mid-way between Vienna, Berlin and Paris, he told Minna, and within easy reach of Mainz, Wiesbaden, Darmstadt, Frankfort, and Karlsruhe, in all of which towns he had friends to supply the cheerful society of which he was always in need. To Biebrich, accordingly, he betook himself at the end of February. He rented a small first-floor flat in a villa near the Rhine,[12] had his furniture sent from Paris, installed a portion of it in the flat, sent the remainder a little later to Minna in Dresden, and prepared to settle down in earnest to the composi-

---

[12] Of Wagner's three rooms, one, the drawing room, overlooked the garden, with a view extending to the Grand Duke's Schloss; the other two faced the Rhine.

tion of the *Meistersinger*. Unfortunately things did not turn out in Biebrich quite as he had expected.

First of all his peace was disturbed by Minna. He had seen little of her since she left Paris, and though there was more or less of an understanding between them that they were to set up house together again as soon as that should prove practicable, he had long ago become convinced that life with her, except perhaps for a few days at a time now and then, was no longer possible. His letters to her touch frequently on the subject of a reunion; and it is difficult to say how much he was influenced by the subconscious longing to have a home of his own again, managed by Minna with her usual efficiency, and how much merely by the necessity for humouring the woefully sick woman. She, for her part, had obstinately set her mind on recapturing him, not because of any genuine affection for him but because it flooded her narrow soul with gall and bitterness to think of his finding any sort of happiness away from her, among people whom she mostly hated. On the subject of his relations with other women she had become a monomaniac. Her bourgeois up-bringing and her limited intellectual capacity had necessarily made her feel out of place in the cultured society that gathered about Wagner in Paris; and for the feminine portion of that society in general, and for the charming Blandine Ollivier in particular, she was possessed by a comprehensive hatred. To female friends of her own type she never tired of pouring out her grievances, real and imaginary. Wagner could hardly show the smallest liking for this or that young woman's society without Minna converting it into what she invariably described as a " love affair ". For this hopeless small-town German bourgeoise, every woman whom she was incapable of understanding and of whom she disapproved was " common "; she alone stood for the higher decencies and eternal moralities. Of her husband's exceptional greatness she had not the smallest perception, while her own mental poverty made it frankly impossible for her to understand that a man of his type might have intellectual necessities which it was a wife's duty to tolerate even if she could not share them. In everything that concerned the pair of them she now saw and felt only for herself. She had become one of those women whom Nietzsche has limned in a biting sentence or two — the women who are " perpetually intriguing in secret against the higher soul of their husbands, whom they would cheat of their future for the sake of a painless, comfortable present." [13] For Minna, *Tristan* was not one of the world's supreme achievements in music, nor was it even hallowed for her in any way by ordinary human comprehension of, and ordinary human sympathy with, the spiritual pangs which even she must have known accompanied its birth. For her it was merely a work written when her husband was " in love with " Frau Wesendonk, something, therefore, to be hated with a passion at once blind and foul.[14]

And with it all went, in these latter days, a technique of annoyance that was the product half of the invalid in her knowing how to play on her pitiful condition to obtain everyone's sympathy, half of the semi-maniac who had completely lost the power to see things as they were but had developed a super-cunning in the perverse misrepresentation of them. Wagner was despairingly conscious of being caught in a net of misunderstanding and misrepresentation from which there was no escape. " What *won't* appear in my biography some day! " he wrote to her in May, 1862. " Whoever finds letters from *you* among my papers will find there, in black and white, that my wife describes myself and my behaviour towards her as ' heartless ', ' coarse ', and ' common '; so no doubt all this will get into my biography also! Well, I can't prevent it! " And in truth a comparative examination of his letters to Minna and of Minna's letters to friends of her own peculiar type shows how much right he had to complain at this time of her falsification of the evidence against him. To read Minna's letters only is to get the impression that she was fettered for life to a callous brute who not merely delighted in inflicting mental torture on a poor innocent woman but hardly hesitated, on occasion, to use physical violence towards her.[15] But if she wished posterity to share her opinion of

[13] *Menschliches, Allzumenschliches*, VII, 434.

[14] On the very day that should have seen the first performance of *Tristan* in Munich, in May, 1865, Pusinelli telegraphed Wagner that Minna was on the point of death. No one acquainted with her correspondence as a whole can doubt that this seizure — from which she recovered — was something rather more than pure coincidence.

[15] In 1861 she assured a correspondent that when she was handing Wagner a letter from Frau Wesendonk he gripped her arm so brutally that the blue marks of his five fingers on her flesh were visible for weeks after. Three years later she tells the same story again; but by now the five finger marks have multiplied to ten!

Wagner she ought to have avoided the cardinal blunder of preserving his letters. For we have only to compare these with the impression of them she tried to convey to her correspondents to see how hopelessly perverted her mind had now become.

His letter to her of the 8th May, 1862, for instance, contains nothing but the most soothing common sense about her plan for a joint residence in Dresden. No town in particular, he says, means more to him than any other; therefore let it be Dresden for her sake, since she is most comfortable there among her own friends. When he visits her it will not be for work, but " with the heartfelt wish to find, or re-establish, peace and comfort there." He exhorts her once again not to be perpetually brooding over actual or imaginary wrongs, but to try to create the atmosphere of tranquillity that is so necessary for both of them — for her health, for his work.

> " You see how placably I keep on stretching out my hand, and trying to open out roads towards the best one could wish; so for heaven's sake allow time and experience their rights, do what it behoves you to do, and do not keep on forever disturbing the peace of mind of your husband, who does not belong to you alone but to his art, to the world and to posterity. . . . Do please be sensible, master this eternal mania, which is unworthy of you, for wranglings . . . I beseech you, lay that to heart! "

This sensible and friendly letter she describes to Pusinelli as " abominably heartless "!

5

Not only had such intelligence as the poor creature had ever possessed been corroded by long physical suffering, but the drugs to which she had been addicted since about 1850 had destroyed her original simple kindliness and perverted her moral vision. She saw everything, where Wagner was concerned, with a falsity that one can only call maniacal. From the first Zürich days she had dramatised their situation and cast herself for the part of heroine; and the longer she played the agreeable part before others the more completely she identified it with herself. She wanted to fix him in Dresden not because she cared very much for him, but to administer, as she imagined, a slap in the face to Mathilde Wesendonk (the mere mention of whose name was by this time enough to unhinge her mind completely), and to give an answer to the world which, she morbidly imagined, was despising her as an " abandoned wife ".[16] Nothing that he could say or do was right; and whether he did something or did nothing she was equally convinced that his sole purpose was to afflict her still further. So it had been for many years now. If, under provocation, he lost his temper with her she complained to her friends of his " brutality ". Did he manage to keep a tight hold on himself, and, out of consideration for her no less than for himself, refuse to let a discussion degenerate into a vulgar wrangle? That was an offence of another kind; he could not possibly care for her, or he would not be so cool and so polite! And always it was he who plumbed the depths of marital infamy, whereas she was a model of patience and gentleness under provocation. " You deceive yourself grossly ", she wrote to one of her friends in 1860, " when you imagine that I cavil at Richard, or quarrel with him often, as no doubt is the case with certain people. God forbid! No, with us it is something different. Never a word falls from my mouth about what he does — never do I grumble or sulk. But it is the so-called ' court tone ' that exists between us that I hate."

---

[16] To Cäcilie Avenarius she wrote on the 30th September, 1861, "My husband cannot provide me with a home, and I do not feel unhappy about that. On the contrary, I could wish that circumstances will keep him away for a long time yet. I am afraid of him, and I can bring myself to resolve on a [joint] establishment some day only on other people's account, and with the prospect that he will be very often away from home." HMP, p. 295.

Herzfeld's book contains a number of hitherto unpublished Minna letters. Incidentally it gives us reason to doubt whether her daughter Natalie has been quite fairly judged by posterity. See in particular her moving letter of the 30th March, 1867 — a year or so after Minna's death — to Cäcilie. She had evidently been treated all her life with the utmost harshness by her mother. "In what rough words, and with what wounding inconsiderateness, the fact was flung in my face a thousand times that God had not been kind to me in the matter of looks! I cannot tell you what bitter pain such reproaches often caused me. Believe me, such hard, cold lovelessness, such pitilessness, can turn us ostensibly into something different from what one really is. One becomes, without wishing it, reserved and self-contained; servile fear takes the place of love; in all that one does and says, in one's every attitude, one becomes awkward, clumsy, stupid, a monstrosity to oneself and to others. . . . Yet in the end it is a good thing for me that all my life I have known, instead of love, only the hardest, most grievous coldness. How could I bear now my hopeless loneliness had I been accustomed to love and confidence and kind treatment? God's wisdom sees to it that we learn how to bear the burdens that life is to lay on us." HMP, p. 220.

Not once in the last four years, she tells Cäcilie, has Richard written to her in a tone that she can call even mild. If he had, or if he had treated her with any humanity while they were together, she would be a healthy woman today, for heart troubles such as those she suffers from are caused only by agitations and annoyances, as every doctor knows. Richard, it seems, can hardly wait in patience until she is under the earth. As for herself, she is a saint who knows how to suffer without a word of complaint: " I have behaved so nobly in all his love affairs, never let a word escape me; he could do what he liked; the horrible word ' jealousy ' was no more than a word to me." And at the mere word " jealousy " the incurably jealous woman's mind goes back to Mathilde Wesendonk; and at the thought of Mathilde she becomes once more hardly responsible for anything she does or says.

It was this unhappy creature, whose main occupation now seemed to be the torture of her husband and of herself, by turns a whimpering weakling and a nagging fury, who suddenly descended on Wagner in Biebrich in the third week of February. She did not like the idea of his finding any sort of peace and quiet so far away from her; and probably she suspected that his satisfaction with the place came from the fact that yet another " love affair " was in progress. On what other supposition, indeed, could a mind so diseased as hers account for his saying that he doubts whether so quiet a retreat will suit her as well as it will him, though she will be welcome if she decides to come, in which case he will look out for a house for them both that will be at once comfortable and cheap? She herself confessed a couple of years later, in a letter to Cäcilie Avenarius, that he was rejoiced to see her in Biebrich, and that his eyes filled with tears as they greeted each other. She, for her part, fell foul of him almost at once for having begun the removal of the furniture from the custom-house without waiting for her to come and take charge of the operation.

Then, two or three days after her arrival, occurred the strangest of coincidences. There came a letter and a box of amiable trifles from Frau Wesendonk. In vain did Wagner try to make her see reason: the parcel contained some Christmas presents that had been sent to him by the Wesendonk family nearly three months earlier; arriving in Vienna after he had left for Paris, it had been returned to Zürich; having at last obtained his Biebrich address, Mathilde had despatched the parcel there. Explanations, assurances that his relations with Frau Wesendonk were now only of the ordinary friendly kind, were alike useless: nothing would convince Minna that the " affair " was not in full swing still. Even four months later we find him, sorely against his will, going over the old ground for her once more in reply to her upbraidings, and telling her quietly that

> " between you and me there stands no one — only your own suspicion and the illusion with which you plague yourself and me. . . . It really almost moves me to laughter to see you crazily mistaken; but as this illusion makes you suffer so terribly my laughter dies away, and — as you know from many an experience — absolute despair takes its place, to think that nothing can teach you the true state of affairs."

A letter of his to Cornelius of the 4th March gives us an idea of how near insanity she had brought him in Biebrich. It was as if time had retraced its steps and he was in the Asyl again in 1858 — the same flood of accusations, the same vulgar abuse of himself and Mathilde, the same refusal to listen to explanations, and then, when his patience at last broke down under it all, the same reproaches that he had no consideration for his wife's health, the same triumphant assurance that he would not lose his temper in this way were his conscience clear. " The old madhouse opening out in front of me again! It was enough to drive me out of my mind."

6

When Minna left him, after " ten atrocious days ", he had acquired the despairing conviction that for her sake, even more than his own, it would be better if they were never to meet again; against this eternal self-pity and this ever-smouldering resentment he felt himself to be powerless.

But her perverse soul was now more than ever set on imprisoning by her side in Dresden this man with whom she now could not live a day without plaguing him well-nigh to death, and herself along with him. She had evidently urged him, when she was in Biebrich, to apply once more to the Dresden authorities for a full amnesty.

He was reluctant to do so; but at last, on the 25th March, he brought himself to petition the King of Saxony for clemency, on the double grounds that the important Dresden theatre was beyond his reach while he remained an exile from his native land, and that a permanent refuge for his sick wife was possible only in Dresden. He appended to his petition a long medical certificate from Pusinelli, in which the latter traced the whole history of Minna's health from 1843 onwards. There was no hope, he said, of a permanent cure of her heart disease. The most that could be hoped for was that its development might be checked; nothing would contribute so much towards this result as freedom from mental trouble on Minna's part; and for that an end to her life of wandering, the establishment of a placid home in Dresden, was the prime requisite. This medical report gave the King and his ministers the excuse they had long been in search of for reversing their behaviour towards Wagner. On the 28th March he was formally notified that he had been granted the right of free re-entry into Saxony, plus " exemption from any further prosecution on account of your participation in the treasonable enterprise of May 1849."

Wagner duly thanked the Minister of Justice, von Behr, on the 9th April; he could now, he said, " consider once more the possibility of definitely settling in Dresden next autumn." With Minna also, in one letter after another, he discussed the scheme for an establishment there in which she would be comfortable and happy and where he could visit her occasionally; but for all his desire to soothe the poor self-torturing woman he was honest enough to make it clear to her that for his creative work he would have to live for the most part elsewhere. It is evident that neither the fact of his pardon nor the circumstances accompanying it gave him any pleasure. He resentfully maintained that he could have been pardoned without having been made to humiliate himself — which, indeed, had been the case with certain others of the misdemeanants of 1849: he had no particular use just then for Dresden, apart from the rather dim hope of a production of *Tristan* there; there were few people now in the town the thought of whose company day after day did not repel him; and the amnesty made it harder than ever for him to make excuses to Minna for not setting up house with her again.

She was soon at her old work, indeed, pestering him to return

to her so as to " rehabilitate " her in the eyes of her little bourgeois world; [17] and once more he had to exhaust himself in the effort
to make her see that virtually his very life, to say nothing of her
allowance, depended on his having the *Meistersinger* ready for
performance next winter, and that work upon it was impossible
without a certain amount of peace of mind. Once again he had to
go over the old wearisome ground in an attempt to make her realise
that to himself the pardon meant next to nothing, and that he had
consented to ask for it only in order that she might be able to make
Dresden her home for the future. He spoke of his anxieties with
regard to money and the necessity of his beginning to earn something; she forthwith converted his remarks into " covert reproaches " of herself, thereby compelling him to explain still further. So it went on once more, week after week, month after month,
Minna plaguing and fretting him beyond endurance while at the
same time protesting to Pusinelli that never in her whole life, in
any circumstances, had she behaved otherwise than nobly towards
this deplorable Richard of hers, and Wagner patiently trying again
and again to convince her that all her troubles arose in her own
incurably suspicious mind. Finally it came to the point where he
could write to his sister Klara Wolfram in these bitter terms:

" I have tried to arrange matters alone, without dragging anyone else
into it, with this unhappy woman who is uselessly torturing herself

---

[17] It has been the fashion to credit Minna with a sort of super-nobility of soul for
having worked so hard to procure Richard's Saxon amnesty. In the light of all we
now know of the matter, however, that opinion of her conduct must be revised. It is
only too clear that her central motive was not love of him but hatred of his friends,
a hatred that easily overflowed to himself. She herself wanted to live nowhere but
in Dresden. So long as Richard was banned from Saxony he could plead sheer inability to set up house with her there: by obtaining his full pardon she deprived him
of this argument. If now he went to live with her, she could keep him out of "affairs",
exhibit him triumphantly as her capture, and plague him to her heart's content: if
he still refused, she would have an excuse for endless new embroideries on the theme
of his "brutality", "heartlessness", and all the rest of it.

We have seen her declaring in September 1861 that she could endure the thought
of a reunion with Wagner only on the supposition that he would often be away from
home. Her mentality is revealed again in a remark of hers in the following June.
When the news of Wagner's amnesty was made public, his sister Luise Brockhaus
wrote him in such kind terms as to make him look forward to resuming his rather
impaired relations with some members of the family when he settled again in Dresden.
"Unfortunately", he writes to Pusinelli, "I communicated this feeling to my wife:
at this she immediately expressed herself in a burst of jealousy and envy and hoped
indeed that I would thrive under her care alone. . . . So it always happens with
me!" RWAP, p. 126.

and me to death; but there is no end to be found to the madness. . . . It was solely her painful malady that imposed forbearance on me: her woeful character, which makes her pursue with jealousy and hatred everyone who is associated with me, has long been impotent for that. I see now that I cannot possibly be the right one to have a beneficial influence on her heart-trouble; therefore a continuance or resumption of our domestic union would be the most foolish and preposterous thing that could happen."

7

He had, in fact, been driven to contemplate a legal severance from her. He laid his case frankly before the trusty Pusinelli in a letter of the 14th June, 1862. His one desire in life, he says, is to complete the works he has in hand. For that he needs peace and quiet; but these Minna seems determined not to allow him. No one can imagine what he has suffered, and is still suffering, through her. She gives him credit for no kindness, no good will towards her. If they are together, she drags up the painful past and insults and wounds him, till it all ends in " a scene of the most disgusting sort ". If they are away from each other, " she sends me letters which are often so insane and so filled with vulgar outbursts of rage that as a rule I am incapable of any work for days." Reasoning with her is useless; nothing can overcome her crazy obsessions. Even now he would be willing to live with her if he could persuade himself that his company would be of benefit to her. But this he cannot do: experience has shown him that she is always in better health when she is away from him. He asks Pusinelli for a frank report on her disease. Is there any prospect of its improving? If not, which would be better for her — to go on, with regard to him, as she is doing at present, or to agree that they shall henceforth live apart and correspond as little as possible? Is she well enough at the moment to receive a suggestion to this latter effect, supposing it to be considered desirable to make it? He ends by asking Pusinelli to talk matters over with Luise Brockhaus.[18]

As will be gathered from this summary of his letter, Wagner did not, in so many words, ask his friend to raise the question of a separation with Minna. But it is evident that both the doctor and

[18] RWAP, pp. 123–126.

Luise Brockhaus saw no other solution of the eternal problem than this; and Pusinelli must have written immediately about it to Minna, who was in Chemnitz at the time. Her reply of the 16th, which is packed with the old crazy delusions, the old irrelevant railings against Frau Wesendonk, was a flat refusal to entertain the idea of a divorce. She followed this up on the 30th with another letter in which she once more consoles herself with the self-righteous reflection that she has never had anything to reproach herself with in her behaviour towards Richard, and reiterates that she would rather die — with the implication that the guilt for her death, her health being what it is, will lie at Wagner's door — than consent to "a shameful separation".[19] She was malignantly resolved to keep him tied to her, at whatever cost to his happiness and his work. There was nothing for Wagner to do but resign himself to his chains. It is clear enough from his contemporary letters, by the way, that his memory betrayed him when he said, in *Mein Leben*, that he had asked Pusinelli to broach the question of a separation with Minna. That solution of the problem, one suspects, had been suggested to him in the first place by Luise Brockhaus: this theory would seem to be supported by the fact that he asked Pusinelli to talk the matter over with Luise, and by the further fact that in his letter of July 11th to Klara Wolfram he states categorically that "the idea of a divorce, obvious as it is, did not proceed from me." [20] Pusinelli, indeed, in a letter of the 17th August to Minna (in Reichenhall),[21] assures her that the idea of a divorce emanated from him, and that, as her medical adviser, he still thinks she is unwise not to fall in with it. The context supports the supposition that by "emanates from me" he means only "I raised the matter with you on my own responsibility, after Richard had 'unreservedly laid before me his situation and asked me what I considered best'."

The "medicine", though never administered, worked by suggestion, perhaps for the simple reason that it was so unexpectedly

---

[19] HMP, pp. 313–318.

[20] In *Mein Leben* he says it was Klara who, a short time earlier, had "prescribed the strong medicine" of a divorce as "the best remedy for the patient." For "Klara" we no doubt have to read "Luise".

[21] The letter is now in the Burrell Collection. It was published for the first time in RWAP, pp. 131–133.

strong; it probably made even Minna begin to think when she found not only Wagner's sisters but the honest, faithful Pusinelli siding with Richard against her. The tone of Wagner's letters to her during the autumn of 1862 indicates clearly enough that she had ceased, or almost ceased, to plague him in the old way to the old extent; in September, indeed, he could actually compliment her tactfully on her " kind and entertaining letters ". Of a reconciliation, in the deeper sense of the word, there could, however, be no question, then or at any other time; the most that could be hoped for was a tacit understanding that dangerous topics should be as far as possible avoided. In November Wagner had occasion to enter Dresden again, for the first time since his flight from it in 1849. He stayed with Minna as a matter of course, but each was ill at ease in the company of the other. Minna had evidently been apprehensive of this, for she had invited Klara Wolfram to share her room during Richard's stay; and a long round of visits to and calls from friends old and new, such as the Pusinellis, the Brockhaus couple, old Heine, Karl Kummer (the theatre oboist), and Ludwig and Malvina Schnorr, left Richard and Minna with few opportunities of being alone together for long, while he saw to it that all subjects tending towards the controversial were avoided. Their parting was painful, poor Minna having a presentiment that she would never see him again. It proved, indeed, to be their last meeting.

8

Consideration of the Minna problem in all its bearings has carried us a little ahead of our strict chronological scheme. We must now return to the point we had reached in February 1862, when the Minna question happened to come once more to the forefront.

In Biebrich and its neighbourhood Wagner made several new friends and re-discovered some old acquaintances. Among the latter was Raff, who was now located in Wiesbaden: his wife, an actress at the Court theatre there, had managed to transform the rather feckless Raff who had been so intimate with Liszt in the old Weimar days into the most respectable and prudent of bourgeois. Wagner records in *Mein Leben* that he found him " an uncommonly dry and prosy man, with a great conceit of himself as a thinker, but with no breadth of view "; a description which tallies so perfectly with all we know of Raff from his writings that we have no hesitation in accepting it as accurate. It goes without saying that just as, in the old days, he had demonstrated to the composer of *Lohengrin* what was really wrong with that work, he now showed Wagner precisely where he had gone wrong over *Tristan*, and how much better the thing could have been done had he only been gifted with an intellect like his. Wagner, after a momentary flash or two of annoyance, found the right way to deal with an omniscient of Raff's type; he treated him with a playful irony that puzzled and disconcerted him.

To another old acquaintance, Wendelin Weissheimer, Wagner was more strongly attracted for a while. Weissheimer, who was twenty-four at this time, was something of a trial to him for two reasons: he composed and he conducted. Wagner was never vastly interested even in good contemporary composers, while to composers of Weissheimer's modest calibre he always found it hard even to be conventionally polite. Nor did the young man, who had just been given office at the Mainz Opera, ever show any signs of particular aptitude as a conductor. His memoirs [22] reveal a personality never deficient in self-esteem; but he was thoroughly devoted to Wagner, to whom he was useful in many ways during the Biebrich period. As he was the son of a rich farmer in Osthofen, it is hardly likely that Wagner hurt his feelings at any time by declining small loans from him.

Two women came into Wagner's orbit at this time, one of them destined to pass out of it again very soon, the other to remain a highly-prized friend to the end of his days. Friederike Meyer, an actress, and apparently quite a good one, was the sister of Frau Meyer-Dustmann, of the Vienna Opera. The precise nature of his relations with her is not known, but there are indications that for a brief while she did what she could to console him for the loveless life to which his estrangement from Minna had reduced him. She seems to have been a likable and in some ways rather a pathetic creature, of a type not uncommon in the theatrical world. She was living under the protection of Herr Guaita, the manager of the Frankfort theatre; and Wagner's account of the explanations she

---

[22] WEWL.

THE LIFE OF RICHARD WAGNER

gave him, by way of self-exculpation, of the origin and circumstances of that association appears to indicate that he felt he had
some right to an explanation. She fell ill a little later, lost her looks
and her vitality, and made pitiful and futile attempts to work her
way back to her old position in the theatre. She gradually fades out
of the Wagner record; and her main interest for us today arises
from the fact that Frau Dustmann's resentment at the way Friederike's name had been coupled with that of Wagner was one of the
reasons why, in the end, it became impossible to produce *Tristan*
in Vienna.

Mathilde Maier cuts a very different figure in Wagner biography.
When he first met her in 1862, in Schott's house, she was in her
twenty-ninth year. Her father, a notary, had died young; and
Mathilde was living in modest circumstances in Mainz with her
mother, two aunts, and a younger sister and brother. She was intelligent enough to command the respect of many men of culture,
Nietzsche among them in later years; but her greatest attractions
seem to have been a goodness of heart and a sweetness of disposition that made her the type of person of whom no one is ever heard
to say an ill word. She herself said that at the first sight of Wagner
her heart went out to him because of the profound unhappiness
written on his face; she felt, she wrote to him later, that she would
have liked to summon all the joys of earth to wash away that look
of suffering. There can be no doubt that at one time or another he
thought of marrying her: here and there in his letters of this period,
written under the stress of Minna's malignant warfare on him, the
essentially home-loving man speaks plaintively of his right to
" sympathetic female companionship ". The references are almost
certainly to Mathilde Maier; and no doubt it was the thought of
the sympathy and understanding upon which he could count from
this gentle creature that added to the attractiveness of the idea
of a divorce in the summer of 1862. Mathilde, however, believing herself threatened with hereditary deafness, did not think
herself justified in marrying any man, and least of all a musician.
But though she was not fated to play a leading part in his life she
makes a gracious and lovable figure not only in Wagner's letters
to her, which extend from 1862 to 1878, but, which is a much more
notable achievement on her part, in the pages of *Mein Leben*. Hers

is one of the few personalities that survive the ordeal of his detailed attention in those pages without the faintest shadow falling upon their memory.

How he managed to work at all under the load of anxieties and annoyances laid on him by Minna and others at this time is a mystery to be explained only on the theory of the almost complete insulation of the creative instinct in an artist from his outward circumstances; but work he did for a time. By the third week in April the score of the *Meistersinger* overture was complete, precisely as it stands today, although he appears to have made little progress as yet with the first act of the opera. By the third week in July he had got as far with this as the scene where Pogner introduces Walther to the Mastersingers; then an accident occurred that stopped all work upon the score.[23] The architect who owned the house of which Wagner's three rooms formed a part had a bulldog whose verminous and generally neglected condition aroused Wagner's sympathy. As he had made friends with the animal he thought it safe to hold its head while a servant washed it, only to meet with the fate that so often attends benefactors in this imperfect world — the helping hand was bitten. His right thumb soon swelled to such an extent that work upon the *Meistersinger* score became impossible, and remained so for a good two months. The dog played a larger part in determining Wagner's future fortunes than he could have foreseen when he snapped at him: the enforced delay in the delivery of the score of the opera led to a temporary drying up of supplies from Schott, so that Wagner was compelled, later in the year, to plunge once more into the wearisome business of concert-conducting: and this in its turn threw him into still further arrears with his composition.

9

The reader who has been brought up to believe that with Wagner the words were always written first and the music born of them no doubt wonders how it came about that while the composition of the

---

[23] In *Mein Leben* he gives the date as "about the middle of August"; but in his letter of the 21st August to Minna he says "the day after tomorrow it will be four weeks since I had to suspend my work entirely."

Meistersinger was not completed until February, 1867, the overture — constructed, apparently, out of "motives" derived from
the opera — was ready for performance in April 1862. Until the
whole of his sketches for the opera are published in their proper
chronological sequence we dare not dogmatise as to how much of
the music was sketched in advance of the words. We know, however, that in no less important an instance than that of the Dream
Song in the first part of the third act and the Prize Song in the latter
part he calmly created his melody first and afterwards worked out
a poem to fit it. Weissheimer, who saw a good deal of Wagner in
February and March 1862, tells us that one day " he showed me
a sheet containing the broad working-out of the initial motive [of
the prelude], and, underneath this, the second motive, in E, and the
characteristic *Meistersinger* trumpet passage. He thus wrote the
prelude before he had composed a note along with the text! . . .
and the astonishing thing about the motive in E was the happy accident that later on the words of Walther's Prize Song exactly fitted
this wonderful melody. When writing the prelude he certainly had
not the remotest idea of that Prize Song in the third act." [24] Glasenapp, who never loses an opportunity of being malicious where
Weissheimer is concerned, calls all this " incredibly naïve ". As it
happens, Weissheimer was right as regards the E major theme,
though he did not know the full history of the matter, which has only
recently become available.

The melody to which Weissheimer is referring enters at the 97th
bar of the prelude:

The present-day listener, associating this with the final stanza of
the Prize Song, naturally assumes that Wagner transferred it from
there to his prelude. But in 1862 Wagner had no thought of the
Prize Song either in its present poetic or its present musical form.
We have already seen the type of verse and a specimen of the actual
melody of the song in its original form,[25] and obviously the E major

---

[24] WEWL, p. 94.   [25] See *supra*, p. 172.

theme just quoted cannot have played any part in this. For one thing, it is difficult to see how the lilting six-eight rhythm of the melody quoted by Wagner for Frau Wesendonk's benefit could ever transform itself into the four-four of the melody cited above. For another thing, the words of the final stanza in the 1862 version of the Song cannot be made to fit this melody. We are therefore not surprised to discover that both the words and the music of the Prize Song in its definitive form are creations of a much later date.

Wagner began the composition of the third act at Triebschen in October, 1866. Three or four of the pages — Nos. 19–22 — of the manuscript of the scene between Walther and Sachs present a curious spectacle: the melody of the Dream Song as we know it today is there, but *without any words*, although the full text of each of Sachs's interjections accompanies the music.

On the 25th October, reporting progress with the *Meistersinger* to King Ludwig, Wagner wrote, " I am well into the third act now, and one of these days I shall have to write the words of Walther's Prize Song,[26] the melody of which is already finished; but before I can do that I really must get the masons, locksmiths and carpenters out of the house." The melody had, in fact, begun to take shape in his mind towards the end of September, though Wagner does not record the fact in his " Annals " until the end of the year, — " Journeys to Basel: melody of the Prize Song — without text. At Christmas also the poem: 24 Dec: 12 midnight. (Christmas gift)." [27] The new melody to which he refers here is of course only that of the first two stanzas, commencing respectively " Morgenlich leuchtend in rosigem Schein " and " Wonnig entragend dem seligen Raum ": for the " aftersong ", commencing " Sei euch vertraut ", he went back to the above-mentioned E major theme of the overture (written in 1862), transposed it, to agree with what he had already written, into C major, cast it into three-four instead of common time, and developed it on fresh lines towards the end. A sketch dated the 28th September shows the melody already complete and perfect. The new words did not come to him until nearly three months later. It was the first pencil draft of them that he gave Cosima as a Christmas present: a later copy of it in ink, in his

---

[26] At this stage, of course, the Dream Song.
[27] KLRWB, II, 4–5, 98–99.

handwriting, contains pencil interlineations of the nonsense that Beckmesser is later to make of the words.[28]

A further fact in connection with the Prize Song may as well be noted here, instead of being dealt with later. It was seemingly not until Wagner had almost finished the composition of the *Meistersinger* that he became aware of a prime flaw in the construction of his drama: in each of his Prose Sketches he had made the Prize Song as sung by Walther in the final scene identical with the Dream Song launched by him a little while before in the scene between himself and Sachs. Wagner now realised, Cosima wrote to King Ludwig, " that it was absolutely impossible to have the same poem delivered twice in the same act. But it has to be the same yet different, clear and succinct; besides, it would have gone against the grain with Walther to repeat in this fashion, before the Folk and the Masters, the intimate happenings in Sachs's room! This difficult problem, which has kept the Friend [Wagner] uncommonly busy of late, has been solved, in my opinion, with wonderful success. The second poem is the interpretation of the dream, and an intensification of it: it is the dream become the master-song." [29]

The change was made at the seventh line of the Dream Song; after " Ein Garten lud mich ein ", Walther, instead of continuing, as before, with " Gast ihm zu sein ", and thereby completing the first stanza, now changes these latter words into " Dort unter einem Wunderbaum ", and adds a further six lines before concluding the stanza with " Eva im Paradies ". From that point onwards the Prize Song becomes an entirely different poem, with, of course, corresponding changes in the build of the music. The text of the poem, however (taken down in the earlier scene by Sachs as Walther sang it), had been given to the Mastersingers for them to follow, so that they might see for themselves that Beckmesser's rendering of it had been merely farcical. How is it, then, the spectator might ask, that they do not perceive that Walther is *not* singing the same text from the sixth line onwards? Wagner gets over this little difficulty in ingenious fashion: he makes Kothner, who is holding the script, so overcome with emotion at this point that he involun-

---

[28] See the facsimiles accompanying Otto Strobel's article *Wie Walthers Preislied entstand*, in BFF, 1933, p. 148 ff.

[29] MECW, I, 333.

tarily lets the paper drop: " he and the others ", according to the stage directions, " merely listen, absorbed, to the remainder of the song. Walther seems, without betraying the fact, to perceive this, and he now continues in a free version " [30] [of the Dream Song].

---

[30] In my English version of the *Meistersinger* text, published by Breitkopf and Härtel, I wrongly rendered these last words "with more self-possession". In the light of the context, the full significance of which I had not grasped at the time I made my version, "Fassung" must obviously be taken not in the sense of "composure" but in its other sense of "*Ausdrucksweise*, manner of expression, version, wording, terms", as the dictionary puts it. Wagner's stage direction makes the meaning perfectly clear — as soon as Walther observes that the Mastersingers no longer have the manuscript in front of them he feels safe in departing from the script of his song.

The sentence "Walther seems to perceive this, and now continues in a free version" is not translated at all by Frederick Jameson, no doubt because it does not appear in the original score. Wagner inserted it, however, in the separate imprint of the poem, whence it is now transferred to the score in at least one modern edition — that of Breitkopf.

CHAPTER VIII

SHIPWRECK

1

WHEN HE was not under the painful necessity of thinking about Minna, Wagner found life at this time, on the whole, very agreeable. If he had money in his pocket he gaily spent it; if he had none he borrowed, or obtained whatever he required on credit, his inextinguishable optimism always painting the future in rosy colours for him. He sold to Schott for 1,000 francs the settings he had made in 1857–8 of *Five Poems* by Mathilde Wesendonk. In Biebrich and the neighbourhood he had numerous friends to whom he could read, from time to time, the *Meistersinger* poem and lay down the law on every subject under the sun, a procedure without which life was rarely worth living for him. Bülow and Cosima came to him in July, and one day he was surprised to see his old Dresden friend Röckel walk into the dining room of the hotel: he had been discharged in the preceding March, and, apart from a little greying of the hair, seemed not a penny the worse for his thirteen years' imprisonment.

Wagner would look in occasionally at the Casino in Wiesbaden, where the roulette tables and their devotees seem to have had a certain fascination for him. He had the common experience — though, it goes without saying, he regarded it as wholly peculiar to himself — of playing like one inspired so long as he merely staked mentally. Twice in succession, one day when he was there in Weissheimer's company, he foretold, without staking, the winning *plein*: his own explanation of this achievement was that he felt himself overcome by a spell. Weissheimer, unwilling to see a gift for divination like this being wasted, naturally urged him to plunge; he refused. Still possessed, he tells us in *Mein Leben*, by that curious feeling of oracular guidance, he solemnly explained that " if I were to introduce my personal interests into the game, the gift I

have proved myself to possess would at once disappear." The incident and the remark were delightfully characteristic of him. Whatever happened to Richard Wagner, even though to the ordinary
eye of man it might look very much like what was happening daily
to millions of other people, had a profundity of significance which
one had to be a reader of the stars to fathom. It was so, for instance,
in later years when a son was born to him: from what he had to say
on that commonplace subject one gets the impression that the
cosmos had surpassed itself on this occasion, and that he gave it
generous credit for having done so. He would have scouted the
idea that the trifling success he had in the Casino on another day —
when, by flinging a few pieces on the table, he retrieved what Cosima
had lost — was merely the " beginner's luck " that Casinos everywhere benevolently keep in store for the stranger in their midst.

It was during this summer that he met his future Tristan for
the first time. He had been in communication with Schnorr — who
was now attached to the Dresden Opera — as early as November
1861, hoping to persuade him to obtain leave of absence for the
following three months in order to sing Tristan and other Wagner
parts in Vienna. Apparently the tenor had replied that, for all his
enthusiasm for the new work, he still regretted to have to confess
that, as in 1859, the third act was beyond his physical powers;
whereupon Wagner assured him that for the first few performances
he would not insist on this act being given without cuts, though he
was confident that that would prove possible later. (He apparently
thought also that the act in its complete form would be more than
the average audience could assimilate at a first hearing). It proved
impossible for Schnorr to get the desired leave from Dresden at
the right time, then or later. When Wagner heard that the tenor
and his wife were to be " guesting " at Karlsruhe in May (1862) he
seized the opportunity of hearing Schnorr for the first time. His
memory seems to have been at fault when he said, in *Mein Leben*
and in the *Recollections of Ludwig Schnorr von Carolsfeld*, that,
fearing that his impressions might be unfavourable, and therefore
wishing to avoid making the singer's personal acquaintance, he
attended the performance of *Lohengrin* (on the 26th May) in secret,
having obtained a ticket from Kapellmeister Kalliwoda: actually
he had asked Schnorr himself to get a ticket for him and address it

to him at the Hotel " Zum Erbprinzen ", where he expected to stay. He found, within a few minutes of Schnorr's entry as Lohengrin, that his fears had been groundless: the voice, the art and the spiritual quality of the man were such as to leave the spectator undistressed by his corpulence. All that Wagner had to criticise in him was a few immaturities of conception and style. Schnorr called on him at the hotel afterwards: the two men took to each other instantly, and a bond was sealed between them that was to be broken only by death.

The Schnorr couple happened to take their summer holiday that year by the Rhine at the time when Bülow and Cosima were with Wagner in Biebrich. With Hans at the piano, Schnorr and Malvina sang long stretches of the Tristan and Isolde parts: and Wagner taught them, as only he could do, how to overcome the occasional physical strain of the music by a completer understanding of the words and the situation.[1] They sang for him also the opening scene of the third act of *Lohengrin;* and Wagner, to Bülow's accompaniment, initiated them into so much as was already written of the *Meistersinger.* In *Mein Leben* Wagner hints that he and Cosima had to suffer occasionally during those summer months from Bülow's irritability and depression: poor Hans was, as usual, a very sick, exhausted man, whose jangled nerves required something else to restore them than the constant excitement in which Wagner kept everyone in his company. But the *Meistersinger* was a joy to him — " a real masterpiece ", he wrote to Richard Pohl: " half of the first act sketched out — immense wealth of musical ideas — a humour that makes Shakespeare's seem in comparison a trifle threadbare. Overture C major — high-spirited (at the end four motives combined), scoring finished." Tired as he was, he could not refrain from making a copy of so much of the score of the opera as was already written — " 145 quarto pages ", he tells Pohl: " I have worn out my fingers over it at the rate of eight hours a day for five days, in this appalling heat! " And Wagner the man exercised the old irresistible fascination over him: " Don't think it ill of me ", he adds, " that I can't work up the faintest interest in Alkan and Heinze just now; to have Wagner as a neighbour means

---

[1] In the *Recollections* he nowhere mentions Malvina. The reasons for this shabby treatment of her will appear in a later chapter.

that everything else shrivels into insignificance, becomes utterly childish, null and void."

2

By the autumn, when it had become evident that Schott would disgorge nothing more until further progress had been made with the *Meistersinger*, Wagner had to make up his mind to resort once more to the tiring and distasteful work of concert-giving in order to raise a little money. It occurred to Weissheimer that for a concert of his own compositions in Leipzig — to be given at his own expense — the co-operation of Wagner and Bülow would be an added attraction. He accordingly engaged the Gewandhaus and its orchestra for the 1st November. Bülow played the solo part in Liszt's second piano concerto [2] (in A major); Wagner conducted the first performance anywhere of the *Meistersinger* prelude and closed the concert with the *Tannhäuser* overture. At that time Leipzig surpassed even Berlin as a hot-bed of anti-Wagnerian prejudice. There seem to have been exceedingly few people in the Gewandhaus that evening, apart from a handful of Wagner's friends. He was conscious, at first, that the orchestra was cool towards him to the point of unfriendliness; but first the prelude (which had to be repeated) and then the overture won the players over in spite of themselves, and they gave him an ovation at the finish. Financially, of course, the concert was a failure: poor Weissheimer, instead of being able to hand over something to Wagner as he had hoped, had to draw heavily on his father to make good his own loss.

Wagner himself was by this time completely out of funds; and only an unexpected windfall of 1,500 marks from the Grand Duke of Weimar — who, Wagner believed, hoped by this gift to conciliate Liszt and induce him to settle in Weimar again — enabled him to renew his tenancy of his Biebrich apartment, which he did not want to lose, and to make a round of visits in Dresden, Mainz and elsewhere before setting out once more for Vienna. In Dresden, as has already been said, he saw Minna for the last time. The town

---

[2] Wagner, in *Mein Leben*, describes it as "a new piano concerto by Liszt." It had been finished, however, apart from a few "improvements" in 1861, as long ago as 1857, and performed for the first time in Weimar on the 7th January of that year, with Bronsart as the soloist and Liszt conducting.

had changed somewhat in its outer aspect since he saw it last in 1849, while for Wagner his old haunts seemed mostly peopled by ghosts. Reissiger, Lüttichau and many of the older members of the orchestra were dead or retired; Lipinski, the one-time leader, had left the town long ago; there was a new King, and a new set of ministers. Wagner dutifully called on Behr, the Minister of Justice, and on Baron Beust, the President of the Council, to thank them for their good offices in the matter of his pardon. He found the former a little doubtful about the wisdom of that step: he feared that Wagner's popularity would make it easy for him to work up a democratic demonstration, and was greatly relieved when he learned that he had no intention of showing himself in the theatre during his stay in Dresden. The oily-mannered Beust disconcerted him by confronting him smilingly with that compromising letter of his that had been found in Röckel's pocket at the time of the latter's arrest in 1849,[3] and which had been the prime cause of the issue of a warrant against Wagner. It took him completely by surprise, for he had not known until then that the letter had fallen into the hands of the Saxon authorities; and he had to confess to Beust that he must regard the amnesty as a pardon for his " imprudent conduct " in the past.

3

In Vienna, meanwhile, the old comedy, which was now degenerating into a farce, had begun again. *Tristan*, he was assured, was being " earnestly studied ", and his presence would be welcomed. He arrived there on the 15th November, accompanied by Friederike Meyer, who was going to fill some " guest " engagements at the Burg Theatre. Frau Dustmann was at once up in arms: she resented, in the first place, the presence in Vienna of the sister who was regarded as the bad girl of the family, and in the second place the fact that Wagner was friendlier with her than she thought desirable. From this time, it is generally supposed, Frau Dustmann's enthusiasm for Wagner and for *Tristan* began to decline rapidly. Ander could already be written off as merely a liability; as the weeks wore on it became more and more evident that nothing was

---

[3] See Vol. II, pp. 64, 109.

to be expected of this " blasse, blonde, blöde Brillenträger", as
Schnorr alliteratively described him.[4] And now a further obstacle
in the path of *Tristan* arose.

Hanslick, the music critic of the *Presse*, whose musical attain-
ments seem to have impressed no expert who came into contact
with him,[5] and who would be almost forgotten today were it not for
the touch of comic relief he adds to Wagner biography, had managed, partly by means of a readable style, partly by an unscrupulous use of his power, to make himself not only read but feared in
Vienna to an extent that is quite incomprehensible to us today.
There are reasons for doubting whether even his own public took
him very seriously as a critic, for there was hardly a contemporary
work of genius or high talent in connection with which he did not
demonstrate, at some time or other in the course of his career, the
limitations not merely of his intellect but of his taste — from *Tristan* to *Aïda*, from *Carmen* to *Die Fledermaus* he was consistently
wrong. But singers, instrumentalists, conductors all stood in awe
of him; and even the Opera management used to become apprehensive when it became known that Hanslick was prejudiced against
the composer of a new work. After beginning as an admirer of the
early Wagner, Hanslick, for some reason of his own — perhaps not
unconnected with the article on *Judaism in Music* — had developed into one of his bitterest and most unscrupulous enemies.

Wagner was too intelligent ever to think very much of " musical
criticism ", too contemptuous of the critics ever to pay the slightest
court to them, and too uncompromising to make even a pretence
of politeness when he happened to be thrown into the company of
one of the fraternity. There are indications, however, that Hanslick
was willing to make friendly advances to Wagner, whose position
in the musical world, he could not help recognising, was very different from when the pair had first met in 1845. The Vienna company also spared no effort to bring them together. Each attempt of
the kind broke down, however, in the face of Wagner's scornful

[4] "This pale, blonde, purblind spectacles-wearer".

[5] See, for example, the contempt for him expressed by Wilhelm Kienzl, the composer of *Der Evangelimann*, who spent some time, as a student, under this "Professor
of Musical History and Aesthetic" at the University of Vienna. (*Meine Lebens-
wanderung*, pp. 68–72). Brahms found Hanslick useful, but evidently had no great
opinion of his musical capacity.

[197]

aloofness. At the rehearsal of *Lohengrin* in May, 1861, to which he listened on the stage, someone took it on himself to present Hanslick, apparently at the critic's request. Wagner, as he says in *Mein Leben*, " greeted him shortly, like a perfectly unknown person ". Thereupon Ander presented him a second time, adding the remark that Herr Hanslick was an old acquaintance of the composer. Wagner replied curtly that he remembered Herr Hanslick perfectly well,·and then turned his attention to the stage again. In the following autumn Laube, who knew everyone in Vienna, invited them both to dinner, naïvely believing they would be " particularly interested " in each other. Again Wagner ignored the critic completely.

A little later Frau Dustmann, who was also obsessed with the idea that in Wagner's own interest it was of the utmost importance to conciliate Hanslick, " introduced " the two men once more at an evening party. Being in a good temper just then, Wagner tells us, he managed to " treat Hanslick as a superficial acquaintance." The critic drew him aside for an intimate talk, during which he assured him, " with sobs and tears ", that he could not bear to be misunderstood by him any longer — that if he had sometimes been guilty of extravagance in his judgments of Wagner this was due not to malice but to his own limitations, which he ardently desired to remedy. Moved by the passion of this outburst, Wagner became for the moment not only soothing but sympathetic; and he heard later that Hanslick had afterwards been so loud in praise of his amiability that the Opera management thought it safe to summon him once more to Vienna in the autumn of 1862. All this, though we have no confirmation of it from any other quarter, seems credible enough. Wagner *did* receive a fresh call to Vienna about that time; and it was no doubt because it was generally assumed that Hanslick and he were now " reconciled " that Standhartner, in November, 1862, invited the critic to a party at his house at which Wagner was to read the *Meistersinger* libretto.

But by that time Wagner had lost whatever small sympathy he may have felt for the tearful Hanslick at their last meeting; and Standhartner's well-meant gesture only made matters worse. Wagner tells us that as the reading went on the critic became ever paler and more ill at ease, nor could he be persuaded to stay a minute after it was over. " My friends ", says Wagner with a charming assumption of innocent wonder, " all agreed that Hanslick regarded the whole poem as a lampoon directed against himself, and felt our (*sic*) invitation to the reading to be an affront." He fails to mention that the name he had originally given to the Marker in his play was " Hanslich ". Even if he gave the Marker another name, or no name at all, during his reading, there must have been dozens of people in Vienna who knew of the " Hanslich " joke. The report had probably reached the critic's ears, and his presence at Standhartner's may have been primarily due to the desire to know the worst. That after listening to the libretto he should be convinced that Wagner was deliberately caricaturing him is not at all surprising. As a matter of fact, though Hanslick was not aware of it, the essential features of Beckmesser as a hidebound opponent of the new art, who becomes ridiculous as soon as he tries to practise himself what he presumes to teach, were already embodied in the Sketch of 1845, long before Wagner had any reason to complain of Hanslick's unfriendliness. One little touch of 1861, however, was undoubtedly motived by the desire to work off some of Wagner's dislike and contempt for his enemy. " Anyone more mischievous " [*boshaft*, malicious], Wagner makes Sachs say as the Marker goes off with the song that has been palmed off on him in the second act, " I have never known. But in the long run he can't get away with it." [6] But there has been nothing in Beckmesser's conduct so far in the drama to make us regard him as particularly *boshaft*. He has merely been stupid and pompous: we keep laughing at him, but we do not dislike him. The *boshaft* is an epithet which we shall perhaps not go far wrong in assuming to have been inserted during the writing of the poem, with special reference to Hanslick; and we can easily imagine Wagner giving particular point to these lines of Sachs's as he read them. Anyhow, Hanslick had seen and heard enough that evening to warn him what an immortality of ridicule was in store for him as soon as the *Meistersinger* began its public career; and even Wagner could not have felt any surprise at what he calls the critic's " intensified hostility " towards him after that.

[6] The reader will pardon, I hope, the colloquialism of the translation.

And Hanslick, in one way and another, could do a great deal of mischief in Vienna.[7]

4

In the autumn of 1862 Wagner was at loggerheads with his publisher Schott, who sturdily refused to part with any more money until he received delivery of more of the *Meistersinger* score. On the 20th October Wagner wrote to him in acrimonious terms, blaming *him* for the delay in the completion of the work: it was the publisher's duty, it seems, not only to keep the composer provided with funds but to see that nothing happened to disturb his equanimity. " You are making a mistake, my good Herr Schott! " he said. " You are altogether in error in your notions of how a man like myself should be treated. Many things can be wrung out of one by hunger, but not works of the higher kind." His letter, the angry tone of which he himself recognised, he described as " the effusion of a sleepless night ", which " the eternal laws of righteousness " forbade him to spare the peccant publisher. Schott replied with a tartness matching his own. He would prefer, he said, to pass over in silence " the effusion you favour me with of one of your sleepless nights, my good Herr Wagner, because, although I know how I ought to behave towards artists, I will not tell you what I expect from an artist. . . . Speaking generally, a music publisher cannot provide for your requirements; that could only be done by an enormously rich banker, or by some prince with millions at his disposal."

Sobered, perhaps, by this plain speaking, Wagner, at the end of 1862, plunged into the none too congenial business of concert-giving, with the object not only of raising a little money but of breaking down the barrier interposed by the opera houses between the musical public and the knowledge of his latest works. He began with three concerts in Vienna, given in the Theater an der Wien, the next largest theatre in the city after the Opera House. At the first

---

[7] Hanslick had persistently pooh-poohed the enthusiasm shown for Wagner by the Vienna public during and after the *Lohengrin* and *Flying Dutchman* performances of May 1861: it was mere sensation-hunting, mere sympathy with the one-time exile, merely a side-blow at the French for their rejection of *Tannhäuser* — anything, in fact, but honest and rational approval of Wagner's bad music. For his own and other contemporary Vienna criticisms of Wagner see BWSW, p. 51 ff.

concert, on the 26th December, the programme consisted of extracts from the *Meistersinger* — the prelude, Pogner's Address (sung by Hrabanek), and the Gathering of the Mastersingers; from the *Valkyrie* — the Ride of the Valkyries, Siegmund's Spring Song (sung by Olschbauer), and Wotan's Farewell (sung by Mayerhofer); and the *Rhinegold* — the second part of the first scene (described as the " Rape of the Rhinegold "), and the Entry of the Gods into Valhalla. Ovation followed ovation for Wagner; the Vienna public, like that in virtually every other town except Berlin and Leipzig, showed itself utterly unaffected by the almost universal enmity of the critics towards him. The second concert took place on the 1st January, before a smaller audience than that of the first, owing to the preoccupation of the Viennese with other pleasures that day. For this concert Wagner went to the extra expense of constructing a sound-board behind the orchestra — an admirable idea in itself, but adding another 230 gulden to the cost of the evening. The programme was the same as before, with the addition of Siegfried's two forge songs. Wagner, of course, conducted everything by heart, and wrote his own " programme notes ". Superficially the two concerts were a solid success for him, not only in the musical but in the social sense: the Empress herself had been present at the first, and the Minister Schmerling at the second. But financially it was quite another story: the receipts, good as they were, came nowhere near covering expenses.

To retrieve the situation he gave a third concert on the 8th January, to which once more the Empress and the ladies of the Court lent their patronage. This time Wagner omitted the *Rhinegold* pieces from the programme, substituting for them the *Faust Overture* and the overture to *Tannhäuser*. The enthusiasm was greater than ever, but the financial result, presumably, not much more satisfactory than before: and Weissheimer, who had attended all three concerts, shook his head over the reckless extravagance of the dinner which Wagner gave to the leading performers and some of his friends after the third — in spite of the fact that he was already heavily in debt to the landlord of his hotel. His way of dealing with situations of this kind was the simple, and, to a great extent, sound one of calling on champagne to banish dull care. One evening, after depressing Weissheimer and Tausig with his talk about the hopelessness of his position, he suddenly jumped up from the sofa on which he had been reclining, rang for the waiter, and ordered two bottles on ice. The young men were horrified; but Wagner made them an eloquent speech on the absolute necessity of champagne to mankind when things looked black. " Drink with me ", he said, " for *we* are the victors, *ours* is the world! " And sure enough, the next morning he showed Weissheimer in triumph 1,000 gulden which had been sent him, Weissheimer surmised, by the Empress.

The success of these three concerts led to an invitation to give a similar one in Prague. Friends there took charge of the business arrangements for him, with the result that he came away with more than 1,000 florins clear profit. The programme for this concert, which took place on the 8th February, 1863, consisted of the *Faust Overture*, the *Meistersinger* prelude, the *Tannhäuser* overture, the *Tristan* prelude, Siegmund's Spring Song (Bernard), the Gathering of the Mastersingers, and Pogner's Address (Rokitansky). Prague was as enthusiastic over the new works as Vienna had been; there was even talk of a production of *Tristan* there in the course of the summer. This project fell through because of the impossibility of the co-operation of Schnorr; while in Vienna, although the Opera management had been stirred to fresh efforts — or the semblance of them — by the success of the concerts there, not a yard of real progress was made either then or later. Ander not only became more and more scared of his part but kept supplying the journalists unfriendly to Wagner with inside information calculated to damage the prospects of the work. Frau Dustmann's zeal diminished week by week; and the Opera personnel in general began to grumble at the amount of work demanded from them for an undertaking which they all foresaw was doomed to failure.

5

Wagner's incurable optimism sustained him through it all, however. To Minna he summed up in a single phrase the situation of that winter as he saw it — " things are at the same time moving and stagnant." It took him a very long while and many bitter experiences to realise that the Opera people were not playing straight

with him as regards *Tristan,* while he could always persuade himself there would be a fall of manna from the sky before long —
money from concerts, help from friends, a commission for *Tristan*
or the *Meistersinger* from Weimar or some other theatre, a pension
jointly provided by their Highnesses of Baden, Weimar and Prussia, and so ad infinitum. Ironically enough, his salvation that winter came not from Germany but from Russia. In November, 1862
he had received an invitation, made, apparently, at the instance of
his true friend Mme. Kalergis, to conduct two Philharmonic concerts in St. Petersburg. Thither he betook himself in the following
February, his preliminary expenses having been happily provided
for by his concert in Prague. Travelling by way of Berlin, where
he was able to spend a few hours with Bülow and Cosima, he arrived
in St. Petersburg towards the end of the month. There he found at
his service a fine orchestra of more than a hundred and twenty
players — many of them Germans — culled from all the imperial
theatres, and a public no less enthusiastic than that of Vienna. In
Russia he made several new friends and met again one or two old
ones, among the latter the composer-critic Serov.

At the first concert, on the 3rd March, his programme consisted of
the *Lohengrin* prelude — with no fewer than sixty violins — Senta's Ballad (sung by a Mme. Bianchi), the overture and the Sailors'
Chorus from the *Flying Dutchman,* the *Tannhäuser* overture, Wolfram's romance (Soboleff) and the " March " from the second act
of *Tannhäuser,* and the Eroica symphony. At the second concert, a
few days later, he substituted Beethoven's C minor for the Eroica,
and made one or two small changes among his own works. These
two concerts were under the auspices of the Philharmonic Society.
A third he gave on his own account, the programme being devoted
entirely to his own works — the *Tannhäuser* overture, the *Lohengrin* prelude, and the now customary selections from his earlier
operas and from the *Ring.* From St. Petersburg he went on to
Moscow, where he had been engaged, on handsome terms, to give
three concerts with the same programmes as in the capital. Returning to St. Petersburg he gave two more concerts, one on his own
account and one for the benefit of those imprisoned for debt — a
cause which perhaps struck a responsive chord in his bosom. The
simultaneous announcement of these two concerts had precisely the

result he might have foreseen: the charity affair, which was under the patronage of the Court, was sold out in advance, while for his own concert he merely managed to cover expenses.

His sojourn in Russia had been one long triumph; the Court, and more especially the Grand Duchess Helene, took, or appeared to take, a warm interest in him; he read to her and her ladies no less than four times the whole of the *Ring* libretto, from the proof sheets of the public issue of the poem which the publisher J. J. Weber, of Leipzig, then had in hand.[8] For a while he thought he had found in the art-loving Grand Duchess the patroness, at once intelligent and rich, he had long been looking for: she sent him 1,000 roubles by way of compensation for the receipts he had been balked of in connection with his last concert in St. Petersburg, and, according to him, promised him the same amount annually until his circumstances improved. When, however, he suggested returning each year to place his services at her disposal, and when he further threw out a broad hint that although he would like to build a house for himself in Biebrich he feared the cost would eat up all he had so far made in Russia, and leave him with nothing to live on, she seems to have become what he calls " evasive ". Perhaps, like so many other patrons, she had begun to feel that it was imprudent to encourage Wagner too far.

6

If the Russian expedition was of no significance whatever in his development as an artist, it at any rate provided him with a neat little capital of some 12,000 marks after all expenses had been paid. Any other man would have found this ample for his maintenance until some fresh source of revenue had been discovered; but the money passed through Wagner's fingers like water through a sieve. He gave up the idea of building in Biebrich, removed his furniture from there to Vienna, and in mid-May rented the entire upper part — carrying with it the exclusive right to a fairly large garden — of a house in near-by Penzing belonging to one Baron von Rackowitz. The rent was 2,400 marks a year. He took into his service the Bohemian Franz Mrazeck and his wife Anna, who

---

[8] The *Meistersinger* poem had been published by Schott in December, 1862.

afterwards served him so well during the Munich period, spared no expense in making the place not only comfortable but handsome, laid in a store of excellent wine, and settled down, rich in nothing but optimism and debts, to enjoying life as he had rarely enjoyed it before. Perhaps the serenade and torchlight procession to which the members of various Male Voice Choral Societies treated him on the 3rd June, in rather belated celebration of his fiftieth birthday, contributed not a little to make him feel that Vienna was wholly devoted to him, and that he could safely make the town his home until at least *Tristan* had been produced and the *Meistersinger* score completed.

But soon the old disharmony between receipts and expenditure began to show itself. On the 23rd and 28th July he was compelled to give concerts in Pesth, with programmes of the type of those he had given in Vienna, Prague and Russia. The audiences were wildly enthusiastic, and his profit amounted to about 1,000 gulden. Everywhere he went, indeed, he was cheered and fêted; but the one thing he most desired — a production of *Tristan* — persistently evaded him. A new opera house was nearing completion in Vienna, and in anticipation of its opening Wagner gave the Viennese the benefit of a lifetime's thinking about opera, its problems and its ideals.[9] As usual when he gets on to a subject solely concerned with art, he talks the soundest of sound sense on these and cognate topics. He exposes the weaknesses of the ordinary German methods of opera production and shows how these might be improved; and he enlarges on a favourite thesis of his, that while the provision of theatrical amusement of the ordinary kind can safely be left to the entrepreneurs who are keen to make money out of the public, a State institution should see to it that the theatre, in the matter of the quality both of its performances and of its repertory, plays its proper part in the elevation of the community's manners and the purifying of its taste. His words, of course, fell on deaf ears, in Vienna as everywhere else.

The early winter of 1863–4 saw him still trying, by means of concerts, at once to raise funds and to get into touch with the musical

[9] The treatise, running to some twenty-five pages of print, arose out of a conversation with his friend Uhl. Wagner's first intention was to write an article for Uhl's paper, the *Botschafter;* but he ultimately issued his work as a brochure, in October 1863.

public. He gave two concerts in Prague, on the 5th and 8th November, two in Karlsruhe, on the 14th and 19th, and one in Breslau on the 6th December. In all he spent some five weeks exhausting himself in this manner, generally with disappointing financial results. On the whole the audiences were keen enough about what at that time was bafflingly new music; but necessarily many of the fragments he gave them failed of their full effect through dissociation from their context. We find Tourgenieff, for instance, who was fairly representative of the cultured non-professional music lover of the period, going into ecstasies over the Ride of the Valkyries but declaring himself " revolted " by Wotan's Farewell.[10]

Wagner was back in Penzing about the middle of December. On the 27th of the month he took part in a concert given by Tausig in Vienna, his own contribution comprising the *Freischütz* overture in addition to some pieces of his own. He found, even at this late date, and even in Vienna, the orchestra accustomed to taking the overture in the old senseless way against which he had protested, both with his pen and by his practice, in his Dresden days — the opening adagio, for example, being converted into an easy-going andante. It was not without considerable trouble that he managed to have the work played as he imagined it and as Weber had conceived it.

In the opening months of 1864 the clouds were rolling thick and fast towards Penzing. Wagner's passion for luxury and his faith in his star had seduced him into incurring great expense in the furnishing of his house. In the end, the ordinary sources of credit having dried up, he had recourse to moneylenders; and as Tausig had been indiscreet enough to back a bill for him, the catastrophe, when it came, threatened to involve him also. Inside his pleasant Penzing home Wagner could generally forget the outer world in the congenial company of Tausig, Standhartner, Gustav Schönaich and Cornelius, especially the last-named. Peter was perhaps never a whole-hearted Wagnerian. For a long time he could not see beyond *Lohengrin:* he was smitten almost dumb by the imaginative power and the technical resource of *Tristan,* but he was slow to become convinced with regard to it as a whole. In the *Ring* he

---

[10] MMKB, p. 124. Tourgenieff had attended the Karlsruhe concert in the company of Mme. Kalergis.

jibbed, as so many worthy people did at this time, at the " incestu-
ous " love of Siegmund and Sieglinde. But Peter's wide culture,
his intellectual honesty and his pawky humour appealed greatly to
Wagner; while perhaps it was the very strain of independence that
Cornelius manifested now and then that attracted him to the younger
man. For Cornelius was always admirably detached and commendably plain-spoken. He made no secret of his determination not
to allow his own modest aspirations as a composer to be sacrificed
to the ruthless egoism of Wagner. He never cherished the smallest
illusion as to certain weaknesses in the great man's character. " I
say in a word ", he noted in his diary on the 3rd February, 1863,

> " that his morality is weak and without a true basis. His whole life-
> course, along with his egotistic bent, has ensnared him in ethical
> labyrinths. He makes use of people for himself alone, without any
> real feeling for them, without even paying them in return the tribute
> of pure piety. Within himself he has been too much intent on making
> his mental greatness cover all his moral weaknesses; I fear that pos-
> terity will be more critical." [11]

The " oriental ", " satrapic " luxury with which Wagner's enemies in Munich were to reproach him later is evident enough in the
way he celebrated the Christmas of 1863. Though he had little
cash just then, he airily informs us in *Mein Leben*, he was thoroughly sanguine as to the future; so on Christmas Eve he invited his
particular friends to his house, gathered them round the tree, and
gave each of them what he calls " an appropriate trifle ". For light
on the " trifles " we have to turn to Cornelius's letter of the 11th
January to his sister Susanne. " The mad Wagner ", he writes,

> " had fixed up a big Christmas tree, and underneath it a royally rich
> table for me. Just imagine: a marvellous heavy overcoat — an elegant
> grey dressing gown — a red scarf, a blue cigar-case and tinder-box —
> lovely silk handkerchiefs, splendid gold shirt studs — the *Struwwel-*
> *peter* — elegant pen-wipers with gold mottoes — fine cravats, a meer-
> schaum cigar-holder with his initials — in short, all sorts of things
> that only an Oriental imagination could think of. It made my heart
> heavy, and the next day I gave half of them away, and only then was
> I happy — to Seraphine the gold studs, to Ernestine a lovely purse
> with a silver thaler inside, to Gustav Schönaich a sash, to young Ruben
> the cigar-holder, to Fritz Porges the pen-wiper, something to each of

---

[11] CABT, I, 698.

my house people, a yellow handkerchief to Marie, a red one to Frau Müller . . . to Herr Müller the tinder-box, to Karl Müller a new waistcoat from myself, in place of which I kept the one from Wagner."

All this for Peter alone! What Wagner's other guests received is not recorded in history.

To all this there could, in the nature of things, be only one end.[12] Wagner's optimism had been largely based, apparently, on the fantastic prospect of a marriage with a wealthy widow — Frau von Bissing, the sister of Frau Wille, — a plan that came to nothing, and on the perhaps not quite so fantastic idea of a profitable visit to Russia in the following spring. This latter scheme seems to have foundered owing to a delay in the post to Russia: a letter which he despatched to Moscow on the 2nd February did not arrive until the 23rd March, when it was too late to have any relevance to the concert season of the spring and summer of 1864. It was probably in consequence of the collapse of this plan that, as he confessed to Pusinelli later, he " lost his head "; perhaps more than one creditor had been induced to stay his hand only because of what Wagner had promised him after his return from Russia. In the early days of March he was making desperate efforts in every quarter to raise enough to stave off the disaster he now saw to be impending, but all in vain: friends and acquaintances alike seemed to be tired of him. At last there was nothing for it but flight if he was to escape the imprisonment to which defaulting debtors were still liable in Austria.

On the afternoon of the 23rd March he left Penzing for Mariafeld, feeling that Frau Wille was one of the few people who could and would offer him shelter till his fortunes changed. He spent a couple of days in Munich. He found the town in mourning for the late King, Maximilian II, who had died on the 10th. On one of his walks through the gloomy streets Wagner saw in a shop window a photograph that attracted him mysteriously: it was that of the

---

[12] Even the pretence of hoping to give *Tristan* at the Opera had been abandoned long ago. Vienna did not hear the work until after Wagner's death.

We read everywhere of *Tristan* having been "given up in Vienna after seventy-seven rehearsals" — a phrase without any real meaning. If "rehearsals" is to be taken in the ordinary sense of the term, seventy-seven is a ludicrous exaggeration. If the hours devoted to the coaching of the singers are to be taken into account, seventy-seven is perhaps an under-statement.

singularly handsome boy who had succeeded to the Bavarian throne, and who, unknown to him as yet, held in his hands the destiny of Wagner and of his art.

Wagner had still enough vitality left in him to write, while in Munich, a humorous epitaph for himself:

> Hier liegt Wagner, der nichts geworden,
> nicht einmal Ritter vom lumpigsten Orden;
> nicht einen Hund hinter'm Ofen entlockt' er,
> Universitäten nicht 'mal 'nen Dokter.

It was his last gallows grin at life for some time. In Mariafeld he remained until the end of April. The head of the house had been abroad when Wagner arrived there: on his return he made it unmistakably clear that he had no intention of harbouring the fugitive indefinitely. Frau Wille did everything in her power to heal Wagner's wounds. He tried to occupy his mind with books; but his soul was gangrened with bitterness against the world, which, in his opinion, had cruelly denied him the simple right to live.[13]

---

[13] See a typical outburst recorded by Frau Wille, quoted in Vol. II, p. 408.

CHAPTER IX

THE RESCUE

1

DURING THOSE tortured weeks in Mariafeld, Wagner, as he said later, had a kind of mystical intuition that a dramatic turn in his fortunes was bound to occur before long. It was unthinkable that he, Richard Wagner, should go down to final defeat and extinction; and the nearer the Fates edged him towards the abyss the more convinced he was, in spite of all his misery, that something would happen to save him from the ruinous fall. Certainly his position had never been so desperate. After the fiasco of the *Tristan* rehearsals in Vienna it was unlikely that any other theatre would take up that seemingly impossible work, while belief in the ultimate impracticability of the still unfinished *Ring* was by now fairly general, even among his friends and well-wishers. His debts were by this time colossal for a man in his circumstances; and after the publicity given to them by his flight from Vienna it was unlikely that he would enjoy much credit anywhere in the future. Vienna itself, as a place of residence, was henceforth closed to him; and the Vienna Opera happened to be, after Berlin, the most important institution of its kind in the German-speaking countries. Most of his friends, especially those who had any money, were tired of him and a little afraid of him; they had come to regard him as congenitally incapable of running his life with ordinary prudence, and they dreaded any further demand on their purses. Wille had shown him conclusively that he wanted nothing more to do with him. The Wesendonks obviously would not house him, though they were willing to provide him with 100 francs a month during his stay at Mariafeld: this, however, he declined to accept. According to *Mein Leben*, as soon as he heard of the offer (presumably from Frau Wille), he " announced to Frau Wesendonk his immediate departure from Switzerland, and requested her, in the friendliest fashion, to consider herself as relieved of all anxiety concerning him, as he had arranged his affairs in accordance with his own wishes." He heard later, he tells us, that " this letter, which she [Mathilde] may possibly have considered compromising ", was returned by her to Frau Wille unopened.[1] It all points to the plainest reluctance on the part of Otto and Mathilde to open a fresh chapter of embarrassments for themselves through personal contact with him. He was within a few weeks of his fifty-first birthday, without much prospect of income except by concert conducting, which repelled and exhausted him. He had in a drawer, precisely as in 1860, three complete new works and two-thirds of a fourth, with no apparent possibility of the production of any of them. From whatever point of view he looked at his life, it must have seemed a complete and irrevocable failure. Yet the very hopelessness of it all kindled a mystic hope

---

[1] Nothing is known at first hand of the contents of this letter: but in an article *Uber einen unbekannten Brief Richard Wagners an Mathilde Wesendonk und seine Geschichte*, in BFF 1937, pp. 152–158, Dr. Strobel gives us some hitherto unknown details of its after-history. It appears that Mathilde declined to receive from Frau Wille the letter which Wagner had left behind him at Mariafeld for her. He did not hear of this until some weeks later, when Frau Wille passed on to him a letter in which Mathilde gave her reasons for having acted as she did. In his reply he says that his Mariafeld letter to Frau Wesendonk had been "a last letter, a holy letter:" "Let her exert herself, then", he continues, "to find me again: she had me at one time and knew me; that she could lose me and misjudge me I can understand but not excuse. Let her atone for it!".

In October 1865 Frau Wille at last persuaded Mathilde to accept the letter: the contents of it made Mathilde feel that it was imperative that she should write to Mariafeld about it. Frau Wille, in her turn, thought it her duty to send this letter of Mathilde's to Wagner. He read it first alone, then in company with Cosima. He returned it to Frau Wille with a letter of his own of the 22nd October, in which, in his now well-known fashion, he attributes everything that had gone wrong in May, 1864 to the "weakness" of Mathilde. On the evening of the same day he went to Vienna, leaving behind him this letter of his to Frau Wille, either because he had forgotten to post it or because, on further reflection, he had decided not to do so. Cosima came upon it, and apparently the terms of it gave her a fair notion of those of the undelivered "last" letter of May, 1864. She seems to have given strong expression to her wounded feelings in a letter to Wagner, who replies in an entry in the "Brown Book" of the 24th. In this he admits he was in the wrong as regarded her, confesses that he ought never to have shown her Mathilde's letter, and, in his customary style, mobilises all the resources of his dialectic to justify himself from first to last vis-à-vis Mathilde. Further entries in the "Brown Book" show that Cosima was not easily appeased; and so in December we find him writing in his worst vein to Frau Wille: "I cannot and should not leave that letter, that last letter, in those hands [Mathilde's]. I cannot, after all I have borne and suffered, allow that positive lie to continue to exist that flourishes there as a deceptive atonement." Presumably Frau Wesendonk then returned him his letter through Frau Wille. This episode, of course, marked the definite end of the old relations between Wagner and the Wesendonks, though the outward courtesies were always maintained between them.

in him. Only where there are graves, as Nietzsche says, are there resurrections.

And already, unknown to him, his saviour was planning his rescue. The unexpected death of King Max II on the 10th March, 1864, at the age of fifty-two, had placed on the Bavarian throne a youth of eighteen-and-a-half [2] who had long ago adopted Wagner as his idol. As we have seen,[3] the boy, when not yet thirteen, had been thrilled, in February 1858, by the accounts given him by his governess of the Munich production of *Lohengrin;* this world of romantic idealism was the one in which he himself already lived and moved and had his being. Three years later, at his urgent request, his father had commanded a performance of the work in Munich (on the 16th June, 1861), in which Schnorr von Carolsfeld, " guesting " from Dresden, sang the title-part. This, however, was not, as is generally supposed, Ludwig's first acquaintance with *Lohengrin:* his letters to Wagner make it clear that he had heard the work in Munich some four months earlier, on the 2nd February, 1861, the Lohengrin being Moritz Grill. It was not until the 22nd December, 1862 that Ludwig heard *Tannhäuser.* In February, 1864, shortly before his accession to the throne, he himself had been instrumental in bringing about a further performance of *Lohengrin* in which Niemann sang as " guest ";[4] and with each hearing of the work the boy plunged more and more ecstatically into the world of Wagnerian romance. Meanwhile he had studied Wagner's prose writings perhaps more ardently than anyone else in Germany or Austria outside the small circle of the elect. On his Uncle Max's piano he had found Wagner's *Art-Work of the Future* and *The Music of the Future:* these he read and re-read. He learned the texts of the Wagner operas by heart: and there still exists a list of Wagner's published prose works drawn up by a Munich bookseller, Christian Kaiser, on the 19th November, 1863, at the request of the young Crown Prince. One of the Ministerial Councillors assured Gottfried von Böhm that Ludwig's tutor, Professor Steininger, presented him at Christmas 1858 with *Opera and Drama* — strange

---

[2] He was born on the 25th August, 1845 — in the *Tannhäuser* year, as Wagner loved to remind himself and his friends.

[3] See Vol. II, p. 540.

[4] Niemann sang also in two performances of *Tannhäuser* during this "guest" engagement.

reading for a boy of thirteen! The *Lohengrin* saga, and Wagner's operatic treatment of it, had a peculiar fascination for him: he had been drawn to it, no doubt, by the pictures dealing with the legend which adorned one of the rooms of the castle of Hohenschwangau, in which a good deal of his childhood had been spent. Even as a boy he sealed his letters with a cross and a swan. So thoroughly had he assimilated the Wagnerian style that in his letters to Wagner he was liable at any moment to break out into profuse alliteration in the manner of the *Ring*.

2

There had also come into his hands a copy of the public issue (1863) of the *Ring* poem, in the preface to which Wagner had enlarged upon the hopelessness of his trying to get an adequate performance of the work under the ordinary conditions of the degenerate German theatre of the day, and had sketched his plan for a production, under festival conditions, in one of the smaller towns. The German theatres, he had said, had no sense of style; all the nation could boast of was a few singers of distinction, who, however, were scattered about in the various opera houses. For his purpose not only these singers but the right kind of stage designers and machinists would have to be gathered into the one focus and trained by himself for the new tasks with which they would be confronted in the *Ring*. He wanted, again, an invisible orchestra; and this would be practicable only in a provisional theatre designed for that and other special purposes of his own. Furthermore, the audience he had in view for the creation of this new national artwork would be one that had escaped, for the time being, from the conditions of ordinary opera-going in the large towns, where, tired out by their day's work, people went to the theatre merely for an evening's amusement. In time, he hoped, these model performances of a work in which the drama was as important as the music would bring about a much-needed change in the attitude both of theatre producers and of the public towards the existing masterpieces of opera: they " might give the impetus to a genuinely German style of musico-dramatic production of which there is not the slightest trace at present."

The means for the production of the *Ring* could be provided only in one of two ways, he had continued. A number of German art-lovers might combine to raise the necessary funds; but when he looked round upon his fellow-countrymen he could indulge himself in small hope of this. A German Prince with some conception of his duties towards German art, however, could, without much difficulty, realise the new ideal in his Court theatre. " Will this Prince be found? " were Wagner's final words: " In the Beginning was the Deed! " [5]

This despairing cry had reverberated in the head and heart of the ardent young Crown Prince of Bavaria; he had resolved that if ever it should lie in his power to do so he would convert Wagner's dream into reality. Suddenly, in March 1864, the boy found himself King, legally of full age, free to indulge himself in any fancy. He had had no training whatever for the responsibilities of state that were so suddenly thrust upon him; and as yet no one had more than the barest inkling of the unusual individuality that was soon to reveal itself. The future reckless spender of millions on fantastic architectural plans had been limited, as a boy, to pocket money of a few shillings a week. Even as a child, however, he had a strong sense of his importance as heir to the Bavarian throne; he kept his younger brother Otto strictly in his place, even in their games. In later years he was to develop decided leanings towards absolutism, Louis XIV of France being his ideal. From the first he had shown signs of being a visionary; the inner world of his imagination was already more vital for him than the outer world. By the time he ascended the throne the main features of a character that was eventually to puzzle or amuse all Europe were already beginning to define themselves. He loved the country and hated large towns [6] — his own capital in particular, in which the air stifled him and the sight and sound of the mob nauseated him. He was constitutionally out of tune with his relations, especially his commonplace mother,[7]

---

[5] The Foreword will be found in RWGS, VI, p. 272 ff.

[6] "Oh how I envy you your quiet untroubled retreat in dear Triebschen!" he wrote to Wagner in 1869, after having been nearly five years on the throne. "Oh how I long to escape from the horrible bustle of the town into my beloved mountains! For freedom is in the mountains — is everywhere, indeed, where mankind does not break in with its misery."

[7] He could never quite forgive her for being a Prussian.

whose " prose ", as he put it, used to spoil for him the poetry of the solitude of his favourite Hohenschwangau. He believed that it was best to keep majestic mountains unravished by railways and unsullied by the trippers they were sure to let loose on nature's sanctuaries. He had a strong distaste for the pompous ceremonial of Courts, and suffered agonies of boredom at the official dinners and other functions he was sometimes compelled to attend. He preferred the talk of men of culture to the chatter of women, and had no use for the fripperies of the sex-comedy. He had no liking for the conventional royal mountebankery of playing at soldiering. He suffered scheming priests and politicians and other knaves and fools anything but gladly. He had not only the intellectual but the physical *pudeur* of the sensitive solitary, so that he enjoyed the theatre in general, and Wagner's works in particular, most fully when he could listen to the performance either quite alone or in the company merely of a few choice spirits built more or less on his own model, who would not break in upon his dream with the customary gabble of theatre-going humanity.[8] In short, he exhibited so many signs of exceptional sanity that it was a foregone conclusion that the world would some day declare him to be mad; for the majority of men always find it difficult to believe in the sanity of anyone who is not only markedly different from themselves but betrays no great desire for their company, and shows the most uncompromising contempt for their standards of value. His " madness " has accordingly become a legend; yet there is no proof, and there never was any proof, that he was insane in either the strict medical or the strict legal sense of the term.[9]

---

[8] Ernst von Possart, Regisseur (later Intendant) of the Munich Court Theatre from 1872 to 1887, tells how the King sent for him one day and said in an angry tone, "I can no longer get any illusion in the theatre with people staring at me all the time and following every movement of my face with their opera glasses. [The reader may need to be reminded that in those days the lights were not lowered during dramatic or operatic performances]. I want to see the spectacle, not to be a spectacle myself for the multitude." On one occasion Ludwig left the theatre in the middle of an act because of the way he was being stared at. All this was particularly annoying to him in the small Residenz Theatre. See Possart's reminiscences, *Erstrebtes und Erlebtes*, 1916, p. 256, etc.

[9] See Appendix II.

The story goes that the Cabinet Secretary, Franz von Pfister-meister, noticing one day that the young King was pensive and un-happy, asked him if there was anything he particularly desired; whereupon Ludwig said, " Find Richard Wagner for me! " The version given by Pfistermeister himself in later years to the his-torian Gottfried von Böhm [10] was to the effect that in the first weeks of his reign Ludwig used to examine the Munich Strangers' List closely, asking many questions about it, and evidently being in quest of something. One day he asked Pfistermeister why Wagner's name was not in the list. The Secretary replied that there were many Wagners in the world: which of them had the King in mind? Ludwig's answer was that for him there was only one Wagner — Richard Wagner; and Pfistermeister was ordered to find him. Little did the poor Cabinet Secretary know, when on the 14th April he set out upon his search, what a plague he was about to bring on his own head! [11]

Julius Fröbel, writing his memoirs some twenty-five years after that date, was of the opinion that the call of Wagner to Munich had really been the work less of the King himself than of the politicians — Ludwig, so to speak, had had the card they wanted him to draw " forced " upon him by the conjurers.

"From first to last", says Fröbel, "the artist was the puppet of po-litical intrigue: it was this that not only drove him out but had brought him there in the first place. Originally he was regarded by the spon-sors of the political plan hatched in Regensburg as the most suitable instrument for working upon the young and inexperienced King who felt such enthusiasm for him. [The story of the Regensburg plot will

---

[10] BLKB, p. 43.

[11] Only six days before, Wagner had written to Peter Cornelius, "My situation is an extremely anxious one: it is poised on the slenderest balance: a single jolt, and all is over, to the extent that nothing more can ever come out of me, nothing, nothing! A *light* must show itself: a *man* must arise who will help me energetically *now:* then I shall have the strength to repay the help: otherwise, I feel — nothing!" RWFZ, pp. 372, 373.

On the 9th May, a few days after the news of Wagner's rescue had become public, Cornelius wrote prophetically to his brother Carl: "Just imagine: only a few weeks ago I was saying, 'Well, the first Ludwig occupied himself with painters, King Max with savants and poets: what if the present King were suddenly to become interested in music, and infatuated with Wagner?" CAB, I, 766.

be told later: see p. 396]. In order to make him [Wagner] useable for this purpose, Pfistermeister, with whom the plan did not originate, was induced to bring him to Munich. The King's longing for the creator of the musical masterworks he so much admired merely played, in this affair, the same rôle as, in other cases, the sensual desires of a prince whom political intrigue provides with a mistress." [12]

Fröbel may have been to some extent right in this surmise, far-fetched as it may seem at first sight. We have to remember that he himself was an expert in political wire-pulling, that he knew personally most of the leading politicians of the day, and that his own political work in Munich and elsewhere brought him into the closest touch with Pfistermeister and the other ministers in the years immediately following 1864.

Pfistermeister traced Wagner to his Penzing house, but found that he had left it a fortnight or so before. The Cabinet Secretary wanted to take back with him a photograph for the King; but as the servant would not allow him to do so he had to content himself with annexing a pen and a pencil. It seems to have been Pfistermeister who told Böhm [13] that in the cellar of the house were a hundred bottles of champagne which the creditors, assuming them to belong to the landlord, had not seized; they found it difficult to believe that all this wine could have been laid down by a man so impecunious as Wagner notoriously was. The Secretary informed the King by telegram of his failure to find the composer: Ludwig's answering letter of the 17th, dated from Schloss Berg, was recently found among Pfistermeister's papers: [14]

---

[12] FEL, II, 406–7. We may perhaps see a partial confirmation of Fröbel's theory in a passage in a letter of the 12th May, 1864 from Count Blome, the Austrian ambassador in Munich, to his chief in Vienna. After saying that the composer of *Lohengrin* has come to Munich, that he has been granted a stipend by the King, and that there is a good deal of feeling in the town against Wagner, Blome continues: "No doubt Wagner will cost the King a good deal of money; but it would be a sad thing if at his [Ludwig's] age he could not do something foolish. Much more serious, in my opinion, is the fact that his entourage has already begun to tell him how handsome he is, and how handsome the women find him." The politicians were no doubt ready and willing to experiment with more than one technique in order to induce the boy to leave political matters entirely to them.

[13] BLKB, p. 44.

[14] HNBJ, p. 601. Pfistermeister died in 1912, at the age of ninety-two. His diaries, memoranda and other papers, if ever published in full, will no doubt throw much new light on the Ludwig-Wagner story. They were drawn upon to some extent by Arthur Hübscher for his article HNBJ.

"Baron Moy and I had just started on a walk in the park when your telegram was brought to me. The contents horrify me! My resolution is quickly taken. Go after R. Wagner as quickly as possible, if you can do so without attracting attention. I hope this will be possible; it is of the utmost importance to me that this long-cherished wish of mine shall soon be gratified."

4

Having learned from Friedrich Uhl,[15] the editor of the Vienna *Botschafter,* that Wagner was now in Switzerland, Pfistermeister returned to Munich and reported to King Ludwig on the 20th. Owing to the Court mourning after the death of Princess Augusta it was not until the 30th that Pfistermeister received the order to resume his search for Wagner. On the 1st May he called at Mariafeld: he happened to be already acquainted with Wille. Wagner had left on the 29th April, however, for Stuttgart, where his friend Kapellmeister Karl Eckert was at the head of the local opera.[16] From Basel, where he had broken his journey, he had written to Frau Wille saying once more that he would some day return to Mariafeld, and asking her to preserve for him " his lodging and her friendship ". She had to reply frankly that to her great regret she could not fall in with his plan for a return. This must have been the last bitter drop in his cup, though he mastered himself sufficiently to reply from Stuttgart, on the 2nd May, that he now shared her view of the matter. " My immediate future is still uncertain ", he continued. " A doctor whom I have consulted recommends Cannstadt." The Eckert family was well disposed towards him, he said — Eckert's wife, by the way, had a comfortable income of

---

[15] See *supra*, p. 205, and Vol. II, p. 37.

[16] "He would first of all, he told my husband, go to some spa or other to restore his health", says Frau Wille: "then he would have a look at the theatres in Stuttgart, Karlsruhe and Hanover, to see if a performance of any of his works would be possible there." He had talked cheerfully of coming back and occupying, apparently, a smaller house in the Mariafeld grounds: he would summon Bülow and Cosima to him there, and during the summer they would make much music together. "Wille was astounded, and said neither Yes nor No."

On the eve of his departure he said to Frau Wille, "My friend, you do not know how great my suffering is, nor the depths of the misery that lies before me." She could only reply, "No! not misery! Something will happen. I do not know what, but it will be something good, something different from what you think. Have patience: good fortune will come." RWEW, pp. 84–5.

her own — and he had hopes in connection with Baron Gall, the Stuttgart Theatre Intendant, though, he added, a performance he had seen at the local opera the day before had put him woefully out of tune. As a matter of fact, Gall at once promised him a performance of *Lohengrin,* and paid him the fee for it in advance.

In Stuttgart, where he had arrived on the 29th April, he put up at the Hotel Marquardt. With his usual ache for companionship he had telegraphed to Wendelin Weissheimer, who was at the moment in Osthofen, asking him to come to him at once. Weissheimer joined him the next day: he found Wagner fretted and anxious, apparently at the end of his resources in money and in friends, and dreading arrest at the instance of his creditors. He wanted to find some quiet place in which he could hide himself till the storm had blown over, and perhaps make enough progress with the composition of the *Meistersinger* to extract a further payment from Schott. Weissheimer suggested the Rauhe Alb, and undertook to share his solitude there. As Wagner wished to attend the matinée performance of *Don Giovanni* [17] on Sunday, the 1st May — no doubt to see if there was any likelihood of the Stuttgart company being equal to *Tristan* — their departure was arranged for the following Tuesday.

5

On the Monday evening Wagner was at Eckert's house: there the card of someone describing himself as " Secretary to the King of Bavaria ", was brought to him. Disturbed to find that his presence in Stuttgart was known, and probably suspecting a ruse on the part of some relentless creditor or other, he sent word that he was " not there ". On returning to his hotel he was informed by his landlord that a gentleman from Munich wished to see him on urgent business. He reluctantly made an appointment for the next morning at ten o'clock: he slept badly that night, nerving himself to meet the misfortune he was sure was impending. In the morning Pfistermeister was shown up to his room: he announced himself as

---

[17] The part of Don Giovanni was sung by Angelo Neumann, "guesting" from Vienna. In later years this Neumann, then an impresario, was to render signal service to Wagner by giving a series of complete performances of the *Ring* (the first outside Bayreuth) with a touring company.

the Cabinet Secretary [18] of the young King of Bavaria, expressed his pleasure at having found Wagner at last after having pursued him through Vienna and Mariafeld, told him he had instructions to take him back with him at once to Munich, and handed him a photograph of Ludwig and a ring. Wagner is in error when he says in *Mein Leben* — in a passage dictated in 1880 — that these gifts were accompanied by a letter from the King. Pfistermeister brought him only a verbal message to the effect that Ludwig was his " most ardent admirer ", knowing his writings by heart, that everything he needed would be placed at his disposal in Munich, and that the *Ring* would be produced there. Weissheimer's summary of the message can be trusted, as it was taken from a letter he wrote to his fiancée on the 4th May.[19] It was arranged that Wagner should leave with Pfistermeister the next day. On the morning of that day Wagner wrote a grateful letter to the King, in which the very accent and colour of their later correspondence are foreshadowed:

> " These tears of the heavenliest emotion I send to you, to tell you that now the marvels of poetry have come as a divine reality into my poor, love-lacking life. And that life, its last poetry, its last tones, belong henceforth to you, my gracious young King: dispose of them as your own property."

Wagner lunched with the Eckerts and Weissheimer on the 3rd; during the meal, by one of those dramatic coincidences in which his life was rich, the news came that Meyerbeer had died in Paris in the early hours of the 2nd. According to *Mein Leben*, Weissheimer " burst into boorish laughter over the strange coincidence that Meyerbeer, who had done me so much injury, had not lived to see this day." We may conjecture that the coincidence had not

---

[18] This term may possibly set up false connotations in the mind of the English reader. The Cabinet Secretaryship was a peculiarity of the Bavarian system of administration. The Cabinet Secretary was a confidential official attached to the person of the monarch. Some of the parties in the State held the institution to be unconstitutional; under Ludwig II, in particular, there was at times a good deal of discontent because the King mostly kept in touch with public affairs through the reports of his Cabinet Secretary instead of by direct contact with his ministers. The post was obviously one of great influence; hence Wagner's desire, in later days, to have it occupied by someone devoted to the royal interests as Wagner conceived them. An explanation of the working of the institution of the Cabinet Secretariat, with a historical account of its origin, is given in BLKB, pp. 82–87.

[19] Weissheimer's story of the happenings of those days will be found in WEWL, p. 259 ff.

failed to strike Wagner also. During the next three or four days, while the still dazed Wagner, now in Munich, was at last realising that he had not been dreaming all this time, Meyerbeer was lying on his bier with bells on his hands and feet, and watchers always present to catch any sign of returning consciousness, for he had always had a morbid fear of a seeming death and premature burial. But Meyerbeer was dead in all truth, and with him had died an epoch in the history of opera. The future was with his younger rival.[20]

At five o'clock on the afternoon of the 3rd, Wagner left Stuttgart with Pfistermeister, not without a touch of comedy in the proceedings, if we are to believe Weissheimer's account of what happened at the railway station. Pfistermeister, it seems, was already in his first-class carriage when Wagner arrived, not long before the train was due to start. The penniless Wagner had assumed that his own ticket would be provided for him; discovering that he had been mistaken, he ran after the departing Weissheimer and asked him to obtain one for him. Weissheimer bought one at his own expense, chased back down the platform, and just had time to throw the ticket into the compartment as the train went out. According to Weissheimer, Wagner had brought no money with him to Stuttgart: he had paid his hotel bill with a snuff-box which had been presented to him by someone of high standing in St. Petersburg. Weissheimer asked Wagner why he had not handed *him* the snuff-box, which was very valuable, to convert into cash: Wagner's reply was that henceforth he would be free of money cares.

6

Pfistermeister arrived in Munich with his charge that night, and the next afternoon Wagner had his first audience, lasting an hour-and-a-half, with the young King. Each was deeply moved — Ludwig, for all his sense of the dignity of his office, feeling a slight

[20] In the Gare du Nord, where the coffin halted for some hours on its way to Germany, speeches were made in the dead man's honour. The address "in the name of the French nation" was given by no less a person than Wagner's friend Emile Ollivier! Meyerbeer's music, he declared in the best official style, had shown the nations that they were brothers: he had forged a bond that linked "the fatherland of Beethoven, Mozart and Meyerbeer with that of Hérold, Halévy and Auber."

embarrassment in the presence of this man of genius who had been his ideal for so many years, while Wagner was touched by the youth and virginal beauty of the King, the ardour of his boyish idealism, and the pathos inherent in his obvious inexperience not only of kingship but of the world. The generous-hearted boy felt curiously and nobly shamed by Wagner's thanks for the assurance given him that not only would it be made possible for him to complete the *Ring* but that he could count on a production of it answering in full to his desires. " He bent low over my hand ", the King said a few days later to his cousin, the young Archduchess Sophie Charlotte,

> " and seemed moved by what was so natural: he remained a long time in that position, without saying a word. I had the impression that our rôles were reversed. I stooped down to him,[21] and took him to my heart with the feeling that I was taking an oath to myself to be true to him to the end of time." [22]

" Rest assured ", the King wrote to Wagner on the 5th,[23]

> " that I will do everything in my power to make up to you for what you have suffered in the past. The mean cares of everyday life I will banish from you for ever; I will procure for you the peace you have longed for in order that you may be free to spread the mighty wings of your genius in the pure aether of rapturous art. Though you were unconscious of it, you were *the sole source of my delight* from my tenderest youth onwards, my friend who spoke to my heart as no other did, my best teacher and educator. I will repay you everything to the best of my ability. O how I have looked forward to the time when I could do this! I hardly dared indulge myself in the hope so soon to be able to prove my love to you."

Alone among the German princes he showed, now and later, a real comprehension of the man he had to deal with. " He has the

---

[21] Ludwig was over six feet in height.

[22] HRWV, p. 13. Julius Hey was at this time music teacher to the family of Duke Maximilian, the father of the Archduchess Sophie. His conversation with her took place shortly after the King had given her his first impression of Wagner. Ludwig, it seems, had been struck by the composer's animated manner and his unconquerable will. At this first audience he had talked of his opponents with humour rather than with bitterness. His greatest trouble, he said, was always with the singers and the Kapellmeisters; the latter made no distinction between him and Verdi and Meyerbeer.

[23] This is the letter — the first in the long chain of their correspondence — which Wagner, in later years, wrongly imagined to have been presented to him by Pfister-meister in Stuttgart.

profoundest understanding of my nature and my needs ", Wagner wrote to Mathilde Maier on the 5th May: " he offers me everything I want for my life, for my creative activity, for the production of my works. I am to be simply his friend: no appointment, no functions. He is the ideal fulfilment of my desires." And there was something mystical for him in the thought that his ship had been saved in the very hour when the waves and rocks seemed to have been bent on utterly destroying it.

7

It was the King's wish that they should be able to commune alone with each other in the country; Pfistermeister was accordingly commissioned to find for Wagner a house somewhere on the Starnberg Lake, in the near neighbourhood of the royal residence of Berg. The Pellet villa [24] at Kempfenhausen, near Starnberg, proving to be the ideal thing for the purpose, the King rented it for his new friend's use during the summer months. Before settling there, however, it was necessary for Wagner to take the first step towards settling his affairs in Vienna. He left for Vienna on the night of the 9th, provided by the King with enough money to meet his more pressing needs there. His letters to various friends during the first week or two after his summons to Munich show him tackling the question of his debts and his finances in general with the energy and dexterity customary with him when matters of this kind engaged his serious attention. We see, too, how grievously the thought of the loss of his Vienna belongings still rankled in him. He even managed to persuade himself that his friends there were directly answerable for all his misfortunes! Had he not taken their advice in March to flee the city, he told them, King Ludwig's emissary would have found him in Penzing in the middle of April, and much suffering and expense would have been spared him.

He had convinced himself by now that had he *not* left Penzing he could have come to an amicable arrangement with his creditors; none of them, he was certain, would have proceeded, after hearing his explanations, to extremes against either his person or his property. He had even contemplated returning from Mariafeld to talk

[24] Later the property of Prince Baratinsky, and known as the Villa Seehaus.

to them. But this scheme had been ruined, according to him, by the hurried sale to which his friends had consented in order to avoid the publicity of a distraint. His curiously perverted sense of logic made it appear to him that nothing could have been so calculated as this sale to set the law in operation, as it merely encouraged the smaller creditors to make trouble! There would have been no sense, therefore, in his returning from Switzerland: with what " face ", he asked Standhartner, could he have stood up to his creditors after that? How could he have hoped to impress them with his eloquence in a room stripped of its furnishings? The forced sale had brought shame on him without doing much good to anyone else: it had realised absurdly little for the creditors, and now he would have to buy back his favourite chattels at much higher prices. He is gracious enough now and then to admit that the friends whom he had entrusted with plenary powers when he left Vienna had done what seemed best to them according to their lights; but his anger with them is unmistakable. That he had given them, and was now again giving them, an immense amount of trouble over matters which were really no concern of theirs, never seems to have crossed his mind.

He asked one of these Vienna victims of his, Heinrich Porges, to have his beloved Erard piano sent to Starnberg. Dismayed to find that it had been sold, he urged Bülow to persuade Bechstein to present him with one of his pianos. Bechstein was kind enough to do so. The purchaser of the bulk of Wagner's belongings seems to have been a Herr Rebel. With this gentleman he had an interview on the 11th that left him in so agitated a state that he could not bring himself to see his good friend Standhartner: it would appear, however, that in the sequel Herr Rebel behaved towards him in a way for which even he could manage to find a word or two of praise. Like the consummate strategist he was, he keeps all the complicated threads of his affairs in full view at every moment. No move is made in one direction without consideration of its possible effects in another. His creditors, he tells the Vienna friends, are to be assured that all his debts will be fully paid before long; but no one is to be told as yet that he is now under the King of Bavaria's protection, lest that should cause the creditors to insist on more in ready cash. We even find him doing a bit of smart financial jug-

glery in Dresden. On the 7th May he tells Porges that he will be
in Vienna on the morning of the 10th, bringing with him " a small
contribution towards what is most pressingly required for putting
my affairs in order " — the said " small contribution " being no
less than 4,000 florins, granted him as a free gift by the King; by
this time, too, he must have known that a yearly stipend of 4,000
florins had been, or soon would be, assigned to him. On the 8th he
telegraphed in high humour to Standhartner that he would be in
Vienna on the 10th with " the necessary musical material for the
concert on the 11th ". Yet on the very day — the 7th — on which
he announces to Porges his coming with the " small contribution "
he writes to his Dresden friend Pusinelli asking for " a little more
patience regarding your loan of 100 thalers ", which he " hopes to
repay shortly "; he furthermore begs Pusinelli to continue to co-
operate with Frau Tichatschek in " taking care " of Minna for
" only a very short time still."

Manifestly he intended to employ a certain amount of the King's
bounty not in extinguishing his debts but in providing himself with
a few luxuries — a procedure he was to repeat more than once on
a later occasion. And he is shrewd enough, as always, to adapt his
technique to the local circumstances. To his Vienna friends, who
have to repel the assault of his hungry creditors, he lays stress on
his favourable situation as the protégé of the King of Bavaria.
But to Pusinelli — and to the other Dresden people, of course,
with whom Pusinelli is his intermediary — there is not a word,
not a hint, of this. He does indeed tell Pusinelli that he will probably be spending " this summer in the Bavarian highlands for the
benefit of my health and my work ", " at the invitation of the
young King of Bavaria "; but he says nothing at all about
the substantial financial help he is receiving from Ludwig. On the
contrary, he tries to make it appear that he hopes to reimburse
Frau Tichatschek and Pusinelli himself out of the profits of a quite
mythical concert tour in Russia in the near future.

From subterfuge of this merely negative kind he was soon to
pass, where the good Pusinelli was concerned, to bland perversion
of the truth. The newspaper reports of his good fortune in Munich
soon brought a number of old creditors knocking at his door. Frau
Kriete, for instance, imagining, as he plaintively put it in a letter

of the 2nd October to Pusinelli, " that I am swimming in money here ", demanded " 1,822 thalers interest on the principal of 2,000 thalers that was refunded." The mere suggestion of this barbarous purpose is sufficient to unlock the floodgates of his self-pity. " It is madness ", he tells Pusinelli, " to lay claim to such a thing now: it *is* possible that the time will come when I shall really be rewarded for my work and suffering: in order to obtain this, I must now still have great patience." Should not " Herr Musikhändler Müller be persuaded, for honour's sake, to pay over something more to Frau Kriete? "

His " monthly income — in addition to free residence — is 100 florins. With that I am content. Naturally I can only pay my wife's annual allowance of 1,000 thalers out of my occasional receipts from other quarters." These, however, come in irregularly; so he asks Pusinelli to see that she gets her 250 thalers punctually at the quarter dates, " in return for which I would at once send you whatever I receive from abroad. . . . If such an arrangement were possible, how much would it contribute to the peace of mind that I need so badly! " [25] His allowance from the King, however, was not 1,200 florins per annum but 4,000. This he had been receiving as from the 1st May: in addition he had had from the King free gifts of 4,000 florins on the 10th May and 20,000 florins [26] on the 10th June; while he must already have been negotiating with the King and the Treasury the agreement of the 18th October, under which he was to receive, only a fortnight after this letter of the 2nd reached Pusinelli, a further 16,500 florins under the contract for the completion of the *Ring*. It is not often that we find Wagner stooping to deliberate untruth; but in the present instance we must find him guilty. The fact was, of course, that he had no sooner begun furnishing his fine Briennerstrasse house than the poor man found himself without a florin in the world for anything but satrap luxuries. But even while heroically tightening his belt and biting on the bullet in this fashion he was benevolently determined that Minna should not suffer with him; her allowance should never be a single day overdue so long as there was a gulden left at the bottom

---

[25] Needless to say, this letter was not included in the official reprint of letters from Wagner to Pusinelli. It was published for the first time in RWAP, pp. 167–169.
[26] 4,000 florins of this were for his removal expenses.

of Pusinelli's purse. And to do him full justice, he informed his old Dresden friend, as soon as the terms of the *Ring* contract were settled, that for the next three years he would be able to pay Minna's quarterly instalments regularly.[27]

In order to round off the story we have had to leap forward a little in time and space. Let us return to the Munich days of mid-May.

Wagner was back in Munich on the morning of the 13th, bringing with him his servants Franz and Anna Mrazeck, their three-months-old child, and the old dog Pohl; and the next day he went to the Villa Pellet, where he remained, for the most part, until the early part of October. On his birthday, the 22nd May, he received from his royal friend a portrait in oils for which, during the last few weeks, the King had given special sittings to the artist.

Those were idyllic days: the King's carriage called for him each day to take him to Berg, a matter of a mere ten or fifteen minutes' drive. The conversation of the pair turned mostly on Wagner himself, his vicissitudes in the past and his plans for the future: he was astonished to find that Ludwig knew his writings as perhaps no other man did, and regarded himself as his pupil. Wagner read and expounded some of his works to the King, who looked upon him as the last word in human wisdom. " You cannot believe ", he wrote to Wagner on the 28th May,

" how super-happy I am to see at last, face to face, the man whose sublime nature attracted and captured me with irresistible might from my tenderest youth. I used to long incessantly for the time when I should be able to compensate you in some degree for the many cares and sufferings you have had to endure; now, to my delight, the moment has come, now that I am wrapped in the purple mantle; and now that I have the power, I will use it, so far as I am able, to sweeten life for you. You shall wear no bonds: you shall be free to devote your-

[27] RWAP, p. 171. This letter of the 15th October also appeared for the first time in Mr. Lenrow's volume. It will be observed that Wagner still does not give Pusinelli the smallest hint of how much he had received from the King during the last five months. "Above all", he writes, "I thank you for your efforts to bring Madame Kriete to reason. I confess that my breath almost fails me when I see myself again and again exposed to calamities of this sort. One should first only grant me peace of mind again, so that I could bring about, and profit by, favorable conditions for the performance of my new works: if then I should be rewarded only to some extent according to my deserts it will be a pleasant duty for me to settle every obligation of the past." The letters relating to the Vienna visit of the 10–13th May will be found in RWFZ, pp. 383–398, KLRWB, V, 3–5, and RWAP, pp. 161–163.

self to your magnificent art solely as the spirit moves you. When, as lately, I see you before me, deeply moved, and I can say to myself, ' Through you he has been made happy and contented ', then I am so happy, and more than happy, so borne aloft on exquisite emotions, that I imagine heaven to have come to earth. You often say to me that you owe me much; but all that is the merest nothing in comparison with what I have to thank you for." [28]

8

By the end of the month of their first meeting, Wagner had sketched out for the King, at the latter's request, a " programme " for the pair of them for the coming years. During the summer of 1864, while the Court was still in mourning, there were to be private auditions of scenes from the *Ring*, with Bülow or Klindworth at the piano: in the autumn he himself was to conduct in the Munich Court Theatre selections from his as yet unperformed works: the winter was to see a production of *Lohengrin*, if a local tenor adequate to the name-part could be found — if not, they were to wait until the right man could be engaged as " guest ". In the spring of 1865 *Tristan* was to be given (with Schnorr von Carolsfeld), and in the early winter the *Meistersinger*. *Tannhäuser*, in the Paris version, was to follow in 1866, the complete *Ring* in 1867–8, *Die Sieger* in 1869–70, *Parsifal* in 1871–2, and " my happy death " in 1873.[29] It will be seen that at this time he still contemplated writing *Die Sieger*, and that his intention was to finish the *Meistersinger* before setting to work again at the *Ring*. " The *Meistersinger* ", he had written to Schott on the 6th May, " *must* be produced next January." One reason, of course, for his desire to

---

[28] KLRWB, I, 12.

[29] This "programme", the original draft of which is still in the Wahnfried archives, is repeated almost literally in a letter of the 1st June to Bülow. He is blissfully dead to the world, he tells Hans: the price he has to pay for this death is the fulfilment of certain "solemn promises" which alone bind him now to life. "What has befallen me here is something heavenly, undreamed-of, incomparably splendid and beautiful. It is beyond understanding, because it has *never* happened before; and only to me could anything of the kind have happened. I myself have begotten it for myself out of the depths of my longing and my suffering: and a Queen had to bear this son for me."

In the letter to Bülow, but not in the plan drawn up for the King, he talks of giving *Lohengrin* as well as *Tannhäuser* in 1866. It is interesting to note that just then he had Therese Tietjens in his mind for Isolde. On this point something will be said later.

complete the work quickly was to receive payment for the score
from Schott. It was apparently in the late summer of 1864 that he
decided to complete the *Ring*, which " alone is now sympathetic to
me ", before taking up the *Meistersinger* again: just then, he told
Bülow, he was " too highly-wrought to concern myself with Beckmesser and Pogner." [30]

Wagner spent the 11th to the 14th June in a second visit to
Vienna, putting the final touch on his business affairs there — or a
touch as approximately final as was possible to a man who could
never quite square up to the hard realities of his finances. King
Ludwig, as we have seen, had given him a fresh gift of 20,000
gulden; and he had already been granted, as from the 1st May, a
yearly stipend of 4,000 gulden. (The amount was understated for
public purposes, partly not to arouse envy, partly for fear of encouraging Wagner's creditors to be unpleasantly importunate). [31]
The allowance, plus a rent-free house wherever he might choose to
live, was a liberal one: according to Stemplinger, the highest salary
at that time of a Bavarian Councillor of the Supreme Court of
Justice was only 2,800 florins, of a grammar school head master
2,200 florins, of a Royal Councillor 1,800 florins, and of the head
of a ministerial department, after eighteen years' service, 3,900

[30] Letter of the 23rd September, 1864, in RWHB, p. 223.

[31] The salary was given out as 1200 florins (a florin was the same as a gulden) by
the *Neuer Bayrischer Kurier* on the 10th May.

Bavaria was at that time a relatively small state with no more than 7,000,000
inhabitants and a comparatively small revenue. The King's Civil List was fixed at
about 2,000,000 gulden, but a quarter of this was earmarked for the still-living
Ludwig I (the grandfather of the young King), who had abdicated in 1848. The
private fortune of Max II, being held in trust, was not at Ludwig's personal disposal.
After provision had been made for all necessary expenses, such as the maintenance
of the Court, the payment of household servants, the upkeep of royal buildings, and
so on, the Civil List showed a disposable surplus of only some 300,000 florins. (RLW,
I, 76; SWM, p. 21). The reader should bear these figures in mind as the story of
Wagner's financial relations with Ludwig unfolds itself. The politicians soon became
disturbed over what a writer in 1868 called the "galloping consumption" that attacked the King's purse after Wagner came on the scene. As early as the 25th June,
1864, before the more grandiose schemes of the pair had taken definite shape, Kapellmeister Esser (who had learned a good deal about Wagner in Vienna), wrote to Schott
"His Bavarian Majesty will soon find that he is not in a position to cope, out of his
modest means, with the Wagnerian passion for prodigality."

We have to remember, in justice to Wagner, that he regarded, or almost managed
to convince himself that he regarded, the grant of 16,000 gulden as merely an advance
on his future earnings from the German theatres, which would all be hypothecated
to the Crown. He makes this point perfectly clear in his letter of the 6th June to
Pfistermeister. See KLRWB, IV, 37.

florins.[32] Munich at that time was a town of only 166,000 inhabitants, with a very modest standard of living, as may be gathered
from the earnings of the smaller fry of the musical profession. A
young student who might take to teaching would receive no more
than six kreutzer an hour. Joseph Rheinberger thought himself
lucky to make 8 gulden a month by twenty lessons. As Court organ-
ist he received 60 florins a year, as teacher of the piano at the
Conservatoire 300 gulden a year — later increased by 100 florins
a year as professor of composition. In 1864, at the age of twenty-
five, he was made solo-repetitor (coach) at the Opera; his yearly
salary for this was only 600 florins, but he was well pleased
with it.[33] The economic standards of the town being what they
were, it is little wonder that there was considerable resentment in
some quarters as the full extent of the King's expenditure upon
Wagner became known during the next year or so.

Apart, however, from the large sums granted him at various
times for special purposes, such as the payment of his debts, there
was little or nothing to justify unfriendly comment, either then or
now, in the financial side of Wagner's relations with the King. He
set forth his position in detail in the memorandum already referred
to which he submitted to Pfistermeister on the 6th June; the draft of
it is still at Wahnfried. It was the King's express desire, he said,
that henceforth he should be relieved of the necessity of earning his
living in the ordinary way, in order that he might devote himself
exclusively to the completion of the big works he had in hand.
Such chance receipts as might accrue to him from outside sources
in the coming years he could apply to clearing off his debts, the
outstanding balance of which he estimated at 16,000 florins. The
grant of this lump sum to him he would regard, therefore, only as a
loan. The best course, were that possible, would be for him to obtain this sum from a private lender; but as that would be difficult

---

[32] SWM, p. 22. For the rough English equivalents of the currency of those days
see Vol. I, p. 20. Wagner himself, when sending the good news to Mathilde Maier
on the 18th May, describes his allowance as "enormous for Munich"; a year's salary
was to be paid to him at once.

It will be observed that while he could tell Mathilde Maier, as early as the 18th
May, the correct amount of his stipend, as late as the 2nd October he was assuring
Pusinelli that it was only 1,200 florins per annum. Mathilde, presumably, was not a
creditor; Pusinelli was.

[33] See KJR, pp. 33, 35, 67, 68.

for him without the formal guarantee of the King, a loan from the latter would amount to the same thing in the end and would save everyone's time and trouble. Henceforth, to the end of his days, he, and those of his works which were still unwritten or unperformed, would belong to King Ludwig and no one else. The manuscripts would be the King's property; it would be for the King to decide when and where and how the works should be produced; the King alone could grant to other theatres, or withhold from them, permission to perform the works.

It had always been a source of profound grief to him, Wagner continues, that he had had to deliver up, for mere existence' sake, his earlier works to the German theatres, where they were produced in a manner of which he could not approve, as merely part and parcel of the common opera repertory.[34] The King agreed with him that he ought to be spared this ignominy in future: the projected Munich productions of his new works were to be models for the rest of the world, and the King would have it in his power to refuse permission for their performance to any other theatre that could not, or would not, guarantee an adequate production on the Munich lines. Cutting himself off, therefore, as Wagner would necessarily do, from the ordinary sources of income open to him as an operatic composer, it was obviously only right, he argued, that the King should advance him what was required to pay off his debts. It was hardly a commercial relation of the common kind: it was simply the outward and visible form of the spiritual bond between them. Furthermore, to devote himself henceforth entirely to the service of the King would mean that he would be unable to earn money, as he had done in the past, by giving concerts of his own works: this would be impossible in any case, on a scale that would really matter, anywhere except in Russia and England, and that would involve

---

[34] "The King's pure and lofty mind knows, and feels deeply", Wagner tells Pfistermeister, "the distress and humiliation in which I, with my earnest, ideal striving, find myself in my relations with the modern theatrical public. One of the main sources of my sufferings has been that hitherto I have been compelled to treat my works merely as merchandise to be sold to the opera houses: these works of mine have, at bottom, attained general currency only in so far as they could be dragged down to the level of the common opera repertory; and to every fine mind that witnessed this distortion of my purpose it must have been a profound sorrow to see the degradation to which I am always exposed when I am compelled, merely for a pittance, to hand my works over to the theatres."

a drain on his time and his strength which would impair his ability to complete the works he had pledged himself to complete for the King.[35]

9

All this was not only plain common sense on Wagner's part but the simple statement in formal terms of the King's own views as expressed in the talks between them. It is impossible to understand the nature of the future relations between the pair unless one realises from the start that it was never a case of " royal patronage " of the usual German kind; again and again, in their correspondence, they both smile at the vulgar notion that theirs is merely the ordinary story of a benevolent King and an " opera composer " who was to grace his Court with the fruits of his labours. We of today may be unable to comprehend how any man could attribute such significance to the theatre as a seminal factor in civilisation as Wagner did: [36] but of the fact that he did so there can be no dispute, nor of the material sacrifices he was always willing to make for his ideal. It was only the sheer necessity of living that made him consent to what he regarded as fundamentally misrepresentative performances of his works; he looked upon almost every sale of them to the commercial theatres as a degradation of himself and of them; and more than once he refused them to the theatres at the cost of his pocket. Verdi held that the box office takings were the " only infallible thermometer " of the success or failure of an opera. There can be no quarrel with that point of view; Verdi, like all sensible artists, held that if the public wanted to benefit by the work of his brain it should be prepared to pay for it as it would have to do for any other commodity, and therefore the more it had paid the more " successful " the work must be judged to be. But this was not Wagner's view. He did not look

[35] KLRWB, IV, 37–40. The document was first given in full in SWMZ, pp. 300–303. In the latter, the amount asked for by Wagner (16,000 florins) appears, by a printer's error, as 6,000.

In his answering letter of the 9th June (KLRWB, IV, 40), Pfistermeister tells Wagner that he is delighted to inform him that the King freely and willingly grants him the 16,000 florins, which he can either collect at the royal treasury or have in the form of a draft on Vienna. "The King", Pfistermeister adds, "wants you to be free from anxieties, and gladly lifts the present burden from your shoulders."

[36] On this point see Vol. II, p. 125 ff.

upon himself merely as an " opera composer ", turning out operas in order to live, and competing in the open market with other opera composers for the public's money. He felt that he had a mission — that of regenerating Germany through the theatre. Had he possessed an income which would have raised him above material cares he would never have wished for much more than a few performances of his works that should serve as models not only for operatic production but for operatic composition. In the early 1870's, when the tide had definitely set in his favour, he could have had as many performances as he liked, and on his own terms.[37] Why then, at that very time, when the ball was at last at his feet, did he part company from the King — painful as the separation was for him — and shoulder, at the age of nearly sixty, the colossal burden of creating a theatre of his own? Simply because the experiences of the last few years had shown him that even Ludwig and Munich could not be trusted to realise his ideal in all its uncompromising purity.

But in 1864 he and the King were in perfect accord. Ludwig shared his contempt for the ordinary theatre. This was well enough as a place of entertainment for the generality, but neither of them had much interest in the philistine crowd, or in the theatre as just an easy entertainment for tired people after a day's work. The whole object of the King's patronage of Wagner was to preserve him henceforth from the necessity of commercial and artistic compromise with the ordinary theatre; and as this would of necessity involve his surrender of the sources of income normally open to him as composer and conductor, manifestly he was entitled to an allowance that would secure his material existence while he completed the huge creative plans he had in hand — especially as the Bavarian state, through the King, was acquiring a series of ultimately valuable properties in return. And though even this reasonable and equitable arrangement would have excited envy and brought Wagner enemies,[38] human nature being what it is, neither

---

[37] See his letter of the 5th May, 1870 to King Ludwig (KLRWB, II, 306), in which he speaks of the new generation that has sprung up, a generation formed by himself, largely composed of young people who not merely admired his music but shared his view of the cultural importance of music drama.

[38] Many of Wagner's bitterest opponents in Munich belonged to the circle of minor poets and littérateurs who had basked in the favour of King Max, but suddenly found themselves of no account with his successor.

the envy nor the hatred would ever have attained mass and momentum enough to have brought about his downfall had his hands been quite clean in all other respects. But his hands, unfortunately, were not quite clean, nor was his head always quite clear. Undoubtedly he went, bit by bit, too far in his personal, as distinct from his artistic, demands on the royal purse; his intellectual influence over the King threatened, before long, to make matters difficult for the latter's ministers; while he was soon to compromise himself gravely by his association with Cosima von Bülow. Had he had a good case in each of these matters he would still have found it hard enough to beat off the attacks of the more irreconcilable of his enemies in the Press and elsewhere: with a case so weak at many points as his, the fight was lost almost as soon as the battle was joined.

10

During the first few weeks of his call to Munich, however, there was hardly a cloud on the horizon. Pfistermeister was so far friendly; the politicians watched and waited; the Press, in spite of the prejudice still existing in some quarters against Wagner on account of his " revolutionary " record, sheathed its claws out of consideration for the boy King; the older members of the royal family, the Queen Mother and Ludwig's uncle Maximilian in particular, and with them the nobility, viewed with a certain apprehension this " infatuation " on the inexperienced young monarch's part with a man of Wagner's political past and unsavoury reputation in money matters, but as yet they saw no danger either to themselves or to the country in this " infatuation ". The politicians were unaware as yet of the strength of Wagner's hold upon the King's mind, and in any case, they thought, a boy so unversed in affairs of state, and with his head bursting with romantic notions about art, would prove to be easily manageable by them in everything that really mattered. And so, for a time, all went well. Wagner and the King swam in a sea of mutual admiration and delight; each of them was convinced that, thanks to them, a new era was dawning for humanity in general and for Bavaria in particular.

It was only gradually that the situation defined itself for outside observers, some of whom began to have a dim sense that both their own interests and those of the state were likely to be threatened before long. Wagner was sometimes indiscreet enough to talk of his enormous influence on the young King; and though, at first, he was tactful enough to refrain from any act that could excite suspicion,[39] more than one of his friends sensed the possibilities of trouble. It was a necessity to him, personal and artistic, to gather round him as many of his old associates as he could attract to Munich: he needed them at the moment to pour his ardent talk into, and he would soon need them also to help him in his plans for reorganising the musical life of the capital. He made strenuous efforts all through the summer to induce Cornelius to leave Vienna and settle in Munich; but it was not until the end of December that the exceptionally clear-sighted younger man could be persuaded to take the plunge. Bülow being essential to Wagner for the model performances that were in the offing, he secured for Hans a post as pianist to the King, as preliminary to a more important appointment in Munich. Other friends and satellites from abroad were to follow; and it was not long before the local musicians who until then had had all the threads of Munich musical life in their hands began to feel that their dominion was threatened. They would have been more than human had they not closed their harried ranks against him.

For a while, however, such public comment as there was upon him was good-natured enough, mostly making play in humorous fashion with the already standard theme of the absurdity of his libretti. On the 26th June, 1864 the Munich *Punsch* came out with a parody of a kind that was not uncommon in those days. " Richard Wagner ", it said, " has already sketched, during his residence by the Starnberg Lake, a new opera, about which we are able to give some information. It is entitled —

---

[39] "You can imagine ", he wrote to Weissheimer on the 20th May, "the prodigious envy I have to face: my influence on the young King is so great that all who do not know me are very uneasy. The large salary that the King has settled on me will therefore be designedly given out as less than it really is. For my part, I keep quite in the background, as indeed my nature and my necessity dictate; and I spread calm in all directions, so that bit by bit the fear will die down. Lachner can already be twisted round my finger. Like myself, the King *despises* the *theatre*. We let everything go along here and wait for the time when we can give this also a nobler direction in the right way."

STARNBERG LAKE MYSTERIES,

A Grand Future-Musical Trilogy consisting of three operas:
1. Salmon and Salmon-Maiden. (Romantic Genre).
2. The Bleeding Lake-Nixy, or the Fateful Nail at the Bathing-Place. (Historical Genre).
3. A Mad *Waller:* Ichthyopsychological Soul-Picture. (Mixed Genre).

With an After-Play:

An Antediluvian Church-Dedication, or The Stab with the Stone Knife. A Picture of Men and Morals in the Pile-Work Period."

There follows a clumsy burlesque of the *Ring* as the philistines of that day saw it, though some of the touches are not without humour: the Young Salmon, for instance, commences his monologue thus:

" Ha! (*A chord*) — How? (*A stronger chord*) — Oh! (*A long stretch of music*) ";

and the sketch ends with the words: " The whole work presents no scenic difficulties, and can be easily produced, given good-will and no intrigues against it." [40]

The humour, it will be seen, is a trifle heavy-handed and splay-footed; but there is no real malice apparent in it, and the parody was not likely to stir up any ill-will against Wagner. This attitude of good-humoured toleration, however, was not to last long.

[40] The sketch will be found in full in RLW, I, pp. 69–70.

CHAPTER X

WAGNER AND LUDWIG

1

THE PRESENT-DAY reader of the Ludwig-Wagner letters must not be misled into drawing wrong conclusions from the effusively romantic tone in which most of them are pitched. The constant protestations of undying " love " on both sides must be viewed in the light of the period, the race, the language of the race,[1] and the peculiar circumstances of the King and the composer — the eager boy lavishing on the great artist the wealth of affection that had been suppressed in him by his cold family life, the older man profoundly touched by not only the fine qualities of the youthful King's nature but the pathos of his difficult position. In view of Ludwig's homosexuality in later years it is perhaps not surprising that malicious gossip should have hinted that his relations with Wagner were of that nature. For this gossip there was never the slightest foundation in fact. Wagner never had any leanings whatever in that direction; among the documents preserved in the Wahnfried archives, indeed, is a jotting of his of 1873 in which he notes that " there is one thing about the Greeks that we shall never be able to understand, a thing which separates them utterly from us: their love — pederasty." [2] And when writers like Aldo Oberdorfer try to make out that Ludwig was subconsciously and by second remove, as it were, attracted to Wagner because he found in *Lohengrin* " the perfect incarnation of the masculine ideal ", that " the desire for a beautiful form already ran in his blood: it drew him downwards, to the flesh, however much he might believe that he was in search of it for the redemption of his spirit ", the only suitable comment is

---

[1] A number of German words expressive of affection or esteem do not necessarily carry, in the original, the same significance as they would in English in a literal translation. Thus when Wagner addresses Pfistermeister in one of his letters as "Theuerster" it does not at all imply that the Cabinet Secretary was the object of his ardent love.   [2] KLRWB, I, xv.

that this is " psycho-analysis " getting drunk on its own words. Ludwig's letters show him to have been much more interested in certain other works of Wagner than *Lohengrin:* his passion for *Tristan* and for *Parsifal* and his constant urging of Wagner to carry out his plan for *Die Sieger* are in themselves proof sufficient that what drew and held him to Wagner was not the under-workings of a perverted sex instinct but a community of idealism and mysticism.

Nor is there any foundation whatever for Oberdorfer's summing-up of the situation as a boyish illusion on the one side and cunning calculation on the other, a shrewd insight on the composer's part into the real source of the innocent young King's " infatuation " and a still shrewder determination to use him for his own ends. All this reads impressively enough so long as we do not submit it to the test of facts: the trouble is that it has no congruence whatever with the realities of the matter as revealed by the correspondence of the pair, which, by the way, was not available in full when Oberdorfer wrote his book. It is only in novels, or in " best-seller " biographies infected by the spirit of the novel, that human beings are constructed on quite such simple lines as these. Wagner's mind and motives were infinitely more complicated. Still less truth is there in Oberdorfer's theory that Cosima was even more the King's " evil genius " than Wagner was.

> " More coldly egoistic than he [Wagner], Cosima, now at his side as accomplice and ally, helped him to torment this sick brain [Ludwig's], conscious of the evil she was working. Yet it was not for this reason that Ludwig showed so manifest an antipathy towards her: he saw in Cosima a rival, one who contended with him for the heart of Wagner: he felt towards her the immensely simple and complex sentiment to which we give the name of jealousy." [3]

All this is mere novelistic fantasy. It is contradicted at every point by Ludwig's letters: his brain was not in the least " sick " during the years now under consideration; and he had the sincerest regard for Cosima from the first day of their acquaintance to the last. Nor is there any evidence whatever that Cosima's attitude towards the King was merely " coldly egoistic ". Believing, with Wagner and with the King, that the Wagnerian ideal of art was of supreme im-

---

[3] OIRF, pp. 58–60.

portance to humanity, she naturally did all she could to bring it to full realisation. Like Wagner, she too did some indiscreet things when the question of art pure and simple became inextricably interwoven with questions of politics and the party moves of politicians; but she was no more " coldly egoistic " in these circumstances than anyone is who throws his whole energy into the attainment of an end which he believes to be of the first importance to humanity.

Montaigne, in his whimsical way, wondered whether, in his games with his cat, it was he who was using the animal for his own purposes, or vice versa. Writers of today who take the easy line that Ludwig was " used " by Wagner and Cosima might profitably ask themselves whether the " using " — if we are to employ that objectionable term — was not reciprocal. No one was ever able to " use " Ludwig for purposes of his own if those purposes did not happen to be also Ludwig's; not a single instance in his career can be adduced of anyone, in politics or in private life, having succeeded in doing that. The central spring of his being, indeed, lay in his proud sense of himself and his office: he was quick to resent any encroachment, real or suspected, on these; and the mistrustful look which more than one observer noted in his eyes in the early years of his reign was no doubt a hint of a swift instinctive mobilising of his defensive resources against a dimly apprehended danger — young as he was, he knew already that his very youth would cause more experienced people to regard him as an easy prey. Some of the politicians, indeed, made that mistake at the outset of his reign: with a boy of less than nineteen years old on the throne, who had had no formal training at all for his office, they saw themselves prospectively as the unhampered rulers of the country.

" All the ministers ", says Fröbel, " had offended the young King by the crude way in which they tried to terrorise him: Schrenck [the Minister for Foreign Affairs] had been particularly rough and inconsiderate. The whole crew had, as a matter of fact, mutinied, hoping that the inexperienced young monarch lacked the spirit to show a judgment and a will of his own. It was actually an attempt at a bureaucratic insurrection." [4]

They soon discovered, to their mortification, that they had completely misread Ludwig's character; as Fröbel says, the last part

[4] FEL, II, 315–6.

the young King had any intention of playing on the political stage was that of a mere super. Already there was strong in him that tendency to absolutism which became so marked in his final years. In the earliest days of his reign he had told his grandfather, the ex-King Ludwig, and his uncle, the Grand Duke of Hesse, that he would not be kept under — that the only position worthy of a prince was one like that of the Tsar of Russia.

The simplest reading of the situation so far as Wagner and the King were concerned would seem to be this — that even as a boy Ludwig had had a romantic vision of himself, as King, leading the German people along ideal paths, and that the Wagner writings simply happened to strike into that vision at the critical time and with tremendous impact. It was not that he first became fascinated by Wagner's operas and then used his power as a king to realise them in the theatre, but rather that in Wagner he saw the artist who had given, and alone could give, substance and form to *his* vision of the ideal: in furthering Wagner's aims he was really accomplishing his own. It is significant that his letters to Wagner, from the very commencement, speak not of " your " ideals and purposes but of " ours " — of " our intentions ", " our activities ", " our work ", " our furthering of art ". " The world does not understand us ", was his constant cry in his letters — " us ", be it observed, not " you ". The stupid world could see in their association only a king " protecting " a composer: it missed the very essence of the brotherhood — that composer and King were equal co-partners in the great emprise, that it was not a mere case of an artist providing the works and a monarch the patronage, but of a monarch finding his very self realised in an artist. " When we two have long been dead ", Ludwig wrote prophetically to Wagner in the early days of their union, " our work will still be a shining example to distant posterity, a delight to the centuries; and hearts will glow with enthusiasm for art, the God-given, the eternally living! " *Our* work, not Wagner's alone! That was written in August 1865, in the full flush of Ludwig's happiness at having at least brought *Tristan* into being in the theatre. Three-and-a-half years later, in February 1869, at a time when fate had sundered them physically and each had suffered grievous disappointments and disillusionments in the sphere of mundane reality, we find the King again assuring Wagner that it is their common ideal alone that gives him strength to go on living.

"I *implore* you, dear Friend, to do what you can to make this performance possible [i.e. the *Rhinegold* in Munich]: oh, I need joys of this kind if I am not to perish in the whirlpool of trivial everyday life. Yet I do not withdraw myself from this; I even take pleasure now in the fulfilling of my kingly duties, which formerly I hated; I am interested in the affairs of government; even for the dry ministerial communications and reports of parliamentary debates I have been able to acquire as much taste as possible; it is a sad necessity. It is the prospect of the accomplishment of what I yearn for, the realisation of our ideals, that gives me strength for *everything:* we shall not go under, dear Friend! We shall accomplish everything, everything: I know it, I am as sure of it as that I live and breathe." [5]

To bear this in mind is to understand better how Ludwig succeeded as he did, often in most difficult circumstances, in distinguishing between the man and the artist in Wagner, and how little his occasional displeasure with the former could affect for any length of time his devotion to the latter. He could not, indeed, had he tried, have torn Wagner the artist out of his soul, for Wagner's art was only his own soul made manifest to him. It was perfectly natural that his vast love for Wagner's mind and art should overflow into love for the man himself, and sometimes find extravagant expression. But the love was never wholly blind; on every occasion when it became necessary to make a distinction between the man and the artist, and to translate that distinction into action, Ludwig acted promptly and firmly, often to the astonishment and discomfiture of Wagner.

2

In spite of all that has been written about Ludwig, an adequate study of his strange personality is still to seek. His complexities and contradictions make it very difficult for us to " compose " him. The easiest solution of the problem, of course, is to call him " mad " and leave it at that; but apart from the fact that, as we have already had occasion to observe, his " madness " was never in the smallest degree *proved* in either the strict scientific or the strict legal sense of that word, merely to call him mad does not help us very much

[5] KLRWB, II, 255.

towards a real understanding of him. The occasional inconsistencies of his nature and of his actions leap to the eye; but there may possibly, for all that, have been a unity underlying them which none of his biographers have been psychologists enough to discover. Some of them have made merry over those portraits of his in the early days of his kingship in which the grandiose ceremonial clothes of the monarch or the soldier seem not merely figuratively but literally too big for the meagre chest of the boy; the temptation is almost irresistible to see in it all a symbol of his pathetic impotence in a world of hard reality. But he was never a weakling, either physically or mentally; in his early thirties he developed physically into a powerful giant,[6] while mentally he often showed himself to be of harder stuff than some of the people who had thought they could twist him round their finger had bargained for.

Bismarck, who was no bad judge of men, had considerable respect for Ludwig's political judgment.[7] There is contemporary evidence enough of the attention he devoted to public affairs in the earlier years of his reign, and of the respect his ministers had for his quick grasp of things and his promptness and firmness of action when

---

[6] He was six feet three-and-a-half inches in height at the time of his death in 1886. One who was present at the post-mortem declared that he had "never seen such gigantic shanks", and that "auch die Geschlechtsteile seien wohlangebildet und gross gewesen." BLKB, pp. 635–6.

[7] The pair met only once, in August, 1863, when Ludwig was still Crown Prince; but "from the time he came to the throne", Bismarck writes, "to the end of his life our relations were good, and I was in fairly frequent correspondence with him: he always gave me the impression of a clear-headed ruler with a German-national outlook, though with a particular care for the maintenance of the federative principle in the German constitution and for the privileges of his own country within that constitution." Bismarck, *Gedanken und Erinnerungen*, I, 352 (1898). "His consciousness of his kingship", said Bismarck further, "was not mere vanity, his many-sided knowledge was not a mere showy pretence of omniscience, his statesmanlike activities were not foolish." The personal as distinct from the official correspondence of the pair during the 1870's and 1880's has not yet been published.

Prince Hohenlohe, who in December 1866 became Bavarian Minister of Foreign Affairs and President of the Council, and was in later years (until 1901) the German Imperial Chancellor, noted in his diary on the 15th April, 1865, "As regards Bavaria . . . we have the most amiable and engaging sovereign I have ever beheld. His is a noble and poetic nature, and his manner is so particularly attractive because one feels that his courtesy is the natural expression of a truly kind heart. He has plenty of brains, and character to boot. I trust that the tasks he has before him may not be beyond his strength." (HSM, I, 138).

In 1870, in a conversation with Delbrück, the King impressed this level-headed agent of Bismarck by his "astounding knowledge of canon law" [the question at issue was the recent promulgation of the doctrine of papal infallibility] and "the clearness and elegance" of his exposition.

action was called for. The popular notion of him as merely a phantast, an unpractical idealist who fell a victim to the wiles of Wagner, who spent his life indulging in fireworks and moonlight sleigh-rides and private theatrical performances, to the neglect of his duties as a king, who was slightly mad from the start and finally had to be put away because his insanity had become manifest and incurable, has no correspondence at all with reality. If his life went to pieces in his later years, it was not for lack of character in him but, in large part, from the fact that his very circumstances as a king, with absolute power in many matters, allowed certain elements in his nature to assert themselves disproportionately. But as to his inborn ability in practical matters there can be no question. One of his ministers, Düfflipp, assured Gottfried von Böhm [8] that " the King's apprehension of things was rapid and easy. It was not difficult to transact business with him; and I could not have wished for a better and at times more amiable master if now and then his unfortunate hobby-horses (*Liebhabereien*) had not got the upper hand of reason, and made a methodical conduct of business impossible." [9] On his accession to the throne he showed a keenness in his judgment of men that everyone found astonishing in one who had been brought up in such seclusion from the world.[10]

His inexperience in politics at the time of his accession was easily remedied; there he was quickly and rather cruelly schooled by hard facts. Part of his tragedy was that while he was equally inexperienced in other worldly matters, especially that of sex, in these his very position, no less than his own exquisite shyness, barred him both from friendly counsellors and from the easy initiations that come of themselves to young people in humbler walks of life. He was singularly ignorant in his early manhood's days of some of the commonest facts of life: he had once to ask for an explanation of the terms " natural son " and " rape ". It is probable, however, that his innocence and reticence in matters of this kind came funda-

[8] Böhm, whose biography of Ludwig (1921, second edition 1924) is the standard one, spent a long life in the official political world of Bavaria. As a boy he lived in Munich through the stirring Wagner days of the 1860's, and recorded his impressions of events in his diary. His later duties brought him into close contact with many of the personalities, from Pfistermeister onwards, who figure so largely in Wagner-Ludwig biography.

[9] BLKB, p. 14.

[10] See Paul Heyse's *Jugenderinnerungen und Bekenntnisse* (1900), p. 282.

mentally not so much from a deficiency of sexual vitality as from obscure sensual promptings which the lonely boy was too shy to discuss with others, and against which his longing for purity made him instinctively rebel at a time when he was too young even to be clearly aware that two sides of his nature were already at war with each other. It may well be that his passion, when no more than a child, for the texts of Wagner's operas was rooted in the dim feeling that they resolved for him certain moral difficulties which he did not as yet quite realise to be such, but which were none the less subtly operative within him. On this point his diary — or so much of it as has been published — which has been so unintelligently used to support the facile theory of his " madness ",[11] gives us, rightly considered, some curious and valuable clues.

3

The diary, which, in its published form, begins in December 1869, is largely the pathetic record of his lapses into homosexuality and his struggles against the vice, his bitter self-reproaches, tortured regrets, and frenzied vows of amendment. It has apparently escaped the notice of anti-Wagnerian readers of these sad pages that it is almost invariably Wagner and his opera texts that Ludwig summons to his aid to steel him in his hard fight.[12] " Accursed be I and my ideals ", he writes on the first page of the diary, " if I fall again. God be praised, it will not be possible again, for I am protected by God's holy will, by the King's august word! Only spiritual love is permissible: the sensual is accursed. I call down solemn anathema upon it "; and he quotes, for the heartening of himself, the words of the high-minded Wolfram in *Tannhäuser* —

> Du nahst als Gottgesandte,
> ich folg' aus holder Fern':
> so führst du in die Lande,
> wo ewig strahlt dein Stern.

---

[11] Its "editing" by Edir Grein is a deplorable exhibition of pseudo-psychiatry.

[12] At the time of the commencement of the diary Ludwig and Wagner had been already separated for three-and-a-half years. They met very rarely, indeed, in the years between the King's surreptitious visit to Triebschen, in May, 1866, and Wagner's death in 1883.

("Thou comest as a messenger from heaven, I follow from afar: thou guidest me into the land where deathless shines thy star.") Later he cites Wolfram's words to Tannhäuser —

> Ein Engel bat für dich auf Erden —
> bald schwebt er segnend über dir,

linking them up with the final lines of Wolfram's song to the evening star —

> Wenn sie entschwebt dem Thal der Erden,
> ein sel'ger Engel dort zu werden:

("An angel prayed for thee on earth; soon will it hover over thee with its blessing" . . . "When she soars beyond the vale of earth, there to become a blessed angel.")

That the Wagner whom the world had torn from him in December 1865 was often in his thoughts in these moments of anguished struggle with himself is shown by the quotation, on the 11th January, 1870, from *Lohengrin* (Elsa's confession of faith in her deliverer): though Ludwig quotes only the last two of the six lines, the preceding four were certainly also in his mind at the time —

> Mein Schirm! Mein Engel! Mein Erlöser!
> der fest an meine Unschuld glaubt!
> Wie gäb es Zweifels Schuld, die grösser,
> als die an dich den Glauben raubt?
> Wie du mich schirmst in meiner Noth,
> so halt' in Treu ich dein Gebot.

("My shield, my angel, my deliverer, who doubts not of my innocence! What greater guilt could there be than doubt that would rob thee of faith? As thou dost protect me in my need, so am I true to thy command.")

So it goes on throughout these moving pages. Years before, on the 13th September, 1865, the King, in a letter to Wagner, had quoted a line that had struck him in the first Prose Sketch of the *Parsifal* poem — "Great is the magic power of him who craves: yet greater still of him who renounces." "What greatness, what shattering truth there is in these words! O Parsifal! O Redeemer!" he had then cried. Did he already in 1865 feel within himself the necessity for the renunciation of cravings the meaning of which was as yet not clear to him? In August, 1871 he notes in his diary, " Redeemed September or October?!!!! ", following this up with the very words from the *Parsifal* sketch quoted above.

A bitterly regretted lapse on the night of the 14–15th October, 1872 is followed on the 16th by a citation from Elisabeth's appeal for Tannhäuser —

> Der Muth des Glaubens sei ihm neu gegeben,
> dass auch für ihn einst der Erlöser litt!

(" May he be strengthened again by the faith that for him too the Redeemer died! ") [13] This is immediately succeeded by two others of Elisabeth's lines —

> Um deiner Gnaden reichste Huld
> nur anzufleh'n für seine Schuld:

(" To pray the richest favour of Thy grace for his guilt.")

In a later entry the distracted man quotes once more from Wolfram's plea for Tannhäuser:

> O Himmel, lass dich jetzt erflehen,
> gieb meinem Lied der Weihe [Rache] Preis!
> Gebannt lass mich die Sünde sehen
> aus diesem edlen, reinen [hohen] Kreis!
> Dir, hohe Liebe, töne
> begeistert mein Gesang,
> die mir in Engels-Schöne [Engelsthönen]
> tief in die Seele drang! [14]

(" O heaven, I implore thee, consecrate my song. Let me see sin banished from this pure and noble company. By thee, O highest love, let my song be inspired, by thee, who struckest deep into my soul in angelic beauty.") This is followed by another citation of

---

[13] Ludwig gives the last line as "Dass auch für ihn einst der Erlöser *lebt*."

[14] The words in brackets represent the King's variants from the original. He knew the texts of the Wagner dramas by heart, and frequently cited them in his letters to Wagner. We can never be quite sure whether a slight departure from the original in the diary or in a letter was due to a slip of Ludwig's memory, or whether the change was deliberately made to match his train of thought of the moment more closely. Here and there the discrepancy is the result simply of Edir Grein's misreading of the King's script and of his ignorance of the source of a quotation. He gives, for instance, "Geburt" — which is pure nonsense — for "Gebannt" in the third line of the above quotation, puts a full stop after "Rache", and lets the "Preis" run straight on to the "Geburt"!

the lines already quoted on page 244, "Du nahst als Gottge-sandte ", etc.), and these again by the words, "Past for ever! I, the King! "

The year 1877 he hails as his " year of redemption ". " The royal lily triumphs and makes relapse quite impossible. LR [Louis Roi] . . . 1877 Redemption Year! . . . (*Nibelungen* year) RW and LR. . . ." Wagner is in his thoughts again a little later, when he quotes (with many modifications) the eight lines in which Lohengrin describes the yearly descent of the dove that brings with it the blessing of the Grail upon the Knights — the Grail, that preserves its chosen ones from earthly evil; it is to be observed that the King deliberately alters the final line from " who looks upon the Grail is safe from the night of death " to " safe from the might of sin ", — " der Sünde Macht " in place of " des Todes Nacht " — underlines this " Sünde Macht ", and adds a threefold " Amen! "

At the end of October, 1880 Wagner, passing through Munich on his way from Italy to Bayreuth, spent a few days in Ludwig's capital. On the 10th November he sat with the King at a performance of *Lohengrin,* and on the 12th — destined to be their last meeting — he conducted in private, at the King's request, two performances of the *Parsifal* Prelude: the poetic contents of the music he explained to his royal friend in a " programme note " that has since become famous.[15] " Profoundly significant ", the King notes in his diary for that day, evidently applying the lesson of sin and salvation to his own case. Two or three days later he left Linderhof for Hohenschwangau with his minion of the moment. There followed the usual lapse and the usual contrition: " Never again! Never again! Never again! " we read in the diary: " newly sworn in the octave of Good Friday." [16] Once more, then, the aspiration towards purity is associated with Wagner and with Wagner's poetic creations. On the 17th he wrote to Wagner telling him how deeply he had been moved by the Prelude and the programme note. He had just been re-reading the poem of *Parsifal* in surroundings that harmonised ideally with it — in the " Gurnemanz hut " which he had

---

[15] It will be found in RWGS, XII, 347.
[16] The various passages cited in the text will be found in TALKB, pp. 3, 5, 9, 21, 39, 53, 63, 67, 81.

had built in the woods a few years before, in an entrancing natural setting of meadow and lake and stream that was the counterpart of the Good Friday scene in the opera. There, no doubt, he pondered despairingly on the analogy of his own case with that of Amfortas. " This was the right place for it " [i.e., for the reading of *Parsifal*], he tells Wagner; " there too I see the holy lake in which Amfortas seeks healing, there I hear in spirit the sublime trombone tones resounding from the Gralsburg." [17]

4

It is manifest, then, that in the long, agonising combat between the body and the spirit — a combat the record of which reminds us of the self-rending confessions of some of the flesh-haunted monks of the Middle Ages — it was to thoughts of Wagner, and to the Wagner texts dealing with similar conflicts of the soul, that he fled for aid against his lower self. Even after Wagner's death it was to his memory that he clung for hope of salvation from his vice: the entry in the diary for the 13th February, 1886 — only some four months before his own death — runs thus: " Three years since the death of Richard Wagner: swore by his imperishable name, and before the image of the Great King, never again (sensual kisses)." [18] The conclusion seems warrantable that from the beginning of his adolescent life it had been the lofty spirituality of characters like Wolfram and Elisabeth and Elsa that had appealed to this boy who already felt dimly that the world of sense is at constant war with the world of the ideal. All through his letters to Wagner in the first period of their friendship there runs an unbroken thread of reference to this war, of aspiration towards the ideal. On the 11th December, 1864 he wrote to Wagner, after hearing fragments of the latter's works,

" I was borne aloft into super-terrestrial spheres; I drank in immeasurable bliss. But why do I try to describe this beatitude? For that, the poor toneless word does not suffice: I can only adore you, only praise the power that led you to me. More clearly and ever more clearly do I feel that I cannot reward you as you deserve: all I do, all I can ever do for you, can be no better than stammered thanks. An

---

[17] KLRWB, III, 189.   [18] TALKB, p. 113.

earthly being cannot requite a divine spirit. But it can love, it can venerate: you are my first, my only love, and ever will be."

Then follows, as usual, a citation from one of the operas, this time Wolfram's song in praise of purity in love —

> Da blick' ich auf zu einem nur der Sterne,
> der an dem Himmel, der mich blendet, steht:
> es sammelt sich mein Geist aus jeder Ferne,
> andächtig sinkt die Seele in Gebet:

(" I look aloft to one bright star in the blinding sky: my spirit finds itself: my soul is sunk in devout prayer.")

The evidence might be multiplied a hundredfold. The boy, as yet ignorant of life, was instinctively anxious to escape the soilings of ugly reality; and the evangel of his simple religion he found first of all in Wagner's poems, then in the man himself, with his manifest elevation, so far as art was concerned, over the murk and moil of common life. When, in December, 1865, Wagner was torn from him by the crude realities of the world, the centre-pin of his own existence was broken.[19] Had Wagner been permitted by Fate to spend the remainder of his life in Munich, the King's personal destiny for certain, and possibly the political history of Bavaria, would have been different from what they subsequently were. But whatever view we may take of Ludwig as he was in himself, one fallacy pure and simple must be discarded once for all — the fallacy that Wagner merely acted from first to last a part with the King, cunningly flattering him and encouraging him in his romantic illusions in order that he might the more efficiently use him for his own selfish purposes. Whatever seeming basis there might formerly have been for that superficial reading of the pair has ceased to exist since the recent publication of the hundreds of new documents bearing on the relations between the King and Wagner

---

[19] Oberdorfer would have us believe that it was the sight of Schnorr von Carolsfeld as Lohengrin in 1861 that played a decisive part in making Ludwig a Wagnerian — that is to say, in plain terms, that the boy was already homosexual *in posse*, and the stage figure ministered to his secret desire to find his ideal in the male form. But this is too far-fetched. Both Schnorr and Tichatschek were so corpulent that they repelled him physically: he felt that they clashed with his inner ideal of the super-sensuality of the Wagner characters. His passion, dating from his boyhood days, for the dove and the swan — he had them reproduced for him in a thousand ways, in seals, in figurines, in decorations and so on — had its roots in the potency of them as symbols of purity. He was a Wagnerian in spirit before ever he saw Schnorr.

which we owe to the editorship of Dr. Otto Strobel. The true explanation of Wagner's attitude towards Ludwig has been missed,
indeed, because of its perfect obviousness and complete simplicity:
Wagner was entirely sincere in his expressions of affection and admiration for the King. Each of them was right when he said that
they two understood each other but no one else understood either of
them and the true nature of the bond between them. Wagner had
been conscious from the beginning that the young Ludwig, ignorant
as he was of the world, had instinctively arrived at a simple truth
that had evaded all the other notabilities with whom Wagner had
come into contact, precisely because of its simplicity, perhaps —
that so exceptional an artist needed exceptional treatment if the
world for which he could do so much was to get the best out of him.
All the others, the German princelings and dukelets, even the Emperor Napoleon, could imagine no other way of helping him than
the ordinary one of making an occasional place for one of his
operas in the ordinary theatre repertory. It had touched Wagner,
at his first meeting with the King, to discover that Ludwig wanted
no service of the customary kind from him. He was not to be a
Kapellmeister; he was to hold no office, waste himself in no routine
duties of any kind; he was simply to be Richard Wagner, fulfilling
his mission to German culture in his own way; his works were not to
form part of the current repertory, to be handled in accordance with
the alien traditions of that repertory, but to be treated as something
apart from and superior to the usual theatrical routine.

5

The references in Wagner's letters to the King's perfect comprehension of him are many and varied, and they occur in all kinds of
contexts that rule out any and every suspicion of acting on his part.
The most convincing references of all are found in his " Brown
Book " — a depository of self-communings never intended for any
other eyes than his own and Cosima's. In August, 1865 he was
alone in the mountains, Cosima having gone with Bülow to Buda-
pest. The unhappy man confided his most secret thoughts to his
diary. " Oh heaven! " he wrote in it on the 20th. " Which of us understands the being by his very side? What do our dearest friends

know of us? Unless it [i.e., knowledge and understanding of us] comes from the stars, as with Parzival,[20] no one can learn out of himself alone who the other is." And a few days later, *à propos* of a visit of Cosima's to Liszt's friend Baron Augusz, " I also have made the Baron's acquaintance. It is the most charming people who are the most dangerous: we credit them with depth, a divine ' must ', — and then we blush for ourselves at some time or other for having gone much too far. One man only have I ever come upon with this divine ' must ' in his soul — my Parzival, my son in the Holy Spirit." [21]

It is a curious reflection today that Wagner and Ludwig were each of them really and truly understood only by the other and by one woman in addition. In the King's case the woman was his cousin, the beautiful and intelligent Empress Elisabeth of Austria, whose life was as tragic as his own; [22] in Wagner's case it was Cosima. The strain of melancholy and the sense of frustration in Elisabeth gave her, and her alone in his immediate circle, the key to Ludwig's unhappiness: her comment when she heard of his death in the Starnberg Lake in 1886 got nearer the heart of the matter than all the pseudo-scientific maunderings of the " psychiatrists " of that day or since — " He was not mad, but just lonely." As for Wagner, there can be no doubt that he understood the young King as no one else in Bavaria did. From the documents now available with regard to the period from 1864 to about 1868 it is easy to see what his counsel would have been had his advice been sought.

" None of you politicians and priests ", we can imagine him saying, " understand the King, because he is first and foremost what none of you are — an artist; an artist, it is true, in conception rather than in projection, whose impulses and intuitions are far beyond his capacity for expression. He cannot realise himself through himself, as the creative artist can, but only through an-

---

[20] His name for the King.

[21] KLRWB, I, LVII, LXI.

[22] She was born on the 24th December, 1837, being the daughter of Duke Maximilian of Bavaria. She married the Austrian Emperor Franz Josef at the age of little more than sixteen, in April, 1854. In January, 1889, at Mayerling, her son, the Crown Prince Rudolf, shot himself and a young actress, Marie Vetsera, with whom he was in love. In September, 1898 Elisabeth was assassinated at Geneva by an anarchist, Luigi Luccheni, who nonchalantly informed his judges that he had gone out that morning determined to kill some ruling person or other, it did not matter whom!

other — in this case myself. He is drawn as he is to me because in my work he finds himself as much as he finds me. He is very young, and the difficulties that in any event would confront an inexperienced youth so suddenly called upon to govern a kingdom are complicated and multiplied in his case by the fact that, at present, the ideal world counts for more with him than the real. You are anxious, to the verge of distractedness, to bring him to realise more fully the responsibilities and duties of his position. In that you are quite right, but the way you are going about it is entirely the wrong one.

" Let me remind you of one or two of the maxims of a wise Spaniard who understood human nature as few men have done. ' Find out each man's thumbscrew ', he has told us. ' It is the art of setting their wills in action. . . . You must know where to get at any one. . . . All men are idolaters, some of fame, others of self-interest, most of pleasure. Skill consists in knowing these idols in order to bring them into play. Knowing any man's mainspring of motive you have as it were the key to his will. . . . First guess a man's ruling passion, appeal to it by a word, set it in motion by temptation, and you will infallibly give checkmate to his freedom of will.' Apply now these precepts to your handling of the King.[23]

" His mainspring of motive, at present, is the desire to realise, chiefly through me, his youthful and necessarily somewhat vague ideals of mankind's regeneration through art. Give this mainspring free play for the time being and you will be able to influence the

---

[23] The politicians did discover later, when the burning question of Bavaria and Prussia came to the forefront, that the way to work upon Ludwig was by "knowing his mainspring", "finding out his thumbscrew" — in this case his sense of his own dignity as head of a state with fourteen centuries of unbroken political unity behind it. "When it became a matter of sovereignty and independence", says a modern historian, "he [Ludwig] manifested at an early date a lively interest in affairs: this developed with the years, and became so notorious that those who wanted to influence him made it their starting-point." (M. Doeberl, *Bayern und die Bismarckische Reichsgründung*, [1925], pp. 4–5). They could have worked upon him with equal ease, in the critical years between 1864 and 1867, had they realised that the way at that time to the King's "thumbscrew" lay through Wagner — not so much, all in all, through Wagner the individual as through Wagner as the living embodiment of Ludwig's own dreams of art. The trouble was that the politicians, not being artists themselves, were completely lacking in understanding of a nature like the King's. They should have made use of Wagner as an artist. But for that they were too unsubtle: they made the mistake of trying to use him simply as a politician; and when they realised that he had no intention of being their pawn in mere political intrigues they resolved to destroy him.

King, subtly, insensibly, in spheres *other* than that of art. Make him happy by letting him feel that he is doing some good in the world in the way that seems to him, at the moment, the most important: keep his spirit healthy by allowing his immense energy to find for itself its natural outlet. Do this and you will keep him so in tune with himself and the world that he will be quite accessible to the suggestion that, great as art is, it is not the whole of life, and that a monarch in particular must devote himself seriously to other things as well. You may some day succeed in making of him an ardent politician and administrator as well as an artist; but you will fail utterly if you try to make him these things at the cost of his self-indulgences as an artist.

" You are making every mistake that men in your position could possibly make. Instead of leaving the King's mainspring free to work first of all in its natural way, merely standing by in order to help him to make good other use of such tension in it as may not be necessary for his artistic purposes, you are dislocating the spring by your clumsy attempts to direct it. You are merely making him hate politics and mistrust not only politicians but mankind in general, for young as he is he is intelligent enough to see people like you for what you are, and not to believe blindly in any of you. So exquisitely delicate an instrument as this young King calls for a special technique, a superfine touch in performance on it: you are attempting to play on it with a touch and a technique developed in you by contact with human instruments of a much harder and coarser kind. I warn you that if you persist in your present courses you will not only not get the kind of music you want but you will destroy the instrument: either the King will abdicate in order to surrender himself entirely to his dreams, or he will try to run his material affairs, and those of Bavaria, on the principles of his ideal life, and crash in the impossible attempt."

That this was the correct reading of Ludwig's mind, and that Wagner knew it to be such, is evident enough from their correspondence; witness the passage already quoted from a letter of February, 1869 in which the King confesses that the gratification of his heart's desire to hear a Wagner opera has given him a new heart for duties of state that were formerly abhorrent to him.[24] But the politicians

---

[24] Passages of this kind abound in the King's letters — in that of the 8th November,

and the priests were inveterate in their mishandling of him because, in the first place, they were not psychologists enough to comprehend so exceptional a nature as Ludwig's, and in the second place because there was so much in Wagner that aroused their dislike and distrust — his " revolutionary " past, his vast ambitions, his ruthless driving power, his lack of conscience where money was concerned. Wagner himself was regarded by many people in that epoch and later as " mad " with egoism, vanity and lust for power; and in some quarters there was a quite honest fear of the possible evil effects of such a man upon the mind of a youth so unlike the average young Bavarian of his day as Ludwig was.[25] The King's plan for an expensive Wagner Theatre in Munich caused considerable alarm; many worthy people honestly believed that the Satanic pride of this visitant from abroad would accomplish in the end the financial ruin of the Bavarian state. And so, for one reason or another, some good, some bad, some honest, some corrupt, some quite disinterested, some nakedly selfish, the politicians and their accomplices in the Press and the Church gradually concentrated on the one great objective of separating the King from Wagner. To the latter they did no great ultimate harm: it is tolerably certain, indeed, that by compelling him to substitute Bayreuth for Munich as the hearth and home of his art they unwittingly did both him and the world a service. But Ludwig they ruined. By depriving him of the society and the stimulus of the one man with whom he felt he had a soul in common they exacerbated his mistrust of humanity, drove him in upon himself, increased not only his sense of singularity but his passion for solitude, made him seek an outlet for his artistic impulses in fantastic architectural schemes, and deprived him of every influence that might have steadied him in those critical years. It is on the politicians' and journalists' conscience, not on Wagner's, that the guilt for the ruin of the King's soul lies.

1864, for instance, where he writes, after an illness of Wagner's, "The thought of you eases for me the burden of my calling: as long as you are alive, life for me also is glorious and blessed." He repeatedly assures Wagner that he will not survive him.

[25] The naïve belief that it was Wagner who had actually driven the King "mad" was common even in non-"psychiatrist" circles. After the death of Ludwig in 1886, three years after that of Wagner, a Paris journal, Le Triboulet, came out with a picture of Wagner, in the Elysian Fields, reading in a German paper the announcement of the King's tragic end and saying to himself, "Am I not the real murderer of this poor prince?"

CHAPTER XI

AT THE VILLA PELLET

1

WHILE WAGNER was at the Villa Pellet the Fates were shaping for him one of the major crises of his inner life. On the 18th June the Starnberg idyll had been interrupted by King Ludwig having to go to Kissingen to meet some Russian, Austrian and other royalties. It was nearly a month before he returned to Berg, and during that time the solitude of the villa became an intolerable burden to Wagner. As we have seen, from the 11th to the 14th he had been in Vienna, where, besides making the arrangements with his creditors that were necessary for the release of his household belongings, he had vainly tried to induce Cornelius and Heinrich Porges to leave all and follow him to Munich. Back in Starnberg again, and alone, his eternal need for sympathetic companionship began once more to assert itself. The long hours of talk with the King were compounded of ecstasy and fatigue for each of them: the boy sometimes found it a strain on his immature faculties to keep pace with Wagner's quick-fire conversation, that touched on every subject under the sun; while Wagner, for his part, sometimes felt that his young adorer was inclined to keep him too constantly hovering in the empyrean. " I am frightfully lonely ", he wrote to Frau Wille on the 30th June; " it is only on the highest mountain peaks, as it were, that I can maintain myself with this young King." There were other elements in his complex nature that were calling out for satisfaction; he no doubt felt the need at times to give free play to the pungent man-of-the-world humour that was characteristic of him in moments when his head was not in the clouds.

So he made desperate attempts to gather some of his friends round him at the Villa Pellet: as he put it in one of his letters to Porges, " I must have my Penzing in Starnberg." Porges and Cornelius he felt to be particularly needful to him in different ways;

and so, before the end of May, we find him moving heaven and earth to persuade Heinrich to settle in Munich as his secretary — to deal with his business correspondence, keep his manuscripts in order, and so on. Porges, he said, would still have ample time for his own literary work, and even for teaching, if he could find pupils worth his while. But Porges was not to be persuaded, while with the level-headed Cornelius Wagner had still more trouble.

On the 31st May, exasperated at being unable to bring Peter to a decision, or even, at times, to get an answer to his letters, Wagner sent him what was almost an ultimatum. As usual, he saw no side of the case but his own; needing Cornelius as he did, it was Peter's plain duty to leave all and follow him. " I am trying ", he writes, " to balance my account, to discover definitely what I have and what I must renounce. The point in my life at which I have now arrived demands this: I must organise my peace of soul, either, as I have said, by the way of possession or by that of renunciation." He reminds Cornelius that he has offered him everything he can desire for an ideal life with him — leisure for his own work, a piano, a box always full of cigars. " This, Peter, is *zeal!* It calls for reciprocation or — it goes to pieces completely." Cornelius, it seems, has had the effrontery to inform him, through Porges, that having still three months' work to do at his opera *Der Cid* he prefers to remain in Vienna for at least that time. Wagner is frankly, naïvely, astonished at such a point of view: " Which is better, now, dear Peter ", he asks him,

> " for us to talk about this singular behaviour of yours, or — to keep silent about it? I am almost driven to believe that silence would be best, for manifestly there is something hidden here that will not be made clearer by discussion, but, on the contrary, only distorted and stifled."

He reminds Peter how shamefully he had failed him once before:

> " exactly two years ago I was longingly awaiting you in Biebrich; for a long while I received no news at all, and then I suddenly learned, through a third party, that you had allowed Tausig to take you off to Geneva. You never knew how deeply that put me out.[1] Nothing of

---

[1] The young men's conduct on this occasion evidently still upset him when he was dealing (about 1879) with the Vienna period in his autobiography. "I had", he naively records, "a grudge against them both for their behaviour during the pre-ceding summer, which had put me in a very bad humour. I had intended to invite

that kind must happen this time: we must come to some arrangement
with each other as men."

Far from their plans for composition interfering with each other,
he will take an interest in Peter's work. But a decision must be
come to at once;

> " either you accept my invitation immediately and settle down for the
> rest of your days to some sort of domestic life-bond with me — or, you
> reject my proposal with scorn, and so expressly disclaim the wish to
> unite yourself with me. In the latter case I, for my part, renounce you
> wholly and absolutely, and try no more to draw you into my scheme
> of life. On the degree of your confidence with regard to the grounds
> you have for your conduct it will and must depend whether fate has
> it in store for us that our relations shall remain friendly. You will
> see from this how sorely I need *tranquillity*. For that, I must know
> definitely where I stand. My present connection with you is a fright-
> ful torment to me: it must either become complete, or break alto-
> gether." [2]

Wagner had probably never heard of Sheridan, of whose Sir
Anthony Absolute he often seems to have been a re-incarnation:
" Hark'ee, Jack; — I have heard you for some time with patience
— I have been cool — quite cool; but take care — you know I
am compliance itself — when I am not thwarted; — no one more
easily led — when I have my own way; — but don't put me in a
frenzy. . . . . . . Now damn me! if ever I call you Jack again
while I live! . . . . I give you six hours and a half to consider of
this: if you then agree, without any condition, to be everything on
earth that I choose, why — confound you! I may in time forgive

---

the Bülows and the Schnorrs to come to me in Biebrich, and my warm interest in
these two younger friends [Cornelius and Tausig] led me to invite them too. Cornelius accepted immediately, and I was therefore the more surprised to get a letter
from him one day from Geneva, whither Tausig . . . had carried him off on a summer
excursion which was no doubt more important and pleasanter. Without the least
mention of any regret at not being able to meet me that summer, they merely told
me that 'a glorious cigar had just been smoked to my health'. When I met them
again in Vienna I could not refrain from pointing out to them how insultingly they
had behaved; but they seemed unable to comprehend what I could have objected
to in their preferring a nice excursion to French Switzerland to visiting me in Biebrich. They obviously regarded me as a tyrant." His attitude towards all his friends,
in fact, was, "Be my brother, or I'll protect you!"

[2] RWFZ, p. 406 ff. Of all his male friends, Cornelius was the one he needed most.
"Wagner", Bülow writes to his mother on the 28th December, 1864, "is in sore
need of Cornelius's happy humour, for his own incessant ill-health, which he in-
tensifies by his impatience, puts him out of tune and pulls him down." BB, IV, 10.

you. — If not, zounds! don't enter the same hemisphere with me! don't dare to breathe the same air, or use the same light with me; but get an atmosphere and a sun of your own! . . . . . I'll disown you, I'll disinherit you, I'll unget you! And damn me! if ever I call you Jack again! "

But Cornelius, knowing his man as he did, quietly kept to his resolution not to exchange Vienna and independence for Munich and Wagner until he had finished the *Cid*. It was in a towering temper that Wagner had arrived in Vienna on the 11th June. When Seraphine Mauro innocently asked him what he had come to Vienna for, he replied grimly, " To quarrel with my friends! " He made a scene with the Porges brothers, reproaching the absent Cornelius, with tears in his eyes, for having rejected his offer of a piano, cigars, and what not. Standhartner advised Peter, if his mind was really made up, to keep out of Wagner's way for the present, otherwise a total breach was certain. So Peter wrote at last to Wagner, apologising for his long silence, and assuring him that he would fall in with his wishes when his work was off his hands. " To this ", Cornelius writes to his brother Carl on the 15th,

> " no answer! Standhartner approaches him again on my behalf; Heinrich Porges writes him — ' Reconciliation with Peter, otherwise: Egoist! '. He dashes off a letter to Porges — ' Don't call on me today ', and to Standhartner, ' Don't come to me till tomorrow ', etc., etc.; and when they all go the next day he has left the town. So one can put it bluntly that he has treated his best friends in Vienna like bootblacks."

To Reinhold Köhler, nine days later, Cornelius wrote that Wagner merely wanted him to be his Kurveral: " he does not understand that I have many qualifications, even to dog-like fidelity, for that rôle, but unfortunately also a trifle of independence in my character, and too much talent to be merely the nought behind his one "; and to his sister Susanne on the 24th, giving her a résumé of the affair, " In Wagner's house, I knew, I could not have written a single note. I should be merely a piece of intellectual furniture for him, without the slightest influence on his deeper life." Profoundly as he admired Wagner, and sincerely attached to him as he was, Cornelius had no illusion about his overmastering egoism. It was all very well, he wrote to his brother in September, for Wagner to promise him a good post at the Munich Conservatoire or with the King. " If he has any real good will towards me, what he should do is to look after my *Cid;* that is the most important thing to me now. But salvation will not come to me from *that* direction: Wagner never gives a moment's serious thought to anyone but himself." [3]

True to his resolution, Cornelius did not go to Munich until the end of the year, when the King guaranteed him a yearly salary of 1,000 gulden in order that, as Wagner put it in his letter of the 7th October, he might live for his art, be at the service of the King for special purposes, " and be helpful, as a friend, to me, your friend." Ludwig had been influenced by Wagner's assurances that Cornelius was indispensable to their joint plans for music and the theatre in Munich.

2

Frustrated, for the moment, in his desire to gather his male friends about him in Starnberg, Wagner turned, in his dire need for domestic companionship, to another quarter. " Child! " he writes to Mathilde Maier on the 22nd June,

" I am hunting myself to death and can find no peace! I must have someone with me to run my house! Though it may be a shock to you, I have to disturb your peace with the question — will you come and take charge of it? "

He is appalled by the prospect of the autumn in Munich with no one but his servants.

" I, of all people! No woman by my side! No cultivated person in the house to talk to! Obviously that can't be! Nor King nor Kaiser is any use to me if things are not right in the house! I shall have no peace. I am looking again for a woman who will keep my things in order.[4] . . . It can't go on like this."

---

[3] CABT, I, 770–784.

[4] "The derelict state of my household affairs, the compulsion to deal solely by myself with things for which I really have no aptitude", he wrote to Frau Wille about this time, "paralyses my vital forces: I have now to transplant myself once again to Munich, to set up house, to bother about knives, forks, dishes, pots and pans, bed-linen and so on!"

Will not Mathilde come to him? he asks. He knows her reluctance to leave her mother, but, as he sophistically argues, would she not have to do so if she were to marry, for example? In Munich, as in Starnberg, he will have a house on two floors — the lower for himself, the upper for her.

> "You see how it is! For a long time I have been struggling with myself to write to you about this, but now my patience won't hold out any longer: it is too disgraceful that I have to look after myself all the time in this way! It really can't go on; a decision must be come to, and I fear you will one day lose me if you don't come to my help. Talk and letters are no use in a case like this. Good heavens! I am scared already at the excitement into which this will throw you; but I can do nothing else than pour out my distress to you. There's no peace for me; my days, my life, are a torment if things remain as they are. This was my main trouble all last year, the reason why I could not work. . . . I implore you, come in September, come to my help: make any conditions you like, so long as I have you."

He follows this up on the 25th with a letter to Mathilde's mother in which he dwells again on the impossibility of his enduring existence without a woman to take charge of his house and provide him with pleasant, cultured company. So dire is his need for domesticity, he says, that he had seriously considered for a time whether to ask Minna to rejoin him! Experience tells him, however, that this would be a mistake; his friends, too, warn him against it. As for a divorce, Minna could never be brought to consent to that; while he himself is barred from taking any steps towards it by consideration for the critical state of her health. He is of an age to adopt a daughter; but there is the risk of his making a mistake in his choice of which he would afterwards have reason to repent. But there is Mathilde, who is sympathetic and who understands him. True, she is not young enough to be a daughter to him: but are there not other degrees of relationship among human beings? He has nieces of Mathilde's age who, if he cared to invite them, would gladly come to him, and to whose presence in his house no one could make any objection. Could not Mathilde come as a quasi-niece, or something of that kind? It fills him with bitterness to think that all that stands in the way of his happiness is the evil mind of the world. His intentions towards Mathilde, he assures her mother, are strictly honourable: she will occupy her half of the house, he his own. Full to the brim and running over with self-pity, he implores Frau Maier to save his very life by sending him the only woman who can redeem it. And in a covering letter to Mathilde herself he assures her that he can think of no one who could take her place.

Mathilde evidently shrank from giving her mother Wagner's letter; and before she could do so we find him writing to her, on the 29th, in a very different strain. He would never forgive himself, he says, if he were to bring a catastrophe on them; he must solve his problem in another way. He now asks Mathilde neither to show her mother his letter of the 25th nor to speak to her about it; wretched as his condition is, it would become intolerable were he now to be plunged into an emotional storm that would rob him of his peace of mind for ever.

> " What shall be my salvation must come to me as a gentle, peaceful, unstained happiness, like the sun after a storm — as my King came to me in the night of my life. I could no longer bear any convulsions of grief or any silent heart-ache — for I have already suffered more than any man's due, and my strength in these matters is at an end. So do not fear any aberration on my part. Friends are coming to visit me: in the autumn I will perhaps bring Vreneli [5] from Lucerne; the running of my household will then be at any rate taken off my hands, and for the rest, no doubt, I shall be helped by having a lot of work to do and by being occupied with performances. And so — peace! Adieu, my child! Take care of yourself, and love me in spite of everything." [6]

Thus airily does he fade out the now superfluous Mathilde.

3

The Fates had decided the matter for him that very day. What had been his innermost relations with Cosima von Bülow since that day in November, 1863 when, as he was later to say in *Mein Leben*, " with tears and sobs we sealed our confession to belong to each other alone ",[7] we have at present no means of knowing; though

---

[5] His Lucerne servant of 1859: see Vol. II, p. 584. She became his housekeeper in Munich in September, 1864.

[6] RWMM, p. 162 ff.

[7] See *infra*, p. 303.

it may not be without significance that in her diary for 1877 Cosima sings the praises of that 28th November, 1863 as " the day when we found each other and were united in the unhappiness-of-death-in-love " (" *in Liebes-Todesnot* ").[8] (They had not met since that day).

From the 25th May, Wagner had been urging Bülow to come to him in Starnberg, and he was confidently expecting him by the 20th June. On the 9th, however, he invited not only Hans but Cosima and the children to spend the summer and early autumn with him at the Villa Pellet:

"You have no idea how well things are going with me; only — my house is lonely! But it is large: three complete floors . . . a whole floor for you and your dear family . . . a sitting room with a balcony and a magnificent view: two bedrooms, a room for the children, and one for your maid . . . for heaven's sake, Children! No ' *No* '. I could not bear it. Telegraph me."

But for one reason or another Bülow could not or would not come just then, and on the 21st we find Wagner telegraphing him to postpone his visit to the end of the month. The next day, as we have seen, Wagner, finding his solitude unbearable, wrote to Mathilde Maier in the terms quoted above. He is shortly expecting the Bülows, he tells her, to stay with him for a few months: " this will help me for a time." Apparently it was with Mathilde that he contemplated, just then, a more or less permanent domestic bond. But on the 29th June Cosima, a servant, and the two little children, Blandine and Daniela, arrived — without Hans, who, on the verge of a breakdown in health, did not come until the 7th July. In that week of *solitude à deux* Wagner and Cosima found each other, never to be separated in heart and soul again: the child (Isolde) that was born to Cosima on the 10th April, 1865 was not Bülow's but Wagner's. She and Wagner were fully conscious that their whole future lives were now decided for them. In " the little village of Starnberg, by the Lake ", Cosima wrote to her confidante Marie von Buch on the 2nd July,

"everything seems remote from me; it is as if I were forgotten by the whole world, and I myself forget the world. When I have once explained it all to you, you will not misunderstand my words. I have

---

[8] MECW, I, 813.

been here three days, and it seems as though it were already a century and would last I do not know how long! And so my spirit is steeped in peace, and I have an infinite longing never to see or hear a town again." [9]

4

King Ludwig returned to Berg on the 15th July. Before he had left for Kissingen he had asked Wagner to set forth for him in what respects, and to what extent, his ideas on social and political matters had changed since the publication of the treatises of 1849–1851. Wagner fulfilled the commission by writing during these weeks of separation a long essay, *On State and Religion*, the beautifully written manuscript of which, dated 16th July,[10] he presented to the King on the latter's return. The essay is a highly metaphysical and mystical exposition, of a type not uncommon in Germany, of the origin and function of the State; of the difference between religion and dogma; of the illusoriness of " public opinion " as represented by the Press; of the sublimity and at the same time the tragedy of the position of a King as the symbol of a State ideal which, the world being what it is, is not realisable in practice; of the evil condition of the Church as a mere institution of the State; and of the necessity for an inner reconciliation of the two in the soul of the King. It is to be hoped that Ludwig understood it all, though one takes leave to doubt it. He had no gift for metaphysics or for close formal dialectic of any kind: he had only lofty ideals and a fervent desire to realise them. It certainly did Wagner, the tortured artist who had somehow or other to provide himself with some mystical reason for going on living and working, a world of good to rid his soul of all this perilous stuff; but what its bearing on practical politics or practical religion could be it would perhaps have puzzled even him to say had he been challenged. If the Bavarian politicians saw the essay, as no doubt they did, or even if Ludwig only attempted to paraphrase it for them in his own way, they could well be forgiven for feeling that Wagner was likely to

[9] MECW, I, 233.

[10] It is still in Munich, among the papers left by the King. The Wahnfried archives contain both Wagner's original draft and a clean copy, dated 1st August, made by Cosima. The essay does not seem to have been printed until 1873, when it appeared in the eighth volume of Wagner's collected works.

be a bad influence on the young monarch, in that, however pure his artistic motives might be, he was filling the boy's head with cloudy metaphysics instead of leaving him free to learn the practical business of his post. Ludwig's bent towards the visionary was already strong enough to make it undesirable that he should fall, anywhere else but in matters of art, too much under the spell of an artist who, while the essence of practicality in his own professional sphere, was an obvious phantast in most others. Only one thing worse than being born a metaphysician could happen to any king — for him to give his soul into the keeping of a word-intoxicated metaphysician with an incurable itch for meddling in affairs of state without understanding them. There is no evidence, however, that Ludwig ever took Wagner's political lucubrations very seriously for very long after reading them. For the moment, no doubt, the rush of words acted like a spell: but Wagner himself confessed to a friend later, in a moment of pique, that whenever he got on to politics in their conversations Ludwig would look up at the ceiling and whistle softly to himself.

For Ludwig's birthday, the 25th August, Wagner had written the *Huldigungsmarsch,* intending it to be performed before the King as an act of homage on that day. The work was rehearsed in Munich, under Music Director Streck, by a military band of eighty players who journeyed on the 24th to Füssen, where they were met by Wagner, and where they stayed the night. The plan of performing the March at Hohenschwangau on the 25th had to be abandoned, in consequence of the presence there of the Queen Mother, with whom Wagner was never *persona grata.* (It was at Augsburg, on the return journey, that a humorous little incident occurred that has been erroneously connected with Munich. In Augsburg railway station Wagner had an altercation with the guard on the subject of his luggage, which was overweight. The guard sent for the station master, whom the irate Wagner brushed aside with the epithet " stupid fellow! " This constituted, in the Germany of that period, the grave offence of *Amtsehrenbeleidigung* (" an insult to the honour of one's office "). The station master, one Haug, lodged a complaint in court, and Wagner, in the following June, was condemned to a fine of 25 gulden). It was not until the 5th October that the March could be performed for the King, in the courtyard

of the Munich Residenz, along with selections from *Tannhäuser*
and *Lohengrin;* two days later Wagner presented Ludwig with the
exquisitely written manuscript, during the course of a two hours'
audience at which the production of the *Ring* was discussed between them. Though Wagner himself had taken the rehearsals of
the March, the performance was conducted by Siebenkäs. A light
on Pfistermeister's private attitude towards Wagner is shed by a
brief note in his diary after the celebration: " All humbug! " [11]

During the weeks that followed Ludwig's return to Berg in July,
much music, principally Wagner's, was made for him by Bülow
and Klindworth; Wagner had persuaded the latter to come to him
for a little while from London. Bülow's health was shattered by
overwork and worry in Berlin and elsewhere. It was partly to
rescue him from his Berlin misery, partly to make certain of him
for the projected " model " Wagner performances in Munich, and
partly to ensure himself as far as possible against separation from
Cosima, that Wagner obtained for Hans in September a preliminary engagement as " Vorspieler " to the King — to initiate Ludwig, as Wagner put it to Mathilde Maier, " in the right way into
good musical literature " — [12] at a salary of 2000 florins.

---

[11] FKLB, p. 85.
[12] The general impression is that Ludwig's mind was not really musical. "He
knows no music", Wagner said in the above-mentioned letter to Mathilde Maier.
In an angry moment in later years he more than once described the King as "quite
unmusical"; to the tenor Georg Unger, for instance (the first Bayreuth Siegfried),
he wrote in 1876, "The King is completely unmusical: he is endowed only with
poetic feeling"; and he told Cornelius that though Ludwig liked his [Wagner's]
music, it was all the same to him how it was performed. Ignaz von Döllinger, who
had been Ludwig's mentor during his boyhood, denied him the possession of "a
musical ear". The Countess zu Leiningen-Westerburg, speaking from personal knowledge of him, said that "what fascinated him in Wagner's art was not so much the
music as the texts of the operas. He was absolutely unmusical. His piano teacher
often assured my father that he did not know a Strauss waltz from a Beethoven
sonata. It was the romantic substance of Wagner's poems that constituted their
tremendous attraction for him." (See SWM, p. 28).
As against all this, however, there has to be set the facts that (1) Ludwig used
to enjoy performances of such operas as *Aïda*, the poetic contents of which could
hardly have been the main attraction for him; (2) of all the Wagner works he had
heard by 1872, *Tristan* was his favourite—and a man who had not the root of the
musical matter in him could hardly have sat through one performance after another
of *Tristan* with delight; (3) in a letter of the 27th August, 1872 he assures Wagner
that "only the heavenly, god-born art of music was able to make clear to me the
blissful emotions that fill my soul: the eternal cannot be laid hold of in words; to
try to do that would be a profanation." (KLRWB, III, 6).
It seems to stand to reason that the King would not have been so anxious to see

Towards the end of the summer of 1864 Wagner and Liszt met again. From the 22nd to the 26th August a festival of the Allgemeiner Deutscher Musikverein had been held at Karlsruhe: it should have been conducted by Bülow, who, however, was too ill to make the journey. Liszt had attended the festival, though somewhat reluctantly: he was unwilling to quit his Rome retreat to plunge into German musical politics once more, he had made Bülow's co-operation a *sine qua non* of his own attendance, and he had been anything but pleased at Wagner's lack of interest in the affair.[13] Cosima had kept her father company during the festival; and at the end of the month she took him back to Munich with her to see Hans, who was now lying desperately ill — temporarily paralysed in both legs and one arm — at the Bayerischer Hof Hotel. Bülow had been in a deplorable state of health the whole time of his stay at Starnberg. " Poor Bülow ", Wagner wrote to Frau Wille on the 9th September, " came here at the beginning of July [14] with his nerves shattered: the weather was cold and wretched all the time, the house, in consequence, unhealthy; and he got over one sickness only to fall into another. . . ." [15] The supposition cannot be ruled out that his breakdown may have been the result, in part, of a frank revelation by Wagner and Cosima of the new domestic situation that had suddenly arisen; [16] and Cosima's journey to Karlsruhe on the 19th August may possibly have been not for the simple purpose of keeping Liszt company during the festival but in order to make the situation clear to him also. Unless the need to see her father had been extremely urgent, it is difficult to account for her leaving Starnberg on the very day that Hans, ostensibly on the grounds that his illness had become vastly more serious, also left Starnberg and Wagner to take up his abode in a

---

and hear the works in their entirety — even to the point of braving Wagner's displeasure by his premature productions of the *Rhinegold* and the *Valkyrie*, — unless the music meant something to him. If all he was sentitive to was the poem, he could surely read this for himself as often as he liked!

[13] In any case Wagner's relations with the King would have made it impossible for him to be absent on Ludwig's birthday.

[14] Actually on the 7th.

[15] There seems to have been an editorial cut made in the letter at this point.

[16] See, on the general question of the triangle, Chapter XXI, *infra*.

Munich hotel! [17] " Cosima arrived here on Friday " [the 19th],
Liszt wrote to Princess Wittgenstein on the 21st.

> " I had refrained from writing to her, as I did not wish to influence
> her in any way — and I did not quite grasp the position of Hans at
> Munich, relatively to Wagner, etc. She discovered through a third
> party that I was here; and she imagined I had stopped at St. Tropez
> or Paris, where she telegraphed and wrote me news of the serious ill-
> ness of Hans." [18]

We further discover from Liszt that for the preceding fortnight
Bülow has been at the end of his physical and mental resources,
that he wants to return to Berlin, and that " possibly Cosima will
return to him tomorrow to look after his health." Once more we
may remark that it is curious that she should have left him at such
a time, miserably ill as he was, and that he should have preferred
a hotel in Munich to the hospitality of Wagner in Starnberg.[19] In
the light of all we now know of the Wagner-Cosima-Bülow triangle,
we may perhaps not unreasonably assume that the perturbed Cosima had gone to Karlsruhe, without waiting for an invitation from
her father, to put him *en rapport* with the crisis that had recently
come about, and to ask for his counsel and help.

She arrived in Munich with him on the evening of the 28th August. He remained two days with Bülow, who, he told the Princess,
was in a sad state, — the paralysis had already lasted a week. Cosima, on the 29th, went to Starnberg, perhaps to report to Wagner
the result of her Karlsruhe conversations with Liszt. She and Wagner returned to Munich the same day. On the afternoon of the 30th
Wagner and Liszt went to Starnberg. Liszt was back in Munich on
the 31st; Wagner followed him there on the 2nd September. On
the morning of the 3rd Liszt left for Stuttgart; and on the evening
of the same day Hans and Cosima went back with the children to
Berlin. We learn from Liszt's letters to the Princess that although

---

[17] There may be some concealed significance in the entry in Wagner's "Annals"
relating to this episode: "Cosima to Karlsruhe. Hans to Munich: ill and furious
in hotel." (KLRWB, I, 4). The equivalents of "wüthend" given in the dictionaries
are "furious", "frantic", "foaming", "raging", "infuriated". The reader can take
his choice of these. With Hans in this condition, Cosima, instead of accompanying
him to the Munich hotel, goes off the same day to Karlsruhe to see her father, and
does not return till nine days later!

[18] LZB, VI, 35.

[19] In Munich, however, he could probably get better medical advice.

Bülow's relations with King Ludwig had been of the happiest and most flattering kind, he was obstinately bent on returning to Berlin for a while " to take the ' Roman baths ' there and complete his cure far away from Munich ". One suspects that the world has been told a good deal less than the whole truth, and occasionally something other than the truth, about the Starnberg episode of July 1864.

Wagner and Liszt met, at Bülow's bedside, for the first time in three years; and though, as Wagner said to Cornelius, had it not been for the accident of Bülow's illness the meeting would not have taken place at all, something of the old cordial relationship was re-established for the moment. During Liszt's brief stay in Starnberg Wagner talked to him about the marvellous change in his fortunes, and showed him the King's glowing letters. " As for Wagner's position, it savours of the prodigious ", Liszt wrote to Princess Wittgenstein; " Solomon was wrong: there *is* something new under the sun! " At bottom, he found, there was nothing really changed between him and the Glorious One, as he calls Wagner. He went through so much of the *Meistersinger* as was already written, and declared it ' a masterpiece of humour, wit, and vivacious grace — lively and beautiful, like Shakespeare." He played his own Beatitudes (from *Christus*), with which Wagner seemed to be highly pleased.[20] Weissheimer also came to Starnberg, a few days after Liszt had left; like every other friend who had known Wagner in the days of his despair he was dazzled by the dramatic change in his fortunes.

As the summer wore on, however, the sky began to darken for Wagner. As yet, indeed, there was no cloud upon his relations with the King. On the 16th September he sent Ludwig a poem of seven eight-line stanzas — *An meinen König* — in which he poured out his love and gratitude to his benefactor; [21] three days later Ludwig replied with a versified effort of his own — *An meinen Freund* [22] —that gave ardent expression to his faith in Wagner and the triumph of their joint cause. But already there were hints of bad weather in the distance: on the 19th there appeared in the

[20] LZB, VI, 36 ff.
[21] It will be found in RWGS, VIII, I, and KLRWB, I, 22.
[22] KLRWB, I, 24.

Augsburg *Abendzeitung* (reprinted from the Berlin *Nationalzeitung*) a message from the Munich correspondent of the latter paper, in which Wagner was characterised as " a man swollen with vanity and presumption ". The powers of darkness were already at work in Munich.

Within himself Wagner was not happy. Bülow, as we have seen, had taken Cosima with him when he returned to Berlin on the 3rd September.[23] Wagner found the separation from her intolerable. He had fully realised now that henceforth she would be indispensable to him; yet there seemed to be no way by which she could become completely his in the eyes of the world. On the 1st October he secretly communed with her in a poem — *An Dich!* — the original manuscript of which is still at Wahnfried. In this he hails her as the star [24] that has at last risen in the dark night of his life.

To Bülow on the 30th September, he wrote in what at first sight seem mysterious terms:

"I too am uneasy about Cosima's ailing condition. Everything relating to her is extraordinary and unusual: her due is freedom in the noblest sense of the word. She is childlike and profound — the laws of her being will always lead her to the highest only. No one will ever help her but she herself! She belongs to a peculiar world-order which we must learn to grasp through her. You will have, in the future, more propitious leisure and freedom of your own to consider this, and to find your noble place by her side. And that too is a comfort to me." [25]

It is generally opined that this must have been " incomprehensible " to Hans. Perhaps; but in view of all we now know about the matter we may take leave to doubt it. The sacrosanct biographical legend that Wagner and Cosima " deceived " Bülow for some two years from July 1864 hardly survives critical examination today. Every sentence in this citation from Wagner's letter is consistent with the theory that the pair had frankly made Bülow acquainted

---

[23] He was definitely appointed Vorspieler to the King on the 12th.
[24] Es winkt der Stern der Sonne, dass sie bliebe;
Nun steht sie still. Ich bin geliebt, und liebe!

    'Ich bin geliebt'—blinkt mir der Stern hernieder —
Die Braut, der nie sich winden soll der Kranz!
'Ich liebe'—glüht der Sonne Strahl darwieder —
Der Bräutigam, der nie Dich führt zum Tanz!
[25] RWHB, p. 226.

THE LIFE OF RICHARD WAGNER

with the new situation from the very first. Why, we may ask, should Wagner console Bülow with the reflection that he (Hans) may in the future be able to find his " noble place by Cosima's side ", unless Bülow had already been given to understand that the " place " could never again be the old one?

The whole truth of the matter will not be known until the Wagner-Bülow-Liszt-Cosima correspondence is published in full, and the passages restored that have been deleted from some of the letters so far vouchsafed to us. In his letter of the 21st October, 1864 to Bülow (from Rome), Liszt says that while not presuming to offer him advice, he nevertheless urges him to settle without delay in Munich: " a complicated task and painful duties await you. You will succeed in them; in so doing your public career will be enlarged, and your *interior* self will rise to its natural height." [26] How, we may ask, could the mere *duties* that would confront Bülow in Munich, first as pianist to the King, then, in the somewhat remote future, as conductor of the Wagner operas, be forecast as " painful ", except in so far as they involved daily association with Wagner and Cosima in the changed circumstances that had arisen? How could his settling down in Munich help his *interior* self (the word is underlined by Liszt) to " rise to its natural height " except in that way? And when we observe that the editor of the Liszt-Bülow correspondence admits having suppressed the passage that immediately precedes the one quoted above, we may be excused the suspicion that the two men had been discussing other matters than the merely *external* aspects of the Munich appointment. In Liszt's next letter, of the 12th November, he exhorts Bülow — manifestly in reply to something Hans has been saying to him — to overcome his habit of regarding himself as being to blame, and to have confidence in his " real worth of heart, character, intelligence and talent ". It is difficult to believe that Liszt would be stressing these virtues of Bülow's if it were a mere matter of Hans going to conduct and play the piano in Munich instead of in Berlin; and we are confirmed in our scepticism when we discover that once more the editor of the correspondence has thought it advisable to suppress something in the letter after the next sentence, which runs, " Try then to leave your migraines and rheumatisms of every kind [*sic*]

[26] BLW, p. 321.

[270]

in Berlin with your old furniture — and to make a fresh start in Munich." [27]

6

To the discovery of each other by Wagner and Cosima in Starnberg we owe, even if at a rather long remove, no less a work than the *Siegfried Idyll*.

The analysts have always assured us that the *Idyll* is based on two themes from Brynhilde's part in the duet in the third act of *Siegfried:* the first of these is sung by her to the words " Ewig war ich, ewig bin ich " —

and the second, a few bars later, to the words " O Siegfried, Herrlicher! Hort der Welt! " —

The use of these themes in *Siegfried,* however, is so peculiar — for Wagner — that even before we had learned the real provenance of at any rate the first of them some of us had a vague feeling that something was wrong.

(1) The whole musical texture of the pages commencing with " Ewig war ich " is somewhat alien to what has gone before: the expansive lyrical flow of this section is in marked contrast to the general style of the third act of *Siegfried* and of virtually the whole

---

[27] BLW, p. 321. It may be permissible to point out to the reader that the first of these two letters was written while Liszt and Cosima were together in France, and the second between the date of Cosima's return to Bülow in Berlin (2nd November) and the definitive migration of the pair to Munich (20th November).

of the *Götterdämmerung*, where the texture results from the incessant interweaving of short, pregnant motives.

(2) The six-bar phrase in the bass clarinet which introduces No. 1 is manifestly only a makeshift bridge-passage that has no organic part to play in the total design.

(3) No one has ever been able to find a convincing reason why, after this bridge-passage, the strings should first of all give out No. 1 in the major (eight bars), and Brynhilde then sing her opening words to the same melody in the *minor*.

(4) The " declamation " of the words right through this episode is not in the genuine later Wagnerian style, in which melodic accent and speech-accent are organically one: here we find syllables spaced out to cover several notes of the obviously pre-conceived melody, and sometimes the words, thus constrained, fall awkwardly from the tongue. Occasionally the words and the music go so ill with each other, even after the former have been twisted about to suit the latter, that we are astonished at Wagner's ever allowing them to appear in the score in this form. For example, the words he had originally put into Brynhilde's mouth at this point were —

> Ewig licht
> lachst du aus mir
> selig selbst dir entgegen.

Finding that the music he wanted to use here (No. 1) did not fit these rhythmically symmetrical lines he altered them to " Ewig licht lachst du selig dann aus mir dir entgegen ", to which he adjusts his pre-conceived melody as well as he can, but not conspicuously well. It is to be further observed that in the later public issue of the *Ring* poem he printed at this point, not the lame words he had set to music — or to be more accurate, which he had manufactured merely for the music — but the original lines, as given above, from *Young Siegfried*, merely inserting before the " selig " a "dann " which does not improve matters at all. Evidently he was not proud of " Ewig licht lachst du selig dann aus mir dir entgegen " as a poetic, or even a metrical, effort.[28]

---

[28] His reasons for pulling the lines about as he has done are obvious. Had he kept to his original "Ewig licht lachst du aus mir selig selbst dir entgegen", the strong melodic beat of the bar would have coincided with the "aus". To avoid this absurdity he transferred "selig" to the position formerly occupied by "aus"; in this

(5) The analysts have always been puzzled what names to give to the two musical motives quoted above, and no wonder, for as a matter of fact they are not really motives at all in the true Wagnerian sense: No. 1 is never employed again in the *Ring*, while No. 2 makes only a transitory appearance at two points in the *Götterdämmerung*. The desperate and inadequate best that the analysts have been able to achieve is to call the two " motives " by names derived from the words to which they have been sung by Brynhilde — in the one case the " Peace " motive, in the other the " Treasure of the World " motive.

Something unusual has obviously happened at this point of the *Siegfried* score, something, it is not going too far to say, quite un-Wagnerian. We find the explanation in a passage in Cosima's diary for 1878. The score of the *Idyll* had recently been published, and both she and Wagner were amused by the " discoveries " the commentators were making in connection with it, one of them fancying he had found an echo of the Forest Murmurs, another of the scene between Siegfried and Fafner, and so on. As Cosima was playing the *Idyll* on the piano one day, Wagner said to her, " *We* know quite well what is the origin of it all." " He told me ", Cosima adds, " that he had written down the first theme that time when I visited him in Starnberg." As a matter of fact he had told her this already — in December, 1870, not long after the composition of the *Idyll*. It appears that in Starnberg, in the summer of 1864, he had intended to write a string quartet for Cosima, and our No. 1 was designed to be the first subject of this: in 1870, when he took up the melody again in order to produce a work specially for Cosima, he had, as he said, interwoven with the original strain such motives as that of the bird in *Siegfried*.[29]

way he could smuggle in the relatively unimportant "aus" on a weak beat at the end of the bar, thus allowing the more important "mir" to take the strong beat of the next bar. But this procedure, in its turn, virtually forced on him the insertion of a "dann" before the "aus" and a "dir" after the "mir." (A reference to the score will make these points quite clear to the reader). Then, when he came to print the poem apart from the score, he quite unnecessarily worked in the "dann" which he had been constrained to adopt for his purely musical purpose. In the original *Young Siegfried* the two lines

> selig selbst dir entgegen,
> froh und heiter ein Held!

match each other in rhythm. The added "dann" is superfluous both rhythmically and from the point of view of sense.

[29] See MECW, I, 546, 819.

So far there is no direct evidence that the second main theme of the *Idyll* — our No. 2 — was also conceived in 1864, but the indirect evidence points strongly in this direction. The two melodies have obviously been planned not only to flow naturally into each other but to go with each other in double counterpoint, i.e., with either of them as the upper part to the other. Now there is no particular reason why Wagner, having, supposedly, in June 1869 made Brynhilde sing " Ewig war ich, ewig bin ich ", etc. to the melody of the Starnberg quartet, and then, after these eleven bars, having to invent a melody for " O Siegfried, Herrlicher! ", should so shape this other melody that it will go in double counterpoint with its predecessor, not, be it observed, in the *opera* — where it is not so employed — but in a work the idea of which only occurred to him some eighteen months later. The conclusion seems inescapable that not only our quotation No. 1 but our No. 2 formed part of the quartet drafted in 1864. It must be recalled that Wagner's son Siegfried was born on the 6th June, 1869, at the very time when he was engaged on the closing scene of the third act of his opera. Nietzsche called for the first time at Triebschen in mid-May, 1869. While waiting for his name to be taken to Wagner he heard the latter repeating again and again some poignant harmonies which Nietzsche afterwards recognised as those accompanying Brynhilde's words " Verwundet hat mich, der mich erweckt "; presumably Wagner had just reached that point in his composition. The remainder of *Siegfried* — occupying some twenty-five pages of an ordinary vocal score — was completed in about a month from then, on the 14th June. Only five of these pages are required to carry Wagner from " Verwundet hat mich, der mich erweckt " to " Sieh' meine Angst " and the bass clarinet solo mentioned above. Are we to believe that the composition of these five pages alone occupied three weeks, from the 15th May to the 6th June — the day of Siegfried's birth — and that Wagner then crammed the writing of the final twenty pages into the mere week between the 6th and the 14th? That is to say, was the four-page section commencing " Ewig war ich " conceived in its present form in the ordinary sequence of events? Or did Wagner, having discovered that at last, on the

6th June, he had managed to produce a long-desired son — a feat which he seemed to regard as of well-nigh cosmic importance — write these four pages some time after he had received the assurance of his good fortune, using for this purpose the quartet material in fond retrospect of the Starnberg days? [30] As soon as this stylistically irrelevant section is off his hands — at the words " vernichte dein Eigen nicht! " — Wagner settles down again, for the final seventeen pages of *Siegfried*, to his normal method of leading-motive manipulation. There *must* be some purely personal reason for his having spatchcocked into his score this four-page episode in a style that has neither an inner musical nor an inner dramatic logic of its own.

What is perhaps evidence of another kind is furnished by a facsimile of No. 1 in its full form, given by Dr. Strobel in BFF, 1933, p. 176. Dr. Strobel describes it as " the earliest known recording of the ' Peace' theme of the third act of *Siegfried*". The manuscript appears to be dated " 14th Nov. 1864 ". At first sight, it is true, the 4 in the " 1864 " might be taken for a 7. But, as it happens, a number of facsimiles of Wagner manuscripts have been published containing both 4's and 7's; and from these it would seem that his practice was to write his 7's with (a) a preliminary " up-take " stroke, (b) a small cross-stroke, in the fashion common on the continent, through the long tail of the figure. Both these peculiarities are lacking in the present instance. The length of the final downstroke of the figure gives it a faint suggestion of a 7; this long down-stroke, however, is a characteristic of many of Wagner's 4's. Moreover, while it was not until March 1869 that Wagner began work on the third act of *Siegfried*, " 14th Nov. 1864 " fits in with all we know from other sources as to the date of the conception of the string quartet.[31]

---

[30] The reader, by the way, must not be misled by a passage in Wagner's letter of the 12th January, 1870 to Pusinelli, in which he says he "finished the composition of *Siegfried*" on "that day last summer when a handsome son was born to more-than-happy me", i.e., on the 6th June. (RWAP, p. 225). The correct dates are as given above.

[31] It may be added that no words are included in the sketch of the theme.

Dr. Strobel would no doubt be able to say definitely whether the sketch belongs to 1864 or 1867; but the war makes it impossible for me at present to refer the point to his courteous consideration.

CHAPTER XII

COSIMA

1

OF ALL the characters in the Wagner story, Cosima is the one who most successfully evades ultimate analysis. Her father, Liszt, was half-sincere, half-poseur, but his assumptions and discardings of the actor's mask are mostly so obvious that we cannot be in the least doubt as to which was mask and which was face, or as to the true features of the latter. In Cosima's case, partly by natural constitution, partly by long self-discipline and the moulding force of circumstances, face and mask were almost from the first so perfectly modelled to each other that it is difficult for us to say on any given occasion which was which; not only did she consciously assume the mask before others but one suspects that she sometimes found a subtle secret pleasure in merging mask and face even in her own contemplation of herself in the glass. Hence it was, no doubt, that most people who were not irresistibly attracted by her could not even begin to like or even endure her; Houston Stewart Chamberlain, who knew her well, said that men of talent either made obeisance to her or fled from her. In the case of some of the men of talent their flight may have been due to their specialist knowledge of their own subject making them resent her too-assured amateur generalisations about it, a habit of mind in respect of which she was a true Wagnerian long before she came into Wagner's sphere of intellectual influence; but many of them disliked her for more broadly and simply human reasons. On the one hand we have the highest tributes paid to her mind and character not only by men like Wagner, Bülow and Nietzsche, who were certainly not fools, but by other people, men and women, who knew her less intimately, but, from what they saw of her, measured her coolly by the critical standards they applied to humanity in general. On the other hand, many people felt an instinctive, unconquerable repulsion from her. Here and there this was because of the French cast that her personality and her manner had acquired from her earliest environment. It rubbed a few of the blunter Germans the wrong way; there was something in her polish which they felt to be fundamentally alien to them and their race. " What all of us had to grow accustomed to in her ", says Ludwig Schemann, who saw a good deal of her from 1877 onwards,

> " was a certain foreign element, traceable in part to her origin, in part to her French education, and making itself evident in several characteristics of her being, her speech and her style. Many of our circle were particularly struck by her fundamental antithesis to Wagner's nature, which was German to the point of inconsiderateness; and in proportion as this trait was personal to the beholder himself he found her nature a stone of stumbling, especially as her powerful, irresistible influence gave its tone to the whole circle. Essentially Germanic natures such as that of Plüddemann [1] rose in energetic revolt against this element in her that was so foreign to them; even more moderate people could be heard complaining of the etiquette, the salon atmosphere, the ' regimen of women ', and other things of that kind that reigned in Wahnfried." [2]

But it was not merely the French traits in her mental heredity and the French nuance in her social manner that made some dyed-in-the-wool Teutons a little doubtful about her; they were sensitive also, says Schemann, to something in her which they called, according to their point of view and the nature of their experience of her, " Jesuitry ", " heartlessness ", " cruelty ", " serpent guile "; [3] and they mistrusted or detested her accordingly. Schemann, of course, is speaking of the Cosima of the later years of

---

[1] Martin Plüddemann (1854–1897) is generally regarded as the successor of Loewe in the German ballad. He joined the Wahnfried circle in the late 1870's. Ludwig Schemann has devoted a volume to him as a composer — *Martin Plüddemann und die deutsche Ballade* (1930).

[2] SLD, pp. 134–5. Cosima told Houston Stewart Chamberlain, in 1891, that not only had she become by that time alienated from French literature in general but she was losing her sense of the niceties of the French language — the distinctions, for example between *ai, è, é, est, ée*, and so on. Her only love now was German, probably, she said, "because it is wedded to song, which is the life of my soul." "My children", she continued, "are now in a choir that is to sing in Bach's St. John Passion: and in this work I feel I have my home, my tongue, my faith, — in short, my everything, because here I see a foreshadowing of [Wagner's] works, which descend as naturally from it as Siegfried from Wotan." WHSC, 222–3.

[3] SLD, p. 137.

Wagner's life and of the period immediately following his death, when the care of Bayreuth lay heavily on her shoulders. But, as he truly says, no one can carry any great work through in this world without a certain amount of Jesuitry, nor can anyone who pursues unrelentingly a single fixed purpose be perpetually under the critical and often hostile eyes of others without the shadows as well as the high lights of his character becoming noticeable. The waters of diplomacy can never be quite clean; no one can bathe daily in them for many years and preserve an absolutely spotless skin. And Cosima had very often to be diplomatic, for Wagner's sake and Wagner's work's sake as well as her own. Furthermore, there was something in her serene self-assurance, her always urbane but immovable egocentricism and Wagner-centricism, that made many people who did not dispute her spell edge away from her instinctively in defence of their own liberty of thought and action; while her social technique was of such consummate perfection as to raise doubts of her complete sincerity. This happened with the French writer Edouard Schuré, a passionate admirer of Wagner, who spent three days at Triebschen at the end of October 1869. " My impressions have been curious and diverse ", he afterwards wrote to his friend Gottfried von Böhm, the later biographer of Ludwig II:

> " this is because Madame de Bülow is a singular creature of the strongest type, impenetrable and unfathomable in her purposes, and for that reason disturbing. . . . If you were to ask me whether she is an *intrigante* or a heroine I should not know how to answer you. . . . Perhaps both, I would say between ourselves; the human heart is complex enough for that to be possible. These doubts and a thousand strange thoughts assailed me during those three days, sometimes causing me a kind of inward and silent martyrdom; not to see clearly into people, down to their foundations, is a torment to me." [4]

2

Between the Cosima whom the older people of our own generation knew, however, and the Cosima of 1864, many years had gone by. She was born on the Christmas Day of 1837; she died, in her ninety-third year, on the 1st April 1930, having survived Wagner

---

[4] BKLB, pp. 201–2.

a full forty-seven years. What kind of woman was the Cosima of twenty-six-and-a-half whose life became so inseparably interwoven with his in 1864?

She was no more than seven, her elder sister Blandine no more than nine, and her brother Daniel only five, when, about 1844, the ways of her father and mother began to diverge for good. Liszt resumed his vagrant virtuoso career through Europe; the Countess d'Agoult settled with the children in Paris. There they remained, for the most part, in the care of Liszt's mother; Liszt did not wish them to see too much of their own mother, nor, fighting as she was just then to regain her social position in Paris, was it possible for her to impose, as constituent parts of her own household, three illegitimate children, each of them the product of an extra-marital association with a mere piano virtuoso, upon her aristocratic family and on the high French social world of that day.[5] For years at a time the children never saw their father, who was little more than a grandiose, fantastic figure of legend to them. As time went on, and Liszt's hatred of Marie d'Agoult increased, he used his authority more and more to sequestrate and estrange the children from their mother, who, under French law, had no legal rights in them. This hatred of his was fanned by the woman with whom he had cast in his lot in 1847, the Princess Carolyne von Sayn-Wittgenstein, who detested Marie for three excellent feminine and Carolynian reasons — she was beautiful, she was intelligent, and Liszt had once adored her. Liszt's worship of his worshipping Princess combined with his resentment at Marie's unkind exposure of his human weaknesses in her novel *Nélida* (1846) to turn him completely against his former love; and the hand of the Princess is plainly evident in his unfriendly dealings with Marie in the matter of the children.

---

[5] The modern reader needs to be constantly reminded that in Paris and London in the first half of the nineteenth century, and even later, it was difficult for the ordinary musical performer to get himself accepted on terms of equality in high society. Adolphe Adam tells us that the Countess d'Agoult, who upheld the "rights of talent", scandalised good Parisian society by asking the conductor Pasdeloup to dinner with Littré, Carnot and Grévy, and by inviting an opera singer to lunch with Paul de Saint-Victor. See, for further evidence of the low social status of the musician in general in those days, NML, *passim*. Liszt's notorious kowtowing to titles was largely the product of his secret resentment of the humiliations to which his pride had been subjected by the aristocratic world in his younger days.

In October, 1850 Carolyne brought it about that they were re-moved from Madame Liszt's house and placed completely in the charge of her own former governess, Madame Patersi, who was brought from Russia to Paris for that purpose. They seem to have had no child companions, no games, and few pleasures appropriate to their age. From Madame Patersi and her sister Madame de Saint-Mars, two acidulous old ladies of over seventy, they received an education of the strictest possible kind, being allowed to come into contact with nothing but what was held to be most admirable in literature, in music, in the theatre, and in the museums. They worked hard at their piano-playing, as became the children of Franz Liszt; they learned English and German in addition to French. From Madame Patersi, again, the main occupation of whose life had been bringing up the children of Russian aristocrats, they received a thorough schooling in the manners, deportment and forms of address of high society. To the end of her days Cosima carried about with her an atmosphere of the finest breeding; more than once, in this or that assembly of aristocrats by birth, beholders who did not know who she was singled her out as the most aristo-cratic of them all; Dr. Bayersdorfer, the Director of the Munich Pinakothek, whose gallery she visited one day in the company of several princesses and countesses, described her afterwards as " *the* princess —the others were simply her suite ".[6] She was long and lanky, with a figure that only her perfect poise enabled her to carry off successfully; her nose was too long for feminine beauty. But she had beautiful golden hair that was to be Wagner's delight; her voice was deep and richly resonant.

3

Those childhood years in Paris determined Cosima's character in its essentials for the rest of her life. In spite of all the efforts of Liszt and Carolyne, the children, as they grew older, saw their mother fairly frequently, and the more they saw her the more ir-resistibly they were attracted by her. Probably because they had little or no physical outlet of the customary kind for their youthful

[6] SFCW, p. 95.

energy they bent their minds as few children could have done, or would have had need to do, to the understanding of the strange situation in which they found themselves between their mother — with her beauty and her charm, her cultivated intelligence, her delightful library, and her circle of acquaintances which included all that was most distinguished in the literary, artistic and political worlds of the Paris of that day — the dried-up, thin-lipped old dragon of a Madame Patersi, without a particle of tenderness in her composition — " Merely water! " she would say when their eyes filled with tears, and " Just like their mother! " when one of them did something of which she disapproved — their father, a severe, remote figure, who had no understanding of children, and least of all of his own,[7] and who wrote them letters that often did little more than modulate between sternness and downright harshness — and, in the background, the gushing but venomous Carolyne, with her blue-stocking habit of mind and her over-blown literary style, doing all she could to bring them to regard herself as their true " mother ".[8] They saw not only their own letters to their father and the Princess censored by their governess but their mother's letters to them " tapped " by her and the contents passed on to Weimar.[9]

There were plentiful occasions here for thought, and the two little girls, being unusually intelligent, did a good deal of quiet thinking about their situation and the personalities by whom they were surrounded. About Blandine, who died young, we know little except that she developed into a woman of exceptional charm and some coquetry. But of Cosima we can be certain that the peculiar circumstances of her early life went far towards making her what she afterwards became. The child's clear intelligence seems to have pierced to the roots of the distressful conflict that was for ever

---

[7] " It was quite a novelty to me ", says Wagner in *Mein Leben* à propos of his first meeting with the children in Paris in 1853, "to see my friend [Liszt] with these girls, who were already growing up, and to watch him in his intercourse with his son, who was passing from boyhood to youth. Liszt himself seemed astonished by his situation as father, only the cares of which, and none of its compensating feelings, he had known for many years."

[8] At that time both she and Liszt believed that she would be able to obtain a divorce from her husband and marry Liszt, in which case, of course, the children would some day take up their abode under her roof. It was Madame Patersi's task to mould them into the right shape for that contingency.

[9] See on this point Vol. II, p. 497.

raging in the divided soul of Liszt. " I know ", Cosima wrote to King Ludwig in 1866,

> " that your Majesty's love for the Friend [Wagner] is not mere ' youthful enthusiasm '; I have caught the deeper meaning of it, and I know also that my own truest sentiments, those that have ruled my whole life, were intuitions of my first youth. Even as a child I *knew* that my father suffered — the father whom I was accustomed to seeing only in the splendour and the intoxication of triumph; I *knew* it, and I suffered with him, secretly and silently, like a child, but without end." [10]

From her own childish difficulties and sorrows and from those of others she learned two lessons she was never to forget — first, that wisdom counselled saying least about the things that hurt her most, second, that the smoothest way through life, and the way most likely in the end to achieve her own purposes, was to see every difficult situation calmly as a problem that could be " managed " in terms of an understanding of the personalities involved in it. Her instincts, her intelligence, her breeding and her early experience of the social world combined to impress on her that the secret of handling men was to reveal to them no more of herself than was necessary, and to turn them into her unconscious instruments by making them believe that in following her they were acting precisely as they themselves would have chosen to act. The subtle Gracian — the seventeenth century Spanish Jesuit who, in his *Art of Worldly Wisdom*, has given the world its completest manual for the skilled ordering of one's life [11] — would have been astonished to find that this young woman, who had assuredly never read a line of his, had worked out for herself most of what was vital in his teaching. Precept after precept in his book might almost have been framed in anticipation of Cosima's diplomatic technique: " A bad manner spoils everything, even reason and justice; a good one supplies everything, gilds a ' No ', sweetens truth. . . ." " Fine behaviour is a joy in life, and a pleasant expression helps out of a difficulty in a remarkable way." " Courtesy is the politic witchery of great personages." " You should learn to seize things not by the blade, which cuts, but by the handle, which saves you from

---

[10] KLRWB, I, 255.

[11] It was Schopenhauer's favourite book: he translated it into German and discussed it lovingly. There is an excellent English version by Joseph Jacobs.

harm: especially is this the rule with the doings of your enemies. A wise man gets more use from his enemies than a fool from his friends." " Do not show your wounded finger, for everything will knock up against it; nor complain about it, for malice always aims where weakness can be injured." " Avoid familiarities in intercourse: neither use them nor permit them . . . the stars keep their brilliance by not making themselves common." Cosima brought to the conduct of Wagner's affairs a Jesuitical art of worldly wisdom in which he himself had for the most part been sadly lacking until then.

4

That there was a good deal of the Jesuit in her cannot, indeed, be denied. But even Jesuitry, like most other things in this complicated life of ours, is neither good nor evil in itself, but only with reference to the uses to which it is put. Cosima put her own Jesuitry, for the most part, to lofty uses. She no doubt found delight in the consciousness of the perfection of her technique, for there can be no expert handling of any instrument whatever without a feeling of satisfaction in one's skill; and often, over and above the plain pursuit of her aim in this letter or that of hers, we are conscious of the artist luxuriously savouring the virtuosity of her own finesse. But she generally worked for ends that were in essence greater than herself, however much she had made them part and parcel of herself. A combination of talent and will such as hers could easily have been put to uses dangerous to mankind: she chose deliberately to devote herself, in the main, to fine causes. She, if anyone, knew the meaning of the word self-sacrifice: she had sacrificed herself for Bülow's sake in marrying him, and her life both with Wagner and in the lonely after-days when the huge burden of Bayreuth and its cultural mission lay on her sole shoulders was one long ecstatic sacrifice to an ideal which she thought supreme among the things of this world.

Her defects and her virtues, as with all highly dynamic characters, nourished each the other's blood and fed the other's flames. What she saw in any field of life she saw with an unclouded, unwavering, bird-like gaze that narrowed it down at once to what for her were its essentials, profiting by, though sometimes paying the penalty for, the cutting-out of whatever there was in its surroundings that might have blurred the sharp definition of its outlines, and so delayed the speed and energy of her reaction to it. In spite of her wide reading and her inexhaustible interest, almost to the end of her long life, in the pageant of the world, hers was a one-track mind; whatever entered it took on instantaneously the shape and colour of it, and was accepted or rejected according as it squared or failed to square with her own immovably fixed prepossessions and prejudices. She was astonishingly like Wagner in her way of referring everything to the touchstone of a few convenient formulae of her own; she complacently simplified every problem, however complicated, in history, in politics, in literature, in art, in life, by submitting it to the test of conformity or nonconformity with a few principles that were as fixed for her as the constitution of matter or the courses of the stars.

The Cosima our generation knows best is, of course, the Cosima of the second half of her long life, in connection with which the first-hand documents are the most abundant. But she was of a piece throughout: she was always Cosima, and the strong light we have on her in her later years illuminates her for us also as she must have been in her youth. She was the natural counterpart and pre-ordained ally of Wagner if only because his own habit of putting the most complex questions into some three or four test tubes of his own, and submitting them to a stereotyped personal reaction by which they had to stand or fall, was native to her also. Like him, she solved, in her own estimation and to her own satisfaction, no end of problems by tracing them back to " the Jews ", an admirably simple procedure that easily passed current for wisdom in Germany, with the lunatic doctrines of " race " that were current there even at that time, but led to the most ludicrous results when applied to the affairs of other countries. " Cherchez le Juif! " might have been her device. In 1893 Prince Ernst zu Hohenlohe-Langenburg, who was at that time attached to the German Embassy in London, wrote to tell her of Henry Irving's curious version of *Faust:* she was not astonished at this perversion of Goethe, she wrote back, for she understood that Irving was a Jew! [12] That, of course, explained everything: no Jew could possibly understand Goethe, and

[12] BCWH, p. 45.

conversely a misunderstanding of Goethe pointed strongly to the criminal being a Jew.[13] Race, for Cosima, explained most things: she was a firm believer in Gobineau's fanciful doctrine of the inherent superiority of certain races and the inherent inferiority of others. " The race most capable of culture ", she assured Hohenlohe-Langenburg, " is the Germanic, which on that account is destined to dominance " [14] — a doctrine, it is needless to say, not seriously disputed by any intelligent person anywhere in the world today, except, perhaps, outside Germany. She attributed the fact, or supposed fact, that " art is absolutely alien to England " — the England of Chaucer, Shakespeare, Milton, Purcell, Dowland, Byrd, Constable, Elgar, of a thousand rare spirits in literature, painting and music! — to the " Normans " having pushed " the artistic element " into the background for the benefit of " the state-organisation ", the " Puritans " having later " completed the ruin ". She saw some slight hope for the French only if they could develop " the sense of the ideal " by assimilating German culture in general and that of Goethe and Wagner in particular:

> " if we may assume that the religious sentiment in France still possesses strength enough for a re-birth, the influence of our own art could contribute immeasurably to this blessing: in this sense I welcome everything that has been told me about the *Meistersinger*." [15]

But the French, she said, repeating a famous saying of Blücher's, " are repugnant to me ": she could not read " love scenes " in a French novel because in France " an honourable feeling between man and woman is impossible ". Sarah Bernhardt in *Tosca* struck her merely as " an old she-ape ". [16] In the Home Rule struggle of

---

[13] Writing to Houston Stewart Chamberlain in December, 1899, during the Boer war, she regretted that so many men on both sides had to die "just for the Jew Rhodes". (WHSC, p. 586). Neither Irving nor Rhodes, as it happened, had any Jewish blood in him; but Cosima, like so many other people in Germany in her day and after her, ceased to be a rational human being when Jews were mentioned.

Long after Nietzsche's death she thought she had discovered the secret of his shortcomings as a man and as a philosopher in the fact that he was of "Slav origin". (WHSC, p. 502). Frau Förster-Nietzsche, however, has declared her brother's theory of the "noble Polish ancestry" of the family to be a myth.

[14] BCWH, p. 45.

[15] BCWH, p. 160. The *Meistersinger* had just been successfully given in Paris for the first time (1897).

[16] BCWH, pp. 191–2. The French novel that had given her so unfavourable an opinion of the French was Anatole France's *L'anneau d'améthyste*, which had been published about that time (1899). Cosima was convinced that it was "unbearably characteristic of the decomposition going on there".

the 1890's her Germanised eye saw all kinds of mysterious and sinister forces at work which were providentially concealed not only from the purely British spectators of the events of those days but from the purely British participants in them. When the Liberal Government of Lord Rosebery fell in the summer of 1895, largely because of its Home Rule leanings, Cosima gravely asked herself and her correspondent " whether its activities were merely ' ridiculous ', as one of the electors thought, or whether it was the Jewish instinct, or perhaps a Catholic plan for the ruin of England." [17]

The Jews and the Catholics, but especially the Jews, accounted, in Cosima's opinion, for most of Europe's ills, as well as for most of the opposition to Wagner. For her to know or to suspect that a man was a Jew was sufficient to deprive her of all capacity to see him steadily and see him whole. " The names of the leaders in the [Russian] anarchy — Lenin and Bornstein-Trotsky! " — she wrote in 1918, " prove to me once more that at all times and in all places the Semitic element is the undermining and disintegrating element. My son says jestingly that Robespierre and Marat must have been really Rubinstein and Marx." [18] But if Cosima was incapable of reasoning lucidly where Jews were concerned, she had no more objection than Wagner had to making use of them when they could serve her own and the Wagnerian purpose. It was, to be sure, a redeeming feature in any Jew's character that he should devote himself to Bayreuth; but even then the poor man could not escape the curse of his race. Both she and Wagner made abundant use of Hermann Levi — it was he, indeed, who conducted the first performance of the highly Christian *Parsifal* at Bayreuth in 1882; but when he died in 1900 the best she could find to say of him was this:

" Though he could not get away from his extraction, and numerous failings of his race showed themselves markedly in him, yet he distinguished himself by his great fidelity to Bayreuth, and I confess that the Jewish element in him often amused more than it irritated me, because it showed itself with such diverting openness." [19]

---

[17] BCWH, p. 123.
[18] BCWH, p. 368.
[19] BCWH, p. 203. Weingartner gives us, from first-hand experiences, a painful picture of the contemptuous rudeness of the Wagner family towards Levi in the years following Wagner's death—merely because he was a Jew. One would not

For so upright a Jewish artist as Joachim, however, she could never
find a good word, for Joachim had *not* " distinguished himself by
his great fidelity to Bayreuth ". For Cosima he was always "the
apostate " [20] who had turned his back on Wagner and Liszt. In
1877, when in London, she saw Watts's masterly portrait of him.
" The whole biography of the excessively vile person ", she wrote,
" lies open to me in this portrait. The painter had no intention of
this; and his artistic talent reveals itself precisely by the fact that
he has represented the truth without being aware of it, while meaning, indeed, to express something splendid." [21] When, some years
later, she met Joachim's daughters in Bayreuth, she could not fail
to admit it as a good point in them that they were interested in
Wagner, but still she could not help seeing their race in them: " I
cannot say ", she wrote to a friend,

> " that they have anything Germanic about them, but in them the Orien-
> tal cast expresses itself in the most singular softness and submissive-
> ness. When I thought of the connections of the father and then looked
> at these children I was deeply moved, particularly because it occurred
> to me that the vileness of the ancestors lay like a veil or a check upon
> the mind and the bent of the children. I can say that both these girls
> won me over." [22]

5

It was a mind insatiably avid of knowledge and experience, but
fundamentally limited. She read widely and indefatigably: but
hardly one of her thousand comments upon literature, art, history
or politics reveals her as anything more than an earnest, self-
assured dilettante, with nothing of her mother's fine sense of values.
As a child she had been encouraged, nay, forced, to commit to

have thought Cosima's Wahnfried capable of such an exhibition of ill-breeding. See
WL, I, 264–5. On one occasion the youthful Weingartner ventured to protest to
Cosima against her behaviour to Levi. "She heard me out quietly", he says, "and
then replied that no bond between Aryan and Semitic blood was possible." WL, I,
266.

[20] MECW, II, 774.

[21] MECW, I, 802. The ordinary person looks in vain in the Watts portrait for
the revelation of an "excessively vile" personality. Du Moulin Eckart's commentary
on the above passage is equally rich: "The sight of Joachim's portrait, awakening
as it did all her unpleasant memories of this enemy of her father and of her first and
her second husband, and revealing him clearly as a felon", etc.

[22] MECW, II, 428–9.

writing her opinions upon what she had recently read or seen; and she retained all her life the habit of stuffing her letters with little essays that show no more basic understanding of the subject she happens to be discussing than any paper read by any young lady at any meeting of any provincial literary society might do.

As a child of thirteen she dutifully wrote to her father:

> " I have read Augustin Thierry's *La Conquête de l'Angleterre par les Normands,* which interested me very much and was very useful for understanding the history of England. I like the Saxons far better than the Normans, but I have never liked Harold. I do not regard it as good to swear to free one's country and then not to give it freedom. At Grandmamma's I had a dispute on this point with an Englishwoman, who preferred the Normans, which I could never understand."

A year or so later she writes, " I do not like Chateaubriand's character. For me his soul is too dry, too cold, and moreover egotistical." There is no essential difference between that naïve kind of thing and this of half a century later, à propos of Gladstone and the Irish:

> " When now I remember the impression made on me by Mr. Gladstone's physiognomy in Lenbach's living portrait of him, it seems to me that once again we have before us on the one side humanitarian phrases, the passion for popularity, and the levity that goes along with these, on the other side the concern for the maintenance of the highest interests of a nation and the appearance of sternness, even cruelty, that is always allied with this concern ";

or this about the elder Dumas:

> " He represents a side of the novel — adventure, invention — which is in a certain sense just what we ask for in a novel, and the antithesis of which is the minutely psychological heart-analysis typified by Richardson in *Clarissa Harlowe* and by Rousseau in *La Nouvelle Héloise,* and, unfortunately, inevitably made somewhat wearisome there ";

or this, after reading, about the same time, Zola's *Lourdes* and Scott's *Fair Maid of Perth:* the latter

> " is indeed something quite different, and we fully understand the admiration so often expressed by Goethe for this fine work. Here Walter Scott reveals himself as a real artist in the way he holds together the most extensive action and shows us each small part, however remote it may be from the others, as belonging to the whole. His

figures, whether they be princes, peasants or burghers, are of extraordinary pregnancy, and not one of them bears a label, or is dissected before our eyes. And the whole thing moves along quietly and animatedly, like a lovely river, as it were the Rhine at Basel, which I saw lately, and that once more made a great impression on me." [23]

Or take her little essay on Cromwell, in a letter of about 1892:

" It is very difficult to speak of this man, before whom we stand as before a phenomenon of nature. He is the only case known to me of military genius without previous training in that line. Whereas Napoleon, Frederick the Great and Moltke had pursued a military career from their youth up, and revealed their vocation precisely by this choice, Cromwell, their peer, comes out of a tranquil agricultural life, and shows himself superior to them in that he first of all had to make an army; and he was so conscious of his earthly mission that he opposed to the principle of the monarchy and of an aristocracy by birth the idea of faith. But as this monarchy regarded itself as instituted by God, we see here the revolt of innermost cognition against everything that is taken for granted, against hallowed convention. And the unique feature of this phenomenon, it seems to me, is the fact that the hero felt within himself the strength and title to oppose misused right, as the executor of the will of God." [24]

And so on. There are pages and pages of this kind of thing in her letters, from first to last the mere ink-spilling of a literary schoolgirl who has never grown up, the sort of stuff which any English magazine editor, were it sent to him, would consign straight off to the waste-paper basket. It passed current, however, and apparently still passes, for the highest wisdom in the inner Wagner circle, where, indeed, Wagner himself had been accustomed to talk with the same assurance and as little understanding about matters in which he was only a cultivated dilettante.[25] The vast majority of Cosima's comments upon men and books and events, contemporary and historical, never rise above this dead level of complacent platitude; and, apart from the naturally wider range of literary clichés in the mature woman, there is little intellectual

---

[23] The quotations from the mature Cosima are all from the Hohenlohe-Langenburg correspondence (BCWH).

[24] MECW, II, 438–9.

[25] One evening in 1879 he assured Cosima that in *Lohengrin* "he had given a complete picture of the Middle Ages". Not to be outdone in dilettantism, she capped this nonsense with "*Lohengrin* is the *one and only* monument of the Middle Ages." (MECW, I, 878).

difference between what she wrote when she was fifteen and what she wrote when she was seventy-five.

But if she exhibited no intelligence above the ordinary as a critic of literature and art or as a student of politics and history, she was endowed with a mind and a temperament of the ideal kind for her pre-ordained mission in life — to be a companion to Wagner and to further the interests of his art. She had everything that he desired, and nothing that jarred on him. She was intelligent enough to be able to place herself at his point of view in everything, but very rarely intelligent enough to have a point of view of her own that might distress him by conflicting with his. She was a past mistress in the rare and delicate domestic tact which Edmund Gosse, *à propos* of his own father and mother, has described as " that artful female casuistry which insinuates into the wounded consciousness of a man the conviction that, after all, he is right, and all the rest of the world is wrong." She believed as firmly as Wagner did in not only the all-importance of his work but the all-rightness of his judgment upon practically every subject under the sun. She was the perfect and complete Yes-man before the Americans ever thought of that human automaton. She saw the whole contemporary world, as Wagner did, under one sole aspect, as something to be conquered for Wagnerian art, and that not so much because it was Wagner's art but because it was the only means to the salvation of European culture. She brought to her task a persistency as indomitable as his own,[26] and several qualities in which he was notoriously lacking — a self-poise that nothing could

---

[26] Walther Siegfried gives an amusing example of her quiet inflexibility and resource. At the rehearsals for a *Tannhäuser* production at Bayreuth (after Wagner's death, of course), the young woman who was to play Elisabeth used to emphasise the heroine's greeting of the Hall of Song by entering with her arms stretched out as if to take it to her bosom. In this she was aided and abetted by her teacher, a former Elisabeth who had found this style of entry very "effective" in her own theatre. Cosima insisted that it would be more in keeping with the mediæval milieu and with the un-selfconscious nature of Elisabeth for the singer to enter quite simply, with her arms by her side. It all ended with a secret understanding between the singer and her teacher that the former was to humour Cosima at the rehearsals but to do the thing in the "effective" way "on the night", the teacher amiably promising her pupil that she would wring her neck if she disobeyed her. After the performance, in which Elisabeth had greeted the Hall of Song with her arms in repose, the teacher furiously demanded an explanation; she learned that when the girl had dutifully tried to raise her arms she had found that Cosima had had the sleeves of Elisabeth's mantle sewn up in such a way as to make it impossible. SFCW, pp. 89–90.

disturb,[27] a consummate knowledge of how to manage people, an instinct for diplomacy and a command of the subtler nuances of the language of diplomacy that few German politicians have ever possessed. Wagner was heartened by her unshakable belief in him, not only as an artist but as a man; [28] their perfect community of thought made it possible for him to delegate the most delicate tasks to her in full confidence that they would be carried out precisely as if he had handled them himself; while her social polish gave his household a distinction that was of the utmost benefit to him in his later years. It is doubtful whether without her he could ever have completed his creative work or achieved the triumph of Bayreuth: it is practically certain that but for her Bayreuth would have perished not long after his death.

6

The route by which she gradually came to him is not easy to map out in detail, for lack of some of the necessary first-hand documents. Liszt had had no grandiose ideas with regard to the settlement of his children in life. As he had ceased to earn money as a pianist and a great part of the fortune he had made in earlier years had been dissipated in high living and in benefactions of all kinds, public and private, the dowry he could promise the two girls was relatively small. For all his own adoration of titles and his inveterate tuft-hunting, he seems to have had the sense to perceive that a sober bourgeois marriage would in the long run be the best thing for their happiness. He had no desire to fetter their choice when the time should come for them to exercise it; he only hoped, he said, that it would fall on neither a musician nor a doctor. That Cosima's first husband should be a musician was decided by the Fates, ironically enough, through the Princess Wittgenstein. Her last decisive act in her warfare with Marie d'Agoult had been to persuade Liszt to remove the girls from Paris (in September, 1855),

[27] The only instance in which she can be seen to have lost her head completely was that of her desperate appeal to King Ludwig to vindicate her "honour" by means of a letter, intended for publication, to Hans von Bülow. See infra, p. 547.

[28] See her testimony to "his pure nature, which is as lofty as the glaciers", in Vol. I, p. 431.

and place them in the charge of Bülow's mother in Berlin.[29] Bülow was entrusted with their musical education. He taught them the piano himself; and he has left us his testimony to Cosima's ability as a pianist.[30] Theory she studied with Weitzmann, one of the most distinguished musical scholars of that epoch. Bülow had made many enemies in Berlin musical circles by his propaganda for Wagner and Liszt. At one of his concerts he conducted the *Tannhäuser* overture. It was hissed. Bülow's nerves snapped under the

---

[29] New light has recently been thrown on Cosima and Wagner by the *Erinnerungen an Richard Wagner* (HERW) of Princess Marie zu Hohenlohe, the daughter of Liszt's Princess von Wittgenstein, and the "Child" of whom Wagner was so fond in the 1850's. (Marie was some ten months older than Cosima, having been born on the 18th February, 1837.] She married in October, 1859 Prince Konstantin von Hohenlohe-Schillingsfürst, who later became Obersthofmeister at the Court of the Austrian Emperor Franz Joseph. She died on the 20th January, 1920. The few pages recently published containing her reminiscences of Wagner — evidently written about 1889 — are now in the Richard Wagner Museum in Eisenach. They are not signed, but the handwriting is hers, and the paper on which they are written bears the Hohenlohe coat of arms).

Princess Marie, as the reader will remember, was one of the small company to which Wagner read the *Ring* poem in October, 1853, partly in Basel, partly in Paris. (See Vol. II, p. 393). She admits that she did not understand very much of it, while evidently its peculiar phraseology was rather too much for Blandine and Cosima, whose German was not far enough advanced at that time to enable them to cope with this kind of thing. Marie, who had been brought up from infancy in the larger social world, saw Blandine as a pretty girl already rather pleased with herself, and Cosima as an awkward *Backfisch*, "tall and angular, with a sallow complexion, a wide mouth, and a long nose — the image of her father": she had beautiful hair, however. "In the poor child's heart", continues Marie, "a volcano raged. Obscure stirrings of love pulsated within her, along with an overweening vanity: and now and then her lips would curl mischievously with the inborn mockery of the Parisienne." Wagner, it seems, "had no eyes for the ugly child."

Marie further informs us that Frau von Bülow had reluctantly accepted the charge of Blandine and Cosima, but had been unable to refuse to take them after all that Liszt had done for Hans.

Apparently Wagner and Marie did not meet again, after her marriage in 1859, until 1876, in Vienna: one surmises that at some time in the intervening years he had tried to borrow money from her and had been refused — perhaps at the instigation of the Prince.

There was a mild estrangement for a while between Cosima and Marie over the publication of Liszt's letters to the Princess Wittgenstein: the property in these was vested in Marie under her mother's will, but Cosima held that she had a certain *moral* right in them. (See MCEW, II, 327, 511, 625, 778, etc.).

[30] "You ask me, dear Master", he wrote to Liszt on the 30th September, 1855, "for news of Mesdemoiselles Liszt. It would have been impossible for me to send you any until now, in the state of stupefaction, admiration and even exaltation to which they had reduced me, especially the younger one [Cosima]. As regards musical disposition they are not talents but geniuses. They are truly the daughters of my benefactor, quite exceptional beings." (BLW, p. 152). In Cosima's playing he recognised "ipsissimum Lisztum". Wagner, in later years, praised Cosima's Beethoven playing.

strain: he fell into a faint after the concert, was attended to in the artists' room, and did not arrive home until two in the morning; Liszt accompanied him to the door but did not go in with him. Frau von Bülow, Cosima and Blandine had been at the concert. On their return, Cosima, who had been stirred to her depths by sympathy for Bülow, proposed that they should all wait up for Hans. The others refusing, she kept vigil for him alone. She consoled the broken man, and, it is generally supposed, offered him her hand in pledge of comradeship in his fight for an ideal that was also hers. Liszt had no basic objection to the marriage, but merely stipulated for a longish delay, which was natural enough in the circumstances. Cosima and Bülow were married on the 18th August, 1857. She did all she could to encourage and fortify him in his artistic mission, not only as a performer but as a composer.

Marie Hohenlohe, who, as Liszt's step-daughter (in a sense) and the friend of Cosima and Hans, can be taken as representing the views of the inner Lisztian circle on this matter, gives the following account of the situation before and after the marriage.

" Cosima remained in Berlin [after Blandine's return to Paris]. She had developed into an imposing personality, acute and self-conscious, but still filled with obscure urgings of affection. Her relations with the duenna [Frau von Bülow] who had been forced upon her necessarily became hostile: Frau von Bülow was perpetually scolding and complaining about her son, who would not share her petty interests: and this was reason enough for Cosima to bestow her full sympathy on Hans. The ailing, nervous, essentially dry Bülow was not the Siegfried who in the long run could subdue this young Valkyrie. But he felt flattered by the favour of the gifted young woman, and it particularly answered to his ambition to become the son-in-law of his universally admired master; while Liszt, on the other hand, was rejoiced to see his favourite child safe and settled. Marriage for her meant freedom and redemption from her dubious social situation [as an illegitimate child]. And so this marriage, which contained so much combustible material in it, was concluded to everyone's satisfaction. . . . Cosima strove honourably in the early years to be the faithful, valiant comrade of her husband. . . . She was an excellent housewife, energetic in every department, bearing cheerfully with her husband's morbid whims and his perpetual peevishness. Not that the fairies had endowed her in her cradle with mildness and gentleness: on the contrary, by her lofty self-confidence and her inborn sharpness she offended most women and many German men of her acquaintance, who complained that she was unfeminine. In later years she became the most affectionate and solicitous of mothers, and remained so throughout all the storms of her life." [31]

<h1 style="text-align:center">7</h1>

We know comparatively little of the details of Bülow's and Cosima's life together during the years immediately following their marriage. Whether there was ever much romantic affection between them is doubtful: romance of that kind was perhaps not in Bülow's constitution. But he had the profoundest respect for Cosima's mind and heart, a respect, indeed, that was not far from awe. Paradoxically enough in so obstinate and quarrelsome a man, there was a strong inferiority complex in him: it accounts not only for Wagner's immense hold over him but for the curious confessions in his letters and conversations of his sense of Cosima's superiority. As early as June, 1856 he had written to Jessie Laussot,

"These two wonderful girls have a right to their name; they are full of talent, spirit and life — interesting phenomena such as I have seldom met with. Anyone else but myself would be happy to associate with them. Their obvious superiority, however, embarrasses me; and the impossibility of appearing sufficiently interesting in their eyes prevents me from appreciating the pleasure of their society as I should like. This is a confession the candour of which you will not deny. It is not flattering for a young man, but it is out-and-out true." [32]

In the noble and moving letter he wrote to Cosima on the 17th June, 1869,[33] after she had definitely severed her life from his, he not only stressed once more his obligations to her — without her, he said, he was now a " bankrupt " — but expressed his regret at having " very badly, very ill-naturedly recompensed you for all the devotion you have lavished on me in our past life "; *her* life, he said, he had " poisoned ". Precisely what lies behind that self-reproach we do not know; we can only guess at it, or at part of it. All his life Bülow was an ailing man, his nerves constantly in tatters through the strain he put upon them in his public work and through the violent enmities he roused, wherever he went, by the sharpness of his tongue and his ruthlessness in the pursuit of his ideal. We of today who have been taught to see him only as the sincerest of artists and a great gentleman in more than one difficult situation do not see anything like the whole of him. With his peevish furies and his equally peevish despairs, his nervous storms and his wounding sarcasms, he must have been at times a sore domestic trial.[34] " Hans von Bülow ", says Du Moulin Eckart,

> " was not the kind of man who is made for marriage. His violence was often so great that, long before the entry of Wagner into the Bülow household, a Berlin doctor had said that it was marvellous that Frau Cosima could stand such a state of affairs at all. But she was too much of an artist's child not to be able to do so. She knew the violence of her own father, and was able to see beyond the indefinable exasperation that was the result of Hans's artistic production and activity: she managed to get through the most passionate scenes with a certain coolness, and even with the display of a certain humour." [35]

" Cosima achieves a marvellous work of art by managing to endure life with me ", Bülow confessed to his sister in June, 1862.

> " My own nature inclines to the feminine; my wife is strong-minded, and unfortunately has so little need of my protection that on the contrary she bestows hers on me. Thank God that you haven't an artist for a husband, and particularly a musician! " [36]

---

[34] The recent publication, for the first time, of the letter Cosima had addressed to Hans on the 15th June, 1869 — to which the letter of Bülow referred to above is the reply — raises the suspicion that she had suffered woefully from his ironic bitterness of speech in those hours of frustration and depression that were frequent with him. She begins her letter by saying that she has heard that before he leaves Germany he desires to hear from her with regard to the children and to the future generally. "This gives me courage", she continues, "to send you a few lines: I do so in great timidity, begging you not to be irritated if they come at an inopportune moment. I have never been very fortunate in my conversations with you: when I have tried to re-establish an honourable peace between us you have answered me with irony: when I have asked for a definitive separation you have refused to listen to me. Today I beg you to listen to me in a kindly spirit, retiring into yourself and forgetting external things, and recalling what we have suffered in common for so many years." "The memory", she says later, "of our domestic life together from the second year of our betrothal onwards has always been with me to prove to me that, however sincerely I have tried to do so, I could not make you happy. Nothing that I did was right. How many times, when you were ill, you have sent me away from your bedside without my understanding why! You will remember, too, that when I was enceinte with Loulou [Daniela] I did not dare to tell you of it, as if my pregnancy had been illegitimate; I revealed it to you in a dream." KLRWB, V, 115 ff.

[35] MECW, I, 419–20. Du Moulin Eckart no doubt derived a good deal of his information about Bülow from his own father, who knew Hans well, having gone to Berlin in April, 1857, on Wagner's recommendation, to study music with him. See Bülow's letter to Liszt of the 19th April, 1857, in BLW, p. 205.

[36] Quoted in SHB, p. 15.

Even before his marriage, Bülow seems to have doubted whether he was doing altogether right in tying Cosima to him for the rest of his life — a point which we shall do well to remember when, in a later chapter, we shall have to try to elucidate the Wagner-Cosima-Bülow triangle. In the letter in which he formally asked for Cosima's hand he wrote to Liszt: " I swear to you that, strongly as I feel bound to her by my love, I would never hesitate to sacrifice myself to her happiness — to set her free if she should discover that she has been deceived in me."

Cosima appears also to have suffered greatly in the Berlin days from the cold, hard nature of her mother-in-law; her second child was actually born without a doctor in attendance, Frau von Bülow having callously left her alone in her travail. Cosima bore all her trials with the marvellous patience — or appearance of patience — and self-command that were characteristic of her throughout her life: it was not for nothing that she had absorbed the teachings of Thomas à Kempis in her childhood. One may doubt, as Du Moulin says, whether she ever felt " a real passion " for Bülow: such bond as there ever was between them was perhaps purely intellectual. But it is unquestionable that she faced the domestic and external difficulties of their early life together with unwavering evenness of spirit, and that Bülow knew himself to be deeply in her debt for her courage, steadfastness and devotion.

8

It was probably only by slow stages that she succeeded in " composing " herself after the fashion of some work of art by a painter or a sculptor, a " composition " that was later to make it difficult for the world to see her just as she was. The letters of her early twenties, especially those to Georg and Emma Herwegh, have a lightness of touch, a gay humour of observation and a springiness of step that tended to disappear from her writing as she grew older and more German. In part, of course, the greater *verve* of these early letters may come from the fact that the language of them is French; but even so, the livelier tempo of her mind at that time is manifest enough. There is abundant testimony to her youthful gaiety also, especially when she was with Blandine. There must have been a good deal of dangerous substance in her that she only gradually learned to face squarely and to fight down. Her mother wrote of her in 1857, in a letter to Emma Herwegh,

" I too have often and very vividly experienced the *double* impression which you describe for me so strikingly. She [Cosima] is a quite extraordinary creature to be living in the present day, this child of passion and liberty. There is goodness in her, and grandeur. Judgment often fails her, but that will come only too soon, perhaps with the sad experience of life." [37]

In the preceding October also she had diagnosed both her daughters accurately. " Blandine ", she wrote to Madame Herwegh,

" is beautiful, witty, very cultivated, and charms everyone by graces that are eminently feminine. Cosima is a girl of genius, very like her father. Her powerful imagination will take her out of the ordinary routes. She feels the *démon intérieur,* and will always resolutely sacrifice to it everything it may demand of her. Circumstances have pushed her into a marriage in which, I fear, there will be no happiness for anyone." [38]

That there was a wild strain in Cosima which, in her earlier years, was liable to break through the restraints she had learned even by then to impose on her feelings, is shown by the episode to which reference has already been made, in another connection, in the Foreword to Volume One of the present Life. As the reader will remember, Bülow and Cosima visited Zürich in August, 1858, during the last melancholy days of Wagner in the Asyl. Leaving Hans with Wagner for a few days, Cosima accompanied her mother back to Geneva, where they were to meet Blandine Liszt; Karl Ritter escorted them, and remained a little while with the sisters. Early in September Karl came to see Wagner in Venice, where he told him the curious story which Wagner passed on to Frau Wesendonk in his letter of the 4th — a letter which was suppressed in the public issue of the Wagner-Mathilde correspondence. At Geneva, it seems, there had been a passionate scene with Karl. Cosima had asked him to kill her: he, who was unhappy in his own marriage,

---

[37] HAPD, p. 181. A few days later her mother writes: "I have a predilection for her which *circumstances* have made more painful than joyful. But the poor child also has suffered greatly, in spite of her courage and her youth."
[38] HAPD, p. 167.

offered to die with her. She wanted to throw herself from a boat into the Lake, and desisted from her purpose only because he swore to follow her. "So it has all been left in a passionately unclear suspense", says Wagner: "they parted with the understanding that at the end of three weeks they were to give each other news of their circumstances, their mood, and their further resolution. The outcome of this conflict remains to be seen."

Writing again to Mathilde on the 30th September, Wagner says that at the end of the three weeks Cosima wrote to Karl regretting her vehemence, of which she was now ashamed, and asking him to forget what had happened. Millenkovich-Morold's reading of the episode strikes one as correct — Karl having opened his heart to Cosima about the miseries of his marriage, that revelation had given her an intolerable sense of the unhappiness of her own: thereupon Karl had crudely assumed that here was the promise of an "affair" which would compensate him for his own bad fortune, as to which Cosima, having regained command of herself, had to disillusion him. "He feels bitterly offended", says Wagner to Frau Wesendonk, "and will not reply to her." Wagner is puzzled about Cosima, whose melancholy had impressed him during the Asyl days: what had really happened within her, he says, he does not understand: "I regard her, however, as the higher nature." Then comes a passage in the letter that throws some light, however faint, on the non-success of her marriage with Bülow.

> "If she can hold out — for Hans, who is a good, talented being, but not a significant, decisive and wholly absorbing one, does not suffice for her — I shall watch her inner development with profound interest. She deserves your consideration. Through this matter I have once more experienced a thorough horror of youthful marriages; except in the case of wholly insignificant people, I have never yet come across *one* the radical error of which did not reveal itself in time." [39]

The probability is that both Ritter and Cosima, in their several ways, had been made additionally conscious of their own marital unhappiness by the distressing scenes between Wagner and Minna

---

[39] Ellis and others assumed this last sentence to refer to Karl Ritter's marriage. We now know that it had reference to Cosima's. This particular passage appears in the official edition of the Wagner-Mathilde letters; everything else cited in the paragraph above from Wagner's letters to Mathilde of the 4th and 30th September has been suppressed in that edition. The full text will be found in Julius Kapp's article on *Unbekannte Wagner-Dokumente*, in the *Berliner Illustrierte Nachtausgabe*

at the Asyl. On the 16th August, the day before Wagner left the Asyl for ever, Bülow and Cosima took leave of him, Hans, he tells us in *Mein Leben,* bathed in tears, Cosima gloomy and silent. From the suppressed passage in the letter to Mathilde of the 4th September we learn that after the return from Geneva

> " Cosima was in a strangely excited state, which showed itself especially in convulsively passionate tenderness towards me. At our parting the next day she fell at my feet, and covered my hands with tears and kisses: astonished and alarmed, I gazed into this mystery without being able to find the key to it."

Her feelings were no doubt as much a mystery to Cosima herself as they were to him. At the root of them, no doubt, was simply a dumb sense of his misery, which seems to have become symbolical for her of hopeless human suffering in general; and from this the transition to revolt against her own unhappy condition would be natural.

9

Before that time she does not appear to have been particularly attracted to Wagner as a man. The reader will remember that Cosima and Hans had previously stayed at the Asyl for some three weeks in August and September, 1857, immediately after their marriage. Something in Wagner's nature, or perhaps even more in his none too polished manner, seems to have jarred on the finely-bred young woman at that time and to have left her decidedly cool towards him afterwards; for on the 18th January following we find him telling Hans that Cosima's reserve towards him disturbs him:

---

of the 25th November, 1930. This and other expansions of the official Wagner-Wesendonk text were set forth later by Kapp in KUD, pp. 877–883.

It had been Wagner's wish that Mathilde should destroy his letters: she could not bring herself to do so because she felt that they belonged to the world as much as to herself. Her desire was that they should be published unexpurgated. Cosima, however, appears to have insisted on the deletion of certain things. That she should have objected to the publication of such passages about herself as those just quoted, and of others in which the Wagner of 1858 had enlarged on the contrast between the commonplace Ritter-Cosima episode and the ideal nature of the Wagner-Mathilde union, is easily understandable. A few other passages here and there in the letters, containing remarks by Wagner about certain people that are harmless enough in themselves but that might have given pain (in 1904) to those concerned, if still alive, oɪ to their descendants, were also rightly deleted; and Cosima's filial piety no doubt made her shrink from publishing to the world a disparaging remark or two of Wagner's about certain little weaknesses in Liszt's character — his tuft-hunting, for example.

" should my manner have been too singular in her eyes, should she have been hurt now and then by a rough expression on my part, by a slight scorn (with regard to the Herweghs, etc.), I should be justified in regretting having let myself go a trifle too far in my confidences. . . . My completely regardless familiarity with those who are sympathetic to me has already estranged many people from me: may your dear young wife's estrangement not last long! "

She had evidently not approved of his treatment of the Herweghs, to whom she felt particularly drawn at that time: while recognising Minna's intellectual unfitness to be Wagner's life-companion, she had a good deal of plain human sympathy for her: and there was something in Wagner's way of ordering his life that grated on her. When, in the spring of 1857, a subscription was being raised for Lamartine, who, after a life of sacrifice for humanity, had fallen on evil days, she wrote to her young friend Marie Wittgenstein,

" It makes one angry that one cannot have the mines of Peru to place at the feet of this greatest of poets and citizens. For my part I confess that I would give them to him rather than to Richard of Zürich. . . . I have come to the conclusion that the famous bankruptcy of Wagner is happily covered by this modern Beatrice [Frau Wesendonk], who opens out to her poet the heavens of material tranquillity and easy luxury — perhaps the only heaven in which he believes! "

A little later she was annoyed with him for having " almost threatened " to take the *Tristan* piano transcription from Hans and give it to " the Jew " Tausig: " Wagner n'est pas gentil ", she says. His peculiar brand of Saxon humour she appears to have found lacking in delicacy. " Did I tell you ", she writes to Marie Wittgenstein in July, 1858, just before her second visit to the Asyl,

" that a few days ago I had a letter from Zürich, a letter the ' humour ' of which approached the ridiculous? Richard, in an access of gaiety, writes me *à propos* of nothing and talks to me as if I were a child of three months old, so that I felt inclined to ask him if he had not made a mistake in the address — whether the letter was not intended for Herwegh's [bâby] son. I did not reply: I put this facetious *entrain* down to a paroxysm of passion for la belle Mathilde."

She judged him at this time with an objectivity that decidedly inclined to harshness. " What you tell me ", she wrote to Emma Herwegh on the 21st June, 1858,

" of our very illustrious friend Richard's situation distresses and sur-
prises me to some extent. Although I knew of the sad scenes between
the wife and the husband, I did not know that matters would go as
far as this; and I can see only sadness and prose in the conflicts of a
love [i.e. Wagner's and Mathilde Wesendonk's] born of ennui, vanity
and the need for money! Like you, I am sorry for Madame Minna,
yet at the same time unable to blame Richard, who, consumed by the
necessity of the ideal and of repose, and weary of the monotonous and
incessant worries of his life, flies for a morsel of happiness to a pale
and sickly creature [40] who is as incapable of living energetically a
simple and straight life as of breaking her existing ties in order to
abandon herself to love and support her lover. Let us hope that equi-
librium will be re-established by simple means and without too many
scenes." [41]

That was her view of Wagner before the fateful journey to
the Asyl in 1858. She had gone there that summer for Hans's sake
rather than her own, expecting to be half-entertained, half-bored
by Wagner's domestic and other infelicities. "When I get to
Zürich", she had promised Marie, "I will tell you all about the
tragi-comedies of which I shall be the witness and perhaps, alas,
the confidante." What she found there was not the tragi-comedy
she had anticipated but a pure tragedy of the most heartrending
kind: for the first time, one gathers, she pierced below the superficial commonnesses and uglinesses of Wagner's situation and
realised how much of his suffering was the result of his inability
as an artist to find anchorage in the world of reality.

10

We know too little of their attitude towards each other in the
years immediately ensuing to permit of more than the most tenta-
tive psychologising about it. We see them meeting occasionally in
Reichenhall and elsewhere, sometimes in the company of Liszt and
Blandine; and perhaps in Wagner's " confidentially jesting " remark about Bülow to Liszt in Weimar — " There was no need for
him to have married Cosima "; to which Liszt " replied, with a

[40] In the preceding summer Cosima had found Mathilde, as we gather from a
letter to Marie Wittgenstein, "fort gentille, quoi qu'un peu sentimentale."
[41] For the letters to Marie Wittgenstein see BLE, p. 162 ff., and for those to the
Herweghs HAPD, p. 210 ff.

slight bow, ' That was a luxury ' '', — we may find a hint not only
of a widening gulf between Cosima and Hans but of a rapprochement between her and Wagner. At the parting from Cosima and
Blandine in Reichenhall in August, 1861, he tells us rather mysteriously, she gave him " an almost timid look of enquiry ". The few
remaining references to her, direct or veiled, with which we meet
in *Mein Leben* have obviously an esoteric significance upon which
the minds of both of them were dwelling retrospectively when they
were at work upon the autobiography. In Frankfort, in 1862,

> " Cosima seemed to have lost the shyness that had struck me a year
> before in Reichenhall; it had changed into something very friendly.
> One day when I was singing Wotan's Farewell to my friends I noticed
> the same expression on her face as I had seen, to my astonishment, at
> that farewell of ours in Zürich in 1858,[42] only the ecstasy of it was now
> serenely transfigured. It was all veiled in silence and secrecy; but the
> belief that she belonged to me grew to such certainty within me that
> in moments of strange excitement I fell into the most unbridled
> exuberance."

He was reminded of this " expression " once more in November,
1863. He had spent the night of the 28th under Bülow's roof in
Berlin, on his way from Mainz to Löwenberg. While Bülow was
attending to the preparations for his concert of that evening Wagner and Cosima went for an afternoon drive. " This time ", he
says in *Mein Leben*,

> "there was no jesting for us silent ones: we gazed speechless into
> each other's eyes; and an intense longing for the fullest avowal of the

---

[42] He had apparently forgotten, when dictating this passage, that in his account
in *Mein Leben* of the parting at the Asyl he had said nothing about any such expression on Cosima's face: he had merely said that she was "gloomy and silent". The
gap in our knowledge at this point has now been filled in by the restoration of the
deleted passage in Wagner's letter of the 4th September to Frau Wesendonk.

That they had felt some sort of vague mystical attraction to each other even in
1858 is shown by several remarks of his in later years. "I ought to have taken you
with me to Venice that time in Zürich [1858]", he told her in 1878. "I had finished
with my wife, the situation as far as Hans was concerned was not yet so clearly defined, and you had no children. But I was as stupid as Tristan, and you were Isolde,
a *dumme Liese* [a goose]. We could have stayed in Italy, and it would all have been
sensible and rational." Again when they were in Taormina in 1882—"We should
have fled here in 1858, and so spared ourselves many, many a needless pain." And
yet again, a few months later, "Why did you not say to me then, in 1858, 'I will
live for no one but you'? Then I should have known what to do." He often lamented
to her that they had "found each other fifteen years too late". See MECW, I, 806,
840, 880, 963, 974.

truth overpowered us, to the point of a confession, not needing to be put into words, of the infinite unhappiness which weighed upon us. A load was lifted from us; in a mood of profound calm we found the necessary cheerfulness to attend the concert without a sense of oppression."

From the official edition of *Mein Leben,* however, a sentence has been omitted between the passage that ends with " weighed upon us " and the one commencing " a load was lifted from us ": it runs thus in the privately printed version of the autobiography: " With tears and sobs we sealed our confession to belong to each other alone." [43] Manifestly this was a decisive moment in the lives of both of them. Wagner spent the night under Bülow's roof, and left the town the next day. " The farewell ", he says,

> " reminded me so strongly of that first marvellously moving parting from Cosima in Zürich that the intervening years vanished like a confused dream between two days of the utmost importance in one's life. If on that earlier occasion a mysterious, uncomprehended presentiment had compelled silence, it was now no less impossible to give expression in words to what was tacitly acknowledged." [44]

This is the last occasion on which reference is made to Cosima in *Mein Leben.* No one acquainted with Wagner's way of saying just enough to permit of himself and Cosima indulging openly, as they laid their heads together over the autobiography, in the luxury of reminiscence, but not enough to let the reader into this or that secret between them, can have the least doubt that his carefully chosen words conceal even more than they reveal about the relations of the pair between about 1861 and 1863. We are told of Cosima's " almost timid look of enquiry ", of her " shyness " changing into " something very friendly ", of an ecstasy of expression which, for all the " veil of silence and secrecy ", gave him the certainty that she belonged to him. The words " silence " and

[43] KPWA, pp. 730–1.
[44] An entry in Cosima's diary for 1877 shows that for her the 28th November was the anniversary of the day "on which we found each other and became united." A telegram of hers of the 17th May, 1867 to Wagner, who was at that time in Triebschen, runs thus: "November-day, 10 April, Good Friday, 17th February . . ." which, being decoded, shows her to have been reminding Wagner of (a) the 28th November, 1863, (b) the date of Isolde's birth in 1865, (c) a certain oath of truth and fidelity to each other and the King taken on Good Friday, 1866, (d) the date of Eva's birth in 1867.

" avowal of the truth " recur like leading motives. There is assuredly some hidden significance, again, in his account in *Mein Leben* of his meeting with Marie von Buch [45] after his concert in Breslau early in December, 1863, when she happened to express her sympathy with him in his many anxieties. On his return to Vienna he sent her, at her request, a contribution to her album. " In recollection of the convulsive emotions that had accompanied my departure from Berlin " (obviously referring to his parting from Cosima), he tells us,

> " and at the same time as a revelation of my spiritual mood to one who was not unworthy of it, I added Calderon's words ' Things about which it is impossible to be silent, and impossible to speak out '; by which I felt I had conveyed, in a way clear to no one but myself, to a friendly soul, in a sort of happy obscurity, the one thing that had life within me."

One surmises from this that Cosima had already made Marie von Buch her confidante: and the reader will recall that it was to her that Cosima, immediately after her and Wagner's fate had been decided in Starnberg, wrote her the letter quoted on pages 262–3, between the lines of which the already initiated Marie would easily be able to read.

11

The strangest thing of all in these backward glances of Wagner and Cosima during the dictation of *Mein Leben* is a passage he inserts in his account of his brief visit to the Bülows in Berlin at the end of February, 1863. Cosima was nearing her second confinement. (Her daughter Blandine was born on the 20th March).[46] Bülow was a little hesitant about letting Wagner see Cosima, as he had once expressed his aversion from the sight of a woman in advanced pregnancy: Wagner gaily reassured him with the remark that nothing could possibly disturb him where Cosima was concerned. What hidden motive, we ask ourselves, could he have had

---

[45] One of Cosima's greatest friends and most trusted confidantes, both in the early Berlin days and afterwards. She married, about this time, Baron Schleinitz: later she became Countess Wolkenstein.

[46] Not on the 11th, as stated by Du Moulin Eckart and others.

for adding to his story, for transmission to posterity, so completely
unnecessary and tasteless a detail as this? As the eyes of the pair
met across the writing table during the dictation of that passage,
in the mind of each of them, perhaps, was the recollection of something to which they alone had the key, the luxury of which memory
they meant to savour even at the cost of the introduction into the
autobiography of something so paltry and irrelevant as this.[47]

The mystery deepens when we recall Wagner's adventures with
Friederike Meyer and other women during this period of his life,
his project, in 1864, for the restoration of his fortunes by a rich
marriage, and his later attempt to induce Mathilde Maier to throw
in her lot with him at Starnberg. Cosima, of course, must have
seemed unobtainable and almost inaccessible to him all this time,
married as she was and apparently located for good in Berlin; they
presumably resigned themselves to that " silence and secrecy " of
which he is so fond of speaking. Their week alone together in
Starnberg at the end of June and beginning of July, 1864 decided
the matter for them dramatically; and with the possibility of now
settling Bülow as conductor in Munich the way to something like a
solution of their problem at last became clear. Of their immense
love for each other there can be no question — Wagner's self-communings in the " Brown Book " are proof enough of that; while in
Cosima, moreover, he found the ideal collaborator, who made his
interests in Munich entirely her own. The situation there appealed
to her also because at last she had before her a field in which all her
gifts of energy and diplomacy, her love of power, and her unwavering persistence in pursuit of a single aim could find their full
outlet and their supreme satisfaction. The sense of her power, indeed, must have been an intoxication. It does not fall to the lot of
every young woman of twenty-six-and-a-half not only to have in
her hands the main threads of the most vital artistic movement of
an epoch, but to make her voice heard in a King's councils not
merely along with those of his ministers but often above them. And,
to do her justice, no other woman in Europe would have been equal
to all the tasks now and later put upon her.

Her technique in the Munich days was not quite perfect, espe-

---

[47] The passage in question was dictated about March, 1880.

cially where Wagner was concerned. Already she had an immense influence over him, but as yet she did not use it altogether wisely, or even tactfully. In later years she achieved her amazing success in the wise regulation of his life by creating about him the domestic environment most calculated to keep him happy — an environment of admirers for whom his will was law and his judgment in all things infallible: unpleasant people and things she mostly either kept away from him altogether or allowed them to reach him only after they had spent much of their force on her polite diplomacy. In the Munich days she had to take Wagner's personal environment as she found it; and there is abundant evidence of the resentment of some of his old male friends at her wedge-driving between him and them. Cornelius gives us a piquant vignette of a scene in the Briennerstrasse in October, 1865. The trouble began with Wagner, grown sentimental under the influence of wine, saying pathetically, " I have one friend — Bülow." Cornelius and Porges took the blow in silence; but Cosima was " beside herself because he had not said, ' I have one friend — Liszt '. She bickered with him the whole evening and opposed him in everything." The conversation turned afterwards on Vienna, and Cosima, who, according to Cornelius, had " a special talent for converting a conversation into an endless dispute ", so that she might have the pleasure of " bringing Richard under the slipper ", abused the Vienna public (which she hated), although she knew — or perhaps because she knew — that the others, including Bülow, had an affection for it. Later still she was forgetful enough to become enthusiastic over Schubert, whereupon Cornelius blandly pointed out to her that Schubert was the very incarnation of Vienna. " Ah, bah! " said Cosima, " you will be saying next that Wagner has some connection with Leipzig." Harmony was restored by Wagner, who — perhaps it was the wine again — was in jovial humour that evening. " Of course I have! " he said: " think of the Leipzig of those days — the first town that had regular concerts in the Gewandhaus, and was a centre of intellectual attraction."

It is pleasant to discover, from intimate little revelations of this kind, that at this time Wagner and Cosima were not always occupied in handling the King, manoeuvring against the politicians, and abusing the journalists. They could spare a little time occa-

sionally to be not historical figures but ordinary human beings.
As the years went on, Cosima made Wagner live up more and more
to what was expected of him as a historical figure. Male friends of
the Cornelius type, at once artists and men of the world, admiring
the great man but preserving their mental and spiritual independence as against him, enduring much from him but never failing to
show their resentment when he presumed too far on their indulgence, disappeared in time from the Triebschen and from the
Bayreuth hearth: Cosima came more and more to " compose "
Wagner as she did herself. There was a touch in her also, as she
herself admitted, of that obsequiousness to titles that was so characteristic of Liszt: this too became more pronounced as time went
on, and most pronounced of all in the years after Wagner's death,
when Bayreuth had become the centre of the artistic world. " It
is in the nature of things ", says Ludwig Schemann,

> " that in one's dealings with the children of this world it is not the
> noblest qualities that are developed and come to the front. For in-
> stance, Frau Cosima herself would have been the last to deny what it
> pained faithful people in full harmony with her to observe — that a
> commoner of standing had often to give way to some insignificant
> *Hochgeboren* or other: to one of her closest friends, indeed, she once,
> half in jest, half in earnest, described this *Fürstendienerei* [knee-
> bending to princes] as an inheritance from her father."

Immature in so many ways, however, as Cosima was in the
1860's, still she was Cosima, — sometimes, as her more discern-
ing friends saw, a danger to Wagner, but in the main a devoted and
highly capable ally.

CHAPTER XIII

SETTLING DOWN IN MUNICH

1

WITHOUT THE summer, rich as it had been in experiences, having brought him the improvement in physical health he had been hoping for, Wagner had to return to the town in the autumn of 1864 and make a start with the vast plans upon which he and the King had agreed. He seems to have left Starnberg on the 3rd October; on the evening of the 5th, as we have seen, he serenaded the King in Munich with the lately-written *Huldigungsmarsch*. First of all, of course, there was the question of his material future to be settled. A house — No. 21 in the Briennerstrasse, the long, broad street running from the Residenz to the Propyläen and the Glyptothek — had already been found for him by the King's orders. Wagner signed the agreement in respect of the lease on the 27th September; the owner is described as a " Frau Agnes Wagner, by a previous marriage Leinfelder." "I am on the point", he wrote to Mathilde Maier exultantly the same day, " of acquiring for the remainder of my life an extraordinarily fine house with a glorious garden, in the best part of the town."

On the 6th October he writes to Ludwig that he is now ready to dedicate himself to annihilation, his work to birth, and his King to the heritage of his fame. He feels elevated and inspired, he says, as he has never been before: now that the time for action has come he is able to comprehend the magnitude of the tasks he has undertaken. " I ask for three years of your royal grace, and on the twenty-second birthday of my noble Lord the work [the *Ring*] will be produced, and, through him, disclosed to the German nation "; he requests an hour's audience in which to talk over certain necessary preliminaries. At that audience — on the 7th — it was settled that Wagner was to have everything he might require for the completion and stage production of the *Ring*. The next day he set forth the terms of the proposed contract in a letter to the Cabinet Treasurer, Julius von Hofmann. To secure for him three years of leisure and comfort for the finishing of the *Ring*, he was to have (1) the Briennerstrasse house rent-free (the rent was 3,000 florins a year) from the 1st October, 1864 to the 1st October, 1867; (2) an addition of 2,000 florins a year to his present salary during those three years; (3) an immediate sum in cash of 15,000 gulden, in part for the suitable furnishing of the house, in part for the liquidation of old liabilities. He gives Hofmann " the well-considered and definite assurance " that this large additional grant, which he has asked for only in consideration of the fact that he will have to devote three years of the most intensive effort to his work, will be sufficient for all his necessities and his desires, and that no further demands upon the royal treasury need be feared; after all, as he airily points out, " altogether it only amounts to what can be made by a famous singer or dancer in three months, or what St. Petersburg pays for a new Verdi opera." [1] What it all amounted to was that he was to receive, in addition to his basic stipend of 4,000 florins, a total of 30,000 florins for the completion of the *Ring* within three years. No one, least of all Wagner himself, could have foreseen that it would be another eight years before the great work was finished.

The formal contract was signed by Hofmann and Wagner on the 18th October: the essential features of it were (1) that a copy of the score of each of the four operas was to be delivered to Hofmann within three years; (2) the work was to be the property of the King; (3) Wagner was to receive in all 30,000 florins — (a) an immediate payment of 15,000 florins, (b) 9,000 in six equal payments of 1,500 florins between the date of the signing of the contract and the 24th April, 1867, and (c) 6,000 in thirty-six equal monthly payments of 166 florins, 40 kreutzer, from the 1st November, 1864 to the 1st October, 1867; [2] (4) Wagner was to bear the whole expense

---

[1] The letter is given in full in RLW, II, 209–210.

[2] Sebastian Röckl, to whom we owe our knowledge of this document, creates some slight confusion by giving clause 3 (b) as "6,000 florins in six equal payments of 1,500 florins." The 6,000 is obviously a misprint for 9,000; while the "1st October, 1876" in Röckl's statement of clause 3 (c) should of course be the 1st October, 1867.

On the 6th December clauses 3 (a) and 3 (c) were amended by mutual agreement: Wagner was now to receive an extra 3,000 florins in immediate cash, but for the thirty-six monthly payments of 166 florins 40 kreutzer (6,000 florins in all) there were to be substituted thirty-six at 83 florins 20 kreutzer—a sum total of 3,000

THE LIFE OF RICHARD WAGNER

of preparing and copying the scores; (5) he was to render a statement, at the end of each contractual year, of the progress made with
the work; (6) an extension of the agreed-upon three years would
be permitted only in case of a long illness on his part, the stipulated
payments, in that case, to be adjusted accordingly; (7) should the
work be completed and delivered in less than three years, the balance of the total amount due to him under the agreement was to
be paid him in a lump sum, subject to the consent of the Treasury
to that course; (8) " should Herr Richard Wagner not observe the
within-mentioned terminal date, or any other such date to be mutually agreed upon later, Herr Hofmann is authorised to demand the
return of the honoraria paid to him,[3] and Herr Richard Wagner
hereby expressly renounces the right to protest against the enforce-
ment of this counterclaim "; (9) if Wagner should die before completing the work, so much of it as was finished was to be the property of the Treasury without claim on its part with regard to the
payments so far made, and without liability on its part to any third
party for any further payments.[4]

---

florins. Apparently Wagner had found that he needed more than 15,000 florins for
debts and furnishing, and was content to have his monthly payments docked accordingly—and to trust to something turning up during the next three years.

[3] Wagner, of course, would cheerfully sign his name to any stipulation of that
kind: in the first place he had no doubt, at the moment, that he would be able to
complete the *Ring* within the specified time, and in the second place he never worried
much about a hypothetical future. What he needed was always money there and
then. As a matter of fact the clause, as might have been expected, proved to be a
dead letter.

[4] RLW, II, 210 ff. After the founding of Bayreuth, for the express purpose of
presenting the *Ring* in a theatre of his own, Wagner came to regard this old contract
with the King as non-operative; but the Minister Düfflipp reminded him of it in
1877 when, as a means towards the liquidation of the debt of the 1876 festival,
Wagner was contemplating selling the performing rights of the tetralogy to some of
the larger German theatres, including Vienna. Glasenapp tries to make out (GRW,
V, 344–5) that the contract of 1864 was "never taken seriously" by either party,
the sole object of it being to enable the King to make Wagner an allowance without
antagonising public feeling in Munich. Ludwig, of course, consented, when the question was raised in 1877, to regard the agreement as null and void so far as the rights
conferred by it on him were concerned. But the ministers, in that year, were perfectly justified in taking the line they did. Nothing could be more definite than the
fact that Wagner had legally assigned his property in performances of the tetralogy
to the King; the latter's rescript of the 11th October, 1864 distinctly says: "My
Court Secretariat is accordingly to conclude an agreement with Richard Wagner
whereby the property in the composition named is assured to me." The ministers
were therefore within their legal rights in contending that Wagner had parted with
his theatrical property in the work.

2

Wagner entered upon possession of his new house on the 15th October. He describes it in his letter of the 30th September to Bülow as a " very expensive and enviable property, consisting of a very elegant residence, a beautiful garden, and a garden house suitable for a small family." In view of the high price put on it, a purchase of it is not to be thought of, at any rate for the moment; so the King is merely renting it for him for the present. Anyhow he will not leave it, he says, except for a house to be specially built for him; but " perhaps a way will be found for me to keep this property until my death — for which I long heartily in the depth of my soul, and which, I hope, will crown the production of my *Nibelungen*." The garden house, consisting of a drawing room and two bedrooms — together with a mews containing a pleasant room for the children — he offers to Hans and Cosima for the summer; in the winter they would occupy a house of their own which he has in mind for them in the Ludwigstrasse at a rent of 600 florins. (In May 1865 the King bought the Briennerstrasse house outright for Wagner, each of them being convinced, at that time, that Munich would be the composer's headquarters to the end of his days). He will be well looked after by his servants, he assures Bülow, and he is longing passionately to resume his activities as an artist. He is marvellously in tune for the third act of *Siegfried*, especially for Wotan's first scene: " this will be a prelude, if you like! — brief, but with accent." Pfistermeister had warned him that his occupation of such a house would draw on him the envy of the Müncheners; but Wagner had assured him that he was no Lola Montez.[5] It was not long before it was precisely as the successor of Lola — with the nickname of Lolotte — that his enemies were to hold him up to public opprobrium.

The winter of 1864–5 was spent by Wagner and the King in maturing their plans for operatic productions. As the singers with the necessary qualifications for the *Ring* could not at present be found, they would have to be made; and for this purpose Wagner per-

---

[5] It was largely because of the scandal of his infatuation with the pseudo-Spanish adventuress Lola Montez, whom he had ennobled with the title of Countess Landsberg, that Ludwig I had thought it wise to surrender his throne in 1848.

suaded the King to bring to Munich a Leipzig teacher of singing, Friedrich Schmitt,[6] of whose methods he had a high opinion. But the singers, of course, were only half the battle: for the full realisation of the Wagnerian ideal there would have to be a reorganisation of Munich musical life from the foundations upwards. This could only be done by bringing into being a new type of Music School, planned on the most thoroughgoing lines. The basic features of Wagner's ambitious scheme for the School will be set forth later. The prime essential of all for the *Ring* was a new theatre to be constructed in accordance with Wagner's revolutionary ideas. The King's resolution to build such a theatre was taken in November, 1864: the story of the vicissitudes and the ultimate fate of the scheme will be told in a later chapter.

Meanwhile, partly to gratify the King's burning desire to hear one of Wagner's works, partly in order to see how far the normal resources of the Munich theatre were likely to be adequate to *Tristan* and the *Ring*, the *Flying Dutchman* was put into rehearsal.[7] Wagner and the King had hopes of being able to secure the cancellation of Schnorr von Carolsfeld's engagement with the Dresden theatre and bring him to Munich for good; he was the only tenor to whom Wagner could think of entrusting the part of Tristan. The utmost they could do, however, was to obtain from the King of Saxony the promise of an occasional long leave of absence for Schnorr. In part to spare Wagner's strength, in part, no doubt, not to stir up ill-feeling in the theatre and in the town, the *Flying Dutchman* rehearsals were at first entrusted to Kapellmeister Franz Lachner. He was temperamentally not in tune with the work: one of his grievances was " the incessant wind that blew out at you wherever you happened to open the score." [8] He began by making cuts, which Wagner vetoed. The performance, originally fixed for

---

[6] The negotiations with Schmitt were concluded at Christmas, 1864.

[7] Almost immediately after his accession, before he had sent Pfistermeister in search of Wagner, the King had ordered the *Flying Dutchman* to be prepared for his first visit to the theatre after the period of Court mourning. The opera had not as yet been given in Munich.

[8] Lachner's own words to Max Zenger. See ZGMO, p. 464, *note*. Zenger (whose book is invaluable for the story of the Munich Opera from the seventeenth century onwards) was at that time living in Munich, and was acquainted with both Lachner and Wagner. The latter gave him a ticket admitting him to the *Flying Dutchman* rehearsals.

the 13th November, was postponed to the 4th December. On the 8th November the King shocked Wagner by telling him that he did not propose to attend the first performance; he feared, he said, that there would be faults in this, and he would prefer to wait until they were corrected. Wagner begged him to reconsider his decision, which, of course, if acted upon, would lead to misunderstanding in the town. Besides, he said, his own experience was that there was something electric in a first performance under his own direction that was apt to disappear later, when the nervous tension of the singers, that made them rise above themselves on these occasions, had given way to all the evils of complacent theatre routine as they gradually came to feel more settled in their parts. The King, of course, at once withdrew his objection.

On the 29th November Wagner appeared at the stage rehearsal, thanked Lachner for his services, and subjected the first act to a thorough revision, especially from the dramatic point of view. Lachner having been given ten days' leave, Wagner took the second act on the 30th and the third on the 1st December. Lachner had cut the final terzet, from the Dutchman's words " Sagt Lebewohl auf Ewigkeit dem Lande! " Wagner restored the deleted section, but to make things easier for the singers allowed the finale, from the words " Segel auf! Anker los! ", to be transposed a semitone lower. On the morning of the 2nd December he went through the first two acts again, taking the third act the same evening. The final complete rehearsal took place on the 3rd December; for neither this nor the first performance were free tickets sent to the Press. Max Zenger still remembered, many years later, the contrast between Lachner's metronomic time-beating and the flexibility of Wagner's melodic line.

As late as mid-day on the 4th December there was a fear that the performance, for which the house, which held 2,000 people, had been sold out long before, would have to be postponed once again, and the scenery for *The Daughter of the Regiment* was mobilised to meet a possible emergency. The performance, which was for the benefit of the theatre pension fund, was conducted by Wagner, although his name did not appear on the bills. The cast was as follows: Senta, Sophie Stehle, who seems to have carried off the vocal honours of the evening; Daland, Karl Fischer; Erik, Wilhelm

Richard; the Steersman, Ferdinand Bohlig; Mary, Emma Seehofer. The first act seems to have fallen rather flat — it must be remembered that Munich had already seen the maturer *Tannhäuser* and *Lohengrin* — but the second and the third were warmly applauded. The scenery and the stage handling appear to have been inadequate; in the third act, indeed, Wagner was more than once so perturbed by the bungling of the machinists that he neglected to give the orchestra its leads. On the whole, however, he seems to have been moderately satisfied. Bülow, who was present, thought the performance " electrifying ". No doubt it was, on the purely musical side; but Bülow, like Liszt, was relatively insensitive to the poetic and dramatic side of opera; his interest was always mainly in the orchestral score. The King perhaps showed a better understanding of the totality of the achievement when he acceded later to Wagner's request not to see any more operas of his until Schnorr could take the tenor parts. For the moment, however, Ludwig was in the seventh heaven of happiness over this first step towards the realisation of his dreams; and the grateful Wagner presented him with the original manuscript of the Orchestral Sketch of the work. From this Ludwig would get some idea of the wretchedness of soul and body in which the opera had been conceived. At the end of the second act Wagner had written, " 13th August, morning; no money again! "; at the end of the third act, " Finis. Richard Wagner, Meudon, 22nd August 1841, in need and care "; and after the overture, " Paris, 5th November 1841. Per aspera ad astra. God grant it! " [9]

The second performance of the *Flying Dutchman* took place under Wagner on the 8th December, the King being again present; and on Sunday, the 11th, at the King's command, a Wagner concert, under the composer himself, was given in the theatre in the place of the usual play: the patrons of the Sunday dramatic performance showed their resentment at the change of bill by staying away in large numbers. The programme consisted of the *Faust Overture*, the *Tristan* Prelude and Liebestod, the Ride of the Valkyries (which

---

[9] See KLRWB, I, 40, *note*, and RLW, I, 61. According to Dr. Otto Strobel, an examination of the manuscript shows Glasenapp to have been wrong in saying that the title page bears the words "In Nacht und Elend" ("In Night and Wretchedness"). The statement to that effect in Vol. I, p. 314 of the present Life should therefore be corrected accordingly.

was encored), the *Meistersinger* Overture, Pogner's Address and the Gathering of the Mastersingers, Siegmund's " Spring Song " and Wotan's Farewell from the *Valkyrie,* and the two smithying songs from the first act of *Siegfried.* The singers were Fischer, Simons and Richard; the programme notes, as we should describe them today, were Wagner's own.

3

To complete the musical record to the end of the year 1864 it may be added that on the 25th December Bülow introduced himself to the Munich public, with great success, at a concert of the theatre orchestra in the Odeon, playing a Bach-Liszt organ prelude and fugue, the C minor Fantasia of Mozart, and the solo part in Beethoven's Emperor Concerto. Lachner, according to Bülow, conducted " quite tolerably ". The classical programme, Hans wrote to his mother, had been specially chosen to " shut the mouths of the numerous croakers who are complaining in advance about the invasion of the music-of-the-future and the destruction of the ancient gods." The concert was manifestly given in order to float Bülow: the King was present — apparently it was the only time in his life that he attended an Odeon concert — and according to an eyewitness he followed the performances with the greatest interest. Bülow himself, however, seems to have had no illusions about him. " He was very charming ", he writes to his mother,

> " but for all that does not appear to want to become really musical. For the moment his musical receptivity is concentrated on Wagner's music. Wagner himself is naturally desirous of making an end of this exclusiveness. We shall probably make, along with Baron von Perfall,[10] suggestions for intimate little Court con-

[10] This Freiherr Karl von Perfall, who was later to become a thorn in Wagner's flesh, was at this time Court Music Intendant. He seems to have been a person of the most comprehensive dilettantism. He had first of all graduated in law: then he had taken up the study of music in Leipzig under Moritz Hauptmann, from whom he was not likely to imbibe much sympathy with Wagner. In 1850, at the age of twenty-six, he became conductor of the Munich Choral Society. When, in November, 1867, the Intendanzrat ("Theatre Councillor") Wilhelm Schmitt was pensioned off, Perfall succeeded him as provisional Intendant of the Court Theatre. In September, 1869 he was made actual Intendant, and in January, 1872 both General Intendant and an Excellency. In the Munich records he figures as the author of a play, *Die*

[315]

certs, which will be confined, at any rate at first, to chamber music." [11]

Bülow, with memories of the bitter opposition he had had to fight against in reactionary Berlin [12] was just then full of hopes for his career in Munich under the Wagner-Ludwig aegis: little did he foresee that Munich was before long — thanks in large part to his own lack of tact — to inflict the torments of the damned on him. For the present, while he knew that there was a fight ahead for the Wagner party, he looked forward to it with glee, confident as he was of being on the winning side. He had the same comprehensive contempt for the Munich " blockheads ", as he called them, as for those of Berlin; " the orchestra is rather better here, though it contains many rotten elements. It goes without saying that it will be radically reformed, but — *poco a poco* ".[13] " It is a good thing that we have power ", he wrote complacently to Bechstein on the 25th.[14] In considerably less than a year he was to realise that neither he nor Wagner had anything like the unlimited power they imagined they were going to have in Munich.

It was, of course, only power for his artistic purposes that Wagner wanted, not " honours " of the conventional kind; so he took but a languid interest in the move that was made in November to obtain for him the Maximilian Order for Science and Art. Three possessors of this coveted Bavarian Order had died during the last

Brüder, which had a dazzling run of three performances. He was no less successful as an opera composer, certain works of his forcing their way by sheer merit into the repertory of the Court Theatre in spite of the fact that the composer of them was the official head of that institution, and receiving between them no fewer than twenty performances in the six years 1881, 1882, 1885, 1886, 1887 and 1889. (See Otto Julius Bierbaum, *Fünfundzwanzig Jahre Münchner Hoftheater-Geschichte*, 1892, pp. 6–7, 24, 36, and ZGMO, *passim*). He functioned as Intendant till the end of 1892. His dealings with Wagner will come into our story later.

[11] BB, IV, 6 ff.

[12] He had gone through hell in his Berlin years, owing less to his championship of Wagner, one surmises, than to his zeal for Liszt. The Wagner cause had for some time been making such headway throughout Germany that the Berlin critics, though unconvinced and unfriendly, were beginning to be a little cautious of opposing it too openly. But the obvious weaknesses of Liszt's music played into their hands; by deriding these weaknesses they could strike venomous side-blows at the whole "music of the future." and at Bülow as the apostle of it. See the full contemporary story in the anonymous brochure *Hans von Bülow und die Berliner Kritik: ein Beitrag zur Zeitgeschichte*, Berlin, 1859.

[13] See his letter of the 20th December, 1864 to Carl Bechstein, in BNB, p. 163.

[14] BNB, p. 167.

few months — Hebbel, Klenze and Meyerbeer. On the 10th October, at a sitting of the Capitular of the Order, it was proposed to confer the honour on Wagner and Semper — Wagner being nominated by Lachner. The King passed them both over — or so it appeared — and gave the Order to the poet Oskar von Redwitz. In fact, however, it was Wagner himself who begged to be excused from accepting it. The renunciation did him little good; it was put down to arrogance, and some worthy members of the Order felt aggrieved. It appears that Wagner had not understood that the honour had been offered him on the sole initiative of the Capitular: he had assumed the suggestion to have come from the King, and he did not wish to add to the envy which he knew to be beating up about him already in Munich by accepting yet another royal favour. When the honour was offered him again nine years later there was no longer any reason why he should decline it.

4

Two things were necessary before a production of the *Ring* could be contemplated either in Munich or elsewhere — a new type of singer, trained to deal with the many novel problems with which the colossal work would confront them, and a new opera house embodying the sunken orchestra and the various stage improvements which Wagner had had in his mind for so many years. Naturally, therefore, he and the King debated these questions in their earliest talks. As early as the 31st May the official *Bayrische Zeitung* had hinted at a coming reorganization of the Munich Conservatoire. As he became surer that the King would stop at nothing for the realisation of their ideals, Wagner began to give concrete form to his plans for canalising the whole of the musical life of the town for his own artistic ends.[15] As yet, he felt, there was virtually

---

[15] With the *sacro egoismo* characteristic of his type of genius, he could see no salvation for musical humanity in any art but his own. As a matter of fact, Munich contained a number of sound musicians and cultivated amateurs of classical leanings. Lachner was a conscientious, hard-working artist who had done a great deal, according to his lights, for the musical life of the town. He had made the opera repertory thoroughly representative of the period: he had formed so good an orchestra that, with one or two exceptions of the sort to be found in even the best orchestras, it was equal to all that Wagner could demand of it in *Tristan:* at his Musical Academy concerts he had produced several notable works, among them the Matthew Passion

no one, apart from Bülow and the Schnorrs, whom he could regard as an efficient instrument for his purposes. " The difficulties ", he wrote to King Ludwig on the 2nd September,

" are enormous. A single conversation with any one of the wretched people who move about like senseless machines in the ordinary ruts of theatrical and musical routine is often sufficient to drive me to flight from the world — to hide myself in some spot where at least I shall not have to endure the misery of traffic of this sort. And yet it has to be! And so — Courage! "

He hopes that the relatively simple *Flying Dutchman* will prove to be within the capacity of the Munich singers. But after the *Flying Dutchman* will have to come *Tannhäuser*, *Lohengrin*, and — *Tristan!* At the thought of this last his heart almost fails him. Since the necessary human instruments for his greater works do not exist, he says, he will have to create them. He had always been convinced, though merely in a general, detached sort of way, that the art schools and conservatoires not only had not helped art but had been a positive hindrance to it. Now, to his sorrow, he feels that he must come to grips with the problem of what to do with these institutions and the " wretched proletariat " of art that infests them. The King, in his reply, fully agreed with him that a School must be founded for the training of a new kind of opera singer and actor; and accordingly Wagner, in the autumn of 1864, addressed himself seriously to this problem.

The first step to be taken, he told the King, was to bring Friedrich Schmitt to Munich and entrust a couple of promising students to him for two years. Their tuition was to be under Wagner's supervision: if within six months neither Schmitt nor the students showed signs of proving equal to the tasks set them, he was to have author-

as long ago as 1842. Though he had little taste for, or understanding of, the music of the New German School, he did his honest best for it when circumstances brought it his way.

Julius Justus Maier, the Custos of the State Library, who taught at the Conservatoire (where Rheinberger was his pupil for harmony and counterpoint), was a sound musical scholar of the older school, though a hard-cased conservative. *Tristan* was utterly beyond him: having to classify the full score of it for the catalogue of the Library he pencilled on the inside of the cover "Mus. th." ("Musica theoretica").

Munich certainly did not lack solid musicians and well-informed dilettanti of the older kind, especially in the sphere of Catholic church music. (See KJR pp. 18–29). But Wagner, of course, was so obsessed with his own culture-mission that he could not see the necessity for any other contemporary art but his own.

ity to make an end of the experiment; if, on the other hand, it appeared to be going well, Schmitt would be allowed to extend the field of his labours. The King, of course, fell in at once with this as with all Wagner's other suggestions; he himself felt it particularly necessary to find a tenor who in due time might be able to replace Schnorr, whose increasing corpulence he viewed with dismay.

It was not until well on in the new year that Wagner was able to put his views on the projected Music School into writing.[16] The *Report to His Majesty King Ludwig II of Bavaria upon a German Music School to be founded in Munich* was published (in Munich) in the early spring of 1865. It was a brochure of some fifty pages, and, like all Wagner's writings that deal with practical artistic matters, packed with the soundest sense; its only fault was that, as with all schemes for reform that proceed by way of pure reason, it took insufficient account of the stubborn realities of things in a world in which pure reason has regrettably little say. Wagner's basic thesis is that the Germans, unlike the French and the Italians, have as yet no style of performance innately correspondent to the nature of their own musical or dramatic art: " the most cursory glance at the history of music in Germany shows us that in the matter of institutions for the practice of this art we are in an utterly un-self-reliant, unripe and wavering condition: in no department do we find the means towards the formation of a style answering to the German spirit." The Italians and the French, on the other hand, have long possessed a style purely their own. Their individual actors and singers are under no necessity to work out that style, each for himself, in order to apply it to the job in hand; they find it pre-existent in the very atmosphere of the institutions in which they are brought up; and as each new Italian or French work is conceived with reference, conscious or unconscious, to that style, the technique appropriate to the task before the performers is second nature to them.

But in Germany there is nothing answering to this pre-established harmony between the thing to be done and the traditional manner

---

[16] The actual document would appear to be largely Bülow's work, though of course the guiding ideas are Wagner's. "Bülow", he writes to the King on the 21st January, 1865, "is engaged in the composition of a very detailed and comprehensive memoir on the subject of the Music School, which we are discussing with the utmost thoroughness." KLRWB, I, 51.

of doing it. The great German creative artists have mostly been either somewhat alien to the contemporary German spirit, or so far in advance of it that they have had to express themselves as best they could through an apparatus as yet undeveloped. Gluck's artistic affiliations, for instance, were largely French, Mozart's largely Italian; Beethoven had to manage as best he could with performers, and with conditions of performance, utterly inadequate to his larger works. His symphonies he had to hurl at the public's head after a rehearsal or two with a scratch orchestra. To these conditions he had always to resign himself where his larger works were concerned; it was only now and then with his chamber music that he could make a serious attempt to infuse into the players something of the style appropriate to the new spirit he was bringing into music — and even here his personal influence extended no further than the Schuppanzigh Quartet. Bach, " the most prodigious enigma of all time ", never had at his service anything like the apparatus necessary for the proper interpretation of his bigger works. In all these matters, says Wagner, there is even today no such tradition of performance as is the common heritage of the French or Italian performer: the right way of rendering the works of Mozart, Bach, Beethoven and the other glories of German music we have slowly to discover for ourselves by intensive thought and indefatigable experiment.

All this, he continues, holds equally good of the German drama — indeed, the evil is still more manifest there. For the proper contemporary performance of Gluck's and Mozart's operas, the German singers of those days could at least study the established styles of singing and declamation in France or Italy. But the contemporary actors of the purely German Goethe or Schiller had no foreign model to which they could resort for guidance, while there was nothing in their own experience to direct them. Brought up as they had been on naturalistic drama, they were completely at a loss what to do with the more idealistic productions of the two great Germans. Any budding French or Italian singer or actor had only to frequent his local theatre to imbibe unconsciously the style proper to the works in which he himself would one day have to appear; but the German actors who were called upon to play Goethe or Schiller were so lacking both in the instinct for German verse and in models for the delivery of it that they fell helplessly between two stools — they either flattened out the verse into prose, or, vaguely aware that there was a rhythm in it somewhere, they mouthed the lines in a monotonous sing-song.[17]

5

The Germans, in short, have as yet no style of performance truly answering to their own national art. That style, therefore, will have to be made. The basis of all good musical rendering is song: if melody does not *sing* it is nothing. The later Beethoven works remained for so long a closed book to performers and listeners because of a clodhopper manner of performance that deprived the melos of its inner life. Once the secret of this melos has been discovered and made plain, these works of Beethoven spring into amazing life; and oddly enough it was the French who, by sheer persistence, had attained to the secret of them. The orchestra of the Paris Conservatoire, under Habeneck, found the Ninth Symphony at first an insoluble riddle; they only solved it by three years' unremitting rehearsal, during which the meaning of the music became increasingly clear to them as they learned how to give life to Beethoven's melody. At the present time, says Wagner, it is to a French Quartet — he evidently means the Maurin-Chevillard — [18] that a German musician has to go to hear performances of the posthumous Beethoven quartets that make these great works not merely intelligible but electrifying.

The secret of revelatory performance, then, even of instrumental works, having to be sought in song, it is upon singing, in the widest sense of the word, that the energies of the new Music School should be concentrated. Without this singing style, nothing can be done with music; with it, most other things follow as a matter of course. In Wagner's view, a Conservatoire should not, *qua* Conservatoire, address itself to tuition in individual instruments; that should be done by the teachers in their private capacity. The central object of a Conservatoire should be to teach performance, especially in

---

[17] It sounds like a description of the present-day English actor or public reader faced with the problems of English verse!

[18] See Vol. II, p. 364.

ensemble — by careful training under people who understand their business, and by regular combined practice. As for singing in the more purely technical and limited sense of the term, the German finds himself in peculiar difficulties, owing in part to the structure of his throat, in part to the incalcitrant nature of his language. He must, of course, study singing by and for itself in order to acquire beauty of tone and ease of production; but having done that he must not ape foreign models but translate what he has learned from them into terms of his own language and his native musical and dramatic idiom.

The main objective of the new Music School should be a dual one — to cultivate the right way of rendering the great German music of the past, and so to establish a style that will make it easier for living German creative artists to realise their ends. Prizes should be offered for works which, " while related in this way or that to the classical art cultivated by the School, shall yet present new problems of performance and [stage] production." These works would be given model performances in the new model theatre that Wagner has in mind; moreover, this theatre would give each year " festival " performances of the masterpieces of German art that would serve as a standard to the other German theatres. Finally, the education of the students is to be completed by a musical journal expressly founded for that purpose, which will have the double object of discussion, by the teachers, of the many technical problems with which the students have to deal, and, so far as wider questions of style are concerned, of forming a link between the performing artists and the public. Wagner hits out with all his force against " musical criticism " as practised by the newspapers, Hanslick, no doubt, being particularly in his mind. " The unexampled levity, the unpardonable indifference, with which the most conscientious editors of our newspapers abandon the rubric of ' Music and the Theatre ' to the most unqualified gabblers, if only they know how to amuse the public, is no secret to any dispassionate observer." [19]

The whole plan, it will be observed, is in its origins and its ends Wagnerian: since the performers capable of undertaking the *Ring* do not exist, they are to be made; and since the ordinary opera

---

[19] RWGS, VIII, 125–176.

house, built for general purposes and catering nightly for all varieties of public, lacks the apparatus and the atmosphere for a work of the size and character of the *Ring*, a new theatre must be built for it. Entirely rational, therefore, as the scheme was in itself, and vastly beneficial as the realisation of it would have been to German opera, it is clear at a glance that it could be carried out only in a world rather less imperfect than ours. A dozen vested interests at once felt themselves to be threatened. The Munich teachers of music saw themselves discredited and brushed aside; conductors and singers throughout Germany were as good as told that they had no *raison d'être* except to further the special ends of Wagnerian opera; though Wagner expressly disclaimed the intention of wishing to interfere with the ordinary theatrical entertainment of the plain man [20] — for whom, for profit's sake, he said, there would always be sharp-witted entrepreneurs enough — the average theatre-goer would resent the suggestion that only Wagnerian opera mattered, or ought to matter, in a truly civilised community; and the proposal that the finances of the Bavarian State should be drawn upon to provide Wagner with a theatre of his own looked at that time like the very insanity of egoism. It is small wonder, then, that as the full implications of his hold upon the King's mind became apparent there should be a strong reaction in many Munich circles against them both.

6

The politicians, for their part, were now becoming a trifle alarmed; not only was their own influence over the young King threatened but they had some reason to fear the results of all these airy schemes on the public purse. It had not taken many months to

---

[20] The King was entirely of Wagner's way of thinking in this matter. The theatre as an entertainment for the tired business man made no appeal to him: either it should be a focus of culture or it was not worth serious consideration. "My purpose", he wrote to Wagner on the 8th November, 1864, "is to bring the Munich public into a more thoughtful, more elevated frame of mind by the production of earnest and significant works such as those of Shakespeare, Calderon, Goethe, Schiller, Beethoven, Mozart, Gluck and Weber, to help it to wean itself gradually of the liking for common, frivolous 'tendency works', and so to prepare it for the marvels of your own works and facilitate its understanding of these by first of all putting before it the works of other notable men; for everyone must be filled with a sense of the *seriousness* of art."

convince a number of people that Wagner, as the " King's favourite ", was going to play a part not merely in Munich music but in
Bavarian politics. In these circumstances it behoved the Wagner
party to walk warily if it was not to make a fatal false step: the
average Bavarian was none too well disposed towards even German " foreigners ",[21] and the normal opposition to Wagner the
artist was likely to be intensified if the artist seemed to contemplate stepping out of his proper sphere into that of politics.

Wagner himself showed, for a time, commendable prudence.
He made no secret to his friends and correspondents of his power
over the King's mind, but at first he had no intention of using this
power for anything but strictly artistic ends. The relatives of a
man condemned to death sought his intervention with the King:
Wagner refused. In the summer of 1864 the Socialist Ferdinand
Lassalle had appealed for his aid. Lassalle was in love with
Helene von Dönniges, the daughter of the Bavarian chargé d'af-
faires in Geneva, who would have nothing to do with the brilliant
Jew. In the early days of August the lovers had been driven to
desperation by the arbitrary conduct of Dönniges, who not only
opened his daughter's letters but confined her to her room, though
she was of full age according to Bavarian law and therefore did
not require her father's consent to her marriage. Lassalle had
many influential political and social friends, among them the Bavarian Minister for Foreign Affairs, Baron von Schrenck; and he
set them all to work on his behalf. He had been intimate in Berlin
with Bülow, with whom he had many intellectual interests in com-

---

[21] The reader must bear in mind that at that time Bavaria was the second largest
of the German states, and that the majority of the population disliked and distrusted
Prussia and was opposed to Bismarck's plans for welding Germany into one. Bavarian nationalism — or "particularism", as it was called locally at that time — was
the most popular of all the party creeds. A modern German historian, dealing with
the events that ultimately led to the unification of Germany, describes Bavaria as
"the oldest of the German, and indeed one of the oldest of European, states, . . .
which, in the opinion not only of Bavarian statesmen but of Bismarck himself,
possessed in the highest degree everything that entitled it to an independent existence
— an immensely ancient political tradition, a fourteen-centuries-old political unity,
a dynasty that had been part and parcel of the land and the people for a thousand
years, a population with an intense political self-consciousness, an indigenous,
firmly-rooted, vigorous people with an ancient culture of its own, with its own
markedly individual characteristics of social and of business life. . . ." (M. Doeberl,
Bayern und die Bismarckische Reichsgründung, pp. 1–2). More than one good
Münchener resented the Wagnerian "invasion" on purely political grounds.

mon (Bülow had presented him with a copy of the *Ring* poem in
1863); [22] and as both Lassalle and Helene were ardent admirers
of Wagner it was natural that the former should suggest to Bülow
that his now " powerful friend " might lay his case personally
before the King and ask for protection against Dönniges. " Adieu,
dear friend ", he ended his agitated letter to Bülow; " life is just
a comedy of dogs and apes . . . everything mean and filthy, an
absolute *dégoût*. Adieu! Adieu! "

The distracted man, having heard that Bülow was in Starnberg,
arrived there on the 17th August. He found a somewhat unsympathetic listener in Wagner. " He [Wagner] was not insensible ",
says Glasenapp in his equally unsympathetic story of the episode,
" either to the unusual talents of the intellectually very gifted man
or to his quick wits or his remarkable fluency; but at the same time
he was conscious in Lassalle of an excess of ambition and a vain
belief in himself that made him feel he was entitled to use everyone
and everything for his private concerns " — a singular reproach
for a partisan Wagner biographer to bring against any man! Be that
as it may, Wagner evidently did not particularly warm to Lassalle,
in whom, he wrote to Eliza Wille on the 9th September, he saw
" the type of the significant man of our future, which I would call
the Germanic-Jewish ", nor to his trouble of the moment, which
struck him as merely " a love affair of pure vanity and false
pathos." [23] Wagner may have been set against him by Cosima,
whose anti-Semitic prejudices had already shown themselves in her
attitude towards Lassalle in Berlin. The utmost that Wagner would
do was to hold out a half-hope that he would bring the matter before the King on the latter's return. Lassalle went back to Switzerland more distracted than ever. A few days later he telegraphed to

[22] At Lassalle's request, Bülow set to music in 1863, under the pseudonym of
"W. Solinger", Herwegh's poem "' Bet' und arbeit'! ruft die Welt", which was
adopted by the German Workers' Party as its "anthem". Bülow's setting — for
male chorus, in four parts — is given as a supplement to the third volume of BB. It
is a stirring piece of work, that called, however, for a more advanced harmonic sense
than any proletariat but the German was likely to possess. Bülow never lost his
admiration for Lassalle. Writing to a friend in 1877, thirteen years after the catastrophe, he said that in his Berlin days "when I was at Lassalle's house I had neither
eyes nor ears for anyone but the heroic man who was so sympathetic to me, — all
the others present were for me merely 'supers', *figurants*, shadows, daylight ghosts."
BB, III, 345.
[23] RWEW, p. 104.

Wagner a withdrawal of his request for help, on the grounds of
" the total unworthiness of the person " (Helene). On the 28th he
was wounded by his rival, Prince Janko Rackowitza, in a duel, and
on the 31st he was dead.[24]

Apart from his personal dislike of Lassalle, Wagner was of
course right in walking warily in the matter of a personal intervention with the King; the only result of his interference would have
been to give his enemies at Court a handle against him, and this he
was anxious to avoid. For the first few months after his call to
Munich he seems to have forborne scrupulously to use his favour
with the King for any ends but those concerned with his art, though
he was well aware of the danger threatening both Ludwig and himself from certain political quarters. " All the Ministers ", says
Gottfried von Böhm,

> " had by their insolent rudeness vexed the King, whom they thought
> they could terrorise; Schrenck in particular, a man of small intel-
> lectual capacity, had behaved inconsiderately and unbecomingly. The
> whole company of politicians had in fact mutinied against the King,
> hoping that their inexperienced monarch would not have the courage
> to show a judgment and a will of his own. A plot was hatched for a
> bureaucratic revolt. They were completely wrong, however, in their
> estimate of the King: the last rôle he would want to play would be
> that of a mere political supernumerary." [25]

The time was to come when Wagner, not only in his own interests
but in those of Ludwig, felt it necessary to take a hand in the game
of politics; but for the present he moved with becoming caution,
making no parade of his influence over the boy's mind among the
politicians, however much he may have plumed himself on it in
private letters to his closest friends. It is true that he once made

---

[24] A slender volume of Lassalle's letters to Bülow was published, with Bülow's
consent, in 1893. See BBFL. Most people no doubt know that George Meredith's
novel *The Tragic Comedians* is based on Lassalle's story. The reader who is interested
in the truly extraordinary affair may be referred to Helene's own account of it in
later years — *Meine Beziehungen zu Ferdinand Lassalle*, von Helene von Rackowitza,
geb. von Dönniges — on which Meredith's novel was mainly founded, and to the letters
of all the parties concerned, which were published in 1868 under the editorship of
Lassalle's friend Bernhard Becker — *Enthüllungen über das tragische Lebensende Ferdinand Lassalles*. Elizabeth E. Evans's *Ferdinand Lassalle and Helene von Dönniges*
(1897) is a convenient summary of documents and events for English readers un-
acquainted with German.
[25] BLKB, p. 32.

Pfistermeister's eyebrows go up by a reference to the King as " mein Junge ", [26] but this was probably an isolated verbal indiscretion. In his first Munich period he seems to have had all his wits about him. His adherents, however, were not so prudent: some of them were already beginning to provoke resentment in the town. On the 1st January, 1865 Ludwig Nohl [27] had been appointed Ehren-professor of musical history and aesthetics at the Munich University. Bülow, writing to a friend on the 4th January, immediately after a visit from Nohl, described him as a " dull, shallow bab-bler ",

> " a renegade who now, like many others, wants to turn Wagner's favour to his own profit; he is trying to ingratiate himself with the King as an intimate of the ' favourite ', and threatens to throw the odium of his appointment — which, one hopes, can still be cancelled — on Wagner, who is quite innocent in the matter. In days gone by the reactionary music-professorial party unceremoniously spat Nohl out when he swore allegiance to it." [28]

It was not long before Nohl had to leave Munich, his charlatan self-assurance being too much for the King; but meanwhile he did Wagner no good in social and literary circles by his patronising airs towards the Müncheners. Nor was Wagner's cause better served by certain others of his imported henchmen. Schmitt's rough manners set the local pedagogic world by the ears. Bülow, here as every-where else, was singularly successful in making trouble for him-self and therefore for Wagner. His ideals were always of the high-est, his intentions always of the best; but he was too superior to the Munich musical environment in general not to feel a certain con-tempt for it, a contempt he had not the tact to conceal, especially in moments when, owing to his ill-health, his nerves got out of control and his tongue with them. He soon made himself universally dis-liked in the town, in part as a personality, in larger part as a Prus-sian; he revealed too frankly that it was the ultimate intention of his party, relying on the support of the King, to utilise the main forces of Munich musical life for the sole benefit of " the music of

---

[26] See *infra*, p. 342.
[27] He came from Heidelberg. He is remembered today, if at all, chiefly by his biographies of Beethoven and Wagner and by his editions of Beethoven and Mozart letters.
[28] BB, IV, 15.

the future ". Every interest in the town, theatrical, musical, artistic, literary and political, began to feel itself threatened by these
invaders from abroad. Only Cornelius, clear of eye, steady of
brain as usual, saw the impending trouble and steered his prudent
course accordingly. Bülow, with the knowledge of all that Wagner stood for with the King, could complacently write to Carl Bechstein, on the 25th December, 1864, " It is a good thing we have
power; it can be put to good account in all sorts of ways." Before
many weeks were out he was to be made to realise that neither
Wagner's power nor his own was as assured as they imagined it
to be.

CHAPTER XIV

TROUBLE BREWING

1

A T THE beginning of 1865 Wagner seems to have been unaware of the storm-clouds that were already drifting up towards him. He was ostensibly settled in Munich for the rest of his days, with his livelihood ensured, free to complete the works he already had on the stocks and then to embark tranquilly upon *Parsifal* and *Die Sieger*, and certain of a production of each fresh work answering to his desires, so far as that would be possible in the Germany of that day. Early in January he drafted for the King's benefit a scheme for the re-issue of his literary works in several volumes: the scheme was to include all the larger treatises, such as *Opera and Drama*, the brochures and occasional articles from the first Paris period onwards, the programme analyses, the sketches for *Die Sarazenin, Jesus von Nazareth* and *Wieland der Schmied,* and the texts of the *Flying Dutchman, Tannhäuser, Lohengrin, Tristan,* the *Ring* and the *Meistersinger*. (It is interesting to see, from the list he drew up for the King, that he already had in his mind the famous treatise on conducting that was not to come into being until nearly five years later). Like so many other plans of Wagner's, this one had to wait some years for its realisation: it was not until 1871 that he began the systematic re-issue of his works.

He also outlined for Ludwig, probably in January, their joint plan of campaign in the theatre for the next nine years: it will be observed that it differs at several points from that of May, 1864, given on page 228. The new time-table is as follows:

May and June 1865. *Tristan* in the Residenz Theatre, before an invited public: three to six performances, with Schnorr and his wife (Dresden), Mitterwurzer (Dresden) as Kurvenal, Beck (Vienna) as Marke, and Sophie Stehle (Munich) as Brangaene.

May and June 1866. Repeats of *Tristan*, and completely new productions of *Tannhäuser* and *Lohengrin* in the Residenz Theatre, " or, under particularly favourable conditions, in the
large Court Theatre ", with the above-named singers, " or perhaps with some newly-trained forces."

(His phraseology suggests that he intended to work afresh over
Lohengrin as he had already done with *Tannhäuser*).

August 1867 The *Ring* in the new Festival Theatre.
August 1868 Repeats of the *Ring*.
August 1869 The *Meistersinger*, with possibly *Tannhäuser* and
Lohengrin.
August 1870 *Die Sieger* and the *Meistersinger*.
August 1871 *Tristan*, the *Meistersinger* and *Die Sieger*.
August 1872 *Parsifal*, with repeats of some of the other works.
August 1873 *Tannhäuser*, *Lohengrin*, *Tristan*, the *Ring*, the
Meistersinger, *Die Sieger* and *Parsifal*.

The solitary item in all this to be realised according to plan was
the production of *Tristan* in the summer of 1865. *Die Sieger* was
never written: [1] the *Meistersinger* was completed before the *Ring*,
and given in 1868: the *Ring* was not produced in its entirety until
1876, and then not in Munich but in Bayreuth: *Parsifal* first saw
the light in Bayreuth in 1882 .

On the morning of January 13th, Peter Cornelius, barbered regardless of the expense, and arrayed in his indigent best, was
shown into an antechamber of the Munich Residenz, where, noticing
that the sole of his right shoe was split, he had to sit with the dilapi-
dation turned all the time groundwards; " It must have given me ",
he notes humorously in his diary, " in consequence of my immo-
bility, something of the appearance of a statue." Discovering, after
waiting awhile, that he could not be received in audience until
half-past twelve, he rushed off to a shop in the Briennerstrasse and
spent seven gulden on a new pair of shoes: " it did not run to a

---

[1] We may doubt whether Wagner ever thought seriously of composing such an
opera; he never got as far as writing the poem, or even an extended prose sketch
of the very short outline he had drafted in May, 1856. The subject however, appealed
enormously to the King—perhaps in their conversations Wagner had enlarged on
the theme; and almost to the end of Wagner's days we find Ludwig urging him to
write the work in which he was so passionately interested.

new hat as well." Back in the Residenz again, he had a brief talk with one of the adjutants, who innocently wondered what influence Wagner's amazing good luck would have on his works: Cornelius gravely assured him that as things of this kind developed subconsciously from spiritual germs of long ago, later mundane events could have no influence on the creator of them. At last he was admitted to the audience. He was profoundly impressed by Ludwig's dignified appearance and by the simple human-kindness that seemed to radiate from him. " The secret fear that I should find something ailing or over-excited about the young King disappeared at once, and completely. He is healthy, robust." Cornelius, who was a penetrating reader of men, left the presence convinced that here was a soul of exceptional beauty and nobility.[2]

In the autumn and early winter of 1864–5 it must have seemed to both Wagner and the King that there was little to do but to steer their great treasure-laden ship slowly and smoothly into port. They left out of account two powerful inimical forces, the politicians and the meaner Press — the former actuated to some degree by genuine solicitude for the state, to a greater degree by anxiety for their own interests, the latter ready and eager, as always and everywhere, to pull down anything or anyone elevated by nature above it. Wagner might possibly have won his fight had he had only the politicians to contend with; but from the moment that the baser Bavarian journalists took the field against him he was lost. It was not long before their hostility towards him became manifest.

At first the politicians, dubious as they must have been with regard to the possible influence over the King of this stranger in their midst, were not markedly unfriendly: and no one can blame them for keeping a watchful eye on the finances that would have to bear the burden of the far-reaching royal plans for the furtherance of Wagner's art-aims. They seem to have done what they legitimately could to keep these plans private until more light could be thrown upon them: they even went to the extent of denying, through the Press, the reports as to the construction of a new theatre which soon became current as the natural result of Semper's audience of the 29th December, 1864 with the King. The denial caught the architect's eye. He was naturally perturbed, and as naturally wrote at

---

[2] CABT, II, 14–16.

once to Wagner asking for his verbal agreement with the King to be reinforced by a formal commission on the part of the Cabinet. This, however, Wagner did not think it would be tactful on his part to suggest.[3] In that unsatisfactory condition the matter remained for the present: the first points of what was destined to prove a long game had gone to the opposition.

The situation was not improved by the conduct of some of Wagner's supporters. His old friend of the Paris and Dresden days, Friedrich Pecht, who was at this time practising as a painter and general art-authority in Munich, was indiscreet enough to publish in a Vienna paper, with Wagner's approval, an article on " King Ludwig II and Art " in which he exhorted the King to proceed with his plans for the new theatre without regard to the " intrigues ", the " stupid opposition ", the " miserable nativism " of the Munich Press malcontents. The only result of this was to bring from the Augsburg *Allgemeine Zeitung*, on the 7th February, a further denial of the rumour that a festival theatre was in contemplation.

The storm broke, in somewhat unexpected fashion, in February, 1865. On the surface the sea had been, to all appearances, smooth enough. Pfistermeister, whatever his private reflections may have been, was outwardly friendly. He lunched more than once at the Briennerstrasse house, sometimes in company with some of Wagner's intimates. Wagner was at this time convinced that " the trusty Pfistermeister ", as he calls him in a letter to the King, would support him in all his artistic plans. The Cabinet Secretary, however, was evidently playing a diplomatic part until he could be sure which way the cat was going to jump: in his diary he wrote, on the 31st December, " Dinner this afternoon at Wagner's, with Semper, Bülow, and Cornelius. Unfriendly impressions." Perhaps the talk of the company had been a shade too self-assured to please him.

In purely political circles things were manifestly going none too well. Professor Huber, whose duty it was to make reports to the King upon events of the day, was suspicious of the possible influence on him of Wagner's supposed republicanism and free-thinking. Ludwig had perturbed Huber by telling him that even in his Crown Prince days he had resolved, when he became King, to put into practice, as far as might be possible, Feuerbach's theory of the

---

[3] The full story of the festival theatre will be told in Chapter XVII.

State; and now that Wagner was said to be encouraging the boy to read Feuerbach again, Huber foresaw trouble with the clerical party. Wagner's obvious intention to instal his own nominees in musical and journalistic key-posts in Munich necessarily made trouble for him in literary and artistic circles; and no matter how careful he may have been at this time to refrain from active intervention in purely political matters, it was no secret that his intervention was being sought by interested parties; even if the town gossip outran the facts, as it generally did, the effects of the gossip remained. It needed only the semblance of an indiscretion on his part to bring his Press enemies down on him; and their first great chance came early in February. It was the first organised move in a battle that was to end in his decisive defeat some ten months later.

2

As is the case with so many crises, that of February, 1865 was immediately precipitated by a happening absurdly disproportionate to the effects that resulted from it. The King had presented Wagner with a portrait of himself in oils, and, desiring one of Wagner, had expressed the hope that he would sit for it to the painter Joseph Bernhardt. Wagner demurred to this, on the reasonable ground that it was no use his sitting for an artist who did not know him. In days gone by, he said, he had driven casual painters to the verge of distraction by the changes in his face wrought by the fluctuation of his moods from day to day; they were dismayed to find a different man confronting them at each sitting. Having talked the matter over with Pecht, they agreed between them that the latter was to make a portrait of him which, if it turned out a success, could be sent to the King by way of an agreeable surprise. On the 30th January Ludwig found the picture in one of his rooms at the Residenz. He was enchanted with it, and sent Wagner his " warmest, most heartfelt thanks " in a letter of the same day.

A week later Pfistermeister asked Wagner what was to be done in the matter of paying the artist. The simple facts of an affair that has been greatly misrepresented are now known to be as follows. It had never occurred to Wagner that the King would regard the portrait as a *gift* from him: the offer of such a gift would have seemed to him at that time a breach of etiquette. (The King's original intention, indeed, had been to commission a portrait, at his own expense, by Bernhardt: in what respect, then, Wagner might well ask himself, was the situation altered by the substitution of Pecht for Bernhardt?). When Pfistermeister raised the question of payment with Wagner, the latter naturally told him to proceed in that regard precisely as he would have done had Bernhardt been the artist concerned: between himself and Pecht the subject of money had never been so much as broached. As soon as Wagner realised that the King preferred, for reasons of his own, to look upon the portrait as a present, he arranged the matter of a fee direct with his friend: he paid him, in the following July, 500 gulden, 100 of which Pecht voluntarily returned to him.[4] Stories such as that of Fritz Linde [5] — that " Pfistermeister shrewdly perceived the weak point of his secret adversary [Wagner], and underlined his mistake: instead of the agreed-upon 500 gulden he paid Pecht, ostensibly on Wagner's suggestion, 1000. Ludwig was revolted ", etc., — are sheer fiction of a type only too common in Wagner biography.

It seems to be beyond question that in some way or other, whether by accident or design, it was Pfistermeister who was responsible for the trouble. According to a contemporary letter from Schnorr to his mother, Pfistermeister had told the King that *Wagner* " wanted 1000 gulden for the picture "; this was said to have enraged the King so much that he declared that while he would scrupulously carry out his pledges with regard to the *Ring* he would break off personal relations with the composer; and he authorised his " reader ", Legationsrat Leinfelder, to let this be known. The town already knew that Ludwig had not been present at a performance of the *Flying Dutchman* on the 5th February. This was wrongly interpreted as a public demonstration of his displeasure; the fact was that after the *Flying Dutchman* performances of the previous December, with which Wagner had not been satisfied, it had been agreed between them that until *Tristan* could be produced in

---

[4] See Wagner's letter of the 13th July to Pecht, enclosing the 500 gulden, and Pecht's acknowledgment of the 14th, in KLRWB, IV, 68.

[5] LIK, p. 64.

" model " style, in the summer of 1865, the King would not attend any more Wagner performances. The combination of fact and fiction in the situation created by the Pecht portrait afforded rich matter for gossip in the town; and it was to put a stop to this that on the 12th February Ludwig, repenting of his momentary irritation, had a rather lame *démenti* published in the *Neueste Nachrichten:*

> " The report in various quarters that Richard Wagner is in disgrace can be characterised as unfounded. Wagner's position is bound up with the duty of talking to the King about music when leisure and circumstances permit. The preparation of legislative plans for the coming Landtag makes, however, more than normal demands on the King's time just now; moreover he has entered upon the study of jurisprudence. So that if the composer has not been summoned to the King during the past month for a discussion of music, this is because his Majesty has had even weightier things to occupy him: meanwhile the King did not fail to express his highest praise to the composer after the private performance of some of Wagner's music in the Residenz Theatre on the first of this month."

It could hardly fail to be known in the town, however, that on the 6th February Wagner had been refused access to the King at the Residenz, though permission to call there had been granted him in response to a petition on his part on the previous day.[6] The hounds were now in full cry after him. On the 14th February the Augsburg *Allgemeine Zeitung*, in a paragraph from its Munich correspondent, as good as told its readers that it did not credit the semi-official *démenti* of two days before:

> " Munich, 12th February. In today's *Neueste Nachrichten* appears a statement, to all appearance inspired by an interested party, that there is no truth whatever in the report current in various quarters that Richard Wagner is in disgrace with the King. Notwithstanding this, I can positively assure you that Richard Wagner has completely forfeited the favour so richly bestowed on him by our monarch, and truly in such a way that nothing now remains but to hope that mis-

---

[6] Wagner refers to this episode in his letter of the 9th March to the King: "At one o'clock in the afternoon of the 6th of last month the dreadful experience befell me of being turned away from the door of my exalted Friend — to which I had come on his gracious invitation — and conducted back to the courtyard. I was told that the reason for this repulse was not that my King was unwell but that he was profoundly displeased with me." KLRWB, I, 69.

trust has not been sown all too soon in the good and noble heart of our young King." [To this sentence there was appended a footnote by the editor of the paper: " From another quarter we have received detailed information about Richard Wagner and his associates, about which we prefer to say nothing at present, but which more than fully justifies this decision of the King."]. " I hear that Herr Wagner has left Munich. There can therefore be no question of any more ' reports on music to the King when leisure and circumstances permit '."

This of necessity brought Wagner into the field. The next day the *Allgemeine Zeitung* printed the following denial on his behalf:

" While correspondents from Munich persist in saying that there has been a fundamental change in the personal relations of Richard Wagner with the Court, we have received from the gentleman in question the following *réclamation:* ' Solely to reassure my friends abroad I characterise as false the communication from a Munich correspondent relative to myself and my friends in the town, which appeared in yesterday's issue of the *Allgemeine Zeitung*. Richard Wagner.' "

3

The situation, in fact, had already changed in his favour so far as Ludwig was concerned. On the 12th, Wagner attended a performance of *Tannhäuser* that moved him so deeply as to revive his temporarily drooping belief in his artistic mission. Associating it all with the King's loving care for him, he wrote to Ludwig the next day a letter expressing his gratitude; " He [the King] understands me, and I — live! " He told him also that Semper had suggested moving cautiously at first in the matter of the acoustic and scenic apparatus planned for the new theatre the King had in mind: Semper's idea was to put up a cheaper provisional construction in a wing of the Glaspalast in which the new arrangements could be tried out; if successful, they could easily be incorporated later in the definitive theatre. This letter probably completed the process of repentance that was already going on in the King's mind. On the 14th he wrote to Wagner expressing his delight at the good effect the *Tannhäuser* performance had had on him, and hoping that the time was not far distant when the ideal production they both had in view would be possible.

" As regards Semper's plan for a provisional theatre in the Glaspalast ", he continued, " I am in full agreement with this, though I am consumed with longing to see his plan for the festival theatre that is so ardently desired both by yourself, beloved Friend, and by me. . . . Miserable, shortsighted people who can talk about ' disgrace', who can have no conception of our love! ' Forgive them, for they know not what they do! ' They do not know that to me you are, have been, and will unto death be everything, that I loved you before I ever saw you; but I know that my Friend knows me, that his faith in me will never fail. O write to me again! I hope to see you soon! "

On the 15th Wagner sent Pfistermeister, of the sincerity of whose friendship he was apparently still convinced — or at any rate not excessively doubtful, — a letter in which he explained the misunderstanding with regard to the portrait. He looked to Pfistermeister, he added, to do whatever might be necessary — by means of an official public *démenti* in the name of the government department concerned — to put an end to current rumours of his " shameless demands ", rumours as injurious to the King as to himself.[7]

Two days later, as we learn from an entry in Wagner's " Annals " — " 17. Audience: assurance of innocence. Pfisterm." — he was received by Ludwig, to whom, presumably, he had no difficulty in making the position clear. After the audience Wagner wrote rather sharply to Pfistermeister: he told him — which was quite true — that paragraphs such as that in the *Allgemeine Zeitung* of the day before could not possibly appear without the complicity of the Cabinet. The *Allgemeine Zeitung*, in fact, had been at its unfriendly work again. In a message from its Munich correspondent dated the 14th, and appearing in its issue of the 16th, it had said:

" That His Majesty knows well, in the Richard Wagner affair, how to distinguish between persons and things, is shown by the latest resolution of the King, notwithstanding all that has happened, to assure the poet-composer, as before, the means to enable him to finish in Munich, free of care, his great work the *Nibelungen*. We ought to add, by the way, that a definite time-limit is in view for the completion of the work mentioned. Anyone who knows the firm will of the King will understand that this means that there is now an end not only to the wide-reaching and chimerical artistic plans cherished, if not by Wagner himself, at any rate by his associates and spread abroad by them, but also to any further relationship — which these people, it appears, have abused — between themselves and the Court."

---

[7] The letter is printed in KLRWB, IV, 43, from Wagner's own draft, which is still in the Wahnfried archives.

Wagner could put only one interpretation on this — that the politicians, or somebody closely connected with them, had not been playing quite straight with him. In his letter of the 17th he tells Pfistermeister that

> "There cannot be the least doubt that a simple order from the Cabinet would suffice to refute these offensive statements and to silence them. Since, as you will agree with me, they affect in an unpleasant manner his Majesty himself, I shall have no alternative, if no contradiction follows and these calumnious reports are continued in the Press of all countries, but to assume an agreement with them inside the Cabinet itself, against which, as I well understand, I cannot keep silence with you, my honoured friend. The means by which I am to defend my own and my friend's [Pecht's] deeply wounded honour are not at the moment quite clear to me; in any case you, my honoured friend, would then be free of the many vexations you have experienced through my hitherto having failed to comprehend your presumably very difficult position between sharply opposed interests.[8]

He makes his meaning still clearer in a further letter to Pfistermeister the following day.

> "The expression 'Royal Cabinet' used by me was only a euphemism for a person (whose name I have already given you) or for several persons, who alone, in virtue of their position in his Majesty's service, could have access to such matters as constitute the basis of public rumours and publicised statements. The exceptionally well-weighed wording of the communication concerning me in the *Allgemeine Zeitung* of the 14th February conveys to all readers, in its statement of my present relations with his Majesty, the impression of having come from a confidential source: it was obvious to me that there exists somewhere an interest bent on representing these relations in such a way as to make it virtually impossible for me to issue a public contradiction, since . . . upon one matter I cannot say anything in my own justification, namely, his Majesty's gracious disposition towards my person."

He assures Pfistermeister that he is not to be taken as suspecting the Cabinet Secretary himself of " duplicity and dishonesty ", and expresses his gratitude for all Pfistermeister has done for him in difficult times, but he hopes that something can be done to save him from the attacks of the " interests " to which he has referred:

[8] KLRWB, IV, 45.

" it is impossible that my exalted protector should abandon me for long to such a state of affairs as that of the past fortnight, in which I am daily hounded to death." [9]

Whether, or to what extent, Pfistermeister personally had been secretly double-crossing him we have no means at present of knowing. There can be no question, however, that ammunition for the Press campaign against Wagner must have come either from within the Cabinet itself, or from Court circles, unfriendly to him, in close touch with the Cabinet.

4

If Wagner believed that with his restoration to the King's favour his public troubles were over he was quickly disillusioned. The *Allgemeine Zeitung* now unmasked its batteries. On the 19th February it printed a long article entitled " Richard Wagner and Public Opinion "; the article was anonymous, but it is known to have been the work of the Munich poet Oskar von Redwitz — described by Schnorr as "the banner-bearer of the priests ". The article repeats and presses home the previous attacks on " Wagner and his associates ".[10] It refuses to accept Wagner's *démenti* of the rumour of his disgrace, and hints that the earlier communication of the Munich correspondent of the *Allgemeine Zeitung* had been based on information from a quarter in the closest touch with the facts. The writer professes to know, on the best authority, that Wagner, entirely on his own initiative, after having had his portrait painted by his friend Pecht, had deposited the picture in the King's

---

[9] KLRWB, IV, 45–7.

[10] The German word is "Genossen" — companions, associates, company, partners, etc. There is no doubt that as applied by the paper to the inner Wagner circle it was meant to be offensive, and it was hotly resented by Wagner's bodyguard; it particularly rankled in Bülow's mind, and that it stung Wagner to the quick is shown by the entry in his "Annals" for that date — "Allgemeine Z. 'Genossen'." Bülow, with his unique gift for doing and saying the injudicious thing, fell foul of Pfistermeister over the expression, and evidently gave an exhibition of temper for which he was sorry later, so that Cosima had to write the Cabinet Secretary one of her tactful letters the next day. Pfistermeister, in his talk with Bülow, seems to have taken the sensible line of telling him not to trouble his head over anything the Press might have to say on any subject. But Bülow, says Cosima, did not resent criticism of himself as an artist, but as a "man of honour". Cosima's letter, which was found among Pfistermeister's posthumous papers, is given in HNBW, p. 604.

antechamber along with a bill for 1,000 gulden. The King had refused to pay the bill, partly out of resentment at Wagner's conduct, partly to mark his displeasure with Pecht over the latter's article on " King Ludwig II and Art " [11] and the attempts of the Wagner-Pecht party to make it appear that he had already sanctioned the Semper plan for an expensive new theatre. Wagner's denial of the disgrace is not accepted: manifestly the talk of the withdrawal of the King's favour had its foundation in (a) information from someone at Court as to Ludwig's refusal to see Wagner on the 6th February, (b) a mistaken interpretation of the King's absence from the performance of the *Flying Dutchman* on the 5th February and that of *Tannhäuser* on the 12th.

We now know Redwitz's account of the affair to be untrue. But manifestly the whole story, such as it was, could have come only from some one of two or three people in the innermost circle of the Residenz. Let us summarise the course of events. The King finds the portrait in his room on the 30th January, and sends Wagner an exuberant letter of thanks for it the same day — a fact which disposes of Redwitz's assertion that " along with the picture was the bill for 1,000 gulden." On the 31st, Wagner writes to the King with reference to the programme for a private concert of his works in the Residenz; Ludwig, in his reply of the 1st February, goes into ecstasies over the prospect, and hopes to see Wagner soon. On the 5th, Wagner asks for an audience, which is granted him for one o'clock the next day. But on presenting himself at the Residenz on the 6th he is refused admission! Clearly, then, the King's mind had been poisoned against Wagner between the afternoon of the 5th and mid-day of the 6th. Who had done the poisoning? Presumably either Pfistermeister or the King's " reader ", Ministerialrat Leinfelder. Pfistermeister's diary contains the following entries:

" 6th Feb. Wagner not admitted. I had to tell him and console him.
" 7th Feb. The King apparently angry with Wagner, because Leinfelder has been telling him all kinds of things about him.
" 12th Feb. A rumour that R. Wagner is in disgrace."

(As a matter of fact the 12th was the day on which the " disgrace " was semi-officially *contradicted* in the *Neueste Nachrichten*, so that

[11] See *supra*, p. 332.

the rumour must have been set going at least a couple of days earlier).

All in all, one inclines to the theory that the prime source of the King's misunderstanding was Pfistermeister. Schnorr's account of the matter (which he evidently had from Wagner) is that a week after the King had received the picture, Pfistermeister called on Wagner and asked him " how the matter stood as regards payment ", whereupon it was agreed between them that Pfistermeister should settle this direct with Pecht. " Meanwhile, however, [i.e., before seeing Pecht] Pfistermeister goes to the King and tells him that Wagner (*sic!*) wants 1,000 gulden for the picture." As Wagner, in his temperate letter of the 15th February to Pfistermeister, makes no charge whatever against either the Cabinet Secretary's sincerity or his veracity, the presumption is that at that time he had no reason to believe that there had been anything but an honest misunderstanding of the Pecht situation on Pfistermeister's part. But that someone inside the Residenz had been doing some rather dirty work between the evening of February 5th and the 8th simply cannot be doubted. On the one hand this person had poisoned the King's mind; on the other hand he had fed the Press, directly or indirectly, with inside information, — for Wagner was perfectly right in his contention that the information, true and false, supplied to the Press and set circulating in the beer-houses could have originated only from someone stationed at the very centre of things.

Pecht, in a letter that appeared in the *Allgemeine Zeitung* of the 21st February, denied categorically that he had made any claim whatever on the Treasury for payment for the picture, either directly or through any other person. In his memoirs [12] he tells us that " at the first opportunity " he spoke to Pfistermeister about the matter " in Wagner's presence ". Pfistermeister informed him that *he* had suggested to the King that the latter should express his gratitude to Pecht for the fine portrait *and* send him a fee of 1,000 gulden. But in that case why did the King become so furious with *Wagner* on the morning of the 6th? It is difficult to resist the conclusion that Pfistermeister had not been quite straight either with the King, with Wagner or with Pecht.

---

[12] PAMZ, II, p. 138.

It is possible, however, that the immediate cause of the King's anger may have been something even more trifling, in itself, than the misunderstanding over the portrait. Wagner's " Annals " contain the following brief entry for the 6th February: " Pfisterm.'s morning visit ('Mein Junge'). Sent away from the King's door." [13] Let us now try to reconstruct the events leading up to this entry.

On the 5th, Wagner had sent a brief note to the Residenz to the effect that he would lose interest in everything if he did not soon have a meeting with his " animating guardian angel "; and he asked for an hour's audience. This was granted him for one o'clock the next day. Clearly there was no feeling whatever on Ludwig's part against Wagner when he sent his Secretary to him with that message on the morning of the 6th. In his talk with Pfistermeister, Wagner, perhaps out of sheer high spirits, was indiscreet enough to refer to the King as " Mein Junge "; [14] this, apparently, had given offence to the Court official in Pfistermeister, and he had called Wagner to order. Almost exactly a year later (on the 7th February, 1866) we find Cosima writing to the King, " I recalled with a certain uneasiness Herr Pfistermeister's visit of just about a year ago to the Friend [Wagner], during which he advised him to use only becoming expressions when speaking of your Majesty! Our [15] horrified amazement at the time, the Friend's indignation and fury with the Councillor, who had certainly taken the worst for granted, have remained vividly in my memory — as well as the results of this strange proceeding." [16]

Now why should Wagner have troubled to record the " Mein Junge " in his journal unless consequences of some importance had followed from his use of those words? Would Cosima, again, a year later, have had so lively a recollection of the incident unless the immediate results of it had been of exceptional moment? And would her letter have been intelligible to the King if *he* did not already know the " unbecoming expression " of Wagner's to which

---

[13] KLRWB, I, 5.
[14] The episode and the expression itself constitute further proof that as late as the morning of the 6th there was no cloud on Wagner's relations with the King.
[15] Cosima, of course, had been present at the interview.
[16] KLRWB, I, xlvi.

she was referring? We have abundant testimony, including Wagner's own, to his inability to control his tongue in moments of temper: it is more than probable, then, that he had replied abusively and offensively to Pfistermeister's admonishment to him to refer to his Majesty in more becoming terms. The interview, we can readily believe, ended with " indignation and fury " on Pfistermeister's side as well as on Wagner's.

It would take the Cabinet Secretary only a few minutes to get back from the Briennerstrasse to the Residenz. Is it not probable that, angry as he was, he repeated Wagner's incautious expression to Ludwig, and that it was *this* that was the immediate cause of the refusal of the audience? For Cosima leaves us in no doubt that the words " Mein Junge " had dire " results ": and as there is equally no doubt that the King's displeasure with Wagner sprang up some time in the brief interval between Pfistermeister's departure to the Briennerstrasse on the royal commission and Wagner's presenting himself at the Residenz shortly after mid-day, is the supposition too far-fetched that the prime cause of the trouble was the unfortunate " Mein Junge "? We have seen Wagner's reference to the matter in general in his letter of the 9th March to Ludwig — " I was told that the reason for this repulse was not that my King was unwell but that he was profoundly displeased [17] with me." We have seen also that it was Pfistermeister himself who had to announce the refusal to Wagner and " console him ". This entry in Pfistermeister's diary, made the very day of the incident, makes no mention of the matter of the portrait, nor does it even hint that, as yet, Wagner is " in disgrace ". It is not until two days later that we learn from the diary that the King is angry with Wagner because of things that Leinfelder has been telling him about him, and not until the 12th that Pfistermeister refers to the " rumour " of Wagner's " disgrace ". It all fits in perfectly with the supposition that the King's feelings towards Wagner were of the usual friendly kind until, on the morning of the 6th, his Secretary told him of the " Mein Junge "; that in a flash of resentment at this he refused to receive Wagner; and that Leinfelder and others, quick to see their opportunity, took advantage of this resentment to prejudice the King

---

[17] "Dessen grosse Verstimmung gegen mich". "Verstimmung" implies, literally, being "out of tune with".

still further against his favourite by telling him the fable of Wagner's " demand " of 1,000 gulden for the portrait.

An angry reaction to an expression that seemed to him lacking in respect for his kingship would be quite in keeping with all we know of Ludwig's character. An incident from his later life may be adduced by way of illustration. In 1880 he conceived a great admiration for the young Meiningen actor Joseph Kainz, who had made a " guest " appearance at Munich in September of that year, and who joined the Court Theatre company in the following month. Ludwig entertained him frequently at his castles, loaded him with gifts, and even went so far as to address him, in conversation, as " Du ". In the summer of 1881 he took Kainz with him on a fortnight's tour of the Lake Lucerne neighbourhood, where they visited Tell's Chapel and other places of legend dear to the King's romantic heart. All went well until the night of the 11th July, when they reached the Rütli. There Ludwig asked the actor to read to him the Melchthal scene from Schiller's drama *Wilhelm Tell*. Kainz, who was of plebeian origin, had a good deal in his manner and his speech that jarred on the King: all this, however, he could overlook when things were going smoothly. On this occasion Kainz, after commencing the reading, suddenly stopped and said he was too tired to go on with it.

" This seemingly insolent refusal vexed the King all the more because he had not expected it. He looked at Kainz quite disconcerted. He felt that to acquiesce would be to compromise his dignity too deeply. He rose to his feet in some irresolution. ' Very well! ' he said at last, with tears in his eyes, ' If you are too tired, go and rest '. Then, resolved on a breach, he turned on his heel and walked across the meadow to the landing place. Hesselschwerdt [his groom] and Aschwanden [a local ranger] followed him to the boat. When the King had gone on board, Aschwanden said to him, ' Herr Marquis, Didier isn't here '. [18] The King replied, ' Let him be: we will start '. So the boat went without Kainz. . . . It was four in the morning before Kainz could find a small boat to take him to Brunnen: he went to his bedroom in the villa without anyone knowing he was there. He awoke in the late afternoon, and, with rather an uneasy conscience, looked about for the King: he found that the latter, in obedience to a sudden resolution, had

---

[18] The King and Kainz were travelling as the Marquis de Saverny and Didier respectively — characters in Victor Hugo's play *Marion Delorme*.

left the Villa Gutenberg for ever, excusing himself on the plea of indisposition for not taking personal leave of his host, Herr Benziger." [19]

Kainz followed after him, astounded and dismayed. He received en route a letter from Hesselschwerdt, telling him the direction he was to take. He rejoined the King at Lucerne, and they travelled back to Munich together. The King was in a magnanimous and courteous mood again and seemed to have forgiven Kainz for his *faux pas:* the pair were photographed together, and the actor read selections from Hauff. On his return to Munich the King wrote to Kainz, expressing his joy that the disagreeable impressions of that night on the Rütli had been removed — " so far as is possible ". A second letter followed a few days later, and that was the end of the friendship: Ludwig could neither forget nor forgive Kainz's over-stepping, even for a moment, the boundary line fixed by nature between the King and the commoner. Ludwig never troubled about him again until Kainz's final appearance in Munich in April 1883, when he sent him a message of warm praise, as of old, and, as of old, some costly presents.

6

Having cleared up, as best we can, the mystery of the King's sudden exasperation with Wagner, let us return to Redwitz's attack on the latter in the *Allgemeine Zeitung.*

The news of Wagner's disgrace, Redwitz continues, had been joyfully received in all Munich circles except that of a certain composer's partisans who held that his genius as an artist elevated him above criticism as a man, and that of the political party which admired Wagner as " the one-time barricades man ", and thought it could now turn his influence at Court to its own profit. Public opinion, unanimous as to Wagner's genius and his devotion to his ideal, does not grudge him the King's favour for purely artistic ends. But Wagner does not know, and never will know, how to be duly grateful for a royal benevolence such as has fallen to the lot of no other artist.

" His demands in matters of ordinary life and comfort seem to be of so exquisitely sybaritic a nature that truly an oriental *grand seigneur*

[19] WKLW, p. 209.

need not recoil from the prospect of putting up permanently in his house near the Propyläen and sitting as guest at his table. The ugly trait of ingratitude for benefits received that is so evident in Wagner's behaviour towards his former gracious royal Maecenas, the noble Friedrich August of Saxony — in comparison with which, in our opinion, his political aberration is wholly pardonable — this misuse of princely favour and liberality has moved the Bavarian people for months past to suppressed as well as open, and more than justified, displeasure. Or is it perhaps worthy of a really great and noble artist-nature that Wagner, in his luxurious house-furnishing here, should spend thousands on carpets alone, for instance — out of the purse of his generous benefactor — in the ostentatious rôle of a modern Croesus? And previously to all this prodigality it happened, as is well known, that his royal protector had terminated the old familiar conflict, in Vienna, between Wagnerian receipts and Wagnerian expenditure by the grant of so incredibly large a sum that Mozart and Beethoven, Wagner's much greater predecessors, would have been heartily grateful to any prince for the gift of the mere interest on this debt-capital for any year of their anxious life."

On top of all this there is Wagner's excessive belief in himself, his contempt for his great forerunners, the arrogant attitude of his hangers-on towards Munich " musical barbarism " and " Bavarian stupidity ", and the natural public exasperation at the way the noble young King has become involved in this degrading business. Is it any wonder, therefore, that

" we who have so profound a regard for this young and lovable monarch and would gladly protect his head from the smallest shadow, ask ourselves whether, without descending at all to ignoble *Schadenfreude*, we ought not to have rejoiced when we learned that the King, enlightened by all this abuse of his grace, has now determined to keep his enthusiasm for Wagner's music separate from the personality of the composer, and to restrain the unconscionable financial and artistic demands of the latter within reasonable limits, which henceforth Wagner will go beyond only to his own damage.

" This is the mild interpretation we put upon the much-discussed ' disfavour ' of the King. How many a great artist who starved his whole life through would have been supremely happy to have suffered such ' disfavour ', even if it had brought him only a quarter of what Wagner can still enjoy, thanks to this disfavour! Let us repeat, however, that we are really not so pitifully envious as to grudge Wagner the means to a decent, comfortable, free existence as that term is understood by ordinary people. Nor would any true Bavarian wish to deprive his King, on whose young shoulders so heavy a burden of office has fallen, of his enthusiasm for Wagner's music. . . . We ask only one thing — that Richard Wagner shall not again overstep, in fresh blindness, the limits now set to his demands, and that both he and 'his friends here' will learn that they must no longer, by their continual brutal disdain for what in our modest opinion is our very worthy situation, even in matters musical, thrust themselves between us Bavarians and our beloved King, like a false note that pains our piety. Otherwise we shall have to praise the day when Richard Wagner and his friends, this time really and truly ' overthrown ', will have to turn their backs on our good Munich and on Bavaria itself. For however exalted Wagner and his music may be, our King and our love for him stand, for us, a hundred times higher." [20]

The first public result of this savage attack — the prime purpose of which was obviously to alienate the King from Wagner by representing the latter as an object of universal opprobrium — was to bring the *Allgemeine Zeitung* a fiery challenge from the invariably indiscreet Bülow. On the 21st February the paper printed the following letter from " Baron von Bülow, ' Doctor of Philosophy, Royal Prussian Court Pianist, Pianist to his Majesty King Ludwig II ' " — the editor apparently reproducing with gleeful irony Bülow's parade of his titles either on his note-paper or on his visiting card:

> " A Munich correspondent of the *Allgemeine Zeitung,* in its issue of the 16th February, accuses the so-called ' associates ' of Herr Richard Wagner of the abuse of their connections with the royal Court. As among the said ' associates ' I, the undersigned, alone have the honour to possess any such connections, I avail myself of my right to characterise the anonymous originator of this aspersion as an infamous slanderer. Munich, 18th Feb. Hans von Bülow." [21]

To this there was appended an editorial note to the effect that Herr von Bülow was mistaken in his assumption that he alone, among

---

[20] The long article is reproduced in full in KLRWB, IV, 47–51.

[21] A sharply satirical poem on Redwitz, in twelve stanzas, which appeared soon after in *Kladderadatsch* under the title of "Ritter Amaranthus", seems to have been from Bülow's pen. (See his reference to it in his letter of the 14th April, 1865 to Carl Bechstein, in BNB, p. 176). Redwitz, a pious dilettante with liberal leanings in politics, was best known by his epic poem *Amaranthus* (1849); and the term "amaranthine", as Richard M. Meyer says in his *Die deutsche Literatur des neunzehnten Jahrhunderts,* "had rightly become a derisive equivalent for insipid sentimentality." Bülow's lively poem, which is too long to be quoted here, will be found in RLW, I, 104–5.

Wagner's friends, had any connection with the Court; for the rest, the editor left it to his Munich correspondent either to give further details in support of his original statement or to ignore Bülow's letter. The editor added that he had received an intimation from Wagner himself that a reply of his own to the article of the 19th was on the way; and he finished up by saying that " from several other quarters we hear that Herr Wagner has received the assurance that the royal grace has not been withdrawn from him — as was already hinted in yesterday's communication from Zürich."

7

Wagner's lengthy rejoinder, which was concocted with the aid of Bülow, Cornelius and Pecht, appeared in the issue of the 22nd.[22] He began by protesting against the intrusion of the Press into his private affairs. In London and Paris, in days gone by, he had been attacked in his art and his theories, but in these alone; it had been reserved for his enemies in Munich, to which place he had been called by the King in his hour of direst need, to commit the baseness of holding him up to public execration as a man. The King had contracted with him for the completion of his *Ring*, on terms intended to compensate him for loss of income from other sources during the time necessary for its completion, but in no wise exceeding those paid by other Bavarian monarchs for works of art. Regarding himself, then, not as a " favourite " but as an artist receiving legitimate payment for his work, he denied the right of anyone to demand from him an account of how he spent his earnings. He corrects his anonymous critic on certain points of fact and on the conclusions he had drawn from these. Etiquette bars him from dealing in public with matters private to the King and to himself: but he assures his critic that the King's absence from the performance of *Tannhäuser* was in no wise due to displeasure

---

[22] Cornelius tells us that they sat up over it until one in the morning, he and Bülow taking down from Wagner's dictation, and a lively debate sometimes arising when they counselled moderation. Bülow's suggestion for the closing sentence was accepted—"Not to me, but to public opinion, does my opponent owe an answer to these questions."

with him, but to reasons already agreed upon between them. He derides the alleged " confidential " information of his accuser with regard to his demand of 1,000 gulden for the Pecht portrait: there is not a word of truth in the whole story, as his critic can easily discover by applying to the official department concerned.

His accuser is wrong, again, in his statement of the present position of the scheme for the new Semper theatre. Wagner ironically rejoices over Redwitz's eulogies of him as a composer, but regrets that he should couple these with a charge that as a man he is " frivolous ".

> " In Paris it was the other way about: there people found my art and my tendencies ' detestable ', but they pointed me out as an example of a man who willingly, without a moment's weakening, sacrificed the brightest chances of ' making a fortune ' to the seriousness of his artistic convictions, and thereby landed himself in a situation that was worsened by a three years' utterly helpless residence in his German fatherland to such an extent that a year ago he had lost all hope either of producing his later works or of continuing the practice of his art at all, so that he had resolved to disappear completely."

His critic has no right to put the complexion he has done on Wagner's debts: the fact is that the advances made to him in respect of these are to be repaid out of future receipts from performances of his works. He resents his accuser's references to his household luxury; the artist, he contends, is justified in providing himself with the objects and the atmosphere he requires for his work and his happiness; all this is, or should be, a private matter pure and simple. He repels the charge that he is contemptuous of the local musical world. His opinion of the low estate of public music in Germany as a whole he has never concealed, but it is precisely in Munich that he places his hopes for betterment — Munich, in which Franz Lachner has rendered such good service. He dexterously turns against Redwitz the latter's remarks about the harm that is being done to the King by the association of his name with " all these true and false reports ". In so far as the reports are true, says Wagner, they can only redound to his Majesty's honour and fame. As for the false reports, who is it puts them into general circulation but people like the anonymous author of this article? Redwitz is misinformed as to the state of mind of the Bavarian people in general: from all quarters Wagner has received assurances of glad recognition of the great work that the King has done for him.[23]

Minna, it will be remembered, complained to her friend Emma Herwegh that in her disputes with Richard she was helpless against his " wonderful blarney " (*seine vortreffliche Suade*).[24] Both he and Cosima had an incomparable gift for making any case in which they were interested look precisely as they wanted it to look; Pfistermeister and the other politicians, in their correspondence with the pair, often seem, in comparison, like mere amateurs in the art of diplomatic manoeuvring and word-spinning. Wagner's letter to the *Allgemeine Zeitung* is a masterpiece of its genre. It wins the average reader's support for a general proposition that is not in dispute — the right of the private man to run his private affairs according to his own notions, — and so distracts attention from what is the real point at issue — the right of a particular private man to incur huge debts by extravagant living and then have them liquidated out of public or semi-public funds; nay, not even to use the King's gifts (which were quite another matter than payments in advance for artistic services to be rendered) for the settling of old debts but for lavish new expenditure, while at the same time, as so many people knew, fresh debts were being accumulated for which there would have to be a day of reckoning some time or other. Sebastian Röckl rather obscures the issue when he says that " the Münchener of that epoch, even the Münchener in good circumstances, lived so simple a life that any kind of luxury looked to him like criminal extravagance or folly: it was impossible for him to understand that richly-coloured surroundings that flattered the senses might be of importance to an artist." Here again, while the general proposition might be true enough, it was the particular application of it, and the manner of its application, that concerned the Müncheners. All over Europe, even in circles which fell prostrate before his genius, Wagner was in evil repute as an insatiable borrower and a most reluctant payer; and the grievance of the Müncheners against him was not so much that he was living more

[23] The article is reproduced in full in KLRWB, IV, 52–56, and RWGS, XII, 295–301.
[24] See Vol. II, p. 543.

luxuriously than they, but that, as they saw the matter, he was doing so, directly or indirectly, at their expense.[25] His letter to the *Allgemeine Zeitung* no doubt won him the sympathies of many, though perhaps the general verdict of the jury was that of an Irish judge in a recent trial — " The defendant leaves the court without a stain on his character, beyond those that were there when he came in."

8

But if his enemies were no match for Wagner in dialectic they had in their armoury a weapon against which the best case is often powerless — that of irony and burlesque. And so the local laugh must have been against him when, less than a week after his open letter, the Munich *Punsch* came out with " A Morning in the Life of a New German Composer ", the application of which was obvious to the dullest intelligence. The article is worth reproducing in full for the light it throws on the Munich situation as many people saw it in 1865.

The setting is as follows:

---

[25] A cartoon in the Munich *Punsch* gave expression to public opinion on this matter as early as 1864. The cartoon shows a Bavarian military officer taking the necessary expenditure on the army, in the form of bags of coin, out of a chest marked "Royal Bavarian Treasury". Standing by him is Wagner, who says, "Dear Friend, don't take it *all* out. Leave a few gulden to cover the cost of my Conservatoire of the Future." Another picture in the same journal (1865) shows us Wagner seated at an instrument that seems to be a combination of a piano and an organ: round him are dancing, to his music, a number of money-bags each marked "1000". The text informs us that "The Orpheus of old set rocks in motion; the new Orpheus charms pieces of metal." In a third *Punsch* cartoon we see Wagner skating on the ice, blissfully unconscious that right in front of him is a thawed patch inscribed "Ungnade" (Disgrace). A Münchener standing by warns him that if he carries his head so high in the air he will fall into the hole. Yet a fourth picture of 1865 presents us with a burlesque of Pecht's portrait of Wagner, with a label attached to the frame, marked "1000 florins." All these cartoons are reproduced in KFW, p. 34 ff.

Wagner and Bülow, indeed, were just then and for long afterwards godsends to the Bavarian comic papers. The novelists followed close on the heels of the cartoonists. In 1868 appeared August Becker's novel *Vervehmt* (4 vols., Berlin, 1868), in which Wagner appears in the character of a director of the ballet who reduces the private purse of the King to a "galloping consumption" to gratify his artistic ambitions. Oddly enough, Becker's work is not mentioned by Miss Anna Jacobson in her exhaustive study of the novels dealing with Wagner and his operas — *Nachklänge Richard Wagners im Roman*, Heidelberg, 1932. These novels constitute by now a small library. Three or four of them, perhaps, repay the trouble of reading today. I myself have made a heroic start on quite a number of them, but have found it impossible to continue with more than half a dozen to the end.

" A magnificent bedroom: velvet hangings, silk curtains, wool carpets, mirrored ceiling with frescoes by Pecht and Kaulbach. Towards
the window a small orange grove, in which, from time to time, a ripe
fruit falls to the ground. The wash-hand-stand is in a rocky grotto
planted with sweet-scented moss, ivy and box. Out of the rock two
streams, one cold, one warm, flow into two crystal basins. Left and
right grow the finest sponges; Paris soaps are seen in mother-of-pearl
shells. From behind prismatic glasses a flamelet projects over the
whole group a rainbow, which, however, since the beautiful rosy rays
of morning are streaming into the room, looks a trifle pale.

Rumorhäuser, the great composer, awakes, stretches himself, *aber
nicht nach der Decke, sondern nach der Länge*,[26] looks round, and tugs
at the bell-pull. At once the trumpet signal from *Lohengrin* is heard.
A Valet in shoes and stockings enters.

Rumorhäuser.   Don't stamp about like that; you know I can't bear
               the least noise; my ears get more sensitive every day.
               Bring my socks.

(The Valet bows apologetically, glides out on his toes, and returns
with a silver salver containing six pairs of socks of various colours).

Rumorhäuser (looking them over).   Hm! not much choice! MORE
               SOCKS! (Lies back).

(The Valet goes out again circumspectly, and soon returns with a
larger salver, on which there are twelve new pairs of socks of various
colours).

Rumorhäuser (looking them over).   Hm! nothing there to take my
               fancy. I will wear yesterday's again. (Puts them on).
               Bring me the catalogue of my silk dressing-gowns.
               (The Valet does so). I want the violet-blue one with
               the yellow embroidery, the one in which I recently
               composed the big tenor aria for the giant Fafner:
               there will never be anything like that; it is the *ne plus
               supra* of all arias. (He gets up). My brown skull-
               cap — the one on which the Princess Vitzlibutzli em-
               broidered the laurel wreath in green silk.

(He slips into his morning things and walks up and down).

Valet.   Who is to have the honour of bringing the Herr Di-
               rector his coffee today?

Rumorhäuser.   Can't you remember anything, you booby? If I am
               having black coffee, the negro brings it. If it is a
               mélange, the mulatto brings it; if it is white, *you*
               serve it. We'll see about that later. Now I will wash.

---

[26] An English equivalent is impossible. Literally — "not according to the coverlet,
but lengthways." But "sich nicht nach der Decke zu strecken" is idiomatic for
"not to cut one's coat according to one's cloth", or "not to live within one's income." The application to Wagner is obvious.

	(Goes into the grotto-boudoir and looks at the little stream). What's this? How is it there are so few goldfish? How trumpery! The water must be gay, lively! Bring some more goldfish!
Valet.	Excuse me, Herr Director, they are very difficult to get just now.
Rumorhäuser.	What's that? Difficult to get? For me difficulties don't exist. Just send round to the royal winter garden and give them the message that I NEED GOLD-FISH, and it will be all right.
Valet (bowing).	Very well.
Rumorhäuser.	Is the antechamber ready and properly warmed? Is it just the temperature I require when I have to write a duet? Donnerwetter, what's this I have stepped on? What wretched sort of a carpet is this? The weaving is so full of knots and lumps that one ruins one's feet.
Valet.	Paris goods, supplied by Schneider and Diss, laid by Steinmetz.[27]
Rumorhäuser.	What do you mean, Paris goods? Who today would give himself corns on a Paris carpet? What's the object of the present-day easy communication with the East? I have never been able to endure any but Indian carpets, or at any rate Persian. Tomorrow I must stand on something else: you understand? You simple Europeans will have to asiaticise yourselves a bit, or else we shall never get on with each other. (He washes).
Valet.	That's just the marvellous thing about it — that your Excellency, for all your oriental tastes, is the authentic representative of sturdy German music.
Rumorhäuser.	We Germans came from Asia originally: we belong to the Indo-Germanic race, see?
Valet.	Well, well; I have often thought I must belong to a race, and I am glad to hear it's the Hintergermanic.

(Rumorhäuser goes into the antechamber and looks at the big flower-stand).

Rumorhäuser.	Hm! Not so bad. Camellias, azaleas, violets, carnations, the best that can be done just now. But you must put more laurel trees in here. I can never see enough laurels. And tell the Court gardener that I want some rhododendrons and edelweiss growing in front of the windows.
Valet.	That's hardly possible, because of the temperature.

---

[27] Munich furnishing firms of the period.

THE LIFE OF RICHARD WAGNER

Rumorhäuser.   It's got to be possible! A man who composes such long operas as I do can't bother about temperature. (Throws himself on to a sofa). That's a bell-pull on that wall, isn't it? I would like some other kind of mechanism in its place. When I ring, it must strike like a big drum; that disturbs me less when I am composing than a tinkle does. Penkmayr, the theatre machinist, has been instructed to fit up what is necessary here. Now let me have some black coffee.

Valet.   That means the negro! (Rushes out).

Rumorhäuser (hums to himself some new arias).

      For tenor: Oho! Ohe! Ha, Hi! Ha, Ho!
                    Ollaho! Ollahe! Ha, Hu!
                    Heijoh, Hollahehahi!
      For Soprano: Eia pupeia,
                    Tralala, walala
                    Wugala weia!

(A negro enters with breakfast and a pipe: on a silver tray is No. 50 of the *Allgemeine Zeitung*.[28]

Rumorhäuser (has lit his pipe, sips his coffee, and takes up the paper).

      Richard Wagner — what? Richard Wagner and — and what? — and Public Opinion! (Opens the paper and reads). Ha, disgraceful! And what a style! — Debts in Vienna — pitiable! Sybaritism — ludicrous! The people's love — one can't believe one's eyes — this kind of thing can only happen in Munich! (Throws his pipe at the negro's head, goes into his bedroom, and bolts the door behind him).

Valet (hearing the noise, rushes in in dismay and tidies up).

Rumorhäuser (from within).   Send for my old friend Pecht! [29]

9

If Wagner himself was guilty of a tactical error about this time by flaunting his luxury before the Müncheners' eyes, some of his imported " associates ", as the *Allgemeine Zeitung* called them, were not improving matters for him. Nohl, towards the end of January, had got on the wrong side of the King. The vain and foolish fellow had probably done no more than kindle a mild sur-

---

[28] The number containing the article *Richard Wagner and Public Opinion*.
[29] RLW, I, 97 ff.

prise in Ludwig when he submitted to him a document in which he proved, to his own satisfaction, that the King " need not do any-thing *in extenso*, as everything was implicitly contained in music ". But when he went on to say that he, Ludwig Nohl, being gifted with second sight, had known of the coming death of King Max some weeks before it happened, Ludwig lost his temper and said, " See that this swindler never crosses my threshold again! " On the 1st February the papers announced that Nohl, in disgrace with the King, had gone to Switzerland; whereat everyone who had mis-takenly coupled the " swindler " with Wagner rejoiced.

Some excuse for Nohl's aberrations may be found in his notori-ous weakness of intellect; but another explanation must be sought for Bülow's indiscretions. The report of Wagner's " disgrace" having appeared in many of the German papers, Weissheimer wrote agitatedly to Bülow asking if it were true. Bülow replied in characteristic style on the 19th February, prefacing his letter with the music of the shrill laughter of the sailors in the *Flying Dutch-man:*

" So you have fallen into the trap? " he wrote. " But what are news-papers for? Why does the proverb say ' To lie like print? ' Just calm yourself at once, for with the attachment and friendship of a man like you one doesn't need to practise hocus-pocus. . . . The reports that have upset you so much are *our own invention*, put about to save, to some extent, Wagner and even my small self from the shameless im-portunity of the beggarly crew who, from far and near, pester us like bugs or summer flies with requests for protection. . . . Since the sun-shine of the royal favour merely entices and breeds this sort of vermin, the only possible insecticide to use in such cases is . . . an eclipse of the sun.[30] The effect has been grandiose, Bengal-lightish. We had in-fernally little trouble over it; and in twenty-four hours the ' confiden-tial information' was *non plus ultra* public. . . . Not merely the Bavarian papers but the middle, north and south German ones, and even the French, Belgian and so on, are full of the ' disgrace'. The aristocracy is furious at being constantly ignored by the splendid King: to the recent concert of a week last Wednesday in the Residenz Theatre (where everything sounds almost as well as in the Paris Con-servatoire), his Majesty admitted no one but Wagner's special friends — not even the Intendant's wife. The architects are boiling over with rage over the summons to Semper; the sculptors are spitting poison

[30] Bülow's style was always personal and peculiar.

over Pecht's official article (in the Vienna *Botschafter* and the Munich *Neueste Nachrichten*) in which Hähnel's engagement was hinted at; the poets, the journalists have had deadly wounds dealt to their vanity — well, orchestrate this *Jubelsinfonie* for yourself!

" Now we are at peace, unbothered; even the chamber musicians no longer come to play their trios for us, which is a mercy to my ears, that have been martyred by their wretched fiddling; and so on. *Per contra*, one order after another on his Majesty's part to Zumbusch, who can do nothing now but make busts of Wagner; Pecht's excellent portrait of Wagner hung by the King alongside the portraits of his ancestors; Echter working at illustrations of the whole of the Wagner operas; Schmitt smithying at tenors and sopranos; *enfin, enfin*, everything *charmant* and better than before, when the papers were *not* lying and consequently caused us a lot of trouble." [31]

That Wagner had other troubles at this time besides the politicians and the Press is beyond dispute. Forgotten creditors were beginning to gather round him affectionately again: tradesmen in more than one far-off city were opening their ledgers at the bad-debts-written-off page and wondering wistfully whether, by a little gentle pressure on their part, some of the gulden that King Ludwig was believed to be pouring into Wagner's pocket might possibly be diverted in their direction. On the 11th February Wagner offered Schott the " Young King of Bavaria's March " — i.e., the work now known as the *Huldigungsmarsch*. It is scored for a large military band, he says, but any skilled military band conductor will be able to adapt it to smaller forces: he himself is already arranging it for an ordinary orchestra with strings. He is confident that it will be very popular, and that Schott will be acquiring a valuable property. Wagner is in need of an immediate 1,000 francs, " which I still owe someone in Paris: unfortunately I had forgotten all about it, and at the present moment it is extremely inconvenient for me. Please give your Paris agent instructions to pay this 1,000 francs to Monsieur Jules Malsis, tailor, 4, Rue de la Bourse . . ." This debt must obviously have been incurred some four or five years earlier. As Schott did not do anything immediately in the matter, Wagner wrote him again, this time more urgently, on the 10th

---

[31] WEWL, pp. 333–336. Hähnel and Zumbusch were sculptors. Echter was a painter, much in favour with Ludwig II.

March. Everybody believes, he says plaintively, that he can draw as much as he likes from the royal treasury; the consequence is that his creditors hàve become unreasonably importunate. There has been a bit of a public rumpus over it all — this, of course, refers to the attack on his " luxury " by Redwitz — and he simply cannot ask the King for more money for some time to come, as that would be pouring fresh oil on the flames. At the same time he really must be free of all these worries if he is to get on with his work. If Schott cannot see his way to make him the advance on his future sales, will he let him have the 1,000 francs as a loan pure and simple, to be paid back by the end of the year? It ended, of course, in Schott paying the Paris tailor.[32]

We can readily believe that M. Malsis was not the only creditor who was expressing at this time an ardent desire to refresh his tired eyes with the colour of Wagner's money. It was quite true also that, as Bülow told Weissheimer, a " beggarly crew " of all descriptions was trying to make use of Wagner's influence with the King for purposes of its own. But were it not for the fact that Bülow was a Prussian, and, indeed, something of a Junker, one would almost be tempted to doubt whether he was accustomed to drawing a very fine line between truth and fiction when it suited his purpose better not to do so. We know now that there *was* something in the report of Wagner's disgrace, that that report was *not* set going by Wagner himself and his friends in order to keep this " Bettelvolk " at a safe distance, that the Wagner party was *not* delighted with the success of its brilliant strategy,[33] and that in Munich all was decidedly *not* for the best in the best of all possible worlds. The interest of Bülow's letter lies mostly in the light it throws on his mentality. He could be, on occasion, as sophistical or as untruthful as any of them — a point to bear in mind constantly when we are trying to understand his attitude in the Bülow-Cosima-Wagner affair; and

---

[32] See RWBV, II, 80–83.

[33] The conspirators could not even agree among themselves as to which story they were to tell! We find Bülow, on the 12th February, assuring Weissheimer and other foreign friends that the story of the "disgrace" had been put about by the Wagner camp itself, in the hope that it would be accepted as gospel and so ward off creditors and other tiresome people. Yet on the 15th, as we have seen (p. 336), Wagner, in the columns of the *Allgemeine Zeitung*, "characterised as false" the report that he was in disfavour at Court!

THE LIFE OF RICHARD WAGNER

both the matter and the manner of his letter to Weissheimer make it easier for us to comprehend how and why he managed to achieve the unpopularity he did in Munich.[34]

---

[34] Rheinberger, who saw a good deal of him in the Munich days, and sincerely admired his gifts, wrote to his parents, in May, 1865, that Bülow was "more Wagnerian than Wagner himself, just as there are Catholics who are more Catholic than the Pope. Bülow is actually a Berliner, but in disposition a Mecklenburg Junker who regards every public as merely *canaille*; hence the famous *Schweinehunde* [see *infra*, p. 370], which has already brought him some bitter experiences." KJR, p. 82.

It was one of the oddities of Bülow's character that, Junker as he was, he was a democrat of the Left in politics. One would have thought, a priori, that a man with such contempt for the human *canaille* in general as he had would have found the mob particularly objectionable. But in 1848 he was all for the social revolution; in the 'sixties, in Berlin, he was all in sympathy with Lassalle's plan for a "workers' republic"; and in 1871 he could write to his friend Spitzweg, "The events in Paris are to me, as Lassalle's friend, in the highest degree important: I have the greatest respect and admiration for the Commune, while the Parliament moves me to the profoundest disgust." (BB, IV, 481). As has been the case with so many other aristocratic intellectuals, his contempt for the faults of the kind of people he knew best made him exaggerate the virtues of the kind of people he knew hardly at all.

CHAPTER XV

THE "TRISTAN" PRODUCTION

1

IF, HOWEVER, his enemies imagined they had done him any real damage in the King's eyes they deceived themselves. On the day on which the *Punsch* article appeared, Wagner sent Ludwig, without any accompanying comment, an adaptation of Lohengrin's words to King Henry (in the second act of the opera, in which he replies to Telramund's attack on his honour), followed by Lohengrin's appeal to Elsa to have faith in him.[1] Ludwig grasped his meaning, and, equally avoiding any overt reference to the recent trouble, replied with a poem of his own which he linked up with Elsa's cry of trust in her deliverer and her invincible love for him.[2] " O that I could protect you against the lies of slanderers! " he concluded.

" Some day, my dear one, it will be seen by everyone that the bond between us is pure, holy and eternal. . . . Some day their astonished eyes will behold the wonders that you and I together have dedicated to a better age than this. And so, have courage! Let us have faith in each other: love's work is for all eternity." [3]

Four days before this, a " fey " old woman whose name, we now learn from the " Annals ", was Frau Dangl, had called on Wagner to talk to him, as she said, about himself and the King. According to her, the two previous Kings of Bavaria had done themselves no good by failing to follow her advice. " Do you believe in the

---

[1] The passage in the opera may be paraphrased thus: "Not to thee [Telramund] who hast been so forgetful of honour, do I owe a word. The evil man's doubt is impotent against me: the pure one he cannot destroy. . . . Yea, against even the King can I stand, and all the princes of the earth: not they will increase the load of doubt, for they saw my deed, how good it was. . . . In thy hands, in thy faith, lies the pledge of our happiness."

[2] "With what greater guilt could doubt be charged than that of destroying faith in thee? . . . My rescuer, who brought me salvation! My hero, in whom I must cease to be! My love shall endure against all the might of doubt!"

[3] KLRWB, I, pp. 60, 61.

stars? " she had asked him. " It is written in them that this young King is called to great deeds. I want him to have peace, and you, Herr Wagner, must guard him against the machinations of evil men who would ruin him as they ruined his father and grandfather." Wagner, in his highly-wrought mood of the moment — it was the day on which his indignant letter to the *Allgemeine Zeitung* appeared — was impressed by the old soothsayer, whose opinions harmonised so perfectly with his own. " The fate of this wonderful, unique youth, who is profoundly linked with me by a mystical magic ", he wrote to Mathilde Maier the next day,

"is entrusted to me, *me*. There is a lofty, marvellous significance in his love. To abandon him to the scum of intrigue and corruption would be a treachery against the reproach of which I would have no defence. The profound meaning of my duty to the King, which is of significance to a whole people, nay, to Germany itself, has been revealed to me through an almost supernatural experience. I ask myself now, ' Why this cup to *my* lips? I, who want only peace, peace, liberty to belong to myself. I to hold in my hands the destiny of a nation, of a glorious, indescribably endowed King! ' Grasp the sense of what I am saying to you, and ask yourself how I face my task, what is going on within me, in what unrest I sigh and suffer! " [4]

This extraordinary letter, as has been said above, was written the day after Frau Dangl's " revelation " of his " mission " to him. We may wonder why he took the old crone's chatter so seriously; but of the fact that he did so there can be no question. " My position, my destiny ", he tells Mathilde, " is becoming very *serious;* it has assumed a significance that almost overwhelms me." Three days later he writes to Frau Wille in the same strain. He tells her, as he had told Mathilde Maier, that there had been " one insincerity " — he uses the same word, *Unaufrichtigkeit,* in each letter — in his reply to the *Allgemeine Zeitung:* he had deliberately, for

---

[4] To Mathilde Maier, 23rd February, 1865, in RWMM, p. 200. Wagner's own story of the visit of Frau Dangl, as told by him to Fröbel in October of the same year, will be found in RLW, II, 217 (quoting from Fröbel's unpublished diary). "Wagner", Fröbel adds, "is possessed with the idea that his connection with the King, which seems to him very intimate, imposes on him great and lofty duties. In this he is right. He conceives the matter, however, in a purely poetic, almost theatrical, way." Fröbel is dealing with the period, of which more will be said later, when attempts were being made to induce him to settle in Munich as editor of a new journal which was to be the mouthpiece of Wagner's (and therefore the King's) views on the interrelations of politics and culture.

prudence' sake, made out his relations with the King to be more limited than they actually were: he only wishes, for his own peace of mind, that it were so, he assures both his correspondents in almost identical terms. But, he tells Frau Wille, the King's affection for him is " marvellously profound, fatalistic ". " If, for the sake of my own peace, I renounce the rights that this affection gives me, I do not know how I can justify it to my heart and my conscience to shirk the duties it imposes on me." The agitation against himself, it seems, is merely a blind: it is the King who is actually being aimed at, and Wagner " shudders " at the thought of " abandoning him to his environment." Why, he asks Frau Wille, as he had asked Mathilde Maier, is this cup presented to *his* lips — to *him*, who longs only for quiet leisure for his work? Why is " the welfare of a divinely gifted being, perhaps even the well-being of a country ", placed in his hands? To the King is lacking any man who can really help him.

> " The outer moves of the intrigue amount to nothing; they were merely intended to make me beside myself, to betray me into an indiscretion. But what energy — and at the utter and eternal cost of my tranquillity — would I require to tear my young Friend for ever from his surroundings? He remains true, touchingly fine, to me, and now turns his back on it all."

The politicians were now plainly anxious, for reasons of their own, to minimise in public Wagner's alleged influence over the King. On the 25th February there appeared in the official journal, the *Bayerische Zeitung*, a brief announcement that the truth of the much-debated matter lay between the two extremes — that while the King admired Wagner as a composer, the latter's " influence " was confined to the ideal sphere of art. The communiqué was no doubt directed to Wagner as much as to the public; between the lines lay a hint that it would be well for him not to cherish " hopes " and " illusions " that were in conflict with the realities of the situation. He was manifestly a little put out by this, for he forthwith sent to the Cabinet Secretariat a detailed statement, drafted by himself, which he requested should be published officially. It appeared, though with some alterations which annoyed him, on the 27th. In essentials it adds nothing to the previous communiqué; it reiterates the assurance that Wagner talks to the King only about matters connected with his art, and adds that no one who knows the King will require to be told that the latter is not in the habit of " letting the initiative be taken out of his own hands ", or of being " influenced " in any way.[5]

Whatever conclusion the general public may have come to about it all, it is clear that the King's restored confidence in Wagner was now not to be shaken: Schnorr, who, with his wife, had arrived in Munich at the end of February to discuss the arrangements for the coming *Tristan*, wrote to his mother on the 4th March that

> " the main object of our journey here is achieved: the *Tristan* project now stands on firm ground, and Wagner has taken heart again: he needed this, after having been so basely treated in Munich, where he could not find *one* man to understand him. The King, an idealistic, high-minded, finely-strung being, whose love and enthusiasm for Wagner know no bounds, is the *only* one here who loves him. He loves him without understanding him: for that he is as yet too young. It is all a marvel."

The situation during the weeks immediately following the February storm was summed up in a few words in an entry in Cornelius's diary on the 11th March:

> " Since then the tempest has died down: the upshot of it all is that while Wagner and the King write each other the friendliest letters imaginable they have hardly once met in person. They could hardly do that: the water was much too deep ":

which may mean either that the " disgrace " had left some slight personal embarrassment behind it for both the King and Wagner, or that they thought it as well not to do anything that would be likely to attract unfriendly attention to themselves and start another journalistic campaign.

The King had long been all impatience to hear *Tristan;* and as Schnorr was the only possible tenor for this, Ludwig used his personal good offices with the King of Saxony to obtain a three months' leave for him in the summer. Wagner asked the King to command an immediate performance of *Lohengrin* with Schnorr as Lohengrin and Malvina as Ortrud, and a private concert in the Residenz Theatre, under Wagner's direction, in which the pair could sing the duet from the second act of *Tristan* and fragments from the *Val-*

---

[5] RLW, I, 103–4.

kyrie and *Siegfried*. After consulting the Intendant the King found, to his regret, that all this would be impossible at the moment; but a performance of *Tannhäuser*, under Lachner, was arranged for the 5th March. At the solitary rehearsal Wagner was astounded by Schnorr's understanding of all his intentions in the work: he had even restored that vital passage in the second act which all previous tenors had shirked because of its difficulty; [6] and more than ever Wagner was convinced that he had found the ideal man for his *Tristan*. Schnorr, for his part, regarded himself as Wagner's spiritual debtor, and found his highest satisfaction in serving him. There was never the smallest trace in this great artist of the ordinary operatic tenor's naïve self-esteem and opinionativeness. "Wagner's influence on me", he wrote after the rehearsal to his mother,

> "is immeasurable: if I already answered to his intentions in the main, the rôle has taken on some new features by reason of certain weighty details to which he drew my attention today, for which I at once thanked him. I cannot tell you how happy I am."

And two days after the performance he wrote to Cosima:

> "I know full well how much is due to me, how small was my part in the success, what driving force Wagner exercised on me: yet I am proud of that evening — from that day I feel myself dedicated as an artist. I have the certainty now that I am not unworthy to have Wagner's spirit breathed into me."

The King, like Wagner, had been delighted to find that Schnorr's generous poundage in no way detracted from the idealism of his performance: one forgot everything in the face of the beauty of his singing and the intelligence of his acting.

2

Apparently it was some time since Wagner had been admitted to the King, and he began to feel some doubt as to his real standing with him. On the 9th March he addressed an appeal to him to make the situation clearer; without Ludwig's love and perfect trust, he

---

[6] See Wagner's account of the rehearsal and the performance in his *Recollections of Schnorr von Carolsfeld*, in RWGS, VIII, p. 180 ff.

said, he could not go on. The King, in his reply, regretted that circumstances over which he had no control — the unwelcome company of his mother, who was an unappeasable enemy of Wagner — made it impossible for him to grant just then the composer's request for a personal meeting; but he begged him not to doubt that his love would endure to his dying breath, and that happier days for both of them would come. Even this did not satisfy Wagner, whose nerves seem at this time to have been near breaking-point. He asked for one clear word from his royal friend:

> " Shall I go? Shall I stay? Your will is mine. If I go it will be to some distant land. I will never return to Germany: for my works I will do what I can; but I will sever completely the connection between the man and the thing. If I remain, my glorious Friend has given me strength to have patience, to bear every trial; for my faith is unassailable. So it is for the Friend to decide: one word, and joyfully I accept my fate. But the decision must be made, and today. My spiritual forces are at their utmost tension: I must know by which decision I can bring peace to my dear one."

The veiled threat of losing Wagner was too much for Ludwig, as it was to prove on more than one occasion in later years. His reply was prompt and brief: " Dear Friend, remain here, remain here; everything will be as glorious as before. My work presses. Till death, your Ludwig." A troubled chapter was thus closed: a new one was about to open, rich in promise but destined for a tragic ending.

" I live again! " was Wagner's joyous answer to the King's letter. His courage restored, he took up once more his plan for the Music School, and addressed himself seriously to the question of the presentation of *Tristan*. He would have to stipulate, he told the King, for control of all the main rehearsals; but as he was physically unequal to the actual conducting, as he could not ask Lachner to accept a subordinate post under him, and as no other local Kapellmeister could be regarded as satisfactory, the work would have to be entrusted to the only man upon whom he could wholly rely — Bülow. He accordingly begged the King to confer on Bülow, for their present joint purpose, the rank of " Court Kapellmeister for special services ". Ludwig at once gave the necessary order, and asked for news of his darling project — the new festival theatre — which the Cabinet was evidently impeding all it could, for financial and other reasons.

Meanwhile Wagner was busy working at the cast for *Tristan*. For his Tristan and his Isolde, of course, there could be no question of anyone but Schnorr and Malvina. In view of the later shabby attempts of Wagner and Cosima to minimise Malvina's share in the success of *Tristan*, a special interest attaches to a letter of Cosima's to Malvina written, evidently at Wagner's prompting, from Starnberg about the end of July, 1864. Wagner, we learn from this, " builds firmly on you and your husband ": he is always talking, it appears, of the Biebrich days of 1862, when " the exceptional artist pair, as he calls you ", had proved to him that this " impossible " work of his was after all possible. Then comes a curious passage that throws a new light on Wagner's attitude towards his own operas in the theatre.

> " While I am on the subject of impossibility ", says Cosima, " I may tell you that Wagner has become very accommodating in the matter of cuts. He told me yesterday that there is a great distinction between the artistic conception and the theatre performance, and that one must take this fully into consideration and sacrifice many details for the strengthening of the whole; he went so far as to say that *Tristan* could finish with the second act; the ' curse of love ', the whole of the big monologue in the third act, he is prepared to cut. I tell you this between ourselves, in case your husband should feel some well-justified apprehension as to excessive strain." [7]

Cosima may not have rendered Wagner's meaning quite accurately [8] here and there, but we may take it for granted that he *had* hinted at his willingness to make liberal cuts in *Tristan* — which is rather surprising in view of his general attitude towards his own

---

[7] KLRWB, V, xxix–xxx.

[8] Her German at this time was not as good as it became later; she herself apologises to Malvina for her "fremdes Deutsch". Dr. Strobel prints the letter just as Cosima wrote it, with all its sins against the German language. It is very difficult to believe that Wagner ever said that in the theatre *Tristan* could end with the second act!

It seems certain, however, that in later life he recognised that in the fury of creation he had occasionally been cruel to the singers. Weingartner tells us that in the Munich theatre's score of *Tristan* two cuts had been noted by Hermann Levi as sanctioned by Wagner. "Levi further told me", says Weingartner, "that on one occasion, after hearing *Tristan* on one of his journeys, he [Wagner] cried out quite excitedly, 'Cut out the trombones in the duet! It is all too heavily orchestrated!'." WL, I, 249–50.

works. Dr. Strobel surmises that he may have been anxious to re-assure Malvina on Schnorr's behalf: we know how carefully she watched over the health of her ten or eleven years younger husband. Perhaps, however, Cosima's remarks were also intended to convey delicately to Malvina that Wagner would raise no objection to necessary cuts in the part of Isolde as well. Malvina was now on the brink of forty, so the presumption is that her voice was not in its first vigour or brilliance: it stands to reason also that if her rôle in *Lohengrin* was Ortrud there must have been more than one passage in the part of Isolde that lay rather high for her. There were no doubt several German sopranos just then with better voices; but none of them had Malvina's sum of qualifications for Isolde.

For Kurvenal there was Mitterwurzer, of Dresden — the original Wolfram in the Dresden *Tannhäuser* of 1845: for King Marke Wagner would have liked to have Beck, of Vienna, but as Beck could not obtain the necessary leave, Wagner looked next to August Kindermann, of Munich: Sophie Stehle, also of Munich, would do, he thought, for Brangaene. In the end, the part of Marke had to be given to Zottmayer, of Hanover, and that of Brangaene to Anna Deinet, who had joined the Munich opera not long before.[9]

Schnorr, who now had leave of absence from Dresden for the whole of April, May and June, arrived in Munich again with his wife on the 5th April, and the rehearsals began immediately. From the 10th of the month onwards there was an instrumental rehearsal of one kind or another in the Residenz Theatre under Bülow every morning, and a piano rehearsal every evening at Wagner's house; and by an ironic freak of fate it was on the day of the first rehearsal that Cosima presented Bülow with Wagner's daughter, Isolde Ludowika Josepha.[10] On the 14th, announcing this happy domestic event to his friend Carl Gille, Bülow could say that things already

---

[9] Max Zenger describes her as having a bright voice with a good coloratura technique. In 1868 she married Ernst von Possart, at that time an actor at the Munich Court Theatre, of which he became later the famous Regisseur and then Intendant. See his eulogies of her in his autobiography, PEE, pp. 182 ff., 231 ff. She appears to have been very pretty, a good pianist and something of a musician. Zenger, who knew both ladies, thought the deeper voice of Sophie Stehle would have been more suitable for Brangaene. It was said that she had declined the part because of its "difficulties"; but this appears not to have been the real reason.

[10] She married the conductor Franz Beidler, and died on the 7th February, 1919. The "Ludowika" was obviously in honour of King Ludwig.

augured well for the opera, the first performance of which had been fixed for some day between the 10th and the 17th May; " the two Schnorrs are divine, Fräulein Deinet very capable, Zottmayer weak in the head but strong in the lungs, and of a good presence." [11]

3

The King wanted *Tristan* to be given in the large Court Theatre, holding about 2,000 people. In his opinion the Residenz Theatre was " unsuitable for the performance of such huge works as this "; and for once at any rate he was right, as against Wagner, on a matter of art pure and simple. Wagner implored him not to press the point.

"I beg you ", he wrote to him, " to let us stay in the cosy Residenz Theatre! You have no idea how happy we all feel there; it is as if we were already beyond the reach of the common world. Music sounds wonderfully beautiful there — more beautiful than in any other theatre or hall in my experience. The singers are delighted with the way their voices sound; everything is easier for them; even the most difficult things succeed. This is a complete enigma, but it is always so with acoustics, which are still a mystery. The tone, to be sure, is not great in volume, but it is remarkably clear and luminous: the words are particularly easy to follow — to this I attach infinite importance, especially in this case. As for the stage action, there are no masses of useless choristers to think about; it is simply a matter of the portrayal of the purely-human. The happenings are all of a delicate, intimate nature: every quiver of the face, every movement of the eyes, must tell its tale. Only in such a theatre, in such conditions, would *Tristan* — *Tristan* of all works! — be possible. . . . If later we must make a sacrifice and transplant it to the large theatre, it will mean the ruin of the purity of the representation, to which I shall have to resign myself. I beg you to preserve this purity for me as long as possible — at least for the first three performances! "

---

[11] "How Wagner", says Max Zenger, who lived in Munich at that time, "could have selected this singer, the uncouthness of whose movements was surpassed only by that of his singing, for a part in every way so difficult and perilous [as that of King Marke] was simply incomprehensible to the people in the theatre, including myself. It can only be assumed that a combination of unfortunate circumstances made it impossible to find an artist who could be taken seriously, and Bülow had to put the best face he could on a bad business." (ZGMO, p. 481). In his letter of the 14th April to Carl Bechstein, Bülow says that Zottmayer "has a good voice, but it is not yet properly trained."

Bülow was of Wagner's opinion; he too was enchanted with the resonance of the little theatre.

The King, of course, gave way; but he had hardly done so when Wagner himself was compelled to change his mind.

" I have now realised clearly ", he confessed to Ludwig on the 1st May, " how necessary the new theatre [i.e., the projected festival theatre] is for my new works. My temporary flight into the Residenz Theatre, I now see, has not brought me into haven. The material, sensuously strong sound of the orchestra, which I cannot contrive any apparatus to dampen, and against which no care in the playing is of any avail, drives me with my dear singers out of this noisy little place back into the larger theatre. But there I labour under two disadvantages from which I would gladly escape if I could — the too great distance, so far as the miming is concerned, of the actors from the spectator, and the disturbing effect of a large audience: for the first performances I had wished for a smaller and more select company. I have to give up this in order to achieve musical clarity. Oh for my invisible, sunken, transfigured orchestra in the theatre of the future! "

Presumably what had happened was that so long as sectional rehearsals alone were being held, with the singers using only half-voice, the resonance was ideal; but the more the rehearsals approximated to a performance at full physical tension, vocal and orchestral, the more out of scale the work became in the smaller theatre. On the 2nd May Schnorr wrote to his mother:

" Unfortunately we shall have to give the first performance in the larger theatre; the acoustics of the Residenz Theatre are too coarse and sensuous for the *Tristan* orchestra. The tone is not sufficiently refined, and so it completely covers the voices. The root of the trouble is that the orchestra is a couple of feet too high, a disadvantage that unfortunately cannot be corrected, because the orchestral podium rests on a vault. When one is sitting in the pit the lamps of the desks come up to the knees of the characters on the stage."

Wagner's original intention was to give at the most five performances, not simply because his leading " guest " singers would not be available after June, but also because he wished the production to be regarded not as merely one more item in the ordinary theatrical repertory, but as a demonstration of Wagnerian aims and a model of Wagnerian style. The 15th May was at last fixed upon for the first performance; by the 6th of that month, Bülow had already had eighteen orchestral rehearsals, in addition to many others at the piano.

Meanwhile, on the 18th April, Wagner had addressed to his friend Friedrich Uhl, the editor of the Vienna *Botschafter*, an open letter concerning the coming production. In this he tells the story of the years-long difficulties in connection with the floating of *Tristan,* in Karlsruhe, Vienna and elsewhere, and of the change in the fortune of the work effected by the King of Bavaria. He announces " perhaps only three performances ", which " are to be regarded as art-festivals, to which I am allowed to invite the friends of my art from far and near: they will consequently be remote from the character of ordinary theatre productions and will stand outside the usual relations between the theatre and the public of our day." To these " friends of his art ", then, he issues an invitation to Munich. To the possible insinuation that his object in doing so is to fill the theatre with people already well-disposed towards him he quietly replies that " this time it is not a question of pleasing or displeasing — that marvellous game of theatrical hazard! — but merely whether artistic problems of the kind I have set before me in this work can really be solved, and in what way, and whether the solving of them is worth the trouble." By this he does not mean discovering whether this kind of production will make money — which is what the ordinary theatre understands by success or failure — but solely whether excellent performances of this type can produce the expected effect on cultivated people. His concern, then, being solely with an artistic problem, the presence is not sought of those who are not seriously interested in this and similar problems. Should it be solved on this occasion, the question will then open out more widely: it will be made clear what is being done in Munich to give the public proper a share in the highest and deepest things of art, even though the theatrical public as it is now does not come into the reckoning.[12]

At the rehearsal of the 2nd May, Bülow, who had worked himself, as was his way, to the verge of a nervous breakdown — he actually fainted at one rehearsal — was guilty of one of those fatal

---

[12] This letter is not included in RWGS. It was printed in the BBW of June 1890. Ellis's translation will be found in the eighth volume of his English version of Wagner's writings.

indiscretions for which he was notorious, and of which the *Neueste Nachrichten* made the most in its issue of the 7th. He had wanted the orchestral area to be enlarged: the theatre machinist, Penkmayr, had told him that this would mean sacrificing thirty stalls: whereupon Bülow burst out with " What does it matter whether we have thirty *Schweinehunde* more or less in the place? " The paper, after reporting the incident, obligingly offered Bülow the hospitality of its columns for a reply. This appeared on the 9th. He had to admit that he had made use of " a most unparliamentary expression ", which, however, had a " much more brutal sense ", perhaps, in Munich than in other places. He hastened to assure the readers of the paper that he never intended the defamatory term to be understood as applying to the " cultivated Munich public " as a whole. For it is to the public that the artist has to look for support; and indeed both he and his " highly honoured friend Richard Wagner " had been well supported by the Munich public. The term he had the misfortune to use on the spur of the moment was meant to apply, therefore, only to those malevolent theatre-goers who were suspected of having intrigued against and slandered the Master. In any case he had never anticipated that this ejaculation of his, made in the half-dark theatre but evidently overheard, unknown to him, by people for whose ears it was not intended, would have to face the harsh light of publicity in the Press.

The *Neueste Nachrichten* accepted the lame apology courteously; but other journals were not so accommodating, while threats and attacks, signed or anonymous, poured in upon Bülow from private correspondents. The *Volksblatt* was particularly truculent. " If Hans von Bülow, this typical specimen of truly Prussian self-esteem and insolence, were to commit an indiscretion of this kind in the patriotic rooms of the Hofbräuhaus, the ' Zervierteln ' would be the least that would happen to him. ' Go abroad ' is the motto of the old-Müncheners. But Hans Bülow and his clan do not go; nor would his spiritual affinity Lola Montez go — but she went all the same." The *Neuer Bayerischer Kurier* displayed every day for a whole week the provocative slogan, " Hans von Bülow is still here! ", the size of the letters increasing from day to day. The plain object of this campaign was to drive Bülow out of the town and so make the performance of *Tristan* impossible. The " Schweine-

hunde " was one of the cardinal blunders of Bülow's career; his and
Wagner's enemies in Munich took care that it was never forgotten.
There was a good deal of truth in Pecht's remark that " there is not
the least doubt that Wagner, protected by the King as he was, would
have been able to hold out longer than he did in Munich had he not
brought to the town, in the person of Hans von Bülow, an associate
who had a gift quite out of the common for getting himself disliked
by the Müncheners." [13]

4

One of Wagner's own sins came home to roost at this time. " It is
my strange fate ", he wrote with almost comic self-delusion and
self-pity to the King on the 22nd April,

> " never to meet, in my relations with the world as an ordinary citizen,
> with fine, noble natures, but always to have to do with the common-
> est specimens of humanity. An experience of this sort, of the most
> shameful inconsiderateness, has just fallen once more to my lot, with
> the result that the peace of life which my Friend has secured to me, at
> any rate for a few years, by such real sacrifices, has been disturbed in
> the most offensive way. Anyone who knows what it means, after a life
> like mine, to be able to believe that I have won quietness and an as-
> sured regularity in life's outer mechanism, and then to find all this
> crumbling away just when I am on the point of making use of it for
> my higher mission — anyone who knows this will understand my
> terror over this affair! Even the good Pfistermeister seemed to be
> quite staggered by it! "

— which reminds one of Polly Peachum's " Even butchers weep! "
in her sympathetic pre-vision of the hanging of Macheath.

" Schwabe-Schwind " is Wagner's shorthand note of the affair in
the " Annals ". The reader will recall that in 1860, after the ruin
his three Paris concerts had brought on him, Malwida von Meysenbug had obtained for him about 5,000 francs from a rich widow,
Mme. Julie Schwabe,[14] to whose daughter Malwida was then acting

---

[13] PAMZ, II, 137.

[14] Wagner speaks none too kindly of the lady in *Mein Leben:* he calls her "rather
grotesque", suggests that it was only because her "vanity" was flattered by the
"distinction she obtained from frequenting my salon" that she came to his rescue,
and says that she always went to sleep when his music was being performed. Perhaps his normal inability, when writing his memoirs, to remember benefactors
cordially had been increased in this case by his irritation over the affair of the bill

as governess. Being unwilling, according to his own much later account, to accept the money as a gift, he insisted on giving the lady, although she had not asked for it, a note of hand payable in twelve months. At the end of that time he had to ask for a renewal for a further year, whereupon Malwida assured him — there seems to be no evidence, however, that Mme. Schwabe, who was not in Paris at that time, formally joined in the assurance — that his benefactor regarded the sum not as a loan but as a gift.[15] Several unmet bills of his had from time to time been sold by weary holders of them to speculators willing to take the risk of getting something or nothing for them; and it has always been taken for granted that the Schwabe bill was one of these, the story told in all the biographies being that some enemies of Wagner, having bought the paper, presented it to him just before the *Tristan* production, with the clear intention of disgracing him publicly in the very likely event of his being unable to find the money to meet it. Wagner and his circle always believed that the villain of the piece was the painter Moritz von Schwind, who never made any attempt to conceal his dislike of him: hence the " Schwabe-Schwind " of the " Annals ". The true facts of the matter have only recently come to light.

It is manifest now that the holder and presenter of the bill was none other than Frau Salis-Schwabe herself, who was apparently living in Rome at that time; she had no doubt heard, like the rest of the world, of the large sums Wagner was supposed to have obtained from King Ludwig, and saw no reason why her own five-year-old loan should not at long last be repaid out of them. From a friend in Rome she obtained the name of a Munich lawyer, Dr. von

in 1865. This Mme. Schwabe seems to have been a kindly sort of person; and that she should have chosen Malwida to educate her daughter suggests that she had a mind. Malwida paints an attractive portrait of her in her *Memoiren einer Idealisten*, laying particular stress on her constant readiness to open her purse for any good work; in 1860 she sent out to Italy, at Malwida's request, a large consignment of hospital material for Garibaldi's wounded soldiers. If in 1860 she hardly knew Wagner and was not particularly interested in him as a composer, her readiness to help him to the extent of 5,000 francs seems all the clearer evidence of her goodness of heart.

From Wagner's letter of the 22nd June, 1860 to Malwida it appears that he was much more grateful to Mme. Schwabe at the time of the loan than he was when writing *Mein Leben* some years later. In 1860 he could hardly find warm enough praise for the generosity of this woman, who, without having any personal ties with him, came to his help when everyone else was leaving him to his fate. See MGW, pp. 559–560.

[15] RWML, II, 827.

Schauss, whom she engaged to act for her. When Schwind's name began to be bandied about in connection with the affair he complained to Schauss (in September, 1865) about it; and in a letter of the following December to the Vienna conductor Heinrich Esser he quotes the substance of the lawyer's reply. Schauss could throw no light on the problem of how the rumour regarding Schwind had started; but he informed the painter that it was in the preceding March that Frau Salis-Schwabe had sent him the Wagner bill for collection. He wrote Wagner, he said, " an extremely polite note " on the 20th March, in which he urged him to give serious attention to the matter, as a delay in settlement would compel him [Schauss] to take steps that would be likely to embarrass him during the preparations for the production of " his great opera *Tristan und Isolde* ". [16]

As Wagner could not meet the bill, a provisional distraint was levied on his furniture, apparently on what should have been the day of the first performance of *Tristan*, the 15th May. In his distress he had to appeal to the Cabinet for aid: " Highly honoured friend ", he wrote to the Treasurer on the 15th, " the bearer of these lines [Cosima?] will inform you with what friendliness and consideration I am treated here. It will be impossible for me to survive these days if some powerful helping hand does not protect me today. Spare me the intended ignominy, and may God reward you." The bill was of course paid at once by the Treasury, in whose accounts it figures as 2,400 florins.

5

On the 5th May, which, as has been pointed out on an earlier page, he always regarded erroneously as the anniversary of the King's first letter to him, Wagner had promised Ludwig that as *Lohengrin* had first won him his love, so *Tristan* would strengthen it. Ludwig, for his part, found the days moving on all too slowly to the 15th, the day assigned for the first performance. On the 10th he assured Wagner of his undying affection, and of his unshakable devotion to their joint work.

---

[16] Schauss's letter has only recently come to light. It will be found in KLRWB, V, 229–30.

" We must break through the barriers of custom, shatter to pieces the laws of the base egoistical world; the ideal must and shall come to life! Let us march forward conscious of victory: I will never forsake you, my loved one! O *Tristan, Tristan* will come to me! The dreams of my boyhood and youth will be realised! With the commonness of the world you should have nothing to do: I will bear you high above the troubles of earth! . . . My love for you and your art is ever increasing, and this flame of love shall bring well-being and salvation."

On the fateful 15th Wagner was able to send the King the architect's plans for the provisional theatre. " Everything must be accomplished ", Ludwig wrote back the same day; " I will never relax. The boldest of dreams must be made a reality! " On this one day four letters passed between the Residenz and the Briennerstrasse. Wagner told the King the details of the " Schwabe-Schwind " affair, at which he had only vaguely hinted in his letter of the 22nd April, and Ludwig was full of sympathy and consolation: the world was not wholly vile, he said, in spite of its unkind treatment of his beloved: " there are many good and noble beings in it, to live and work for whom is true joy." And he reached out his affectionate hand to him to soothe yet another grief. Wagner, on the 6th May, had invited Pusinelli to one of the *Tristan* performances, but begged him, if he came, to say nothing of it to Minna: " I have finally come to the state where any contact with her merely wounds and embitters me; she is and will be the only one, truly, who will *never* come to understand me clearly." [17] Pusinelli's reply, which seems to have reached Wagner on the 14th, was a cold douche; it informed him that Minna was dying. But immediately on the heels of this letter came another, bringing better news. Wagner's telegram in reply, sent at ten in the morning of the 15th, is curiously revelatory of his mentality: relieved as he was by it, or as we must assume him to have been, his thoughts were still mainly with *Tristan* and the coming performance. " A thousand thanks for your last news ", he said.

" The sudden change after the most terrible apprehension is only to be compared with my whole strange destiny. Best greetings and wishes for a happy recovery. For the rest you can realise in what excitement

---

[17] RWAP, p. 172. This passage in the letter was omitted from the official publication of the Wagner-Pusinelli correspondence.

I am living just now. But all will be wonderfully fine. Thanks for your true friendship. Retain it for me." [18]

For the great day, the 15th, Wagner's friends and followers had come to Munich from every part of Europe — Gasperini from Paris, Klindworth from London, Heinrich Porges from Prague, Uhl from Vienna, Röckel from Frankfort, Franz Müller from Weimar, Alexander Ritter, Pohl, Lassen, Adolf Jensen, Raff, Carl Gille, Leopold Damrosch, Eckert, Kalliwoda, Draeseke, and others from all parts: Liszt, who had just taken minor orders, preferred to remain in Rome and commune with his soul. Another notable absentee was Cornelius, who was busy in Weimar in connection with the forthcoming production (on the 21st May), of his opera *Der Cid*.[19] Things had been going none too well between him and Wagner for some time: Cornelius had realised that the older man took little real interest in him for his own sake as an artist, and he already regretted having settled in Munich merely to serve Wagnerian ends.

The final *Tristan* rehearsal proper — the twenty-first of its kind — which was really a private full-dress performance before the King and' some six hundred invited guests, lasting from ten in the morning till a quarter past three in the afternoon, took place on the 11th; the King signalised the occasion by granting a pardon to those who had been condemned for participation in the revolution of 1849. Before the prelude began, Wagner came on the stage and, in a voice trembling with emotion, addressed the orchestral players. He expressed his regret that owing to his poor health he was unable to have the honour of leading them himself on this occasion, thanked them for their exertions and their devotion, and expressed his perfect confidence in his second self, Bülow. " As regards the first actual performance ", he concluded,

---

[18] RWAP, p. 175. The draft of the telegram is still in the Wahnfried archives. See KLRWB, IV, 60. How irreparable the breech between him and Minna now was is shown by the fact that even in this solemn moment he did not write to her direct, nor had Minna addressed a word direct to him, although, as is shown by her making her will on the 11th, she had felt death to be near.

[19] On the 21st March he had a conversation with the Grand Duke, who asked for news of Liszt. "I said to him", Cornelius wrote to Hestermann the same day, "'I greatly regret that Liszt has severed his connection with Germany; I regard his settling in Rome as the sulking of a privileged spirit, and he ought not to sulk'." CABT, II, 49.

" there remains to be seen only the effect on the real public — for today is merely a rehearsal before invited listeners. I feel no anxiety
over this contact with the real public. It was the German public that
everywhere upheld me against the hostility of the factions. Yet perhaps hatred cannot everywhere be extinguished: let us employ against
it the means that Tristan and Isolde have taught us. Isolde believes
that she hates Tristan, and so hands him the potion of death; but destiny changes this into the potion of love. To the poison-filled heart
that perchance may come to our work let us tender the love potion.
With you it rests to achieve this magic of love: I leave its work in your
hands."

" I can still remember as if it were yesterday ", says Max Zenger,
who was present at the performance, " the spontaneous applause
which these final words of Wagner's wrung from me." The general
emotion, according to Zenger, was too deep for anyone to be struck,
at the time, by the discrepancy between Wagner's mystical words
and his very realistic appearance.

" Wagner was not in everyday clothes but in the most festal-formal
costume, in deep black from his chin to his elegant patent leather
shoes: it gave a more remarkable prominence than ever — an almost
uncanny prominence — to his head. There was thus no lack of the exquisite in his outer presentation. But precisely this exquisite, of which
the audience soon became conscious, brought a certain disenchantment
with it. People asked, ' Where then are the poison-filled hearts to
which we must hand not the potion of death but the potion of love? '
With the exception of a few raven-black journalists no one was poison-
filled, no one had come there in the expectation of a party conflict:
all were keyed up to discover what impression would be made by the
new and virtually unknown work." [20]

Wagner was followed by Bülow, who also spoke in great agitation. He thanked the orchestra and the singers warmly for their
long self-forgetting labours, which alone had enabled him to fulfil
the trust reposed in him by Wagner. At the end of each act there
were calls for Wagner, who, however, did not appear. According

[20] ZGMO, pp. 483–4. Josephine von Kaulbach (the wife of the painter), who
was present at this performance, described Wagner's speech, in a letter to her
husband, as "excellent, modest, simple and heartfelt." "I wish I could say as much
of the opera!" she added. The duet in the second act she describes as three quarters
of an hour without any melody, and expressing only "utterly barbaric passions, I
might even say the passions of some antediluvian race: too much for our feeble
nerves and ears." BLKB, p. 59.

to Zenger, the effect of the performance on the average spectator was one of complete mental and physical exhaustion, which made it impossible for him to retain in his memory a single detail when it was all over. Not only was the music difficult to follow, but the peculiar diction of the poem created difficulties. On the 13th an extra rehearsal, to which no one was invited, was held in order to put the finishing touches on the performance.

6

The 15th must have seemed to Wagner, in retrospect, one of the most tragic days of his life. It was on the morning of that day that the bailiffs invaded Briennerstrasse 21 and he had to send Cosima in post haste to Treasurer Hofmann with an appeal for 2,400 florins. That unpleasant matter could hardly have been settled when Schnorr arrived at the house with tears in his eyes, to tell Wagner that a performance that evening would be impossible, Malvina having suddenly become hoarse. So hard-hit had Wagner been, however, by his earlier experience of that morning that, as he told the King in his letter of the same afternoon, he did not feel this second blow. " I am fit for nothing more in this world ", he said wearily. " My life was too long at the mercy of the base: my glance into the hearts of men shows me an abyss that all my hopes will henceforth be unable to fill! "

The postponement of *Tristan*, the announcement of which was made publicly in the late afternoon, provided the town with a first-class sensation. Rumour was soon busy with its thousand tongues — Wagner and his abominable music had ruined Frau Schnorr's voice; Bülow dared not appear in the theatre, certain students having laid in a large stock of rotten eggs and apples to pay him out for his " Schweinehunde "; Bülow had bought, for ten gulden worth of beer, the secret of the plot of some frenzied local patriots to assassinate him; the whole orchestra, with the exception of a clarinettist and a hornist, had struck for more pay, at the instigation of two other hornists, Sendelbeck and Strauss; [21] and so on *ad infinitum*.

---

[21] The father of the composer Richard Strauss. Bülow used to call him "the Joachim of the horn". A musical conservative of the first water, he made no secret of his detestation of Wagner and "the music of the future"; but for all that he played magnificently in the Wagner operas. Even Wagner seems to have been a little

Those of Wagner's friends from abroad who could afford it stayed on for a week or so in the hope of a performance, spending many happy hours in Wagner's house, where Bülow and Wagner himself initiated them into the scores of the *Rhinegold* and the *Meistersinger*. A well-known photograph, taken in the Bayerischer Hof Hotel on the 17th, showing fifteen of the faithful grouped round the master and his dog, is today a precious document for the student of the coats and trousers, the neckties and the beards of that amazing epoch.

Most of the guests, however, had to return home without hearing *Tristan*, for Frau Schnorr's hoarseness — the result of her having taken a vapour bath on the morning of what should have been the first performance — took some time to cure. It was Wagner and the King who suffered most from the postponement, because of the sudden and painful collapse of the nervous tension in which they had lived daily for so many weeks. The more unfriendly section of the Bavarian Press exulted boorishly over the catastrophe: the *Volksbote* opined that the new opera was now more than ever the music of the future, and that the most disappointed of all was Bülow, who " had been looking forward so eagerly to an ovation from the Schweinehunde." On this occasion, as on many similar ones, we might be able to forgive Wagner's German compatriots for disliking the man and feeling no enthusiasm for his work; what we find it difficult either to forgive or to understand is the sheer baseness of soul that could rejoice so maliciously over the misfortunes of an artist, and the loutish vulgarity in the expression of its malice. A small local theatre came out with a parody of the opera

---

afraid of this tough old Münchener. Bülow said of him, "The fellow is intolerable, but when he blows his horn you can't be angry with him." At the end of one long rehearsal, Strauss said bluntly that he could play no more. "Then take your pension!" said the irritated Bülow. Strauss picked up his horn, went to the Intendant, and asked for his pension "at the orders of Herr von Bülow". As he was indispensable, Perfall had to use all his diplomacy to smooth the trouble out. The hornist could safely permit himself liberties and impertinences that his fellows would have shrunk from, for he was economically more or less independent, having married a daughter of the rich brewer Pschorr. His antipathy towards Wagner endured to the end of his days, and on the morrow of the composer's death in 1883 it showed itself in a most unpleasant way. Before commencing a rehearsal under Hermann Levi the orchestra stood up in silence to show its respect for the dead master: Strauss alone boorishly kept his seat. With Bülow, however, the incorruptible irreconcilable became quite reconciled in the early 'nineties — after Bülow had taken up the promising young Richard Strauss.

—Tristanderl und Süssholde — which, if it corresponded in any degree to its playbill,[22] must have been a model of clumsy grossness. *Punsch* added to the general merriment by printing a parody of the text of *Tristan.*

7

Malvina, accompanied by her husband, went to Reichenhall to recover. Wagner tried hard to induce Schnorr to return and take part in a performance of the *Flying Dutchman* on the 28th May, and one of *Tannhäuser* on the 1st June, which he hoped to set before his friends from afar as some sort of compensation for the loss of *Tristan;* but Schnorr could not be persuaded to leave his wife. The pair did not return to Munich until the 6th June; rehearsals were held on the three following days, and on the 10th the great work came at last to a public hearing, eight years after Wagner had first embarked on it, six years after the last note had been written. The audience included Anton Bruckner, who had come all the way from Linz for the occasion — the first expression of a doglike devotion to Wagner that endured to the end of Bruckner's days.

The performance was timed to commence at six o'clock. At ten minutes past the hour the handsome young King, looking his most romantic, took his place in the royal box: it was characteristic of him that he chose to occupy it alone, although elsewhere in the house were several notabilities so closely allied to him as the old King Ludwig I, Duke Max, and Prince Luitpold (the King's uncle) with his two elder sons. Bülow raised his baton immediately after Ludwig had taken his seat. During the playing of the prelude the audience kept streaming into the pit and gallery; the reason for permitting this, apparently, was to frustrate any attempt at a " Schweinehunde " demonstration against Bülow. The hissing heard in some quarters after each act was drowned in the applause of the great majority. At the final fall of the curtain, close on eleven o'clock, Wagner appeared on the stage between his Tristan and his Isolde; he wore a black coat and white trousers.[23]

---

[22] Given in RLW, I, 155.
[23] The King was in ordinary civilian dress.

The impossible had been accomplished; the unperformable opera had been performed. Even in the Press approving voices were heard here and there during the next few days; but on the whole no injustice was done to the character of the journalistic criticisms by Schnorr's description of them in a letter to his mother:

> " Perhaps about no other theatrical production has so much nonsense ever been written as about *Tristan and Isolde.* The poor lovers would not have let themselves be awakened in their graves had they known how maliciously the world would behave towards their awakener, and consequently to themselves. To the devil with these wretched notices! I have read some eight or ten without finding in a single one of them the faintest evidence that the writer of it had read the poem, let alone understood it."

Schnorr was no Niemann; he was an artist and a thinker as well as a tenor. He knew the innermost meaning of the work he had studied so conscientiously for so many years; and knowing it, he knew also that even when, as occasionally happened, the scribes praised, they did not really understand. Schnorr's thought, from first to last, was not for himself but for Wagner. " Mingled with our [his own and Malvina's] immense happiness ", he wrote to his mother *à propos* of the applause they had received at the end of the performance, " was a good deal of downright pride. . . . We have accomplished something which others cannot imitate: we have at last attained the great, great goal." On the 12th the King sent Wagner, from Berg, a letter overflowing with joy at what had so far been done and confidence in what was yet to do: he begged Wagner to convey his warmest thanks to the Schnorrs. Wagner's heart was too full for eloquence: he could write the noble couple only a line or two in a tone of friendly banter; what he really felt he expressed in another way — by presenting them with the King's letter.

A second performance followed on the 13th June, and a third on the 19th. The King was not present at the latter; even *Tristan* he preferred not to hear at all to hearing it in the uncongenial company of his uncle Otto, the King of Greece, a gentleman notoriously not overburdened with intelligence, whose conversation, Ludwig no doubt felt, he would find it hard to endure with patience at such a time. The performances as a whole gave Wagner the ecstatic sense of hearing a work of his for the first time virtually as he had con-

ceived it. It is true that the worthy Mitterwurzer occasionally over-
acted as Kurvenal, and Zottmayer was not the ideal Marke. But
the Brangaene seems to have been very competent, Frau Schnorr
proved a great Isolde, while for his Tristan Wagner could never
find language, then or later, adequate to express the admiration,
love and gratitude he felt.[24]

One of his griefs was that few even of the people who had waxed
enthusiastic over this work of his at its first performance could
have had any real understanding of it — which, indeed, is very
much the state of affairs at any performance of *Tristan* in any
theatre today. But even worse was it to be snatched out of his ideal
world of beauty into the world of ugly reality as he must have been
by some of the baser happenings about him. " You are satisfied,
dear one, are you not? " we find the King writing him anxiously
on the 17th June. " Why be so sad and dispirited because there are
people who malign you, who do not understand you? " Had Wagner, perhaps, in his distress, passed on to the young King a letter
he had just received from one of those people whose strangely perverted mentality finds peculiar pleasure in trying to inflict pain
behind the safe shield of anonymity? Dr. Strobel prints the letter,
which is still preserved in the Wahnfried archives — or, to be more
accurate, parts of the letter, for some of it, it appears, is too gross
for publication. " Your *Tristan* ", wrote this fine flower of Munich
culture,

" has now been given here twice. Enough incense will have been
strewn around you; here is something to sober you. . . . Your chief
fault is your monstrous arrogance, that makes you despise everything
previous to you and around you. . . . You have talent; but your arrogance prevents you from recognising the measure and the limitations
of it, just as it prevented you from studying properly and forming
yourself on good models. In addition there is your moral, or rather
immoral, constitution. . . . You have known how to insinuate yourself or force your way here as you have done in other places. At present you are the evil genius of our young King. . . . Now for a word
more particularly about your *Tristan*. The libretto, especially in the
second act, is a monstrosity of indecency. . . . The music is a chaos

---

[24] "We are all in a dream-state over the extraordinarily complete success, and
especially over the public's increasing sympathy", Bülow wrote to Raff on the 21st
June. "It is the greatest success that a new Wagner work has ever had anywhere.
The Schnorrs were unbelievable; all the others quite tolerable; orchestra excellent."

of sounds . . . it struck me as the ravings of a madman with some lucid intervals. . . . Time will judge; before the present generation has passed away you and your music will be spoken of only as curiosities. . . . They call you the musician of the future. Compose for the best minds of the present day, and you will then have composed for the future: otherwise, your music will have no future." 25

8

While we are on the subject of *Tristan* it may be as well to clear up a little misunderstanding with regard to Wagner's opinion of analysis by way of " leading motives ". It has latterly come to be taken for granted that this term was the invention of Hans von Wolzogen, and that it was never sanctioned by Wagner. Mr. G. A. Hight, for example, tells us that

" as the originator of these books [the " Guides " to the Wagner operas] was the editor of the *Bayreuther Blätter*, it has been supposed that they were published by Wagner's authority, or, at least, that he gave them his approval. This is a mistake; he never gave them any sort of approval; on the contrary, he said they were worthless for a musician. . . . I infer from the published correspondence that he [Wolzogen] once wrote asking Wagner to say something about his books, probably thinking that a line from him would be useful as an advertisement. Wagner's reply was, ' Don't ask me about the impression which your writings make upon me; I am only interested in yourself'. In other words: ' I like *you,* but the less said about your books the better! ' The term *Leitmotiv* is nowhere used by Wagner, and was not invented by him." 26

This is not quite correspondent with the facts, and it does some injustice to Wolzogen, who did not settle in Bayreuth until October, 1877. Wagner's momentary petulance in his letter of the 23rd November, 1876 was obviously the product of a reading of his youthful admirer's book *Der Nibelungenmythus im Sage und Literatur* (1876); 27 there is no warrant for assuming it to have been called

25 KLRWB̌, I, 107.
26 G. A. Hight, *Richard Wagner*, I, 168–9.
27 See the letter in RWSK, pp. 375–6. Wolzogen had been indiscreet to mention, in the same breath as Wagner, the third-rate poet Wilhelm Jordan, whose *Die Nibelunge (Sigfridssage* 1868, *Hildebrandts Heimkehr,* 1874) had achieved enormous popularity about that time. Wagner resented being coupled with "this literary-poetic charlatan", as he calls Jordan in his letter to Wolzogen.

forth by Wolzogen's thematic analysis of the *Ring* in another work altogether.

Nor is Mr. Hight correct in his assertions (a) that Wolzogen was " the originator of these books ", and (b) that " the term *Leitmotiv* is nowhere used by Wagner ". Heinrich Porges' book on *Tristan und Isolde* (1906), that is at once a " Guide " and an aesthetic discussion, was published for the first time in the *Bayreuther Blätter* in 1902–3 [28] — some years, that is to say, after Wolzogen had begun (in 1876) his series of " Guides " to the Wagner operas. But Porges' work had been written as early as 1866–7, apparently for the benefit of King Ludwig.[29] Now not only does Porges analyse *Tristan* throughout in terms of " motives " — " Hauptmotive " (Principal Motives) as he sometimes calls them — but Wagner himself employed that very term [30] in the letter of congratulation he addressed to Porges after having read the section of the manuscript dealing with the second act of the opera: to show how carefully he has gone through it, he says, he would point out that Porges is not quite accurate in his analysis of King Marke, and has failed to observe that the closing orchestral bars of Act II, which are " formed melodically out of Marke's Hauptmotiv (of good will), consequently contain the Motiv of self-reproach, which appears to overcome Tristan." As early as 1867, then, Wagner himself was explaining his score, musically and dramatically, in terms of " Hauptmotive ". Perhaps we shall not be far astray if we assume that it was he himself who, in his conversations with Porges and others of his circle, had started the employment of this term.[31]

---

[28] Porges died in 1900.

[29] See the King's references to the manuscript in his letters to Wagner of the 18th July, 1866, 7th March, 1867, and 12th July, 1867 (in KLRWB, II, 73, 149, 184), and in Ludwig's letter of the 4th September, 1867 to Düfflipp (KLRWB, IV, 191).

[30] The difference between a "Leitmotiv" and a "Hauptmotiv" is, of course, merely verbal.

[31] Wagner's letter is given in RWFZ, p. 484, and again in Wolzogen's foreword to Porges' book. It is all the more curious that Mr. Hight should have overlooked it as he includes Porges' *Tristan und Isolde* in the Bibliography of Wagner literature consulted by him, though, it is true, he gives the date of the book as 1896 instead of 1906.

CHAPTER XVI

AFTER "TRISTAN"

1

W AGNER, IN later years, used to look back wistfully upon those *Tristan* days of 1865 as in some respects the happiest of his life: for the first time he had realised to the full what the King could do for him in the matter of the production of those new works of his that most people had hitherto regarded as impossible. But, as was generally the case with him, the brief halcyon hour was only the prelude to fresh storm and shipwreck. Within six months of his triumph with *Tristan* he was to be driven out of Munich, never to enter it again except as the visitor of a day.

In spite of the large number of contemporary documents bearing on this period that we now possess, it is still far from easy to fathom what had been going on beneath the surface of events in Munich during the first six months of 1865. Wagner, as we have seen, had been received there, in the summer of 1864, if not effusively, at all events with toleration; the politicians and the Court party, if by no means unmindful of his record in the Dresden rising of 1849 and of his later preachings of " revolution ", do not seem at first to have apprehended any particular danger to the young King on that account. No doubt it all looked to them, at first, as just one more case of a Wittelsbach monarch patronising a deserving artist; and if this passion for art were to absorb the boy King to the extent of making him leave the main threads of public affairs in the hands of the professional politicians, so much the better. But it must have gradually dawned on them that things were not working out quite as they had expected. Ludwig manifested, for a while, an unexpected zeal and energy in the discharge of his duties, and an equally unexpected resistance to pressure from his elders in either private or public matters.[1] At first the politicians may have

---

[1] Count de La Rosée, who was Ludwig's "governor" until he became of age in 1863, said of him at that time, "He is lively and very gifted. He has learned a good

thought that the King's " patronage " of Wagner would be confined, so far as finance was concerned, to granting him a comfortable allowance, liquidating his debts, and incurring now and then a little extra expenditure in connection with the production of one or other of his operas as part of the Munich repertory. To see all this good Bavarian money going into the pocket of an alien was no doubt mildly annoying, but had that been all it would not have been very serious.

But in the early part of 1865 it had become evident that it was to be by no means all. Though the descent of Wagner's " associates " — Bülow, Cornelius, Porges, Schmitt, Nohl — upon Munich must have created a good deal of resentment in professional musical circles, it is hardly likely that the Court and the Cabinet Secretariat were seriously perturbed over that: it was part of the Munich tradition to have German " foreigners " imposed from above upon the artistic and literary life of the town and to dislike the intruders heartily. Even the plan for the supersession of the Conservatoire by a Music School on Wagnerian lines might in and by itself have left the officials relatively unmoved. But the scheme for a grandiose new theatre to be devoted exclusively to rare performances of Wagner's operas was another matter altogether: the building itself would be very expensive, the running of it quite uneconomic; and the politicians were right in trying to keep the King's expenditure within prudent limits, however dubious may have been some of the devices they adopted to achieve their ends.

It is difficult to say precisely what had been the prime cause of the trouble in February 1865. We may perhaps assume that the politicians were primarily bent on scotching the Semper scheme. But that scheme was the King's own, the darling of his imagination: it certainly could not be used to drive a wedge between him and Wagner. Perhaps, again, the Press agitation had been worked up by the politicians less as a punishment of Wagner for anything he had already done than as a warning to him not to overstep in the future the line they had drawn for him. There was no suggestion

deal, and already has a range of knowledge far beyond the ordinary. He has a wealth of imagination that I have seldom met with in so young a man. But he is hasty and passionate: an exceptionally developed wilfulness points to an obstinacy which he has probably inherited from his grandfather, and which it will be difficult to master."

in Redwitz's articles of out-and-out enmity towards him: on the contrary, a plain hint had been given him that there would be no interference with the contract already made with him for the production of the *Ring*, but that he must henceforth refrain from making " immoderate financial and artistic demands " on the royal purse; that reference is obviously inspired, and is as obviously to the Semper theatre.

Had the politicians any reason, at this time, to fear that Wagner's prestige with the King as an artist was leading, or was likely to lead, to a pernicious influence over the young monarch in matters other than artistic? There is no evidence of such a fear on their part, or of the possibility of such a thing having occurred to either Wagner or Ludwig. The correspondence of the pair during the first nine months or so of their acquaintance, from May, 1864 to the passing storm of February, 1865, shows a certain formal reserve on the part of both of them. The King's attitude towards Wagner is in the main that of a young man towards a revered elder to whom he is delighted to be of service. He shows a perfectly clear sense of what the bond of union between them is: Wagner's rôle is to realise his unique powers of creation; that of the King is to make this possible by setting the great artist free from all common cares. They are partners in a vast and noble enterprise; Ludwig, as we have already had occasion to observe, did not look upon himself as merely a tool for Wagner's use, but regarded Wagner, to some extent, as the divinely-sent instrument through which he himself could realise his own romantic dreams of a regeneration of the world through art.

But the relation between them in the early days was, for all that, unmistakably that of sovereign and subject. In spite of Ludwig's outpourings of affection and solicitude for the older man, this relation, with all that it involved, was tacitly recognised on both sides. It was not until later that the distance marked out between them by etiquette gradually narrowed until, apart from the conventional courtesies of address on Wagner's part, the letters exchanged between them might often be those of two people in the same rank of life. Very soon after the misunderstanding of February, 1865 they become for each other, in the signatures to their letters, just " Ludwig " and " Richard Wagner ", plus a few demonstrative epithets

[386]

such as " eternal " and " true ". The tone until then, however, had not been anything like so intimate. The King did indeed sign himself now and then merely " Ludwig "; but the usual ending to his earliest letters was " Your Friend, Ludwig King of Bavaria ", " Your Friend and King, Ludwig ", " Your well-inclined King and true Friend, Ludwig ", with a tendency towards a simple " Your true Ludwig " as time goes on. On Wagner's side the mode of signature during these first few months is always respectfully conformable to etiquette: " Your Subject, Richard Wagner ", or " Your Majesty's most faithful Subject ", or " Your most faithful Subject and thrice-blessed Friend ", or occasionally " Your happy protégé " or " My royal protector's obedient servant ". But after the happy ending to the crisis of February, 1865 we virtually never meet again with an expression such as " subject " or " servant " on Wagner's part.[2]

2

Although, as we have seen, after the visit of Frau Dangl to Wagner in February he became virtually convinced that Providence had entrusted to him the responsibility for the well-being of Bavaria, if not, indeed, of all Germany, he does not seem even yet to have wished to take a hand in the purely political game. His experiences during the February crisis, as well as those in connection with the Semper theatre, had shown him how great was the underground power of the politicians and the Press: and in his remark about the right kind of man being lacking to the King we may see perhaps the first hint of a perception on his part that if his and the King's

---

[2] The letter of March 12th, 1865, which begins with the formal triple allocution,
"Most Illustrious King!
"Most Mighty King and Lord!
"Your Majesty",
and ends, "Awaiting a gracious decision with regard to my most humble petition, I remain in most respectful fidelity and devotion Your Majesty's most obedient Subject, Richard Wagner"—is only the exception that proves the rule. The letter is a request for a royal order that Bülow shall be given plenipotentiary powers in connection with the *Tristan* rehearsals. As this was a matter of theatre routine—implying the temporary supersession of Lachner—it would have to go before the Court Theatre Intendant; and the starched formality of Wagner's style is intended solely for official eyes. In the more personal and private letter that accompanies this same document he signs himself "With love beyond the grave, your Richard Wagner".

plans for art were not to be frustrated there would have to be a change in Ludwig's immediate environment. During the early summer of 1865, however, his hands had been too full with the *Tristan* preparations and performances for him to be able to give much thought, even had it been immediately necessary, to the question of replacing Pfistermeister and certain others by people in whom he and the King could have more confidence. But if he had for the moment forgotten his enemies, they had not forgotten him; and unknown to him, as we have lately discovered, they were debating among themselves what to do with him.

Towards the end of 1864 it had become apparent that Baron von Schrenck, the Bavarian Minister for Foreign Affairs, was hardly equal to the increasing difficulties of his post. Apparently not knowing where to turn just then to find the right man to head the Ministry and take the portfolio of Foreign Affairs, the King, in December, confided these two offices to Baron Ludwig von der Pfordten, who had served under his father from 1849 to 1859. Pfordten, a Bavarian by birth,[3] had been, in the early 'forties, Professor of Roman Law at Leipzig: having begun to dabble in politics he attracted the attention of King Friedrich August of Saxony, who made him his Minister of Education in 1848. The reader will remember that in May of that year Wagner tried unsuccessfully to secure Pfordten's interest in his *Plan for the Organisation of a German National Theatre for the Kingdom of Saxony*.[4] Pfordten no doubt observed with unfriendly interest the Dresden Kapellmeister's revolutionary exploits in 1849; and he remained an irreconcilable enemy of Wagner to the end of his days. Everything in and about Wagner was repugnant to him — his music, his political ideas, his personality, his success with the public: in 1858 he had assured the actor Emil Devrient that " if the princes would only hold together as the democrats do, Wagner's music would not be given anywhere." He had tried to persuade King Max II not to allow *Tannhäuser* to be given in Munich: the young Crown Prince heard of this and is said never to have forgiven Pfordten for it. Ludwig disliked his new minister for several other reasons, chief among them being Pfordten's exasperating habit of lecturing him:

[3] He had been "ennobled" by King Max II in 1854.
[4] See Vol. I, p. 499.

for Pfordten had been a professor, and most professors find it hard
to shake off the academic habit of talking down to everyone they
meet as if he were a junior class. Even his associates in the Bavarian
Ministry found Pfordten's *de haut en bas* manner rather trying.
" Though his bearing was anything but aristocratic ", says one modern German historian, " Herr von der Pfordten was full of self-
importance: he comported himself more like a principal than a
colleague. One was always conscious that he had arrived too rapidly at a high position, without any preliminary training in the
greater world." As a politician no one, in his own day or afterwards, ever regarded him as one of Germany's most commanding
intellects; the best that either friends or foes can find to say for
him was that when in office he worked hard, spoke well, if a trifle
pedantically, and did his duty according to his lights.[5] In 1866 he
had the misfortune to come into collision with Bismarck, was badly
worsted and humiliated, and soon afterwards disappeared from
the political scene for good. Bismarck's contemptuous description
of him in later years was " a worthy and learned but politically
not clever German professor ".

During the weeks of the preparations for *Tristan* the politicians
had become more than normally concerned at the closeness of the
bond between Wagner and the King. The latter had asked that
two semi-official rescripts should be drawn up and sent to all the
Bavarian legations; in one of these it was to be announced that he
could undertake no journeys that year on account of his health,
while in the other his relations with Wagner were to be set forth
clearly for the public benefit. Pfordten consented to the former,
though everyone knew that physically there was nothing wrong
with the King, and nothing mentally apart from his distaste for
humanity in the mass and his desire to live the kind of life that
happened to give him most pleasure, that is to say, planning with
Wagner the culture of the future. But Pfordten could not draw up
the second circular, he wrote to Pfistermeister on the 28th May,
until he himself knew precisely what the relations of the King
and the composer now were, and what they were to be in the future.

---

[5] A critical summing-up of him will be found in Karl Alexander von Müller's
Bayern im Jahre 1866 (Munich, 1909), pp. 11–16. The utmost possible credit for
what he strove to do and what he succeeded in doing is given him by a later historian, Michael Doeberl, in his *Entwicklungsgeschichte Bayerns*, Vol. III.

He had been waiting to get *Tristan* over, he says. Now that the performance seems to be postponed indefinitely by the illness of Frau Schnorr he thinks it his duty — Pfordten was always strong on his duty; it was one of the traits in him that maddened Ludwig — to

> " set forth the misgivings which the Wagner-Bülow situation arouses in everyone who sincerely and faithfully loves the King and would fain preserve him from a damage that is unhappily drawing only too near. . . . My conviction is that Bülow must be discharged by his Majesty, and the sooner the better. As regards Wagner, all contracts made with him are to be observed, but personal relations between him and the King must be put an end to if his Majesty is not to be prejudiced both at home and abroad."

Grants to liquidate Wagner's debts must cease; the King must not let his kindness be abused. The King seems to have replied curtly and acidly to this in a note to Pfistermeister: he had no objection to Bülow being induced to leave Munich for a while after the *Tristan* production, but he meant to retain Wagner there. On the 3rd June Pfistermeister told Pfordten that his Majesty would like a public announcement to be made that during the last four months he had received Wagner in audience only once — on the 22nd May — " and so it would be in the future."

This called out all that was most official, most professorial and most paternal in the soul of the worthy Pfordten. He sees, he writes to Pfistermeister on the 5th, that the King does not desire any further discussion of the Wagner-Bülow matter. He too will be silent about this, as he has neither the right nor the presumption to interfere there. But it is his duty to draw attention to the dangers of which, he fears, the King is unaware, lost as he is in his ideal seclusion from the world of actuality.

> " I am prepared to issue a circular despatch if his Majesty commands it. I would like, however, to remind you of the old adage, ' Qui s'excuse s'accuse '. If Wagner, as man and as artist, is worthy of the royal enthusiasm and support, then there is nothing blameworthy in personal contact with him as well. If this latter be disputed, then the question arises why the former should continue. The difficulty centres precisely in the difference of opinion as to the worthiness of the individual and of his endeavours. Therefore I must ask you to furnish me with the whole contents of the proposed circular — not merely the

negative parts of it but the positive as well — and to authorise me to announce that the despatch is issued by the royal command. The difficulty referred to above will become more evident when it comes to the actual drafting of the despatch. For that, in any case, an exacter knowledge of the circumstances is requisite than I possess."

The letter is completely typical of Pfordten's professorial pseudo-logic, of his complacent way of imagining he had disposed of a complex problem when he had reduced it to a neat verbal antithesis or two, and of his habit of behaving towards the King like an all-wise father instructing a little boy who could not be expected to know better at his age. Ludwig's sole rejoinder to the letter was to let the whole thing drop.[6]

In all this it is still impossible to detect any trace of a suspicion of Wagner's exercising direct *political* influence over the King, although Pfordten and the others may perhaps have felt that there was always a danger of its coming to this. Bülow's position is still harder to understand. He had practically no communication with the King, personal or epistolary; why then this desire to get him out of Munich? One can only suppose that it was in part because he had made himself disliked everywhere by his rough tongue and his overbearing manner, and in still larger part simply because he was a Prussian. So far as Pfordten was concerned, his unfriendliness towards Wagner probably had its roots in nothing more rational than his old dislike of the man. Pfistermeister's case was somewhat different. As the official most frequently in contact with both Wagner and the King, and therefore having the fullest knowledge of their artistic plans, he must have realised fairly soon after Wagner's coming to Munich that his own job would depend to some extent on the composer's favour. For some months in the autumn of 1864 and the early part of 1865 each of them was secretly mistrustful of the other, though Wagner was perhaps the less suspicious of the two. The outer forms of politeness were maintained between them, however, until the affair of the " disgrace " of February 1865, when each of them bared his claws, and Cosima's diplomacy had to be called in to soft-pedal their antiphonal growlings. By the summer of 1865, in all probability, Pfistermeister had no friendliness

⁶ RVPW, pp. 536–7, and FKLB, pp. 86–7. Both Röckl's article and Frantz's are based on previously unpublished letters and memoranda of Pfordten and Pfister-meister.

at all left towards Wagner: it is amusing to discover that at the very time when his apparent willingness to assist in the *Tristan* preparations was earning the warm gratitude of Wagner, to his diary he was confiding such private expressions of opinion as those of the 17th June — " This accursed *Tristan!* " and " The devil fly away with the musicians! " [7]

3

Being manifestly a trifle perturbed by the reports that were reaching him of a set-back in his popularity, the King turned for further information from Pfordten to Pfistermeister. The latter sought the counsel of one who might be assumed to have his finger on the pulse of public opinion in the capital — Baron Sigmund von Pfeufer, the Munich Chief of Police. This gentleman, who, from what we can learn of him today, seems to have been a clear-sighted and commendably plain-spoken official, replied to Pfistermeister's enquiries in a letter of the 31st May, following upon a conversation between them on the preceding day. Pfeufer is inclined to pooh-pooh the feeling in some quarters that " the Lola times are come again "; the political parallel between 1848 and 1865, he objects, does not hold good. But there is undoubtedly a general feeling of dissatisfaction with regard to Wagner and Bülow; and the reasons for this are threefold. Some people are set against Wagner because he is an alien and a Protestant: these malcontents, however, are merely the " nativists ", the Ultramontanes, and others of the sort who, for the last fifty years, have made Munich not so much famous as notorious. Then there are the people

" who reckon up the thousands that Wagner has already cost his Majesty and will continue to cost him, and cannot imagine what profit Wagner's music will bring. This view is the least dangerous one, because it is the least justified. The matter of cost is the concern of the King and no one else — an opinion shared by rational people who, although enemies of Wagner, fully recognise the King's right to spend when and how he chooses. The so-called Finance Party, which would like to make political capital out of this matter of expenditure, is therefore not to be taken seriously. It is quite another story, however, with the third group, which reckons up the days and hours spent by his

[7] FKLB, p. 86.

Majesty in seclusion and says, ' Our King lives almost entirely to him-self; he rarely sees anyone belonging to the official, military, learned or artistic classes. The man who is responsible for this seclusion is Richard Wagner, who has brought it about that the King feels at ease in no society but his, communes with him by the hour, if not verbally at all events by letter, pays homage to his poetic and musical trend alone, and feels no interest in the remainder of mankind '. This point of view has the largest and most influential following in all sections of society, of the aristocracy, and of the bourgeoisie. And the longer the opinion of this section prevails the more dangerous becomes the situation of the King, since there comes a slackening in the love and veneration without which no ruler can really rule.

" You will now ask ' What is to be done? Must the King drive Wag-ner away? ' This would be asking too much of a young, noble, poetic, romantically-inclined heart. Therefore I reply ' No ' to the question. Richard Wagner can remain if the King will decide to give up his hermit's life and come into closer contact with individual officials and personalities. The Court officials, the Ministers, the upper officials and officers, savants and artists should be invited oftener to Court; the present etiquette, which rules only in Spain, Austria and Bavaria, should be abolished or modified; the King should go to the Odeon concerts, and not confine his visits to the theatre to Wagner operas; the higher ranks of society should be diverted with Court balls and concerts ":

in short, the King should try to make himself popular with all sec-tions of his subjects by behaving as subjects everywhere expect their Kings to behave — not at all a difficult thing to do, says the shrewd and pleasantly cynical Pfeufer, seeing how large a part the vanity of the individual citizen plays in public life and how respon-sive people are to the amiabilities and condescensions of a mon-arch. He is " completely convinced ", he says, that if the King will only cease to be so " exclusive " the association with Wagner will recede into the background and cease to be the subject of dis-cussion and cavil.[8]

Once more we have to observe that in all this there is not so much as a hint anywhere that Wagner has been misusing the King's par-tiality in order to pursue *political* aims of his own. The grievance, in fact, is, in the last resort, less against him than against the King. All the weaknesses and petty vanities and jealousies of human na-ture in general, and Munich human nature in particular, had been

---

[8] FKLB, pp. 94–5.

stirred up by Ludwig's curtailment of the ceremonial of the Court, his sensitive self-seclusion, his contempt for most of the public mountebankery of kingship, and his preferring Wagner's art to that of the crowd of mediocrities and nonentities who had been wont to sun themselves in the favour of the worthy but commonplace King Max. There was, of course, a more serious side than this to the matter. Ludwig was already showing himself reluctant to meet his fellow-sovereigns and to grant foreign ambassadors audience; and there were too many clouds on the international horizon just then for his ministers to be anything but anxious over this developing trait in him. But for everything that had happened and was happening Wagner was made the scapegoat. We of today can be wise after the event: we can see, what the Pfordtens and the Pfister-meisters and the rest of them could not see, that Wagner stood in an entirely different category from the other musicians of his epoch, that in his own way the King was also a personality irreducible to the common denominator, and that the association between the two men was a phenomenon to which nothing in the politicians' previous experience of the world had given them the key. The results of their failure to read the situation rightly, however, were destined to be fatal. If only one of them had had the sense to see that the right way to handle the young King was to leave him, for the first year or two, perfectly free to follow his artistic ideals as he chose and to keep what company he liked, not only might Munich have become what it was left to Bayreuth to be, but the tragedy of the Starnberg Lake in 1886 would have been avoided. As it was, their stupidities, their jealousies, their chicaneries, and even the honesty of such of them as happened to be honest all combined to drive the King down the very road from which they were trying so hard to head him off. For their opposition to himself and to Wagner, and the means by which some of his officials tried to render that opposition effective, made him increasingly mistrustful of his advisers and intensified his passion for solitude. The more we study his case and that of Wagner the more evident becomes the truth of their claim that only they two in the whole world understood each other; and Wagner was perfectly right when he said, at a rather later date than the one we are now dealing with, that the surest way to get the King to devote himself more closely to public affairs, as the politicians desired him to do, would be to make it possible for him to recall the exile to Munich.

4

All in all, Wagner was more sinned against than sinning in the spring and early summer of 1865. Even at the end of that year he was still somewhat puzzled to account for the storm that had broken over his head in the previous February: he could only assume that " they wanted to find out exactly where they stood with me, it having become evident that the King's love for me could not be shaken." [9] " Finding out exactly where they stood with him " meant, of course, for some of them, finding out which side he could be bribed to take, or advise the King to take, in the intrigues with which the political world of the capital was honeycombed: judging him by themselves, it was purely and simply incredible to these people that he meant just what he said when he declared that his interests were solely artistic, and that he had no desire either to become involved in Bavarian politics or to use his favour with the King for " power " of the commoner kind. Probably what had happened in February was that one Court section, misunderstanding Wagner's attitude, and fearing that he would throw in his lot with a rival section, had tried to undermine him as a politician by publicly defaming him as a man. He more than once refers in his letters to the King to the " net of lies " in which they were both enmeshed. It was Wagner's opinion, at that time, that even Pfistermeister was caught in this net. The Cabinet Secretary's private jottings show no cordiality towards Wagner; but the latter seems to have had rather more belief in Pfistermeister's sincerity than it is possible, in general, for us to share today. Cynics might say that the friendliness of his approaches to Pfistermeister was purely the

---

[9] See Wagner's letter of the 15th December, 1865 to Fröbel, in RLW, II, 1.

In a letter of the 15th July, 1865 to Pfistermeister (RLW II, 214) Wagner indicates the Cabinet Treasurer, Hofmann, as the hidden hand in the troubles of the preceding February: Hofmann, it appears, had been opposed to certain of the King's "wishes and schemes"—by which we may particularly understand the Semper scheme—of which he imagined Wagner to be the instigator. This seems very probable; as it was mainly on the ground of the expense of Wagner to Bavaria that Redwitz had attacked him, one of the likeliest quarters to have supplied the journalistic opposition with the necessary information was the financial department most immediately concerned.

result of calculation; but that explanation will not hold good when we find him referring to the Secretary in the most appreciative terms in his letters to the King. His view of the crisis of February — a view perhaps a little too favourable to Pfistermeister — was that the Secretary had been caught in the same " net of lies " as himself, yet, in spite of that, had behaved loyally towards him; and Wagner assured him, in his letters of the 17th and 18th February, of his " truest friendship and gratitude " for his good will " in particularly difficult circumstances ".

Pfistermeister's temporary good will, such as it was, seems to have been motived by a lively sense of favours to come. For his own position was being threatened at this time; and believing, as everyone else did, that Wagner could be persuaded to use his " influence " with the King for ordinary political purposes, he was not at all unwilling to have that influence exerted in his own favour. In the third week of February an intrigue that was partly aimed at himself came to a head. Prince Max Taxis, father of the King's adjutant, Prince Paul von Thurn und Taxis,[10] had conceived, in collusion with Prussia and the Bavarian Ultramontane party (the Jesuits), a plan for carving out a kingdom for his eldest son in the Westphalian Rhineland with the addition of half Belgium; at the same time a bank was to be founded through which pressure could be exerted, by financial methods, on the choice of representatives in the Bavarian and other German parliaments;[11] Prussia was to be bought off by certain territorial concessions in north Germany, and Bavaria by some in the south. At the end of February, 1865 Prince Max Taxis had sent two of his agents, Baron von Gruben and

---

[10] Prince Paul, who was a couple of years older than the King, plays a considerable part in the Wagner-Ludwig story of the next two or three years. He appears to have had neither political abilities nor political ambitions, but to have commended himself to the King by sharing all the latter's artistic enthusiasms, especially his admiration for Wagner. Paul offended his father by forming a misalliance with a soubrette of the Munich Volkstheater, a niece of the composer Kreutzer. In January, 1867 he left the army and surrendered his princely title for an allowance of 6,000 florins per annum: the King, however, elevated him eighteen months later to the "personal nobility" under the name of "von Fels". He found his true vocation in managing a theatre in Switzerland for some years. He died of consumption at Cannes. See BKLB, pp. 496–8.

[11] "This project, with its far-reaching Jesuit plans", says Glasenapp, "found a short-lived realisation in the notorious Landgrand-Dumonceau Bank, which cost the Taxis family several millions." GRW, IV, 52, note.

Staatsrat Klindworth, from Regensburg to Munich to sound Wagner as to his possible co-operation in this plan. (The reader will remember that Wagner made the acquaintance of Klindworth, who was a seasoned diplomatist, in Brussels in 1860).[12] In his later account of the matter in a letter of the 15th December, 1865 [13] to Julius Fröbel, Wagner says that the emissaries called on him on two occasions, on the second of which they were reinforced by Klindworth's daughter Agnes Street, an old friend of Cosima. " I remained dense ", he says: he diplomatically affected not to understand them when they offered him their future support in his artistic schemes if he would persuade the King to dismiss Pfistermeister and install Klindworth in his place.[14]

We now have an expansion of the story in a recently-published letter of Wagner's of the 16th December, 1865, from Vevey, to August Röckel, in which he gives further details of the events that preceded his fall. " The Jesuits ", he says bitterly,

"who had had experience of my unshakeable power over the King, have made my path to whatever I might want so plain before me that truly I have been guilty of a perfidy towards my art-ideal in not showing myself more accommodating. Prince Taxis, through two agents whom he sent to me from Brussels and Regensburg during the first Cabinet struggle of last winter, made me a singular offer of funds — in the form of free shares in a big financial enterprise; Pfistermeister, whom the Prince wanted to remove, bid against him with the Music School, the Semper theatre, the purchase of my house,[15] and all the credit I could desire — all for a definite assurance that I would duly place myself at the service of the reaction." [16]

[12] See *supra*, p. 24, and RWML, II, 833.
[13] I.e., after his banishment from Munich.
[14] FEL, II, 404 ff.
[15] I.e., at the expense of the Civil List. See Wagner's parallel letter to Fröbel.
[16] KLRWB, IV, 116. Lutz also, he says, "came out [at a later date] with an open request to me to support, 'out of love for the King, of an increase of whose power it was now a question', the plans of the reaction, which he set before me in exact detail."
On the 19th February Pfistermeister confides to his diary, "Prince [Paul] Taxis describes my position as precarious"; and on the 20th, "Leinfelder brings me an instruction to pile on the compliments" [or "to bow more deeply"]. This evidently refers to Wagner: and it is the fullest confirmation imaginable of the truth of the story, told in his letter, of the attempts of the politicians to bribe him to work with them. (See HNBW, p. 605). Bülow, writing to Carl Bechstein on the 4th March, says that "the Cabinet is tottering, and Pfistermeister is eagerly hooking himself on to Wagner, who remains firmly fixed, though, alas, violently attacked." (BNB, p. 171).

Wagner, however, remained uninterested and unmoved; he made it clear to Pfistermeister that all he was concerned with was his artistic plans for Munich; he may possibly have reflected that everything that Pfistermeister or anyone else offered him he was tolerably certain of obtaining through the King, without plunging, to his own danger, into the muddy waters of foreign politics.

That the Munich politicians were anxious to have him, at any cost, as a pawn in their game is beyond question. Their general object seems to have been to regain for the monarchy, for their own ends, the quasi-absolutist power it had had before the 1848 revolution. That idea could be presumed to appeal to the King; and as this power would naturally be exercised by him for the furtherance of Wagner's artistic plans, it must have seemed to the politicians a foregone conclusion that Wagner would help them by " influencing " Ludwig politically. Their antagonism towards Wagner was sometimes the result less of an honest objection to this mere musician's interfering in politics than of a selfish fear that the side he might take would not be theirs. They assumed him to be made of the same material as themselves: " When I said ' No ' to their offers ", he told Röckel, " but instead merely advised the King to look about for some upright people, they of course took this to be simply masked democratic agitation on my part, since they could not bring themselves to believe that I was just stupid." Röckel, he says, is fortunate in that he can still believe in liberalism and democracy, for which Wagner now feels only a comprehensive contempt. As for the politicians who have been trying to bribe him, the fact that they are stupid, slow and lazy does not cause him so much concern as the fact that they are dishonest: " Just look at those sheep and foxes, how they plume themselves on having something in common with me; to them I am nothing but the luxurious musician! "

5

Wagner does not appear to have met the King between the 17th February and the 22nd May, when he was invited to celebrate his own birthday in Berg. For a little while after his return to Munich we find him expressing the hope that he and Ludwig may meet oftener in the flesh, for there is so much connected with their common ideal that needs to be discussed; but there is never any mention whatever of politics in his letters, and not the slightest evidence that he was directly interested in them. The reason that Ludwig gives him for not being able immediately to grant his request for more frequent meetings is that circumstances still make it necessary for him to be cautious — the " circumstances " being the normal inability of his family and his officials to realise the true nature of the bond between them. "Entirely for you, ardently loved one, did I come into the world: this I see more clearly every day ", he wrote to Wagner on the 9th July.

> " For you and art will I live. . . . Do not lose faith in present-day humanity. It will, I know, some day understand you fully: we will work together for that. Do not despair: do not withdraw from the world: a brilliant success will crown steadfastness. Precious fruit ripens slowly: the struggle with the small-mindedness of the multitude will be difficult, but do not grudge the painful fight. . . . We must meet and talk soon: if it rested only with me I would be with you always. Could we but free ourselves of the world and its wearisome laws! . . . I hope that when [Semper] comes to Munich again he will choose the site for the theatre. I will defy the world, I will be brave, for our great aim,"

— and so on. And again,

> " What can it signify to you when wretched worms try to attack or injure you? . . . I conjure you again — I regard it as my duty to do so — look forwards, forget the world, follow the spirit that heaven has implanted in you."

For his part, Wagner is conscious of little else but a vast weariness and a desire to forget the world and be forgotten by it: " I have less and less to say to the world. To anyone who desires to understand me I have said enough: I am heartily tired of the present day, and would like to be able soon to repose in the bosom of the future." Two people less occupied with the chicaneries of politics could hardly be imagined: the main immediate concerns of both of them, but more especially of the King, were the scheme for the Semper theatre and that for the Music School.

It was for an object far removed from politics that Wagner was trying to get the King to exercise his authority in June, immediately after the production of *Tristan*. One of the most shameful features of the musical life of the day, he said, was the way in which the real musicians, as he always called them — the orchestral players — were bled to the bone for the financial benefit of the " star " singers. When he surveyed the German theatrical world he could find any sort of promise of adequate performances of his works only in the orchestras. But the players, in general, were so grossly underpaid that their life was one of constant hardship and anxiety; and he asks Ludwig to remedy this deplorable state of affairs so far as the Munich Opera is concerned. He suggests that Bülow, Perfall and himself shall be instructed to form a committee to enquire into, and report upon, the present remuneration of the orchestral players and the chorus and the possibility of improving it. And here, for the first time in the correspondence, we find him squaring up, though at first only tentatively, to the obvious fact that his and the King's new plans will require a new type of official to put them into execution. He laments the insufficiency of Perfall as the Court Music Intendant, just as in days gone by he had had to lament the insufficiency of Lüttichau. " I know ", he writes to the King,

" that you, my glorious Friend, were sent to me by God so that my faith might become religion. To establish our foundations we need a complete breach with the old ways of looking at things. No one can advise you on a matter which he himself does not understand: but I will never suggest to my King anything that is not at once right and reasonable, well-based on practice, and for that very reason feasible. No one, however, can judge of the practicableness and feasibility of measures the meaning and significance of which he cannot grasp."

Evidently the officials were bristling once more at this suggestion of their own inadequacy for Wagnerian ends, and at the mere hint of opening the royal purse an inch further, even to pay the poor orchestral players a decent wage. But the King once more found himself frustrated. " O if only I could always gratify your wishes! ", he wrote in reply:

" what grieves me is that I too cannot free myself from the restraints, the irksome bonds which the ' world ' lays on me: I too have to take others into consideration. But I promise my unique one that I will do everything that is possible and advisable in connection with the matter of his lately-expressed wish."

[400]

His and Wagner's " chief enemies ", Wagner wrote to Mathilde Maier on the 12th July, had assured the King that the proposals were impracticable. As regards the raising of the players' salaries nothing appears to have been done: the King no doubt felt that if there was to be war with his ministers over questions of expenditure, he had better reserve all his forces for the two schemes that would at once be the most expensive and the most difficult of all, that of the festival theatre and that of the Music School.

The opposition to the former was increasing in official quarters. Pfistermeister, in his temporary gratitude for the negative service Wagner had been to him in the Taxis affair, had been so cordial and helpful all through the period of the preparations for *Tristan* that Wagner, long after the gulf between them had become un-bridgeable, could still praise his " uncommon energy and trusti-ness " during this brief period, the understanding he showed of his demands, and the scrupulous way in which he carried out the King's orders.[17] But the more apparent it became that the King was bent on carrying the Semper scheme through, the more open became the opposition of Pfistermeister to it. And now we see Wagner's patience beginning at last to break down. It was obvi-ously impossible for real progress to be made with any artistic scheme when the official medium of communication between him-self and the King was an official who had no understanding of either of them or of what it was they were working for. We see Pfistermeister and Wagner snapping politely at each other in the third week of July — primarily over a letter in which Wagner had declined the King's offer of a grant for a holiday in Switzer-land — Wagner making no secret of his dislike of officials, and Pfistermeister acidly assuring him that it is no satisfaction to *him* to be mixed up in matters which, strictly speaking, lie outside his province as Cabinet Secretary. On the 20th Cosima had to exert her diplomacy. " Believe me, honoured sir ", she wrote to Pfister-meister,

> " Wagner knows full well the value of the services you have rendered him with indefatigable zeal and the most sympathetic friendliness. He has always regretted that not only his nature but his very far-reaching

[17] See Wagner's letter to the King of the 12th January, 1870.

plans have drawn you into a sphere that has meant a good deal of un-
pleasantness for you. I know how quick his temper is when he is not
wholly understood; but I know also that it is easier to *divine* than to
understand him, and that often his manner misleads those who are
friendly disposed towards him. I cannot tell you, dear Herr State
Councillor, how it would distress me if your relations with Wagner
were to be disturbed. No one knows better than I do how friendly
your intentions have been and the enormous difficulty of your task;
and if *I* know that, you may imagine that Wagner is conscious of it
also." [18]

6

Wagner, however, with his jangled nerves near snapping-point,
was not so disposed as Cosima to toy with the niceties of diplomacy.
We gather that it had been against Cosima's better judgment that
he had sent Pfistermeister his letter of the 15th, for on the rough
draft of it that is still in Wahnfried he has scribbled, evidently for
her, " Forgive me! I have just sent this letter off to Pfistermeister! " He felt that the time had come to short-circuit the devious
currents running between himself and the King. He was depressed,
he wrote to Ludwig on the 22nd July, by the letter of " friend
Pfistermeister " that had accompanied the Semper plans; the " poor
man ", it seems, does not understand him and has taken offence
where no offence was intended. God himself, he tells the King,
could not bring about accord where spiritual comprehension is
totally lacking. Confusion is inevitable when two men of fundamentally different views in matters of art have to try to come to
some sort of agreement as to procedure; and there is a limit, which
limit he is near reaching, to what he can endure in this line. The
worthy Cabinet Secretary whom the King has inherited from his
father is qualified neither by nature nor by culture to form the sole
personal link between " the highly poetic royal Friend " and " the
so-called ' opera composer ' Richard Wagner, whom few of his
contemporaries as yet understand."

He gives Pfistermeister all credit for zeal towards the King and
honesty of intentions towards himself. Unless, therefore, the King
has good reasons of his own for removing Pfistermeister altogether
from his post, he himself does not desire that to happen; but he

[18] KLRWB, IV, 72.

ventures to advise Ludwig to restrict his Cabinet Secretary in future
to the true duties of his office. (He believes, for his part, that
Pfistermeister's long occupancy of that post has led to an importance becoming attached to it that is not wholly consistent with
the royal interest). He suggests that Ludwig shall now appoint a
Court official — a " General Intendant of the Civil List " — whose
special duty it shall be to see that the royal wishes and orders in
connection with artistic plans shall be properly carried out, instead
of being sacrificed, as at present, to " common personal interests ".
He has heard the King speak favourably of Baron Moy: he accordingly suggests that Moy shall be appointed Intendant of all the
departments of the royal household that are concerned with art;
he is to be made the head of the theatre and the orchestra, with authority to draw up a new budget for the maintenance of both of these
and of the chorus; and he is to see that the royal intentions with
regard to the reorganisation of the Conservatoire and the erection
of the provisional theatre in the Glaspalast are carried out.[19]

Though Moy had the confidence of both Wagner and the King,
nothing came of this plan to make him Intendant, owing, apparently, to it having been divulged too soon to the Press. Wagner,
indeed, seems to have become weary, for the moment, of this struggle with the official world, and to have longed only for peace of
soul so that he might sink himself in the scoring of the second act
of *Siegfried*. For the Fates had dealt him just at that time the cruel-
lest of blows.

After the third performance of *Tristan*, on the 19th June, the
Schnorrs went to Tegernsee for a rest. The King being impatient
to hear another performance of the work — it will be recalled that
he had not been present at the third — the two singers returned to
Munich on the 30th, and the performance took place the next day.
The King having obtained an extension of Schnorr's leave from
Dresden, the *Flying Dutchman* was given under Bülow on the 9th
July, with Schnorr as Erik, and on the 12th Wagner himself con-
ducted for the King, in the Residenz Theatre, a number of pieces
from works old and new of his — the prelude to the third act of
Tannhäuser, the prelude to *Lohengrin*, the *Tristan* prelude and

---

[19] As regards this provisional theatre see Chapter XVII.

Liebestod,[20] the Ride of the Valkyries, and the *Meistersinger* over-ture; Schnorr sang the two tenor songs from the first act of *Siegfried* and Siegmund's " Love Song " from the first act of the *Valkyrie*, besides taking part with Zottmayer and others in the final scene of the *Rhinegold* and the scene of Walther before the Mastersingers in the first act of the opera. Simons contributed Wotan's Farewell. An effective touch — an act of grateful homage on Wagner's part — was the performance of the *Huldigungsmarsch* by an invisible military band of eighty players immediately after the prelude to the third act of *Tannhäuser*, the final E flat of the prelude merging without a break into the opening E flat chord of the March. Besides the King there was present only a small select audience of some twenty or thirty people, so placed as to be invisible to him.

7

On the 28th June — that is to say, after the third performance of *Tristan* — Wagner had told the King that he had had several requests for the work from the German theatres, but that he was firmly resolved to withhold it from even the best of them: he re-garded it as belonging only to his royal benefactor. " In this way ", he wrote, " I will preserve my work from stain or perversion of any kind, and thus do something for the honour of our noble but profoundly debased German art." The King, in his reply, com-mended his resolution — *Tristan*, he agreed, should never be pro-faned, never serve merely to gratify the idle curiosity of the ordi-nary seeker after theatrical diversion. It might have been as well for everyone concerned had the King himself been content with the three performances already given.

The circumstances of Schnorr's death are still involved in some obscurity,[21] but it is clear enough that by at any rate the third per-formance he was complaining bitterly to Wagner of the failure of the theatre authorities, in spite of his remonstrances, to screen him from the icy draught that swept over him from the wings while he

---

[20] It is interesting to observe that for Wagner the "Liebestod" was the *prelude:* "Liebestod and Verklärung" is his description of the two pieces in his letter to the King.

[21] More will be said on this subject later.

was over-heated from his terrific exertions in the third act. That
he had had a foreboding of trouble is plain from Wagner's own
words — " As we noticed no symptoms of a catarrhal cold in him,
he hinted gloomily that chills had other and more dangerous consequences with him. During his last days in Munich his excitability
took on an ever darker tinge "; and in the *Flying Dutchman* on the
9th July he had sent a shudder through everyone by the gloomy
intensity of his playing of Erik. He opened out his heart to Wagner that night in a tone of depression of which there had been no
signs until then: the distasteful idea of going back to Dresden to
sing in *Trovatore* or the *Huguenots* had suddenly filled him with
pessimism as he realised how hard was the fight still before Wagner and himself.[22] Plainly the man was already ill.

He had recovered his spirits at the concert of the 12th, as the
result, apparently, of his contact with the newer products of Wagner's genius. On the 13th he and Malvina returned to Dresden.
During the days immediately following, Wagner twice visited the
King in Berg, on the 13th and the 16th, and on the 17th he began the
dictation of his autobiography [23] to Cosima. Four days after that
came the shattering news that Schnorr was dead.

At a rehearsal for *Don Giovanni* on the 15th the singer was in
excellent voice and seemingly in good spirits. The performance
should have taken place the next day, a Sunday. But on the morning of that day a general rheumatism set in, centreing mainly in the
knee, which gave him agonising pain. He grew rapidly worse during the next couple of days, the heat, abnormal even for July, setting up a fever that culminated in delirium; and on the morning
of the 21st an apoplexy of the brain brought his short life to a

[22] Herr Garrigues, who is never wholly sympathetic towards Wagner and Cosima,
is inclined to pooh-pooh the idea that Schnorr was unhappy at the thought of going
back to Dresden to sing parts like Manrico and Raoul again. It is clear enough,
however, from the passage from the last letter Schnorr ever wrote that is quoted by
Herr Garrigues himself, that the great singer despised the taste of the public as a
whole and was thoroughly out of tune with his theatrical surroundings. "I was
drawn to the theatre", he wrote, "by genuine, lofty enthusiasm and youthful ideals.
Those feelings are still not extinguished in me, but what I had hoped to find there
faded out into a miserable nullity, and so I conceived an aversion to the standpoint
of our theatres so vast that my very joy in life is threatened. If I am to follow up
the alluring prospect that now opens out before me, I cannot any longer wear, like a
merry-Andrew, the motley robe of a present-day opera singer." (GIS, p. 286).
[23] It was begun at the instigation of the King.

sudden close. As early as the 18th he had sensed the coming end
and taken farewell of his family. Five hours before his death he
burst into a paroxysm of song; but the final two hours were peaceful. His last words were, " Farewell, Siegfried! [24] Console my
Richard! "

When Wagner heard by telegraph that Schnorr was dead he
wired back to Dresden enquiring " which Schnorr? ": [25] so far was
he from apprehending any evil to Ludwig. At midday on Saturday
the 22nd, dazed and sick at heart, he set out with Bülow for Dresden. He had been told that the funeral was for nine on Sunday
morning; and he had telegraphed to Malvina to delay it for half
an hour so that he might look on his Tristan for the last time. The
intense heat, however, and the congestion of the railway station by
visitors to a festival of twenty thousand German choral singers, had
made it necessary to advance the burial by some hours. Wagner
and Bülow arrived in the town at eleven o'clock, too late to do
more than drive to the house and hear from the distracted Malvina
the story of Ludwig's last hours. Within two hours of their arrival
in Dresden they were on their way back to Munich again. " He was
a fine, noble being ", Wagner wrote to the King three days later,
" consecrated to me, faithful to me. The richly-gifted *artist* became a theatre singer to be of service to me, to be able to further
my work. My King, in this singer I have lost much! "

8

At the end of July we find him once more plunging into questions
of politics and finance. To the King, on the 30th, he wrote that it
was painful to find himself in the position of seeming to mix himself
up with administrative affairs from which his innermost nature
bade him keep aloof. But he has no choice. Every intention of
the King and himself is delayed, frustrated or diverted into the
wrong channel by the officials, partly from malevolence, partly
from sheer stupidity. They want to give the plan for the Music
School, for instance, a shape that will ruin it. Great as the strain

[24] Meaning either the part of Siegfried, which he had hoped to be the first to
play, or King Ludwig, whom Wagner sometimes referred to under that name.
[25] The singer had several relations in Dresden, where his father, the painter, was
now settled.

upon him would have been, he went on to say, and seriously as it would have interfered with his creative work, he had been willing to undertake the direction of the School himself, solely to ensure its fulfilling the purposes for which it was to be called into being: the senseless proposal of the Commission, however, had been that Perfall was to be made director. The School was an indispensable part of the ideal which the King and he himself had in view, and more indispensable than ever now that Schnorr's death had deprived them of the singer who should have been the model for the students. The opponents of the plan for the festival theatre kept asking him sceptically who were the artists who were to perform in such a theatre. The answer to that was, " The artists whom the new School is to form "; indeed, he says, without the preliminary work of the School there is no sense in the theatre scheme. And in the face of this, they do all they can to make the School impossible! Nor can he make the slightest impression on the officials with regard to the amelioration of the lot of the ill-paid orchestral players, though the resources of the opera house are cheerfully squandered on " the most utterly useless, superfluous singers and actors, who can never be of any service to noble ends." He finds the situation even more grievous than that against which he had revolted in Dresden in days of servitude gone by: " there my musicians and chorus had at least a decent livelihood secured to them, whereas here I am depressed by the spectacle of a misery which my heart cannot endure " — especially as, in the eyes of the world, his own financial position is so enviable a one. But, he adds, he feels the need to recur to a matter that has evidently been the subject of conversation between himself and Ludwig — a " more thorough and independent establishment of my own affairs if I am to remain worthily by my King's side, free and exempt from care."

This is the first hint in his letters of those new financial demands of his upon the King that were to be one of the prime causes of his downfall within four months of this date. Ludwig, at the end of July, had offered him a further subvention in order that he might keep a carriage: Wagner had been at Berg again on the 28th, a few days after his return from Schnorr's funeral, and it must have been evident to the King that the loss of his only tenor had had a dire effect on Wagner's health. On the 1st August we find him telling the King that he had found it impossible to bring himself to sign the document relating to the carriage which the Treasury had put before him. He does not make his motives for the refusal clear; but we gather from his letter that he is even more sick in mind than in body. On the 4th the King again begged him to accept his offer. This time he gave way, and an addition of 1,200 gulden per annum for the upkeep of a carriage was made to his allowance as from the 1st August: the new total of the latter thus became 6,200 gulden. Four days later he put before the King a series of elaborate proposals for the permanent settlement of his financial affairs.

CHAPTER XVII

SEMPER AND THE FESTIVAL THEATRE

1

A GOOD DEAL of Wagner's time and the King's during 1865 and the years immediately following was taken up with the scheme for building a Wagner festival theatre in Munich. To avoid interrupting the main biographical narrative at one point after another in order to set forth the vicissitudes of this scheme, and to enable the reader to get a connected view of the shameful treatment of Semper by virtually everyone concerned in the affair, it will be convenient at this point to tell the long story from start to finish without a break.[1]

The idea of a grandiose festival theatre originated with the King: the passion for building was in the Wittelsbach blood. The first mention of the plan is in a letter of the 26th November, 1864, from Ludwig to Wagner:

> " I have decided to have a large stone theatre built, so that the production of the *Ring* may be a perfect one. That incomparable work must be presented in a place worthy of it. . . . I will go further into the matter of the theatre verbally with you; briefly, those words of yours in the Foreword to your *Ring* poem shall come to life: I proclaim — ' In the beginning be the Deed! '." [2]

Wagner's thoughts at once flew to his old Dresden friend Semper, who, as we have seen, had been Professor of Architecture at the Zürich Polytechnic since 1855. " I have finished the music to the *Rhinegold*, and begun that of the *Valkyrie* ", he had written to

---

[1] Our main first-hand sources of information regarding the matter are the 1906 book (SMF) of the architect's son Manfred Semper, and the correspondence, especially that between Wagner and the King, in KLRWB. The latter contains a quantity of new material.

[2] "Will this Prince be found?" Wagner had asked in the Foreword. "'In the beginning was the Deed!'". See *supra*, p. 214.

him as long ago as August, 1854: "without your help I cannot think of a performance some day." He now writes to Semper, on the 13th December, 1864, asking him to undertake this great new work.[3] Being the soul of practicality in all matters of this kind, he had urged upon the King the desirability of first of all constructing a provisional theatre in wood and brick. A host of new technical problems, he knew, would confront both himself and the architect — the problem of the amphitheatrical form, that of the sunken orchestra, that of the apparatus for a new type of scenery, for a new system of lighting, and so on; and, as he explained to Semper, it would be better for both of them to experiment first of all with a relatively cheap provisional building in which he could tentatively stage a few performances after his own heart of his already existing works: in the light of the experience thus gained both he and Semper would be better able to decide upon the definitive structure of the more expensive permanent theatre.

Towards the end of December Semper came to Munich; he had several conversations with Wagner, and on the 29th an audience with the King, who definitely commissioned him to proceed at once with the great work, to which he was to devote all his spare time and the sum of his artistic powers. The site for the monumental theatre was selected — the Gasteig hill, adjacent to the Maximilianeum. The lofty, commanding position was ideal from the aesthetic point of view, while the fact that a good deal of the ground was royal property would make it easier of acquisition.[4]

---

[3] "My young protector", he tells Semper, "has a profound faith in the truth of my ideal of a dramatic art-work radically and momentously distinct from both the modern stage play and the opera. In order to achieve intelligible performances in this style he intends, with me, to abandon entirely the attempt to make them part of the ordinary theatre repertory; he proposes to define exactly the exceptional nature of such performances by giving them not in the everyday opera house but in a special theatre constructed solely to that end and destined for no other."

It will be remembered that at this time both Wagner and Ludwig believed that the Ring would be ready for production in the summer of 1867.

[4] The scheme involved the cutting of an imposing new street — corresponding in some degree to the present Prinz-Regenten Strasse — from the Hofgarten to the River Isar. From this a new bridge across the river would lead to the Gasteig, on the heights of which the theatre was to be set. See Semper's model opposite p. 426.

The ultimate plan, as agreed upon between Wagner and Ludwig, is set forth in detail in Wagner's letter to the King of the 13th September, 1865: "King Ludwig II ... will make a street in Munich, as his noble father and grandfather have done. This will be an affair of the future, but already we can consider the plan for it. The street will be a prolongation of the Briennerstrasse, running past the palace, through the

Semper set himself immediately to grapple with his problems, it being Ludwig's desire that the theatre should be ready by the summer of 1867. Naturally the architect would have liked to be given a definite contract; but on the 12th January, 1865, and again on the 15th February, we find Wagner urging him, not without reason, not to press for this. The King, he said, was King, and would not be influenced or turned aside by anyone; but it would be tactless, Wagner hinted, for Semper to insist on a contract, which would be equivalent to doubting the royal word.

> " My experience of this richly gifted young King is that he is profound, high-minded, and firm. But on one point he is very sensitive — he does not like to be regarded as too young and not fully competent. It would put him sorely out of tune were I to press him to supplement his orders to me with others of the official business kind."

All this, in and by itself, was rational enough: a King's word being concerned, the situation was a delicate one for both Wagner and Semper. But manifestly a new theatre would be to some extent a concern of the Cabinet and the country: and the politicians, as well as the royal family in general and the Court party, were against the scheme from the first.

Their objections to it were not, at that time, wholly unreasonable: the building would be expensive, there was no guarantee that what they regarded as the young King's " infatuation " for a composer who was still looked upon by many people as half-mad would endure, and, lacking the experience of Bayreuth to guide them, they could not see the necessity for a theatre to be devoted exclusively to Wagner's works, especially those still incomplete or not yet begun. Nothing, however, can excuse the chicanery of the politicians in their handling of the matter, a chicanery of which the

---

royal garden, straight on to the Isar: a bridge will be thrown over this to the elevated bank of the river, on the lofty terraces of which the ideal festival theatre will rise up in its pride. This is the complete plan, to be carried out according to time and circumstances. For the present just the theatre will be erected on the spot indicated, environed by the finest promenade in Munich, at an appropriate distance from the Maximilianeum; later it will be connected with the Residenz by the bridge and the new street." Wagner advised the King to find out from his Finance Minister exactly what funds could be devoted to the purpose, and then lay aside a definite sum per annum for it. The theatre could not be completed in less than four, probably five, years, and Wagner estimated the total cost at "perhaps a million and a half" gulden. He suggested "economies and preparations" during 1866, and the erection of the *provisional* theatre in 1867; it might open in the winter of that year with *Lohengrin*.

victim throughout was not Wagner but Semper. With an impudence that cannot be explained except on the assumption that they thought the King too young and inexperienced to oppose them effectively, they fed the Press with lies and half-truths from the beginning. They publicly and mendaciously denied, in the *Allgemeine Zeitung*, that Semper had had an audience with the King on the 29th December. It was as a counterpoise to tactics of this kind that Pecht, in collusion with Wagner, published his article on *King Ludwig II and Art* in the Vienna *Botschafter*, the object of which was to urge the King not to be deflected from his purpose by the " miserable nativism " of certain Munich circles. To this the *Allgemeine Zeitung* replied, on the 7th February, with a point-blank denial that there was any thought in high quarters of going on with the festival theatre scheme — this after the King had assured Wagner of his intention of carrying it out! It is not to be wondered at that Semper, in these circumstances, should press for a watertight official contract. Sebastian Röckl conjectures that it was at the suggestion of the Cabinet that Wagner assured his friend that the King would be put " sorely out of tune " by a request to place the commission for the theatre on a more business-like footing. That is quite possible: the Cabinet had at its fingertips every trick of evasion and misrepresentation and procrastination, and never hesitated to employ them against Wagner, Semper, the King, or all three together.

2

For a long time after this the architect was left more or less dangling in mid-air. The King could not fail to take account of Wagner's arguments in favour of a provisional theatre to be erected in the Glaspalast, a huge glass building which was mainly used for exhibitions.[5] But he was both too impatient and too inexperienced to give their proper weight to the many technical considerations involved: his heart, both as dilettante builder and as Wagner enthusiast, was set on a magnificent temple of art that should be at once his own joy, his enduring monument, and the pride of Munich. Semper had the utmost difficulty in obtaining the necessary

[5] It was burned down on the night of the 5th–6th June, 1931.

preliminary details — dimensions, elevations, and so on — of either the Glaspalast or the Gasteig terrain. In the end he had to call in the technical assistance of Pecht and the local architect Gottfried Neureuther, who unselfishly placed their services at the disposal of their distinguished colleague. The Cabinet were practising the delays and evasions that are the stock-in-trade of politicians all the world over: they pretended to approve the idea of a provisional theatre, in which other operas besides those of Wagner could be given if desired, but even as regards the realisation of this subsidiary scheme they placed every possible obstacle in Semper's way.[6] In March, 1865 Wagner informed his friend that he had had an interview with Pfistermeister, who had told him that the King was now resigned to confining himself, for the present, to the provisional theatre, postponing the more ambitious plan until ampler funds should be available: Semper was to come to Munich at Easter, however, to make the needful reconnaissances in connection with the grander scheme. Wagner insisted on Pfistermeister's writing to Semper direct; he had evidently no desire to be entangled any more than he could help in this rapidly spreading network of Cabinet intrigue.

The first official letter the architect received on the subject was Pfistermeister's of the 8th April, 1865. The King, said the Cabinet Secretary, now wanted the provisional theatre, but at the same time it would be highly agreeable to his Majesty to have " completely worked-out plans " for the monumental festival theatre. Pfistermeister assured Semper that he had already written him to this effect three weeks earlier, but had now discovered, to his horror, that the letter had been incorrectly addressed. But this, as Semper's son points out, is hardly credible: the envelope would have borne not only an official inscription but the Government seal, and would consequently, in case of a wrong address, have been returned promptly to the Government office. (Nor, it may be added, is it easily believable that a letter directed anywhere at all in Zürich

---

[6] Glasenapp (GRW, IV, 38) quotes Pfistermeister as confessing that the agitation against Wagner "began the day when the plan for a great model theatre was mooted, a plan which seemed to threaten the interests of the Civil List." Glasenapp adds that "the warm interest taken by the Cabinet Secretariat in the Civil List" sprang from the fact that "since the reign of Ludwig I it had been the custom in Bavaria for a certain percentage of the annual superfluity of the funds of the Civil List and of the whole private royal fortune to go to the Cabinet officials."

[413]

to so distinguished a resident of so small a town could possibly fail to be delivered to him). In spite of the fact that Pfistermeister was a professional politician, one is not necessarily bound to believe that nothing but the truth ever passed his lips; and it is difficult to resist the conclusion that on this occasion he was evading direct contact with the truth.[7] The contents of the letter of the 8th April confirm the impression that the Cabinet was merely playing with Semper. Pfistermeister asks the architect if he is willing to send the King a set of plans: yet he must have known quite well, from his conversations with both Wagner and the King, that Semper had been busily engaged upon such plans, at the King's own request, since the preceding January.

Between the dodges of the politicians, the vacillations of the King — who was torn between the desire to endow Munich with the theatre of his dreams and the logic of the arguments in favour of the smaller scheme as a commencement, — and Wagner's increasing reluctance to mix himself up in the Cabinet intrigues which he knew were going on, Semper had a sorry time of it. Nobody could or would supply him with the technical details he needed: how could he design and plan a building on the Gasteig without the most elementary data as to either the area or the contour of the land on which he was supposed to build? However, on the 10th May he sent Wagner two carefully worked out plans for a provisional theatre in the Glaspalast, accompanied by a long explanatory letter. The problem evidently bristled with difficulties of all

---

[7] Böhm, who was himself, at a later period, an official in the Bavarian Government service, says that "Pfistermeister often told me and other people the reason why he refused to co-operate in the [theatre] plan. The reason was simply this, that as the King had no private fortune his resources were confined to the Civil List. But out of this he had to pay his grandfather, Ludwig I, 500,000 florins a year, while the Court establishment absorbed 1,200,000 florins. There consequently remained to the King only 300,000 florins, which would have been reduced by one-half had he to pay the interest on a capital debt of 3,000,000." (BLKB, p. 141). With that point of view one can wholly sympathise; it was manifestly Pfistermeister's duty to protect the enthusiastic young King against the possible evil consequences of his inexperience in financial matters. But it does not excuse the chicanery of the politicians' dealings with Semper. Böhm himself, after saying what he can in defence of Pfistermeister and Düfflipp — a later Court Secretary — has to admit that "neither of them can escape the grave reproach that in this question of the festival theatre they deceived their royal master by means of subterfuges and ambuscades, and tricked and fooled the great architect year after year. Their conduct was unworthy of the advisers of a King."

kinds: not only had the existent building and its surroundings as a whole to be preserved for their original purposes as an exhibition ground and a place of popular entertainment, but the theatre itself had to be designed with special reference to Wagner's novel demands with regard to seating, stage machinery, and a concealed orchestra. To insert a theatre in an existing structure would be a much harder task than the erection of one on a virgin site would have been. Public feeling in general, it soon appeared, was against the diversion of a State building such as the Glaspalast to any use but its original one. Apart from that, there were technical problems such as land drainage to be considered: the Minister for Trade reported to the King that the excavations required for the theatre stage would be incompatible with the present drainage system of the Glaspalast as a whole. Semper's covering letter of the 10th May to Wagner shows what infinite trouble he had taken to plan an efficient theatre with the minimum disturbance of existing conditions.

3

He heard nothing more about the matter from anyone for several weeks. Wagner had duly passed the plans on to the King: his silence in the matter was no doubt due to his growing conviction that between Ludwig on the one hand and the Cabinet on the other his own position in the affair was rapidly becoming an impossible one. As the mouthpiece of the impulsive King he had committed Semper to a tremendous undertaking the difficulties of which were increasing every day; and now the King, harassed on every side, was obviously shrinking from making any decisive move. Wagner himself could manifestly do nothing; he could neither advise Semper to think no more about the matter, nor bring the King to settle it finally one way or the other, nor fight against the underground machinations of the politicians. So he took refuge in silence so far as Semper was concerned, feeling, and rightly so, that it was for the King, and the King alone, to clear up a situation which had been purely of his own originating. Wagner's personal sympathies, as an artist who knew to his cost what it meant to struggle against the inertia of the official world, would be entirely with the great fellow-artist whom he had unwittingly dragged into this morass; but he could do nothing, either one way or the other, to help him out of it.

At last Semper wrote to Pfistermeister: the latter replied on the 14th July — two months after the plans had been despatched to Munich! The King, he said, had gone over the plans with great interest, but " has not yet come to any decision in the matter, as his Majesty has had his energies occupied in another direction, through the meeting of the Bavarian Parliament." The King would be grateful, however, if Semper would now send him not detailed technical plans but " a general view or sketch of this architectural undertaking, from which his Majesty could get an approximate idea of it as a whole." He would like Semper to come to Munich, " to look for a provisional site in case the building should come to realisation "! Ten days later another official, Councillor Leinfelder, wrote to Semper at the King's command: would the architect send him a rough preliminary estimate of the cost of a monumental theatre? Semper's reply was that he would come to Munich in the first days of September, bringing with him, for the King's information, the designs for a large theatre he had in hand for Rio de Janeiro, which could serve as a basis for an estimate such as the King desired. Pfistermeister replied that it would be agreeable to his Majesty if Semper would come to Munich " to make the appropriate studies in connection with a site for the projected theatre ", and, after finishing his business there, go to Hohenschwangau to lay the designs before the King and discuss the matter further. Ludwig had by this time evidently reverted to his original intention of constructing the monumental stone theatre. On the 1st September Semper received a telegram from Secretary Lutz expressing the impatience of his royal master to see the drawings he had requested of such a theatre. The architect's patient reply was that he had been engaged upon that very task ever since he had received the King's commission some nine months ago, but that he could not complete his work until he heard what Wagner had to say about the solution of the technical problems put forward in the plans sent to him in May; it had been understood that a try-out of these plans in a provisional theatre was a necessary preliminary to an application of them to the definitive theatre, for the very form of the latter — and therefore the pictorial design for which the

King was now pressing — would depend upon which plans were adopted.[8]

4

Semper spent his September holiday in Munich, only to be informed by Pfistermeister, writing from Hohenschwangau on the 7th September, 1865, that while the King had been greatly inter-

[8] In his covering letter of the 10th May to Wagner, Semper had said that the first of the two plans he was submitting related to a theatre in amphitheatrical form, to seat about 1,000; in the other plan, marked B, "the stage is an independent structure completely separated from the auditorium, as in the ancient Greek theatre, whereas in plan A both structures are comprised in one, on the Roman model." Plan B would give a seating accommodation of about 1,500. Apart from all other technical considerations, the novel problem of concealing the orchestra from the view of the spectators would call for different perspectives in the structure according to whether plan A or plan B were adopted. "I have prepared", Semper continues, "the sketch for the monumental theatre on the high bank of the Isar, not far from the Maximilianeum and to the right of this. But before I give these their definitive form I would like to have your opinion upon the suggestions I have made in connection with the projects now enclosed."

Further light on the architectural way of approach to the new problems of the Wagner theatre is thrown by Semper's formal memorandum on the plans for the monumental structure, given in SMF, p. 107 ff. It is obvious that the guiding ideas were Wagner's; and we can readily imagine that he and Semper must often have discussed the subject in Zürich in the 1850's. Especially interesting is the suggestion, in the memorandum referred to above, of "a second, higher and broader, proscenium, to be placed fifteen feet in front of the actual stage-proscenium, making a huge frame, a recess, behind which, sideways and above, are concealed the gas-jets for the lighting of the real stage." This forward stage-proscenium was to be so planned as to be in all respects like the hinder one except that its special proportions would give rise to "a perspective illusion, since the eye will be unable to distinguish the actual differences in dimensions from the differences due to perspective. . . . In this way will be achieved the desired annihilation of the scale of distances, and along with it the separation of the ideal world of the stage from the reality of the world of the spectators. There will be the further weighty advantage that when the actors come right forward to the front line of the stage they will appear to be of more than life-size, because the eye will be led to measure them according not to the actual scale but to the diminished scale of the smaller inner proscenium. In this way there will be achieved something resembling what the Greek tragedians aimed at when, by means of masks, the cothurnus, and so on, they made the performers of heroic parts appear to be larger than life." We shall probably be safe in seeing Wagner's mind and hand in all this: from the beginning of his work on the *Ring* he could hardly fail to have been occupied with the problem of making his gods and heroes look not like ordinary men and women but like the gods and heroes of a saga. No such illusion, of course, is possible in the ordinary opera house.

It is interesting to discover that in 1865 the literary historian Georg Reinhard Röpe, in a discussion of "The Dramatic Treatment of the Nibelung Saga in Hebbel's *Nibelungen* and Geibel's *Brünhild*" — à propos of the recent production of Hebbel's play, — had said that the drama "made an unwarrantable demand on the imagination of the audience, by reason of the contradiction between the gigantic nature of the characters and the ordinary stature of the actors." See R. M. Werner's Foreword to his critical edition of Hebbel's *Die Nibelungen*, p. XXII.

ested in the information the architect had sent him as to the probable cost of the festival theatre, he regretted that he could not see him as he had hoped: he had been unwell, and his physician had advised him to go still further away into the quiet of the mountains. Nor, apparently, was the architect, about this time, receiving the support he was entitled to from Wagner. This is evident from the comments of Peter Cornelius, who was in close touch with Wagner. " Since then ", Cornelius wrote to Bertha Jung on the 28th August [i.e., since the King's and the composer's first enthusiasm for the festival theatre scheme],

> " Schnorr has died; the *Ring* is still far from completion; supposing, then, the theatre to be ready, what could one do with it? Wagner himself rather dreads the too brilliant fulfilment of his wishes. Furthermore, he recognises that this theatre is a particular stone of stumbling for the people who will have to defray the cost. What he desires most of all just now is a year's rest, complete recovery of his health, and the maintenance of the comfort secured to him by the King; and he sees that all these are likely to be disturbed or made problematic by plunging into this affair. Consequently his attitude towards these matters is one of braking rather than pushing ".

Wagner was, in fact, carefully watching his step just then: he was trying to pump a large sum out of the royal treasury for his personal benefit, and until he had this safely in his pocket the last thing he would want to do would be to scare the officials with the prospect of having further to finance the festival theatre plan. Three weeks later, on the 20th September, Cornelius tells his fiancée that Semper has had to leave Munich without seeing the King, and that " Wagner, in his heart of hearts, is damnably little concerned about the scheme coming to anything, because the building will be very expensive, and it might easily become a stone of stumbling to him in his own affairs." [9]

The architect, of course, was blissfully unconscious of all these cross-currents in the background of the affair. Though he may have suspected that the King's " indisposition " was merely of the diplomatic order, he replied politely on the 14th that he was busily engaged in collecting a mass of important data without which it

---

[9] CABT, II, 244, 257.

would be difficult for him to make any further progress with his plans. Most urgent of all was it that he should have accurate measurements of the site near the Maximilianeum, details of its " profile ", and so on. His own time being short, he says, Neureuther has promised to help him in this matter; but first of all it is essential that the Court gardener, in whose jurisdiction the grounds about the Maximilianeum lie, shall be instructed to allow the necessary measurements to be taken. He has seen Wagner, he adds, and has come to an agreement with him over the plans for the definitive theatre. It appears, then, that during all the months in which Semper had been urged by the King to submit his plans for the monumental theatre, nothing whatever had been done by the officials towards supplying him with the pre-requisite particulars of the ground on which he was to build! Manfred Semper is no doubt right in his theory that the reason for this was the passive resistance of the higher officials, who were playing a double game of intrigue and delay with both Semper and the King. When, on the 1st October, Neureuther was at last able to send him the information he required, Semper probably thought his troubles were nearing their end. The poor man was deceiving himself: they were merely beginning again in a new form.

On the day of his departure from Munich, the 20th September, he received, through Wagner, a message from the King, expressing an ardent desire to see a " plastic model " of the festival theatre; once more it becomes evident that Ludwig was too impatient to see his darling architectural project in front of him in the round to have much time or inclination for the study of mere dry technical details. Henceforth Semper is bombarded with requests for the model. In November Cosima was able to inform the King that Wagner had received a " long letter " from Semper, together with sketches for both the provisional and the monumental theatres. This letter has recently come to light in the Wahnfried archives.[10] The plans referred to in Semper's letter to Wagner of the 10th May, which have been summarised above, had evidently been taken back by him to Zürich in September, to be worked over afresh with the most conscientious care.

---

[10] It is given in full in KLRWB, I, lxxx ff.

From this "long letter" (of the 26th November, 1865) one gathers that the King had asked for a detailed estimate of the cost of the provisional theatre, to include the stage machinery and decorations, lighting, heating, the fitting up of the auditorium, the various room-furnishings, and so on. Although some of these matters hardly come within the functions of the architect as such, Semper has addressed himself to them. He asks Wagner to consult, on their joint accounts, the Munich theatre machinist with regard to the stage apparatus — to get him to fill in, as well as he can, the technical details for which Semper has left blank places in the plans, and to draw up an estimate of the probable cost of the machinery. Semper has now modified to some extent the plans he had sent to Wagner in May. In his "new project", as he calls it, he will need the assistance of an architect on the spot; but he hesitates to make such heavy demands on the time of Neureuther or any other Munich artist without official authorisation. His "new project" shows a further subtilisation of the scheme of a double proscenium, together with a number of technical suggestions with regard to the stage lighting, etc., with which we need not concern ourselves here: the earlier plan of the definitive theatre has also been modified in some particulars. Semper wishes Wagner to assure the King that he is throwing himself heart and soul into both the plans and the plastic model: he is being perpetually faced, he says, with new problems that call for much study and take up a great deal of his time. His labour and his zeal certainly deserved something better than the ingratitude they were to meet with in the end.

But in the midst of all this the King once more begins, no doubt under the pressure of the Cabinet, to vacillate between the provisional and the definitive theatre. On the 14th October Pfistermeister writes to Semper: "His Majesty would like to know whether you regard the erection of a provisional theatre in the Glaspalast as absolutely necessary, or whether the expense of this could be avoided. In case you are not of the latter opinion, his Majesty would like to know when the erection of the provisional theatre could be begun." Semper, in his reply to this, points out the many technical problems involved in Wagner's scheme for an invisible

orchestra and the complete separation of the real world of the auditorium from the ideal world of the stage, and says that as his work
has progressed he has become more and more convinced of the
necessity of testing the new ideas in a provisional structure before
embarking on the definitive one. He points out that a theatre in the
Glaspalast need not necessarily be a white elephant: it could be
used for other than Wagnerian performances — for concerts, exhibitions, etc., — and so virtually pay its way. He is working, he
says, at the plastic model of the monumental theatre, the construction of which could be started the following spring. " The most
difficult and most expensive part of it will be the stage equipment."
From the King he received a personal letter expressing his delight
at the prospect of seeing first of all the model and later the actual
theatre, the product of " the co-operation of the greatest poet and
musician and the greatest architect of the century, a work which
will long endure, to the fame and the blessing of mankind. And so
I cry out to you from the depth of my soul, ' Success to your
work! ' "

The situation, then, by December, 1865, when Wagner was driven
out of Munich, was simply this: that for a whole year Semper had
been working without intermission at plans for both the provisional
and the definitive theatre without having a proper commission for
either of them from anyone, without any financial terms being
agreed upon, with the King always unable to make up his mind
which of the two schemes to put into execution, and with the Cabinet placing every possible obstacle in the way of all parties.

On the 16th December the King, evidently anxious to set the
architect's mind at rest, instructed Pfistermeister to inform him
that the royal intentions were not at all affected by Wagner's departure — at this time, of course, Ludwig thought the exile would
be only temporary — and that it was his wish that the provisional
theatre should first be erected: Semper was accordingly to continue
his labours in connection with this, and the King would be glad to
know approximately when the building could be completed. Pfistermeister was unaware that a set of plans had been sent to Wagner
at the end of November; and perhaps Wagner himself had not
been able to give them much attention. On the 7th December he

had received notice of Ludwig's desire that he should leave Munich for a few months. He left on the 10th; and it is understandable that in his agony of mind, and with the thousand preparations he had to make, he should have neither the time nor the heart to devote himself just then to the question of the theatre. It turned out later that the plans had been locked up, with a number of other papers, in a chest which had been left temporarily in the house in the Briennerstrasse, the key being given into Cosima's keeping. They did not come to light again until the middle of February, 1866.

5

By that time Semper's model for the provisional theatre had reached the King, who seems to have given orders for the scheme to be proceeded with at once. This made it necessary for the politicians to resort to new tactics. They now began to harp upon the expense of the building. Pfistermeister set the rumour going that it could cost about 800,000 florins: when, in March, Semper's estimate was received — about 200,000 florins, provided that the scenic apparatus did not call for quite exceptional sums; and anyhow, as Semper pointed out to Pfistermeister, with this part of the matter an architect was no more concerned than with any other expense connected with actual theatrical productions — the politicians took the line of affecting to doubt the accuracy of an estimate over which both Semper himself and the experts whom he had consulted in Paris had taken exceptional trouble. On the 16th March, 1866 Pfistermeister wrote Semper that he had discussed the estimate with Lutz, who, he said, was convinced that the King would now order a beginning to be made; the matter was consequently being put into the hands of Hofmann, the State Treasurer. But only six days later came a cold douche for Semper: Hofmann, said Pfistermeister, could hardly hope to be able to give the matter his attention at present, as his hands were full with the financial arrangements for providing Prince Otto with an establishment of his own. " I cannot very well tell you in writing ", continued Pfistermeister hypocritically,

" why the affair thus seems to be at any rate postponed: it would appear, however, that very many people are concerned in it, and that for all kinds of reasons they are doing their best to persuade the young King from the project. I sincerely hope that I am wrong in supposing this, and that sooner or later the definitive theatre will come into being."

No one knew better than Pfistermeister who was at the bottom of this last of the many " postponements " the scheme had had to endure.

Manfred Semper is no doubt right in supposing that had either Ludwig or Wagner intervened energetically there would have been a summary end to all these " postponements ". But Wagner's interest in the theatre was now relatively slight, and was becoming slighter still as the months went on: determined, as he already was in his heart, that he would never return to Munich, never again allow himself to be dragged into the political and theatrical hell of that or any other capital, of what concern to him could a theatre be which, while ostensibly intended solely for his works, would now have to produce them without his own constant guidance and control? What ultimate distinction would there be, in practice, between such a theatre and the many others whose mutilations and misunderstandings of his works he had had to deplore so long as the productions were left to the local Kapellmeister and his forces? [11] As for the King, although by now he had the model of the provisional theatre before him, his interest in this part of the scheme had faded: his thoughts now ran solely on the definitive theatre. About the provisional building Semper from now onwards heard virtually nothing more from the Cabinet. So complete was the indifference shown to this part of the architect's labours, says Manfred Semper, writing in 1906, that " when, a few years ago, a search was made, for a particular purpose, for the plans

---

[11] All along his contention had been that the first real step towards the realisation of his ideal was the foundation of the Music School, for the new Wagner theatre would have been of little use without the new type of Wagner singer and actor it would have been the business of the School to train. But now, even with Bülow at the head of it, the School could never become what he had intended it to be under his own supervision. It is understandable, then, that the longer he remained at Triebschen, the more adamant his resolution became never to live in Munich again, and the more he realised that the growing political anxieties of the time would combine with the machinations of the politicians to distract the King's attention and weaken his purpose, the more certain he would feel that in the end the festival theatre scheme was doomed either to a half-life or no life at all.

and model of the provisional theatre, neither of them could be found." [12]

Not a word reached Semper from Wagner in all these months — not even a card with his new address; and though Wagner had been more than once in Zürich or its neighbourhood he seems studiously to have avoided his old friend, perhaps from pure shame at the course events had taken and despair of ever being able to bring order into the chaos. At the end of May the architect had to ask Frau Wesendonk for Wagner's Lucerne address: he wanted to find out, he said, whether Wagner would wish to see the plans, now completed, for the festival theatre, with the bridge leading to it and the lay-out of the surrounding streets, and indeed whether the composer had any further interest in the thing at all. " I do not know where I am ", he wrote to Mathilde, " for even from Munich itself I hear nothing whatever about the matter." A letter of the 4th June to Wagner, written after Semper had received the Triebschen address from Mathilde Wesendonk, has recently come to light.[13] Semper tells Wagner that the complete plans have long been finished. He does not know what to do next, he says; it is urgently necessary that he shall have a talk with him. He will bring the plans with him if Wagner would like him to do so. (Manfred Semper says " it cannot be ascertained whether Semper had an opportunity to show Wagner his plans for the monumental theatre "; but we now know from Wagner's " Annals " and from Frau Wille's reminiscences that Semper *did* go to Triebschen at this time: his visit coincided with one from François Wille, who had gone there to try to induce Wagner to use his influence with the King to remain neutral in the dispute between Austria and Prussia).

On the 13th June (1866) he sent word to Munich that they were ready, and asked for instructions with regard to them. On the 19th he was asked to send them to the Cabinet Secretariat, and at the same time urged to make all possible haste with the model, which the King was growing more and more impatient to see. Mere plans,

---

[12] The original model of the provisional theatre is now in the Ludwig II Museum in Herrenchiemsee Castle: that of the monumental theatre is in the Bavarian National Museum in Munich. Herrenchiemsee also contains a model of the latter theatre, made in 1927 from Semper's design.

[13] KLRWB, V, 32.

with their complicated and often incomprehensible technical details, evidently repelled Ludwig: a model was something upon which he could at once feast his eyes and let his romantic fancy play.

6

Upon the model, accordingly, Semper now concentrated. It was finished in December, 1866, and after being not only shown to Wagner — in Zürich on the 1st January, 1867 [14] — but exhibited for a few days in a hall of the Zürich Polytechnic, it was sent to Munich in the early days of January. The King, in his enthusiasm, summoned Semper to demonstrate it to him in detail: he expressed his delight with it, and gave the architect his word, accompanied by a handshake, that the work should be carried out. Semper now saw Lutz, who turned him over to Düfflipp. They both assured him that the building had been definitely decided upon and that steps would at once be taken to acquire the necessary land. While the negotiations in connection with this were in progress — they would necessarily take some time — Semper was to occupy himself in working out detailed estimates of cost, so that everything would be ready for a start upon the building. He was urged, both by the politicians and by the King himself in person, to leave Zürich, settle for good in Munich, and enter the Bavarian service. To this suggestion he had to postpone a definite reply, on account of his obligations in Zürich; and taught by his previous experiences he wondered, as he wrote to his young son, whether " some obstacle or other would not still be placed in the path of the scheme." He asked Düfflipp for an official contract, but had to be content with the bland assurance that this would be sent to him later in Zürich:

[14] Wagner was so moved by the beauty and grandeur of Semper's plan and by the thought of the ideal purpose it enshrined that, as he informed the King some eighteen months later, he made a vow that if ever the theatre and its *Ring* production became fact he would match "so great a prize" with "a great oblation" on his own part: he would "remain far from the festival, deny myself the prodigious effect of the dedication, but humbly pay homage in secret prayer to my good genius, my godlike Friend and Fulfiller. Such was my oath. Shall I live to have to keep it?" That this was not mere rhetoric for the King's benefit is proved by the entry in his diary on the 1st January, 1867: "Zürich. (Semper. Theatre model—Homeward journey: Vow)."

[425]

meantime he was to set confidently to work. A contract, however, he never received, either then or later, although Düfflipp called on him in Zürich, by order of the King,[15] to discuss the theatre with him. He could not even extract from the crafty politician so much as a written memorandum of agreement; he was assured that a proper contract would be sent to him from Munich immediately on Düfflipp's return there. But all that Semper received, on the 17th February, was a note from Düfflipp protesting that unexpected difficulties had arisen in connection with the purchase of the site, the demands of the owners of some of the land required having soared to such a height that another terrain would have to be sought for.

It was now suggested that the theatre should be erected on the site of the old barracks in the Hofgarten — a site already considered by Wagner and Semper long ago and rejected by them in favour of the one by the Maximilianeum. That a new site would mean Semper's having to begin his plans all over again from the commencement does not appear to have disturbed the politicians. Perhaps, indeed, they counted on this to make him refuse, in sheer exasperation, to proceed any further with the matter. There is little doubt that all along they were playing a double game, feeding the Press with information, true or false, calculated to prejudice public opinion against the scheme for the new theatre, weakening Ludwig's resolution every now and then by representing to him the difficulties and objections, financial and other, about which everyone in Munich was alleged to be talking, and then using the distracted King's vacillations as an excuse for putting Semper off. Manfred Semper's language about it all is not a whit too strong — "nothing in this letter of Düfflipp's but untruths, phrases, empty assurances; fresh evidence of how consummately Royal Cabinet Councillor von Düfflipp understood how to keep Semper on the hook without in any way binding either himself or the Cabinet."

[15] On the 14th January, 1867 the King had written to Wagner saying that the building of the monumental theatre would commence in the spring. It would take four or five years; the *Ring*, he hoped, would be completed well before then, and the theatre would open with this: "the Music School will by that time have created a Wotan and a Siegfried for us — perhaps a Parsifal."

Meanwhile fresh trouble was drifting up from other quarters. On the 27th January, 1867 August Röckel sent Wagner a long letter in which he favoured him with the latest news from Munich. It was a solid fact, he said, that the projected new street for the festival theatre would be a public calamity. The Müncheners had made the grave mistake, when developing the town, of diverting it from the river and making a host of new streets to the west and north, where speculators had put up at inflated prices large numbers of houses that were mostly unlet; and many people were now paying the penalty for this mistake. What was done could not be undone; but if the King were to force this scheme through, values would immediately decline still further in the speculative area, and Ludwig would be blamed not only for this but for destroying all hopes of a future recovery. The result would be in the first place a general outcry, not so much against the King as against Wagner as the prime cause of all the trouble — the proposed new street had already been baptised, in the town, the Richard Wagner Strasse — and in the second place renewed criticism of the King for having considered other interests than those of the community as a whole. Moreover, it would be quite impossible for Ludwig to carry the theatre scheme through on his own account and at his own expense; some public money would be necessary, while the law would have to be invoked to authorise certain expropriations. The finances of Munich were in none too good a condition; a loan of 4,000,000 gulden had recently been raised with some difficulty and on onerous terms. Economy was now necessary; and public opinion would be strongly against expenditure on a grandiose building plan that would obviously damage many interests. Only three alternatives were held to be possible for the King: he could give up the scheme for the new street and build the theatre elsewhere, or he could postpone the whole affair until a more favourable time — and when would that time come? — or, which would be best of all, he could set himself to hasten the coming of this better time by promoting the general welfare of the capital in accordance with the new political and economic conditions of the day. The business men of the city felt that Munich was ripe for new industrial developments, but no one could see precisely, at the moment, what form they should take. In short, and in plain language, virtually every interest in the town was set against the new theatre scheme.[16]

Thus Röckel. Wagner's reply of the 29th strengthens the impression that if ever, after December, 1865, he had been really enamoured of the plan for a Wagner theatre in Munich his enthusiasm for it had now waned. The King's " rapidly-formed resolution to carry out this scheme at once ", he told Röckel, had " terrified " him; and now he [Wagner] " had other things in his mind than a Wagner theatre and a Wagnerstrasse." His resolve never to return to Munich was by this time unshakable; the theatre project had virtually ceased to interest him; no doubt his tireless brain was already at work on the question of a Wagner theatre of his own elsewhere.

He turned over to Cosima the difficult task of forwarding Röckel's letter to Semper, a task which she fulfilled with her usual smooth diplomacy. " You will see from Röckel's letter ", she wrote, " that the most vexatious tittle-tattle continues to pour in upon the King concerning his great plans; and it would probably have pleased him if he could have heard something heartening, hope-awakening from you. According to Herr von Düfflipp it is to be assumed that the building will be begun in the spring." [17] Semper's reply to Cosima of the 31st January, from which Manfred Semper quoted no more than a few lines in 1906, has only recently become available in full. He begins with some acid remarks about his and Wagner's old Dresden friend Röckel: his long imprisonment, he says, has done him a world of good physically but seems to have damaged him mentally. He resents Röckel's pedagogical tone, and wishes he had kept out of a matter in which his interference can achieve nothing but harm. As for the calamitous re-

---

[16] KLRWB, IV, 175–6.

[17] Düfflipp had been in Triebschen a few days before this, and had assured Wagner that the necessary economies were in view to allow of a start being made shortly and to "carry on *doucement* for five or six years. For the present it is a matter only of the theatre: bridge and street to be reserved for a more convenient future." Thus Wagner to Röckel on the 29th January: "I had nothing to say against this", he adds. Reading between the lines, we surmise that he did not take Düfflipp's assurances very seriously, though he seems to have liked the man personally as much as it was possible for him to like any politician.

sults that Röckel prophesies if the new street is constructed through the St. Anne suburb, there are, says Semper, three alternatives: (1) " the new street-line will have no particular influence on the neighbourhood or on the business of the town as a whole, in which case Röckel's apprehensions for the well-being of the Philistines with houses in the west and north quarters are groundless "; (2) the opening out of the, at present, sequestered Isar quarter may give the traffic of Munich a new direction; the population will decide the matter for itself, regardless of the interests of the speculators in another part of the town; is the natural development of Munich to be impeded for the benefit of these people? Why not embark now upon the new lay-out of the district in its broad features, and then leave the development of it to time and common sense? — i.e., not plunge at once into a huge expenditure on showy and costly buildings and monuments for mere ornament's sake, as has been done already in the Maximilianstrasse; (3) it is quite possible that by opening out the " labyrinthine confusion of the St. Anne quarter to industrial communication this part of the town will become the centre of a new population, without there following, as a necessary consequence, the depopulation of other parts; rather will the new activity contribute to the revival of the streets at present isolated."

This third possibility, he prophesied, is one that will some day be realised: " sooner or later the unnaturally constructed Munich of the west and north . . . will attain, for the first time, to a real organic being from the new impulse from the east and south." Wagner should not listen to a mere doctrinaire like Röckel, who means well, but is only "an Epimetheus with his finger always at his nose ". If, however, the worst comes to the worst, if the momentary unpopularity of the scheme, considerations of economy, and so on, really make it necessary to place the festival theatre elsewhere, he would prefer the site of the dilapidated barracks at the eastern end of the Hofgarten, near the Residenz — that is to say, the site occupied today by the Bavarian Army Museum. A theatre there would of course lack the ideal character of one on the Gasteig; but if it was simply a question of a conflict of interests between the north-west of the town and the land by the river — in which latter direction, as he foresaw, and as the later cutting of the Prinz-

Regentenstrasse was to prove, the future of Munich lay — all this lay outside his province as architect.[18]

The architect's reply to Cosima had evidently irritated Wagner, perhaps because, in his heart of hearts, he was tired of the whole affair, was conscious that it would come to nothing in the end, and did not quite know how to face Semper now. In his answer of the beginning of February, the confused style of which shows the impatience with which it was written, he professes to have been disturbed at not having heard from Semper since they had met in Zürich, on the 1st January, to view the model of the theatre, while he, for his part, he says, had been doing all he could to further " our great affair ".

> " God knows that my zeal is not for the furthering of my personal interests; were I to regard only my personal peace and security I would straightway dissuade the King from the now resolved-on realisation of the scheme, for, as I need not tell you, every odious construction that can be put upon it and turned to account will be laid to *my* charge, while all the glory of the undertaking will fall solely to you."

He speaks of how grievously he has suffered because of the misunderstanding of his artistic ideals by the German world, and especially by the Press, but consoles himself with the reflection that sometimes good comes out of evil — it gratifies him to think that these sufferings of his will have been the means of calling into being Semper's " incomparably beautiful building."

> " This reflection is so consoling to me that with all my zeal I decided to take an active part in the game as the only power that could help to realise your art-work — a realisation which depends entirely on the young King's faith in me and my art — in spite of the fact that, as I have just told you, my personal interest would in no way drive me in that direction, especially because in order to do justice to my own art-tendency I must now address myself to preliminary creations which at the moment lie far remote from a monumental edifice."

And once more he tries to put upon Semper the odium of having neglected *him* in unfriendly and inconsiderate fashion by not writing to him earlier.

Replying to Wagner on the 4th February, 1867, Semper sets forth the latest details of his struggle with the King and the offi-

---

[18] Semper's letter will be found in full, together with a further letter from him in reply to one of Wagner's, in KLRWB, V, 54–56, 58–61.

cials. He had recently spent ten days in Munich. The King had already had the model of the theatre installed in one of the rooms of the Residenz, whither Semper was summoned on the 11th January. In an audience lasting more than two hours he explained the model and the plans in full. Ludwig enquired if he was willing to undertake the realisation of the scheme: he replied that he would feel honoured by such a command. The next day there was a further audience, at which Ludwig went closely into the matter of the site and the proposed lay-out of roads.

> " His Majesty seemed to decide for the plan that was your [Wagner's] first idea — a prolongation of the Briennerstrasse through the Hofgarten, past the north side of the Residenz, through the St. Anne suburb, then joining up both banks of the river by means of the bridge, and ending with the festival theatre on the eastern height on the further side of the river."

In reply to a question of the King's he had said that while it was inadvisable to hurry over the building of the theatre, the sooner a start was made the better; speaking offhand, he estimated that something like six years would be needed to complete the whole scheme. Since that second audience he had not seen the King; but on the 13th Lutz brought him a command to survey the site with the Court gardener and to help the Court photographer, Albert, to take photographs of the designs and the plastic model. These tasks kept Semper occupied for several days. He was anxious to get back to his duties in Zürich, but Lutz advised him to wait and see if the King desired his presence again. On the 19th Lutz assured him that his Majesty, having decided to proceed with the plan, had ordered either Hofmann or Düfflipp to get to work at the preliminaries, especially the purchase of the necessary ground. Thereupon Semper saw Düfflipp, who, as usual, was most friendly, but, again as usual, distressingly vague; he still, he said, had no orders in writing from the King, and therefore could not as yet enter into any official negotiations with the architect.

That is how the matter stands now, Semper tells Wagner. He is hurt by Wagner's suggestion that if the work is now put in hand the danger will be all his and the glory all Semper's: he can see no particular danger to Wagner, he says, while he himself will not profit much by the work, at any rate during his lifetime: he creates solely for the pleasure of creating, and his enthusiasm for the festi-val theatre has been in large part the product of his desire to serve Wagner, whose dramatic conceptions, he feels, are too vast to be realised in an ordinary theatre.

Cosima seems to have thought Semper's tone rather sharp. We, on the other hand, would not feel any astonishment had it been sharper, for apart from the fact that the whole burden of the work had fallen upon him for more than two years, and that he could win no certain footing in the morass of chicanery on the part of the politicians and of vacillation on the part of the King that had been slowly spreading round him all that time, it must have been exasperating to be told by Wagner, in effect, that from first to last he had been dependent on *his* good will and influence with the King. Semper himself had not taken up arms against Wagner; he had merely replied to some remarks of Röckel's which, after all, there had been no necessity for Wagner to pass on to him, except on the assumption that he secretly welcomed them as an excuse for his own secret cooling-off towards the theatre scheme. Semper could not fail now to see that the end of it all was near: on the margin of Wagner's letter he noted, evidently at some later date, " After the receipt of this letter it was clear to me that it would turn out as it has done."

The King's interest in the affair was apparently weakening just then, as a result partly of increasing political anxieties, partly of the despairing recognition that Wagner was really determined never to take up his residence in Munich again. The matter lapsed more and more completely into the hands of the politicians, and they knew well how to deal with it. The written contract promised Semper by Düfflipp in February never came. For seven months, indeed, Semper had no communication from him; then he received a letter explaining that Düfflipp had delayed writing, week by week, until he should have good news for him, and suggesting a meeting in the Zürich railway station to talk matters over; the wary politician was evidently reluctant to commit himself to anything on paper. Semper, however, was in Paris, whence he wrote to Düfflipp on the 21st September;

" I see dissolved in mists before my eyes the noblest of dreams, in the realisation of which I have believed for three whole years, and to which I have dedicated all my thought, all my endeavour, my very being itself. But even yet I do not quite give up the hope of seeing the work, which is now complete in every detail and ready to be put into execution immediately, called into life. I rely on the generous, faith-keeping mind of the royal art-protector and on a certain inner conviction of the worth of the idea which it was his Majesty's purpose to call into being."

Semper once more pressed for a statement in writing of " the real position of the matter ". But a couple of months more having gone by without his receiving any communication from either Düfflipp or Wagner, in November he sent his young son Manfred, armed with all the documents of the case, to Munich. Manfred was received in the friendliest fashion by Düfflipp, who assured him that the theatre would be put in hand as soon as certain political and economic difficulties had been cleared out of the way; moreover, Semper was to be asked to take up his residence in Munich with the post of Oberbaurat (Chief State Architect) and Director of all buildings erected under the Civil List. He was given to understand that only the assent of the King was required for the settlement of all the financial questions involved, including that of the theatre. On the 30th November Düfflipp went to Hohenschwangau to consult the King, and a further conference with Manfred Semper was fixed for the 3rd December. On that day Manfred received the official assurance that the arrangements had the King's approval in every respect, and that Düfflipp was to proceed with them forthwith: Düfflipp promised to send the necessary papers to Zürich in a few days. Young and relatively inexperienced as he was, however, Manfred did not take all the politician's smooth words at their face value: he went to a Munich attorney, Herr von Schauss, before whom he laid the whole history of the case. Meanwhile Semper was willing to accept Düfflipp's offer. Wagner, who seems to have had word of the proposals direct from Munich, urged him to do so, as in Munich he would be able to render valuable aid to the new ideals. Wagner relied, he said, absolutely on the King: " he will become ever stronger, and in the end everything will be carried through. And so, a handshake on it! Accept! "

But again the weeks went by without the promised documents arriving in Zürich.[19] On the last day of 1867 Cosima wrote to Semper that she had had an interview with Düfflipp, who, good man, was lost in innocent wonder at the news that the architect was still waiting to hear from him; he had written to him in full, he said, on the 8th December, and posted the letter with his own hand! This was the first time, he assured Cosima, he had ever heard of a Cabinet letter being lost in the post; as Manfred Semper ironically remarks, had he consulted the files he would have discovered that precisely the same miracle had happened in connection with precisely the same Semper a couple of years before. However, said Düfflipp, a duplicate of the lost letter would be sent to Zürich in the early days of January. By the middle of January 1868, no communication being even yet forthcoming from Munich, Semper had once more to turn to Cosima for information. She wrote to the King, who ordered Düfflipp to go to Triebschen to see her. The latter's excuse now for not having kept his promise of some weeks before to Semper was that events had taken a new turn: he had been told in various quarters that it was his " patriotic duty " to advise the King against summoning the architect to Munich. This patriotic duty he had fulfilled, with the result that Ludwig had ordered the matter to rest where it was for the moment. At last, on the 25th January, 1868, Düfflipp, at Cosima's urging, wrote to Semper; but his long letter contained nothing but evasions, untruths about the " lost " letter, flatteries, cajoleries, and pious hopes for a better future. Semper's opinion of it all was expressed in a letter of the

---

[19] The King had evidently instructed Düfflipp to transmit the offer of the new engagement to Semper: on the 11th March, 1867 he had written to Wagner, "Düfflipp is writing today to Semper about his call here." But Düfflipp did not write! The póliticans were manifestly working not only against Semper but against Ludwig: they probably feared that to establish the great architect in Munich would merely be to feed still further the King's passion for building. Apparently the first hint Semper had of the "call" was in the following November; and on the 10th of that month Ludwig wrote to Wagner that he would have to postpone the commencement of the theatre until the following year, on account of the expense to which his engagement to the Archduchess Sophie was putting him.

Wagner not only cordially approved the plan for settling Semper in Munich but advised the King to issue a similar invitation to Liszt.

28th February to his son: " Vile is the lie of the personally-posted and lost Cabinet letter: the whole business is vile. I am sick and tired of it all: I have lost all hope, even of payment."

He vouchsafed no reply to Düfflipp's letter, but put the matter at once into the hands of the lawyer Herr von Schauss, who presented the demand for settlement of Semper's account to the Treasury on the 27th March. His covering letter reviewed, in temperate language, the history of the affair of the theatre, and spoke of Semper's profound disappointment, as an artist, at the annihilation of his hopes of endowing Munich with a building worthy of it and of himself: " three years of painful effort, of study, of care, of doubt, of the most intensive work have gone by, without Herr Semper having received the slightest recognition, let alone compensation, for all his trouble." There followed a formal statement of account, based on the recognised standards of the epoch for this kind of work. For the provisional theatre, two per cent on the estimated cost of 80,000 florins, amounting to 1,600 florins. For the model of this theatre, 316 florins for cost of materials and a mere 100 florins for labour, in all 416 florins. For the plans, estimates, etc., of the monumental theatre, one-and-a-half per cent on the estimated cost of 2,568,299 florins, amounting to 38,524 florins. For the model, 1,215 florins for material and 550 florins for incidental expenses — in all 1,765 florins. Total 42,305 florins, less 5,000 florins already received. Schauss added that there were other considerations, on which, however, he would not insist, that could hardly be assessed in terms of money, to say nothing of the fact that Semper's preoccupation with the Munich scheme for the last three years had hampered him in his general work. The lawyer concluded by saying that he was confident that " the great and noble heart " of the King would be better able to do justice to " the ideal side of the matter " than the " dry jurist " would.

The politicians, of course, at once began to practise the regulation delays and raise the usual objections. On the 1st June Schauss entered an energetic protest against these tactics: " My patience is exhausted ", he wrote to Semper, " and I now advise legal action." Semper, however, was reluctant to take this step, although as late as November the Cabinet was still shilly-shallying.[20] It was not until the 20th January, 1869 that the long and disgraceful episode was closed by the satisfaction of Semper's claim.

Wagner now chose, as the King also had done, to regard himself as in some way or other aggrieved by Semper's conduct. On the 24th April he wrote his old friend a sour letter, in which, while admitting the final success of the politicians' intrigues, he spoke bitterly of Semper's " want of confidence " in *him*; he had given the King, he said, a full and frank account of the intrigues, and it had " shamed " Wagner to be told by Ludwig that he too " found it impossible to have any faith in a man [Semper] who has behaved towards me, in this matter, with such mistrust." That the King, in his ignorance of the worst aspects of the affair, should have felt some resentment against Semper is just conceivable; but the modern reader searches the records in vain for any justification of Wagner's theory that Semper had behaved badly either to him or to Ludwig. Semper treated this letter in the way it deserved: he merely pencilled on it, " This letter, of which I could make neither head nor tail, I left unanswered." [21]

[20] The King, one imagines, could hardly have known the trials and indignities to which the architect had been subjected when he wrote to Wagner, on the 14th September, 1868, "I beg you to use your influence with Semper to pacify him: he persists in his stubbornness. He has forfeited a good deal of my regard by his attitude." Wagner prudently ignores this passage in the letter in his lengthy reply to the King on the 14th October.

If the date in Hefner-Alteneck's memoirs is to be trusted, the King's alienation from Semper dated from long before this time. Hefner-Alteneck says that in an audience of February, 1868 Ludwig asked him whom he regarded as the greatest architect. "I think your Majesty has already found him", said Hefner; to which the King replied, "I know whom you mean: I greatly value his art; but I have had further enquiries made about him. Do not mention his name to me again." (See BLKB, p. 144).

The King's resentment endured to the end. In December, 1873 he sanctioned the conferring of the Maximilian Order on Wagner and five other notabilities, but refused to allow it to be given to Semper.

[21] Glasenapp, of course, takes the dutiful view that Wagner, as always, was without blemish, and that Semper had been guilty of the heinous offence of "a lack of confidence" in him. To talk, as the Wahnfried bodyguard used to do, of Semper having "threatened" the King is to part company with the facts. Schauss's formal statement of Semper's case was a model of restraint. It was only when the officials took refuge in further delays and chicaneries that Schauss felt it necessary, in his client's interest, to adopt a firmer tone; and even then, as his letter of the 25th March to Wagner shows, he made it clear that he drew a distinction between the King and the politicians, and sympathised with the former as much as he did with Semper.

In his "Annals" for March, 1868 Wagner records thus the train of events immediately following Schauss's presentation of Semper's claim and his letter to Triebschen: "Düffl [ipp],—Soon after, Schauss *re* Semper; on the point of going to Zürich to dissuade S. [emper], conferences with Schauss (advoc[ate]:—also for Schwabe!) and Düfflipp. The King breaks with Semper. Theatre done with." (KLRWB, II, 9). From this it appears that Schauss had been the lawyer employed to present to him Madame Schwabe's ancient promissory note in May, 1865 — a circumstance which would hardly endear him to Wagner, or help him to take a calm objective view of the present matter! Glasenapp, needless to say, finds something sinister in the coincidence — it could hardly have been more than that — that the lawyer recommended to Semper, no doubt by some friend in Munich, happened to be this Schauss. For Glasenapp, "this lets us see into the depths of the combination to which Semper's simplicity on the one side, and his want of faith on the other, necessarily made him a sacrifice"!

It is perhaps a minor matter, but one surmises that to Wagner, just at this time, *any* lawyer was as a red rag to a bull. The entry in the "Annals" immediately preceding that cited above runs thus: "Arrest- visit: Advocate Simmerl. (Klepperbein's ancient debt)." It seems that ever since 1847 Wagner had owed a Dresden lady, Frau Wilhelmine Klepperbein, 1,000 thalers, a bagatelle that had no doubt slipped his memory when he was obtaining large sums from King Ludwig for the ostensible purpose of paying his debts. On the 18th March, 1868 she brought an action against him, in Munich, for the repayment of this loan with accrued interest, and on the next day obtained judgment, through her Munich lawyer, Simmerl, for 2,197 gulden, 32 kreutzer. The Court order is still preserved among Wagner's papers at Wahnfried: it authorised his "personal arrest" and imprisonment in the local Neuthurm unless payment was made forthwith. Wagner paid up on the 20th. See KLRWB, II, 9, note 60.

CHAPTER XVIII

"VINCERE SCIS, HANNIBAL"—

1

IT WAS hardly to be supposed that a man who, like Wagner, was in the habit of indulging himself handsomely in luxuries when he had hardly a penny he could call his own would by preference live the Spartan life when he was comfortably provided for. While he was at Starnberg in the summer of 1864, before he had made sure that all his debts were liquidated out of the 15,000 gulden given him by King Ludwig, he had already begun to run up fresh bills with the Viennese milliner Bertha Goldwag — who had helped him to decorate his house in Penzing — stipulating that he was to settle these and future ones of a similar kind at the end of each year. He commissioned her to send him his favourite brown and red and blue and yellow and pink satins, which he could not obtain to his liking in Munich. His imagination dwelt as lovingly on fabrics and shades as ever it did on the harmonies and colours of his orchestra; he betrays real anxiety lest Bertha shall confuse the dark fiery pink which he now wants with the violet pink she had supplied him with in Vienna. Thereafter we read of pink satin counterpanes lined with white, of silk jackets and breeches and dressing-gowns, and other little self-indulgences.

The Briennerstrasse house he could regard as his home for the remainder of his life; here the *Meistersinger* and the *Ring* were to be completed, and *Parsifal* and perhaps *Die Sieger* written. Naturally, therefore, he at once set about providing it with all that was necessary, he being Richard Wagner, to stimulate his artistic powers; soft tissues and rich colours were to kindle his creative imagination and to give him the pleasant feeling of insulation from the outer world. " In the centre of the first floor ", says Röckl,

" there was a large room in which stood Wagner's piano. A door on the right led to the so-called ' Grail ' or satin room,[1] which was about

[1] It was apparently Cornelius who gave this sanctuary the name of the "Grail".

eleven feet six inches high, fourteen feet six inches broad, and sixteen feet long. The walls were covered with fine yellow satin, finished
off with yellow vallances of the same material. The two blunt corners
of the long wall that faced Count von Schack's house were broken by
iron galleries; the resulting recesses, about 27 inches deep, were covered with pink satin in folds. Each of the iron galleries was masked
by two wings of white silk tulle, trimmed with lace. The white curtains and their draperies were also adorned with delicate artificial
roses. The room was lighted by a window in the narrow wall at the
left of the entrance. The curtains of this window were of pink satin,
interlaced with pink and white satin draperies. In the middle of the
broad wall was a mirror, and on the narrow wall opposite the window
a reproduction of Murillo's Madonna. The cornice of the window curtains, the frame of the mirror and that of the picture were puffed out
with pink satin and tied back with white satin bows. The ceiling was
also bordered on all four sides with similar pearl-grey ruches strewn
with artificial roses. The centre of the ceiling was adorned with a
rosette of white satin about 12 inches in circumference and 10 inches
in depth, trimmed with narrow blond lace and with roses like those
on the ceiling. The floor was covered with a soft Smyrna carpet. In
the middle of the floor was a soft and springy couch, covered with a
white flowered moire." [2]

It was perhaps to conceal his luxury as well as he could from
Munich's sober bourgeois that he ordered all or most of these materials from Bertha in Vienna; she told Ludwig Karpath that she paid
two visits to the Briennerstrasse in connection with the decorating
of the house, taking with her goods to the value of about 10,000 gulden. " On Wagner's orders I travelled incognita ", she said: " in
Salzburg, where the customs examination was made, I gave it out
that the silk shirts, dressing-gowns, counterpanes and so forth were
intended for a countess in Berlin." [3] It is hardly surprising that
as early as April, 1865 we find Wagner compelled to stave the
milliner off with a small payment of 500 florins on account, and
then, in August, airily explaining to her that she must still exercise a little patience, as it would go against him were he to seek to
anticipate the quarterly payment of his pension that is due in September.[4]

His expansive and expensive way of living could of course be no
secret from Pfistermeister and the other officials who had occasion
now and then to call on him; and it was presumably from these peo-

[2] RLW, I, 245–6.   [3] KBWP, p. 29.   [4] BRWP, p. 39.

ple that the satirical journalists derived their ammunition against him. His passion for luxury soon became a byword, and long remained so. Baron Otto von Völderndorff, who was employed in the Bavarian Ministry of Foreign Affairs during the Hohenlohe régime, has left us an ironical account of a visit to Wagner at a rather later date. The King had commissioned Völderndorff, through Hohenlohe, to get a statement from Wagner of his political opinions. " So I went one fine afternoon to the house at the corner of Barerstrasse and Arcostrasse in which the Master was staying just then. That day he was in a violet mood. The window was covered with a heavy curtain of violet velvet: he was sitting in a violet velvet robe in a violet velvet armchair; on his head was a violet velvet cap, which he raised ever so slightly as he rose on my entry." [5]

The biographer, unfortunately, finds himself unable to take the view of Wagner's luxury during the Munich period which he himself insisted upon in his reply to the attacks of the *Allgemeine Zeitung*. He was not, as he tried to make out, a purely private person, entitled to run his expenditure according to his own fancy. He was being maintained at the King's expense and the country's; and common prudence ought to have told him that in these circumstances his way of living would be matter for malicious observation. He had a Europe-wide reputation as a gay contractor of liabilities and a most reluctant liquidator of them. It was known that the King had given him large sums specifically to discharge his debts, and it must have been fairly obvious to many people that he had only partially used the money for that purpose, while at the same time he was living in a style that could only lead to further debt, with, as its logical ending, further benefactions on the King's part. We must not blame the Müncheners of that time for not being able to see Wagner and his contribution to German culture as the world of today sees them: the general contemporary view was, and could only be, that a foreigner of admitted distinction in art but of dubious repute in other fields had suddenly planted himself upon Munich, where he not only lived more handsomely upon the royal bounty than any other artist had ever been known to do

    [5] Quoted by Röckl (RLW, II, 223), from an article by Völderndorff in *Velhagen und Klasings Monatshefte*, 1900.

but was trying to land the town in the expense of a new Music School and of a new theatre intended exclusively for the performance of his own works. Wagner's line of defence, of course, would have been that what he was receiving was not bounty but the simple cash equivalent, in advance, of certain future operas of his. To that, however, the Cabinet officials would probably have replied that Wagner's part of the three-years' agreement of 1864 with the Treasury obviously stood little chance now of being carried out by him within the time, that he was therefore getting more from the King than he was morally entitled to, and that his luxurious way of living was making a further appeal for another large sum, to liquidate debts old and new, a practical certainty before long.

Towards the end of the summer of 1865 he seems to have felt the strategic necessity of consolidating his position in Munich along a more advanced line. The King, he knew, would carry out every one of their joint schemes so far as it lay in his power to do so: as regards the Music School, for instance, the only effect of official opposition to the plan as drafted by Wagner was to make Ludwig resolve that the existing Conservatoire should be taken out of the hands of the Ministry of Culture and be financed from the Civil List. It was as evident to him as it was to Wagner that, as he wrote on the 4th August, " our intentions, our exertions for the furtherance of hallowed art are understood by only a few choice spirits." Wagner, for his part, saw that they would never be able to move at more than a snail's pace so long as communications between them had to go through the ordinary official channels. He accordingly pressed the King hard at this time to accede to his request for frequent and undisturbed personal contact between them. As he rightly argued, there was no longer any reason, so far as the world was concerned, why this should not take place. Though the world in general would never rise to the comprehension of the ideal meaning of their bond, it at least knew well enough by this time that a bond of some kind there was. Let the King, then, boldly cut the official knot: let him publicly announce that he had commissioned Wagner to put into execution the ideas elaborated in his Report on the Music School, and that it would be necessary, for this purpose, for Wagner to confer with him frequently. Wagner would be the artistic head of the School, functioning, as it were, as the spiritual trustee of the King: to the Cabinet officials would be left simply the administrative business of the institution.

At the same time, he tells Ludwig in his long letter of the 8th August, he is anxious to have his private affairs placed on a new and solid basis. When, in the autumn of 1864, he had entered into an agreement for the completion of the *Ring* within three years, he says, he had told the King that a secret motive had been operative in him — as he had no desire at that time to live longer than the three years he regarded as necessary for his task, to plan beyond that period seemed to him preposterous. Now, however, matters are different: for one thing, *Tristan* has been realised on the boards. Intoxicating himself with his own words, as he was generally able to do when he wanted, he argues that the former Richard Wagner died with Schnorr, leaving behind him in the world another Richard Wagner who knows that he " can carry out everything — more than the *Ring*, everything — if it be made possible " for him to do so. Another, however, must will this, " since my will no longer belongs to me ". He has carefully surveyed the conditions necessary for his mere terrestrial existence. " If they are refused me, then is my will crippled. I am no longer capable of desiring anything in itself, for myself . . . I repeat: I desire nothing. I say it without the least bitterness, gently, earnestly, calmly." The King has offered him his lodge on the Hochkopf. Thither the renouncing philosopher is going the next day, accompanied by his servant Franz and the old dog Pohl, for rest of body and refreshment of spirit: his reading will be the *Ramayana*.

2

Once more, then, we observe, he was stoically facing a supreme renunciation. Without the least bitterness, gently, earnestly, calmly, this much-enduring man desired nothing at all — except a mere 200,000 gulden more of Bavarian money. As was so often the case with him, he felt that there was no abiding place for him in this hard world that misunderstood him so grievously. Blithely would he leave it; but if death needs must come to him just then, he seems to have reflected sadly, better that it should claim its emaciated prey in a room hung about with pink and white satin than on an uncomfortable pallet in an insanitary hovel. His preference in this respect, however, the Stoic does not communicate to the King; while to Fräulein Bertha, a few days later, he is expressing his regret that he cannot keep his promise to liquidate his large account with her in August.

The reader will recall the terms of the contract of October, 1864 between Wagner and the royal Treasury: he was to deliver the complete score of the *Ring* within three years, against an immediate lump sum of 15,000 florins and a further 15,000 in payments spaced over three years. In a formal document accompanying his letter of the 8th August, 1865 he reminds the King that his original yearly stipend had been fixed at 4,000 florins on the supposition that all he would require would be a residence of the ordinary type in Munich. For the perfect quiet that would be necessary to him during the writing of the *Ring*, however, he needed a house with a garden — an expensive luxury in Munich; and the contract of October, 1864 had provided for a special additional grant to him on this account. During the *Tristan* rehearsals there had been a little trouble with the owner of the Briennerstrasse house, he reminds the King, and for a time it had looked as if he might have to surrender his tenancy. He had poured out his worries into the sympathetic ear of Pfistermeister, who had represented the matter in such a way to the King that the latter had ordered the secret purchase of the house outright. But oddly enough, this arrangement, far from improving Wagner's situation, has actually worsened it! How that has come about is explained to the King in one of the finest examples we have of Wagner's *vortreffliche Suade*. It appears that in the early months of 1865 things were going so badly with him that only three possible courses presented themselves to his distracted mind. The first was to give up the house and leave Munich altogether. (The mere suggestion of that, he well knew, would terrify the King). The second was to remain in the town but take up his abode in a small apartment in Bülow's house. (In this there was implied another threat to the King: were he to leave Munich altogether, he explains, he might still hope to complete his works, but in a small lodging he would have to sacrifice this ambition and restrict himself to looking after the Music School). The third was to ask for a new arrangement with regard to his finances. From this his sensitive soul had shrunk, if only because it would mean his coming into contact once more with the officials who had already shown such marked unfriendliness towards him whenever matters of finance came on the carpet.

However, he feels now that the third of these alternatives is the only one he ought to consider seriously. In any case something really should be done at once as regards his finances, for he is in a position, one gathers, calculated to draw tears of pity from a sabre-toothed tiger. To the casual observer he appears quite well off, no doubt; but alas, the casual observer does not know how much it costs to run a house like the one in the Briennerstrasse as it should be run: [6] the garden is in a sadly neglected condition, and winter heating and other little things of that kind are more expensive than he had ever thought possible. Moreover, his too tender heart bleeds at the thought of the friends of old who had helped him in his need and whose debts he cannot repay, although some of these poor creatures are now in very straitened circumstances. Finally, if the new arrangement goes through he will be able henceforth to make Minna "regularly and without intermission" an allowance of 1,000 thalers (about 1,500 gulden), "without disadvantage to my personal competency."

The contract of October, 1864, he goes on to say, was based on the assumption that the terms of it would be operative for only three years, during which period he was to receive, in addition to his annual allowance, a grant of 3,000 florins per annum in respect of his rent. There is no sense in this latter clause now that the house has become royal property. He accordingly puts forward two new proposals for consideration by the King and the Treasury. (1) His Majesty is to grant him the rent-free occupancy of No. 21 Briennerstrasse for the remainder of his life. (2) A capital sum of 200,000 gulden is to be set aside for his benefit — also for the duration of his life — in the form (a) of an immediate cash grant to him of 40,000 gulden, to be employed as he may decide, (b) of a sum of 160,000 gulden which is to be under the control of the Treasury

---

[6] It was a handsome house, rich in amenities. In the garden was a lofty ash tree under which Wagner used to sit and read: his faithful satellites, remembering their *Ring*, dubbed it, of course, the *Weltesche*. There was a "garden room", linked with the garden by a veranda with a balcony. In the garden Wagner kept a pair of peacocks, who occasionally made themselves at home in the rooms of the house.

so far as the capital is concerned, but the interest on which, at five per cent per annum, is to be paid to him in quarterly instalments of 2,000 gulden each: this new arrangement is to cancel all previous ones with regard to allowances and grants to him from the King, " as well as the stipulations connected with them " — which looks like a request on his part not to be held to a too pedantic legal interpretation of the obligations he himself had undertaken in the preceding October. He expresses, as usual with him on occasions of this kind, his airy confidence that this will be the last time he will have to trouble the Treasury with his financial affairs — that he has, so to speak, no further territorial demands where Bavaria is concerned. He is certain that on 8,000 gulden a year, the interest on the 160,000 gulden capital, he can maintain a decent existence in the (rent-free) house near the Propyläen, and thereby win for himself the peace of mind so necessary to him if he is to fulfil his obligations to his Majesty in respect of his new works.

As for the 40,000 in immediate cash, that would be applied to liquidating old debts and to lightening the burden on him of certain old contracts, such as that with the Dresden publisher. This 40,000 gulden he would hand over to the trusteeship of an experienced and trusted friend — presumably he had in mind Pusinelli; and while there is no doubt that from time to time the fund will be diminished, it is just as likely also to be from time to time increased, as he intends to pay into it all sums accruing to him from outside sources. His optimism increasing as he spins his web of words around his subject and himself, his prophetic eye sees the fund " swelling wisibly " by royalties " from, for instance, the Paris performances of my works ". Nor does his generosity end even here. As the King is to be made legal heir of whatever he may be possessed of at the time of his death, " the assumption — flattering to me, perhaps — that this fund of 40,000 gulden, undiminished if not actually increased, will return to him after my death, perhaps does not wholly lack foundation." But in any case the interest on this capital will allow him to come to the rescue of the needy as he would so much like to do, but which he cannot do at present, at any rate without " a real prejudice to my domestic economy ".

3

It was on the 8th August that Wagner laid this new case of his before Ludwig, enclosing with his private letter the more formal document intended for the Treasury officials. The next day, accompanied only by his servant Franz and the dog, he went off to the Hochkopf, to a royal lodge in the mountains overlooking the Walchensee, 3,000 feet above sea level, which Ludwig had affectionately placed at his disposal in order that he might recuperate after the excitement of the *Tristan* production and the shock of Schnorr's death. There he remained until the 21st, when he returned to the capital. Cosima and Hans had left Munich about the same time as himself: they had gone to meet Liszt in Pesth, where the first performance of *St. Elisabeth* was to take place on the 15th, to be succeeded by other Liszt works during the following fortnight. The pair did not return to Munich until the 13th September. In the solitude of the Hochkopf, in much discomfort and in weather that was mostly bad and that in the end drove him back to the town earlier than he had planned,[7] Wagner sank himself in a reading of the *Ramayana* and in broodings upon his own and Cosima's wretchedness.

If ever it is published in full, the "Brown Book" — a diary bound in brown leather that had been presented to him by Cosima — should prove, judging from the extracts so far vouchsafed to us, one of the three or four most interesting of all the Wagner docu-

---

[7] The living conditions in these mountain retreats of the King were evidently of the most primitive kind. Ludwig, a hardy young giant with a passion for walking and climbing and riding, no doubt thought roughing it good fun. The sybaritic Wagner did not. Night had descended, he notes in the "Brown Book", before he reached the hut, in advance of the others. He had a big bunch of keys with him; having found the right one he stumbled into the hut in the darkness, found the King's sleeping-place, and lay down exhausted, bathed in perspiration. The luggage bearers arrived at last, but it was some time before Franz could get a light. "Extraordinary confusion. At last with Franz alone. An absolute wilderness. No water to be found anywhere. Where is there a spring? We had omitted to enquire. We went groping for one on the mountain, in the wood. In vain! A laborious change of clothes. What a mess! At last we find bread, wine and sausages. But no water! We had to unpack the mineral water brought for my cure. Then a bright idea. Franz had packed my white dressing-gown. Enveloped in this splendour I roamed once more over the wooded heights, looking for water. The moon came out: I must have been a marvellous sight!" (The excerpts from the "Brown Book" will be found in KLRWB, I, li–lxv: they cover not only the Hochkopf period but the first few weeks after Wagner's return to Munich on the 21st August).

ments.[8] It is a new Wagner that we meet with here. His prose works and many of his letters suffer from a plethora of words and an often unbelievable clumsiness of construction, the result, perhaps, of too great an anxiety to convince his audience. But in the " Brown Book " he had no audience, for these pages were meant for no eyes but his own and, later, those of Cosima. We see him communing with himself; and for the first time we get an inkling of how it was that his conversation exercised such compelling power over all who were by nature in tune with him. For as he writes in the " Brown Book " so, one imagines, he must have talked, in short, pointed sentences which, for all the load of knowledge and experience and reflection they carry, travel on the swiftest of wings. On the 10th September we find him musing upon the " eternal return " — to employ a term made familiar to us later by Nietzsche — that seems to govern the lives of men. It was just a year ago, he notes, that Cosima had left him in misery: now she has obeyed another call to her father: and a year hence, no doubt, he will be separated from her again. The thought sets his mind running on varieties of life and character as expressible in terms of musical form:

" In the canon is reflected the ordinary life of the average man — a theme that repeats itself unchanged, rounding itself off solely by means of itself: a character that is always the same, and therefore maintains everything around it the same. Then there is the fugue: the theme remains fundamentally the same throughout, but it has free contrapuntal counter-subjects, which permit it to show itself in one new light after another; it shortens and extends itself, it modulates; the course of the fugue cannot be determined in advance, like that of the unalterable canon; and it finishes only on the organ point of Death. The great and rich character gets no further than the theme of a fine Bach fugue: at most it acquires a fine counter-theme, and then it triumphs; and when the double fugue shows the two themes always

[8] The story of the substitution of the "Annals" for the "Red Book" has been told in Vol. II, pp. 157-8. To that record it should be added that the "Annals" summarising the period from Easter 1846 to 1867 were written in the "Brown Book" in February, 1868. After that, apparently, the pages of the "Brown Book" reverted to their original purpose for a time; but at the end of 1868 Wagner entered in it the "Annals" for that year. There are no entries in the "Brown Book" for the years 1874-9. Wagner took it up again in August, 1880 and used it at intervals between then and the early part of 1882 for the recording of stray thoughts on various subjects. See Otto Strobel's article on *Richard Wagners "Braunes Buch"*, in BFF, 1934, pp. 113-122.

distinctly recognisable and always significant, then life acquires its highest beauty. The two intertwine, separate and re-unite, as in the dance. . . . We two [himself and Cosima] live as a good Bachian double fugue.

" Your father's [Liszt's] life-course expresses itself, for me, in variation form. Here there is simply the original theme, always repeated, yet always unchanged; ornamented, embellished, now the virtuoso, now the diplomat, now the warrior, now the ecclesiastic, always the artist, always charming, always himself, at bottom utterly unlike anyone else, and therefore presenting himself to the world only in variation form; always the personality in the forefront, clearly perceivable, always so posed that it shows to the best advantage, as it were in a prism; always unique, always surprising, yet always the same — and, it goes without saying, after each variation, applause: then comes the peroration, the apotheosis — the coda of the variations. I have nothing against this form: I know that by means of it Beethoven has called into being the most marvellous shapes — the adagios of his quartets, the finale of the Eroica, the andante of the C minor symphony are all constructed in the variation form. But I myself am no good whatever in this form: I can't vary a theme at all! " [9]

The diary shows him longing to make Cosima his wife in all men's eyes and to retire with her into a solitude in which he can devote himself entirely to creative work. Here and there we come upon a sentence or two that throws a faint light on the " triangle " and increases our already legitimate doubt whether Bülow was as " deceived " as the accepted legend makes him out to have been.[10] Cosima has apparently written to Wagner that in Vienna, on their way to Pesth, Hans had refused to go with her to Penzing — where,

---

[9] He is speaking half-ironically, of course, his eye being on the variation-form of human life and character rather than on variation-form in its purely musical sense. Strictly speaking, his own art in its maturer manifestations is constituted of endless thematic variation. But, as he well knew, "abstract" variation, variation for variation's sake, was not his line. He could not spin new musical tissues out of a theme unless it represented, for him, some aspect of the soul or of the world: then, as we know, his creative imagination could play endlessly upon it. In 1871 he was comically angry with himself for having begun the *Kaisermarsch*, a species of composition which he knew to be utterly alien to his genius, and which he was well aware would result, in his case, in little of any real value. He could do nothing in the way of musical "development", he told Cosima in effect, unless he could link up a theme with "ideas", and once he began to do that, the thing proliferated *ad infinitum*. "A march is an absurd affair; at most it can only be a Volkslied, yet it isn't to be sung — it's nonsensical! I must have my big thread from which to develop my music. I can't do anything in this mode." MECW, I, 550.

[10] For a discussion of this subject see Chapter XXI.

as we can readily imagine, she wanted to see the house in which Wagner had joyed and suffered so greatly — but had taken her instead on a round of the Vienna shops: Bülow was perhaps in one of his difficult moods, and, wanting to hurt Cosima, chose the most effective way of doing so — through her affection for Wagner. " This fool, this Hans! " exclaims Wagner in his diary. " Can one believe it? And yet this man is now my sole friend! O blöde Herzen! blinde Augen!! [11] . . . Only *you* have any rights over me: no one else knows me at all. O heaven, how long yet must we endure this existence? And yet — did we not find each other in it? "

4

Now and then he confides to the pages of his diary a reflection on his art. We realise what agonies of ecstasy he had gone through during the *Tristan* performances, and how he shrank from the thought of undergoing such experiences again, even had such a thing been possible now that death had taken Schnorr from him.

> " O fate! . . . no longer to feel in the depths of my being any joy in my own work! How can I think of the only pleasure I have ever had from any of my works, how can I think of *Tristan*, without renouncing all joy henceforth for ever? I shudder when I think of *Tristan*! And that was the only time, the only time, when I was happy! "

Here, as in many other passages in the diary and in his letters, we cannot be quite sure whether by his " Tristan " he means his opera or Schnorr: at that time, indeed, the two concepts were hardly separable in his mind. But apart from the crushing blow of Schnorr's death, his spiritual anguish came from that peculiar weariness of himself as an artist that seems to have taken possession of him more than once in after years, especially after a period either of intensive new creation or of almost equally intensive re-creation of an older work of his in the theatre. As he told Cosima at a much later date, a new work was finished, for him, when, after years of brooding upon it, sketching for it, organising the material as a whole and spinning each finest thread of it in detail, he could at last see the

---

[11] Isolde's words (in reversed order) to Brangaene in Act I of *Tristan* — "O blinded eyes! O foolish hearts! —"

thing with his inner eye as an organic entity: after that, to have to spend long hours and days at his desk merely in order to put all this on paper in a form in which it would be accessible to others was little more than drudgery for him. It was in some such mood as this that in August, 1865, torn between the desire to forget the crude outer universe, to plunge once more into the inner world which he felt to be his own, and the repulsion of his sick nerves and tired body from the thought of facing once more the long slavery of composition on paper, that he noted in the " Brown Book ",

> " Muse as I will, in the end I turn away from it all with a certain weariness, because I feel that I have thought it all before. I keep lighting on ideas I already had: the charm of discovery has disappeared completely, and there remains to grip me nothing but the working-out of the form, the purely artistic joy of bringing the idea to full realisation. I hope to find a good deal of satisfaction in this; though to be sure I shall be subject to the disturbance of always having to cast a side-glance on the translation of it into actuality through the medium of the ordinary sort of performer. Schnorr's death constitutes an at present immeasurably significant dividing line in my life. In front of just *what* it signifies I stand as yet astonished and dazed, without power to think, and hardly to feel. I cannot grasp it, still less fathom it. A vast change will and must take place in me: up to that point I could go upon a possibility — now this is exhausted, and ' possibility ' has no further meaning for me."

The subconscious impulse within him to seek salvation from his physical and mental miseries in creative work turned him first of all in the direction of the *Ramayana,* in which, for a moment or two, he half-managed to persuade himself that he had found the subject for a new drama, just as a previous absorption in the Indian world, in his Venice days, had given him the idea of *Die Sieger.* This mood does not seem to have lasted long with him; perhaps the figure of Rama and its environment resembled those of Savitri too closely for his imagination to be able to give individual form to them both. He took up *Siegfried* again, though we cannot be sure whether it was to continue with the scoring of the second act or to add a few pages to the fair copy of the full score of the first act which he had begun eight years ago in Zürich.[12] A little while later,

---

[12] He may have occupied himself with both these tasks. See KLRWB, I, liv, and V, 169.

after his return to Munich, his thoughts turned in yet another direction. By a curious coincidence, the King had broached the subject of *Parsifal* at virtually the very time when Wagner's own mind had spontaneously reverted to it. " How marvellous! ", he notes in the " Brown Book " on the 26th August, " the King ardently desires to hear about *Parzival.*" [13] It was on the 21st that Ludwig had written him asking him to " communicate his plans concerning *Die Sieger* and *Parcival* ". The letter had been addressed to the Hochkopf. On the 21st, however, Wagner returned to Munich, where the King's letter seems to have caught up with him on the 26th. He began his long Prose Sketch for the drama on the 27th, and by the 30th it was finished: although, as he told the King, he had not consulted the sources of the story since the idea of an opera on the Parsifal subject had first occurred to him in 1845, the theme had taken such deep root in him and proliferated so luxuriantly during his many years of brooding on it that the two days he had first allotted to the carrying out of the King's wish had proved insufficient. [14]

One entry in the " Brown Book " on the 15th August raises our curiosity only to defeat it: " I have received an announcement of poor Zahlberg's death. What a fate! " From a passage in Wagner's letter of the 20th August to the King we gather that this Zahlberg was a young musician, a Münchener by birth, who lived in Karlsruhe — apparently as a member of the Opera orchestra. He

---

[13] It was not until 1877 that Wagner finally discarded this and other spellings of the name for that of "Parsifal".

[14] The Sketch, which runs to nearly twenty closely-printed pages, will be found in RWGS, XI, 395–413. It is not included in the English edition of the Prose Works.

A recent biographer of King Ludwig, who is largely indebted to his imagination for his facts, has described for us, in such detail as to suggest that he was a privileged eye-witness of it all, how Wagner, obeying Ludwig's call, "met him in the hunting lodge on the Hochkopf," how the pair spent "a sun-drenched day" together on the "wonderful flower-strewn alpine meadow", how, "stretched out by the young man on a hillock, the idea of the *Parsifal* poem suddenly (*sic!*) came to the Master", how he "wrote it down at once in a detailed sketch", and how he sent the completed draft to the King "some weeks later". The truth is that Ludwig was never once on the Hochkopf during the twelve days that Wagner spent there, that the *Parsifal* subject had been occupying the latter's attention, off and on, for some twenty years, that the sketch was not made on the Hochkopf but after Wagner's return to Munich, and that he did not send it to the King "some weeks later" but the day (the 31st August) after the completion of it — a delay just long enough to permit of his making a fair copy of it for the King in his famous calligraphy.

This fair copy, by the way, differs somewhat from the original as set down in the "Brown Book". It is the original, apparently, that has been reprinted in RWGS.

had called on Wagner in Munich in the preceding February, impressed him by his lofty idealism, and shown him an orchestral work of his that convinced Wagner that he had " great talent ". Wagner had planned to transplant him to Munich as a teacher in the Music School. Earlier in August he had obtained from the King a grant of 100 florins for Zahlberg, apparently by way of help in his illness. Wagner so rarely praised the music of his younger contemporaries even to their face that we cannot help feeling there may have been something out of the common in a young composer whom he could describe to others as possessing " great talent ". Zahlberg's name seems to be quite unknown to musicographers.

5

Between his arrival in Munich in May, 1864 and the point (August, 1865) at which we have now arrived, Wagner had had from the royal treasury in gifts alone, independently of his stipend, no less a sum than 26,400 gulden.[15] He was now coolly asking for a further gift of 40,000 gulden — for a gift pure and simple, of course, he intended it to be; all his fine talk about the sum being a loan, repayable to King Ludwig after his death, meant nothing at all — plus an assured income henceforth of 8,000 gulden per annum from the income on the capital sum of 160,000 gulden that was to be allocated for his benefit, plus, again, the free occupancy, for his lifetime, of the large house in the Briennerstrasse. Evidently his pre-Munich liabilities had been enormous, while his latest scale of living was so generous that if fresh debts were not to be piled up the King would some day have to dip still more deeply into his pocket. Wagner could hardly have been so blind as not to see that these new demands of his on the King would generate further unfriendliness towards him in ministerial quarters; yet he persisted in them, in the teeth of all opposition, until his objects had been completely attained. Perhaps he had recognised, by August, 1865, the advisability of making his financial position fully and finally impregnable. We seem to catch a faint hint here and there in his letters of a suspicion that some day he might be forced to leave Munich, if

[15] A summary of his cost to Bavaria between 1864 and 1867 will be given later. See *infra*, pp. 466–8.

not, indeed, Bavaria. There were times, no doubt, when he longed to be done with all this intrigue and fighting and come to a reckoning with the too-long neglected artist within him. In October, 1865 there is a wistful entry in the " Brown Book " that supports this conjecture. " O Cosima! ", he writes,

" will it ever come about that I can tranquilly complete my works and enter with you into the promised land of peace? How that longing keeps surging up again and again! It seems as though I desire the most unnatural condition of things, which the world simply will not grant. I am full of care: one strain, one agitation, succeeds another, within me and without. The King's love is a veritable crown of thorns. Treachery lurks at the centre of things, lying in wait, ready for the spring, and our gentle longing for peace is no match for it. . . . O heaven, could I but be happy with you and little Isolde! Happy!! Yes, we *could* be so. . . ." [16]

As for the King, while Wagner never had much reason to doubt that his loyalty would survive every test, there were two contingencies to be taken into consideration — Ludwig might die before him, or, in one of his fits of frustrated idealism, he might abdicate; in either case the politicians would be fairly sure to close down on Wagner as soon as the contract of October, 1864 reached its legal term.

That agreement had been for three years only, during which period Wagner was to complete and deliver the *Ring* against certain payments. Ten months had gone by since the contract was made, and though it is not true, as Stemplinger alleges, that Wagner had done no work at all at the *Ring* during all this time — as we have seen, he had scored part of *Siegfried,* — it was becoming less probable each month that the whole tetralogy would be finished by October, 1867; and article eight of the contract had stipulated that if Wagner had not carried out his part of the agreement within three years the Treasury was to have the right, without the possibility of appeal on his part, to demand repayment of whatever money he had drawn under the contract. He could afford to smile at this and other conditions of the agreement so long as Ludwig remained King; [17] but he must sometimes have reflected that it

---

[16] See BFF, 1937, p. 156.

[17] The King did indeed, some four years later, go so far as to hint at withdrawing Wagner's allowance; but that was in a passing fit of exasperation not merely with

might be no smiling matter for him were his protector to die or ab-
dicàte. We cannot blame him for being anxious to ensure his material well-being fœ the remainder of his days. His earlier operas,
in spite of their huge popularity, brought him in next to nothing
now. There seemed no future for *Tristan* now Schnorr was dead,
nor had he any desire to hand this work over to the tender mercies
of the ordinary German theatre. The *Meistersinger* and the *Ring*
were incomplete; the music of *Parsifal* had not even been begun,
apart from an odd sketch or two. He was unshakably true to his
artistic ideal, and to his conviction that his mission was not to provide the German theatres with lucrative box-office attractions but
to promote German culture by means of a few model performances
of his works in a theatre of his own. The King had brought him
to Munich on the specific understanding that he was to pursue their
common ideal secure henceforth from anxiety about his livelihood:
he was entitled, therefore, to take all reasonable steps to ensure
his economic safety for the remainder of his days. The mistake he
made was the dual one of asking for much more than was reasonable, and then working indefatigably for the removal from office
of the politicians who stood in the way of his getting it. But here
again the matter was by no means as simple as it appears to be on
the surface: Wagner had ultimately managed to convince himself
that in intriguing against the politicians as he did he was serving the
King's interests no less than his own.

It was not until the 18th October that he was given the 40,000
gulden he had asked for on the 8th August, and not until the 26th
November that his allowance was raised to the desired 8,000 gulden
per annum. The dates of themselves indicate that difficulties had
sprung up in official quarters. A major crisis had in fact developed
about the middle of October, when we find Pfistermeister telling
Cosima, with a certain amount of temper, that Wagner has just
shown with regard to him a mistrust such as he had never met with
elsewhere in his twenty years of office; [18] in consequence he has felt

Wagner but with things in general. There was never the least likelihood of his actually doing anything of that kind.

[18] Wagner's nerves had evidently gone to pieces about this time. Peter Cornelius,
in his letters of September to Bertha Jung, speaks of his irritability, and reports him
as saying, "I can't talk to anyone, can't see anyone: if I talk with the least excitement for half an hour, I get an attack of hysteria." He has told his servant to deny

compelled to ask to be relieved of the duty, in future, of acting as intermediary between his Majesty and Wagner; this request the King has granted. What had happened was that on the 10th October Cosima — who seems to have carried on most of the negotiations connected with these latest financial proposals of Wagner — had been officially informed by Pfistermeister of the result of his latest conference with the King on the matter. At the end of September, it appears, he had reminded Ludwig that as a new Bavarian financial year would begin on the 1st October it was high time the government department concerned received definite instructions regarding the suggested additional grants to Wagner. The King had replied that the matter was to stand over for the present, as he intended to discuss it verbally with Wagner when he (the King) returned from Hohenschwangau to Munich. When Pfistermeister broached the subject again, apparently at Cosima's urging, on the 5th October, he received the reply that his Majesty himself had written to Wagner to assure him that the necessary instructions would be given " as soon as might be feasible ", which, however, was not at present.

Pfistermeister raised the question with the King once more on the 6th. Ludwig's reply, which Pfistermeister passed on to Cosima in his letter of the 10th, was to the effect that obviously Wagner wanted the 40,000 gulden for the liquidation of old liabilities, that his Majesty had already given him substantial sums for similar purposes, and that he positively would not pay any more of his debts. The King's object had been, and still was, to " maintain the distinguished and beloved poet-composer in a position in which he would never again have to worry about his livelihood "; and Wagner had assured him, in the preceding autumn, that the contract of that date would provide for all his requirements then and in the future. The King is willing now not only to increase Wagner's yearly allowance to 8,000 gulden but to present him outright with

his door to everyone — he has gone away, he needs quietness, complete seclusion, and so on. But, as was always the case with Wagner, these moods of depression alternated with outbursts of the gayest spirits.

Cornelius had returned to Munich in August after some five months' residence in Weimar. He found on his return that Wagner had gone very grey in the face: it was "not a good colour", Cornelius comments. The two things that had hit Wagner hardest were Schnorr's death in July and the four weeks of separation from Cosima in August and September.

the Briennerstrasse property, which means, in effect, the addition of a further 2,000 gulden a year to his income; and with all this, he thinks, Wagner ought to be satisfied. Wagner should let his creditors know not merely that this is the full extent of his resources, but that these royal benefactions are not liable to legal attachment in respect of debt. But his Majesty simply will not discharge any further Wagnerian liabilities, since no one can be sure that still others will not come to light after the grant of this 40,000 gulden. The King had repeated these remarks to Pfistermeister yet again on the 9th. Wagner, in a fury, passed this letter of the Cabinet Secretary on to the King, whereupon, as we have seen, Pfistermeister as good as told the latter that he would no longer concern himself with Wagner and his affairs.

6

Wagner's temper was unmistakable in a highly sophistical letter of the 17th October to the second Cabinet Secretary, Johann Lutz,[19] in which he spoke so slightingly of Pfistermeister's honour that Lutz, in his reply of the 24th, was compelled to administer a solemn reproof. The official Wagnerians have always maintained that Pfistermeister played a double game with Wagner in this affair. The documents now available do not support that charge. If anyone was to blame it seems to have been the King, who obviously had his doubts as to the wisdom of presenting Wagner with a fresh 40,000 gulden outright, but who seems to have been guilty of at least one verbal indiscretion as the result of which Wagner was led to believe that the money was as good as in his pocket. The King, during this autumn of 1865, was even fuller than before of affection for him; again and again he assured him that he need have no fears about the future — that not only should he be set above all care as to his livelihood but the schemes for the Music School and the festival theatre would be carried through as quickly as possible. He told

---

[19] Like Pfistermeister, this Johann Lutz — in 1866 an Oberappellationsgerichtsrat (judge in a high court of appeal) — was a village schoolmaster's son. He was the Vicar of Bray of Bavarian politics: each ebb and flow of the tide deposited this crafty schemer a few yards nearer his goal each year. By 1886 he was Baron von Lutz, Minister of Culture and President of the Ministerial Council, in which capacity he played a prominent part in the plot for the arrest and deposition of the King.

Cosima, also, that it would have been a crime not to have rescued Wagner. But from motives either of personal delicacy where Wagner was concerned or of prudence where his officials were concerned he shrank from discussing the sordid details of these financial demands with Wagner himself. Those details he went into with his Cabinet Secretaries, who were then instructed to communicate the royal intentions to Wagner, or, as was more often the case, to Cosima.

It can be conceded, in justice to Wagner, that it was quite natural for him to regard Pfistermeister's letter of the 10th October to Cosima as being in flat contradiction with a previous letter to her of the 26th August. Finance, as Pfistermeister more than once reminded Cosima, was not within his official province as Cabinet Secretary, a matter on which he congratulated himself. He was merely, as he put it, the speaking-tube between the King and Wagner. His Majesty, Pfistermeister had said in his letter of the 26th August, had ordered him to say that he would grant Wagner " (1) the free use of Briennerstrasse No. 21 . . . ; (2) a capital sum of 40,000 florins under his own administration, the interest on which is to be at his own disposal, but the capital itself is to revert to his Majesty on Wagner's death; (3) a yearly stipend of 8,000 florins payable by the Cabinet financial department." On the face of it this looks like giving Wagner everything he had asked for in his petition of the 8th August; but if we examine Pfistermeister's words a little more closely we see that it is not quite the same thing. Wagner, it is true, is to get the 8,000 gulden a year he had asked for, but it is not to be provided for by the permanent ear-marking for his benefit of a capital sum of 150,000 gulden: it is to be paid annually out of the Treasury, and, as Pfistermeister expressly points out, it is to be subject, like the two other clauses, to the usual pro forma condition that the grant is to continue " until his Majesty orders otherwise ".

Clause 2, again, is so carelessly worded — the Treasury lawyers assuredly would never have allowed it to go out in this form! — as to be susceptible of two interpretations. Wagner could be forgiven for taking it to mean that the capital of the 40,000 gulden was to be given straight away into his absolute control — which is what he had suggested in his petition. But manifestly if that were to happen there was no assurance whatever that the capital would be intact at his death. He himself had said that he proposed to draw upon it from time to time for sundry purposes of the moment, such as the payment of old debts, but that he hoped to make up deductions of this kind by paying in to the fund any chance receipts that might come his way, such as royalties for performances of his operas. No lawyer and no financier, of course, would take vague talk of this kind seriously. The clear implication of Pfistermeister's second clause is that the full capital sum shall beyond question revert to the King after Wagner's death. But this in turn implies either that it should not be subject to diminution at Wagner's caprice, or alternatively that whatever might be taken out of it at one time should as a matter of course be returned to it at another. As there is no provision made for either of these contingencies, the inference is that the King did not really contemplate the capital of 40,000 passing into Wagner's unfettered control. In view of the loose wording of the clause, however, it is not surprising that Wagner looked no further than the words " a capital sum of 40,000 florins under his own administration ", took them at their face value, and believed he had been granted all he had asked for. We can understand, therefore, that Pfistermeister's announcement, on the 10th October, that the King would *not* give him 40,000 gulden for the liquidation of his debts, and indeed would not be answerable for any further debts of his, must have been a great shock to him.

7

To his letter of the 15th to Cosima, in which he refuses to have anything more to do with Wagner's financial affairs, Pfistermeister adds a curt and acid postscript: " His Majesty has just this moment charged me to say that in my last letter [i.e., that of the 10th, which Wagner, in his fury, had passed on to the King] I did not express his royal opinion quite accurately. I hereby carry out this command." Evidently Ludwig still shrank from discussing finance in detail direct with Wagner, and more especially from being personally concerned in the blank refusal of his request for an out-and-out donation. So once more he evades the real point at issue. In his personal letter to Wagner of the 12th, written after having

received from him Pfistermeister's letter of the 10th, he says no
more about the matter than this:

" What unexampled confusion! But forgive the poor man [Pfister-
meister], who thought he was serving me in so pitiable a way. My
dear one, nothing will separate us, not even death itself. Nothing can
shake my faith in you; and I know that yours in me will never waver.
Once more, do not bear him a grudge for his clumsiness."

It will be observed, however, that while trying to smooth Wagner
down by making it appear that Pfistermeister had been lacking in
tact, he does not say a word in repudiation of the material facts in
the Secretary's letter of the 10th October. Had that letter *not* expressed his own views as to the undesirability of once more giving
Wagner a large sum for the payment of old debts and thus encouraging him to contract new ones, nothing would have been easier than
for him to say so now.[20] And that his Secretary had done no more
than faithfully pass on to Cosima the opinions expressed by his
liege lord in their conversation of the 7th is further proved by
Lutz's letter of the 14th to Cosima. The second Cabinet Secretary,
who is manifestly dealing with the matter now because the first has
asked the King to excuse him from having any further communication, direct or indirect, with Wagner, is writing, it will be observed,
two days after Ludwig has half-apologised for the phraseology
of Pfistermeister's letter without in the smallest degree repudiating
the substance of it. Lutz's letter is in effect simply a repetition of
Pfistermeister's.

---

[20] Arthur Hübscher (HNBW, pp. 607–8) says that Wagner raised the question
of the 40,000 gulden personally with the King at their meeting in Munich on the
2nd October, that Pfistermeister "urgently warned Ludwig against granting the request", and that "the King, half-convinced, told him to send Wagner a refusal, but
afterwards, suddenly changing his mind, wrote to Wagner that what Pfistermeister
would say to him was quite contrary to his own [Ludwig's] view and his liberal intentions, and that Wagner was to have patience — he would receive the desired
amount."

The King had indeed returned from Hohenschwangau to Munich for the "Octo-
berfest" on the 2nd October, and had granted Wagner an audience. There is at
present no evidence, however, that the matter of the 40,000 gulden was then discussed between them, that Pfistermeister "urgently warned" the King against giving Wagner this sum, or that, having instructed Pfistermeister to send Wagner a
refusal, Ludwig told him, behind the Secretary's back, that the letter would not be
the expression of his real views. The subject is not mentioned at all in the King's
letters to Wagner in October. Hübscher presumably bases his story on the evidence
of Pfistermeister's unpublished diary. It would be interesting to have the relative
entries at first hand in full.

" While I was making my report to his Majesty yesterday he communicated to me, with regard to the financial affairs — still in a state of suspense — of Richard Wagner, some remarks which he considers necessary for the elucidation of this matter. His Majesty said that so far he had hesitated to give an order to the Cabinet Treasury Department for the payment to Herr Wagner of the 40,000 gulden under discussion; nor are the misgivings that operated with his Majesty yet removed. It is necessary for his Majesty to point out that he has gladly offered Herr Wagner everything necessary to enable him to fulfil his great artistic mission, and to guarantee him, for that purpose, freedom from outer cares; and it would be superfluous to remark that there has not been the smallest change in the convictions that determined him to act thus. If therefore his Majesty has hesitated as yet to hand over to him the desired 40,000 gulden, it is not merely out of consideration for the Cabinet Treasury but from the conviction that this course is in the best interests of Herr Wagner himself, and that for the following reasons. All that has happened in the meantime has convinced his Majesty that the 40,000 gulden are intended, at all events for the most part, to liquidate earlier liabilities of Herr Wagner. If, however, the means for so doing are to be given him again and again, then the object in view — to secure peace for Herr Wagner — will certainly not be attained.

" His Majesty believes that a much better way of achieving this purpose is to grant him an annual endowment which will be secure from legal attachment by creditors. . . . More than once already his Majesty has helped Herr Wagner to discharge ancient liabilities, in the belief that all matters of the past would thus be put in order. It would be fatal for his Majesty if, notwithstanding all this, still more liabilities should come to light, calling for new and larger sums for their liquidation, especially as his Majesty has no assurance that when these have been dealt with still other claims will not make their appearance later which Herr Wagner has overlooked at the moment.[21] His Majesty has reason to fear that acceding to Herr Wagner's requests would necessitate a regrettable curtailment of the amounts necessary to, and intended for, the realisation of the great artistic ideals which they have in common; these amounts, like all other things, are definitely

---

[21] Perhaps the King had been reminded of Wagner's letter of the 6th June, 1864 to Pfistermeister, in which, asking for 16,000 gulden to pay his debts, he had said he was sure that he could in time make this good out of the royalties to accrue from his as yet unperformed works; he would therefore regard the 16,000 gulden "in no wise as a gift, but as a loan" to be repaid to the King. Now, in August, 1865, he was asking for a further 40,000 gulden, once more not as a gift but as a loan, and once more promising, or at any rate hoping, to replace any sums withdrawn from that capital out of these still problematical royalties. Could Pfistermeister, or the King, or indeed anyone in his senses, persuade himself that the solemn comedy would not be staged yet a third time as soon as the 40,000 gulden had disappeared?

limited. Consequently his Majesty earnestly hopes that you [Cosima] will once more go into this matter thoroughly with Herr Wagner, and be good enough to let me know whether the economic affairs of Herr Wagner cannot be put in order without the payment to him of the 40,000 gulden under discussion." [22]

8

There can be no doubt that the King entirely agreed with his officials that it would be better for everyone, in the long run, that help for Wagner should take the form of a handsome yearly allowance unattachable for debt, rather than a large capital sum to be given into his absolute keeping, with the practical certainty that it would mostly be spent on personal indulgence, leading in due course to more pressure from creditors, more public scandal, and further calls on the bounty of the King. If the suggestion came originally from Pfistermeister, it shows a regard for Wagner's interests, as well as those of the state, for which he ought to be given proper credit. If, as is at least equally probable, the suggestion was the King's, it constitutes a further proof that Ludwig was far from being the mere " dupe " of the current legend, whose adolescent inexperience of the world was basely exploited by Wagner. Whenever it became necessary for the boy to discriminate between Wagner the man and Wagner the artist he had little difficulty in doing so. Vast as were his respect and affection for him, it is perfectly obvious that, as Gottfried von Böhm says, it was the artist, even more than the man, that he adored; and this youth of twenty, whose sanity some people professed to doubt, even in those days, whenever he did something or other that was incomprehensible to them, was keeping a commendably level head all through the developing crisis of the autumn of 1865, and, for all his romantic enthusiasm, seeing the situation as a whole much more realistically than Wagner did.

Wagner's psychology is no easier to understand in this episode than in many others of his strange life: well might he say that " the world did not know how to comport itself with regard to a man like him because it had never met with one like him before ".

---

[22] KLRWB, IV, 88.

It is often impossible to draw a clear dividing line between sincerity and play-acting in his conduct. Perhaps we are even guilty of a psychological crudity in calling him an actor at all, convenient as that facile simplification of him is, as Nietzsche, for example, dis-covered. He was primarily a dramatist, one of whose most com-plex psychological creations was himself. Even in his moments of deepest emotion and profoundest conviction he saw himself, in part, as a projection outside himself; and this projection he manipu-lated both consciously and unconsciously in accordance with the best rules of dramatic art. He had to an extraordinary degree the national faculty for duping himself with his own words, for mistak-ing his artfully constructed verbal fantasies for objective realities, for seeing only what he wanted to see, and convincing himself of the truth of whatever it suited him to believe at the moment. He would not merely have denied indignantly that he was going beyond the limits of strict sincerity or veracity: he would have been frankly unable to understand how such an idea could enter any reasonable person's head. All through the summer and autumn of 1865 he was at one and the same time protesting to the King that he was weary of the world and more than half in love with the idea of retirement from it into poverty, and fighting furiously to secure the handsome fortune on which he had set his heart. A nature like his could be perfectly sincere in both courses. There is abundant evi-dence that after the production of *Tristan,* when the long emotional tension was at last relaxed, and when the death of Schnorr had not only shaken him to the depths as a man but destroyed, for the time being, his dream of a new era in the theatre, he felt a longing to seclude himself from the world and forget his miseries in the joys of creation. Upon that fascinating psychological theme the artist in him could enlarge *ad infinitum,* and the more eloquent he became upon it the more convincing he would find his own eloquence. But in his heart of hearts he knew perfectly well all the time that the King would never allow this charming poetic fancy of his to be transmuted into harsh reality; and so, step by step with his tearful protestations of a sensitiveness that unfits him to make a stand against the cruel world of facts, he presses untiringly his claim to a bounty which, according to his present notions, will guarantee him for the remainder of his days not merely immunity from want but an enviably comfortable existence. And so furious and concentrated was his attack that both the royal and the official opposition collapsed before it.

Wagner's angry letter to Lutz was dated the 17th October. On the very next day he was granted the 40,000 gulden,[23] in spite of all the brave protestations on Pfistermeister's and Lutz's part that the King was not disposed to hand that large sum of money over to him. Why the King surrendered so suddenly and so completely we do not know: perhaps he realised that as Wagner was certain to have his way sooner or later he might as well buy peace at once, even at this price. Over the Cabinet Secretariat Wagner had obtained so signal a victory that the officials could now no longer doubt that either they or he would some day, and that before long, have to come under the heel of the other. From the 20th October to the 1st November the King was in Switzerland; and Hübscher tells us — once more on the evidence, presumably, of Pfistermeister's unpublished diary — that during the royal absence the two Secre-

---

[23] The story of the 40,000 gulden being sent in sacks to the Briennerstrasse with a military escort — the alleged object being to attract attention and stir up public feeling against Wagner — has been told with varying degrees of embellishment in one Wagner Life after another. (See, on this point, Vol. I, p. X). At last we have the simple facts of the matter set forth in two virtually contemporary letters to King Ludwig, the first from Cosima, on the 1st January, 1866, the second from Wagner himself, on the following 9th June.

Cosima, it appears, was with Wagner when the official intimation reached him, on the 19th October, that the 40,000 gulden were at his disposal. She suggested that he should authorise her to collect the sum, her poetic idea being that as it had come to him in the first place from one "friendly hand" it ought to be conveyed to him by another. The suggestion chimed with his own feelings at the moment: he had no particular desire just then to present himself in person to the officials. To the Treasury, accordingly, went Cosima, accompanied by her eldest daughter and the children's governess. She had thought it would be a very simple matter of a handful of banknotes. Evidently, however, the officials were bent on being disagreeable. They told her, according to Wagner, that they had notes only for half the amount: the remainder she would have to take in silver coins. Cosima was quite equal to dealing with a situation of this kind. She calmly sent the governess for a couple of cabs, into which she herself helped to lift the heavy sacks; and she succeeded in shaming even the officials, whose churlish manners improved somewhat as the process of loading the cabs went on. That is all: there is not the slightest suggestion of trouble so far as the public was concerned.

Ironically enough, however, these two accounts of the affair differ on one vital point; whereas Wagner says that Cosima received half the amount in paper money, she herself writes to the King, "To my inexpressible astonishment I was told that I could have no paper money, but only hard cash." Thus difficult is it to arrive at the bare truth about the simplest matter in history, even on the contemporary testimony of the people directly concerned in it!

The letters will be found in KLRWB, I, lxxi, and II, 57.

taries, having discussed the matter together, drafted a document which Pfistermeister placed before Ludwig on his return. The contents of that document — if such a document there was — we do not at present know.

9

When Dr. Johnson said that poverty makes some virtues difficult and others impossible he stated only one half of a great truth. He forgot to add that money has a power of disinterested persuasion far above anything that mere verbal logic can achieve: many a man with a fanatical belief in the cosmic rightness of the communistic principle has suddenly been brought to see the flaws in his reasoning by the simple process of suddenly coming into a legacy. Sydney Smith humorously admitted the compelling force of this logic in his case. The timely death of a brother brought him a substantial inheritance. " This ", he wrote a little while later, " put me at my ease for my few remaining years. After buying into the Consols and the Reduced, I read Seneca *On the Contempt of Wealth*. What intolerable nonsense! " Wagner underwent a similar conversion immediately the 40,000 gulden became unquestionably his own. After a severe struggle with himself, no doubt, he decided that he would deny himself the spiritual uplift of a life of poverty just a little longer, very much as St. Augustine, racked by the flesh in the days of his hot youth, prayed, " Give me chastity, but not just yet! " Poverty and asceticism, Wagner perhaps said to himself, were undoubtedly good for the soul and pleasing in the sight of God: but all the same, 40,000 gulden would buy a lot of the delightful things in which Bertha dealt. And so we hear no more for a long time of his aspirations to follow in the footsteps of St. Francis.

As was more than once the case where Wagner was concerned, from stark mendicity to mild mendacity was only a step. On the 21st October we find him writing to August Röckel in terms decidedly more realistic than poetic; indeed, the only touch of the genuine poetic imagination in the letter is the transformation, by a wave of the magician's wand, of the King's magnificent 40,000 gulden into a modest 10,000. " In order to achieve independence in many things ", he tells Röckel, " and not be dependent on the paltry chicaneries of the Cabinet officials ", he has obtained from his royal patron " a little capital of 10,000 florins, the administration of which is entirely in my hands, but which . . . is to return, under my will, to the King at my death." Obviously he had two reasons for giving the figure as a mere 10,000 gulden — he did not wish the full amount of his good fortune to become generally known, lest the news should attract claims from ravenous creditors and other " old, unhappy, far-off things " (including, perhaps, Minna), and he meant to expend most of the remaining 30,000 gulden on domestic luxuries. He assures Röckel, as he had done the King, that whatever he may take out of the capital sum from time to time will be replaced by means of Berlin, Paris and other royalties. The main object of the 10,000 florins, however, is " to bring up, by means of a good rate of interest, my yearly income to the level indispensable to me." He asks Röckel if he can recommend a banking house that will pay him a high rate of interest and at the same time hold the capital sum at his disposal at a moment's notice. What he has in mind, in fact, is another Aguado — the Paris banker to whom, rather than to the proceeds of his operas, Rossini is said to have owed his large fortune, Aguado having not only invested the composer's money for him to the best advantage but handed over to him the profits of sundry more or less fictitious speculations made in his name. Röckel appears to have found in Frankfort a certain Hohenemser who was willing to look after Wagner's money: whether he proved to be another Aguado we do not know.

On the 22nd October Wagner went to Vienna, ostensibly to consult Standhartner about his health, to receive the attentions of his dentist, and to discuss with Fröbel the plan for settling the latter in Munich; but also, we may be permitted to surmise, to see Bertha Goldwag and place a few substantial orders with her. His presence in Vienna would, on this supposition, account for our having no Putzmacherin letters relating to this period. Apparently he invested a second 10,000 gulden somewhere or other a few weeks later, for at the end of the year we find Cornelius writing to his fiancée — the information having evidently come from Bülow —

" Just imagine, of the 40,000 gulden Wagner has put out only 20,000 at interest: the other 20,000 he has *already spent!* [24] What will be the end of this for him? What poverty may await him in his old age? "

10

This is a convenient place for a summary of Wagner's financial relations with the Bavarian Treasury from the time he settled in Munich to a date rather later than the one we have actually arrived at in our story, a date, however, which evidently seemed to the Treasury officials an appropriate one for calculating his total cost so far to King Ludwig and the state.

Dr. Otto Strobel [25] prints a statement, now reposing in the " Private Household Archives " of the Bavarian State, which purports to set forth the " expenditure on Richard Wagner " from the 10th May, 1864 to the middle of October, 1867. The total is given as 171,390 florins. The entries, however, are incorrect in some respects and misleading in others. The first entry, for instance — that of the 10th May, 1864 — is for 4,000 florins, representing the full annual stipend to be granted to Wagner; but as he drew it only from May 1st of that year, the amount actually received by him in 1864 in respect of that particular grant was only 2,665 florins. There are other overlappings of this kind in the course of the statement that give an erroneous idea of Wagner's actual drawings in respect of his stipend, the amount of which was altered three times between May, 1864 and October, 1865. Again, the 20,000 florins paid by the King as purchase money for the house in the Briennerstrasse figure in the statement as on the 17th April, 1866 — i.e., at the time when Wagner became the tenant of Triebschen; but no mention is made of the fact that when the arrangement was entered

<hr/>

[24] "Ausgegeben", however, may mean "parted with" as well as "spent". A letter of the 20th October to Gasperini shows Wagner sending the latter 3,000 francs to discharge an ancient debt to M. Lucy. (TLFW, p. 276). It appears that Lucy had been dunning him for this since the preceding May. Wagner's good fortune in Munich must have brought many an old-time creditor down on him ever since May 1864. The King, it is evident, was quite correct in his assumption that part at least of the 40,000 gulden would merely pass straight from the Bavarian Treasury into the pockets of creditors.

[25] KLRWB, V, 129. See also V, 230–232.

into with Wagner to cover the rental of Triebschen, the Munich house was returned by him to the Treasury. These 20,000 florins, therefore, really count twice in the statement — once in their simple and open original form as the price of the house, and again as implicit in the substitute transaction carried out later in connection with Triebschen. There are other complications with the disentanglement of which the reader need not be troubled in detail; while one or two items in the account are not strictly pertinent to it — the 1,200 florins, for example, put down as the cost of an ornamental cup presented to Wagner by the King, and 457 florins for the concert of the 5th October, 1864 in the court of the Munich Residenz at which the *Huldigungsmarsch* was first performed.

The essentials of the matter may be stated thus. Wagner's stipend, which was fixed at 4,000 florins per annum in May, 1864, was increased to 5,000 florins on the 1st November of that year, to 6,200 florins on the 1st August 1865, and to 8,000 florins on the following 1st October. In all he drew under the heading of stipend 24,783 florins between May, 1864 and the end of 1867.

The King's gifts to him, for liquidation of his debts or towards removal expenses or the furnishing of his Munich house, were 4,000 florins (10/5/64),[26] 16,000 (gift) and 4,000 (removal) (10/6/64), and 40,000 (18/10/65) — a total of 64,000 florins.

The settlement of the debt to Frau Salis-Schwabe in May, 1865 cost the Treasury 2,400 florins.

Under the contract made in October, 1864 Wagner was to receive a total sum of 30,000 florins for the *Ring*, of which 15,000 were to be paid to him at once, plus 1,500 as the first instalment of an extra 9,000 to be paid in six equal sums between October, 1864 and April, 1867. In April, 1865 he received a second instalment of 1,500 florins under this arrangement.

On the 17th April, 1866 the King granted him 5,000 francs (about 2,333 florins) towards the rent of Triebschen; in March, 1867 Wagner received a further 12,000 florins, and in the following October 6,000 florins, this 18,000 florins representing six years' (1867–1872) rent of Triebschen, at 3,000 florins a year.

[26] Wagner's receipt for that amount, dated the 9th May, 1864, has recently come to light: it will be found in KLRWB, V, 6. This is obviously the "small contribution towards what is most pressingly required for putting my affairs in order" to which Wagner refers in his letter of the 7th May to Heinrich Porges. See *supra*, p. 225.

(The 20,000 florins paid by the King in respect of the Brienner-strasse house do not, therefore, figure in our statement, as the agreement in respect of that house was carried over in a new form into the arrangement made with regard to Triebschen. The total of 20,333 florins granted Wagner for the rent of Triebschen from 1866 to 1872 is roughly equivalent to the 20,000 florins originally paid for the Munich house and presumably received for the re-sale of it after Wagner had returned it to the King in September, 1866).

The grand total of the personal cost of Wagner to Bavaria from May, 1864 to the end of 1867 was therefore some 130,000 florins. His later financial dealings with the King will be set forth in our narrative as occasion arises.

CHAPTER XIX

"—VICTORIA UTI NESCIS"

1

WAGNER'S PERSONAL relations with the King had been particularly cordial all through the summer and autumn of 1865: Ludwig was affectionately anxious to relieve, so far as lay in his power, the suffering that Schnorr's death had caused Wagner, while the latter's attentions to the King about this time were perhaps not entirely unmotived by his desire to make sure of the larger stipend and the gift of 40,000 gulden which he had in mind just then. Cosima also played her part in the cajoling of the King: in August — about the time, that is to say, when Wagner was making his formal financial proposals to the Treasury — she ventured to send Ludwig a " modest piece of work " of her own in which were set forth " the symbols of the great works " which Ludwig had made his own by his generous protection of Wagner. The " modest piece of work " was a cushion on which she had embroidered with her own hand " the Dutchman's ship, Tannhäuser's staff, Lohengrin's swan, Siegfried's sword, and Tristan's cup . . . all on the green ground of Hope . . . and surrounded by the flowers that bloomed so marvellously for Parsifal the Redeemer on Good Friday." [1] This remarkable work of art gave great pleasure to the King. It rejoiced him, he wrote to Cosima, to see the " noble figures from Wagner's blissful works " thus clearly set before him. " Here the luckless Seaman sails over the foaming waves, seeking salvation; here I see a Pilgrim entreating, broken and contrite . . . ; there the god-sent Hero approaches, in a boat drawn by a swan, coming from bliss and splendour into this world of falsehood and evil "; and so on in the romantic style that came naturally to him whenever he thought of Wagner's creations. He exhorts Cosima to co-operate

---

[1] This was Cosima's first letter to the King. It will be found in full in KLRWB, IV, 74–5.

with him in shielding the Unique One from all the world's ills and
helping him to accomplish his divine mission.

Ludwig was even more delighted with the so-called " Wagner
Book " presented to him in October — copies, in Cosima's handwriting, of Wagner's writings during his first Paris period and the
Dresden and Zürich years. He sent the fair scribe, in return, a
sapphire — " the colour of Faith " — " as symbol of the firm faith
and unshakeable confidence that inspire me and give me heart to
do all that it lies in me to do in order to help build the great, the
ETERNAL work."

Wagner, for his part, was equally generous, and at smaller cost
to himself if not to others. At the end of July he had written Otto
Wesendonk a letter that is at the same time one of his masterpieces
of sophistry and an indication of the thickness of skin that helped
him through so many crises in which a man of more delicate scru-
pulosity might have had to confess himself beaten. He does not
deny Otto's " most generous and self-sacrificing sympathy " in connection with the *Ring,* but he assures him that even this had been
insufficient to call the complicated work into being; for that a King
had been required. More than a year ago, he blithely reminds Otto,
he had had to beg him to regard the advances made to him as lost,
there being no possibility of repaying them out of the proceeds of
the publication of the scores. Still, the eternal optimist " does not
abandon the hope of some day repaying you these advances ":
though evidently the voice of honour had never so much as whis-
pered to him that it would be a graceful gesture to offer to pass on
to Wesendonk some of the money he had received, or was about to
receive, from the King. The fact is, he continues airily, that he now
has to ask Otto to " give up all your claims upon my *Nibelungen*
works." " These works should and must belong to the King of
Bavaria ", who has done and is doing so much for him. And so he
hopes Otto will understand, and be kind to him, when he begs him
" to give up, in friendly and liberal wise, the original orchestral
score of the *Rhinegold* which is now in your hands." The noble
Wesendonk, who, in spite of all he had done for Wagner, was destined to be treated in so shabby a way in *Mein Leben,* of course
acceded to this cool request, and was rewarded with an autograph
letter from the King, who seems to have felt some of the scruples

which one might reasonably have expected from Wagner: " Rest assured ", he wrote, " that for my own part I would never have put forward such a claim: the idea of obtaining for me the precious manuscript of the splendid work was Wagner's own."

With another score of his, Wagner was less fortunate. In the Vienna days Cornelius had voluntarily undertaken to make a copy of the new Venusberg scene written for the Paris production of *Tannhäuser*, Wagner's manuscript having by this time become considerably the worse for wear. Somehow or other the original got into the hands of Tausig; and this young man, whose manners were never of the best, and instincts never of the most delicate, took upon himself to make a present of it to Brahms, of all people. To add to the confusion, the copy made by Cornelius was appropriated by Weissheimer, who, while not staking out any legal claim to it, stuck to it, as he himself blandly confesses, in the hope that Wagner had forgotten where it was. For a long time, then, the composer had neither the original nor the copy of this still unprinted music of his. In the spring and summer of 1865, having discovered where the original manuscript was, he made frequent attempts to recover it from Brahms, who behaved throughout with a lack of breeding that today seems excessive even for him. Wagner's assurances that Tausig had never had the smallest right to present him or anyone else with the manuscript had no effect whatever on him. To letter after letter on the subject from Cornelius and Cosima he simply did not reply.[2] In 1875 Wagner, who wished to publish the new Venusberg music, had himself to write to Brahms, assuring him once more that the score had never been Tausig's or Cornelius's to give away, and asking him to return it to him " willingly and in a friendly spirit ". Brahms, in his reply, insisted on his " rights ". Later still he had the assurance to propose a deal — in return for the *Tannhäuser* score Wagner was to present him with a copy of the orchestral score of the *Meistersinger* and some small autograph or other. As Wagner could not obtain a *Meistersinger* score from his publisher he was compelled to buy Brahms off with a copy of the limited edition de luxe of the *Rhinegold*; he accompanied it with a

---

[2] An undated letter from him to Cornelius, printed in CABT, II, 251–2, obviously belongs to a fairly late date. In it Brahms still insists that the score was a gift from Tausig, professes to regard Wagner's reasons for wanting it as insufficient, and flatly refuses to surrender it.

politely ironic and slightly contemptuous letter in which he suggested that Brahms might be professionally interested in following up the development, in the later operas of the *Ring*, of the motives used for the first time in the *Rhinegold*. It had taken ten years to induce Brahms to behave with even this small amount of decency.

2

From Vienna, at the end of October, 1865, Wagner had returned in anything but good fettle, physical or mental, in spite of his agreeable transactions with the Putzmacherin. He had been examined by Standhartner, who prescribed a strict regimen for him. Cornelius found him, on his return to Munich, no less nervy and irritable than in the preceding weeks, falling more and more under the influence of Cosima, with whom he was inclined to bury himself in the Briennerstrasse house, and showing rather too openly that, having no immediate use for old friends like Cornelius and Heinrich Porges, he saw no reason to go out of his way to be particularly gracious to them. In his lassitude and depression he was losing even the art of pretending to feel an interest in his friends; so that Cornelius could say of him in November,

" Wagner concerns himself about people only so long as he has a use for them; he is losing more and more the elasticity that would enable him at least to keep up appearances, and, in general, the kindheartedness that would enable him at least to be fair to everyone and to show a friendly face to those who have deserved it. So it was with the Meyers, so it was with the Wesendonks! "

On the day after King Ludwig had ordered the payment of 40,000 gulden to Wagner he went to Switzerland, not returning to Hohenschwangau until the 2nd November. It is surmised that he had fled to escape from an agitation that was being worked up against Wagner in Court circles, under the leadership of the ex-King Ludwig I. The politicians and officials saw clearly enough by this time that it was their life or Wagner's; and they had already begun in secret to weave around him that web of intrigue in which he was finally caught. One of their underhand moves was to try to terrorise Fröbel, whom Wagner was hoping all this while to bring from Vienna to Munich to edit the new journal that was to be half-political, half-artistic in its aims, and wholly Wagnerian. On the 4th October the Police Assessor Pfister, acting as the mouthpiece of Pfistermeister and others, had written to Fröbel warning him not to have much to do with Wagner, " whose stay in Munich is in any case not likely to last long, and who will drag all his creatures down with him in his fall." Though this letter came into Wagner's and the King's hands some weeks later, for the time being they were blissfully ignorant of it. The King, however, must have been well aware even then of the Court intrigues, and it was no doubt by way of quiet answer to them that as soon as he returned to Hohenschwangau he invited Wagner to be his guest there. Wagner was at Hohenschwangau from the 11th to the 18th November. During that week the train was laid that before long was to blow up his last line of defence in Munich.

All through the year 1865 he had been virtually forced by circumstances to interest himself more and more in politics. It remained as true at the end as it had been at the beginning of this period that what he really had at heart was simply the achievement of his own and the King's cultural aims; but whereas at the beginning he had believed that this could be done without a recourse to politics, in the end he had convinced himself that the two things were inseparable, and that to re-shape the art-life of the community as he desired would mean first of all the creation of a new political atmosphere and of a new type of official to carry out the King's orders. Though as ardent a student of politics as ever, he had ceased for a few years to think that the political world was in urgent need of his personal guidance. He had been as fully persuaded of his capacity in that respect during the European turmoil of the mid-century as of his abilities as a dramatist and composer; but in 1851, as we have seen, the coup d'état of Louis Napoleon had given him so startled a sense of the difference between his own vaporous theorisings and practical politics that he had turned away, disillusioned and apprehensive, from the tough world of reality.[3] By 1865 his confidence in his own political wisdom had had time to recover; and though a few years later he was

[3] See Vol. II, pp. 282-3.

to lose it once more, at any rate for a while, just now his vanity, his economic and artistic necessities, and the adoration of the young King combined to fill him with the sense of a heaven-sent political mission transcending in importance even that of the artist.

Cornelius, who had had a vague notion for some time of what had been going on behind the scenes, soon saw the situation with his usual clarity of vision, and during Wagner's absence in Hohenschwangau in November he confided his fears to his fiancée. Wagner, he said, had definitely begun to aim at playing a political rôle where the King was concerned: he had become a sort of Marquis Posa.[4] The King, it appears, has asked him for his views on German affairs in general; and Wagner has been setting them forth in a series of letters. Moreover Fröbel, with whom Wagner is on friendly terms, is to be brought from Vienna and made editor of the official *Bayerische Zeitung*. . . .

> " When Bülow told me all this . . . I felt a shudder run through me: I sensed in it the beginning of the end. Neither now nor at any other time can any good come of an artist exercising a decisive influence on state affairs in general. And yet, who can be sure! Things are in a really extraordinary condition: everywhere in Germany the outlook is wretched — Bavaria is the most important of the middle states — it might actually come about that an energetic, versatile mind such as Wagner's, pursuing in the main only a noble purpose, could give the impulse a favourable development. Still, until one can see deeper into matters and form an opinion about them, so long as it all looks just dangerous and menacing, one repeats to oneself the old saying, ' Cobbler, stick to your last '; and, applying this to Wagner and the *Meistersinger* he is writing for Schott, we may say, ' Poet, stick to your cobbler! '."

Cornelius's apprehensions proved to be groundless so far as Germany in general and Bavaria in particular were concerned: Wagner was not called upon by the Fates either to co-operate or contend with Bismarck in the creation, for good or ill, of a new German and therefore a new European order. It was he himself, and through him the King, who in the end had to pay dearly for his intrusion into practical politics.

---

[4] A famous character in Schiller's drama *Don Carlos*.

3

It was in mid-September that he began a " Journal " intended for the political education of King Ludwig. They meet too rarely, he explains in his opening lines, and correspondence of the ordinary kind is unsatisfactory, making no distinction, as is the way with letters, between matters of considerable importance and matters of hardly any importance at all. In this Journal, which will be sent off to the King at intervals, he proposes to set down his views on all sorts of matters, practical and theoretical, so that whenever an occasion arises on which Ludwig would like to know what Wagner thinks about this or that, or how he would act in such and such circumstances, all he will have to do will be to turn over the leaves until he lights upon the particular rubric he requires. Thirteen years later Wagner reprinted part of this Journal in the *Bayreuther Blätter* under the title *What is German?* These selections now figure in the tenth volume of his Collected Writings.[5] The full original text is now available, for the first time, in the fourth volume of the *König Ludwig II und Richard Wagner Briefwechsel.*

The central theses of the reflections in the Journal — which was kept up, by the way, only from the 14th to the 27th September, 1865, during which period Wagner managed to write the equivalent of some thirty large pages of print — are that the achievement of his and the King's artistic ideals is inseparably bound up with the general political life of the German nation, that the German princes have failed miserably in their historic duty to their people, that salvation can come only from some prince in whom the sense of duty shall be born again, allied with the natural gifts that will ensure his doing the right thing, and that Providence has cast the young King of Bavaria for this important rôle, — under the tuition and guidance, it is implied if not actually stated, of Richard Wagner. More than one biographer of Ludwig has seen that part at least of his tragedy arose from the fact that he was an atavistic reversion to a mediaeval type of royalty. It was not merely that his general standards of truth and honour were sadly behind the times — the difference between the older and the newer ethical worlds being neatly illustrated by a remark of his and one of Bismarck's,

---

[5] They are translated in Ellis's fourth volume.

Ludwig naïvely pleading that having set his hand to an agreement with another power he must in honour abide by it, the more enlightened Prussian statesman, modern to his finger-tips, coolly asking, " What are covenants when it becomes a matter of ' I must '? " [6] It took Ludwig some years after his accession to the throne to realise that a modern state holds together in virtue of other forces than those that made a mediaeval people and its feudal monarch not simply a material but a semi-spiritual part of each other, that no modern prince, however wise and however good, is qualified to be the nation's leader in all matters of culture, and that no nation as a whole would accept such guidance. When Ludwig did at last realise that he ᴡas a throw-back to the Middle Ages, born out of due time, he shrank inwards upon himself and began to create around him by artificial means the world of romance that reality denied him. And Wagner, from the worthiest motives and with the best intentions, wrought untold damage to the King, in 1865 and 1866, by fostering this belief of the young man in his cultural mission as a Wittelsbach of the historic type.

For Wagner himself was one of those Germans who, with their eyes turned on the past rather than on the future, saw the history of their race mainly as the betrayal by the German princes of the faith the German people had reposed in them. We have seen him in 1849 innocently looking to the King of Saxony for a personal solution, on the best operatic lines, of the problems of that particular kingdom: the King would only have to convert the monarchy into a republic, naming himself as the head of it, and the curtain would rise for a third act of general rejoicing. The Germany in which Wagner was still living mentally in the 1860's was a Germany that was destined before long to pass away utterly, a Germany in which the strongest natural factor of cohesion had been the age-long bond between ruler and people in each of the independent states. He could see, like so many others of the period, that one of the main national difficulties was still the traditional inability of Germans to agree politically among themselves, a difficulty which,

---

[6] Bismarck's view of little things of this sort is further expressed in his reply to Prince Napoleon when the latter asked him whether, in certain stated circumstances, he would fulfil, as against Austria, his obligations to Bavaria under the terms of the offensive and defensive alliance recently concluded between the two countries. "De droit, oui; de fait, non", was the Prussian Chancellor's reply.

as the realists maintained and the course of events was to prove, could be overcome only by some force materially stronger than any individual German state; and it was because of his intuition that Bismarck would ultimately create a new Germany at the cost of so much that had made the older Germany admirable that, as late as April, 1866, he could angrily describe the Prussian Chancellor to King Ludwig as " an ambitious Junker, deceiving his weak-minded King in the most shameless fashion." As he saw the situation, politicians such as Bismarck were " with appalling frivolity playing with the destiny of the noblest, greatest nation on earth ", while " the princes of this nation, these natural, now confused protectors of the Folk, fail to come together, to take counsel with each other, to combine and march on quickly to princely deeds ", but leave it all to the diplomats — " ' German diplomats ' (what an absurdity!) " — " who have not the least idea what is honourable and what is false dealing." At that time he was filled with fury and despair when he thought of the Germany of the future, " an illimitable disorder which no prince will be able to put straight again, but to which the chaos of the multitude, the brutal, needy multitude, will be added: I see my ' Germany ' going to eternal rack and ruin! " He was merely a little previous.

The " Journal " of September, 1865 was not pitched in so highly emotional a key as this, because, at the time of its writing, the danger threatening the rest of Germany from Prussia had not yet fully revealed itself. But the main theme of Wagner's political symphony was in each period of his life much the same — the urgent necessity for the more enlightened of the German princes to become once more the leaders of their peoples if the older and better Germany was to be preserved.[7] Perhaps his reading of his countrymen was correct, for, after all, what he was insisting on was at bottom just another aspect of the " Führerprinzip " which we have seen adopted with such national fervour in recent years. Some of Wagner's remarks about his fellow-Germans suggest that he had no great opinion of their inborn political wisdom, or of their being qualified, as yet, to play a leading part in European politics. In

---

[7] As early as 1617 we find the Prince of Anhalt-Cöthen and a number of other rulers founding a "Fruchtbringende Gesellschaft", the object of which was to set an example to the nation in the purging of the German tongue of all the foreign expressions that had crept into it.

spite of his remark about " the noblest, greatest nation on earth ", he was inclined to be scornfully critical of the bouquets the Germans were even then so fond of handing themselves. He would like, he says, to be quite clear in his own mind what meaning is to be attached to the concept " German ". The patriot is always ready enough to speak of his people with glib admiration: but, says Wagner,

" the greater a nation is, the less importance it seems to attach to uttering its own name with this veneration. We meet much less often, in the public life of France and England, with talk about ' English virtues ' or ' French virtues '; but the German is very much given to talking about ' German depth, German earnestness, German faith ', and so on. Unfortunately it has been very obvious on many occasions that this ascription has not been fully justified; though we should probably be wrong in assuming that the qualities are only imaginary." [8]

The German, as Wagner sees him — and the viewpoint is particularly interesting today — is a man who is best in his native habitat, because he lacks the gift of blending harmoniously with the culture of this or that foreign nation among which his lot may happen to be cast.

" The genuine German, because he did not feel at home in another country, weighed always as a stranger on the alien Folk; and it is a remarkable thing that even to the present day the Germans in Italy and in the Slav countries are hated as foreigners and oppressors, while, as we have to recognise with shame, German national elements willingly go on living under a foreign rule so long as violence is not done to them in matters of language and custom — as, for example, in Alsace."

The true German nature only began to find itself when the ancient idea of a Romish Kaiserdom was abandoned. That having happened, Germany entered on the phase of development that has made German art and thought honoured everywhere:

" but in his yearning after ' German glory ' the German, as a rule, can dream of nothing but a kind of re-establishment of the Romish Kaiser-Reich, the thought of which fills even the best-tempered German with

---

[8] It is piquant to find Nietzsche, some twenty years later, regarding Wagner, in respect of the "illogicality, the half-logicality" of his mind, as typically German, for "with Germans the muddy passes for the profound." See the jottings for a projected work on Wagner in the posthumous *Die Unschuld des Werdens*, I, 159.

an unmistakeable lust for mastery, a longing for power over other nations. He forgets how detrimental to the welfare of the German people the concept of the Romish State had already been: *and he overlooks the fact that the policy of injustice, especially Prussia's, is based purely and simply on this concept that is utterly inapplicable to the German people; it is a policy that is doing incalculable injury to the great* [German] *nation."* [9]

As usual, he solves, to his own satisfaction, the most complex political problems by reducing them to terms of fallacious simplicity. For him the shaping of the ideal constitution for Germany was the easiest thing in the world; all that was necessary was to construct it out of the best qualities of the Germanic peoples! He informs the King that

" the genuine German Folk differs from the other branches of the great Germanic family of peoples in this respect, that its inclinations are not towards the aggressive-revolutionary but towards the defensive-conservative. It is sufficient unto itself; out of its own self it can achieve the loftiest, most purely-human development; it requires as stimulus only the contemplation of what lies outside it; it is not possessed by the passion for making this its own by devouring it. Consequently the German feels no thirst for conquest, and the lust to dominate foreign peoples is un-German.

This makes very interesting reading in 1940. So does this:

" The reason for the political impotence of the Germans is the domination of two German monarchs over territories peopled by non-Germans. To justify this, resort has to be had to a policy of the useless squandering of aggressive force: Prussia and Austria, having to see to it that they do not lose Posen and Venice, have to be continually under arms against all Europe. The consequence of this has been a system of national arming which, on the one side, exhausts the resources of these two countries, while on the other side it estranges the

---

[9] This and other passages italicised in our summary were omitted by Wagner when he prepared the "Journal" for publication in 1878. The successful result of the Franco-German war of 1870 had reconciled him, as it did so many other Germans, to much in Bismarckism and Prussianism that he had formerly loathed.

The omissions are interesting in various ways. Wagner cuts out everything in the original that would reveal the fact that these pages were addressed to King Ludwig and intended for his political education, everything (apart from a brief reference to Fröbel) relating to his and the King's plans in Munich, the foundation of new Press organs to represent their views, the duties of the German princes and their sins of omission and commission in the past, the call to the young King of Bavaria to be the saviour of German culture, etc. The original manuscript abounded in expressions of hatred and contempt for Prussia. These were all omitted from the reprint of 1878.

*people from their monarchs, because it establishes a military caste that
is absolutely un-German and useless, imitated as it is from the warrior-
castes of purely conquering peoples, and inapplicable to our conditions. I do not hesitate to say that the maintenance of huge standing
armies, formed in the interests of the ruling dynasties, will possibly
lead some day to the downfall of the monarchies."*

In place of standing armies he suggests a Volkswehr on the Swiss
model. Such a Volkswehr would provide Germany with millions
of armed warriors as against the few hundred thousands possible
under the present system; moreover it would fill the rest of the
world with confidence and respect, for it would be manifest to other
nations that such an army would never be used to attack them. All
this, innocent as it is, would sound less amateurish in those days
than it does now. Dr. Franz Beidler points out [10] that the German
Radical-Democrats in general advocated a Volkswehr on the Swiss
model as a counterpoise to Prussian militarism. " Contemporane-
ously with Wagner, Johann Jacoby fought for it in the Prussian
Diet, and Wilhelm Rüstow . . . founded in 1864 a ' German Defence Journal ' with the sole object of realising it."

As might be expected, Wagner blames most of the misfortunes
and aberrations of " the German spirit " on the Jews, who, it seems,
have been permitted, through the sloth of the German people and
the incompetence of their princes, to capture the key positions in
every main branch of the nation's mental as well as material life,
particularly the theatre and the Press. Left to himself, the German
desires only to deepen and beautify his inner life: " he covets
nothing from without; but he wants to be left at liberty within. He
does not conquer, but he does not allow himself to be attacked."
He is, in short, one is given to understand, the best of creatures if
only the politicians, with their un-German notions and aims, will
leave him alone. But alas, the Jews, everywhere in Prussia and in
Austria, have seized upon the virtuous German spirit and cor-
rupted it.

*" The industrious German, busy with his trade, a citizen in the truest
sense of the word, inventive, contemplative, artistic, sees himself
hemmed in between the Junker and the Jew in all that concerns his*

---

[10] In a review of Werner Richter's book, *Ludwig II König von Bayern*, in the *Neue
Zürcher Zeitung* of the 20th Dec., 1939.

national life — as is most unmistakeably evident in the Prussian political system ";

and all, of course, because the princes have lost touch with the true spirit of the German people. One may be pardoned the comment that the destruction of the Jews in Germany in recent years does not seem to have brought with it a purging of the " German spirit " of the defects it so grieved Wagner to find in it.

In 1865 Wagner had the lowest possible opinion of Prussia in general and Berlin in particular.

" Berlin, the town with an originally dull-witted, backward, brutal Brandenburg population that was despised by Frederick the Great himself, the higher circles in which were filled out by the French emigrants, while the Jews came in from underneath in large numbers to take charge of ' business ' and to ladle out alcohol instead of things of the spirit to the Folk, in order to dissipate their phlegm — this Berlin has become, in these circumstances, the type of the German future."

As all the world now knows, if anything goes wrong in Germany it is never the fault of the Germans or the " German spirit ", which of themselves, Wagner is confident, are the finest things this imperfect earth has yet produced, but of miscreants alien to that spirit — Frenchmen, Jews, Prussians, and other riff-raff by-products of the same sort.

And the upshot of it all is that the true German spirit can be restored only by the shining example of a prince of the type of Ludwig II, in whom all the characteristic German virtues are blended. Ludwig is to behave like a king in a Wagner opera, showing himself all-wise, all-benevolent, a " redeemer " of his race.

" Then will it be seen whether those who were unable to understand the German nature in the Folk will find their darkness lightened when this nature confronts them once more in a prince of their own kind. Their own future destiny will depend on whether they comprehend this prince; if they are blind in this matter also, and oppose this prince as they formerly opposed the Folk, then it is all over with them. For what the Folk lacked it has now found — the German prince to lead it. That the German Folk does not want demagogues it has already shown: it has shown also what it can do when its prince calls. I believe it to be invincible when led by a truly German prince."

To Mathilde Maier, on the 22nd September, Wagner bewails, in his usual fashion, the hard fate that makes it so difficult for him to devote himself to creative work pure and simple just now, when he feels within him a new energy that needs only physical health and freedom from contact with the crude outer world to bring forth marvellously. As far as lies in his power, he says, he has cut himself off from mankind: " the young King alone I am trying to instruct directly." Thus seriously did he take what he had now come to persuade himself was his heaven-bestowed mission. The King, for his part, though his commonsense must have told him that in practical political and economic matters Wagner was the veriest amateur, was only too happy to visualise himself walking the stage in the rôle for which his mentor had cast him — that of the saviour of German culture, the pair of them marching into the new Jerusalem with all Germany following them, with banners waving, trumpets and trombones blaring, after the manner of a grand operatic procession in the last act. " My warmest thanks ", he wrote to Cosima,

> " for having given yourself the trouble of making me a copy of Wagner's new Journal. I have read it with the greatest enthusiasm. Yes! we will show the German Folk what it can do when it is well led: I will not weary in my zeal, my ardent enthusiasm, until the ' Everlasting Work ' is accomplished."

The trouble was that the practical politicians stubbornly declined to see the situation in terms of opera and to line up in the procession as supers.

5

The week that Wagner spent with the King in Hohenschwangau, from the 11th to the 18th November, was one of delirious happiness for them both. For Wagner this mountain retreat was the " Gralsburg ", where he was " protected by Parzival's sublime love ". For the first time, he confided to the pages of the " Brown Book ", he realised to the full the profundity and the beauty of the King's love for him: " He is I, in a newer, younger, lovelier re-birth: wholly I, and himself only to be beautiful and powerful." As the King was occupied with affairs of state for several hours each morning they met only towards mid-day; but before then they had generally managed to send each other greetings in prose or

verse.[11] At meals they were alone together: at other times Prince
Paul von Thurn and Taxis joined them occasionally. On the 13th
Ludwig and Wagner made an excursion into the Tyrol. To Cosima,
on the 14th, the boy poured out the rapture of his warm young
heart. She and Wagner, he says, are the only two beings on earth
who understand him.

" Let us two [himself and Cosima] take a solemn vow to do all it is in
human power to do to preserve for [Wagner] the peace he has won,
to banish care from him, to take upon ourselves, whenever possible,
every grief of his, to love him, love him with all the strength that God
has put into the human soul! O, I know our love for him is eternal,
eternal; yet it makes me happy to think I have entreated a soul so true
in friendship as yours is, honoured lady, to join me in being to him all
that it is possible for human beings to be to an adored one, a holy one.
O, he is godlike, godlike! My mission is to live for him, to suffer for
him, if that be necessary for his full salvation. . . . Now at last must
the profane world open its eyes and comprehend what we are to each
other, in spite of infamous intrigues."

The crowning romantic touch upon their happiness was probably
that of the morning of the 12th, when three groups of military musicians, brought expressly from Munich for the purpose along with
their conductor, Siebenkäs, and posted upon the turrets of the castle,
answered each other across the depths with motives from *Lohengrin*.
For both Wagner and the King the Middle Ages must have seemed
to have come to life again.

Feeling perfectly sure of himself now, Wagner, in his conversations with the King, urged him once more, and this time more
strongly than ever, to solve their central problem by the appointment of a special Secretary to carry out the royal intentions with
regard to matters of art. These intentions embraced (1) the new

[11] Two authentic poems, commencing respectively "Zwei Sonnen sind's" and
"Vereint, wie musst' uns hell die Sonne scheinen", will be found in RWGS, XII,
389. A third poem of four stanzas, described as "Morning Greeting, 16th November,
1865, Hohenschwangau", and commencing "Im Traume sah ich Eure Majestät",
reproduced in RWGS, XII, 418 from RLW, I, 204–5, is almost certainly, as Dr. Otto
Strobel shows, not by Wagner. It does not appear either in his letters to the King or
in the "Brown Book"; no Wagner autograph of it exists; and it does not sound particularly Wagnerian. Röckl is further in error when he says that "the King at once
expressed in writing his thanks for this 'sublime poetic Morning Greeting' ". The
words Röckl has in mind — "First of all my warmest thanks for the sublime poetic
greeting this morning" — occur in the King's letter of the *15th* November, and refer
to Wagner's poem commencing "Zwei Sonnen sind's."

School of Music, which, with Bülow as Director, was to replace the old Conservatoire; (2) a new musical jouℰnal, under the editorship of one Dr. Franz Grandauer, to supplement the work of the School; (3) a new political-cum-artistic journal with Fröbel as editor. Wagner's recommendation for the new office was one of the ministerial secretaries, Emil Riedel.[12] Wagner, as the result of enquiries he had made about him, describes him to the King as a " serious, experienced, and entirely irreproachable man ". Riedel, however, declined the proffered post, partly on the ground of insufficient acquaintance with the ways of the Court world, partly because he wished to devote himself to the study of social questions.[13] The King was indiscreet enough, towards the end of November, to mention Riedel's name to Pfistermeister, who saw at once that Wagner was intriguing to have him removed from his position, or at all events to curtail the powers of his office. And as Pfistermeister and his associates, during Wagner's stay in Hohenschwangau, had been plotting as energetically against him, the stage was now set for the great scene.[14]

Pfistermeister having shown so unmistakably that he wished for no further personal intercourse with Wagner, the King had released him from attendance at Hohenschwangau while his *bête noire* was there. His place was taken by the wily Lutz, who seems to have been well aware of all that was going on in the castle and to have kept Pfistermeister and his associates informed of it. One of the chief anxieties of the politicians now was in connection with the proposed summons of Fröbel to Munich. Fröbel was *persona non grata* to them for more than one reason. He had been acting for some time in Vienna as a political agent of the Austrian Minister

---

[12] In later years he became Bavarian Finance Minister.

[13] The letter in which he did so is now in the Wahnfried archives: the addressee cannot be identified for certain. The document shows Riedel to have been a man of engaging modesty and exceptional honesty. See KLRWB, IV, 104–106.

[14] We may digress for a moment here to draw attention to an entry — "Engineer Bauer" — in Wagner's "Annals" after his return to Munich. This refers to Wilhelm Bauer, the inventor of the submarine, who had called on him on the 24th November. Apparently Bauer had had to complain of general neglect by the German authorities, but had been befriended by King Ludwig, who granted him a pension of 400 thalers a year. Wagner's comment on the new invention, in a letter to the King, is piquant: "If Bauer's work succeeds, it will be a powerful weapon against the absurd Prussian demands for a useless fleet."

Schmerling; and he was held to be in favour of a German Parliament, which suited just then the book of neither Pfordten and his
colleagues nor the King himself. Upon the romantic dreams and
play-acting of the King and Wagner the officials could afford to turn
a merely amused eye: on the 14th we find Lutz, for example, telling
Pfistermeister that " the King is naturally very much with Wagner; . . . he has had another twenty musicians brought here from
Munich to perform Wagner pieces for him, he swims in the old
German sagas and stories of the gods,[15] and all in all is in excellent
spirits." [16]

This is not the whole story, however, of what happened at Hohenschwangau. While Wagner was staying in the castle, Lutz, acting
in collusion with the politicians in Munich, had made yet another
attempt to bribe Wagner. Lutz disclosed to him in confidence the
whole policy of the Government, which was, in brief, to come to
" an arrangement with Bismarck and the new Prussian tendency ",
Austria being considered " untrustworthy " and the idea of a German Parliament " not acceptable ". The main object was to restore
in Bavaria the despotic pre-1848 constitution. It is not unlikely
that, as Wagner suggests, the ultimate purpose of the schemers was
to divert power from the King's hands to their own. To Wagner,
however, Lutz merely put it that their plan would mean the complete restoration of the former power of the throne; and he assumed that " as a particular friend of the King " Wagner would
see eye to eye with the Government in this matter. Wagner, however, was on his guard. He told Lutz there was no point in making
these communications to him, since he had nothing to do with politics as such and was not well-informed regarding Bavarian state
interests; but, he added ironically, he would rejoice to see the King

---

[15] On the 21st November (i.e., after Wagner had returned to Munich), Ludwig
had a grand display of fireworks at Hohenschwangau, arranged by the Munich Theatre machinist, Penkmayr. Afterwards the episode of the arrival of Lohengrin in the
first act of the opera was staged: across the lake came a boat drawn (apparently) by
a swan: in the boat was Prince Paul von Taxis, correctly apparelled as Lohengrin.
He and the swan were electrically illuminated; and the musicians brought from Munich performed the appropriate music from the opera. The scene was re-enacted the
following night.

[16] RRWM, p. 79. This booklet of Röckl's contains a handy summary of the documents bearing on Wagner's eighteen months in Munich, together with one or two
new letters.

possessed of power enough to order the payment of a decent living wage to his poor orchestral musicians.[17]

The politicians, of course, were merely trying to trick Wagner into temporary support of them: he would have been thrown over as soon as he had done what was expected of him in the matter of influencing the King. His downfall had long been decided upon, for it was clear to them now that, sincere as he might be in saying that he had none but artistic aims in view, to achieve these aims he would not hesitate to remove from his path, if he could, any official whom he might find in his way. At the end of October Pfistermeister had received a plain warning from a member of the Court inner circle, Count Max von Holnstein, that " Wagner would stop at nothing to detach him from the King ";[18] and, apart from the secret reports from Lutz as to what was going on at Hohenschwangau in the middle of November, the Cabinet Secretary and his colleagues could be under no illusion as to the danger threatening them now that Wagner seemed to have taken complete possession of the King's mind.

6

That possession, as it happened, was not quite as complete as they imagined. It is true that the King had been so delighted with Wagner's " Journal " as to have a copy made of it for the benefit of Pfordten and the other ministers. But he seems, as always, to have been capable of drawing a clear line, when necessary, between Wagner's plausible political theorisings and the practical application of them; and there is no evidence that he would have allowed the composer to influence him in any purely political matter except in so far as this was bound up with the cause of art. His letters show him to have been commendably cool and cautious with regard to the appointment of Fröbel: he even directed Lutz to obtain

---

[17] The whole story is told in a long letter of Wagner's of the 17th January, 1867 to his Munich physician, Dr. Oscar Schanzenbach, in RWFZ, pp. 468–478. The general accuracy of it is proved by a passage in Wagner's letter of the 26th November, 1865 to the King: "That your Cabinet, in explicit agreement with Herr von Pfordten, is entirely inclined to fall in with Bismarck's wishes, I know from the frank statements of Herr Lutz himself." This, it will be observed, was written within a few days of the conversations at Hohenschwangau with Lutz.

[18] HNBW, p. 609.

Pfordten's opinion on this subject before adopting Wagner's suggestion. And when Wagner, now plunging waist-deep into politics pure and simple, urged him to recall Max von Neumayr and entrust him with the formation of a new Cabinet,[19] Ludwig politely but firmly refused. " I have weighed your advice carefully ", he wrote Wagner on the 27th November.

> " Rest assured, my dear one, that what I am now saying is not the outcome of a momentary superficial emotion . . . No, I am replying to you calmly and after due consideration. I had the best of reasons for dismissing Neumayr and retracting the confidence I had so long reposed in him, and withdrawing my royal favour. It would therefore be quite inconsequent of me now were I to entrust this man — with whom, I repeat, I have every reason to be dissatisfied, — with the formation of a new Cabinet. Pfistermeister is insignificant and stupid; of that there can be no question. I will not let him remain much longer in the Cabinet; but to dismiss him and the other members of it at the present moment does not seem to me advisable: the time for that is not yet. I say this most positively. Believe me, I have my own good grounds for saying it."

Wagner was too deeply involved now in political intrigue to be able to withdraw without loss of power; and it needed only a first-rate indiscretion on his part to put him completely wrong *vis-à-vis* not only the politicians but the King. Of such an indiscretion he was guilty not many days after his return from Hohenschwangau to Munich: it is probable, indeed, that he blundered, from a combination of over-confidence and sheer bad temper, into a trap that had been artfully laid for him.

---

[19] Neumayr had been Minister of the Interior. Some riots in Munich in early October having shaken his position, he was allowed on the 7th November to tender his resignation. Wagner, in his letter of the 26th November to the King, tries to convince him that Neumayr was a capable and honest servant who had been sacrificed by Pfistermeister and Pfordten and the rest of them partly because he would not act as their tool, partly because they were working hand in glove with the Prussian "reaction".

How seriously Wagner took his self-imposed mission to educate the King is shown by his writing a long essay for him, in the style of the "Journal", *à propos* of these riots, in which he explains at great length just why the lower orders do such strange things as threatening the police when they try to arrest a criminal. (The essay was apparently not sent to Ludwig: the manuscript is inscribed by Cosima, "Fragment inachevé et non communiqué." The text is given in KLRWB, IV, 85–7). Cornelius was right: Wagner would have been better engaged in completing the *Meistersinger* than grinding out this verbiage.

It has already been observed that a good deal of discontent existed in Bavaria over the principle of the Cabinet Secretariat.[20] On the 13th November, while Wagner was in Hohenschwangau, an article had appeared in the democratic Nuremberg *Anzeiger*, entitled " Plain Words to the King of Bavaria and his People on the Subject of the Cabinet Secretariat "; the gist of it was that with the King isolated for seven months in the year from his ministers, " encompassed only by the entirely unconstitutional institution of the Cabinet Secretariat ", the nation had good cause to feel as alarmed as it did. At once the other democratic papers took up the hue and cry; and for the moment the reactionary parties were at a loss what tactical line to take, though one journalist hit on the bright idea of protesting that whatever influence Pfistermeister and Lutz and others might have over the King, it had not availed them as against the influence of " another much-discussed personality ". It was left to the *Volksbote* to perceive that in an affair of this kind the best defence is attack, and that however weak the case for Pfistermeister and company might be, that for Wagner was weaker still, or at any rate might easily be made to appear so.

On the 26th November the *Volksbote* came out with an article in which it was craftily hinted, without precisely saying so, that the *Anzeiger* article of the 13th, if not from the hand of Wagner himself, had been written with his connivance, for was he not in Hohenschwangau at the time of its appearance? In any case the *Volksbote* was certain that the agitation launched by the *Anzeiger* was directed not against the Cabinet Secretariat in the abstract but against two of its most prominent members, Pfistermeister and Hofmann: " these two men are to be set aside in order that certain hankerings after the exploitation of the royal Treasury may the more easily be satisfied." Wagner, it was asserted, had cost Bavaria no less than 190,000 gulden in rather less than twelve months, while only a few weeks ago he had demanded a further 40,000 gulden for his " luxury ". The *Volksbote* could moreover testify that Pfistermeister, acting in accordance with his duty, had advised the young King against the granting of this monstrous sum, that Wagner had then written the Secretary a letter that was " anything but polite ", but

---

[20] See *supra*, p. 220.

that all the same he had succeeded in getting his 40,000 gulden.[21]
The paper permitted itself the assumption that the motive of the agitation against the Cabinet Secretariat in general and certain personalities in particular was not, as had been pretended, a truly
" constitutional " one, but in order that " favourites might secretly
make their influence complete, and utilise that influence partly for
financial ends, partly for those of democracy."

The trick succeeded: Wagner was goaded by this attack into an
indiscretion of the first magnitude. He assumed that the *Volksbote*
article had been inspired by someone in the Cabinet. He lost his
temper completely, and with it went his judgment.

7

He and the King were fond of referring to Pfistermeister and
Hofmann, in their letters and conversations, as Mime and Fafner
respectively — two evil beings whom it was to be Ludwig's mission, as the young Siegfried, to destroy. Wagner's own conduct
during the next few days suggests that even his own Mime could
have taught him very little in the way of guile. He was thoroughly
convinced, of course, that his own motives were purity itself; and
no doubt they were, in the main. But he could never see any matter from other people's point of view; and having once got it into
his head that Pfistermeister and the rest of them were nothing more
than a gang of criminals, not only denying him, Richard Wagner,
the peace of mind he needed for his work but dragging Bavaria and
the King to perdition by opposing his cultural plans, he threw every
scruple to the winds.

On the 29th November there appeared in the Munich *Neueste
Nachrichten* a long anonymous article (dated " Munich, 28th November "), professing to tell the truth, the whole truth, and nothing
but the truth about Wagner, the King, and their ideals, and breath-

---

[21] RLW, I, 212 ff. Unfortunately our knowledge of the text of the article is confined to the extracts made from it by Sebastian Röckl for his book of 1913. It seems
that no other file exists of the *Volksbote* for 1865 than that in the Bavarian State Library in Munich, and that even from this copy the pages in question are now missing.
See Otto Strobel's note in KLRWB, IV, 106.

Part of the further contents of the article of the 26th November can be surmised
from Wagner's letter to the King of the same date.

ing fire and slaughter against certain unnamed but easily identifiable political personages. Cornelius, Porges, and no doubt many other people saw at once that the article was from Wagner's pen. The style of it, indeed, is unmistakable; but if there could ever have been any doubt about the matter it is now at an end, for the draft of the article, in Cosima's handwriting, is today in the Wahnfried archives.[22] The article professes to be written in reply to a desire on the part of the editor of the *Nachrichten* to know the truth about Wagner's position and activities. What is put forward by the anonymous contributor as the truth is, as might be expected, only a plausible half-truth. Everything that made Wagner's position so assailable, particularly his demands on the King's purse, is passed over; he is made to appear as the most disinterested of idealists, intent only on art pure and simple. The King is wholly with him in his desire that he shall be able to devote his life exclusively to noble ends, wholly with him in such plans as that for a new Music School and a festival theatre. But they are opposed at every turn by certain people who pretend that their merely personal interests are those of the country. To damage Wagner they will stop at nothing; unfortunately every blow they aim at him injures the King also. " These people, whom I have no need to mention by name, since they are the objects of universal and contemptuous indignation in Bavaria ", are reduced, in order to save themselves, to representing " the King's unshakable friendship for Wagner " as dangerous to the throne.

> " Of one thing you can be quite certain: it is in no wise a question of any principle, any party position, being attacked by Wagner: it is purely and simply an affair of the lowest personal interests, and that on the part of a very small number of individuals: and I venture to assure you ", the article concludes, " that with the removal of two or three persons who do not enjoy the smallest respect among the Bavarian people, both the King and the Bavarian people would once for all be set free from these annoyances." [23]

Such a communication, making free as it did with the King's name at every turn, would have been a blazing indiscretion even

---

[22] According to Dr. Strobel it is dated by her the 25th November; but either, one imagines, this must be a misprint for the 26th or Cosima misdated her manuscript. The article is obviously a reply to the *Volksbote* challenge, which appeared on the 26th.

[23] The whole article will be found in KLRWB, IV, 107–109.

had Ludwig been a party to it. But Wagner was guilty of something worse than an indiscretion: he deceived the King, if not by commission, certainly by omission. He sent him the *Volksbote* article on the day of its appearance, accompanied by a long letter in which his exasperation is manifest. He feels compelled, he says, to exact a promise from Ludwig that no further order relating to their plans shall pass through either the Cabinet or the Court Theatre until fundamental changes have been made in the personnel of those institutions, for he cannot tolerate any longer the confusion they create. He gives the King " one last energetic piece of advice ", prompted by his love for him and by his sense of duty towards Bavaria. Ludwig has made a mistake in dismissing Neumayr, who should at once be recalled and instructed to form a new Cabinet. At the back of the scandalous *Volksbote* article is Pfistermeister, for it must be evident to the King that " the most monstrous indiscretions " in this article — he presumably refers to the figures of Wagner's supposed cost to the country [24] — could have emanated only from the Cabinet itself. The suggestion of his accuser that he was responsible for the article in the Nuremberg *Anzeiger* is false; never has he been behind *any* newspaper article in any form. He asks himself whether he can leave the King without counsel against " the most shameless treachery on the part of your most confidential servants ". Pfistermeister's insolence is due to his believing himself indispensable. That belief should at once be shattered: therefore, once more — recall Neumayr! The King is urged to send Neumayr an immediate summons, in the writing of someone whose hand is not known to Pfistermeister or Lutz, and conveyed by a secret channel. The whole land will rejoice when it hears of this bold action. As for Neumayr, he is to be confidentially informed of the true relations between Wagner and the King. But Ludwig

---

[24] As Wagner pointed out to the King later, the "190,000 gulden" which he was said to have cost the country in less than twelve months was the exact sum mentioned in Pfistermeister's letter of the 18th September to Cosima as the contribution of the Civil List *to music* in 1865. Wagner regards this coincidence as proof that the *Volksbote* attack was inspired by Pfistermeister. It is hardly likely, however, that the Cabinet Secretary would thus make himself publicly responsible for a statement which he knew to be erroneous and capable of refutation. It is much more probable that the figures were supplied to the *Volksbote* by someone in the Treasury who, knowing of the entry of 190,000 gulden "for music", mistakenly assumed that this meant "for Richard Wagner".

must act quickly and silently. Neumayr's return must be " a complete surprise " to Pfistermeister: " send your most trusty groom riding with the letter."

Fröbel, at his meeting with Wagner in Vienna in the preceding October, had seen that " the gifted but unpolitical artist " was honestly possessed by the idea that his confidential relations with the young King imposed an enormous responsibility on him; his aims, indeed, said Fröbel later, were of the noblest kind, " but he saw politics too poetically, I might say theatrically or operatically." [25] Wagner had really managed to convince himself that the future well-being of Bavaria depended on the infiltration of Wagnerian culture into every nook and cranny of the national life through the media of the theatre, the Music School, and a new Press organ or two. Moreover, with his usual faculty for self-hypnosis, he had honestly persuaded himself that Providence had committed the fate of the gifted young King into *his* hands: Fröbel still remembered, some thirty-five years later, the tone of " prophetic exaltation " in which Wagner, in 1865, had repeated Frau Dangl's mysterious words to him. Of his general sincerity all through the events of the autumn of 1865 there can be no doubt: but neither can there be any question that his methods were occasionally underground and tortuous. Short of telling a deliberate lie, he could not have misled the King more thoroughly, and with the plain intention of doing so, than by his assurance that he had " never been behind *any* newspaper article in any form ". On the very day on which he penned that sentence he was drafting his anonymous communication to the *Nachrichten*.

8

The King replied to this letter on the 27th — that is to say, before he knew anything of the *Nachrichten* article, which did not appear until the 29th. The calm common sense of his reply exposes once more the fallacy of the theory that he was merely the pitiful young gull of an older and craftier schemer. He patiently but firmly points out, as we have already seen, the impossibility of his recalling Neumayr just then; nor is this the best moment imagi-

[25] FEL, II, 397–8.

nable, he says, for getting rid of Pfistermeister. " You will be astonished when I tell you that the [*Volksbote*] article did *not* originate in my Cabinet "; an opinion in which he may or may not have been technically right. But his simple good sense is shown in his exhortation to Wagner not to pay so much attention to " Press tittle-tattle ", but to get on with his real work, secure in the knowledge that they two understand each other, and that Ludwig, for his part, will not be turned aside from his purpose by any amount of opposition of this kind. It would have been well for both of them had Wagner been rational enough to take this advice.

But the irreparable mischief, unknown to the King, was already done: the bomb, due to explode on the 29th, had already been surreptitiously placed in position. Meanwhile, replying on the 27th to Ludwig's letter of the same day, Wagner repeats in a more envenomed form his charges against Pfistermeister, who, he says, has for the last sixteen years been filling one office after another with his creatures, and is now, in fact, the evil genius of Bavaria — for cleverer people than he are using him for *their* purposes, which are not those of the King or of the State. " Your Secretary feels himself to be stronger than you: he orders the far-flung hordes of his own favourites to calumniate his supreme Lord; and they do so." [26] There is not a lying rumour current in Bavaria, in fact, of

---

[26] The King, in his reply of the 3rd December, begs Wagner to specify in more detail the "calumny" to which he had referred; but Wagner, answering on the 6th, asks to be excused from doing so. It has of course been assumed in some quarters that the "calumny" had reference to their supposed homosexual relations. There is no evidence whatever to support this assumption; the probability is, as Dr. Strobel says, that Wagner had heard that the Cabinet Secretariat was spreading a rumour of the King's mental aberration in order to have him deposed. It goes without saying that Wagner could not blurt *this* out to the King.

The passage in Wagner's letter of the 27th November in which he speaks of the calumnies propagated by Pfistermeister continues thus: "The most alarming rumours circulate in the town — that you neglect affairs of state, and are addicted to fantastic notions of which *I* make use in order to further my own shameless demands: this is the only aspect in which they can understand our relations!" The reader will do well to bear constantly in mind that many people regarded Wagner himself as mad, and that even the so-called alienists were solemnly declaring, twenty years after the events with which we are now dealing, that he had infected with his own "madness" the brain of the feeble young King, in whose heredity there happened to be a morbid strain on the female side. As everyone in Germany knew of this hereditary flaw, nothing was easier than for the politicians to put out rumours, whenever it suited their purpose to do so, that the King was "mad". On the other hand, to talk of the necessity of deposing a German prince merely for homosexuality would have made everyone in Germany explode with laughter.

which the unspeakable Pfistermeister is not the ultimate source. As for Wagner, what can he do but place all his powers at the service of his King?

> " Be it so! God will give me strength. If I feel called upon by fate to perform a great and noble service for you and your country, this must remain your secret and mine. No one must know that it was I who opened your eyes. Consequently my energetic advice is still the same — dismiss Pfistermeister immediately, and recall Neumayr with a view to the formation of a new Cabinet."

He surpasses himself in sophistry in his attempt to convince the King that by acting thus he will be doing the wisest thing for the land and for himself. But above all, Neumayr is not to have an inkling that he owes his recall to Wagner: " it shall be my loftiest pride to have performed a fine service to Bavaria known only to you and myself." Operatic to the last, he sees the King flinging himself on his horse, riding from Hohenschwangau to Munich without saying a word to anyone, summoning Neumayr, and " like a hero, at once turning everything into the right channel." Thus delightfully simple do affairs of state appear to composers of romantic operas.[27] And all this while, of course, not so much as a sentence that might suggest to the King that the article he would shortly be reading in the *Nachrichten* was from Wagner's pen.

It was not until the 3rd December that the King wrote to him again. He was then preparing to leave for Munich, where, largely as a consequence of the indiscreet article of the 29th, his presence was now urgently required. " That article in the *Neueste Nachrichten* ", he said sadly, " has contributed not a little to embitter the last days of my sojourn here [Hohenschwangau]. It was unquestionably written by one of your friends who thought he was doing you a service thereby; unfortunately, so far from helping you, it has injured you." It is incredible that Ludwig should not have recognised at once Wagner's style in the article; no doubt he was delicately reluctant to let him see too clearly that he had detected the deceit. For the rest, his letter is a lament over the blindness and the evil of the world, and an assurance to Wagner of eternal fidelity to him and their ideal.

---

[27] As Gottfriod von Böhm says, it never seems to have occurred to him that the Bavarian statesmen and officials might have other duties to perform than the mere furthering of Wagnerian ideals of art.

At that time he had not realised the immensity of the harm Wagner had done himself by his article. Other people, Wagner's friends
as well as his foes, were quicker to perceive this. The journals of
the Progressive Party, while glad enough to have Wagner as an
ally against Pfistermeister and the " unconstitutional " Cabinet
Secretariat, had no great belief either in his political wisdom or in
the permanence of his influence in Munich: as one editor put it
in a letter to Pecht, " Wagner's lack of moderation will sooner or
later bring about his fall. All the same, I recognise that it is to
our interest meanwhile to support him as much as possible against
Pfistermeister; and the best way to do this is to launch concentrated attacks on the latter." [28] The non-democratic papers were
delighted to have an excuse to train their batteries once more on
the hated " demagogue " and " revolutionary "; while *Punsch*
rose brilliantly to the occasion with a parody of a once famous document, known to all Bavarians — the Lord's Prayer of Lola Montez:

" Morning Prayer of a Modest Man.
" O Lord! Give me health; let me keep my little house, my little
garden, and the funds needful therefor, and send me in addition a few
more hundred thousand gulden, not all at once, but for me to draw in
small instalments. O Lord! bless all men, but especially a few who
have such big tenor voices that I can use them for my purposes. I
pray Thee to give strength to all the weak; to the sad, consolation;
and to the sick, recovery. Thou mayst, however, visit two or three men
who do not enjoy the smallest respect among the Bavarian people with
a little apoplectic or other fit, so that they shall no longer stand in my
way here on earth, but enter into eternal life. Amen."

Pfistermeister himself joined in the fray on the 30th November
with a disdainful letter to the official *Bayerische Zeitung* — a letter
which he would hardly have ventured to send without the sanction
of the King — denying the allegations and insinuations of the
Nachrichten article, " the authorship of which is evident enough
from the style and the construction." Yet in spite of everything
the Munich population as a whole seems to have been comparatively
unimpressed by the agitation against Wagner: at all events, whatever it may have thought of the man, it made no secret of its admiration for the artist. On the night of the 1st December he and
Cornelius happened to be at a musical meeting of the Korps Suevia

[28] RLW, I, 220.

in the West End Hall, at which the Sailors' Chorus from the *Flying Dutchman* was performed. He was given an ovation. One of the Munich papers tried to work up a public address expressing sympathy with Pfistermeister: the document received only 810 signatures. Had the matter been left to the judgment of the Munich man in the street, the verdict would probably have been that this latest outcry against Wagner was much ado about next to nothing. The King, however, had to deal directly not with his liege subjects but with his family, the nobility, the Court officials, the politicians, and the heads of the Church; and against their combined assault his defences weakened.

9

They descended on him *en masse* on his return to Munich, filling his ear with artful reports of disaffection among the people, threats of revolution, and doubts on the part of the police whether they could guarantee the safety of Richard Wagner much longer. Wagner's incredible folly had placed all the trump cards in the hands of his none too scrupulous enemies, and they played them promptly and unmercifully. He himself was as yet blissfully unconscious that his luck was at an end. He had prepared, against the King's return, a long letter which he no doubt thought would win the last trick of the game for him; this letter, we may presume, Ludwig found awaiting him on his entry into the Residenz.[29] Wagner is grieved to find the King suffering as he does, when " the simplest exercise of his power " would bring him peace. He protests against the lie of the 190,000 gulden, and asks the King to issue an order to his Secretariat to publish an official correction in the *Bayerische Zeitung,* to which he will append a statement in his own name of the real facts of the royal bounty; and he insists that no third person shall be allowed to water either document down. He concludes with an expression of his perfect confidence not only in the King's love but in his wisdom and his stern will to cut the knot, and a joyous anticipation of the personal meeting which he assumes will soon take place between them.

That meeting never took place; the King had already cut the

---

[29] It is dated the 6th, not, as was formerly supposed, the 7th. It is therefore a reply not to the King's decisive letter of the 7th, but to that of the 3rd.

knot, but in another place than that so obligingly indicated to him by Wagner.

On the 27th November Pfordten had been asked by Lutz to report to the King on the character of a young man of the name of Rudhardt, employed in the Ministry of Foreign Affairs, and his qualifications for the post which Riedel had declined. Pfordten replied a couple of days later to the effect that while he had nothing but good to say of Rudhardt, he hoped the King would think twice before ordering " a reconstruction of the Cabinet according to Richard Wagner's notions ", as that would precipitate a political crisis. On that very day the *Nachrichten* article had appeared, in which Wagner had boasted, " with unheard-of effrontery ", of the King's " unshakable friendship " for him. " Loyal Bavaria ", Pfordten goes on to say,

> " will, although discontentedly, continue to put up with seeing the money that could dry the tears of so many poor people squandered by Wagner and his associates — if that be the King's pleasure; but I am afraid that what Bavaria will not put up with is its King's ' friendship ' for a Richard Wagner. Please, therefore, beg his Majesty, in my name, not to make any decision until he returns to Munich and has heard what I have to say."

The King replied direct to Pfordten on the same day. He has heard, he says, that Munich is much occupied with the Wagner question. But Pfordten is not to take too seriously all this talk about the composer trying to " influence " him and " divorce him from public affairs ": his association with Wagner is confined to matters of art.

Pfordten had already made bold to warn his young master against the danger both to himself and to the State involved in so close an association. Ludwig's letter gave him a pretext for developing this thesis in his reply of the 1st December. He tells the King that the *Nachrichten* article, both by its substance and by its tone, has aroused considerable feeling against Wagner; there is resentment also in Munich over the 40,000 gulden and over Wagner's unwarrantable interference in matters that have nothing to do with art.

> " Your Majesty now stands at a fateful parting of the ways: you have to choose between the love and respect of your faithful people and the

'friendship' of Richard Wagner. This man, who has the audacity to assert that members of the Cabinet who have proved their fidelity do not enjoy the smallest respect among the Bavarian people, is himself despised by every section of the community to which alone the throne can look for support — despised not only for his democratic leanings (in which the democrats themselves do not believe) but for his ingratitude and treachery towards friends and benefactors, his overweening and vicious luxury and extravagance, and the shamelessness with which he exploits the undeserved favour of your Majesty. It is the opinion not of the nobility and the clergy alone but of the respectable middle class and the workers also, who painfully earn their bread by the sweat of their brow while arrogant strangers luxuriate in the royal generosity, and, by way of thanks for this, vilify and deride the Bavarian people and its condition."

Pfordten does not underrate the value of art and music; but these should not be regarded as the first things in the State, " especially in times like these, when the very existence of states and thrones is threatened, and action in the real world is called for rather than dreaming in the ideal." It is the Minister's sacred duty — Pfordten could be trusted not to leave that out! — to tell his sovereign all this, even at the risk of offending him.[30]

Pfordten's plain speaking must have given the King something to think about: it will not have escaped the reader's observation that it was after having received this letter that Ludwig told Wagner, on the 3rd, that whoever was responsible for the *Nachrichten* article had done him more harm than good. As to the general accuracy of Pfordten's indictment of Wagner as a man the King could hardly be in much doubt; and that he could still devote most of his letter of the 3rd to assurances of eternal fidelity to him and to their ideal is one more proof that it was Wagner the artist who fascinated him. And he was wiser than Pfordten in that he could do what was impossible for the honest but narrow-minded minister — he could see that the things of the spirit are so important to humanity that it behoves us not to let our judgment of the personalities serving them be clouded by personal considerations of the commoner kind.

It was Pfordten's letter, however, that mainly determined Wagner's more immediate fate. Ludwig must have done some hard thinking between the time of the receipt of it and his return to Mu-

---

nich in the early hours of the 6th; and it speaks volumes for his native common sense that he recognised almost at once that, for a while at least, his personal feelings must take a second place to political expediency. His first act, on entering the Residenz, was to receive reports from all kinds of people as to the state of public opinion. It has been said that his final decision was mainly the result of fears for Wagner's personal safety; but such documents as we possess from his hand indicate rather that he made up his mind on purely realistic political grounds. " My dear Minister ", he wrote to Pfordten on the 7th, " my resolution stands firm. R. Wagner must leave Bavaria. I will show my dear people that its love and confidence are the first things of all to me. You will realise that this has not been easy for me; but I have overcome."

10

His decision, taken about three o'clock in the afternoon, had been conveyed to Wagner by Lutz in person on the evening of the 6th — a task which it must have given the second Cabinet Secretary infinite pleasure to perform. Wagner was for the moment crushed by the wholly unexpected intimation that the King desired him to leave Bavaria for six months. Then, recovering from the shock, he poured out such a torrent of abuse of Pfistermeister that Lutz had to administer a reproof: " Restrain yourself ", he said: " I am here in my official capacity."

On the 7th, no doubt with a view to softening the blow of the coldly official command, Ludwig sent a personal letter to the Briennerstrasse:

" My dear Friend, Much as it grieves me, I must ask you to comply with the wish I communicated to you yesterday through my Secretary. Believe me, I had to act as I did. My love for you will never die, and I beg you to retain for ever your friendship for me; with a clear conscience I can say that I am worthy of it. Sundered, who can part us? I know you feel with me. I know you can measure the whole depth of my sorrow. I could not do otherwise: be assured of that, and *never* doubt the fidelity of your best friend. It will certainly not be for ever. Until death, your faithful Ludwig."

The postscript — " In accordance with your wish, the matter shall be kept as private as possible " — is no doubt a reply to a passage in a letter of Wagner's of the same day, in which, after asking for a few days' grace to regulate his affairs, he begs that his departure from the town may be accomplished without publicity: it can be announced, he suggests, that he has gone to the Lake of Geneva for his health. He hopes that a correction of the mis-statements about his cost to the State, on the lines he had proposed in an earlier letter, can still be issued, as he would not like this false impression to remain in the public mind: apparently he had not fully realised even yet that the gravamen of the indictment against him was not his financial record but his interference in Bavarian politics. The King, on the 8th, again promised to do all that lay in his power to meet Wagner's wish. His letter shows how grievous was the wound dealt him by the events of the last few days. " That it had to come to this! " he laments. " Our ideals shall be faithfully fostered: of that I need hardly assure you . . . I had to act as I did, for the sake of your peace. Do not misjudge me, even for a moment: that would pain me beyond expression."

For Wagner a last bitterness was reserved on the part of his enemies. On the 8th December the Augsburg *Allgemeine Zeitung*, giving what purported to be an authentic account of the events at the Residenz on the 6th and 7th, assured its readers that the announcement in the official journal that Wagner would leave the country " for a few months " was mere camouflage: they could take it for granted that this meant " for ever ".

At a quarter to six on the morning of the 10th December, looking grey and broken, Wagner left Munich, accompanied only by his servant Franz Mrazeck and the sick old dog Pohl. His departure was as private as he could have wished: he was seen off only by Cosima — Bülow was away on a concert tour — Heinrich Porges and his wife, and Cornelius. Peter, as usual, saw the situation coolly and clearly. He had always been out of sympathy with Wagner's " Marquis Posa " presumptions. He knew the *Nachrichten* article to be a gross strategic blunder, which he attributed to Cosima's influence. He thought it would prove an excellent thing for Wagner, the first shock over, to be compelled to keep out of politics and get on with his real job of writing music. He had no doubt that the King's friendship for him would endure. Of Ludwig's mind and character he had a high opinion; and he was convinced that he too would be all the better, in the long run, for this sobering experience, with its sharp reminder that the ideal world and the real world, though they may touch each other at this point or that, are not identical. It was only in this last respect that Cornelius's cool forecast was not fulfilled to the letter. As long as the King could hug the delusion that Wagner would one day return to him, he could, if not forget his pain, at least brace himself to shoulder his burden. When at last it became clear beyond all doubt that Wagner was determined never to return, Ludwig's inner life was split from top to bottom.

CHAPTER XX

HAVEN IN TRIEBSCHEN

1

WAGNER'S FIRST objective was Vevey, near the eastern end of the Lake of Geneva: travelling by way of Berne, where he spent two nights, he arrived there on the 12th December. He stayed a week at the " Pension du Rivage ", belonging to one Monsieur Prélat; then, on the 20th, he moved on to Geneva, where he occupied a room for two or three days in the Hôtel Métropole. On the 23rd he imagined he had found in the neighbourhood of Geneva the quasi-permanent resting-place he was in search of — a fairly large country house known as " Les Artichauts ". This he rented for three months, until the end of March. He soon discovered that, as with so many " desirable country residences " of its kind, the internal comfort of " Les Artichauts " did not answer to the elegance of its exterior: the place was in poor repair, and he had considerable difficulty in keeping warm. The best thing about the villa was the superb view across the country to Mont Blanc, some thirty miles or more away.

In the third week of January he made for the south of France. Leaving Geneva on the 22nd he was in Hyères on the 24th: the now famous resort seems to have attracted him so little that he set off almost immediately for Marseilles, where he arrived the same evening, putting up at the Grand Hôtel. He is supposed to have been driven out of " Les Artichauts " by a fire in one of the rooms; but the journey to France must have formed part of his plans from the moment of his leaving Bavaria. A letter of the 1st January to a French friend whose name cannot now be determined shows that he already regarded his severance from Munich as final. He asks for his correspondent's assistance in finding some place in the south of France, remote from the world, in which he can devote himself to composition again. What he wants is a small villa somewhere between Avignon, Arles, Perpignan and the Pyrenees: he rules out Nîmes and Marseilles, and indeed every large and busy town. He has in mind a lease of five or six years, with the option of purchase. " Price ", he adds airily, " no object ": the King, he knew, could be trusted to attend to that. " The main thing is to get away from the world into some pleasant spot remote from contact with my terrible recent experiences." This is the only way for him to " rescue " the works he has in hand, which will be lost if he has to spend another year in " convulsions of my usual kind ".[1] But his quest was unsuccessful: by the 29th he was back in Geneva with his problem still unsolved.

While he was away the Fates suddenly intervened in his life in a fashion that was to prove as decisive for his future as the catastrophe in Munich had been.

Minna's health had worsened somewhat during that winter, though it had apparently improved a little when she consulted the faithful Pusinelli on the 24th January: he prescribed a course of treatment, and she spoke of going to Tharand the next day to make arrangements for a holiday there in the summer. That afternoon and evening she was in excellent spirits; neither she nor Natalie seems to have felt any apprehension. At seven o'clock the next morning the servant found her dead, lying half on, half out of the bed, with foam on her lips: apparently she had wakened, with a feeling of suffocation, about two in the morning, had risen and opened the window for air, and had died before she could lie down in her bed again. As Pusinelli did not know Wagner's address he telegraphed the news the same forenoon to Cosima in Munich, asking her to communicate it to Richard and to send him his address. Cosima, not knowing for certain where Wagner was just then, could give no address but " Les Artichauts ". As it happened, Wagner had wired there that same afternoon giving instructions that letters were to be forwarded to Marseilles. Pusinelli's message, re-

---

[1] TLFW, pp. 267–8. The "Monsieur S." of the letter may possibly have been Edouard Schuré, who, as the reader will recall, had become friendly with Wagner in Munich at the time of the *Tristan* production. It would be natural for him, after hearing of Wagner's downfall and his departure for Switzerland, to write and offer his services in the matter of finding a new home — which is what the recipient of this letter had evidently done. "I don't know whom to turn to for information", says Wagner; "but in Paris they know everything, find everything. I was thinking of writing to Truinet when your kind letter turned my thoughts in your direction."

wired from Geneva, reached him in Marseilles the same night; but the wording of it — " ton épouse morte la nuit passée " — combined with the fact that the servant at " Les Artichauts " had not included the date of the Dresden telegram in his transcript of it, left him ignorant of the actual day of Minna's death. In the circumstances he could do no more than ask Pusinelli to make the necessary arrangements for the funeral, and to write him in detail to Geneva, where he would be once more in two or three days' time.[2]

It is to his credit that while humanly grieved both over Minna's troubled life and her sudden death he did not allow himself to drop into any conventional sentimentality about her in his letters of this period. It would have been a pure impossibility for him either to feel or to pretend to feel that he had suffered a loss. Since their final parting in 1862 he had corresponded very little with her;[3] as for Minna, the more she brooded in the last two or three years of her life over her wrongs, real and imaginary, the more rancorous and venomous she became towards him. As late as the end of 1864 we find her describing his conduct to her as that of a " wild beast ", while she, of course, is " a poor, harmless woman " who never did anyone an injury. Her reading of him increased in simplicity as she grew older and crazier — he had been a genius so long as he was in love with her, but had been going steadily to the devil ever since his vanity made him fall a victim to the wiles of such women as Mathilde Wesendonk; and now he was written out. Whereas when living with her he had written the immortal *Flying Dutchman* in seven weeks, he had taken an unconscionable time over the inferior *Tristan*, while apparently he was unable to finish the *Meistersinger*. How different, she said, from Meyerbeer, who had left chest after chest full of manuscripts behind him! After Mathilde the people she hated most were Bülow and Cosima; the latter in

---

[2] His telegram to Pusinelli was despatched at 8.35 a.m. on the 26th. It has been suggested that he could have managed to get to Dresden in time for the funeral had he wanted to. This, however, is stretching unkindness a little too far. It is clear that the Pusinelli telegram did not mention the precise date of Minna's death; nor could Wagner possibly have known at that time that the funeral would not take place until the 28th.

[3] By her will, made in May 1865, she left everything she possessed to her "sister" Natalie. (Wagner had formally conveyed all his Dresden belongings to Minna in order to protect her from distraint by his own creditors).

particular was a monster of " commonness ". A reconciliation between Richard and herself would be for ever impossible, she declared, because she would consent to meet him with a view to an
explanation only if he would confess himself entirely in the wrong
and beg for forgiveness; nor would she settle down with him anywhere unless she were given full powers to rid the house of " a certain kind of creature ".

Crazy as she was on points of this kind, however, she would not
be unjust to him in matters in which she knew his conscience to be
clear. Early in January the Munich *Volksbote* — the clerical organ that was always well to the fore when some piece of blackguardism had to be perpetrated — came out with an insinuation
that all the time Wagner had been wallowing in luxury in Munich
his wife had been left to starve in Dresden. As Wagner himself, at
that time in Geneva, could take no steps to refute this calumny,
Bülow obtained a denial of it from Minna, which was published in
the *Volksbote* on the 16th: she was in receipt, she testified, of an
allowance from her absent husband which guaranteed her an existence quite free from care. The ruffianly journalists of that epoch,
however, were not so easily silenced. A fortnight after Minna's
death — on the 6th February — the *Volksbote* announced that
having its doubts about the communication received from Bülow,
and being virtuously anxious to arrive at the truth, it had made
enquiries in Dresden through " a person of high position " who
was perfectly disinterested in the matter. The " truth ", it now
appeared, was that the recently deceased Frau Wagner had lived
in " the direst penury ", having been reduced, indeed, to accepting
poor relief from the Dresden Corporation: the presumption therefore was that her démenti had been " extorted " from her by means
of " a momentary sustentation on the part of her husband."
" Now ", concluded this disinterested witness, " the grave having
closed over the unfortunate lady, further discussion could lead to
nothing. What has been said above, however, can be taken as
fact." To this the editor of the *Volksbote* added a little contribution
of his own. It had been evident to everyone at the time, he said, that
though the document published on the 16th January was signed by
Frau Wagner it had not been *composed* by her, but had been forced

on her for a particular purpose. The incorruptible *Volksbote* would accept a denial of these new " facts " only from the Dresden authorities themselves.

On the 21st February the paper had to publish an official assurance by the Dresden poor law authorities that Minna had never been in receipt of parish relief and never in need of it, as well as a declaration from Pusinelli that, thanks to her husband, Minna's existence had been carefree and comfortable. To extremities of this kind were decent citizens reduced in those days by the licensed ruffianism of the German Press.

2

For the King, during all these winter months, the one absorbing problem was, " How soon will Wagner return? " For Wagner the corresponding question seems to have been, " How soon can I, and dare I, make it finally clear to him that I have no intention of returning? " Yet neither of them found it possible or practicable to steer a perfectly straight course through this problem of theirs. Of the King's grief at losing Wagner, and of his desire to shorten the period of that grief, there cannot be the smallest doubt. Not only his letters to Wagner himself but those to Cosima are eloquent of his heartbreak. The occasional inconsistency between his personal letters to them and the messages he sends through Lutz is more apparent than real: to Wagner and Cosima he can pour out all his sorrow and all his longing, while the moment he is compelled to discuss the same problems with his Ministers he recognises that the real world has even stronger claims on him, as King, than the ideal. To Cosima he swears that it will cost him his very life if he cannot see Wagner at least on the latter's birthday — the 22nd May. If the Friend is reluctant to settle in Munich again just yet, will he not accept one of his Majesty's lodges, such as that in the Riss, where the King can visit him from time to time? Yet almost in the same breath he can instruct Lutz (on the 12th March) to explain to Cosima that she " must not cherish any illusion — for me to recall Herr Wagner, or grant him permission to return, would mean the instant resignation of Baron Pfordten as Minister for Foreign Affairs " — an event that would have the gravest conse-

quences in the present international crisis.[4] These vacillations are
all to the King's credit; they prove that, as had been the case in
the preceding December, whenever he was called upon to stand up
squarely to the responsibilities of his office he was perfectly capable of putting his romantic predilections on one side and coming
to a vital decision on purely realistic grounds. But the terrible
heartache was there all the time; and in his private letters to Wagner and Cosima he could indulge himself in the sad luxury of
lament.

Wagner's case was rather different, and perhaps, all things considered, more complex. He had fled from Munich pouring curses
on his enemies there, and for a long time afterwards he could never
think of them without hungering for revenge. If anything could
have brought him back it might have been the sweet prospect of
that revenge. He was still unable to visualise what had happened
to him as anything more than a personal matter between the politicians and himself, with the politicians, of course, cast for the rôle
of the villain of the play. He kept on insisting that an official refutation be given of the story of the 190,000 gulden — as if the sole
point at issue had been the extent of his " luxury ", and all he had
to do to rehabilitate himself was to prove that though he may have
dipped his fingers fairly deeply into the royal purse he had never
stooped to picking the royal pocket. It never seems to have occurred
to him that the Bavarian Government had a number of political
problems to occupy it which could be solved only along purely
political lines, and that it saw danger to the State in an amateur
like himself being allowed to determine policies and dismiss and
summon ministers, merely because of the strength of his hold over
the King's mind in matters of art. Early in March, Cosima discussed the question of Wagner's return in a personal interview with
Pfordten. She obtained no satisfaction from him. He began with
one of his typical " without prejudice " double reservations — the
" either-or " gambit of which he was so fond: either what she had
called on him to talk about was a private affair of the King's, with
which, as a minister, he had nothing to do, or it was a matter of
public politics, which, as a minister, he must decline to discuss with

---

[4] War seemed probable between Prussia and Austria just then.

her.[5] All he would commit himself to was the assurance that he would regard Wagner's return, even to some provincial Bavarian town or other, as imperilling the King and the State. Cosima resignedly told the King that she could do nothing with the man, because he had " evidently made a religion of this belief of his ". He really and truly imagined he was serving the King: " in a man of this sort his limitations are his only props, and it was with a narrow mind that I had to deal today." In Cosima's view, as in Wagner's, a conviction held so strongly that it had the fanatical force of a religion was something admirable only when it was met with in *their* camp; in a member of the opposite camp it merely indicated limitation, either intellectual or moral, and perhaps both.

3

One thing cannot be too strongly insisted on — the entire honesty of Wagner's attitude towards the King. The theory that he cunningly, cold-bloodedly and unscrupulously played upon Ludwig's inexperience merely for his own selfish ends must be dismissed as only one more of the many myths that have formed in connection with these Munich years. In entire good faith he identified his own cause with that of Germany; as he himself said, with the survival or the decay of the German spirit his own art must live or die. Whether he was wise in believing that not only social but political man could be " regenerated " through the theatre we may permit ourselves to doubt; but that he did hold this curious belief there can be no question. He believed moreover that in the political sphere he was as necessary to the King as the King was to him in the sphere of art, that it was his mission to stand by the boy's side, not merely as friend but as mentor, until he had learned enough of the ways of men and the evil of the world to take care of himself. The opinion expressed on an earlier page,[6] that had the Bavarian politicians been wiser men — and some of them honester men — they would have seen that through Wagner, and through him alone, the young King might gradually be brought to devote his undoubted

---

[5] See *supra*, pp. 390–1, for another specimen of this favourite gambit of the lawyer-professor.

[6] See *supra*, p. 251ff.

abilities to affairs of state, is amply confirmed by Wagner's letters about this time to more than one correspondent. He not only saw the King, for all the intimacy of his association with him and for all the quasi-paternal affection he had for him, more objectively than Pfordten or Pfistermeister or any of the others did: he saw him more penetratingly. " I regard the young King Ludwig ", he wrote to Constantin Frantz on the 19th March,

" as being quite uncommonly gifted; indeed, the first glance at his very remarkable face would convince you of that. The great question at present is how he will develop as a ruler. An unbelievably sense-less education has managed to generate in the youth a deeply-rooted, and, so far, unconquerable reluctance to occupy himself seriously with matters of state; contemptuous of everyone he meets with in this field, he disposes of these matters, with a sort of nausea, through the existing officials and the established routine. His family, and indeed the whole Court, are repugnant to him; everything that has to do with armies and soldiers he hates; he regards the aristocracy as ludicrous and the mob as despicable; in the matter of religion he is serious and fervent, though clear-sighted and unprejudiced where the priesthood is con-cerned. There is one way, and one way only, to evoke the sympathetic powers of his spirit — through me, my work, my art, which he regards as the truly real world, everything else seeming to him just unreal nonsense. Contact with this one element calls out in him the most sur-prising, really prodigious capacities; here he sees and feels with the most amazing certainty, and manifests for the attainment of my fur-thest-reaching artistic schemes a will that for the present is the expres-sion of his whole being . . . As you can no doubt imagine, this so charming ignorance on his part of real life, an ignorance that is full of promise, is bound to involve the young King in conflicts which, under the pressure of circumstance, drive him to obvious manifesta-tions of weakness. As the only way to act on him is with reference to myself, my removal could only be effected by pretending to him that his love was bringing *me* into the utmost peril. For my part nothing could remain undone that would bring home to him the seriousness of his royal duties; and to achieve this end only one means was possible — to make it a matter of his love for me. In his zeal to serve me he behaved with such blind enthusiasm that he had the pages of my ' Journal ' . . . copied out and passed on to the various ministers with a view to their ' putting into execution ' the ideas expressed there. To what almost diverting confusion this led I need not tell you." [7]

---

[7] This is all very well; but why did Wagner put these precepts before the King if he did not expect him to act on them? As a matter of fact he had said in the first par-agraph of the "Journal" that he proposed, among other things, to "touch *en passant*

He goes on to complain that the King, though he listens attentively to his advice — with regard to ministers, state policy and matters of that kind — rarely acts on it. (This he regards as a sign of " weakness " on the young man's part; to us today it seems just the opposite). So nothing remains for him to do but to work on the King through his love for his Friend's art; and the thought that he can do this fills him with a sense of vast responsibility.

"One thing is now clear to me: with Germany's well-being stands or falls my art-ideal: without Germany's greatness my art was only a dream: if this dream is to become reality, then as a matter of course Germany also must achieve its predestined greatness." [8]

It is certainly the language of a fanatic, but as certainly not of a coldly scheming fanatic. The belief that while this young Wittelsbach could do much for the Wagnerian ideal Wagner in turn could help the King to become the future saviour of all Germany which he fancied he foresaw in him, may have been a complete delusion, but it was a lofty delusion.

4

It is not surprising that Wagner's letters to the King on the subject of his return should exhibit, over a period, a certain inconsistency. In his heart of hearts he had no consuming desire to see Munich again for a very long time, except, perhaps, to do a triumphal dance over the bodies of " Pfi " and " Pfo " — as he and Ludwig used irreverently to refer to Pfistermeister and Pfordten in their private correspondence. But of a return in triumph there was very little likelihood: not only had the politicians beaten him in the field but they had in their hands every means for consolidating their victory. He could not even obtain the small satisfaction of an official démenti of the fable of the 190,000 gulden: Lutz, in reply to a letter of Wagner's which probably did not err on the

on the praxis of life" and to "sketch briefly measures to be adopted, counsels and hints" to which Ludwig could turn for guidance when necessary.

[8] KLRWB, IV, 132–135. Constantin Frantz was a Prussian politician and publicist with whose work Wagner became acquainted in the winter of 1865–6. He found in him a good deal of community with his own ideas as to the future of Germany, and he recommended King Ludwig to read certain works of his. Frantz visited Wagner in Triebschen in the summer of 1866. Wagner dedicated the second edition of *Opera and Drama* (1868) to him.

side of temperance, blandly pointed out to him that an official contradiction of the kind he had in view was impossible, as it would be tantamount to admitting a right on the part of a subject to dictate procedure to the King and demand public " explanations " from him. Moreover, even if the officials saw fit to make a statement on their own account Wagner could hardly expect them to confine it to the lines laid down by him: they would have to set forth his financial relations with the King in full. Not only his direct but his indirect and prospective cost to the State would have to be gone into in the fullest detail. " If an official elucidation is really to elucidate ", said Lutz, " there would have to figure in the account not only the 78,000 florins you have received as capital and the 56,000 florins represented by your house, but the expenditure on opera productions, musical performances, the Music School, subventions to your friends, and so on "; and he was invited to ask himself seriously whether " an explanation of this kind would achieve the end you have in view ", whether, indeed, it would not be much the best thing, in his own interests, to let the whole matter drop. Wagner found himself so thoroughly checkmated that there was nothing to do but to give up the game.

He honestly regarded the King as in danger from the scheming politicians surrounding him, who were hoping to profit by his inexperience of the world; and at a distance he felt powerless to be of any real service to the youth, especially as there was reason to believe that their correspondence was being " tapped ". No one knew the King better than he did; no one, therefore, was in a better position than he to realise that, if he were pushed too far, if the present were made intolerable and the future hopeless for him, he might carry out the threat of abdication which was so often on his lips. That would have suited Wagner's book neither personally nor politically: even if his own economic position were to remain unprejudiced under a new dispensation — which was doubtful — there would be an end to all his dreams of a re-birth of " the German spirit " through this young man who, for one reason and another, he had persuaded himself was the pre-appointed saviour of Germany. From time to time, therefore, both he and Cosima had to soothe Ludwig with words that contained the promise of a reunion, which in any case, the King thought, need not be delayed

[511]

further than the coming May. As against all this was the consideration that Wagner's return to Munich would only lead to further complications and end by weakening the King's position. This also had to be conveyed to the sorely suffering boy, and in such a way as to help him to sustain his belief in himself while not concealing from him the peril he was in.

On the whole, however, Wagner made it as clear as possible to the King, almost from the first, that he did not wish to return. To his other correspondents he made no secret of this. We have already seen him telling his French friend, as early as the 1st January, that he wanted to rent a house in the south of France for five or six years. On the 26th he informs Pusinelli that his one desire just now is to find peace and shelter from the world in order that he may finish the works he has in hand.

> " For this reason I am now compelled to reply most determinedly to my youthful friend the King of Bavaria, who passionately wished to have me near him once more by Easter: for I have resolved only to work, and to produce no more [9] . . . He is disconsolate: I fear that he may bring himself even to abdicating the throne. Judge, then, to what agitations I am exposed by the only solution possible to this situation! Thus everything combines to afflict and alarm my heart! " [10]

Cosima, who was in close touch both with the King and with events in Munich, seems to have thought, at any rate during the first few weeks, that Wagner ought not to decide the question too suddenly. She seems to have tried to persuade him at least to delay his departure from Geneva in quest of a house in France. She was sending him, she said, an important communication. His reply was a telegram — on the 20th January — that left no doubt as to his intentions: " Firmly resolved not to return to Munich, I ask you what communication could be important enough to deter me from the necessary search for an establishment." To this she wired back that she proposed to go to him in Geneva the next day. His reply — the fourth telegram to pass between them that day — begged her not to interfere with his resolution: it would be time enough for

---

[9] I.e., take no part in the production of his works in the theatre.
[10] RWAP, p. 185.

him to discuss whatever it was that was weighing on her mind if his quest proved unsuccessful.[11]

5

If anything could have broken down his resolution it would have been the pitiful letter he had received a few days earlier from the King, a letter that shows how tragically hard the boy had been hit by the severance from his only friend.

"I have not given up hope: better times will come, everything will calm down here, the Friend will return and inspire me with his dear proximity, we will go on with our art-plans, the School will be founded, the festival theatre will rise in its undreamed-of pride and splendour. . . . I hope, believe, love. . . . No, no, what began so divinely shall not end thus! . . . I will do as you desire, will govern firmly, like a King in the fullest sense of the word. But why must we remain apart, each living only for himself? . . . I have a presentiment that you will never find peace abroad. . . . I implore you, let a few months go quietly by, and many things will be quite different. . . . Then, I hope and believe, your return will have no political significance."

But Wagner's mind was made up. "I know what you have suffered on my account", he had replied to the King on the 19th.[12]

"But neither you nor I must go on suffering: you must now *act,* while I *create.* And so, dear one, hear what I have to say: *I will not return to Munich.* Tell this to the wretched people who deceived and betrayed you; but at the same time tell them that you are, and intend to remain, King of Bavaria. Rouse yourself, my noble Friend, and be entirely what destiny has called you to be. . . . We are both of us in need — you of heartening for your royal mission, I of peace for artistic creation. And neither of us can succeed unless we renounce all weakness, each going his own way in the eyes of the world. . . .

---

[11] KLRWB, IV, 124–5. There was reason to believe that telegrams to and from Wagner were systematically communicated by the clerks concerned to his enemies in political circles. To put them off his traces as far as possible he and Cosima had to resort, in time, to signing their wires "Will" and "Vorstel" respectively — the names, of course, being adapted from the title of Schopenhauer's work *Die Welt als Wille und Vorstellung.* The King was referred to as "Arnold". Sometimes Cosima would be "David", and Wagner "Sachs".

[12] It was probably the knowledge of this reply that had made Cosima telegraph him on the 20th to postpone his journey until he had seen her. She was aware that a crisis had been reached.

You know well how dear to me were the house and garden you meant to be mine to the end of my days; and the sacrifice I make in surrendering them will give you an idea of what I hope to win by such a sacrifice — peace, peace, without which, and the assurance of its continuance, I shall go under."

The King is to grant him permission to live for some years in distant retirement, and to take back the Briennerstrasse house, sell it, and make a new home possible for Wagner in Switzerland or southern France. It is the only way: another year such as the last in Munich will mean the end of him and his work.

There were two main reasons for this desire of his to have finished with Munich. He had become absorbed in the *Meistersinger* again,[13] and, as always, found creative work so delightful in itself and so sure a shield against the ugliness of the outer world that he could not bear the thought of abandoning it. And he was consumed with hunger for Cosima. " Enough of words, deeds and sorrows! " he had said in his telegram to her of the 20th January (shortly before his departure from Geneva).

" For God's sake, dear one, no more half-measures! We have suffered enough, without wanting to torment ourselves further. In a month, God willing, we shall be tranquilly re-united, no more talking, through with Munich — final escape! . . . Let me look out for the nest for our peace."

Obviously there was an understanding between them that she was once more to share his home with him; and this would have been impossible in Munich, with its many prying eyes and malicious tongues. The telegram is one more link in the long chain of evidence pointing to some kind of understanding between Wagner, Cosima and Bülow.[14]

But the old tragi-comedy of cross-purposes soon began once more; and by the 3rd February we find Wagner consenting, for the King's sake rather than his own, to return to Munich as soon as that

---

[13] He took up the score again on the 12th January, at the point in the first act at which Beckmesser, after Walther's second song, puts his head out of the Marker's box and asks "Have you finished?" By the 21st February Wagner had completed both the Composition Sketch and the Orchestral Sketch of the first act. It was nearly three months after that before he could find leisure and inclination to begin on the second act.

[14] See *infra*, Chapter XXI.

should prove possible. He made three stipulations, however. (A), his stipend was to be guaranteed him for life; (B), the Brienner-strasse house was to become his personal property, of which he could dispose in his will; (C), he was to be granted Bavarian letters of naturalisation immediately. The King consented at once to A and B: there could be, indeed, no objection to either of these, for if Wagner was to bind himself for life to the service of the Bavarian King, whose property his new works would be, he was obviously entitled to have his livelihood ensured to the end of his days. The third suggestion, however, called forth so much opposition from the politicians that the King had to abandon it. As soon, indeed, as it became a question of translating his own and Wagner's ideal-istic aspirations into prosaic realities the usual difficulties arose. The King once more calls heaven and earth to witness that he will die if he is separated much longer from Wagner; yet the moment his ministers make it clear to him that Wagner's return will mean their resignation, his common sense tells him that even for art's sake he cannot precipitate an internal political crisis at a time of such international tension. So all he can do is to assure the Friend that Pfordten will be dismissed as soon as that shall prove practicable, and that in the meantime he will be true to their ideal and their glorious plans for the future.

As for Wagner, while he was realist enough to recognise the considerations that bound the King hand and foot, he could still see no solution of it all but the excessively simplified one of bidding Ludwig " exercise his royal will ". He protested, as usual, that he was not interested in Bavarian politics and had no wish to interfere in them. He was frankly unable to perceive that advising the King to get rid of certain of his ministers in order that the Wagnerian ideal of culture might have a freer course in Munich *was* interfer-ing in politics: for him it went without saying that any minister who made things easier for Richard Wagner was a good minister, and vice versa. In mid-February we find him reverting to a former suggestion of his for having Baron Moy appointed to the new post of " Intendant of the Civil List for Art-Matters ": he recalled, he told the King, " the warm expression he gave [at an interview with Wagner in the summer of 1865] to his conviction that you must be assured complete tranquillity and certainty as regards the carrying out of your artistic plans, in order that you may win the cheerfulness that will enable you to devote yourself with royal patience to the exacting business of state." All the King would have to do, therefore, would be to nominate Moy and arrange that he was to have no ties with anyone but himself and Wagner! Always he was obsessed by the romantic idea that the " redemption " of Germany could come only through its princes in general — via the theatre — and through the providentially-sent young Ludwig of Bavaria in particular.[15] The King should make it a rule to mistrust his resolutions whenever his heart had no share in them. Shrewdness was nothing: " the highest shrewdness for a monarch is to be great-hearted "; for only genius can find the right way to get things done, and genius is always great-hearted. " The German Folk, the Bavarian land, do not need shrewd politicians: what they need is a real King, a great-hearted, inspired German prince. . . . When will the German Folk find its King? "

But however pleased and flattered Ludwig might have been by this fanciful picture of himself as a typical King of German opera, sitting with his German nobles and his loyal German men-at-arms around him in a German meadow and instructing them, in a few well-chosen words, in the whole art of German policy, his native good sense told him that real life was not at all like that. And so even Wagner's eager eulogy of Baron Moy as the one man suitable for their joint purpose did not blind him to the stark realities of the situation. " We must be very circumspect where this man is concerned ", he wrote back; " I almost believe he rejoiced when you left Munich."

6

Nothing whatever was done, in fact, or could be done as regards Wagner's return to Munich. The only possible solution of the problem that he could think of was that the King should " will " what-

---

[15] "It does not seem to occur to anyone", he wrote in 1867, "that *in this derelict institution* [the theatre] *there lie the seed and the kernel of all spiritual culture in the national-poetic and national-ethical sense, that no other art-branch can ever truly flower, or ever aid the culture of the Folk, until the theatre's all-powerful contribution to this end has been fully recognised and assured.*" (German Art and German Politics, in RWGS, VIII, 60. The italics are Wagner's own.

ever he wanted; yet in his calmer moments he saw as clearly as
Ludwig did that there were limits in practice to what could be
achieved by the theoretic royal " will ". So it is not surprising to
find that, as the weeks went on, his hatred of Munich increased, and
he turned away with more and more bitterness and disgust from
the thought of ever entrusting his fate and that of his art to it again.
" Munich has poisoned me ", he confessed to the King on the 22nd
February. " My King, that is a vile place: never, *never* will our
work prosper there." Munich is not " German ": its people are
led — or misled — by Jesuits and Jews. His thoughts were already
turning in the direction of Nuremberg not only as the ideal home
for so thoroughly " German " a work as the *Meistersinger* but as
the new capital from which the King might rule his kingdom.
He was ill and weary: every nerve in his body cried out for rest
and peace; his every instinct as an artist bade him turn his back on
this sorry world in which *Wahn* reigned supreme, and devote himself in solitude to the creation of those

> Forms more real than living man,
> Nurslings of immortality,

that should be the artist's sole concern. Ludwig himself had to admit that even were the political situation to make it possible for him
to recall the Friend, Munich was not the place in which Wagner
could ever devote himself in peace and quiet to the completion of
his works. Cosima must have come to the same conclusion about
this time; and it must have been strengthened in her, as in Wagner,
by the reflection that now Minna was dead there was one obstacle
the less in the way of their ultimate union, that meanwhile neither
of them would know happiness again until she had resumed the
protectorship over him which, on the whole, had been so much to his
benefit in Munich, and that, if she was to share his house with him
again, the further removed from Munich and its evil journalists
that house was the better.

Cosima, taking with her her daughter Daniela, set out on the
7th March for Lausanne, where Wagner met her; the next day they
were in " Les Artichauts ". On the 9th he was capable of sufficient
detachment from his troubles to begin again with her on the dictation of his autobiography: he worked also at the *Meistersinger* with

such energy that the orchestral score of the first act was completed by the 23rd.[16] It was probably this taste of serene domestic happiness that determined him to finish once for all with the idea of returning to Munich. On the 27th he and Cosima made an excursion to Berne. Three days later, returning by way of Interlaken, they lighted, in the neighbourhood of Lucerne, on a house standing on a promontory a little distance away from the town, with grounds running down to the Lake. Its name was Triebschen, and it belonged to a certain Colonel Am Rhyn. It promised perfect quiet, and it afforded superb views; but it was in such sore disrepair that Wagner hesitated to commit himself definitely over it. Cosima, in fact, returned to Munich the next day without anything having been settled. On the 2nd April Wagner seems to have made up his mind to take the place for a year; and as the owner, in accordance with the local custom, required advance payment of the whole year's rent (5,000 francs), he asked Lutz to arrange for him to receive at once the remainder of his stipend for 1866. The King's reply to this was to order — on the 10th — the despatch to him of 5,000 francs *as a gift*. Already on the 4th, however, having made another inspection of the house and found it, as he said, " very suitable and advantageous ", he had taken it on a year's provisional tenancy.[17] His telegram to Cosima the next day was jubilant: " Big house overlooking the Lake for all of us . . .", from which it is evident that he counted on Cosima settling there with her children, Hans, no doubt, to visit them all from time to time: his professional duties would of course bind him to some extent to Munich, while in the future, as in the past, he would frequently be away on concert tours.

Virtually at the very time Wagner was deciding on Triebschen the King was making him, through Cosima, a last despairing offer

---

[16] It seems to have been during these March days that he heard for the first time, through Corpello, the Italian Consul General in Geneva, that on the preceding 23rd December King Victor Emmanuel II had conferred on him the order of St. Maurizio and St. Lazaro. Wagner, in letters to the King and to Corpello drafted for him in French by Cosima, conveyed his thanks for the honour, but politely explained that he would have to refrain from wearing the Cross in public because of the bad relations between himself and the Saxon Government. See the letters in KLRWB, V, 21 ff.

[17] He entered into possession on the 15th April. In the following September he formally returned his Briennerstrasse house to the King. It was sold, and the proceeds applied to the rental of Triebschen for a further five years.

of the lodge in the Riss, as a temporary expedient until a permanent home could be found for him " somewhere in my country ". " A fortnight ago ", Wagner replied to Cosima, " this letter [of the King] would have changed everything: now it is too late — for the present." He was only being sophistical when he went on to suggest that were he thinking solely of himself he would accept the King's offer and pay forfeit to the owner of Triebschen, but that his conscience will not allow him to create any more difficulties for the King: he " will wait until he can openly summon me to my house in Munich. And so, welcome, Fate! Triebschen be my refuge! " He was merely writing " literature ", merely striking one of his favourite attitudes of " resignation ". He foresaw that in this haven by the Lake he could count on quiet for his fretted nerves and tranquillity for his work: moreover, the place had the dual advantage of being in German Switzerland and lying within easy distance of Munich.

His instinct was sound: in Triebschen he was to spend what were, on the whole, the happiest six years of his life: there he was to complete the *Meistersinger* and *Siegfried,* compose the *Götterdämmerung* [18] and the *Siegfried Idyll,* and write some of the most notable of his prose works, including the *Beethoven,* the treatise *On Conducting,* that on *German Art and German Policy,* and *On the Destiny of Opera.* Above all, it was in Triebschen that Cosima was to become finally his own, and the long-desired son was to be born to him.

---

[18] The scoring of this was done after he had left Triebschen for Bayreuth.

CHAPTER XXI

THE TRIANGLE

1

THIS IS a convenient point at which to devote a few minutes to the examination of a problem that has always been shrouded in a certain obscurity. A final, incontrovertible solution of it is, and perhaps long will be, an impossibility, owing to the fact that a number of letters of the triangle Wagner-Cosima-Bülow have obviously been destroyed, withheld, or mutilated in process of partial publication: we can only try, with the help of all the documents so far available, to piece together events and dates in something like their true sequence, and then permit ourselves the luxury of a broad conjecture as to the conclusion to be drawn from it all.

The central problem is, What was Bülow's real position in the triangle, and what his real attitude — his private, as distinguished from his public attitude — towards it? How much did he know, and at what stage did he begin to know? The universally accepted story is that set forth by Julius Kapp in the following wise. We know that on the 8th April, 1866 Wagner wrote to Bülow asking him to come and settle in Triebschen " for as long as possible " with Cosima and the three children. (Isolde, of course, ranked technically, then and later, as Bülow's child). The house, said Wagner, had three floors: he himself would occupy the middle one, Hans and Cosima the lower, the children and servants the upper: he and Hans could thus work without either of them disturbing or being disturbed by the other.

" This time, too, Bülow acceded to his friend's request ", says Kapp. " As he was detained in Munich himself, he sent Cosima and the children to Triebschen ahead of him, where Wagner awaited the coming of the beloved in an agony of longing. At last, on the 12th May, 1866,[1]

---

[1] This is the date generally given, but it may possibly have been the 11th: on the 10th we find Cosima writing to King Ludwig that "early tomorrow" she will be going

she came to him. But an ardent love-letter from Wagner to Cosima,[2] which arrived shortly after her departure from Munich, was opened by Bülow, he thinking it might contain some communication which he ought to telegraph at once to his wife. It revealed the whole bitter truth to him: the stupendous lie of the last two years suddenly stared him relentlessly in the face."

Added to this, says Kapp, was a renewed Press attack on Wagner and the King, with its accompanying plain speaking about the relations of Cosima and Wagner.

" The only course open to the doubly deceived man ", continues Kapp, " was to hand in his resignation in Munich and go to Triebschen, to get full light on the matter, and above all to silence evil tongues. ' After ten years of a marriage that can hardly have been a bed of roses for him ', says Cornelius, ' Bülow now sees himself compelled to go to Lucerne and put the final question to Cosima — Do you wish to belong to Wagner or to me? What checked and stifled his confidences to me was that it meant questions coming up for discussion which he hardly dared put to himself. Now he sees the papers discussing in the most insulting manner what he did not venture to talk about with his friends, what only once escaped his lips — that Liszt

---

with the children to Lucerne, where she will remain for some weeks. KLRWB, IV, 145, *note.*

Dr. Strobel is now of the opinion that Cosima misdated her letter the 10th instead of the 11th, and that she went to Lucerne, therefore, on the 12th. This necessitates the further assumption that the editor of Cornelius's correspondence has erred in affixing to the [undated] letter in which Cornelius tells his fiancée that Cosima left Bülow "yesterday" the date "Munich, 12th May, 1866". As Wagner's own entries for that week (in the "Annals") are obviously muddled (having no doubt been made much later) the confusion is about as thick as it could be! Dr. Strobel relies on a passage in Bülow's letter of the 13th May to Alexander Ritter, in which he says that Cosima and the children left "yesterday morning". But may not Bülow have misdated *his* letter? It would not have been the first occasion on which he had done that kind of thing. Dr. Strobel further draws attention to the King's telegram of the 13th to Cosima. "The Freundin [Cosima] will by now have joined the dear one." But I see no particular reason to assume that "now" cannot mean anything but the 13th. The whole thing, trifling in itself, is typical of the difficulty that is constantly arising of settling a particular point of chronology in this episode or that in Wagner biography. The documents are plentiful enough to throw doubt on each of two or three conclusions, but just not plentiful enough to decide definitely in favour of any one of them.

[2] I am quoting from the 15th edition of Kapp's book (1929), in which there is some expansion of the story as told in the first-to-sixth edition (1912). In that we read only of "a letter from Wagner to her, which arrived in Munich soon after her departure", etc. In the 15th edition this mere "letter" — of which, the reader will kindly bear in mind, nothing whatever is known at first hand — becomes "an ardent love-letter", as a result of which, so Kapp's 15th edition assures us, "the stupendous lie of the last two years suddenly stared him [Bülow] relentlessly in the face."

had been very angry with his daughter for going to Wagner [i.e., to Geneva on the 7th March].[3] Well, today is the anxious day of decision at Lucerne. I know which way it will go: Cosima will stay with Wagner, for so it must be, for the fulfilment of her destiny! And Wagner's! " [4]

The same story is told in much the same terms by Sebastian Röckl, who seems to have relied upon Kapp: [5]

" On the 12th May Frau von Bülow went once more to Triebschen, ' to keep the unhappy, lonely man company '. A letter from Wagner, which arrived in Munich immediately after her departure, was opened by Bülow in the belief that it contained a communication ' which perhaps he ought to telegraph at once to his wife '. He was horrified by the contents: it revealed to him afresh (sic) the bitter truth of Wagner's relations with Cosima. ' Now I will probably take my farewell and go to Italy ', he said to Cornelius." [6]

2

Cornelius seems to be the ultimate source for the story, such as it is. And what actually does Cornelius say? Merely this (he is writing to his fiancée, by the way, on the 12th(?) May, first before, then after, a visit to Bülow):

" His wife went to Lucerne to Wagner yesterday with the whole family. I have an idea I shall not see her again: I would not mind in the least! I have no longer any relations with her; my nature is altogether alien to her. I said no farewell to her — indeed, I had no official information of the journey. I look forward to enjoying her husband once more this evening, undisturbed, with Mihalovich; for he is so pleasant when she is not there — another man altogether." [7]

One gathers that the letter thus begun was finished the next day, after the evening with Bülow mentioned above: that point, however, is not really material to our enquiry. The final paragraph of this letter of May 12th(?) runs thus:

[3] She had returned to Munich on the 31st March.
[4] JKWF, p. 246 ff.
[5] The first edition of Kapp's book appeared in 1912: Röckl's second volume, dealing with the years 1866–1883, is dated 1920.
[6] RLW, II, 8–9. On a later page (72) Röckl says that from this letter Bülow learned that Wagner and Cosima "were resolved never to part again."
[7] CABT, II, 370. Apparently something immediately following this has been omitted by the editor of Cornelius's letters.

" At Bülow's yesterday we talked about serious things. He had written a very decided letter to Perfall [the Munich Theatre Intendant], complaining bitterly about the bad performance of *St Elisabeth*,[8] demanding four new violinists for *Lohengrin,* etc. He thought it depended on these matters whether he would not refuse his co-operation at the eleventh hour. Just after his family had left he opened a letter — a thing he never does, but he thought he might have to telegraph to his wife at once. But he was really horrified by the letter. He is very much afraid that nothing will come of the Conservatoire and all the rest of it; he may say good-bye and go to Italy. All this is bound up, too, with this departure of the whole family."

At this point also the letter seems to have been cut short by the editor of the correspondence. But such as it is, it is all that Röckl, Kapp, and many others who have dealt with this episode have had to go upon; and the reader will probably ask himself what there is in it to justify what they have all read into it and the remarkable inference they have drawn from it. Cornelius says nothing whatever about an " ardent love-letter ", nothing whatever about this letter revealing " the whole bitter truth " to Bülow, nothing whatever about " the stupendous lie of the last two years suddenly staring him relentlessly in the face ".[9] Cornelius does not so much as say that the letter was from Wagner! We may take leave to doubt, until further and better evidence is forthcoming, that it *was* from him, or at all events that it was " compromising ". In the first place, what sense would there be in Bülow's telegraphing to Triebschen the contents of a letter *from Wagner,* when Cosima would be with the writer of the letter almost as soon as the telegram? Would he not have done what any other man would do in similar circumstances — simply have readdressed the letter? In the second place, is it credible that Wagner, knowing that Cosima was leaving Munich early on a given morning, would send her a letter which was tolerably certain to arrive after she had left? In the third place, is it probable that, in view of the fact that the Wagner-Cosima associa-

[8] Liszt's work had been given in Munich, under Bülow, on the 24th February, 1st March, and 10th May, 1866.
[9] There are no hints of "horror" or "bitterness" in Bülow's reference to Cosima's departure, in his letter of the 13th to Ritter. All he says is, "Yesterday morning my wife took the children to Lucerne for the summer. She will probably stay there over the 22nd [i.e., Wagner's birthday] to keep the poor solitary company, and return here at the beginning of June, when we are threatened with the so-called model performances. Then we will both of us go to Lucerne at the beginning of July."

tion had now lasted for nearly two years, and that not only the personal friends of the parties but all artistic and political Munich either knew about it or suspected it, Wagner would choose precisely *this* letter in which to say something that would, or could, come as a " revelation " to the horrified Bülow?

The internal evidence is not inconsistent with the theory of the letter being from someone else than Wagner, and on some subject unconnected with the " deceiving " of Bülow. For it will be observed that the passage relating to it occurs merely as a link between one sentence of Cornelius's, describing Bülow's dissatisfaction with his job as a conductor in Munich — a dissatisfaction so deep that he contemplates resignation — and another sentence in which Bülow speaks of his further abandonment of hope with regard to the Music School and things of that kind. Is it not possible that the opened letter had something to do with *these* matters, the cumulative effect of it all being that Bülow seriously thinks of leaving Munich and going to Italy? Can any reason be given why Cornelius should suddenly and arbitrarily spatchcock a reference to a fateful Wagner-Cosima letter between two sentences both relating solely to Bülow's professional discontents in Munich? [10] Note also Cornelius's final sentence — " all this is bound up, too, with this departure of the whole family." Surely that of itself suggests that the subject of the opened letter was *not* the relations — hitherto unsuspected by Bülow — of Wagner and Cosima, and that it may even not have been from Wagner to her? Were the construction that the biographers have placed on Cornelius's letter the correct one, the logical sequence of the ideas would have been something like this — Bülow is out of tune with Munich because of the *St. Elisabeth* performance, the quality of the orchestra, the dubious prospects of the Music School, and other matters of that kind, and consequently thinks of turning his back on it all and going to Italy: *in addition,* he has just opened a letter from Wagner that has opened his eyes about Cosima and horrified him.

---

[10] Without a doubt it was these discontents that were taking the heart out of Bülow just then. The third performance of *St. Elisabeth* had been given under him on the 10th. The evening had been a fiasco from every point of view. Bülow himself described the performance as "bad"; Cornelius says that the theatre was empty in spite of the abonnement, and the applause extremely lukewarm. Whether the conversation between the pair took place on the 11th — as is probable — or on the 12th,

The possibility, of course, cannot be ruled out that some day some further documents may be published that will prove this reasoning to be fallacious. For the present, however, we can but exercise our judgment upon Cornelius's letter as we have it, and upon the environing circumstances as we know them; and on the basis of these what conclusion can we come to but that this famous document has not merely been misunderstood by the Wagner biographers, but has been embroidered upon by their fancy to an unwarrantable extent? In passing, the reader will probably have observed for himself that Cornelius does not say that Bülow's weariness of his Munich position is " bound up with " a letter from Wagner to Cosima that brings him the astonishing revelation of the guilty nature of their association, but that the weariness is " bound up with *this departure of the whole family* ". Now that " departure of the whole family " had manifestly been agreed upon between Hans, Cosima and Wagner. Is it not fairly apparent that *already* there was an understanding within the triangle that as Cosima cared for no one now but Wagner, she would in future occupy *his* household, wherever that might be, just as she had done from time to time in the Briennerstrasse? One surmises that all that the trio was anxious about was " saving face " so far as the King and the public were concerned. The illusion that they could do this was soon shattered by the Munich Press; and it was this drastic and unforeseen change in the situation, not the letter of the 10th or 11th May, that made it necessary for Bülow to see the other two and decide on a new joint course of action.

3

A hasty reader of Kapp's story could be forgiven for mistakenly concluding that it was as the *practically direct* result of the opening of the mysterious letter that Bülow was forced to go to Lucerne and put to Cosima the plain question, " Do you wish to belong to Wagner or to me? " But the letter of Cornelius to his fiancée from which *this* part of Kapp's narrative is taken dates from *the early days of June* — some three weeks after the Cornelius letter of the 12th(?)

---

it was within a few hours of one of those disheartening experiences which, as we know from other instances, used to plunge Bülow into the blackest pessimism.

May! [11] Now a good deal had happened in those three weeks, and Bülow's journey was motived by something quite other than the supposed " horror " at having, on the 11th or 12th May, for the first time discovered his wife's long " deception " of him. Bülow's marriage with Cosima, says Cornelius in this (undated) letter of his of " early June ", " was a sacrifice to friendship made for his master Liszt's sake, to give the illegitimate child a brilliant, honourable name, and her father a profound satisfaction and ease of mind. These were Bülow's motives; it was an act of gratitude. This devotion was ill repaid him by Cosima." Then follows the passage already quoted on pages 521–2, commencing " After ten years of marriage ", with its explanation why Bülow has now been compelled to go to see Cosima and put the decisive question to her. Nowhere, in this or any other letter, does Cornelius so much as hint at the crisis having come about through the " sudden " revelation of the opened letter. On the contrary, he treats the situation that arose in June — a situation necessitating Bülow's journey to Triebschen to discuss the matter with Wagner and Cosima — as merely the last inevitable link in a long chain of events; and when we go back and follow up the links one by one we find it difficult to escape the conclusion that the " long deceit " of Bülow is merely one more latter-day biographical myth.

The evolution of the triangle-situation can be clearly traced in the letters and diaries of Cornelius. A letter of his to his Vienna friend Dr. Standhartner, written shortly after his migration to Munich, shows us the state of affairs in January, 1865. He had lately seen a good deal of Wagner and the Bülows, and, not knowing Cosima as well then as he came to do later, he is full of admiration for her: she is " an exceptional being, a genuine Liszt-child, a dear creature, kind and intelligent, possessing not only wit but humour." Wagner is very fond of the Bülow couple, and appreci-

---

[11] The confusion is very pronounced in Röckl, who makes Bülow say, *in propria persona*, "Perhaps I will now [*sic!*] take my leave and go to Italy" *immediately after* Röckl's own "He was horrified by the contents [of the letter]: it revealed to him once more the bitter truth of Wagner's relations with Cosima." The truth is that, as the reader will have observed, there is no "now" in the original Cornelius sentence, and the reasons for Bülow's resolution to leave for Italy, as given by Cornelius, are simply that nothing is likely to come of the Music School and that he feels discouraged about his Munich work in general.

ates all they are to him. But Bülow is in a terrible state; his health is undermined and his whole condition gives cause for anxiety. " Poor Cosima! ", exclaims Cornelius: he is evidently sorry for her, netted as she is in " these tragic complications " — a phrase which seems to hint at a perception on his part that a triangle had already constituted itself. As the months go on, we find Cornelius cooling towards Cosima; he evidently resented the wedge she was beginning to drive between the infatuated Wagner and his old friends, and he watched with regret the gradual extension of her influence over both Wagner's mind and his public actions. (We must bear in mind that Cornelius was in Weimar from the middle of March to the first week of August, 1865: this accounts for the absence of comment on his part on the Wagner-Cosima situation until the autumn). By November, 1865 she had virtually succeeded in isolating Wagner. " He seems now ", says Cornelius, " to bury himself completely with Cosima. The Porges also resign him practically entirely to this comforter. I am mistrustful enough to believe that at the bottom of his heart Wagner already finds the Porges a burden: as he does *me*. For now he looks at everything through another's eyes." By December, 1865, when Wagner is driven from Munich, Cornelius obviously has no doubt whatever as to the real relations of the pair. " There is a downright affair [12] between Cosima and Wagner ", he writes; " one may even conjecture that she will follow him with the children. . . . But what about Bülow? Has he come to a high-romantic understanding with Wagner to hand his wife over to him entirely? Was Wagner's embrace in the railway station his thanks for this? [13] The actual marriage between Hans and Cosima has for some time been only a seeming marriage; otherwise Hans's behaviour would be inexplicable."

It is surely going beyond all reason, after evidence of this kind from the very centre of the Bülow circle, to ask us to surrender our suspicion that Bülow was not only well aware all along of the na-

---

[12] "Ein völliges Verhältnis."

[13] We have no further light on this mysterious "embrace". Shortly before Wagner's fall, Bülow had left Munich on a concert tour: and Cornelius may be referring to something that happened when Wagner saw him off on that occasion.

ture of the association between Wagner and Cosima but acquiesced in it.[14] And the stage of the affair at which we have now arrived, be it noted, is a full five months before the dropping into Bülow's letter-box of that alleged letter of mid-May 1866 from Wagner to Cosima which is supposed to have " opened his eyes ". In his diary Cornelius is even more explicit. His entry for the 9th December, 1865, made a couple of days after the public announcement that the King had requested Wagner to leave Bavaria for a time, runs thus:

> " It is difficult to make the *inner* connection of events in this affair quite clear, because we possess the secret threads of the web of causality only partially, and presented from only *one* side. But I will try to elucidate it. The chief thing is to put the main point in the foreground and group the subsidiary points round it. The main thing is the love affair (*Liebesverhältnis*) [15] between Wagner and Cosima von Bülow. This has developed since the time of my arrival in Munich in January of this year, and it must have come to full bloom at some time or other in the following spring or summer. Since then, Cosima, as third in the alliance, has taken part in the correspondence with the King. Since then, Wagner has been completely and unqualifiedly under her influence. Every day since Bülow went on his concert tour she has been at Wagner's, with or without the two children."

Cornelius's further analysis of the course of events in Munich leading up to Wagner's fall does not concern us here; all that it behoves us to observe is that he speaks in the plainest possible terms of a " love affair " between Wagner and Cosima as having been in existence, to his own knowledge, since the beginning of 1865. To ask us to believe that what was so evident to Cornelius, and not only

---

[14] One would like to know precisely how to interpret an entry in the "Brown Book" on the 20th August, 1865, during Wagner's stay on the Hochkopf. He describes the deadening effect on him of the blow of Schnorr's death, meaning, as it does, the destruction of his hopes for *Tristan*. Can he now feel joy in anything, believe in anything? Cosima, he continues, has still the power to inspire him to go on working. "But give me the necessary peace for that! Stay with me: do not leave me again. Tell poor Hans frankly that without you I simply cannot go on. O heaven, if only you could calmly take your place before the world as my wife!"

Wagner, it will be observed, does not say, "Tell Hans that you and I love each other." He seems to take Bülow's knowledge of that fact for granted: what he asks, apparently, is that Hans shall submit to his destiny and formally relinquish Cosima for Wagner's sake.

[15] The reader who has no German may be interested to know that the dictionary definition of "Liebesverhältnis" is "love, love-affair, amour, intrigue." It will be seen that the interpretation of Cornelius's sentence admits of no dubiety whatever.

to him but to many other people in and around the Wagner-Bülow circle, including the Press and the politicians, was completely hidden, all through 1865 and the first five months of 1866, from Bülow and from him alone, is really to demand too much of our credulity.

One little matter may be mentioned here by way of illustration of that practice of suppression or manipulation of documents that is answerable for so many errors in Wagner biography and Wagner psychology. In the edition of Cornelius's letters and diaries published by his son, Dr. Carl Maria Cornelius, in 1905, the composer's account (in his Diary) of the farewell in the Munich railway station in the early morning of the 10th December, 1865 concludes thus: " Wagner's last words to me were, ' Of course you will remain here, completely tranquil. No one can say or do anything to you: things will be just as they were '." [16] There is nothing whatever in this to suggest that anything has been omitted between this sentence and the next, in which Cornelius glances back at the old happy days with Wagner in Penzing. Twenty years later, however, in his biography of his father (1925), Carl Maria Cornelius lets us see that in the diary the passage quoted above actually continues thus: " The Porges had heard a rumour that Cosima was going to follow Wagner with her children. That would be the third act! " [17] In his biography Carl Maria Cornelius favours us with yet another sentence or two which he had suppressed in his edition of his father's correspondence. The day after Wagner left Munich, Cornelius wrote to Rosa von Milde that in his opinion the exile would prove to be good for him, as he could now forget politics and concentrate on his art. So much we were allowed to know in 1905. [18] But in 1925 we were further told that Cornelius had only one fear for Wagner — that Cosima would follow him to Switzerland: " In that case ", he wrote, " woe to poor Wagner! It will be all up with him! " [19]

Once more, then, we discover that the Wagner-Cosima " affair " was a matter of common knowledge in Munich during a large part of 1865; yet we are asked to believe that the one man who knew nothing at all of it, until his eyes were opened with dramatic suddenness in May, 1866, was Bülow!

---

[16] CABT, II, 318. [17] CPC, II, 69. [18] CABT, II, 313. [19] CPC, II, 70.

Writing to his fiancée on the 4th January, 1866, Cornelius says he has lately spent an evening with the Bülows: " the marriage is going along again in the old way, and there are no signs of a change. They were both of them very pleasant and lively." [20] Cornelius was evidently surprised to find things running so smoothly.

4

It is clear enough now that Cosima's association with Wagner had for some time not only been common talk in Munich but had given grave offence to Liszt. A minor crisis had occurred after Minna's death in January, 1866. Till that happened there had been a double obstacle to Wagner and Cosima coming out, as it were, into the open. Each was already married; and whatever chance there might have been of Bülow quietly consenting in 1864 or 1865 to a divorce at some mutually convenient time or other, there was never any likelihood of Minna agreeing to a divorce from Wagner. But with Minna's sudden death the situation was drastically altered — for the better according to Wagner's view and Cosima's, for the worse according to the point of view of the friends — including Liszt — who sympathised with Bülow and at the same time saw clearly the danger to Wagner personally, and to his artistic plans for Munich, in what would have looked, to the average spectator, merely like the theft of a friend's and disciple's wife.

It was the perception that danger was looming ahead that made Liszt frown upon the idea of Cosima joining Wagner in Geneva. The danger, indeed, must have been apparent to everyone. " Wagner's wife is dead ", Cornelius wrote to his fiancée on the 29th January. (Minna had died during the night of the 24th–25th). " Cosima telegraphed him asking if she should come to him; but he replied that he was going to the south of France. Cosima will soon be with him, however. What will be the outcome of it all? " [21] Cor-

---

[20] CABT, II, 336.
[21] This passage has been completely misunderstood — by Kapp and others — owing to Cornelius's careless phrasing. On the face of it it would appear that Cosima's telegram to Wagner, asking if she should go to Geneva to him, was sent *after* the death of Minna, and as a consequence of that. It was not so. The original telegrams, which have recently been published, show that it was some five days *before* Minna's totally unexpected death that Cosima suggested going to Geneva and Wagner restrained her from doing so, as he was off to the south of France to look for a

nelius was not only a constant visitor at the Bülows' house at this period but, apart from Mihalovich, Hans's sole confidant. His knowledge of the contents of the telegrams and letters passing between the exiled Wagner and Cosima could have been derived only from the latter herself, from Bülow, or from them jointly; and both Cornelius's information and his comments upon it suggest that neither Hans nor his intimate friends were in the smallest degree ignorant of Cosima's passion for Wagner. On the 8th January — only a month or so after Wagner had left Munich — Cornelius had written to his fiancée,

> " Wagner is not in Paris. That was just an error: Frau von Bülow had misunderstood a telegram from him. She has been in touch with developments all the time. God bless the pair if they really love each other deeply, and if poor Wagner, in the evening of his life, has at last found the right woman. It appears that Wagner really loves Cosima: he says that his only solace is the hope of seeing her. If then, for once, he really *loves* — and Cosima, by all appearances, loves *him* ardently — I wish both of them quiet happiness from the depth of my heart. Perhaps, too, Bülow will find a greater consolation and peace alone. I am convinced that he is treading a thorn-set path: he is, God knows, a good and honourable man, who deserved something better."

How, we may ask, could Cornelius have known that Wagner had said that his only solace was the hope of seeing Cosima, unless he had had the information from either Cosima or Hans? We have no letters or telegrams passing between Wagner and Cosima in the early part of January which answer to Cornelius's description; but in the light of a recently published letter of Wagner's of the 20th January to her we have no difficulty in believing that Cornelius was speaking of what he knew. In this letter of the 20th, in which Wagner several times addresses Cosima as " Liebe ", he asks her to excuse him for having negatived her proposal to come to him at Geneva; in another month, God willing, he says, they will be united in peace: " let me only look out for the nest for our peace." He

---

house. He returned to Geneva from his unsuccessful quest on the 29th January. During the ensuing month or so Cosima was busy in Munich with several plans for serving Wagner's interests; and it was not until the 7th March that she could join him in Geneva. Cornelius's "Cosima telegraphed him", etc., is thoroughly misleading, coming as it does immediately after "Wagner's wife is dead". But Cornelius was not giving his fiancée the historical sequence of events; he was merely describing how matters stood psychologically between Cosima and Wagner.

signs the letter "Dein R.". Does not this indicate clearly that it
had been the unconcealed intention of both of them, ever since Wagner had had to leave Munich, to resume their life in common as
soon as he had found a new permanent home? Does not every first-
hand document we possess relating to the triangle at this period
suggest that the love of Wagner and Cosima was a matter of common knowledge to their intimates, their ultimate union being regarded by those intimates as only a matter of time and general
convenience: and can one seriously suppose that until Bülow
opened some "horrifying" letter or other on the 11th or 12th May,
1866, he of all men, and he alone, was in blissful ignorance of what
was manifest to everyone else? The modern throwing of the lime-
light on that letter, of the contents of which, of the very name of the
writer of which, be it remembered, we as yet know absolutely nothing, is pure "theatre".

5

On the 22nd April we find the always well-informed Cornelius
— and once more, in all probability, his information came from
Bülow, for Cosima's relations with Cornelius at this time were not
of so cordial a nature that we can imagine the proud, self-contained
woman making him her confidant — telling his fiancée that Cosima
has accompanied Hans to Amsterdam (where Liszt is to join them),
" for the purpose of making her peace with her father, who, as I
have told you already, was very much annoyed with her for having
gone to Geneva to Wagner " — early in March.[22] That is to say,
even Liszt, in his distant retreat, has heard of the " affair " between

[22] Liszt's admiration for Wagner as a composer never faltered; but for a good
eleven years he kept aloof from him personally, and rarely even wrote to him. They
had met at Weimar in August, 1861. Their next meeting was at the bedside of the
sick Bülow, in Munich, in August, 1864: there can be little doubt, as we have already
had occasion to remark, that it was the newly-arisen Wagner-Bülow-Cosima situation that had brought Liszt there. In October 1867 — (not 1866, as Cosima mistakenly says in her book on her father, WFL, p. 55) — he broke a journey to Munich to
spend a few hours in Triebschen, obviously to discuss the Bülow matter with Wagner.
Then once more, as Cosima herself says, "long years elapsed and it looked as if the
fatal distance between them would result in a complete tacit estrangement. Liszt did
not attend the ceremony of laying the foundation stone of the Bayreuth theatre
[May 1872]. Then the Master broke the ice and visited him in Weimar [September
1872]." Liszt was certainly not on the Wagner-Cosima side in the long-drawn-out
Bülow affair of the 1860's.

Wagner and Cosima. He knows, too, that she has been at Geneva with Richard for more than three weeks in March. He is perturbed about it all, as well he may be. He dreads, we may be sure, a public " scandal ", the certain results of which would be much suffering for Bülow, the rendering of his official position in Munich impossible, the resentment of the King, and a new weapon of the deadliest kind placed in the hands of Wagner's journalistic enemies. Bülow is playing in Amsterdam, Liszt is on his way there from Paris; and Cosima accompanies Hans with the express object of explaining to her father and placating him. Can anyone really persuade himself that Bülow had not the least idea why Cosima had decided to accompany him to Amsterdam, and what was the subject of her conversations with Liszt? — that he had still to wait till May 11th or 12th, and the accident of the opened letter, before he had the smallest inkling of what everyone else in his circle had known and talked about for a year at least?

Dr. Carl Maria Cornelius, who, of course, has knowledge of many matters mentioned in his father's papers that have not yet been fully disclosed to the public, assures us that " Frau von Bülow's journey to Geneva [in March] was merely the prelude to the drama that was completed in May." While keeping up appearances with his other friends — telling them that his wife was going to Geneva for a week " by way of a little company for the poor great lonely one " — to Cornelius Bülow " opened out his heart: he also confided to him that Cosima's behaviour was an abomination to Liszt." [23] The reader may find it convenient to read Cornelius's letter of the 12th May again in the light of all these facts.

Let us look at another aspect of the problem. Unless Bülow were a simpleton of the first order he must from the beginning have had a strong suspicion, if not a conviction, that Isolde could not possibly be his own child. Perhaps we shall not be going an inch too far if we decide outright to call it a conviction. In May, 1914, following on a family quarrel as to the division of the Wagner property, Cosima applied to the German law courts for a legal decision that Isolde was Wagner's child, not Bülow's. " The Court, however, decided against her. The grounds for the judgment were not given; they were to be communicated to the parties in private. Apparently

[23] CPC, II, 81–2.

the piece of evidence that weighed most heavily with the Court was that of Frau Anna Mrazeck, the one-time housekeeper of Wagner. This old lady died on the 11th June, 1914, at the age of eighty, shortly after having made a deposition to the effect that while Frau Cosima was living with Wagner at Starnberg she still occupied Bülow's room during his visit to them. In view of this it was evidently impossible for the Court to declare definitely in favour of Frau Beidler [Isolde]." [24]

The legal nicety, however, has, like so many other legal niceties, no bearing on the plain and simple facts of the case. Cosima had arrived in Starnberg on the 29th June, 1864: Bülow arrived, in a deplorable state of health, on the 7th July. Isolde was born on the 10th April, 1865. Moreover, Cosima herself deposed, at the trial, that " from June 12th to October 12th, 1864, she had lived in intimate relations with no one but Wagner." Can one suppose that when Cosima's pregnancy became evident Bülow could for a single moment be in doubt as to the true paternity of the child? The supposition is not to be ruled out, indeed, that Cosima may have straightforwardly confided in him immediately on his arrival in Starnberg, as she had done with her friend Marie von Buch three or four days earlier; and if this conjecture holds good, Wagner's letter of the following September to Hans is perhaps not so " mysterious " as it is usually held to be. It may even be that Bülow's illness of that July — a nervous breakdown that brought him near death's door — was in part the result of a disclosure made to him by Cosima. A sidelight on the matter of the triangle seems to be thrown by a passage in a letter from Bülow to Raff of the 26th August, 1866. At that time Bülow, after the upheaval of the preceding May and June, was living with Wagner and Cosima at Triebschen, brooding over his broken life, and hinting to various correspondents that he could not tell them the whole story, at any rate on paper.

---

[24] NW, pp. 125–6. I leave unchanged this note (which was based on German newspaper reports of 1914) from a former book of mine. It should be added, however, that it was Isolde Beidler who had asked the Courts to declare that she was not Bülow's child but Wagner's. The regrettable story can be read in full in MMCW, pp. 463–467. Isolde had always ranked technically as Bülow's daughter; she signed herself, until her marriage, "Isolde von Bülow", and she shared in the Bülow patrimony. As she could not adduce any valid legal reason why the Bülow paternity should be negatived, the Court had no alternative but to non-suit her.

" Just as the correct formulation of a problem ", he wrote to Raff, " can be regarded as half the solution of it, so the clear exposition of a scandalous situation is already a halfway point to relief from it. Truly the most shameful part of the case in question was the frightful con- fusion, the difficulty of bringing the fellow-sufferers to a just percep- tion, i.e., to a pessimistically-calm desperation. From February 1865 I was not in the least doubt about the rottenness of things. To be sure I never dreamed to what extent this would develop. Forgive me if I talk in oracles again, and I cannot now consign to the devil those ' con- siderations ' which all along I have wished at the devil! And so — later." [25]

The expression is intentionally obscure, and this obscurity is of itself significant. There would be no need for Bülow to envelop himself in this smoke-screen of words — to " talk in oracles " — were he merely describing to Raff the miseries of his *public* life in Munich in 1864–5: we cannot doubt that he is referring to his relations with Wagner and Cosima. He often discusses Munich musical and political affairs in his letters, but always in unmis- takably direct and robust terms; there would be no reason for him to lapse into a calculated diplomatic obscurity of speech in the present instance were the subject of his remarks merely his profes- sional work, while the references to " fellow-sufferers " and " pes- simistically-calm desperation " can hardly be made to fit any other case than that of the triangle. As for the " considerations " which he wishes were at the devil, what can this refer to but to his efforts all along to conceal the real facts from the world, not only for his own sake but for his wife's sake and Wagner's?

It has to be said frankly that while no valid conclusion as to the triangle can be drawn from Bülow's general silence on the matter, frequently no conclusion can be drawn from what he does say other than the exact opposite of what he would have us believe. By the end of 1868 all the parties concerned had recognised the necessity for a divorce, which had to be delayed, however, for various rea- sons, among them Liszt's displeasure, the peculiarity of the Prus- sian law of divorce, and Bülow's desire to keep the facts as far as possible from the world until he had finished his term of office as conductor in Munich. By way of muzzling scandal he assured his friends in December that Cosima, her health not being good, " is all

---

[25] I have done the best I can with Bülow's peculiar German.

the time in Versailles with her sister, Countess Charnacé; she writes only to the children now and then." [26] This was quite untrue, as Bülow perfectly well knew: on the 16th November Cosima had launched a final defiance to the world and taken up her permanent abode in Triebschen. There is no reason to suppose that this was the only occasion on which, in his perplexity and distress, Bülow had obscured or misrepresented the facts to his friends and correspondents.

Our concern all along in this chapter has been not with the rights and wrongs of the matter but solely with the question whether Bülow knew or did not know before May 1866 of Cosima's love for Wagner. In his long letter of the 15th September, 1869 to Countess Charnacé he says, " Believe me, Madame, I have done all that was humanly possible to avoid a public scandal. For more than three years I have voluntarily submitted to a life of incessant torture: you can form no idea of the agitations that have consumed me without respite." " More than three years " obviously means " since the summer of 1866 " — at which time, however, the ruffianism of the Munich journalists merely dragged into the open what had hitherto been confined mainly to the knowledge of a few. It was at that time, and in consequence of the public dirt-throwing, that Bülow's real torments began: his words do not in the least warrant the interpretation that only in May 1866 were his eyes opened as to the Wagner-Cosima association. And it is worth observing how differently, in this exceedingly moving letter, the unhappy man treats Wagner and Cosima. Against the former the suppressed rage of many years flames up into a sentence the venom of which astonishes us, coming as it does from the pen of Bülow. Only one further sacrifice, he says, could have been asked of him — his life.

" Perhaps I would not have recoiled even from that had I observed on the part of another, as sublime in his works as incomparably abject in his actions, the smallest hint of an approach towards loyalty, the most fugitive suggestion of a sense of honesty. . . . [This] accusation, of which more than twenty years of relations with him have provided me with proof more than enough, is necessary in order to acquit another person, who formerly, as much by the superiority of

[26] To Richard Pohl, in BB, IV, 261.

her intelligence as by the loyalty, the frankness, the nobility of her character, bore such a sisterly likeness to you, Madame." [27]

Bülow, it seems clear, did not make the smallest charge of deceit against Cosima from first to last. Once more we seem compelled to accept the conclusion that she had told him the truth from the beginning.

---

[27] This letter of Bülow's was printed for the first time by Count Guy de Pourtalès in PW, pp. 337–9.

CHAPTER XXII

THE KING AND THE TRIANGLE

1

THE NECESSITY Bülow felt himself to be under of going to Trieb-schen in June, 1866, in order, as Cornelius said, " to put the final decisive question to Cosima [1] — Do you wish to belong to Wagner or to me? " — had no causal connection with the letter of the 10th or 11th May. That necessity was imposed on him by quite a new conjuncture of events: the hands of all three of them had meanwhile been forced by their enemies in Munich.

Unable to bear any longer the separation from his idol, the King had made up his mind to spend Wagner's birthday, the 22nd May, in Triebschen. In the early hours of the 15th he sent Wagner a long telegram:

> " Constantly increasing longing for the Dear One. The [political] horizon is becoming more and more clouded . . . I implore the Friend to give me a speedy answer to the following questions: If it is the Dear One's wish and will, I will joyfully resign the throne and its empty splendour, and come to him, never to part from him again. And when he sits at the mysterious loom and weaves his enchanting works, be it my care to keep him aloof from the world, that is the thief of peace and quietness. For I say it again, to be any longer severed and *alone* is more than I can bear; but to be united with him, above and beyond this earthly existence, is the only thing that can save me from despair and death. . . ."

This was followed on the same day by a passionate, desperate letter in which Ludwig asked Wagner to take a house for the summer near Berg, where they could celebrate the 22nd together: Cosima and

---

[1] Observe Cornelius's wording. Is it not evident from it that Bülow's decision was the result of a much longer pre-occupation with the Wagner-Cosima problem than the three weeks that had elapsed between Cosima's journey to Triebschen and the date of this letter of Cornelius?

the Bülow children, he added, could lodge near by. The King's heart is broken by the loss of his only friend and counsellor:

" The evil world thought it had won its game; it did not know the power of true, holy love and fidelity; it thought we could be severed. Ah, I was forced to wound the swan! [2] It is bitterness to my soul, bitterness, alas! But to my mission I was not untrue. I know whose I am. Without you, my Dear One, I feel so unspeakably wretched that I am ill, inwardly very ill. I cannot endure it long: while we are on this earth let us be together; the day of your death will be mine also."

He implores Wagner to telegraph that he accepts the invitation to Berg and promises that they shall never be parted again; and he repeats the expression of his desire to renounce his throne and spend the remainder of his life with his friend.

Wagner, in his reply, exhorts the King to a half-year's patience, which will steel him for the future; a half-year is also necessary for himself for recovery from his wounds and for the completion of the creative work he has in hand. He counsels Ludwig to let events run their natural course in Munich till his present enemies are overthrown by the simple logic of events. The King is to forget, for these six months, all their joint artistic plans, devote himself energetically to the duties of his post, leave Berg for the capital, show himself to his people, and open the Landtag in person on the 22nd. If, at the end of six months, political events in Germany shall have made it impossible for him to remain King of Bavaria with true dignity, then, indeed, Wagner will see no reason to dissuade him from realising the desire of his heart.

2

The advice was eminently sensible, and as disinterested as it could be in the circumstances; complete disinterestedness, of course, was a luxury Wagner could not possibly allow himself to indulge in, for manifestly if the King were to abdicate and settle permanently in the neighbourhood of Triebschen the Cosima problem would become extremely difficult; and Cosima was almost as

---

[2] A dual reference to *Parsifal* and to Wagner's "banishment" in December, 1865.

indispensable to Wagner as the King. But the hunger in Ludwig's warm young heart was not to be appeased by cold reason; he must see his dear one or die. Surrounded by political wire-pullers whom he could not trust, and faced with a crisis in foreign affairs which, he knew, called for unremitting attention to the most odious realities, he felt the need of at least one deep draught from what was for him the only well of life. In view of the seriousness of the political situation — the differences between Prussia and Austria, into which Bavaria could not fail to be drawn, were rapidly coming to a head — his plan to escape to Triebschen for a day or two had to be concealed from his ministers and his people. On the 17th May he telegraphed to Wagner that his faithful young aide-de-camp Prince Paul von Thurn and Taxis, " the only man in my present environment in whom I have complete confidence ", would soon be on his way to Lucerne; oddly enough, Wagner was at that very time contemplating either going to Berg for a day or two at any cost (a course from which Cosima wisely persuaded him), or asking Ludwig to send some trusty person to Triebschen for an exchange of views. The " treue Friedrich ", as the King used to call Taxis, arrived in Triebschen on the 20th, where he awaited his master's arrival.

In spite of the fact that the contents of the telegrams that passed between Wagner and Ludwig during these few days — there were more than a dozen of them in all — must have been perfectly well known in official circles, where, too, it could hardly have been a secret that Wagner's birthday fell on the 22nd, Ludwig laid his plans so well that he was at Triebschen almost before he was missed from Berg. At five o'clock on the morning of the 22nd he sent Wagner, as a blind, the usual congratulatory telegram, to which Wagner, no doubt by pre-arrangement with " Friedrich ", replied at 9.18, his wire reaching Starnberg at ten past one in the afternoon — by which time the royal bird had safely nested in Triebschen. In the early morning the King had given Lutz an audience. He then went for his usual ride, accompanied by the groom Völk. They galloped to the railway station at Biessenhofen; there they caught the express to Lindau, on the Lake of Constance, where they took the boat to Rorschach, on the Swiss side, a mere fifty miles or so

from Lucerne. Ludwig was in Triebschen by midday. He and
Taxis left on the morning of the 24th; still in the seventh heaven
of happiness he telegraphed to Wagner from Zürich at 9.35 a.m.,
again at 1.40 from Lindau — from the steamboat, which, appro-
priately enough, was named the Wodan, — and once more from
Starnberg at 10.15 the same night.

The secret, of course, was out long before Ludwig's return. He
came back fortified by contact with Wagner and Cosima and full of
good intentions with regard to his royal duties; he promised Wagner, in a telegram of the 25th, that he would open the Landtag in
person on the following day, though, he added, it was only the profundity of his love for the Friend that made possible the performance of so disagreeable a duty. The Bavarian Landtag was actually
opened by him on the 27th; and a telegram of the same afternoon
from the King to Cosima — " Reception ice-cold! Press scandalous! " — gives us a glimpse into the infernal abyss that was already opening out under the feet of the harassed trio.

The times were grave; the very existence of Bavaria was at stake.
The long tension between Austria and Prussia was nearing its
breaking point; and the problem occupying the mind of all Germany was whether Bavaria would or should take sides in the coming
conflict or keep out of it. The position of Bavaria, as the largest of
the German states outside Prussia, was very much that of all half-
detached, half-involved countries that would fain adopt a policy of
isolation in times of international trouble. To neither Prussia nor
Austria did Bavaria feel itself irresistibly drawn. There were
difficulties also in the way of the long-planned Triad — a counterpoise of power to Prussia and Austria, to be created by a confedera-
tion of the southern German states, with Bavaria, as the largest of
them, at its head. For her to ally herself with Austria in the coming
war meant for Bavaria, in case of defeat, the loss of territory, or
the payment of an indemnity, or both; while neutrality would mean,
in the event of a Prussian victory, a Bavaria too weak to face the
rising North German power alone at some near future date. As
was generally the case when he chose to give his serious attention
to politics, Ludwig saw the situation clearly enough: when Hohenlohe, dining with him in April, assured him that " Prussia's only

aim just now was supremacy in North Germany ", the King replied, " *Just now,* yes, but presently she will want more." [3] In proportion as the crisis developed, however, his reluctance to occupy himself seriously with politics increased: his heart was in Triebschen. On the 11th May, the day on which affairs looked so serious that the Bavarian Government ordered the immediate mobilisation of the army and called a meeting of the Landtag for the 22nd, the King retired to Berg; and the country took it ill of him that he should absent himself from his capital at such a time. On the 16th May the Munich Police Director, Pfeufer, complained bitterly to Pfister-meister of the difficulties created on the one hand by Ludwig's aloof-ness from his people, on the other hand by the lame excuses given for this aloofness in the official journals, excuses which were received, he said, with growing scepticism. " In the first year it was the [Court] mourning; in the second year, the condition of the King's health in general; in the third year, his hoarseness. What ostensible sickness, people are asking, will the royal physician find for next year? " It had been officially announced that the distance between Berg and the capital was " negligible ", and that the two places were " in regular connection " — " as if ", said Pfeufer acidly, " every Münchener did not know this already, and every foreigner, too, by means of Baedeker." What the public is asking itself, however, is

" whether it is possible for a train to be available at any moment it may be wanted, for the King to be found at his villa at any given moment, whether now and then there may not be some sudden decision or other on his Majesty's part that cannot be entrusted to the telegraph, and so must suffer delay until the ministers can arrive at Berg. These and other questions are being asked in all walks of life. . . . His Majesty wants to know whether his removal to Berg is deplored. I can only answer ' Yes '; what in ordinary and peaceful times can be regarded as a ' negligible distance ' is looked upon in extraordinary times as a great distance. It is said that on one of the first days his

[3] HSM, I, 145. Prince Chlodwig of Hohenlohe-Schillingsfürst (1819–1901) entered the Bavarian Upper House in April, 1846. On the 31st December, 1866 he became Minister for Foreign Affairs and President of the Council, which position he resigned in March, 1870, to take up his residence in Berlin. From 1870–1874 he was a member of the Reichstag, from 1874–1875 German Ambassador in Paris, and from 1894–1901 Imperial Chancellor. For Wagner students his memoirs and diaries are particularly valuable for the contemporary light they throw on events in Munich between 1864 and 1870.

Majesty was absent till ten or eleven at night, and a few days ago was in Partenkirchen. I do not know what truth there is in this: but the people are asking themselves what would have happened had Pfordten, on one of those days, desired his Majesty's decision on some point or other." [4]

3

Pfeufer's letter, it will be observed, is dated the 16th May. Already, on the 15th, the King had telegraphed to Triebschen his desire to abdicate; and on the 17th his resolution had been taken to go to Wagner at all costs. The Police Director's letter, the contents of which were duly reported to Ludwig by Pfistermeister, no doubt played its part in that resolution. The politicians could obviously have got rid of the King without much difficulty at this time, when the realisation of the vastness of the gulf between the world of his heart's desire and the world of crude reality had for the moment broken his spirit. But they chose to dissuade him, and no doubt they were justified by the circumstances of the time, for the abdication of the King of Bavaria just then would have immensely complicated the political situation; in later years, when they would fain have dispensed with him, he was not to be moved, in spite of an occasional toying with the idea of abdication.

" The King's journey to Switzerland " [5] Hohenlohe noted in his diary on the 31st May,

"has done him much harm there with Munich people. They are said to have shouted abuse at him in the open street, and when he drove to church on the opening day of the Diet there was no hurrahing: they scarcely even saluted him. . . . They tell me the King has refused to open the session personally, so old King Ludwig [his grandfather] and Prince Karl drove over to Berg and lessoned him." [6]

---

[4] FKLB, pp. 97–8. The letter is there given in full for the first time, from the original, which is among the papers left by Pfistermeister at his death.

[5] The German editor of the Hohenlohe Memoirs gravely informs his readers that "the purpose of the journey to Switzerland, where the King visited the scene of Schiller's *Wilhelm Tell*, was misconstrued by the public, who believed that the King went there in order to meet Richard Wagner."

[6] There had been rumours of ministerial resignations, but these proved false. There was also talk of a deputation being sent to Berg to inform the King of the state of feeling in the capital, and to beg him to return there and open the Diet in person; but this plan also was abandoned. At the meeting with Ludwig I and Prince Karl the King declared himself to be willing not merely to open the Landtag on the 27th May but to review the troops and be present at the Corpus Christi Day procession.

Pfeufer, for his outspoken letter of the 16th, was relieved of his post in Munich and transferred to Augsburg. "Instead of entering a protest against this Sultanic encroachment on the part of the Cabinet ", said Hohenlohe,

> "the Minister of the Interior, like the thorough old bureaucratic sleepy-head he is, let it pass without a word. So long as the King is encouraged in his caprices by the sycophancy of the Court and the Government officials, so long will he continue to regard himself as a demigod who can do what he pleases, and for whose pleasure the rest of the world — at any rate Bavaria — was created." [7]

That was the simple fashion in which the matter presented itself to the ordinary observer of the time: no one had the least perception of the boy's spiritual tragedy; to almost everyone it seemed to be merely a case of an ambitious musical adventurer weaving his spells round an unsuspecting boy for his own purposes.

4

Upon Wagner and his friends fell all the odium of the King's flight from politics to Lucerne; and the Press, especially that part of it that was most closely associated with the Cabinet, at once began to pour out the vials of its malice on them. Any stick was now good enough to beat them with, and the dirtier the better. "When one hears ", shrieked and spluttered the *Neuer Bayerischer Kurier* of the 29th May,

> "that the private correspondence of the young King is used by Wagner in the vilest way, subjected to the most disgraceful profanation and the commonest derision; when one knows the pitiful rôle played by ' Herr and Madame Dr. Hanns de Bülow ' in this affair, and the crafty exploitation of the King's private purse, the lies and deceits of all kinds cunningly employed to retain the King's favour for this precious crew, and to isolate him from the society proper to his station; when one sees some residents of Munich so lost to decency as to affront the honourable feelings of the town by the commission of a silver wreath for the opprobrious author of these troubles and by the public exhibi-

---

Böhm, by the way, rather confuses the matter by dating the last sentence quoted above from Hohenlohe's diary "11th April, 1866", instead of the 31st May.
[7] HSM, II, 147.

tion of it for a fortnight; [8] when one is compelled to watch in silence
the direst wounds being dealt the monarchy by a handful of people
of this sort, and the best years of a young, enthusiastic King, with no
weapons as yet against such wiles, poisoned by devilish means and
with the most consummate craft, so that he is tempted to estrange himself from the love of his people; when one remembers that Wagner
has tried to thrust himself as a revolutionary into our constitutional
life; one can only be filled with a glowing and unquenchable hate
against him and all the other workers of such mischief.

" It has already been sufficiently demonstrated that Wagner is impossible in Munich and in Bavaria; yet his most active friends, especially the carrier pigeon, ' Madame Dr. Hanns de Bülow ', and his so-
called teacher of singing, Schmitt, have been able so to arrange things
once more that a return of Wagner to Munich could always be contemplated. So far this has been prevented, thanks to the wise and firm attitude of the ministers and the Cabinet counsellors. It is now — and
our consolation in this catastrophe is the dead certainty that Wagner
will never again dare to show his face in Bavaria — the further and
imperative duty of the counsellors of the Crown to clear also the remaining accomplices of this self-interested man out of the country as
soon as possible, to make their access to the King, by letter or in
person, impossible, and to cleanse the steps of the Bavarian throne of
this species of greedy, self-seeking, branded adventurers."

The *Volksbote* of the 31st May surpassed even this polished effort.

" ' Great is Allah ', say the Mohammedans; and the prophet Richard Wagner has first-rate digestive organs. It is not a year since the
well-known ' Madame Hans de Bülow ' got away in the famous two
cabs with 40,000 gulden from the Treasury for her ' friend ' (or
what?). But what are 40,000 gulden? ' Madame Hans ' ought now to
be looking round for more cabs; for the day before yesterday an action was entered against Richard Wagner in connection with bills to
the tune of no less than 26,000 gulden — a fact absolutely vouched
for to the *Volksbote*. Meanwhile the same ' Madame Hans ', who has
been known to the public since last December by the descriptive title
of ' the carrier pigeon ', is with her ' friend ' (or what?) in Lucerne,
where she was also during the visit of an exalted person." [9]

---

[8] This wreath had been subscribed for by a number of Wagner's admirers in
Munich, and sent to him on his birthday.

[9] The hatred of Bülow in some Munich quarters was partly due to the fact that
he was a Prussian. The Prussians were never popular in Bavaria, and least of all in
1866, when war with them seemed unavoidable. They "needed a sort of Ghetto for
their protection in Munich", Bülow wrote humorously to a friend about this time.
During the Press attacks on him in June a certain other Bülow from Mecklenburg
innocently took up his abode in Munich: confusing him with the musician, a virtuous

The Munich *Punsch* chimed in delightedly, on the 10th June, with an elaborate " Programme for a Grand Future-Musical Procession ", features of which were to be " A herd of *Schweinehunde*, driven in pairs by Dr. Hans von Bülow " (a genial reference to the famous episode during the *Tristan* rehearsals), " Twenty holders of bills of exchange with lighted candles ", and " The Royal Treasury, followed immediately by St. Cosima with the pass-key, and by several members of the Royal Household shaking their heads." [10]

5

It will be seen that the spear-point of this latest assault on Wagner's position was his now notorious relations with Cosima. Obviously it was impossible, after this, for Bülow to maintain his ostrich attitude any longer. He sent a demand for a retraction and " satisfaction " to the editor of the *Volksbote*, Dr. Zander. It was ignored. Thereupon he published, in the *Neueste Nachrichten* of the 3rd June, a philippic against the *Volksbote* which, one is bound to admit, deserved Cornelius's description of it as " exhibiting in every line a mind that has lost its firmness of footing; it was all false irony, feigned cold-bloodedness, and unclearness in the presentation of the facts, and likely only to make a disagreeable impression on every reader, whether he is for or against or completely impartial." All that Bülow's outburst amounted to in actual fact was that as the editor had declined his challenge to a duel there remained only two courses open to him — either to chastise Zander publicly or to seek redress by law; neither was to his taste, " and over matters of taste, as everyone knows, it is useless to dispute." Cornelius was angry with Bülow for having rushed into print in this fashion without consulting him; he would presumably have either helped

---

mob broke into his house, smashed his windows, and destroyed some of his furniture. The trifling error of identification was soon rectified: but, as Hans wrote to Raff, "as a result of this experience Herr von Bülow of Mecklenburg has decided on another place of residence." BB, IV, 134–5.

Bülow was regarded in Munich, especially during the war of 1866, as a Prussian agent and spy, and certain anti-Bavarian articles in the Berlin *Nationalzeitung* were attributed to him. He was a fanatical Bismarckian — in after years he actually identified Bismarck with the "Hero" of the Eroica symphony — and no doubt he had talked indiscreetly about politics in Munich.

[10] The "Programme" is given in full in RLW, II, 14–15.

his exasperated friend to cast his letter to the *Nachrichten* in another
and better form, or would have counselled silence. As it was, Bülow had preferred to go to two of his other friends, Mihalovich and
a certain Lieutenant Schmidt, who, says Cornelius, could see nothing in the *Volksbote* article but the " infamy " of " a democratic
attack on a [Prussian] Junker ". Cornelius himself was manifestly
becoming weary of all this dirty-linen-washing and the waste of life
it meant for everyone concerned.

Obviously something more would have to be done before long
than merely foaming and gesticulating in the newspapers; accordingly Bülow left Munich for Switzerland on the 6th June, probably
with no clearer purpose in his mind at the moment than to discover
if Wagner and Cosima had anything to suggest. It is with reference
to this journey that Cornelius writes to his fiancée that " Bülow now
sees himself compelled to go to Lucerne and put the final decisive
question to Cosima — Do you wish to belong to Wagner or to me?
. . . Today is the anxious day of decision at Lucerne." It is perhaps significant that Hans did not go straight to Triebschen first of
all, but to Zürich, where Cosima met him the next morning. On the
6th, Wagner addressed a desperate letter to the King, imploring
him, in the name of their friendship, to come to the rescue of the
slandered Bülow pair with a personal letter to Hans which the latter
was to be at liberty to publish. Wagner even drafted the lengthy
document, intended for public consumption, which the King had
merely to sign on the dotted line: it spoke of the sacrifices Bülow
had made in coming to Munich at Ludwig's request, and voiced the
King's detestation of the disgraceful attacks on Hans's honour.[11]
" Further ", the draft ran,

---

[11] Either Cosima took a copy of this document with her to Zürich, or Wagner sent
it by post to Bülow. That Hans knew all about it is clear from Wagner's telegram to
him on the 7th, in which he says that "tomorrow" he will "try to get a telegraphic
Yes or No from Berg". As a matter of fact he wired to the King on the afternoon of
the 9th, asking categorically for a "Yes or No" from him after receiving Wagner's
letter of the same day, in which he drives home the points he had made on the 6th.
See KLRWB, II, 52–59, and RWHB, p. 249.

Cosima, by the way, had gone from Zürich to Munich on the morning of the 7th.
She had learned that a number of the King's letters to Wagner had been stolen (by
the politicians, Wagner thought) from the Bülow house, and she wanted to make the
remainder safe. This she did by placing them in the custody of Frau Schnorr for a
few months, after which they were sent to Triebschen. The stolen letters were returned to Wagner in July through the medium of Prince Paul Taxis.

Cosima returned to Zürich on the 8th June.

"as I [the King] have been able to acquire the exactest knowledge of the noble and high-souled character of your honoured wife, who stood as sympathiser and consoler by the side of him [Wagner] who is her father's friend and her husband's exemplar, it remains for me to investigate what is inexplicable in those criminal public calumnies, in order that, having obtained the clearest insight into this outrageous conduct, I may see that the sternest justice is done upon the evildoers."

Wagner carried the bluff a stage further in a telegram of the 8th June to Prince Paul von Taxis, which he knew would be shown to the King: "Should the only too understandable bitterness of my friend B[ülow] not be pardoned, this would lead to a great misfortune, already well prepared for by our enemies. The unheard-of insult to his honour imperatively imposes on me solidarity with him; should the only valid satisfaction, asked for by me, be refused him, then I must share his fate and henceforth be dead even for the exalted Friend [King Ludwig]. I eagerly await the decisive Yes or No." [12] "Solidarity" is good. For the rest, the telegram and his letters amounted, in effect, to blackmail of the King — "Either sign the document I sent you, or be prepared to lose me".

The agitated conspirators at Triebschen could scarcely have cherished, in cooler moments, any real hope that their enemies, with all the indisputable unpleasant facts in their armoury, would be silenced even by such a declaration as this on the King's part. But it was their last sorry card in the game, and they played it with the impudence of desperation. The slowly built-up edifice of deceit had now to be crowned by the worst deceit of all — that of the innocent young King; and what that deceit must have cost Cosima in mental anguish will never be known. Diplomatic usage permits of any and every shade of nuance and degree of subtlety in the presentation or veiling or colouring of the truth in a critical situation; but Wagner and Cosima — and especially Cosima — were now not playing a fair diplomatic game with Ludwig but deliberately lying to him. She herself sent a distracted appeal to him on the 7th:

"For the first and last time I implore you [to act] for us. I fall on my knees before my King, and in humility and distress beg for the letter to my husband, that we may not leave in shame and ignominy the country in which we have desired — perhaps I may say have done

[12] KLRWB, IV, 150-1.

— nothing but good. My dear, exalted Friend, if you make this public statement then all is well; then we can remain here, build once more upon the ruins, bravely and full of comfort, as though nothing had happened — otherwise we must go hence, insulted and abandoned, de-priving him [Wagner] of the only friends who could give him no more than their own existence, fame and repute, and who will now have to build all this up again elsewhere, in order to be able to offer him an abode. My most august Friend, you who came into our lives like a divine apparition, oh, do not consent that we, the innocent, shall be hunted out. Your royal word alone can restore our honour, which has been attacked; it can do so completely; everything will vanish before it. My dear lord, I venture to say what the hero said to the King who had conferred an honour on him: ' *Sire, vous faîtes bien* ': you will do right to take us under your protection, and the people will understand it. . . . You know those mysteriously decisive hours in which the truth stands forth bright as the sun. In the name of those consecrated hours I say: Write my husband the royal letter. . . . If there is a possibility of your gracious letter, then I will persuade my husband that we should return home — otherwise — how could we remain in a city in which we might be treated as malefactors? How could my husband carry on his work in a town in which the honour of his wife had been called in question? My royal lord, I have three children,[13] to whom it is my duty to transmit their father's honourable name unstained. For the sake of these children, that they may not some day inveigh against my love for the Friend [Wagner], I beg you, my most exalted Friend, to write this letter." [14]

6

It was the basest act of Cosima's whole life, something on which she must have looked back for ever after with self-loathing; yet at the moment it was the only way out. And in the turpitude of what she and Wagner did, Bülow must take his share before the tribunal of public opinion; for there cannot be the slightest doubt that he was

---

[13] One of the three was Wagner's. A fourth, also Wagner's, was already on the way; Eva was born on the 17th February, 1867. As Cosima had left Munich for Triebschen on the 11th or 12th May, 1866, and it was the middle of June before Bülow took up his abode in Triebschen, could he possibly have been in any doubt, soon after that date, that Cosima was once more pregnant by Wagner?

In February, 1884, when, a year after Wagner's death, Cosima commissioned Adolf von Gross to discuss the legal aspect of the daughters' inheritance with him, Bülow wrote to Gross, "I feel that I can commemorate the anniversary of the great Master's death by letting his daughter Eva count as mine." See MMCW, p. 364.

[14] MECW, I, 290 ff.

a party to the drafting of the letter which the unsuspecting King was to be fooled and frightened into signing. Ludwig copied out the letter to Hans in full,[15] adding, however, a postscript on his own initiative: " A thousand cordial greetings from a faithful friend's soul to the beloved inhabitants of dear Triebschen." Bülow published the letter in the *Neueste Nachrichten* of the 19th June and the Augsburg *Abendzeitung* of the 20th. It is doubtful whether many people were impressed by it. To anyone in the least acquainted with Wagner's style, his hand was evident enough in its composition: as Cornelius ironically noted in his diary a few weeks later, " This letter was couched in a style too familiar to me for me to be able to mistake it for a moment for the work of the King's secretary." That Bülow was privy to the whole business is further shown by a complacent remark in his letter of the 15th July to Carl Bechstein — written from Triebschen, where he had now more or

---

[15] On the 9th June Ludwig telegraphed to Triebschen that the letter would be sent to Bülow "tomorrow", "with minor alterations which, however, will not essentially change it." Apprehensive as to what this might mean, Wagner replied by telegram on the 10th that he hoped the contemplated variants would not weaken the force of it, otherwise he would prefer the King to hold it over until he had received a second letter from him. "It is a matter of a noble life that is in the utmost peril." Confronted with this fresh ultimatum, Ludwig telegraphed on the 11th that the letter was being sent to Bülow unchanged from Wagner's draft.

Wagner's letter of the 9th, referred to in his telegrams of the 9th and 10th, was a long *pièce justificative*, in which he told the King the full story of Cosima and the 40,000 gulden in October, 1865, and then went on to deal, by implication, with another of those Press "calumnies". When, he said, Lutz came to him in the Briennerstrasse on the 6th December, 1865 to announce the King's wish that he should leave Munich for a time, Cosima and her children were at dinner with him. Cosima was shattered by the news; and as Hans was away from Munich at the time, she took up her abode with Wagner during the next four anxious days, partly because her nerves would not allow her to be alone in her own house, partly because she wanted to help and console Wagner, against whose person, it seems, there had been threats. "I recognised her over-excited, almost visionary condition, and it put my own mind at rest to give her security in my house during those terrible [three] days." His enemies, it seems, have made use of first the episode of the 40,000 gulden, then the fact that Cosima remained in the Briennerstrasse to console him in the dark days of December, 1865, then of the recent visit of the King to Triebschen, to make it appear that "the wife of my friend B. is my ——; that she slept four nights at my house, and paid herself for her caresses with the money-bags she had wheedled out of the Treasury; and that friend B. acquiesced in this, and moreover appropriated to his own use the gratuity intended for the orchestra. That is how the friends of the King of Bavaria are treated in his capital, Munich!" This simplification of the facts of the case does not impose on anyone today; but it was cunningly calculated to ensnare the judgment of the King, who, of course, knew far less about it than we do. Ludwig believed Wagner because he believed *in* Wagner; and so he made himself responsible for the letter to Bülow.

less tranquilly settled down to his part in the curious play, though, as will be seen from the concluding word of the citation, not without a characteristic grimace: " Listen to this, and you will understand a lot; a certain letter that gave you much pleasure was dictated word for word by Richard (Würst)." [16]

The letter had what today would be called a bad Press. " It made a painful impression in all quarters ", said Cornelius,

> " first, that the King, who, in these so difficult times, had given few signs of any energetic participation in public affairs, should devote such exhaustive consideration to this one matter, and secondly that Bülow, the times being what they are, should have made it public."

The *Volksbote*, while professing to regard a letter from the King's own hand as above discussion, calmly added that it stuck to every word it had printed about " Herr Hans von Bülow and Madame Hans von Bülow ". In the serious, nay, dangerous condition in which the Fatherland just then found itself, it continued, it had neither time nor space for any further concern with the doings, how-ever curious, of musicians; as for " insults " and " criminal calum-nies ", the Bavarian courts of justice provided a remedy for things of that kind.[17] That Bülow had not resorted to the law courts in the first place went very much against him with the public; and in many quarters the King's letter was at first regarded as a mystifica-tion. But Munich had little time now, as the *Volksbote* hinted, to waste on the dirty linen of a clique of alien musicians: on the very day that Bülow had sent Ludwig's letter to the papers, Bavaria defi-nitely threw in its lot with Austria and declared war on Prussia. In another month the war was over; after many humiliations at the hands of Bismarck, Bavaria was let off with the payment of sixty million gulden and the loss of certain territories.

" The King sees no one now ", Hohenlohe wrote in his diary on the 16th.

---

[16] BNB, p. 200. This is a typical specimen of Bülow's *Galgenhumor*. There lived in Berlin a composer (of sorts) and critic (also of sorts), by name Richard Wüerst, who was one of Bülow's particular *bêtes noires*. The name seems to have amused him, and at one time he was very fond of introducing it into his letters — for instance, "The whole musical party-scrimmage turns upon two Franz L's and two Richard W's:

Lachner Würst

Liszt   Wagner."

[17] RLW, II, 18.

"He is staying with Taxis on the Roseninsel, and lets off fireworks. Even the members of the Upper House, who were to deliver the address to him, were not received — a case unprecedented in the history of Bavaria. Not to receive addresses of loyalty, and from the faithful Senate, that is a bitter pill for the august Chamber. The Munich people themselves are again making quite justifiable comments. Other people do not trouble their heads about the King's childish tricks, since he lets the Ministers and the Chambers govern without interfering. His behaviour is, however, imprudent, since it tends to make him unpopular."

It certainly did neither the King nor Wagner any good for Bülow to send such a letter, on such a subject, to the newspapers at a time of national pre-occupation with much graver matters.

7

His own and Cosima's and Wagner's "honour" having been vindicated, at any rate to their own satisfaction, by a mendacious letter concocted at a meeting of the conspirators and palmed off upon the unsuspecting King, Bülow took up his residence on the 10th June with Wagner and Cosima at Triebschen,[18] in the naïve belief that this would give a conclusive démenti to the "slanders". At Triebschen he remained for more than two months, bitter, weary, disillusioned, almost hopeless, yet falling completely under Wagner's spell again as he dipped into the manuscript of the *Meistersinger*. "My God!", he wrote on the 31st July to Alexander Ritter, the husband of Wagner's niece Franziska, "all that is still ideal and worth preserving in the German spirit lives in this one head, your uncle's"; and to Raff, on the 12th August, "it seems to me that this work represents the culmination of his genius; it is incredibly vigorous, plastic, richer than *Tristan* in musical detail: I count on its having an immense effect in the national sense." Wagner was now engaged on the second act, and, as always when he was occupied in creation, "full of optimism", as Bülow wrote to Ritter.

---

[18] He brought an action for defamation of character against the *Neuer Bayrischer Kurier:* his assailant was sentenced to three days' imprisonment and a fine of ten florins and costs — about 150 gulden in all. The editor, Peter Rothlauf, had made some absurd charges against Bülow in his capacity as conductor of the Opera orchestra; and it was no doubt mainly in connection with these that Bülow obtained his verdict. Rothlauf appealed, and apparently the sentence was reduced.

But for Hans the future was dark, artistically, morally and financially. Munich was impossible for him just then, although his contract with the theatre ran to 1868. So was Berlin, for several reasons, among them the resentment of the Prussian Court at his having
obeyed Ludwig's call to Munich two years before. Italy attracted
him; he worked at Italian, and sounded various friends as to prospects in Milan or Florence; he would be content, he said, to teach the
piano and do journalistic work, or even play second oboe in an Italian theatre if his lungs were equal to it! Of the Germany of the present he was sick and tired; for the Germany of the future he had little
hope. From an American tour as pianist, and, indeed, in general
from what he called virtuoso-nomadism, he shrank in horror; not
only was his health broken but, with Wagner mostly working at the
Meistersinger from eight o'clock to five each day, he had little opportunity to keep up his piano practice. He was earning little, and
had no immediate prospect of earning more; yet he had his Munich
house on his hands for a further two years. He indulged himself in
the fantasy of a joint bachelor life with Alexander Ritter in Italy,
Cosima and Franziska to live together in Munich next winter; yet
after he had planned to go with Cosima to Munich in August, to
make arrangements with regard to his belongings there, he held
back, for fear of personal violence to them both. He was " music-
tired, future-tired, even present-tired ", he told Raff; his one desire
was to go somewhere and become " obscure ", which was easier,
he said, than to become famous. In the end he decided to settle as
piano teacher and concert performer in Basel, partly because Raff's
brother-in-law Dr. Emil Merian lived there, and Merian was as
fanatical a Bismarckian as himself, partly because Basel was not
too far from Munich, and above all, as he told Bechstein, because
he would be near Wagner. In giving his friends this last reason for
his choice of Basel he may have had it in his mind to give yet another
check to the current scandal. But apart from that, Wagner and his
work exercised the old magnetic attraction upon him; he was still,
in spite of everything, the vassal of the stronger nature and the
greater creative mind.

The strange thing was that he and Wagner and Cosima could
still talk, apparently seriously, of himself and Cosima again setting up house together. Or rather what would seem strange in any

other man in the same circumstances is comprehensible in the case of Bülow. All of them, too, were living on the edge of a volcano. Recent events had appeared to simplify the future for them all, yet each fresh step they took in virtue of this simplification landed them in unforeseen difficulties. Assuming, as we are virtually compelled to do, that there had been in 1865 a tacit agreement within the triangle that Cosima was to play less and less part in Bülow's life and more and more in Wagner's, we can see how the events of December, 1865 and January, 1866 promised, at first sight, to solve their problem for them, at any rate in large part. While Minna was alive there could be no question of anything but an " illicit " association of Wagner with Cosima. Minna's death disposed of that obstacle. The other main difficulty had been that of keeping the association from becoming known to too wide a circle in Munich, where in the first place Wagner's journalistic and political enemies were to be feared, and in the second place the King's suspicions of anything " wrong " must not be aroused. Wagner's exile from Munich, occurring about the same time as the death of Minna, seemed to bring with it at least this advantage, that with Wagner settled in some remote spot in Switzerland or the south of France, Cosima's visits to him would be less a matter of common knowledge than they were rapidly becoming in Munich. It is evident, both from Wagner's " Brown Book " and from Cosima's state of mind as revealed to us in Cornelius's letters and elsewhere, that the pair were determined to belong to each other at all costs: the only question was how to reduce the inevitable cost to a minimum.

There was the material side of the case to be considered as well as the emotional. It was not merely an ordinary human matter of sparing Bülow's feelings as much as possible: even more important, perhaps, than this was the sheer necessity of making no such false step in public as would result in his having to leave Munich. For only in Munich, under King Ludwig's protection, could Wagner's new works be produced in a style at all answering to his ideal: only in Munich could he hope for the establishment of the Music School that was to make singers in his own image: only in Munich could these singers, when fully formed into true Wagnerians, find their place as a matter of course in the royal opera house. It was therefore absolutely necessary to keep Bülow in Munich and for him to retain his standing there as Kapellmeister and as director of the School. Bülow's existence in the town, however, would become a virtual impossibility were it to be suspected that his hands were not quite clean in the matter of the matrimonial " scandal ". Secrecy was a prime necessity, until such time as King Ludwig and public opinion could be prepared for the news of a quiet dissolution of the Bülow marriage: and this secrecy must have seemed at first to be favoured by the distance of Wagner's new home from Bavaria. The immediate cause of the temporary collapse of their plans was no doubt the indiscreet visit of Ludwig to Triebschen in May, 1866. It angered the journalists to find that at the very height of the political crisis the King's thoughts were with his banished " favourite " rather than with his duties as ruler. In their exasperation they savagely turned upon the man whom they looked upon as the young King's evil genius. His artistic schemes had never concerned them greatly, for in these he obviously had the bulk of the public on his side. But they could attack him, as before, for his raids on the King's purse; and when it became known, as it soon did, that Cosima was actually with Wagner at Triebschen during Ludwig's stay there, they had a fresh weapon against him which they would have been more than human to refuse to employ. The vigorous use to which they put it created a whole fresh crop of difficulties for Wagner, Hans and Cosima, and later for the King.

One's final impression from it all is this — that Bülow had been well aware from the summer of 1864 onward that Cosima and Wagner had been irresistibly drawn towards each other, that he himself had no desire to stand in the way of Cosima's choice, but that he acquiesced in their desire to conceal the facts as long as possible from the King and the public, perhaps, at first, out of consideration less for himself than for Wagner and Wagner's work and for Cosima. For all his undeniable force of character, as shown particularly in his refusal ever to compromise either in his acts or in the expression of his opinion where art was concerned, Bülow's mind and his nature were essentially parasitic — using that term, without the slightest offensiveness, to denote the impossibility of his living without attaching himself to some stronger organism than himself. He had found in Wagner and Cosima two natures that were rich in everything he himself lacked — in Wagner the power of original creation, in Cosima the ability to steer a steady course through life undeflected by wind or sea. It is doubtful, as has already been said, whether he had ever felt any deep affection, in the usual sense of the word, for Cosima, whether, indeed, his nature was capable of romantic affection where women were concerned. What had drawn him to Cosima from the first, and what it was in her that kept his admiration and regard for her unshaken to the last, was her strength of will, her clearness of vision, and her indomitable purpose for great ends. He had begun his courtship days by confessing that he felt abashed by the " superiority " of Cosima and Blandine; and to the end of his life this sense of Cosima's superiority, and of the essential rightness of the line she had chosen to pursue, never left him. In 1871, after the divorce had been carried through, he wrote to Carl Bechstein,

> " I was very glad to hear from you that Frau Wagner's health is visibly better. What good fortune it is for this woman, who was *much* too significant relatively to her first husband, to be now parted from him and to be able — which God grant! — to correct the first sad half of her life through a better second half! " [19]

To Adolf von Gross, who called on him, after Wagner's death, to make the necessary legal arrangements for the future of his and Cosima's children, he said,

> " This century has seen three famous men — Napoleon, Bismarck and Wagner — who are not to be held accountable for what was human in them, or indeed for anything. As for Frau Wagner, she is a superior being: for me she is an angel."

As for Wagner, whom, for all his personal faults, he worshipped as the greatest creative genius of his epoch, Bülow would have gone through fire and water to save him from disaster. There cannot be much doubt that, apart from his high regard for Cosima, he kept silence as long as he could before the world because in his heart of hearts he recognised the inner rightness of his friend's claim to Cosima, and was anxious to protect him as long as he could from the Munich Philistines and their bourgeois morality. " Mützelburg and Jensen were here lately ", he wrote to Bechstein in August, 1869;

---

[19] BNB, p. 303.

" It is dreadful what I now have to endure from these friends, discreet as they are. The fact that I myself will come out cleanly, even in the eyes of the evil world, does not compensate me for the fact that a hue-and-cry against the great Master is inevitable. Now, however, I can contribute no further sacrifice." [20]

The theory, then, that Bülow was " deceived " must, on the totality of the evidence in our possession, be ruled out. He had seen for a long time that it was the hand of fate that had drawn Wagner and Cosima together; and it was from the noblest motives that he lent himself to the ignoble deceit it became necessary for all three to practise if Wagner, and with him the prospects of his art in Munich, were not to be brought down in ruin.

---

[20] BNB, p. 260.

APPENDIX I

JOHANNA WAGNER AND GEYER

I AM INDEBTED to Dr. Willi Schuh, the editor of the *Neue Zürcher Zeitung*, for a copy of an article in No. 1299 of that paper (16th July, 1933), which seems to have an inferential bearing on the perennial problem of Wagner's paternity.

The reader will recall that Wagner was born in Leipzig on the 22nd May, 1813, that he was baptised there on the 16th *August*, that his legal father, the Police Actuary Carl Friedrich Wagner, died on the 22nd November, that the widow Johanna married Geyer nine months later, on the 28th August, 1814, and that there must have been cohabitation between the pair by May, 1814 at the latest, as their daughter Cäcilie was born on the 26th February, 1815. The reader will remember also that, although direct evidence is lacking that Geyer lodged as usual in Carl Friedrich's house in the summer and autumn of 1812, there is equally no evidence that during that one summer he was *not* in Leipzig as usual with the Seconda theatrical troupe, of which he had been a member since 1809.[1] In the summer months of 1813 the company was playing, by exception, in Teplitz (Bohemia), " Seconda having decided to play there instead of at Leipzig, about which town the war-clouds were now gathering." Napoleon had defeated the Russian and Prussian forces at Lützen on the 2nd May. The battle of Bautzen began on the 20th May, two days before Richard Wagner's birth. (Bautzen is some ninety miles from Leipzig, and almost due east of it). A truce having been arranged, Napoleon took up his quarters in Dresden (about sixty miles south-east of Leipzig). The truce

---

[1] See Vol. I, pp. 16–18. The Seconda company usually played in Leipzig from Easter to Michaelmas each year. "All in all", as I said in my account of Geyer's career as an actor, "the burden of proof that Geyer, by solitary exception, was absent from Leipzig during the summer theatrical season of 1812 would appear to lie upon those who would fain establish that convenient proposition."

[558]

expired on the 17th August. The battle of Leipzig was fought on the 16–18th October.

Adolf Kolarz, the Kurdirektor at Teplitz, was engaged in 1933 in digging out details of the various visits of Johanna Wagner and Richard to that watering-place from 1817 onwards. (The reader will recall Wagner's trip there with Apel in the summer of 1834). In the course of his investigations of the contemporary Strangers' Lists, Herr Kolarz lighted, to his astonishment, on a hitherto unknown fact — that " Johanna Rosina Wagner, wife of Police Actuary Wagner ", was registered as a lodger in the " Three Pheasants " Hotel on the 21st July 1813. As anything from two to five days used to elapse between an arrival and the published announcement of it, this means that she must have reached Teplitz not later than about the 19th. The Seconda troupe had been playing in the town since the 11th June. With it was Geyer, whose quarters were in the " Golden Three ". At that time the " Three Pheasants " and the " Golden Three " formed parts of one and the same building: they were shortly afterwards rebuilt as the " Prince of Ligne " hotel, which occupies the site today.

Dr. Schuh sums the matter up thus:

" In the summer of 1812 Geyer was in Leipzig, as in other years. Three-quarters of a year later, Richard is born. Geyer's professional duties keep him far away from Leipzig at that time: on the 6th June he writes that he cannot come just now as he has to play in Teplitz. Johanna has scarcely recovered from her confinement when she makes the journey to Teplitz — assuredly, taking into consideration the circumstances and the custom of the epoch, not without her child. Teplitz was no more secure than Leipzig — on the contrary! What then could the object of the journey have been? Only the desire to be with Geyer again and to show him the tiny Richard. After this documentary evidence, doubt as to Geyer's paternity no longer appears possible."

The facts are certainly curious. Why, for one thing, was so long an interval as twelve weeks allowed to elapse between Richard's birth and his christening? Johanna herself, we know, was baptised two days after birth, her son Albert five days after. Mrs. Burrell gives us a facsimile of the page of the official Leipzig register of baptisms in August, 1813 that contains Richard's name. There are

four entries on the page, Wagner's (the 16th August) being numbered 35: the dates of birth of infants Nos. 32, 33 and 34 are 3rd
August, 27th July, and 30th July respectively. Had there been
some special domestic reason why Richard should not also have
been christened shortly after his birth? And was that reason Ludwig Geyer? Had there been trouble between Carl Friedrich and
Johanna over this latest child, which trouble was the cause of the
mother's astonishing journey to Teplitz?

For astonishing it certainly is, having regard to the circumstances of the time. Napoleon's line of communication stretched
westward from Leipzig to Hanau, near Frankfort-on-the-Main. His
headquarters during the armistice were in Dresden, and his armies
were distributed, roughly speaking, north of a line stretching from
Leipzig to Dresden and then beyond the latter. Under the armistice
a neutral territory of some twenty miles had been established between him and the Allies, who were massing in the south and south-
east. Nominally the armistice was to extend to the 17th August,
but the Prussians violated it a few days before its expiry. By the
end of August the most westerly portion of the Allied line ran from
Dresden (which Napoleon had now left) down through Freiberg,
Marienberg, Kaaden and Saaz, whence it branched eastward
through Bohemia. Between Kaaden and Melnik (on the river
Elbe), six allied columns were making their way to Dresden. From
Leipzig to Teplitz is a matter of 150 miles — a considerable journey in those days, even in time of peace. The first ninety miles
would take Johanna as far as Freiberg, through a territory disturbed indeed, but as yet (about mid-July) free from troops. From
Freiberg to Teplitz she would be in the area of the allied armies,
having to pass as best she could through more than one line. Can
anyone imagine that at a time like that, with one campaign barely
ended and another due to commence, a woman who had hardly had
time to recover from her confinement would plan a journey of 150
miles, into the very centre of the field of operations of the allied
armies, merely by way of a holiday or for the sake of her health?
Why, at such a time, should she at all costs make straight for Ludwig Geyer, of all people in the world, unless there had been some
very good reason for such an adventure, some excellent reason why
the objective of it should be just — Geyer?

Even if Johanna went to Teplitz alone, what construction can we put upon her action except that it was a flight from husband and home? The suggestion that she may have gone to Teplitz for safety's sake seems invalid, for other reasons than that Teplitz was decidedly no safer just then than Leipzig. Why should the mother of seven children, the youngest of whom, Richard, was only a few weeks old, while the next youngest, Ottilie, was only two, and the eldest of all, Albert, no more than fourteen, suddenly decide that *she* must escape from Leipzig, even if it meant abandoning her large family and her sorely over-worked husband? Would her departure alone be explicable on any other theory than that of a rupture with Carl Friedrich and a final desperate burning of her boats? On the other hand, if she took the tiny Richard with her, why, we may ask, this child alone? If danger threatened any of the Wagner family in Leipzig, it threatened them all equally. If there was no valid reason why the other small children should not be left behind, what reason could there be for exposing a few-weeks-old baby to the dangers and discomforts of several days' journey through a war area in which transport must have been difficult and food and decent lodging none too easily obtainable? [2] And of all the places and people in all Germany to which she might have gone, why was it imperative that she should go nowhere but to Teplitz, and to no one but Geyer — a struggling actor who could hardly keep himself and could offer her no protection of any kind from the perils of the time? Is it not difficult to resist the conclusion that, in some degree or other, her journey was, in fact, a flight from a home that had all at once become impossible for her, and that in taking only her recent baby with her she was taking from Carl Friedrich something for which he may have believed he had no call to feel any paternal enthusiasm? Taking all the facts into consideration, and looking at them from every possible angle, do they not seem to sug-

---

[2] "About a thousand Cossacks", says Mrs. Burrell, "preceded the Army of the Dwina, and they were 'more feared by the Saxons they came to succour than by the French they came to combat'. [The quotation is from Thiers' *Histoire du Consulat et de L'Empire*.] Even Napoleon himself took them into account and gave orders that by the 15th August . . . there was to be neither a vehicle on the German roads nor a boat on the Elbe, — 'afin que les Cosaques ne trouvassent rien à enlever, et ne pussent piller que le pays', he wrote to Marshal Davout." These were the conditions in which Johanna and her baby had to make their journey back to Leipzig from Teplitz!

gest that the putative father of the child had hinted that she had better betake herself and it to its real father?

Wagner, we may recall, assured Cäcilie, in his letter of the 14th January, 1870, that the old letters between " our father Geyer " and their mother that had recently come into his hands had given him " a penetrating glimpse into the relation between these two at a difficult time ". He now believes he can " see perfectly clearly ", though it is " extremely difficult " for him to put into words the view he takes of " that relation "; he contents himself with saying that it seems to him that " our father Geyer ", by his " sacrifice for the whole family " [in marrying the widow and taking on himself the heavy burden of her many young children], " believed he was atoning for a guilt." But there is little in the very few Geyer letters that have been given to us to account for Wagner's profound emotion, and nothing whatever that could afford anyone " a penetrating glimpse into the relations between these two ", or that could prompt the conjecture that Geyer sacrificed himself to " atone for a guilt ". Some letters have manifestly been either destroyed or suppressed. But why, if there was nothing in them that would not redound to Geyer's and Johanna's credit? One of the letters — that of the 22nd December, 1813 — shown by Cäcilie to Mrs. Burrell for her Life of Wagner, breaks off summarily in the middle of a verb: " the rest of the letter ", says Mrs. Burrell, " was not lent to me." [3] Why was it withheld? It would be interesting to have all the letters in full: they might shed a further ray of light on the vexed question of Wagner's parentage. It certainly looks now, however, as if the gallant opponents of the theory of the Geyer paternity have been defending a lost cause.

---

[3] BRW, p. 32.

APPENDIX II

THE "MADNESS" OF KING LUDWIG

M Y SCEPTICISM as to the " madness " of King Ludwig is the result of many years' acquaintance, frequently renewed, with all the available first-hand documents and most of the literature bearing on the case. An adequate discussion of the subject, however, would necessitate a separate volume. I dealt cursorily with it in an article in the *Sunday Times* of the 19th December, 1937: " It would be impossible ", I said there, " for any of us, in the England of today, to obtain a court order for the destruction of a neighbour's dog by any such methods as sufficed, in the Bavaria of 1886, to have Ludwig arrested and to drive him to his death." He had, of course, become quite impossible as a King; and as he was not disposed to abdicate, the only course open to the politicians who carried out the coup d'état was to get " a few medical tools of their own to declare him incurably insane, on the strength of depositions, mostly by his lackeys, taken in secret and withheld from counter-interrogation or criticism either by the King or his friends." An English judge, Mr. Justice Marshall, in an article dealing with the care which it is the duty of the State to exercise in matters of this kind, has said that " no one has yet been able to give a satisfactory definition of insanity ", that " a person may be quite abnormal about many things without being insane ", and that " the risk of an improper motive operating adversely to a patient obviously occurs where relatives wish to keep a person under detention in order that they may benefit by his property." (*Mental Patients*, in the *Quarterly Review*, January, 1928). The politicians who placed Ludwig under detention had so obvious a motive, proper or improper, for making it appear that he was insane that no court of justice worthy of the name would admit today, without the severest scrutiny, procedure so arbitrary as that by which these gentlemen secretly collected their " evidence " and then acted on it.

The " evidence " collected by the four medical hirelings of the politicians will be found in full in TALKB, pp. 137–155. Not much of it, or of the complacent dogmatisings of the many " psychiatrists " who have written upon the case since 1886, would survive cross-examination in an English court of law today. When we find more than one of these learned " psychiatrists " solemnly attributing Ludwig's " madness " to the " narcotic " influence of Wagner's music on the " cerebral nerves " of the unfortunate King, we can only feel pity for the patients who were subjected to the professional attention of some of them.

In 1872 a certain Dr. Puschmann published a psychiatric study in which he proved, to his own satisfaction, that Wagner was well on the way to complete mental and moral insanity. It was all done on what the proud author of the brochure evidently regarded as the strictest scientific lines: Wagner is made out to be suffering, for instance, from megalomania, from a hatred of present social institutions, from overweening ambition, from the belief that he is a philosopher and politician and economist as well as a musician, " a Saviour, a Messiah who is to redeem humanity afresh "; he wants to " abolish the State and religion and put in their place an opera house from which he is to govern "; his later poems and his later music compete with each other for priority in absurdity; he suffers from persecution mania; his prose style is evidence of a mind diseased — he even manufactures words of his own, which is a fairly sure sign of mental derangement; the specimens quoted by Puschmann " prove that his rational faculty is no longer normal, and that already he suffers from delusions the consequences of which have exercised a deleterious influence on his whole psychical constitution." Wagner is further convicted of a moral perversity that is the certain sign of mental alienation. (See PRW, *passim*).

Dr. Puschmann describes himself on his title-page as " practising physician and specialist in psychiatry in Munich ". One can only hope that a special providence watched over the unfortunate patients of this priceless imbecile. His little book, however, is of exceptional interest today: it should be studied in detail in conjunction with the report of the four " psychiatrists " who solemnly certified King Ludwig to be suffering from " that form of insanity that is well-known, from experience, to alienists under the name of paranoia."

The term " paranoia " seems to have been coined in or about the 1870's as a substitute for " monomania ". It never had either a scientific basis or a surely scientific range of application: it was just one more of those cases, so common in medical terminology, in which a Greek compound is called upon to put a solemn face on professional ignorance. The " alienists " of the final quarter of the nineteenth century complacently solved no end of difficult problems simply by mumbling the magic but meaningless word " paranoia ". Today the term has fallen into discredit even in " alienist " circles. When we find a modern English authority, for instance, saying gingerly that " in its true (*sic!*) form this [paranoia] is uncommon, and has been regarded as perhaps more a morbid unfolding of a peculiar personality than an actual disease ", we get the suspicion that " psychiatry " has no very precise notion of what it is talking about.

The present volume was almost on its way to the printer when there reached me an excellent new study of Ludwig by Werner Richter — *Ludwig II König von Bayern* (Zürich, 1939). Herr Richter seems to have arrived at very much the same conclusion as myself with regard to the certification of the King as a " paranoiac " by the all-wise " alienists " who so obligingly did the Bavarian politicians' dirty work for them in 1886. " Today ", he says in a note to page 358, " the concept of ' paranoia ', which is said in the report of the [Munich] experts to be ' well known to alienists from experience ', seems to have come to pieces. For instance, Lange, in the *Handbuch der Psychiatrie* (1926), says that it was originally intended to include in that work a sub-sectional volume on ' Paranoia ', but that ' paranoia, as a perhaps circumlocutory concept in alienism, has in recent years been particularly roughly treated ', there being in many quarters a tendency to question the justice of the notion that paranoia can be regarded as a particular form of [mental] disease; but that in order not to leave out entirely the projected section of the *Handbuch* there would be a discussion in it of the paranoia *question*. Today, then, paranoia cannot be treated as a clearly characterised and to a certain extent circumscribed phenomenon of [mental] disease; only the paranoia *question* can be dealt with."

It is not often that the medical pseudo-science of today passes judgment upon the medical pseudo-science of yesterday with even such modified frankness as we have here!

THE PUTZMACHERIN LETTERS

THE PUTZMACHERIN letters are of no great account either in themselves or in Wagner biography, but their history is interesting for the light it throws on the ethical standards of some of the anti-Wagnerians of the past.

The letters were first of all published by Daniel Spitzer, with ironical comments, in the Vienna *Neue Freie Presse* of the 16th and 17th June, 1877 — that is to say, during Wagner's lifetime. Apparently there was nothing in the law of Austria to prevent any blackguard from making any malicious and dishonourable use he liked of private letters that had happened to come into his hands. (Spitzer was a well-known humorous journalist and author of that period, a colleague of Hanslick, and an inveterate anti-Wagnerian. It is to him that we owe the novel *Verliebte Wagnerianer*, referred to in Vol. II, p. 612). In 1906 the letters, with Spitzer's running comments, were re-issued in book form by an anonymous editor who is now known to have been the Viennese journalist Paul Taussig. It is to the credit of the Austrian and German Press that most papers of standing either refused to notice this quite needless republication or expressed themselves strongly about it. Indirectly, however, it was the means by which the truth about the whole nasty business was ultimately dragged into the light of day, in the first place by the brochure of Ludwig Karpath referred to in the " Sources and References " as KBWP.

Karpath was for a long time the colleague of Max Kalbeck (the Brahms biographer) on the *Neues Wiener Tageblatt*. He accidently discovered in 1906 that an old man named Ferdinand Goldwag, who for thirty years had brought the Stock Exchange prices to the financial editor of the *Tageblatt* each day, was the brother of Wagner's Putzmacherin, and that she was still alive. Karpath sought her out, won her confidence, and obtained the main facts about the Spitzer affair of 1877 from her. She had been no party to the publication of the letters; she had nothing but good to say of Wagner, who had always been amiability itself with her, and whose debt to her had been discharged in full. She had kept all his letters in a drawer, made up into a packet. One day she missed them. She came to the conclusion that one of her employees had either abstracted them or mistakenly thrown them away as rubbish. It is practically certain, however, that they had been stolen by her ne'er-do-well husband, Louis Maretschek, whose way of life had often landed him in financial difficulties. (He died in 1906). From him they had passed, directly or indirectly, into the hands of one Kafka, a stockjobber who dealt in autographs as a sideline. Spitzer persuaded his editor to buy the letters for 100 gulden. According to Max Morold, they had twice been vainly offered for sale to the Vienna *Deutsche Zeitung*, and also — for a consideration — to Wagner himself: he contemptuously refused to be bled, and the subsequent publication of the letters was merely an act of revenge for the failure of this attempt at blackmail. (See MWK, II, 242).

In the *Neue Freie Presse* of the 10th May, 1908, Hugo Wittmann, a member of the Brahms circle, revealed, in the course of some " Recollections of Johannes Brahms ", that Kafka had first of all shown the letters to Brahms, who read them aloud to some of his cronies at their usual table in the Gause restaurant; they were received, it appears, " with general merriment ". " I do not know ", said Wittmann, " how they came into Brahms's hands, but I do know for certain that it was through his hands that they reached publicity. Michael Etienne, the editor of the *Neue Freie Presse*, bought them and gave them to Spitzer to deal with in an appropriate way. For the satirist they were a veritable titbit, absolutely made for him." Karpath had known all along of Brahms's sorry share in the business, but out of consideration for him he had refrained, in 1906, from telling all he knew, though Brahms had by that time been dead nine years. It was reserved for a gentleman of the composer's own entourage to claim for Brahms the " credit " due to him for having been the instrument through which the Putzmacherin letters were given to the world while Wagner was still living, and with the sole object of raising a Philistine horse-laugh against him.

In his 1934 volume of recollections (KBMG) Karpath disclosed for the first time some information given him long previously about the matter by no less a Brahms authority than the true-blue Max Kalbeck. According to the latter, as soon as Brahms had read the letters he cried out to Kafka, " Ah, this is something for Spitzer. You must take them to Spitzer; he will buy them from you." Kafka went to the journalist, and the letters, as we have seen, were bought by the *Presse* and handed over to Spitzer. Their journalistic purpose having been served, the editor re-sold the letters to one Arthur Faber, a Viennese manufacturer, for the price originally paid for them.

Kalbeck further told Karpath that one day Faber produced the letters and offered to give them to him as a souvenir; whereupon Brahms " flew into a temper, snatched the precious documents out of Kalbeck's hand, and turning to Faber, cried, ' Why should you give these letters to Kalbeck? They are by rights mine.' " Kalbeck asked for only one letter: the other fifteen went to Brahms, together with five letters from Cosima to the Putzmacherin of which Spitzer had not made any use. Brahms intended to bequeath the bulk of his possessions to the Vienna Gesellschaft der Musikfreunde; but as his will was not signed but merely initialled it was disputed by some of his relatives. In the end these Putzmacherin letters of his were sold by these people's trustee; they appeared later in a catalogue of a Boston (U.S.A.) dealer, and were bought for the Library of Congress.

It may have been knowledge of these facts concerning Brahms — who, on occasion, could be something less than a gentleman, — rather than a congenital antipathy to his music, that accounted for the ill odour that later clung to his name in Wahnfried.

INDEX

Franz Josef, Emperor of Austria, 251 (note)

Freischütz, overture at Wagner's Vienna concert, 206

Friedrich, Grand Duke of Baden, 138; discussing with Wagner *Tristan,* 132, 134; Wagner's appeal for financial help, 149

Friedrich, Grand Duke of Weimar, funds to Wagner, 195

Fröbel, Julius, 395 (note), 397, 465, 472, 479 (note), 484 *et seq.;* on Wagner's call to Munich, 216–217; on young King Ludwig, 239–240; on Wagner and King Ludwig, 360 (note), 492

Frommann, Alwine, 52; at Weimar Tonkünstlerverein meeting, 145

Fürstner, Adolph, Wagner rights sold to, 42 (note)

GALL, Baron, promised a *Lohengrin* performance, 219

Garibaldi, 45, 54

Garrigues, on Schnorr, 405 (note)

Gasperini, 108, 466 (note); and Wagner, 4, 7, 143; on Niemann, 62; on Morelli, 63; to Wagner on *Tannhäuser,* 95–97; at first *Tristan* performance, 375

Gautier, Judith, 120; at Paris *Tannhäuser* rehearsal, about Wagner, 120–121

Gautier, Théophile, 120

Geneva, Wagner in, 502 *et seq.*

German Art and German Policy, 519

German Art and German Politics, 516 ·(note)

Germania Marsch (Dräseke), 145

German Workers' Party (anthem), 325 (note)

Germany, Wagner back in, 51

Gevaert, at Wagner's concerts in Paris, 6

Gewandhaus, for Wagner concert, 195

Geyer, Cäcilie, 558, 562

Geyer, Ludwig, evidence for considering Richard his son, 558 *et seq.;* in Teplitz, 559; and Johanna Wagner, 558 *et seq.*

Giacomelli, suggests concerts in Brussels, 22; manages tickets for Paris *Tannhäuser,* 108

Gille, Carl, 366; first *Tristan* performance, 375

Gilman, Lawrence, *A Neglected Page of Wagner's,* 84 (note)

Girard, Narcisse, head of the Paris Opéra, 102

Glasenapp, 61, 110 (note), 127, 396 (note), 436 (note); on Wagner's Munich contract, 310 (note); on the Wagner-Bülow-Lassalle meeting, 325

Glaspalast, suggested for provisional theatre, 336–337, 412 *et seq.*

Gluck, Wagner on production of, 320

Gobineau, race theory, 285

Goethe, Wagner on production of, 320

Goldwag, Bertha, 438–439, 443, 464; on Wagner, 567–569; Putzmacherin letters, 568

Goldwag, Ferdinand, Putzmacherin letters, 567

Gosse, Edmund, 290

Götterdämmerung, 272, 273, 519

Gounod, Charles, 11, 19 (note); at Wagner concerts in Paris, 6

Grab im Busento, Das (Weissheimer), 145

Gräfin Egmont, 150

Grandauer, Dr. Franz, 484

INDEX

Ring (*continued*)
454, 470, 472; financial support
for, 30; production of entirety
or sections of the tetralogy, 137;
publishing rights of, 141;
Schott's financial considerations,
155; slight modification, 160;
extracts in Petersburg concert,
203; libretto, 204; still unfinished, 210; Ludwig gets copy of
poem, 213; Ludwig promises
production, 222; contract for
completion, 226; private auditions, 228–229; parody in Munich *Punsch*, 236; discussion of
production, 265; poem read to
Princess Marie zu Hohenlohe,
292 (note); proposed contract,
309; audience with the King, on,
308–309; negotiations for Munich production, 311–312; 317
et seq., 322–323; copy to Lassalle, 325; Wagner's sum for, 467
Riss, King's lodge offered to Wagner, 519
Ritter, Alexander, 521 (note), 552,
553; Bülow to, 104, 132; and first
Tristan performance, 375
Ritter, Franziska, 552, 553
Ritter, Karl, and Wagner in Zürich,
166; escorting Cosima and Blandine, 297–298; episode with Cosima, 297–298
Robert the Devil (Meyerbeer), 46;
with Niemann in Paris, 128
Roche, 120; translated *Tannhäuser*,
64
Röckel, August, 47, 196, 432; with
Wagner in Biebrich, 192; and
first *Tristan* performance, 375;
Wagner to, on Taxis intrigue,
397–398; informs Wagner on
difficulties for the theatre street
in Munich, 427; Wagner to, on
his capital, 464–465

Röckl, Sebastian, 350; on Wagner-
Hofmann contract, 309 (note);
and festival theatre contract, 412,
413; on Wagner's Brienner-
strasse house, 438–439, 440
(note); on the triangle at Triebschen, 522
Roethe, Gustav, *Zum dramatischen
Aufbau der Wagnerschen "Meistersinger"*, 155 (note)
Roger, Gustave, interested in producing *Tannhäuser*, 125; on Ander, 139 (note)
Rokitansky, 202
Roméo et Juliette (Berlioz), 15
Röpe, Georg Reinhard, 417 (note)
Rossini, 73 (note), 465; in Paris
with Wagner, 12; French singers
trained on, 97
Rothlauf, Peter, 552 (note)
Royer, 115, 126; negotiations for
Tannhäuser performance, 62–64;
suggests "Dance-Intermezzo"
for *Tannhäuser*, 68; Wagner's
ultimatum to, regarding Dietsch,
103; Paris *Tannhäuser* staging,
107 (note); begged for cuts in
Tannhäuser, 114–115; Wagner
to, 117; Wagner asks again for
withdrawal of *Tannhäuser*, 119
Ruben, 207
Rubinstein, 286
Rudhardt, 497
Rudolf, Crown Prince, at Mayerling, 251 (note)
Russia, Helene, Grand Duchess of,
interest in Wagner, 204
Rüstow, Wilhelm, and Volkswehr,
480

SABOUROFF, General von, 76; offer
to Wagner for St. Petersburg,
31
St. Elisabeth (Liszt), 446, 523, 524
(note)

[xxii]

Wagner, Richard (*continued*)
King, 359; to Mathilde Maier on, 360; to Frau Wille on, 360–361; Ludwig's restored confidence in, 362, 364; *Tristan* for Munich, 362 *et seq.*; cuts in *Tristan*, 365; birth of Isolde, 366; wanted *Tristan* in Residenz Theatre, 367–368; to Friedrich Uhl on coming *Tristan* production, 369; financial help from Julie Schwabe through Meysenbug, 371–373; " Schwabe-Schwind " affair, 372–374; Schauss, 372–373; Pusinelli's bad news from Minna, 374–375; *Tristan* rehearsals and performance, 375–377, 377–379, 390; and Bruckner, 379; anonymous letter on *Tristan*, 381–382; and Wolzogen, 382–383; analysis of music by " leading motives ", 382–383; after *Tristan* in Munich, 384 *et seq.*; and the King, 385–387, 392 *et seq.*; and Pfordten, 388 *et seq.*; only artistic, no political interest common with King, 395; Prince Paul von Thurn und Taxis, 396 *et seq.*; Jesuit plans, 396 *et seq.*; to Röckel on Taxis intrigue, 397–398; tired and discouraged, 399; on remunerations at theatres, 400; to Ludwig on Pfistermeister, 402; conducting at Residenz Theatre for the King, 403–404; *Tristan* to be withheld from German theatres, 404; with King in Berg, 405; starts dictation of autobiography, 405; Schnorr's death, 406, 442, 446, 449, 450, 462, 469; plunging into political and financial questions, 406 *et seq.*; Music School and Festival theatre, 406–407; Ludwig's first mention of theatre plan, 409; theatre plan, 410, 414, 415, 422,

Wagner, Richard (*continued*)
427–428; leaves Munich, 421; less interest in Festival theatre, 423; negotiations with Semper and Röckel, 425 *et seq.*; in Triebschen, 424 *et seq.*, 518–519, 520; decided not to return to Munich, 428; to Semper, 430 *et seq.*; Wilhelmine Klepperbein, creditor, 437 (note); luxuries for Briennerstrasse from Bertha Goldwag, 438–439; difficulties in payment, 442; going on the Hochkopf, reading *Ramayana*, 442, 446; contract with royal Treasury, 443; new proposal to Ludwig, 444 *et seq.*; diary " Brown Book ", 446 *et seq.*; " eternal return ", 447; on his art, 449 *et seq.*; seeks salvation of the *Ramayana*, 450; longing to make Cosima his wife, 448, 453; triangle, 448–449; on Bülow, 449; *Die Sieger*, 450; working on *Siegfried*, 450, 453; back in Munich, 451; Prose Sketch for *Parsifal*, 451; on Zahlberg's death, 451–452; gifts from royal Treasury, 452 *et seq.*; intriguing against the politicians, 454; to Lutz, 456; financial demands, 456 *et seq.*, 465; his psychology in the 1865 crisis, 461 *et seq.*; to Röckel on his capital, 464–465; Bertha Goldwag, 465, 472, 567–569; to Vienna, 465; discharging debts, 466; financial relations with the Bavarian Treasury, 466 *et seq.*; relations with Ludwig, 469 *et seq.*; to Otto Wesendonk, 470; manuscript and copy of *Tannhäuser* new Venusberg scene, 471; to Brahms on it, 471; back to Munich, 472; agitation against, 472 *et seq.*; at Hohenschwangau, 473, 482, 485;